# GAMING AND GAMBLING LAW

ASPEN CASEBOOK SERIES

# GAMING AND GAMBLING LAW

*Cases and Materials*

**Kevin Washburn**
Dean and Professor of Law
University of New Mexico School of Law

 Wolters Kluwer
Law & Business

AUSTIN    BOSTON    CHICAGO    NEW YORK    THE NETHERLANDS

Aspen Publishers
Attn: Permissions Department
76 Ninth Avenue, 7th Floor
New York, NY 10011-5201

To contact Customer Care, e-mail customer.service@aspenpublishers.com, call 1-800-234-1660, fax 1-800-901-9075, or mail correspondence to:

Aspen Publishers
Attn: Order Department
PO Box 990
Frederick, MD 21705

Printed in the United States of America.

1 2 3 4 5 6 7 8 9 0

ISBN 978-0-7355-8845-5

**Library of Congress Cataloging-in-Publication Data**

Washburn, Kevin (Kevin K), 1967-
   Gaming and gambling law / Kevin Washburn.
      p. cm.
   Includes bibliographical references and index.
   ISBN 978-0-7355-8845-5 (alk. paper)
1. Gambling—Law and legislation—United States.   I. Title.
   KF3992.W37 2011
   344.73'099—dc22

                                                    2010045592

# About Wolters Kluwer Law & Business

Wolters Kluwer Law & Business is a leading provider of research information and workflow solutions in key specialty areas. The strengths of the individual brands of Aspen Publishers, CCH, Kluwer Law International and Loislaw are aligned within Wolters Kluwer Law & Business to provide comprehensive, in-depth solutions and expert-authored content for the legal, professional and education markets.

**CCH** was founded in 1913 and has served more than four generations of business professionals and their clients. The CCH products in the Wolters Kluwer Law & Business group are highly regarded electronic and print resources for legal, securities, antitrust and trade regulation, government contracting, banking, pension, payroll, employment and labor, and healthcare reimbursement and compliance professionals.

**Aspen Publishers** is a leading information provider for attorneys, business professionals and law students. Written by preeminent authorities, Aspen products offer analytical and practical information in a range of specialty practice areas from securities law and intellectual property to mergers and acquisitions and pension/benefits. Aspen's trusted legal education resources provide professors and students with high-quality, up-to-date and effective resources for successful instruction and study in all areas of the law.

**Kluwer Law International** supplies the global business community with comprehensive English-language international legal information. Legal practitioners, corporate counsel and business executives around the world rely on the Kluwer Law International journals, loose-leafs, books and electronic products for authoritative information in many areas of international legal practice.

**Loislaw** is a premier provider of digitized legal content to small law firm practitioners of various specializations. Loislaw provides attorneys with the ability to quickly and efficiently find the necessary legal information they need, when and where they need it, by facilitating access to primary law as well as state-specific law, records, forms and treatises.

Wolters Kluwer Law & Business, a unit of Wolters Kluwer, is headquartered in New York and Riverwoods, Illinois. Wolters Kluwer is a leading multinational publisher and information services company.

*For Libby, Cole, and Ford, who are the best prizes I could ever win.*

# SUMMARY OF CONTENTS

# CONTENTS

# CHAPTER 2

## THE SOCIAL HARMS OF GAMING/GAMBLING          63

## CHAPTER 3

## PRIVATE LAW AND THE PROHIBITION OF GAMBLING 125

## CHAPTER 4

## FEDERALISM AND DIRECT ENFORCEMENT
## OF GAMBLING PROHIBITIONS                              171

# CHAPTER 5

# THE CHALLENGE OF LIMITING GAMBLING
# IN A PERMISSIVE LEGAL ENVIRONMENT                   273

## CHAPTER 6

## REGULATING LAWFUL GAMING
## THROUGH LICENSURE                                            339

## CHAPTER 7

## REGULATING FAIR PLAY, CHEATING, AND GAMING PROFITABILITY                    425

## CHAPTER 8

### TAXATION OF GAMBLING                                     489

# PREFACE

Commercial gambling has been one of the fastest growing sectors of the economy in the last three decades. Trillions of dollars have been gambled and billions have been lost and earned. Brick and mortar gambling establishments now exist in most American states and illegal sport betting and Internet gaming is, no doubt, occurring in all of them. Indian gaming, which first developed in the 1970s, is now occurring in around 30 states. Most of the states without Indian casinos nevertheless have lotteries, horseracing, bingo, or riverboats. Gambling is ubiquitous in American culture.

What is gambling? The legal boundaries of the term are ill-defined and courts often have difficulty determining how broadly it should reach. Consider the following questions: is the day-trading investor "gambling" when he "plays" the stock market? Is the political candidate "gambling" when she invests millions of dollars of her own and others' money to seek political office, uncertain if she will prevail? Is the patient "gambling" when he chooses surgery over another treatment? Is the average student "gambling" when she attends college, not certain whether there will be a job for her when she graduates? And to draw a finer point, if job opportunities are rare, is a law student gambling when she attends law school? Worse, what about the student earning a Ph.D. in English? Are young parents "gambling" when they pay premiums on life insurance policies so that there will be funds available to raise their children if they die unexpectedly? Is the MIT-trained mathematician "gambling" when he plays blackjack with a predetermined amount of money fully aware of the probabilities in the game and the strategies available to maximize those probabilities to his own benefit?

If betting on an uncertain outcome that is partially determined by luck constitutes "gambling," then most human beings are guilty of gambling many times every day. So why is casino gambling or sports-betting subject to American gambling laws while so many other gambling activities, such as entering the stock market or politics, or choosing medical treatment, investing in an education, or buying life insurance, are not? What are the particular concerns that lead us to apply our gambling laws to activities that happen in casinos, but not to the other activities of life?

Gambling poses numerous riddles in American law and society. In some jurisdictions, gambling is subject to a full and outright prohibition. In others, it is authorized, but only in a very limited manner. In still others, it is legal and even encouraged. Indeed, a majority of American state jurisdictions authorize a particular limited form of gambling, the state lottery, that is not only lawful, but marketed aggressively using public funds. In some of these jurisdictions, state law strongly limits or even prohibits other forms of gambling. Even in jurisdictions in which gambling has been broadly legalized, it is highly regulated. What drives the decision to prohibit gambling or to legalize and regulate it? What are the concerns at work in this calculus? When the decision is made to legalize and regulate gambling, what ought to be the goals of regulation? Indeed, what are the risks presented by the activity and what are the problems sought to be addressed by regulation?

Still another reflection of the enigmatic status of gambling in the United States is this question: what constitutes "fair" gambling? If gambling is a legal and regulated commercial enterprise, what are the responsibilities of the vendor regarding the "game" itself. What is the casino selling? Is it merely providing "entertainment" or is it offering a fair game? That is, must the vendor also provide each player-patron an even playing field as to the game itself? Must the vendor, for example, offer the same gaming opportunity to all patrons, or may the vendor change the rules and even exclude particularly successful patrons from play precisely because they are so successful? May players cooperate with one another to try to minimize the casino's advantage, for example, in a blackjack game in which the game involves players betting against one another and the house? When the patron approaches the blackjack table, is the casino merely offering the patron "entertainment" or is it offering terms that are far more specific? From the patron's vantage point, is the patron merely buying the opportunity to get lucky or is the patron buying the opportunity to use all his skills to make money at the casino?

These are some of the difficult questions that will be addressed in the coming chapters. The first two chapters are closely related. Chapter 1 addresses the fundamental legal question of what constitutes gambling, that is, what is the legal definition of gambling in the laws as interpreted by the courts in the United States. However, the definition of gambling in any given regulatory or prohibitory law is necessarily dependent on the underlying reason for regulating or prohibiting gambling. Chapter 2 takes up the specific concerns that motivate the prohibition or regulation of gaming and thus sheds additional light on how broadly gambling ought to be defined in the law.

Next, the book examines prohibitory approaches to gambling. In Chapters 3 and 4, it explains the legal strategies that have been used to prohibit or discourage gambling in the United States. Chapter 3 takes up private law strategies for discouraging gambling and draws upon the myriad issues that arise from gaming law's nexus with contract law and conflicts of law. Chapter 4 explores federalism and the inherent difficulties in maintaining a gambling prohibition within a nation that has numerous political subdivisions that are authorized to make their own policies about gambling. It also addresses many of the federal laws that were principally developed as tools to prevent unlawful gambling.

Chapters 5 through 8 address issues that arise in efforts to legalize and regulate gambling. Chapter 5 highlights the cross-boundary problems and the difficulties in limiting the expansion of gambling and limiting gambling to certain geographic areas. Chapter 6 takes up licensure, which is the leading regulatory strategy for addressing the potential harms of gambling, and introduces the due process questions that arise in a regime that allows wide discretion for regulators. It also addresses the vexing issues that arise in light of the inevitable and sometimes unhealthy relationship between organized sports and gambling.

Chapter 7 addresses the nature of the regulation of the players and the games themselves, dealing with the relationship between the casino or gaming operator and the consumer. It also addresses what constitutes cheating in the casino context.

Finally, Chapter 8 addresses issues of taxation that are unique to the gambling context and applies many of the principles presented earlier in the course. Taxation requires us to address fundamental questions about the nature of gambling, such as whether the player engages in gambling for entertainment or as a commercial enterprise for profit. Chapter 8 thus brings us full circle and requires us to address the initial questions raised in the first two chapters. What kind of behavior is this and what is the purpose of taxation?

Kevin Washburn

November 2010
Albuquerque

# ACKNOWLEDGMENTS

The genesis for this book was a seminar and then a course at the University of Minnesota Law School. Before joining the faculty at Minnesota, I served as General Counsel of the National Indian Gaming Commission. During my time there, I realized that Indian gaming was regulated much like other forms of commercial gaming across the United States. While some of my Indian law colleagues teach courses on Indian gaming law, most of these courses focus on aspects of federal Indian law and concentrate very little on the general regulatory structure of gambling that occurs inside Indian casinos and in most other American gambling venues. As I taught a course on general gambling law for the first time, I sensed a need for a book that recognizes the common concepts and legal principles that cross all forms of gambling.

In preparing this manuscript, I had tremendous assistance from students and research assistants. At Minnesota, I benefited greatly from the guidance and assistance of Ben Hendrick and Lotem Almog Levy, as well as Julie Strother. I am also grateful to the Prairie Island Sioux Community as well as the Shakopee Mdewakanton Dakota Community for providing my classes back-of-the-house tours of their respective gaming operations, the Treasure Island Casino and the Mystic Lake Casino. I am grateful that then-Dean Alex Johnson and then-Associate Deans Steve Befort and Jim Chen allowed me to explore this new course at Minnesota. Because Minnesota has a robust gaming market and a sophisticated bar, it was a fantastic place to begin.

The manuscript was further refined when I taught the course at Harvard Law School. Approximately 60 students enrolled in the course, the first general course on gambling law ever offered in that school's history. The class benefited greatly by visits from Frank J. Fahrenkopf, Jr., President of the American Gaming Association, former Rep. Jim Leach of Iowa, who was then serving as director of the Kennedy School's Institute of Politics, and Massachusetts State Treasurer Tim Cahill. I am grateful to the Mohegan Tribe of Connecticut which hosted a back-of-the-house tour of its casino for the class, and to then-Dean Elena Kagan and Associate Dean Andy Kaufman for providing generous funding for the course and allowing me to teach it. I was assisted in my work at Harvard by several outstanding students, including Adam Hosmer-Henner, Ethel Branch, Kyle Scherer, Brian Vito, Andrew Woods, and Michael Kaiser.

I last taught the course at the University of Arizona's James E. Rogers College of Law. I am grateful to then-Dean Toni Massaro and Associate Dean Kay Kavanough for allowing me to teach the course, and also to students John Barwell, Leah Lussier, Vanessa Chavez, Trini Contreras, Jason Doucette, Johanna Farmer, Tory Fodder, Erick Gjerdingen, Katie Grounds, A.J. Hart, Mike Ivancie, Tony King, Maria Manibusan, Alex Mayer, Eric Moores, Aaron Nance, Vicki Robertson, Morgan Rodman, and Jesse Sixkiller for helping me to continue to refine my thinking about the course. One of my students, a part-time racing official named Steve May, provided an excellent back-of-the-house tour of the Rillito Downs racetrack. I am also grateful to the Pascua Yaqui Tribe for providing the students a hands-on, back-of-the-house tour of the Casino del Sol.

At the University of New Mexico, I must thank my research assistant Julia Maccini, librarian Ann Hemmens, and especially my wonderful administrative assistant Sandra Bauman for helping me to bring this book to publication.

Over the years, I have learned as much about gaming from teaching the subject with able colleagues and students as I have from studying it alone. From teaching courses with the National Judicial College and the National College of District Attorneys, I have met many colleagues in the field, who have guided my understanding. I am grateful to them.

I am also grateful to the Saginaw Chippewa Indian Tribe of Michigan for appointing me the Chief Judge of the tribe's Court of Appeals in 2008. Through this appointment, I have been exposed to additional issues involving Indian gaming in Michigan, and also helped me to learn the issues faced at the tribal level.

I have several colleagues in academia and the gaming industry to whom I owe intellectual debts for exposing me to, or helping me think through, various problems. These include Montie Deer, Barry Brandon, Penny Coleman, Rick Schiff, and Phil Hogen at the NIGC, as well as Senator John McCain, and many Congressional staffers over the years. These also include numerous attorneys and professors, including, among others, Bradley Bledsoe Downes, Henry Buffalo, Anthony Cabot, Eric Dahlstrom, Skip Durocher, Glenn Feldman, George Forman, Rob Gips, Vanya Hogen, Willie Hardacker, Dan Israel, Danna Jackson, John Jacobson, Mark Jarboe, Professor Tadd Johnson (Univ. of Minnesota-Duluth), Bill Buffalo, Mark Van Norman, Professor Colette Routel (William Mitchell), Heidi McNeil Staudenmaier, Kevin

Gover, Professor Steven Andrew Light (North Dakota), Professor William Rice (Tulsa), Professor Robert N. Clinton (Arizona State), Professor Nelson Rose (Whittier), Professor (and Dean) Kathryn Rand (North Dakota), Professor Ron Rychlak (Ole Miss), Professor Gregg Polsky (UNC), Professor Rebecca Tsosie (ASU), Professor Carole Goldberg (UCLA), and Professor Richard Aaron (Utah).

Judge William C. Canby, Jr., first exposed me to gaming law by assigning me a bench memorandum in what I have since come to recognize as a common type of litigation known as a "a game classification case" while I was clerking for him. He continues to be an outstanding mentor and a role model.

During most all of this work, I have had the generous support of my wife Libby and the love of my sons, Cole and Ford, who traveled all over the country with me to numerous different law schools and cities so that I could pursue an exciting and very rewarding academic career.

Finally, my thanks to the following for permission to reproduce all or portions of their work:

Barbara E. Armacost, *Qualified Immunity: Ignorance Excused*, 51 VAND. L. REV. 583 (1998). Copyright 1998 by Vanderbilt Law Review, Vanderbilt University School of Law; Barbara Armacost. All Rights Reserved.

Cory Aronovitz, *The Regulation of Commercial Gaming*, 5 CHAP. L. REV. 181 (2002). Copyright 2002 by Chapman Law Review; Cory Aronovitz. All Rights Reserved.

Tom W. Bell, *Internet Gambling: Popular, Inexorable, and (Eventually) Legal*, Cato Institute Policy Analysis No. 336, Mar. 8, 1999. Copyright 1999 by the Cato Institute; Tom W. Bell. All Rights Reserved.

Alexandra Berzon, *The Gambler Who Blew $127 Million*, WALL STREET JOURNAL (Dec. 5, 2009). Reprinted by permission of the Wall Street Journal. Copyright © 2009 Dow Jones & Company, Inc. All Rights Reserved worldwide. License number 2540971170669.

AMERICAN PSYCHIATRIC ASSOCIATION, DIAGNOSTIC AND STATISTICAL MANUAL OF MENTAL DISORDERS (4th ed., text revision, 2000). Copyright 2000 by American Psychiatric Association. All Rights Reserved.

Anthony N. Cabot & Louis V. Csoka, *The Games People Play: Is It Time for a New Legal Approach to Prize Games?*, 4 NEV. L.J. 197 (2004). Copyright 2004 by Nevada Law Journal; Anthony N. Cabot; Louis V. Csoka. All Rights Reserved.

Anthony N. Cabot & Robert Hannum, *Advantage Play and Commercial Casinos*, 74 MISS. L.J. 681 (2005). Copyright 2005 by Mississippi Law Journal. Inc.; Anthony N. Cabot; Robert Hannum. All Rights Reserved.

Kathleen M. Sullivan & Gerald Gunther, CONSTITUTIONAL LAW 324 (15th ed. 2004). Copyright 2004 by Thomson Reuters; Kathleen M. Sullivan; Gerald Gunther. All Rights Reserved.

United Methodist Church, *Statements on Gambling*, BOOK OF RESOLUTIONS 2004. Copyright 2004 by The United Methodist Publishing House. All Rights Reserved.

*Should Online Gambling Be Banned?*, WALL STREET JOURNAL ONLINE NEWS ROUNDUP (April 4, 2006). Copyright 2006 by Dow Jones & Company, Inc. Reproduced with permission of Dow Jones & Company, Inc., in the format Textbook via Copyright Clearance Center. All Rights Reserved.

Kevin K. Washburn, *Federal Law, State Policy, and Indian Gaming*, 4 Nev. L. J. 285 (2004). Copyright by Nevada Law Journal; Kevin K. Washburn. All Rights Reserved.

Kevin K. Washburn, *The Legacy of Bryan v. Itasca County: How a $147 County Tax Notice Helped Bring Tribes $200 Billion in Indian Gaming Revenues*, 92 MINN. L. REV. 919 (2008). Copyright 2008 by Minnesota Law Review Foundation; Kevin K. Washburn. All Rights Reserved.

Kevin K. Washburn, *Recurring Problems in Indian Gaming*, 1 WYO. L. REV. 427 (2001). Copyright 2001 by University of Wyoming; Kevin K. Washburn. All Rights Reserved.

# GAMING AND GAMBLING LAW

# CHAPTER

# 1

---

# What Is Gambling?

The common use of the word "gambling" is sometimes very broad. Each of us bets on probabilities and outcomes every day. Dictionary definitions are equally broad. The following definition, edited from the *Merriam-Webster Online Dictionary*, showcases such breadth.

> gam·ble
> Function: *verb*
> Etymology: probably back-formation from *gambler,* probably alteration of obsolete *gamner,* from obsolete *gamen* (to play)
>
> *intransitive senses*
> 1 a: to play a game for money or property
>    b: to bet on an uncertain outcome
>
> 2: to stake something on a contingency: take a chance
>
> *transitive senses*
> 1: to risk by gambling; wager
> 2: venture, hazard.

More specific forms of gambling, however, are often covered more tightly by legal definitions. Consider, for example, the definition of "lottery," a term that appears, undefined, in the constitutions of many American states.

> lot·tery
> Function: *noun*
> Etymology: Middle French *loterie,* from Middle Dutch, from *lot* lot; akin to Old English *hlot* lot
> 1 a: a drawing of lots in which prizes are distributed to the winners among persons buying a chance
>    b: a drawing of lots used to decide something
>
> 2: an event or affair whose outcome is or seems to be determined by chance.

Aside from the basic dictionary definitions, courts have often been required to make their own definitions of these terms. This Chapter will offer more exacting definitions of the term by examining how courts have defined perhaps the broadest and most important term in U.S. gaming law. That term "lottery" is important because many American state constitutions specifically contained provisions banning "lotteries." The term "lottery" has been construed more broadly in courts than it appears in popular usage. As a result, state constitutional prohibitions on lotteries have swept in broader forms of gambling than what might be considered in casual conversation, a "lottery." From repeated cases construing this term as it appears in state constitutions and other state and federal laws, the definition of "lottery" has become, in effect, the general definition of gambling in U.S. law.

## A.  THE ELEMENT OF CONSIDERATION

### GEIS v. CONTINENTAL OIL CO.

**Supreme Court of Utah**
**511 P.2d 725 (1973)**

CALLISTER, Chief Justice:

Plaintiffs initiated this action to recover the prize they claimed that they had won according to the rules in a promotional contest sponsored by defendant. The matter was tried before a jury, and a verdict was rendered awarding plaintiffs general damages of $1,000, and punitive damages of $1,500. The trial court ordered in the alternative a new trial or that plaintiffs agree to a reduction in the verdict from $2,500 to $1,000; the plaintiffs elected the latter. Defendant appeals, urging that the trial court erred when it denied defendant's motion for a judgment notwithstanding the verdict on the ground that plaintiffs had not complied with the rules of the contest by submitting legible entry cards.

Defendant had a promotional contest called "Brand in Orbit." Defendant's service station dealers distributed to customers small cards upon which there was situated spots covered with paper concealing thereunder printing which became visible when the paper was scraped with a coin. The card was divided into two sections, the winning combination in the upper section provided prizes in amounts of 50¢ to $5. The lower portion had one large spot which concealed one word. The object of the contest on the lower portion was to acquire a group of cards which in combination would reveal one of defendant's advertising slogans, such as, "Brand in Orbit," prize $2,500; "Ride the Hot One," $1,000; "Hottest Brand Going," $100; and "Go With Conoco," $25.

The contest was open to all licensed drivers; no purchase was necessary; and the game cards were free. Mrs. Geis was interested solely in the prizes to be awarded in the contest on the lower half of the card. Through her own patronage as well as that of her husband and his employees at defendant's service stations, she acquired 522 cards. According to the testimony of Mrs. Geis, she obtained two cards, which, when scraped, the word "HOT" appeared and then vanished; her husband witnessed this occurrence once. "HOT" was the control word in the slogan "Ride the Hot One." Mrs. Geis took her cards to defendant's agent and claimed the prize of $1,000. Defendant declined to make the award on the ground that the printing was illegible.

During the course of the trial, defendant presented evidence to the effect that there were special markings only discernible under ultra violet light on the control cards, and the two cards submitted by plaintiffs had neither the markings nor the indentations resulting therefrom. Defendant's expert was of the opinion that a sharp instrument had obliterated the printing on the cards urged by plaintiffs to be winners.

The trial court instructed the jury that if it found from a preponderance of the evidence that the two cards in question or either of them had the word "HOT" in the appropriate place and that plaintiffs had complied with the terms of the contest, they were entitled to recover. Furthermore, if they found that the winning cards were deliberately so devised and constructed that when rubbed in accordance with the instructions the lucky word appeared dimly or illegibly and upon further rubbing disappeared, the jury might award exemplary damages.

On appeal, defendant urges that under the rules of the contest, plaintiffs were not winners. Defendant claims there was no evidence that the cards had been deliberately designed so that the winning words would disappear. Defendant cites authority to the effect that the rights of a contestant in a prize contest are limited by the terms of the offer, and there must be compliance with those terms before a contract is formed. The rules of the contest provided that all game cards are void if illegible, mutilated, forged, tampered with or irregular in any way. Defendant reasons that plaintiffs submitted two cards with the printing obliterated, which did not constitute performance of the act required, submitting legible cards; therefore, plaintiffs did not accept in accordance with defendant's offer, and there was no contract.

* * *

[T]he first task facing a contestant seeking to enforce rights allegedly acquired in a prize-winning contest is that of showing that the scheme was legal, for the courts uniformly refuse to lend their aid in the enforcement of an illegal agreement. In other words, since no action can be based on an illegal agreement, no private rights can arise from participating in a prize-winning contest, which is considered illegal, such as a lottery, which has been prohibited by constitutional or legislative provisions. . . .

Article VI, Section 28, Constitution of Utah, provides:

> The Legislature shall not authorize any game of chance, lottery or gift enterprise under any pretense or for any purpose.

Section 76-27-9, U.C.A.1953, provides:

> A lottery is any scheme for the disposal or distribution of property by chance among persons who have paid or promised to pay any valuable consideration for the chance of obtaining such property or a portion of it, or for any scheme or any interest in such property, upon any agreement, understanding or expectation that it is to be distributed or disposed of by lot or chance, whether called a lottery, raffle or gift enterprise, or by whatever name the same may be known.

Thus, the statutory elements of a lottery are: (1) Prize; (2) chance; (3) any valuable consideration. In the instant action the elements of chance and prize are obvious but was there any valuable consideration?

[In *State ex rel. Schillberg v. Safeway Stores, Inc.*, 450 P.2d 949 (Wash. 1969), a state with similar constitutional and statutory provisions, the issue was whether a game called "Bonus Bingo" was a lottery or merely an advertising device of a type widely employed in merchandising.] As in the instant case, to participate in "Bonus Bingo" and to have a chance to win a prize, one received the slips and booklets free of charge without the necessity of making a purchase.

The court observed that the Constitution of Washington prohibited any lottery; and, therefore, it would survey closely any scheme or device which appeared even superficially to be a lottery and to apply the constitutional ban to all of them which in fact amounted to a lottery. The court . . . expressed a belief that [the lottery ban] was controlling in Bonus Bingo, for . . . the fact that prizes were to be won would attract persons to Safeway and to its advertising.

The Washington court explained that the visit to the Safeway Store and a perusal of the promoter's advertising . . . amounted to a consideration moving from player to promoter. The players wagered their time, attention, thought, energy and money spent in transportation to the store for a chance to win a prize — all of which constituted a valuable consideration moving from the players to the promoter.

It is true that in some jurisdictions it has been held that a lottery is a special kind of contract, which requires a special kind of consideration, such as money or its equivalent, which will impoverish the individual who parts with it. However, in light of this state's constitutional mandate and legislative enactments pursuant thereto, this court would be engaging in some type of sophistry to hold that there was consideration present to support a bargain but not to provide the element of consideration to constitute a lottery.

Since plaintiffs cannot establish their claim independent of a transaction prohibited by law, the courts cannot grant them relief. The judgment of the trial court is reversed, and this cause is remanded with an order to dismiss the action. No costs are awarded.

CROCKETT, Justice (dissenting, but concurring in result):

There are some persuasive reasons why I cannot agree to the disposition of this case on the ground stated in the main opinion. . . . [I]t is at least questionable whether the giving away of such cards free for the asking, and the awarding of free prizes, constitutes a transaction so fraught with illegality and moral turpitude that a court should refuse to enforce it. However, assuming that this plan might be held to be illegal, there would arise this further problem: whether the person who created it and accepted full performance, could assert it as a defense against an innocent party who had fully performed. We have previously had occasion to comment on this subject in the case of *McCormick v. Life Insurance Corp. of America*, 308 P.2d 949 (1957). We there stated that in determining whether such a contract should be enforced a number of factors should be considered in each individual case:

> (a) The degree of criminality or evil involved; (b) the moral quality of the conduct of the parties; (c) comparison between them as to guilt or innocence; (d) the equities between them; and (e) the effect upon third parties or the public.

Reflection upon the foregoing in connection with other aspects of the problem will suggest that in all likelihood defendant chose not to assert nor rely upon the defense of illegality for its own good and sufficient reasons. An important one is that it having created and used the extensive and expensive plan of promotion and advertising, and held out the inducement to the plaintiff (and presumably many others) to accept the defendant's offer by performance, its own sense of fairness and good conscience would restrain it from asserting any wrong it may have itself committed as a basis for refusing to fulfill its promises to the public. With that thought I am in hearty accord. If it is to be assumed that the defendant is a wrongdoer, it seems to me discordant with principles of equity and justice to permit it to accept whatever benefits it may have obtained by inducing performance by innocent parties, and then repudiate its promise.[4] It is small wonder that the company never asserted nor relied upon such a defense which would in effect be saying: we are not only wrongdoers, but deceivers and defaulters.

It is unnecessary to establish bad precedents as to both of the propositions I have stated above. It has the potentially troublesome and unfair effect of deciding an important issue without giving the parties an opportunity to present evidence, or to argue and brief the matter, and without giving the trial court an opportunity to rule thereon. This seems particularly undesirable because there are so many advertising and promotion plans of this general character that such a ruling may have such far-reaching effects upon business and commerce. . . .

The plaintiff had to meet one simple and basic requirement: that she obtain, present and exhibit to the defendant cards upon which the required words, "Ride the Hot One," were "legible." There is no evidence whatsoever that when the cards in question were presented the word "hot" was legible. The contention is that the word had been on the two cards plaintiff presented, but that it had disappeared. It is thus plainly and indisputably shown by the evidence that the plaintiff failed to meet the requirement of the defendant's offer.

Inasmuch as the verdict is inconsistent with the observable and incontrovertible facts, I am persuaded that this is a situation where it is necessary that the verdict and judgment be corrected. I therefore agree to the reversal.

## NOTES

1. Under general principles of contract law, the outcome of a decision may depend on the framing of the issue, as will be seen in the next case. Note that consideration is a term well understood in the law. It is also an element of a contract. Indeed, absent consideration, there is generally no enforceable contract. In modern contract law, however, the need for consideration has been watered down

---

4. Where the contract is not so inherently evil or immoral as to be *malum in se* and therefore against public policy, it seems to me that there is no valid reason why its creator should be permitted to urge its illegality. He should be estopped to do so.

substantially, in two ways. First, the scope of what might count as consideration has been viewed very broadly. A mere peppercorn can constitute consideration. Second, under the doctrine of promissory estoppel, a promise that fails to be recognized as a "contract" may nevertheless be enforceable if the promisee has taken action in reliance on the promise. Should consideration be interpreted differently in contract law than in gaming law? Does the element of consideration serve the same purpose in each context?

2. Do "time, attention, thought, energy and money spent in transportation to the store" constitute consideration? The majority placed the plaintiff in a Catch-22. If there was no consideration then there was no enforceable contract. But if there was consideration, it established an illegal contract.

3. How do you think the dissenting judge in *Geis* would have ruled on the legality question if it had been raised properly? Would he have been likely to find the contract illegal under the test that he offered? What is the evil that a gambling contract presents?

## ALBERTSON'S, INC. v. HANSEN

### Supreme Court of Utah
### 600 P.2d 982 (1979)

DURHAM, J.

Plaintiff, a retail grocery chain, filed this action for a declaratory judgment, seeking a determination that its retail sales promotion known as "Double Cash Bingo" was not within the definitions of "gambling" or "lottery" in Sec. 76-10-1101 of the Penal Code.

* * *

Double Cash Bingo was described as a game in which the player is given a bingo-type card and a disc containing numbers under opaque covers. The player uncovers the numbers on the disc. If the numbers can be placed in a winning bingo pattern on the card, the player receives a designated cash prize. The cards and discs were distributed at Albertson's locations free of charge to anyone requesting them. No purchase was required to obtain them and a review of the record does not disclose any circumstance which would prohibit a player from obtaining them by mail and thus participating in the game without even entering upon plaintiff's premises. The record shows further, however, that plaintiff experienced substantial increases in sales which it attributed to the success of the advertising and promotional aspects of the Double Cash Bingo program.

Albertson's was threatened with criminal prosecution, if the game were not discontinued. Albertson's discontinued the game and initiated this action. . . .

The issue before the Court is whether or not the promotional scheme described above constitutes an illegal lottery within the meaning of Section 76-27-9 and Article VI, Section 27, Constitution of Utah. . . . [Section 27 of the Constitution] provides: The Legislature shall not authorize any game of chance, lottery or gift enterprise under any pretense or for any purpose.

This Court has the responsibility of determining the elements of a "lottery" as set forth in that constitutional provision. Those elements have been well established in Utah and are virtually the same as are set forth in the statutory definition of a lottery contained in Section 76-10-1101(2) as enacted in 1973:

> (2) "Lottery" means any scheme for the disposal or distribution of property by chance among any persons who have paid or promised to pay any valuable consideration for the chance of obtaining property, or portion of it, or for any share or any interest in property, upon any agreement, understanding, or expectation that it is to be distributed or disposed of by lot or chance, whether called a lottery, raffle, or gift enterprise, or by whatever name it may be known.

It can be seen that from the above definition that, to be a lottery, this scheme must involve "property" (or "prize"), distribution by "chance," and the payment of "any valuable consideration for the chance." The existence of property to be distributed by chance here is obvious; the remaining question is whether Double Cash Bingo necessitates or involves the payment of any valuable consideration for the opportunity to play and the chance to win.

Defendants argue, and a minority of courts in other jurisdictions have held, that the combination of inconvenience, effort, time, transportation expense and "sacrificed alternatives" (such as traveling to another shopping location) on the part of players, with the increased profits received by the promoter because of the patronage, sales and general goodwill generated by the scheme, constitutes "consideration" within the meaning of the definition of a "lottery" under our statute.

This analysis, however, appears to overlook an important portion of our statutory language. A "lottery" in Utah does not exist merely by virtue of the presence of valuable consideration flowing to or from any element in the transaction. Rather, the statute specifically and directly requires the payment or promise to pay "any valuable consideration *for the chance* of obtaining property." The exchange contemplated is the giving of something of value in return for the chance to win. The dispositive issue, therefore, is not what the promoter receives but what the player parts with. The participant in Double Cash Bingo acquires a chance to win by obtaining a disc and a card. He gives no more for that than the mere request. Although Albertson's received considerable benefits indirectly from the program, those benefits are not given, exchanged, or paid by customers or consumers in order to receive their chance to win. The profits to Albertson's are not "paid . . . for the chance of obtaining property" and thus cannot be part of the "valuable consideration" required by our statute to find a lottery.

Under this analysis, the only remaining elements of valuable consideration are the time, effort, inconvenience, and exercise of choice by participants. A majority of courts in other jurisdictions have found such elements to fall short of the requirements of valuable consideration. *Cudd v. Aschenbrenner,* [377 P.2d 150 (Or. 1962)] is illustrative of the majority rule, wherein the Oregon court presented the following analysis:

> No one could be rendered poor by participating in the plaintiffs' drawings. The worst that could happen to anyone would be that he would buy some groceries. But, if he purchased any, he would do so not in order to qualify himself as a participant in the drawing—for participation was free—but voluntarily. His purchase would not enhance in the slightest degree his chances upon the drawings. Participation in the drawings could not become for him a gambling tendency. There was nothing that anyone could do that would improve his prospects of winning. . . . In order to participate in the drawings it was not necessary for anyone to spend a nickel in the store or in any other place. Tickets for the drawings and tickets to the parking lot (where the drawings occurred) were not for sale. They were free. Anyone who wished to do so could enter the parking lot and watch, free of charge, the drawings take place. This promotional scheme is a mere means of drawing customers to the plaintiff's stores. . . . The scheme is not a lottery although the prize money is distributed by chance. It is not a lottery because there is no consideration which is in any way harmful to the participant. The participant parts with nothing of any value to himself.

The court in that case also observed that nothing can be regarded as consideration unless it is so viewed and treated by both parties, and that, where no purchase is required to participate, neither party to the transaction believed the customer's efforts in participation constituted any valuable consideration.

To find that the effort required to pick up or obtain a card and disc from Albertson's alone is valuable consideration would invalidate any distribution-by-chance scheme for any property whatsoever where the participant is required to expend the slightest effort—mailing of a registration ticket, for example, or presence at a drawing. The "consideration" paid by Double Cash Bingo players would appear to be indistinguishable from that expended by participants in any number of drawings and distributions conducted in this state.[1] Without more, the "*valuable* consideration" required by our statute cannot be said to have been paid or required, and the scheme does not constitute a "lottery" prohibited by the Utah Constitution.

MAUGHAN, Dissenting.

For the following reasons, I dissent. The majority opinion relies on a most novel form of construction, restricting the language of a broad mandatory constitutional interdiction against lotteries to the current statutory definition. The majority proclaims it is the responsibility of this Court to determine the elements of a "lottery" as that term is set forth in the constitution, and then abdicates the responsibility and abandons precedent to restrict the term "any valuable consideration" to further conditions as set forth in the statute. In my view, it is not wise to toy with a term so vital to our law, as consideration. Certainly, we should not judicially redefine it for the purpose of skirting the mandate of the constitution.

This interpretation, which restricts further the meaning of consideration, is antithetical to the command and intent of Article VI, Section 27, Constitution of Utah, viz., the legislature shall not authorize a lottery "*under any pretense or for any purpose.*"

If consideration may be restricted to a pecuniary basis, rather than the legal definition of the term, why may not the legislature declare any amount under fifty dollars shall not be deemed consideration? Why may not the legislature designate that any money contributed to a lottery conducted by a charitable organization be deemed a contribution and not consideration, although a sizeable prize may be awarded? The intent is clear, any scheme involving a prize, chance, and consideration is prohibited, and no matter how cleverly devised or characterized the plan (such as deeming it a promotional game), the blanket constitutional proscription is applicable.... Owing to the societal impact of the issues here presented, I deal with them in extenso....

Under the *Geis* case plaintiff's promotional game would constitute a lottery, although the contestants paid no consideration in the form of pecuniary value to participate. The time, effort, attention and money

---

1. Examples include the common everyday drawings conducted on local television, at church and club socials, as well as *state* drawings conducted to distribute sporting event tickets or game licenses, all of which we can properly take judicial notice[.]

spent in transportation journeying to the store was consideration moving from the players to the promoter. The benefits moving to plaintiff
in the form of increased sales and good will in response to this promotional device also amounted to a valuable consideration. [Plaintiff had
alleged that shutting down the Double Cash Bingo game would cost
them $250,000 per week]. . . .

Plaintiff contends the concept of "valuable consideration" set forth
in *Geis* has been nullified by the subsequent enactment [of Section 76-
10-1101 of the Utah Code,] which provides:

> Definitions.—For the purpose of this part: (1) "Gambling" means risk-
> ing anything of value for a return or risking anything of value upon the
> outcome of a contest, game, gaming scheme, or gaming device when
> the return or outcome is based upon an element of chance and is in
> accord with an agreement or understanding that someone will receive
> something of value in the event of a certain outcome, and gambling
> includes a lottery; gambling does not include: (a) A lawful business
> transaction[.] . . .

> (2) "Lottery" means any scheme for the disposal or distribution of
> property by chance among persons who have paid or promised to pay
> any valuable consideration for the chance of obtaining property, or
> portion of it, or for any share or any interest in property, upon any
> agreement, understanding, or expectation that it is to be distributed
> or disposed of by lot or chance, whether called a lottery, raffle, or gift
> enterprise, or by whatever name it may be known.

> (3) "Gambling bet" means money, checks, credit, or any other repre-
> sentation of value.

Plaintiff urges that to constitute "gambling" under the new statute
the "value" which must be risked is limited to something of pecuniary value as defined in subdivision (3) under the term "gambling
bet," viz., money, checks, credit, or the equivalent thereto. Since
the participants in plaintiff's promotional contest do not risk
anything of pecuniary value, it is claimed that "gambling" is not
involved.

In subdivision (2) the legislature retained the prior statutory definition of "lottery" as contained in Section 76-27-9. In subdivision (1)
of the current statute "gambling" is defined in terms of risking
anything of "value," while the definition of "lottery" contemplates
a person taking a chance and paying "any valuable consideration."
Plaintiff urges the elements set forth in the definition of "gambling"
also limit the elements of "lottery" because subdivision (1) of the
statute provides "gambling includes lottery."

The term "includes" is ordinarily a term of enlargement and not of limitation. The term "including" as a word of enlargement, implies that something else has been given beyond the general language which precedes it; that it adds to the general clause a species which does not naturally belong to it; that it is the equivalent of "also."

Thus the provision in subdivision (1) stating that "gambling includes a lottery" enlarges the definition of gambling insofar as a lottery is concerned to embrace the specific elements of a lottery as set forth in the definition in subdivision (2). In other words, subdivision (1) should be read as defining "gambling" as it is set forth in both (1) and (2). Furthermore, since a type of gambling called a "lottery" is specifically defined, the specific definition controls over the more general definition of "gambling." The new statutory provisions set forth in Section 76-10-1101, do not compel a decision limiting the terms "any valuable consideration" to a consideration of pecuniary value.

Plaintiff contends its promotional device is exempt under subdivision (1)(a) of 76-10-1101 as "a lawful business transaction." Article VI, Section 27, Constitution of Utah prohibits in the broadest language, in mandatory terms, legislative authorization of *any* lottery "under any pretense or for any purpose." If, in fact, any scheme embraces the elements of a lottery, the legislature cannot avoid the constitutional prohibition by vague or inapt definitions or creating exemptions. . . .

\* \* \*

Plaintiff further contends the ruling in the *Geis* case is unsound and should be disavowed by this Court. There is a distinct division of authority as to what constitutes sufficient consideration to support a lottery. Some courts hold any consideration which will support a simple contract is sufficient to constitute a lottery and mere participation in a scheme may provide such consideration. Another group of courts have held although no purchase of merchandise is necessary to participation, if any participants in the promotional scheme are also customers of the sponsoring store, the consideration present is sufficient to render the scheme a lottery as to all the participants. The third group of courts have held the consideration sufficient to support a lottery must have an economic value, and neither participation in a promotional scheme nor the inconvenience arising therefrom constitutes consideration.

The *Schillberg* case [*State ex rel. Schillberg v. Safeway Stores, Inc.*, 450 P.2d 949 (Wash. 1969)] and *Lucky Calendar Co. v. Cohen* [, 117 A.2d 487 (N.J. 1955)] are well reasoned and based on sound public policy; both adhere to the simple contract theory as a basis to find consideration in a scheme alleged to be a lottery. In the *Lucky Calendar* case the court observed the proposed scheme of advertising injected into a natural free market dealing with basic commodities of everyday living all of the distracting consequences of a lottery. The court expressed the public policy as follows:

> It is manifestly not in the public interest to permit the element of chance to control such a vital commodity as food, far-reaching as it is in its effect on the national economy. To do so, in the largest industry in the country would be to encourage a battle of industrial giants for increased business to the detriment of the public[.]

In *Schillberg*, the court stated:

> The antigambling laws are designed not only to prevent loss but to preclude some kinds of gain to the promoter of a lottery from reaping an unearned harvest at the expense of the players; to prevent the wary from preying upon the unwary; and to discourage the overly shrewd from exploiting the natural yearning in most everyone to get something for nothing; and to put a damper on the actions of those who receive from the device much more than they part with in prizes. If, under our mores, it is bad for a man to lose his property on pure chance or lot, it is equally bad for a man to gain property on the same pure chance or lot.

If the evil of gambling be the dissipation of resources which should be devoted to family purposes, then a merchant conducting a promotional scheme, such as, Double Cash Bingo, incites the same evil. A family of limited assets, rather than comparing prices to find the best value, will be distracted by the lure of a prize and patronize the establishment promoting a scheme based on chance. The promotional scheme is a guise designed to inveigle the unwary to spend family funds at one mercantile establishment, without giving adequate regard to the prices of the competitors. The interpretation of this Court in *Geis* of the term "valuable consideration" is consonant with the public policy and should not be disavowed. . . .

CROCKETT, C.J. Dissenting [joining the dissent with additional comments]:

. . . In regard to whether there is a consideration passing from its customers to the plaintiff: it is stated that there is none because the customer is free to choose whether he will go to plaintiff's store, and he pays nothing for the bingo card. I think any fair and realistic analysis of the situation will reveal that there is in fact a detriment to the customer, suffered at the request of the plaintiff, which passes as a benefit to the latter.

It would be fatuous beyond belief for anyone to argue that the plaintiff spends its many thousands of dollars on such a promotion without receiving anything of value therefrom. If the plaintiff does thus receive value in increasing its patronage, and it is absolutely certain that it does, the question arises: whence is derived this substantial material wealth it acquires. If it comes from nothing, the supply would seem to be quite inexhaustible. But in this practical world, the inexorable rule is that it is impossible to make something from nothing. It is equally inexorable that the thing of substantial value which comes to the plaintiff can come from only one source. That is, from the individual customers the game attracts to its store. This has to be true no matter how small the contribution of each individual customer may be.

Suppose two stores, A and B are side by side, and that all other factors which would draw customers are exactly equal. They should normally draw about an equal number of customers. But if store A provided the Double Cash Bingo by which its customers have a chance for a prize, it would draw more customers than store B. Now suppose that the stores are one mile apart. It would take some proportionally greater reward to induce customers nearer store B to go to store A; and as the distance between the stores increased, the inducement offered would have to be proportionally increased. By supposing increasing distances, it should be plain that there must be some real inducement for a customer to go to store A, rather than to store B. The logic is inescapable that in offering its Double Cash Bingo, store A must be giving something of sufficient value to persuade customers to go to its store, rather than to store B; and that each customer gives some benefit of at least equal value to plaintiff, otherwise we may be sure that plaintiff would not operate the game. Further, each customer who is thus induced to enter store A does something he would not otherwise do. Therefore, he thus suffers a detriment to that extent and so contributes his portion, however small that may be, to the total value received by the plaintiff in this Double Cash Bingo plan. It is thus inescapable that there is a consideration on both sides of the equation.

The argument that playing bingo to receive a reward based on chance is not a violation of the prohibitions of the constitution and the law, because it involved but minimal contribution and minor inconvenience to the customers, is simply the old but fallacious argument that a little violation of the law does no great harm and should be tolerated. It seems to me that the mere statement of the proposition destroys the argument. The real evil is that if a little violation of the law is thus countenanced, where and by whom is the line to be drawn between a little and a lot; and where will be the limitation on such schemes.

It is not surprising that due to certain propensities of human nature, the customer may want to get something for nothing, based on chance. But looked at realistically, this is no different in principle than putting a nickel in a slot machine with the same expectation; and this bingo plan can be nothing other than an attempt to delude the customers into believing they are getting something for nothing, based on chance.

A great deal more could be said about what I think are the evils of permitting businesses to depart from traditional values of business competition, based on quality of merchandise and service, and to substitute therefore the specious but hollow allurements of gambling and lotteries. It not only ignores the interdiction of our constitution, but it opens the way for the giants in merchandising, (which seem to be ever increasing in size) to engage in games with each other in attempting to delude the public into thinking they are getting something for nothing. Whereas, it is undeniable that, to the extent money is spent on bingo or other such illusory schemes, the public is actually deprived of that value in merchandise and services. In addition to those direct adverse effects upon the public, the majority decision provides a means for the giant chains to use these deceptive games of chance in unfair competition with the many small and independent operators, and thus drive them out of business, with the concomitant ramifying evils that result therefrom.

*NOTES*

1.  The majority found this to be an easy case, but it drew thoughtful dissenting opinions. Which side has the better argument based on principles of constitutional and statutory interpretation? On principles of contract law? On the "societal impact" of the issue?

2.  In Section 76-10-1101 of the Utah Code, the legislature defined the term "lottery." What is the effect of this definition in light of the use of the same term, undefined, in the Utah Constitution? Did the legislature appropriately define the scope of a term contained within the Constitution? May the legislature narrow the scope of the constitutional term?

3.  Does Albertson's "Double Cash Bingo" game constitute gambling? Why or why not? Are there significant risks that militate toward regulation or prohibition of such activity?

## GLICK v. MTV NETWORKS

### U.S. District Court, Southern District, New York
### 796 F. Supp. 743 (1992)

KEVIN THOMAS DUFFY, D.J.

Plaintiff Barry Glick commenced this civil action against defendant MTV Networks ("MTV") to recover damages for violations of New Jersey's gambling laws.[1] ... The facts are not in dispute. MTV is a division of Viacom International Inc., a corporation engaged in various entertainment and communications businesses. MTV offers several different programming networks, or channels. From August 12 through October 11, 1989, one of those channels, known as VH-1, sponsored a national promotional event in order to increase viewership. That event, a sweepstakes called the "VH-1 Corvette Collection" (the "Sweepstakes"), is the subject of this litigation.

The Sweepstakes was publicized over MTV channels, through the media and through publicity events conducted nationwide. Over 20,000 prizes, including inexpensive watches, T-shirts, hats and key chains, were awarded daily during the Sweepstakes. The grand prize was a choice of either a collection of 36 Corvette automobiles, one from each model year from 1953 to 1989, or a 1989 Corvette plus $200,000 in cash. There were three different ways of entering the Sweepstakes. Participants could: (1) call a "900" number, for which there was a $2 charge; (2) request a toll-free "800" number by mail; or, (3) complete and mail in an official entry blank.

Whichever way they entered, participants could enter as often as they wished, were eligible for daily prizes, and had an equal chance of winning. Over one million people entered the Sweepstakes: 136,506 by way of the mail-in entry blank, 30,094 by dialing the "800" number, and 1,065,624 by calling the "900" number. Bonus prizes were awarded daily by random selection throughout the Sweepstakes. On October 14, 1989, the grand prize winner was selected at random by an

---

1. N.J. Stat. Ann. §2A:40-6 provides:

If the person who shall lose and pay such money, or lose and deliver such thing or things as aforesaid [i.e., as stated in N.J. Stat. Ann. 2A:40-5], shall not, within [6 calendar months after payment or delivery], without collusion, sue for the money or other thing or things so lost and paid, or delivered, any other person may sue for and recover the same, with costs of suit, from such winner, depositary or stakeholder as aforesaid; the one moiety thereof to the use of the person suing for the same, and the other moiety to the use of the state; provided the action is instituted within 6 calendar months from and after the expiration of the time [stated above] for the loser to sue for the same.

independent organization. The winner opted for the collection of 36 Corvettes.

* * *

Glick alleges that the Sweepstakes was prohibited under New Jersey law. Glick argues:

> At the heart of MTV's gambling scheme was the otherwise innocent telephone. In the most basic terms, MTV induced people to place their wagers by simply calling a telephone number with a "900" prefix. Callers to "900" telephone numbers . . . automatically incur a predetermined charge for the call. In this case the charge was $2.00. The charge then appears on the callers' monthly telephone bill as an obligation owed to the carrier that provided the number. Once collected the revenue is split between the carrier . . . and [MTV]. MTV essentially relied upon the telephone company to be its runner in exchange for a cut of the take.

Stripped of its veneer of respectability, Glick continues, the Sweepstakes was nothing more than a nefarious gambling scheme whereby participants were unwittingly lured, by the prospect of a big return, into placing $2 wagers.

Glick argues that the Sweepstakes: (a) was an unlawful gambling scheme under the New Jersey constitution[7] and [laws], and alternatively, (b) was a lottery in violation of New Jersey law. . . .

The current New Jersey criminal . . . code defines "gambling" to mean staking or risking something of value upon the outcome of a contest of chance or a future contingent event not under the actor's control or influence, upon an agreement or understanding that he will receive something of value in the event of a certain outcome[.]

The code defines "lottery" to mean: an unlawful gambling scheme in which (a) the players pay or agree to pay something of value for chances, represented and differentiated by numbers or by combinations of numbers or by some other media, one or more of which chances are to be designated the winning ones; and (b) the winning chances are to be determined by a drawing or by some other method based upon the element of chance; and (c) the holders of the winning chances are to receive something of value[.]

Construing the relevant statutory and constitutional provisions, the New Jersey courts have identified three components of "gambling":

---

7. The New Jersey constitution precludes the legislature from authorizing "gambling of any kind" unless the "specific kind, restrictions, and control thereof" have been approved by the electorate at a general referendum.

chance, prize, and price.[9] The current statutory definitions of both "gambling" and "lottery" require that "something of value" be risked. The criminal code defines the term "something of value" to mean:

> any money or property, any token, object or article exchangeable for money or property, or any form of credit or promise directly or indirectly contemplating transfer of money or property or of any interest therein, or involving extension of a service, entertainment or a privilege of playing at a game or scheme without charge. This definition, however, does not include any form of promise involving extension of a privilege of playing at a game without charge on a mechanical or amusement device, other than a slot machine as an award for the attainment of a certain score on that device. N.J. Stat. Ann. §2c:37-1(d).

Thus, there is no gambling under New Jersey law if the participant is not required to risk "something of value." Historically, the New Jersey courts have struggled to interpret what "something of value" means. See New Jersey Att'y General Formal Opinion No. 6-1983 at n.2 ("Over the decades the courts in New Jersey have struggled to specify the outermost boundary of the 'something of value' concept"). The parties have not cited, and this court has not found, any New Jersey state court decision construing the 1978 statutory definition of "something of value." That the statutory definition is not entirely free of ambiguity only further complicates the task of interpretation. See id. (recognizing ambiguity in current definition).

The New Jersey Attorney General has opined, however, that the current statutory definition of "something of value" seems to encompass money or property, or tangibles or intangibles, including personal services, standing in their stead. Id. This opinion went on to state that the phrasing of the statute indicates that the "legislative intent was to exclude from the statutory elements comprising the gambling offense the sort of personal inconvenience which will constitute consideration sufficient to support a contract." Id. Cf. *Lucky Calendar v. Cohen*, 19 N.J. 399, 117 A.2d 487 (N.J. 1955) (finding consideration not necessary element of "lottery" as defined by then-

---

9. New Jersey has a clear, long-standing and comprehensive policy against gambling. However, New Jersey's sweeping constitutional prohibition against all types of gambling has, over the years, been modified by constitutional amendment approved by a general referendum legalizing certain types of gambling activities. *See, e.g., Atlantic City Racing Ass'n v. Att'y General*, 98 N.J. 535, 489 A.2d 165, 167-170 (N.J. 1985) (tracing history of state's constitutional and legislative actions regarding gambling); *see also Caribe Hilton Hotel v. Toland*, 63 N.J. 301, 307 A.2d 85, 88 (N.J. 1973) ("our public policy no longer can be said to condemn gambling per se. Rather our policy has become one of carefully regulating certain permitted forms of gambling while prohibiting all others entirely.").

existing statute. Alternatively, if consideration were necessary element, consideration present where participant filled in and delivered entry coupon).

For purposes of its motion, MTV concedes that its Sweepstakes was a game of chance in which the winners were entitled to prizes. It maintains, however, that because the participants in the Sweepstakes were not required to give "something of value" (i.e., price) to enter, the Sweepstakes was neither an illegal gambling scheme nor a lottery.

The Sweepstakes' official rules did not require that participants risk "something of value" because alternative cost-free means of entry were reasonably available. One or both of the cost-free methods of entry were publicized in the promotional spots aired several times a day over MTV channels, in the advertisements MTV took out in national magazines, through coverage of the Sweepstakes in newspapers and magazines, and on the free entry blanks distributed through Camelot Music stores and at promotional events.[10] Further, the official rules explicitly stated that no purchase was necessary to enter and that all those who entered had an equal chance of winning. Finally, as many as 166,600 people entered the contest [without charge] through the "800" number or by entry blank.

Glick argues that while MTV may technically have provided alternative means of entering the Sweepstakes, it carefully crafted its promotion so that most entries would come through the "900" number. That approximately 87 per cent of the participants utilized the "900" number, Glick maintains, evidences the success of MTV's promotional slant. Glick further states that, in late September, 1989, he mailed separate requests for a copy of the rules and for the toll-free "800" number. His request for the toll free number was never honored, and he received a copy of the rules only after the contest was over. From these facts, Glick concludes that the "alternate means of entry, while facially supporting an argument that the contest was 'free' did, in fact, either require a participant to give something of value or subjected the participant utilizing the alternate means with a disadvantaged opportunity to win."

The record does not support Glick's contentions. Participants had two months in which to enter the Sweepstakes. Thus, the only people conceivably disadvantaged by utilizing either the "800" number or the mail-in entry forms were those who, having heard about the Sweepstakes in its last days, were not able to meet the October 3 deadline for

10. While there is no question that MTV's promotional information, including its video advertisements, placed primary emphasis on the "900" number, the fact remains that alternative, cost-free methods of entering were available for those who wished to use them.

requesting the "800" number or not able to mail in their entry blank by October 11. In an extensively publicized sweepstakes lasting two months, such a class of people simply are statistically insignificant. More importantly, as all those who entered had an equal chance of winning, there was no risk that certain entrants would secure a more favorable position than others. In sum, Glick has failed to establish the "something of value," or price, element necessary to his gambling claim.[12]

In sum, I do not believe that a $2.00 charge for using a "900" number to phone in an entry to a sweepstakes, when cost-free means of entering are also available, is the type of activity that the State of New Jersey currently proscribes under its gambling laws. While certainly not determinative, that the State chose not to prosecute Viacom or MTV supports this belief. For the foregoing reasons, MTV's motion for summary judgment dismissing the complaint is granted, and Glick's cross-motion for partial summary judgment is denied.

## NOTES

1. MTV and the telephone company earned gross revenues of more than $2 million by virtue of the 900 number. Isn't it clear that the players who play by dialing the 900 number and incurring a $2 charge are paying "something of value" to play a lottery? On what basis is it relevant that others are playing for free? Is this decision correct?

2. A typical state lottery, which involves the sale of chances to win a prize based on a random drawing, clearly involves the three elements discussed above: consideration, chance, and prize. The patron provides consideration in paying the cost of the ticket. Because the numbers are selected randomly, the winning number is chosen by chance. The prize is the jackpot that the player seeks to win. To avoid presenting all three elements, a privately conducted promotional sweepstakes typically offers a chance to play without providing consideration, reflecting the common refrain "no purchase necessary." Because they are based on random drawings and offer valuable prizes, the elements of chance and reward are almost always present. If an offeror of such a sweepstakes required a purchase to play, consideration presumably would be present, and

---

12. Further, while not necessary to my ruling, I would agree with MTV that the "cost" of utilizing the "900" number is the type of "lesser act of personal inconvenience" which is excluded from the "something of value" concept.

the sweepstakes would be an illegal lottery under the laws of most states. See Ronald J. Rychlak, *Lotteries, Revenues and Social Costs: A Historical Examination of State-Sponsored Gambling*, 34 B.C. L. REV. 11, 14-15 (1992). If eliminating consideration in such a fashion as in the *Albertson's* and *MTV Networks* cases can render a sweepstakes legal, what insight does this provide as to the purpose that the consideration element generally serves? What social ill is being addressed by the consideration element? Why did this court conclude that there was no consideration?

3.   While most states continue to prohibit private parties from engaging in for-profit lotteries, a majority of states have state-run lotteries, the proceeds of which are often dedicated to specific educational, social, or environmental state programs. If lotteries are lawful when offered by the state but illegal in other circumstances, what purposes do restrictive lottery laws serve in such a context? Does this provide any further insight about the purpose of the regulation of gambling?

## B.   THE ELEMENT OF CHANCE

### VALENTIN v. EL DIARIO LA PRENSA

**Civil Court of the City of New York, Bronx County**
**427 N.Y.S.2d 185 (1980)**

BLATT, J.

The defendant newspaper herein sponsored a voting contest late in 1979 to determine which of many entrants would be voted the "King of the Infants" or "Rey Infantil." The newspaper is published in the Spanish language and primarily services the Hispanic community of New York City.

Purchasers of the paper at a newsstand cost of 25 cents receive a coupon in each edition which entitles them to vote for the infant of their preference, and to cast 25 votes for each coupon they obtain from the paper. They may vote as many coupons as they purchase. In addition, individuals may go to the offices of the newspaper on Hudson Street in Manhattan and purchase individual pages of the newspaper containing the coupon at a cost of 17 cents. This admittedly was for the purpose of allowing those who did not want to purchase the newspaper in its entirety and whose motivation was merely to obtain extra ballots to vote for their favorite infant. Oral testimony at the trial indicated that large numbers of people came in to purchase quantities of single pages containing the voting coupon.

It is clear that this was a most successful promotion. Defendant displayed a thick sheaf of invoices indicating those who had come in to purchase quantities of single pages containing the coupon with which to cast large quantities of votes for their favorite entrant.

Claimant came into defendant's offices on Hudson Street during business hours on December 11, 1979 and paid $1,000 for single newspaper sheets containing voting coupons. She then subsequently proceeded to vote them all for her son. On that same evening the contest closed. The following day, claimant came back to the offices of the newspaper and demanded her money back. This was refused and she commenced this action to recoup her $1,000. Subsequently, her son won a runner-up prize of $500, which is allegedly being held by the newspaper. The complaint alleges a refusal to return the money after cancellation.

Defendant's memorandum of law contends that the contest as described herein is not a lottery and therefore not against the public policy of the State of New York. It is described as a "voting contest" with no element of chance, and only a mathematical calculation utilized to determine the winner. Cases are cited primarily from sister States, none of which are on all fours with the matter at hand.

Defendant also contends that the prize herein was to go to a contestant, not to a voter and that therefore it cannot be a lottery. They additionally claim that the infant winners furnish no consideration for the prize and that since one of the elements of a lottery is consideration paid by the winner for a "chance," that this cannot therefore be a lottery.

The definition of a lottery in New York State is set forth in a number of cases including *People v. Miller*, 271 N.Y. 44. It indicates that there are three elements necessary to constitute a lottery: (1) consideration, (2) chance, and (3) a prize.

Defendants basically contend that the two elements of consideration and chance were not present, and that therefore, the "voting contest" herein could not be constituted as a lottery.

It is not always crystal clear as to whether or not the element of chance is present. It has been held in our courts that "a business promotion scheme is not a lottery because of the motive for the scheme." On the other hand, if prizes are awarded, and chance determines the winner, a business promotion scheme will be held to be a lottery where, regardless of the subtlety of the device employed, it can be shown as a matter of fact that the scheme in actual operation results in payment, in the great majority of cases of something of value for the opportunity to participate. *People v. Psallis,* 12 N.Y.S.2d 796.

For another example, see *People ex rel. Ellison v. Lavin,* 179 N.Y. 164. In that case it was held that a contest to guess the number of cigars on which the United States would collect taxes during the month of November, 1903, was a lottery, where entrants were required to submit cigar bands to qualify, because chance rather than judgment was the dominating factor in the award of prizes.

There is something clearly analogous in the matter at hand. The critical factor herein is the ability of the public to purchase individual newspaper sheets with the coupon thereon for the price of 17 cents and thereupon "vote" their choice. Logic forces us to conclude that this opportunity to buy single voting coupons in demonstrated large quantities was not in order to vote for "King of the Infants" in an objective sense, but rather in a race prior to deadline to see who could buy the greatest number of votes for their loved one regardless of the contestant's "regal" attributes.

The court feels that the language in part of the last cited case applies; chance rather than judgment was the dominating factor in the award of prizes. The chance was in purchasing and voting more coupons than others. The single sheets provided the opportunity.

Although the complaint asked for cancellation of the contract and did not plead illegality, this does not divest the court of that right when the agreement is antagonistic to the interests of the public. . . .

The winners are not chosen on their personal qualities, but rather on whether or not their loved ones can get together enough money to beat the competition in buying sufficient 17-cent coupons. Here also chance rather than judgment was the dominating factor.

Upon all of the above, the court finds that the sale of voting coupons as described herein is void as against public policy. Judgment in the amount of $1,000 is awarded to the claimant. Since the alleged contest herein has been declared void as against public policy, the award of a prize is nullified.

*NOTES*

1.  *Valentin* is indeed a contest, but is it a game of chance? If not, why not?
2.  Does the activity in *Valentin* present the same kind of harms that are ordinarily present in gambling?

## PEOPLE v. HUNT

### New York City Criminal Court
### 162 Misc. 2d 70, 616 N.Y.S.2d 168 (1994)

SHERYL L. PARKER, J.

Defendant is charged with possession of a gambling device (Penal Law §225.30 [2]) and promoting gambling in the second degree (Penal Law §225.05). The charges stem from allegations that defendant was running a game of three-card monte. Defendant moves to dismiss the accusatory instrument on the ground that it is facially insufficient. For the reasons set forth below, defendant's motion is granted.

The factual portion of the accusatory instrument reads as follows: "Deponent states that he observed the defendant standing alone behind a cardboard box with a small crowd standing around the defendant. Deponent further states that he observed the defendant manipulating cards by shuffling three cards, and encouraging pedestrians to place bets by handing an unapprehended individual a sum of U.S. currency, and stating in substance, 'He won again.' Deponent further states that based upon his training and experience, the defendant was engaged in an illegal street card game commonly known as 'three card monte.' Deponent further states that he recovered three playing cards from on top of the cardboard box."

A person is guilty of promoting gambling in the second degree "when he knowingly advances or profits from unlawful gambling activity." The crime of possession of a gambling device is set forth in Penal Law §225.30, and states that a person is guilty "when, with knowledge of the character thereof, he manufactures, sells, transports, places or possesses, or conducts or negotiates any transaction affecting or designed to affect ownership, custody or use of: . . . (2) Any other gambling device, believing that the same is to be used in the advancement of unlawful gambling activity."

Pivotal to the case at hand is whether the act of playing three-card monte constitutes "gambling" as defined in Penal Law §225.00(2). Gambling occurs when a person "stakes or risks something of value upon the outcome of a contest of chance or a future contingent event not under his control or influence, upon an agreement or understanding that he will receive something of value in the event of a certain outcome." A contest of chance is defined as "any contest, game, gaming scheme or gaming device in which the outcome depends in a material degree upon an element of chance, notwithstanding that skill of the contestants may also be a factor therein."

Defendant argues that three-card monte is a game of skill, and as such falls outside the definition of gambling. The People counter by contending that a commonsense understanding of the game, i.e., that the player has a one in three chance of winning, supports the conclusion that the game is one of chance. The People also argue that the question of whether it is a game of skill or chance is properly resolved by the trier of fact.

Although some games may involve both an element of skill and chance, where "the outcome depends in a material degree upon an element of chance," the game will be deemed a contest of chance.

Three-card monte is a game in which a dealer shows a player three cards and designates one of them as the "court" card. The dealer then turns the cards face down and moves them around on a flat surface. After watching the cards shuffled about, the player attempts to choose the "court" card. If he chooses this card he wins. If not, the dealer wins. The dealer banks on his ability to manipulate the cards faster than the player can track the cards with his eye, while the player stakes his wager on the opposite being true.

Absent trickery or deceit on the part of the dealer, i.e., palmed cards, the contest pits the skill level of the dealer in manipulating the cards against that of the player in visually tracking the card. Played fairly, skill rather than chance is the material component of three-card monte.

In some instances, the dealer has an advantage over the player, even when no trickery is involved. This occurs where there exists a disparity between the players' skill levels. Differing skill levels, however, do not transform the game into a contest of chance. (*People v. Fuerst*, 13 Misc. 304, 307 [Queens County Ct. 1895] [" 'fish pond game' seems to involve no element of chance, and calls wholly for the exercise of skill. . . . In most instances the chances are that the anglers will be found to be unskillful, but that would not make the result of the angling dependant upon chance"].)

By way of example, one could say that an amateur tennis player facing a title-holding champion may not have a "chance" of winning. In that context, the term "chance" denotes the probability of winning that the amateur has, not that tennis is a game of chance as opposed to a game of skill. Similarly, the People's argument, that because the player has a one in three chance of winning, the game is one of chance, rests on a definition of the term "chance" as it relates to probabilities. As almost all games involving either skill or chance, or a combination thereof, can be reduced to a statistical probability, this argument does not address the issue before the court. . . . The court is cognizant of the fact that many three-card monte games involve deception or trickery on the part of the dealer. Allegations of fraudulent behavior bring a dealer within the reach of the criminal law. However, as proof of this behavior may be difficult to secure, the Legislature might want to consider the viability of proscribing the mere act of playing three-card monte, as some States have done. . . .

For the aforementioned reasons, three-card monte is not a contest of chance, and consequently, does not fall within the definition of gambling. As gambling is an element of both counts charged in this case, the People have failed to establish a prima facie case. Defendant's motion to dismiss is granted.

## NOTES

1. Is the distinction between a game of chance and a game of skill real? If so, is it sensible? Does wagering on a game of chance present different social policy concerns than wagering on a game of skill? Does the distinction provide insight into the particular problem that these gambling laws are designed to address?

2. Other courts in New York have taken a different view of the game and declined to accept the chance versus skill dichotomy in the case of three-card monte. According to one of these courts, "the game does not enjoy a reputation for being played fairly even as a game of chance." *People v. Denson*, 192 Misc. 2d 48, 52 (N.Y. Crim. Ct. 2002). "[T]hree card monte masquerades as a game of skill in order to lure players, but in reality, it is *at best* a game of chance." To this court, it is much more likely to be a scheme of fraud than any kind of game. In July 1999, the New York City Council sought to end the confusion surrounding the legal status of three-card monte by unanimously approving legislation to outlaw the public operation of the game and its variants.

3. Assuming that the chance vs. skill distinction is legitimate, all human activities involve some elements of chance. How do we differentiate those activities for which chance is the predominant element from those in which skill predominates? Consider these questions as you read the next case.

## UTAH STATE FAIR ASS'N v. GREEN

### Supreme Court of Utah
### 249 P. 1016 (1926)

THURMAN, J.

[This action addressed the constitutionality of a Utah law which authorized horse racing, created a Horse Racing Commission, and authorized pari-mutuel wagering on those races. The Commissioners of the City of Salt Lake challenged the horse racing act under Section 28 of the Utah Constitution which says: "The Legislature shall not authorize any game of chance, lottery or gift enterprise under any pretense or for any purpose." The trial court found that the horse racing act does not authorize a game of chance in violation of the constitutional prohibition.]

It was stipulated by the parties, and found by the court, that the contention of the plaintiff was that horse racing is a game of skill, while the contention of defendants was that it is a game of chance. . . . Much is said in argument by respondents' counsel to the effect that [the horse racing act] is in conflict with the moral traditions and time-honored policy of the state. Such questions, in some cases, might have considerable weight in determining the probable intent of the Legislature in the passage of particular statutes, but we are unable to perceive what possible relevancy such matters can have in determining the questions presented in the instant case. The immediate question here is: Is horse racing . . . a game of chance? . . . It appears to be conceded that the great weight of judicial opinion throughout the country is to the effect that horse racing is a game. The parties here differ only on the question as to whether [betting on horse races through the use of a pari-mutuel system] is a game of chance.

[In pari-mutuel wagering,] persons can bet severally in denominations of $2, $5 and $10 each on "straight," "place," or "show," as used in racing parlance to indicate the position of the horses at the end of the race as coming in either first, second, [or] third, respectively. . . . As bets are placed with the ticket seller, the operator of [the pari-mutuel] machine registers the bet, and the indicator under the name and number of each horse shows the number of bets placed upon each horse respectively. As bets are received, the bettor is given a ticket indicating the number of the horse upon which he places his money, such number corresponding to the number beside the horse's name on the face of the machine. It also indicates the amount of the bet and the position the bettor has indicated the horse will take at the end of the race, that is, whether "straight," "place," "show," or "combination," of such places. Immediately before the race is started, ticket selling is stopped by the officials of the racing association, and the officials of the pari-mutuel system compute the total amount of money placed in the pool. A commission of 10 per cent of the whole pool is deducted, which percentage is regulated and controlled, and may be changed at any time by the Utah racing commission. Computation is also made to show the ratio the bets on each horse bear to the whole amount of money in the pool, and thus is indicated [by] the odds in favor of or against each horse. The machine records the number of tickets issued on each horse and the total of the tickets so issued on all horses in the race. The odds are indicated and determined on the amount of money placed and the odds or the amount to be paid on any horse cannot be determined until after the last ticket on the race has been purchased. When the race is finished the computers of the pari-mutuel system make announcement of the amount that will be paid on each bet upon the horse coming in first, second or third, and public announcement is made[.] . . . It appears that the pari-mutuel performs no function in determining the result of the game. . . .

In 27 C. J. at page 968, §4, the author says: "The phrase 'game of chance,' it has been said, is not one long known in the law and having therein a settled signification. It is a game determined entirely or in part by lot or mere luck, and in which judgment, practice, skill, or adroitness have honestly no office at all, or are thwarted by chance; a game in which hazard entirely predominates." In 12 R. C. L. at page 716, supra, the same rule is announced in substance, . . . for example, games with dice which are determined by throwing only, and those in which the throw of the dice regulates the play, or in which the hand at cards depends on a dealing with the face down, are instances of games of chance. On the other hand, games of chess, checkers, billiards, and bowling are deemed to be games of skill. This distinction has obtained in all those jurisdictions where the definition of the term "game of chance" has been material under their statutory law. Throwing dice is purely a game of chance, and chess is purely a game of skill. But games of cards do not cease to be games of chance because they call for the exercise of skill by the player, nor do games of billiards cease to be games of skill because at times . . . their result is determined by some unforeseen accident, usually called "luck." The test of the character of the game is not whether it contains an element of chance or an element of skill, but which of these is the dominating element that determines the result of the game."

In [*Harless v. United States,*] the court says: "Penal statutes must not be construed to embrace cases not clearly within their provision. The word 'game' does not embrace all uncertain events, nor does the expression 'games of chance' embrace all games. As generally understood, games are of two kinds, games of chance and games of skill. Besides, there are trials of strength, trials of speed, and various other uncertainties which are perhaps no games at all, certainly they are not games of chance. Among this class may be ranked a horse race. It is as much a game for two persons to strive which can raise the heaviest weight, or live the longest under water, as it is to test the speed of two horses."

Further on in the opinion[,] the court says: "It is said that there are strictly few or no games of chance, but that skill enters as a very material element in most or all of them. This, however, does not prevent them from being games of chance within the meaning of the law. There are many games the result of which depends entirely upon skill. Chance is in no wise resorted to therein. Such games are not prohibited by the statute. But there are other games, which although they call for the exercise of much skill, still there is an intermingling of chance. The result depends, in a very considerable degree, upon sheer hazard. These are the games against which the statute is directed, and horse racing is not included in that class."

. . . In *James v. State*, 63 Md. 242, at pages 252, 253, a system called "mutual pools" was used in connection with horse racing. The system was very similar to the pari-mutuel in the case at bar. [The court held:] "When a man hazards his money on the rise or fall of prices of stocks, cotton, grain, or other commodities, it cannot in the proper use of language be said that he is playing at a game of chance, nor can the place where such ventures are made and registered be designated as a gambling table. Bets are made, and money hazarded on many of the uncertainties and contingencies of life, but in the common use of language, these transactions are not called games of chance. The contingency on which these appellants wagered their money was the result of a race; in one event they would win, in another they would lose. It may be said that many elements of uncertainty were involved in the wager by reason of the various combinations which might be made in the pools. But nevertheless the thing which was to determine gain or loss was the success of the horses chosen. If by any singular subtlety of discourse a horse race could be shown to be a game of chance; by the same reason we must hold that it was played on the race course, and that the horses were the players."

[According to the respondents, however,] "The precise question here is whether the pari-mutuel system of betting or wagering upon horse races where the horse races are operated in connection with and as a part of the pari-mutuel system is a game of chance. In this case it is not necessary to consider whether a horse race by itself is a game of chance or whether the pari-mutuel machine by itself is a gambling device. It is stipulated, and the court has found, that the pari-mutuel system is operated in connection with the running of races; that the commissions and profits derived from the pari-mutuel system of betting or wagering is used in furnishing prizes or purses to the winners, and defraying other expenses incident to the operating of races. It also appears that the same corporation operates both the pool selling and the horse races; that the operation of the races determines who wins in the pari-mutuel pools; that the pari-mutuel pools are operated for the purpose of financing the races. While it is perfectly clear that horse races can be run without the pari-mutuel system of betting or any other scheme of betting, and that the pari-mutuel system of wagering and betting can be used with respect to baseball games, dog races, or other games, yet there is no question here but that both are operated together and that each are an indispensable factor in the operation of the system of betting and wagering[.]"

In *Tollett v. Thomas,* an English case decided in 1871, the defendant was charged with [operating a game of chance for operating a pari-mutuel horse race system]. As to whether it was a game of chance, Chief Justice Cockburn, who wrote the opinion, at page 521 of the report said: "In the present instance, an element of chance is introduced, which, though not having any reference to the main event—namely, the result of the race in the winning of a particular horse—is yet essential in making the wager laid upon the winning horse profitable to the better. The winning of the horse betted upon is of course the primary condition of the wager being won, but whether the winning of the wager shall be productive of any profit to the winner, and more especially what the amount of that profit shall be, depends upon the state of the betting with reference to the number of bets laid on or against the winning horse—a state of things fluctuating from one minute to another throughout the duration of the betting. Now this being something wholly independent of the issue of the race, as well as of the will and judgment of the winner, depending, as it does, on the will or caprice of the other persons betting, is a matter obviously of uncertainty and chance to the individual bettor, more especially in the earlier stages of the betting. There being, then, this element of chance in the transaction among the parties betting, we think it may properly be termed, as amongst them, a game of chance."

In *Miller v. United States,* the District of Columbia case, it was held that book-making on a horse race was a game of chance [within the meaning of a statute. It held:] "This statute of 1883 was not aimed exclusively at any particular game or species of device for gaming, but was intended, as its title and its broad comprehensive provisions declare, more effectually to suppress gaming in this district. The reason and policy of the law, as well as its comprehensive language, apply as well to all games and devices then existing as to all that might be subsequently devised and practiced. That being the object to be accomplished, what could be more grossly obnoxious to the provisions of the statute, or more demoralizing to the community, than the existence of places for the making and selling of books and pools upon horse races, baseball games, foot races, dog fights, cock fights, and all other conceivable contests upon which money may be bet or wagered. The great evil and vice of the thing is not in the horse race, the foot race, or the baseball game, but in the seductive allurements held out to people, young and old, to frequent the gaming table, or the gambling device, and to indulge in excessive betting, and thereby become the victims of the wily and scheming professional gambler. Whether the game or contest upon which the wager is made be a horse race, foot race, baseball game, or what else, it is quite immaterial, if the thing or contest upon which the bet or wager is made be a game of chance. It has from an early time been held that a horse race is a game of chance, and so is a game of baseball, and so a foot race, where wagers have been made upon them[.]" . . .

[This] is a case in which after all, it is necessary to rely largely on the rules of reason and common sense, coupled with such light as may be reflected by adjudicated cases. In the opinion of the court, if games such as horse racing, baseball, billiards, chess, and other games in which there is a basis for the exercise of judgment, learning, experience and skill, must be classed as games of chance, even though there may be an element of skill, then we are unable to determine what constitutes a game of skill as contradistinguished from a game of chance. Unless we apply the rule announced in C.J. and R.C.L., supra, and determine the question by ascertaining which is the dominating element of the game, then there is no reasonable rule by which the question can be determined.

In the instant case it is conceded that the result of the race is determined by the race itself, and not by any machine or other device. Everything else being equal, the fastest horse will be the first to reach the goal. That determines the winners on "straight." The next two in order determine the winners on "place" and "show." If this were all, there could be no reason founded in law, as we view the authorities, for contending that the race is a game of chance. But the amount of each bettor's winnings cannot be foretold at the time he registers his bet. The number of persons who may bet afterwards at the same machine is unknown. This, it would seem, is an element of chance, at least to a limited extent. It is not an element of chance as to the amount he may lose, but only as to the amount he may win. . . . So that the chance feature of the game has nothing to do with whether the bettor wins or loses the race, for as before stated, that depends on the race itself, independent of the pari-mutuel machine. Neither does the chance feature in any manner affect the amount he will lose, for this he can foresee at the time he registers his bet.

[We uphold the trial court's finding that pari-mutuel wagering on horse races is not in contravention of the state Constitution.]

STRAUP, J. (concurring).

I concur. We must take the Constitution as we find it, neither enlarging nor detracting from it. It merely provides that the Legislature shall not authorize "any game of chance, lottery, or gift enterprise." It does not forbid the Legislature authorizing betting, wagering, or gaming. Nor does it forbid the Legislature authorizing any game, except a "game of chance;" That is, the Legislature, if it sees fit, may authorize any game not a game of chance, and at the same time may authorize or permit wagering or betting on it. . . . I am in perfect accord with those who assert that public betting and wagering are pernicious and baneful and ought to be forbidden. But the question of wisdom is one of legislative policy over which we have no control. . . .

It, in effect, is conceded that horse racing within and of itself is like foot racing, boat racing, football, and baseball, a game of skill and endurance, a contest involving skill and judgment, and not a game of chance, and that it is within legislative power to authorize and permit it. That the Constitution does not forbid the Legislature from authorizing or permitting horse racing any more than foot racing, football, or baseball is not seriously doubted by anyone.

Now, from these considerations, I do not see wherein the fact of wagering or betting on the result of a game, or wherein the means or device by which the betting or wagering is carried on or conducted, has anything to do with the determination of whether the game is one of chance or of skill. In other words what does betting or wagering on the result of a game have to do with the character of it? It seems to me a game of football or baseball is a game of skill whether any betting or wagering is laid on its result or not. Nor, as it seems to me, does it make any difference by what method or device the betting or wagering is carried on or conducted. So, too, with respect to horse racing. . . . The device used in the pari-mutuel system of betting is not like a slot machine, or roulette wheel, or other similar device or instrument which by its manipulation or operation itself determines the result. The device merely registers or records and displays the bets as they are made. It is a mere posting of them. They could as well be marked by chalk or pencil on a board or chart displayed in a conspicuous place, and by the use of the one no more than by the other system is the result of the race determined nor the character of it as to skill or chance influenced or affected. Thus I think the respondents misconceive and misstate the main proposition for consideration when they say, as they do, that "the precise question here is whether the pari-mutuel system of betting or wagering upon horse races where the horse races are operated in connection with and as a part of the pari-mutuel system is a game of chance." As I conceive the proposition, it is: Is horse racing a game of chance or a game of skill? If it is a game of chance, that is the end of the inquiry. If it is a game of skill, it is rendered a game of chance by permitting betting or wagering, whether by the pari-mutuel system or by any other method, on the result of the race. Since betting or wagering on the race does not determine or affect the result of it, I think the conclusion inevitable that wagering or betting on the result of a game of skill does not convert the game into one of chance.

\* \* \*

[The plaintiffs argue] that horse racing is not successful—that it is not profitable or remunerative, or interesting—unless betting or wagering on the result of the race or races is permitted. Such considerations have no relevancy. Whether a game is operated successfully or unsuccessfully, profitably or unprofitably, is not a material, nor even a relevant factor in determining whether it is a game of chance or skill. Surely, if a game is operated unsuccessfully, it may not, for such reason, be denominated a game of skill, and, if successfully a game of chance, or vice versa.

### NOTES

1.  Courts sometimes differentiate between a "British rule" and an "American rule" in addressing skill and the element of chance. Under the British rule (also called the "pure chance" doctrine), a game constitutes a game of chance only if the outcome is determined solely by chance. Under the American rule (also called the dominant factor doctrine), a game constitutes a game of chance if chance is the "dominant factor" in the outcome. *See, e.g., Johnson v. Collins Entertainment Co.,* 508 S.E.2d 575, 583 (S.C. 1998) (Burnett, J., dissenting)
2.  In *Hunt,* the question was whether the outcome depended to "a material degree upon an element of chance." In *Green,* the question is whether chance or skill is "the dominating element" in the outcome. Are these inquiries identical? Were they important in determining the outcomes of the cases?
3.  Is *Green*'s approach compelling? Consider an alternative view of the larger question. In *State v. Weithoff,* 51 Mich. 203, 16 N.W. 442 (Mich. 1883), renowned Michigan Justice Thomas M. Cooley famously held: "The word 'game' is very comprehensive, and embraces every contrivance or institution which has for its object

to furnish sport, recreation, or amusement. Let a stake be laid upon the chances of the game, and we have gaming."

4.  In *Green*, the court takes a narrow view of the phrase "game of chance." The court quotes a Maryland case called *James v. State* which suggests that if the game is the horse race, the players are the horses. Is that, however, the only game occurring when a person bets at a horse race?

5.  *Green* also quotes *James v. State* for the following proposition: "When a man hazards his money on the rise or fall of prices of stocks, cotton, grain, or other commodities, it cannot in the proper use of language be said that he is playing at a game of chance, nor can the place where such ventures are made and registered be designated as a gambling table." Why not?


## JOKER CLUB, L.L.C. v. HARDIN
### 643 S.E.2d 626 (N.C. App. 2007)

CALABRIA, Judge.

Joker Club, L.L.C., ("plaintiff") appeals from an order of the trial court, denying its request for injunctive relief against former [Durham County] District Attorney James E. Hardin ("defendant") and concluding that poker is a game of chance that is illegal in North Carolina. . . . Plaintiff filed this action and sought a declaratory judgment that poker was a game of skill, as opposed to a game of chance, and thus not in violation of N.C. Gen. Stat. §14-292 (2005). Plaintiff also sought a temporary restraining order to prevent defendant from enforcing N.C. Gen. Stat. §14-292. The Durham County Superior Court . . . ruled in favor of defendant, concluding that poker was a game of chance . . . [and] denied plaintiff's request for a temporary restraining order.

[This appeal] requires us to determine whether the trial court erred in concluding that poker is a game of chance and thus illegal under N.C. Gen. Stat. §14-292 (2005). That statute provides as follows:

> [A]ny person or organization that operates any game of chance or any person who plays at or bets on any game of chance at which any money, property or other thing of value is bet, whether the same be in stake or not, shall be guilty of a Class 2 misdemeanor. This section shall not apply to a person who plays . . . any lottery game being lawfully conducted in any state.

We first note that plaintiff has not challenged the trial court's findings of fact, and those findings are thus binding on appeal. Here, four witnesses testified for the plaintiff and one for the State. Roy Cooke ("Cooke"), a professional poker player from Las Vegas, Nevada, testified that he had spent most of his adult life studying poker. Cooke testified that there are certain strategies to poker that allow a player to improve his mathematical odds over the course of a game. He indicated that while in a single hand of poker, chance may defeat a skilled and experienced player, the skilled player is likely to prevail when multiple hands are played. Frank Martin ("Martin"), a Florida-based consultant who runs poker tournaments, also testified that skill will prevail over luck over a long period of time in the course of a poker tournament. He further stated that there are certain skills that players can develop to consistently win at poker, including patience, memory, and the ability to analyze odds. Anthony Lee ("Lee"), a casino manager in the Bahamas, testified that there are numerous skills needed for a player to succeed in poker, and that he has failed to develop them himself. Lee testified that patience, knowledge of the odds, the ability to read people, and self-control are all necessary skills. Chris Simmons ("Simmons"), who plays poker in North Carolina, testified that his poker skills have improved greatly since he began studying poker and reading books on winning poker strategies. Simmons stated that in his experience, poker is a game where skill prevails over chance. Richard Thornell ("Thornell"), a North Carolina Alcohol Law Enforcement officer, was the only witness to testify for the State. Thornell, who stated that he has played poker for more than 39 years, testified that while there was skill involved in poker, luck ultimately prevailed. He testified that he had seen a television poker tournament in which a hand with a 91% chance to win lost to a hand with only a 9% chance to win.

The evidence, as presented by these witnesses, establishes that poker is both a game of skill and chance. All witnesses appeared to agree that in a single hand, chance may predominate over skill, but that over a long game, the most skilled players would likely amass the most chips. From the evidence, Judge Hudson was unable to determine whether skill or chance predominated in poker, but concluded that poker is a game of chance. After a careful examination of the case law interpreting North Carolina's prohibition against wagering on games of chance, we agree.

We have held that an inquiry regarding whether a game is a game of chance or skill turns on whether chance or skill predominates. In *State v. Stroupe*, the North Carolina Supreme Court considered whether a certain type of pool was a game of skill or chance. The *Stroupe* Court stated the applicable test as such:

> [T]he test of the character of any kind of a game of pool as to whether it is a game of chance or a game of skill is not whether it contains an element of chance or an element of skill, but which of these is the dominating element that determines the result of the game, to be found from the facts of each particular kind of game. Or to speak alternatively, whether or not the element of chance is present in such a manner as to thwart the exercise of skill or judgment.

*Id.* at 38, 76 S.E.2d at 317 (1953).

The *Stroupe* Court, in articulating its test, relied on Chief Justice Ruffin's classic summary of the law with respect to games of chance. In *State v. Gupton*, Chief Justice Ruffin wrote:

> [W]e believe, that, in the popular mind, the universal acceptation of "a game of chance" is such a game, as is determined entirely or in part by lot or mere luck, and in which judgment, practice, skill, or adroitness have honestly no office at all, or are [thwarted] by chance. As intelligible examples, the games with dice which are determined by throwing only, and those, in which the throw of the dice regulates the play, or the hand at cards depends upon a dealing with the face down, exhibit the two classes of games of chance. A game of skill, on the other hand, is one, in which nothing is left to chance; but superior knowledge and attention, or superior strength, agility, and practice, gain the victory. Of this kind of games chess, draughts or chequers, billiards, fives, bowles, and quoits may be cited as examples. It is true, that in these latter instances superiority of skill is not always successful—the race is not necessarily to the swift. Sometimes an oversight, to which the most [skillful] is subject, gives an adversary the advantage; or an unexpected puff of wind, or an unseen gravel in the way, may turn aside a quoit or a ball and make it come short of the aim. But if those incidents were sufficient to make the games, in which they may occur, games of chance, there would be none other but games of that character.

*State v. Gupton*, 30 N.C. 271, 273-74 (1848).

Chief Justice Ruffin's analysis clarifies the logic underpinning North Carolina's interpretation of the predominate-factor test. It makes clear that while all games have elements of chance, games which can be determined by superior skill are not games of chance. For example, bowling, chess, and billiards are games of skill because skill determines the outcome. The game itself is static and the only factor separating the players is their relative skill levels. In short, the instrumentality for victory is in each player's hands and his fortunes will be determined by how skillfully he use[s] that instrumentality.

Poker, however, presents players with different hands, making the players unequal in the same game and subject to defeat at the turn of a card. Although skills such as knowledge of human psychology, bluffing, and the ability to calculate and analyze odds make it more likely for skilled players to defeat novices, novices may yet prevail with a simple run of luck. No amount of skill can change a deuce into an ace. Thus, the instrumentality for victory is not entirely in the player's hand. In *State v. Taylor*, our Supreme Court noted this distinction.

> It is a matter of universal knowledge that no game played with the ordinary playing cards is unattended with risk, whatever may be the skill, experience or intelligence of the gamesters engaged in it. From the very nature of such games, where cards must be drawn by and dealt out to players, who cannot anticipate what ones may be received by each, the order in which they will be placed or the effect of a given play or mode of playing, there must be unavoidable uncertainty as to the results. 16 S.E. 168, at 169 (1892).

This is not so with bowling, where the player's skill determines whether he picks up the spare; or with billiards, where the shot will find the pocket or not according to its author's skill. During oral arguments, counsel for plaintiff analogized poker to golf, arguing that while a weekend golfer might, by luck, beat a professional golfer such as Tiger Woods on one hole, over the span of 18 holes, Woods' superior skill would prevail. The same would be true for a poker game, plaintiff contended, making poker, like golf, a game of skill. This analogy, while creative, is false. In golf, as in bowling or billiards, the players are presented with an equal challenge, with each determining his fortune by his own skill. Although chance inevitably intervenes, it is not inherent in the game and does not overcome skill, and the player maintains the opportunity to defeat chance with superior skill. Whereas in poker, a skilled player may give himself a statistical advantage but is always subject to defeat at the turn of a card, an instrumentality beyond his control. We think that is the critical difference.

For the reasons stated above, we determine that chance predominates over skill in the game of poker, making that game a game of chance. AFFIRMED.

*NOTES*

1.   The plaintiff likened the chance/skill elements in poker to that of golf, pointing out that an amateur golfer could outscore a professional like Tiger Woods on one hole, just like a lesser-skilled poker player can beat a pro in any single hand. The court rejected this argument, focusing instead on the equal challenge that each

player faces at the outset of a golf game—a condition that the court says does not exist when the game is based on a "turn of a card." Is this a fair distinction for the court to make? Isn't there a high degree of chance in golf when one considers the various natural elements that can affect the velocity and direction of the ball? Can one make an argument that regardless of a golfer's and poker player's respective skills there are elements of chance and luck that may affect both games equally? Is it fair to liken a chance change in wind direction on the golf course that gives a lesser-skilled player an edge to the chance turn of a card that does the same in poker?

2. The Alabama Court of Criminal Appeals recognized that Texas Hold'em poker requires "a certain amount of experience and skill in order to be ... successful[.]" But the court concluded that "poker is fundamentally a game of chance, in that the outcome of the game ultimately depends on a random draw of the cards." *Garrett v. State*, 963 So. 2d 700, 701 (Ala. Crim. App. 2007). That court cited an earlier case that explained its reasoning: "A player may be "skilled" at "playing the odds," but he is still "playing the odds." *State v. Ted's Game Enterprises*, 893 So. 2d 355, 376 (Ala. Civ. App. 2002). But doesn't poker entail more than just "playing the odds"? Did the court take into account the skills required to successfully bluff or to gauge when an opponent might be bluffing when it acknowledged that poker "can be affected by other ... techniques or knowledge ..."? Should those skills make a difference?

3. Similar questions have also raged as to blackjack. *See, e.g., State v. Eisen*, 16 N.C. App. 532, 192 S.E.2d 613 (N.C. App. 1972) (issue whether game of "blackjack" was a game of skill was for jury).

4. Is litigation a game of skill or a game of chance? On what basis could one make either argument? Are contingent fees collected by plaintiffs' lawyers the product of skill or chance? Cf. *Wilson v. Harris*, 688 So. 2d 265 (Ala. App. 1996) (holding that an agreement to pay one-third of a future judgment to a third party in exchange for a cash payment was a gambling contract).

## HUMPHREY v. VIACOM
### 2007 U.S. Dist. LEXIS 44679 (D. N.J. 2007)

CAVANAUGH, District Judge.

Fantasy sports leagues allow participants to "manage" virtual teams of professional players in a given sport throughout a sport's season and to compete against other fantasy sports participants based upon the actual performance of those players in key statistical categories. Fantasy sports have become extremely popular in recent years. They have earned a place in modern popular culture and are the subject of countless newspaper and magazine articles, books, internet message boards and water-cooler conversations. The enormous popularity of fantasy sports can be attributed in part to the services offered on internet websites, such as those operated by Defendants. The websites provide a platform for real-time statistical updates and tracking, message boards and expert analysis.

Fantasy sports leagues allow fans to use their knowledge of players, statistics and strategy to manage their own virtual team based upon the actual performance of professional athletes through a full season of competition. In the early days of fantasy sports, participants compiled and updated the players' statistics manually. Today, the rapid growth of the internet fostered additional services, such as those offered by Defendants, that provide an internet environment and community for playing and discussing fantasy sports. The technology also allows for automatic statistic updates for players and teams and access to expert fantasy sports analysis. As a result, fantasy sports have become much more accessible and popular throughout the country.

Although the rules and services vary somewhat from one fantasy sports provider to another, the websites operate as follows. Participants pay a fee to purchase a fantasy sports team and the related services. The purchase price provides the participant with access to the support services necessary to manage the fantasy team, including access to "real-time" statistical information, expert opinions, analysis and message boards for communicating with other participants.

The purchase price also covers the data-management services necessary to run a fantasy sports team. Using these services, the participants "draft" a slate of players and track the performance of those players in key statistical categories throughout the season. Participants are grouped into "leagues" of as many as twelve teams and compete not only against the members of their own leagues, but can also compete against the winners of the other leagues.

The success of a fantasy sports team depends on the participants' skill in selecting players for his or her team, trading players over the course of the season, adding and dropping players during the course of the season and deciding who among his or her players will start and which players will be placed on the bench. The team with the best performance—based upon the statistics of the players chosen by the participant—is declared the winner at the season's end. Nominal prizes, such as T-shirts or bobble-head dolls, are awarded to each participant whose team wins its league. Managers of the best teams in each sport across all leagues are awarded larger prizes, such as flat-screen TVs or gift certificates. These prizes are announced before the fantasy sports season begins and do not depend upon the number of participants or the amount of registration fees received by Defendants.

Only ESPN, Sportsline and Vulcan Sports Media remain in the case as Defendants. Plaintiff voluntarily dismissed all other Defendants. The Defendants operate separate pay-for-play online fantasy sport leagues. The Complaint alleges that Defendants operate three distinct pay-for-play fantasy sports sites in violation of several states' qui tam gambling loss-recovery laws. . . . Plaintiff claims that the registration fees paid by fantasy sports leagues participants constitute wagers or bets, and he seeks to recover these fees pursuant to the qui tam gambling loss-recovery statutes. In other words, Humphrey concludes that the Defendants' fantasy sports leagues constitute gambling because the participant "wagers" the entry fee for the chance to win a prize and the winner is determined predominantly by chance due to potential injuries to players and the vicissitudes of sporting events in general.

Although the specific elements of the [American] qui tam statutes vary, they share a common origin and purpose. They were intended to prevent gamblers and their families from becoming destitute due to gambling losses—and thus becoming wards of the State—by providing a method for the gambler's spouse, parent or child to recover the lost money from the winner. The statutes were also intended to supplement states' general anti-gaming provisions in an era when local governments' own regulatory and enforcement powers were much less effective than they are today.

Defendants argue that Plaintiff fails to state a claim under New Jersey's qui tam statute because, as a matter of law, the payment of an entry fee to participate in a fantasy sports league is not wagering, betting or staking money. . . . As Plaintiff alleges, Defendants' fantasy sports league participants pay a set fee for each team they enter in a fantasy sports league. This entry fee is paid at the beginning of a fantasy sports season and allows the participant to receive related support services and to compete against other teams in a league throughout the season. As Plaintiff further alleges, Defendants offer set prizes for each league winner and for the overall winners each season. These prizes are guaranteed to be awarded at the end of the season, and the amount of the prize does not depend on the number of entrants. Moreover, Defendants are neutral parties in the fantasy sports games—they do not compete for the prizes and are indifferent as to who wins the prizes. Defendants simply administer and provide internet-based information and related support services for the games. Plaintiff does not allege otherwise.

New Jersey courts have not addressed the three-factor scenario of (1) an entry fee paid unconditionally, (2) prizes guaranteed to be awarded and (3) prizes for which the game operator is not competing. Courts throughout the country, however, have long recognized that it would be "patently absurd" to hold that "the combination of an entry fee and a prize equals gambling," because if that were the case, countless contests engaged in every day would be unlawful gambling, including "golf tournaments, bridge tournaments, local and state rodeos or fair contests, . . . literary or essay competitions, . . . livestock, poultry and produce exhibitions, track meets, spelling bees, beauty contests and the like," and contest participants and sponsors could all be subject to criminal liability. *State v. Am. Holiday Ass'n, Inc.*, 727 P.2d 807, 809, 812 (Ariz. 1986) (en banc).

Courts have distinguished between bona fide entry fees and bets or wagers, holding that entry fees do not constitute bets or wagers where they are paid unconditionally for the privilege of participating in a contest, and the prize is for an amount certain that is guaranteed to be won by one of the contestants (but not the entity offering the prize). Courts that have examined this issue have reasoned that when the entry fees and prizes are unconditional and guaranteed, the element of risk necessary to constitute betting or wagering is missing:

> A prize or premium differs from a wager in that in the former, the person offering the same has no chance of his gaining back the thing offered, but, if he abides by his offer, he must lose; whereas in the latter, each party interested therein has a chance of gain and takes a risk of loss. . . .
>
>   The fact that each contestant is required to pay an entrance fee where the entrance fee does not specifically make up the purse or premium contested for does not convert the contest into a wager.

*Las Vegas Hacienda, Inc. v. Gibson*, 77 Nev. 25, 359 P.2d 85, 86-87 (Nev. 1961). *See also Am. Holiday Ass'n*, 727 P.2d at 810 ("[A] bet is a situation in which the money or prize belongs to the persons posting it, each of whom has a chance to win it. Prize money, on the other hand, is found where the money or other prize belongs to the person offering it, who has no chance to win it and who is unconditionally obligated to pay it to the successful contestant."). Therefore, where the entry fees are unconditional and the prizes are guaranteed, "reasonable entrance fees charged by the sponsor of a contest to participants competing for prizes are not bets or wagers." *Am. Holiday Ass'n*, 727 P.2d at 811.

Plaintiff incorrectly argues that the case law cited by Defendants is inapplicable because it applies only to games of skill. To the contrary, none of the decisions cited by Defendants turn on whether the activity in question is a game of skill or chance. Indeed, courts have made clear that the question whether the money awarded is a bona fide prize (as opposed to a bet or wager) can be determined without deciding whether the outcome of the game is determined by skill or chance. See id., 359 P.2d at 87. ("Whereas we have concluded that the contract does not involve a gaming transaction [because there is no bet or wager], consideration of . . . [whether] the shooting of a "hole-in-one" was a feat of skill . . . becomes unnecessary."). . . .

As a matter of law, the entry fees for Defendants' fantasy sports leagues are not "bets" or "wagers" because (1) the entry fees are paid unconditionally; (2) the prizes offered to fantasy sports contestants are for amounts certain and are guaranteed to be awarded; and (3) Defendants do not compete for the prizes.

## NOTES

1. Does the court successfully distinguish the traditional definition of gambling, and the distinction between chance and skill?
2. The court is undoubtedly correct that the defendants are not seeking to engage in gambling themselves. They do, however, seek to profit. Is this decision correct?
3. In *National Football League v. Delaware*, 435 F. Supp. 1372 (D. Del. 1977), the court held that betting on the outcome of league sports is a game of chance, rather than a game of skill. It ruled as follows:

> The word "lottery" should be interpreted to encompass not only games of pure chance but also games in which chance is the dominant determining factor. The question that remains is whether chance is the dominant factor in [betting on NFL games]. Both the evidence and the case law suggest that it is. . . . Plaintiffs acknowledge that the results of NFL games are a function of myriad factors such as the weather, the health and mood of the players and the condition of the playing field. Some educated predictions can be made about each of these but each is also subject to last minute changes and to an element of the unknowable, or to put it another way, to an element of chance. . . . The evidence tends to show that for the first nine weeks of the 1976 season chance was the dominant factor in the outcome of . . . the NFL games[.] "Jimmy the Greek" is a widely recognized oddsmaker, syndicated columnist and television personality who earns his living in part by predicting the

outcome of NFL games. The record shows that, although he correctly predicted the winner of 101 out of 126 NFL games from September 12 through November 8, if he had bet on both pools of games in "Football Bonus" each week, he would have won only three times. He would never have won the "All-Game Bonus" awarded to those who correctly choose the winners of all fourteen games in a single week. . . . [H]e successfully predicted the point spread in only 38 out of 126 games in nine weeks. This strongly suggests that expertise would not have carried the day. . . . Other courts have likewise concluded that football betting pools and other similar betting schemes based on sporting events qualify as games of chance.

## C.  PRIZE OR REWARD

### MCKEE v. FOSTER
**Oregon Supreme Court**
**347 P.2d 585 (1959)**

ROSSMAN, Justice.

[The plaintiffs brought an action against the state attorney general and the local district attorney seeking a declaratory judgment that their "free replay pinball machines" were not illegal gambling devices under the terms of an Oregon statute that prohibits a person from operating a "device" or "machine" that upon deposit of a coin or other thing "representative of value," dispenses merchandise, money or other representative of value "in varying quantities, depending on chance." The pinball machines offered a free replay to one who could light each of a series of squares on the pinball backboard that corresponded to placement of the pinball in various holes on the pinball machine.]

The cause was submitted to the court upon stipulated facts. . . . The findings contain no assertion that the machine issued to the player anything except a free play. Nor do they contain any recital that there comes to the player something of a tangible or physical nature such as a token, slug or card. The conclusions of law state: "The machine as described in the Findings of Fact does not dispense money, checks, slugs, tokens, credit or other representative of value or evidence of winning capable of being exchanged or redeemed for anything of value, when it returns to the player free plays upon securing a designated score."

The illumination of a part of the machine in the manner indicated by the excerpt which we took from the answer signifies to the player that he has won the right to a free play. In order to avail himself of the right he pushes a button but does not deposit in the machine a coin, slug or anything else. The brief filed by the defendants-appellants (Attorney General and District Attorney) says: "It is this distinctive 'free game' feature which is involved in this case and which incidentally gives this and other similar machines the generic term 'free-play pinball machines.' Such machines thus stand apart from machines dispensing coins, tokens, mints or similar items." In other words, the machine with which this case is concerned issues to the player no slug, coin or other item. Likewise, it awards to the player nothing whatever except occasionally a free play.

The defendants-appellants argue that the plaintiff's machines [are illegal]. They point out that when a player deposits his nickel in a machine the latter may dispense for him only a single play or, if he is lucky, it may give him a sequence of two or more plays. He may thus keep the machine operating upon the deposit of a single nickel as long as his luck continues, or, stated differently, as long as he continues to obtain high scores and win free replays. The defendants-appellants argue that the plaintiff's machines therefore come within this language: "may vend or dispense any . . . other representative of value or evidence of winning in varying quantities or values, depending upon chance." The length of play and hence the "quantities or values" of the play vary in plaintiff's machines, so the defendants argue, according to chance. We may safely assume, since other courts have so held, that a free play is a "representative of value or evidence of winning."

The contention that a free play machine violates [this provision] is fundamentally unsound in our belief. The words "vend or dispense" found in that subsection, if we employ commonplace meanings, describe an ordinary vending machine into which the payer inserts a coin and then stands by while the machine goes through the operation of issuing to him an item of merchandise. The subsection, however, appears to be aimed at machines which, in dispensing mints, gum balls or other items, do so "in varying quantities or values, depending upon chance." Thus, upon one play the patron of the machine may receive a piece of chewing gum and on the next not only gum but also some trinket. The patron of a vending machine stands by idle while the machine goes through the operation incidental to the delivery to him of the desired item. The ordinary "one-arm bandit" slot machine clearly comes under the terms of this subsection. On the other hand, in a pinball game the player actively participates after he has inserted his nickel. And in order to obtain his free play, if one is awarded to him, he must depress a button on the machine so that the play will continue.

[The statute] apparently does not prohibit pinball machines which give free plays if no coin or token is dispensed by the machine. The subsection outlaws only coin operated machines from which "there may be received" some tangible object which "May be deposited in such machine" for a replay. Although "credit or other representative of value or evidence of winning" are among the prohibited class of objects which "May be deposited" in the machine for a replay, we must conclude, if we construe words in their normal sense, that for the purposes of this subsection these things must be of a tactile, tangible character; that is, they must be of a sufficiently corporal nature so that they may be physically "deposited" in the machine. The defendants argue that it would be an absurdity to say that the statute prohibits a machine which dispenses checks or tokens for replay but does not prohibit a machine which permits replays without the use of checks or tokens. If we assume that the argument is unanswerable, the absurdity lies in the statute and not in our interpretation of it. A replay machine which does not issue checks, slugs or tokens is simply *casus omissus* [defined as "an event or contingency for which no provision is made."—ED.].

* * *

[In *State v. Coats*, a pinball machine was held to constitute a lottery.] The patron of Coats' machine or machines, upon inserting a nickel in the device and pulling a lever, set the machine in operation. If chance favored him he could win as much as ten nickels which the machine paid out to him automatically. We see from those facts that the device which was the subject matter of the *Coats* decision was a pay-off machine. It granted no replays. . . . *Coats* recognized that the term "lottery" has no technical or established legal meaning[, holding] that the essential elements of a lottery are prize, chance and consideration. . . . The machine in the *Coats* cases paid to the winner, as we have said, ten times the sum which he deposited [which is] something of a tangible nature[.] A free play, on the other hand, is intangible and, in a sense, of immeasurable value. The manufacturer of the plaintiff's machine assigned the arbitrary value of a nickel to the replay, but in the market place the replay has no such value. The replay cannot be sold. It cannot be carried away. It is intangible in nature and after the mechanics of the replay have been undergone the replay has disappeared for all time. It may appeal to the gambling instincts of some and perhaps is the kind of prize which is a "representative of value or evidence of winning" [in some circumstances]. But there is no reason to believe that *State v. Coats* contemplates "prize" as including a free game within its interpretation of the lottery statute. . . . Since "lottery" has no fixed legal definition it was within the province of the legislature, acting under the constitutional mandate, to provide a reasonable definition of the 'prize' element of a lottery. We believe that the prize must be tangible in nature and have a value in the market place.

*NOTES*

1.  In some ways, this case foreshadows a problem of technology. The court concedes the defendant's compelling argument in *McKee* that it is absurd to hold that a machine that issues a "thing of value" in a tangible form such as a coin or token is unlawful and yet hold that a machine that issues credits in an intangible form is lawful. The court sidesteps the problem by suggesting that the problem is for the legislature to address. In an age of rapidly advancing technologies, should courts follow the spirit of the law, or the letter?

2.  Why did the defendants, the District Attorney and Attorney General, defend this case?

3.  Though it may seem curious today, pinball machines were once the target of serious law enforcement efforts. *See* Brian Lester, *The Free Replay Feature in Pinball Machines: A Fresh Look at the Elements of Gambling and a Revised Method of Analysis*, 41 BRANDEIS L.J. 297 (2002). Lester explains:

    When first introduced, the free replay was awarded based upon the player exceeding a particular score, with subsequent machines incorporating a random match feature to which each participant was entitled once the initial game had terminated. The first pinball machine to contain the free replay was named "Flash" and soon began appearing on machines made by other manufacturers. The free replay feature can still be found in modern versions. The majority of these machines set to award a free replay to those scoring in the top ten percent, while those falling in the random match category providing participants with a seven percent chance or less of matching a random number. Shortly following its introduction, this adaptation proved popular and accounted for the pinball machine becoming the most popular coin-operated amusement game of its time. . . . To further entice participants, soon after the free replay was added, designers and manufacturers placed knock-off switches and replay meters into the hardware of the pinball machine. . . . Even with flippers and the skill element that they presented, many machines prior to the 1950s were equipped with knock-off switches that enabled these machines to be used for gambling. [T]he pinball machine did not directly reimburse the player but did so indirectly through an intermediary, the proprietor, who, in place of the machine, paid the player based upon the number of credits received. Upon "cashing-in," the proprietor would use the knock-off switch to erase the number of accumulated free games credited. The pinball machine owner then would refund the proprietor based on the replay meter's reading of the number of knocked-off replays. The free replay feature could be manipulated in such a way as to record the number of replays given through a registration meter with a knock-off switch attached to erase the number of accumulated credits. [When federal law outlawed these features, technology adjusted]. As some courts began holding that pinball machines with a free replay feature were gambling devices per se, pinball machine designers responded with the introduction of flippers to incorporate the element of skill and thereby avoid a violation of gambling prohibition statutes. In seemingly one stroke, pinball machines became games of skill with one's score closely correlating to one's ability to play the game. Despite the introduction of flippers, the addition of the free replay feature to pinball machines created a division among jurisdictions on the issue of whether these machines initially designed for pure amusement should now be classified as gambling devices. In 1960, to attract players to play pinball machines in jurisdictions in which the free replay was a violation of the law, games were introduced that gave free additional balls to the player rather than free additional games. Jurisdictions that had outlawed free replays embraced free ball machines because this form of an award could not as easily be sold or bargained for as rights to additional games.

Innovations such as those noted by Mr. Lester in the excerpt above led law enforcement personnel to begin to regulate not only activity, but also gambling devices, an issue that will be addressed in a later chapter.

## D. GAMBLING IN OTHER CONTEXTS

### CHRISTINE HURT, REGULATING PUBLIC MORALS AND PRIVATE MARKETS: ONLINE SECURITIES TRADING, INTERNET GAMBLING, AND THE SPECULATION PARADOX

**86 B.U. L. Rev. 371 (2006)**

Risk-taking is a distinctively American value. From the frontier spirit of the settler to the entrepreneurial sense of the founder of a start-up company, Americans have been taught to realize "nothing ventured, nothing gained." This embracing of risk prompts individuals in the United States to participate in two closely intertwined activities: gambling and investing.

To characterize investing as gambling has become a trite and toothless analogy. However, most worn-out proverbs remain in the conventional wisdom because a kernel of truth continues to resonate with those who heed them. In fact, the stereotype of an investor as a gambler seems particularly well deserved. To gamble is to put something of value at risk on an uncertain outcome; in other words, "Wagers are economic choices under uncertainty." Under this broad definition, investors gamble with every purchase of a financial instrument. In making a securities purchase, some investors buy common stock of a corporation because they have studied that company's business plan, find that model to be superior to the company's competitors, and believe that the company's managers will continue to increase profits, thus raising an undervalued stock price. Conversely, some investors buy stock not because they assess positive public information but because they have a good feeling. Others may buy stock merely because they know that others have bought the same or similar stock with some measure of success. Still others choose to buy or sell stocks based solely on a prediction of whether others will buy or sell. In other words, many investors buy stock for some of the same reasons that gamblers may choose certain slot machines, lottery numbers, or squares on a roulette table, or choose to bet or fold a certain poker hand.

Although many investors act as gamblers, both law and society view investing and gambling quite differently. Regulators characterize investing as an enterprise of skill in which the assiduous and diligent may earn deserved rewards. Conversely, gambling is viewed as an enterprise of chance that encourages the lazy and untalented to divert useful capital into a chaotic system whereby an undeserving few reap ill-gotten gains while the vast majority foolishly lose. In stock market investing, the financial intermediaries are viewed as earning modest fees for assisting others to invest wisely, but in gaming, "the house," or the casinos, are detached hawkers who win every game. However, many gambling activities and investing activities can be described equally as speculation, or the assumption of unusual, but considered, risk for the prospect of commensurate gain. Notwithstanding this reality, investing is an activity that the law supports and encourages, but gambling is an activity that the law at least nominally discourages and at most prohibits.

These disparate views of speculation are reflected in the regulation of these two activities. For most of the past century, gambling in the

United States has been illegal by default. Over the past thirty years, exceptions have been drawn to legalize certain types of gambling in certain geographical areas; however, the operation of these legal gambling enterprises is subject to state regulatory control. Buying a passive interest in a corporation, by contrast, is legal by default.

*NOTES*

1.  Could one make a sound legal argument that speculation in publicly traded stocks meets the three basic elements of gambling—consideration, chance, and prize—described in the cases earlier in this chapter? If not, why not? If so, then what other factors are at work to account for why we would nevertheless allow this gambling in another forum?

2.  Note that some courts have sometimes had difficulty finding any difference between gambling and, for example, trading in commodities futures contracts. In futures contracts, traders purchase contracts for commodities, such as corn, or oil, or agricultural goods, that will theoretically be delivered to the holder of the contract in the future. Most futures traders never have any intention of taking delivery of the goods. During the twentieth century, many states enacted specific legislation to legalize commodities futures contracts, at least when made through a legitimate brokerage with an official commodities exchange. *See ACLI Int'l Commodity Services, Inc. v. Lindwall*, 347 N.W.2d 522 (Minn. Ct. App. 1984); *Merrill, Lynch, Pierce, Fenner & Smith, Inc. v. Schriver*, 541 S.W.2d 799 (Tenn. Ct. App. 1976). *Query*: If a state constitution has a lottery prohibition similar to the one common in the cases above, are statutes that authorize futures trading unconstitutional? If so, is the definition of gambling set forth in these cases too broad? Do these broad definitions of gambling reach conduct that ought to be allowed in a modern economy, or are commodities futures contracts truly no different than other kinds of gambling? If commodities trading is no different than other forms of gambling, should it be prohibited? Are there additional factors that courts ought to use in determining whether a given activity is illegal gambling?

3.  Other than market speculators, who is gambling in a futures contract? The farmer who sells a contract, promising to deliver, for example, a bushel of corn next March is not gambling for a chance to win a large prize, but merely to guarantee a fixed price to minimize risk. Likewise, the cereal mill that agrees to

buy the bushel of corn on a futures contract is also seeking to fix a guaranteed price so that it can predict its future expenses and therefore minimize risk. These two types of actors do not seem to be engaging in what we would ordinarily call "gambling."

4. What about an option contract on real estate? Such contracts are often speculative in nature, and executed by the holder of the option only if the land subject to the option rises in value. Do such terms meet the elements of gambling?

5. Now consider insurance, and specifically life insurance. As you read the case consider whether the purchase of life insurance meets the three elements of gambling.

## GRIGSBY v. RUSSELL
### 222 U.S. 149 (1911)

Mr. Justice HOLMES delivered the opinion of the court:

This is a bill of interpleader brought by an insurance company to determine whether a policy of insurance issued to John C. Burchard, now deceased, upon his life, shall be paid to his administrators or to an assignee, the company having turned the amount into court. The material facts are that after he had paid two premiums and a third was overdue, Burchard, being in want and needing money for a surgical operation, asked Dr. Grigsby to buy the policy, and sold it to him in consideration of $100 and Grigsby's undertaking to pay the premiums due or to become due; and that Grigsby had no interest in the life of the assured. The circuit court of appeals, in deference to some intimations of this court, held the assignment valid only to the extent of the money actually given for it and the premiums subsequently paid.

Of course, the ground suggested for denying the validity of an assignment to a person having no interest in the life insured is the public policy that refuses to allow insurance to be taken out by such persons in the first place. A contract of insurance upon a life in which the insured has no interest is a pure wager that gives the insured a sinister counter interest in having the life come to an end. And although that counter interest always exists, as early was emphasized for England in the famous case of Wainewright (Janus Weathercock), the chance that in some cases it may prove a sufficient motive for crime is greatly enhanced if the whole world of the unscrupulous are free to bet on what life they choose. The very meaning of an insurable interest is an interest in having the life continue, and so one that is opposed to crime. And what, perhaps, is more important, the existence of such an interest makes a roughly selected class of persons who, by their general relations with the person whose life is insured, are less likely than criminals at large to attempt to compass his death.

But when the question arises upon an assignment, it is assumed that the objection to the insurance as a wager is out of the case. In the present instance the policy was perfectly good. There was a faint suggestion in argument that it had become void by the failure of Burchard to pay the third premium *ad diem*, and that when Grisby paid, he was making a new contract. But a condition in a policy that it shall be void if premiums are not paid when due means only that it shall be voidable at the option of the company. The company waived the breach, if there was one, and the original contract with Burchard remained on foot. No question as to the character of that contract is before us. It has been performed and the money is in court. But this being so, not only does the objection to wagers disappear, but also the principle of public policy referred to, at least, in its most convincing form. The danger that might arise from a general license to all to insure whom they like does not exist. Obviously it is a very different thing from granting such a general license, to allow the holder of a valid insurance upon his own life to transfer it to one whom he, the party most concerned, is not afraid to trust. The law has no universal cynic fear of the temptation opened by a pecuniary benefit accruing upon a death. It shows no prejudice against remainders after life estates, even by the rule in Shelley's Case. Indeed, the ground of the objection to life insurance without interest in the earlier English cases was not the temptation to murder, but the fact that such wagers came to be regarded as a mischievous kind of gaming.

On the other hand, life insurance has become in our days one of the best recognized forms of investment and self-compelled saving. So far as reasonable safety permits, it is desirable to give to life policies the ordinary characteristics of property. This is recognized by the bankruptcy law, which provides that unless the cash surrender value of a policy like the one before us is secured to the trustee within thirty days after it has been stated, the policy shall pass to the trustee as assets. Of course the trustee may have no interest in the bankrupt's life. To deny the right to sell except to persons having such an interest is to diminish appreciably the value of the contract in the owner's hands. . . . And cases in which a person having an interest lends himself to one without any, as a cloak to what is, in its inception, a wager, have no similarity to those where an honest contract is sold in good faith. . . .

Decree reversed.

*NOTES*

1.  In this case, Justice Holmes discusses the general principle of insurance law that one must have an "insurable interest" in the decedent to be a named beneficiary of the decedent's life insurance policy. Generally, those deemed to have an insurable interest are family members who have no wish for the insured to die, but have a need to be protected against the risk that it will happen. The justifications for the "insurable interest" requirement are well set forth by Justice Holmes, who nevertheless uses general principles of freedom of contract to allow the insured to alienate his interest in his own life insurance policy.

2.  In *Colgrave v. Lowe*, 175 N.E. 569 (Ill. 1931), the court cited *Grigsby* and held:

    > the principal objection to [such a] contract . . . is not so much that it offers a temptation to commit crime as that it is an inducement to speculate and gamble in human life, in which the participants occupy a position directly opposite to that of life insurance companies, all of which are primarily interested in the continued life of each policyholder. The contract under consideration is a wager upon the lives of others in whom the parties to be benefited have no insurable interest, and the use of such a contract to promote the sale of life insurance presents an appeal to the gambling instincts of prospective policyholders that is contrary to sound principles of public policy.

    In other words, to this court, the risk of homicide pales in comparison to the more serious risk that gambling might occur.

3.  Justice Holmes seems to elide the distinction between insurance and gambling. Or, does he? Is there any distinction? If the beneficiary pays the premiums on another's life, are the elements of gambling met? What is the difference between "a wager" and "an honest contract sold in good faith?" Holmes suggests that the reason for the insurable interest requirement in English law was to prevent a "mischievous kind of gaming." Is life insurance for those with an insurable interest nevertheless a "kind of gaming," though perhaps less mischievous?

4.  Did Dr. Grigsby's conduct in this case amount to gambling? Does the fact that the conduct involved the assignment of a pre-existing life insurance policy make any difference in that analysis?

5.  Isn't every life insurance policy simply a morbid lottery ticket? *See Fowler v. Fowler*, 861 So. 2d 181, 183 (La. 2003) (citing Dennis C. Cuneo, *Life Insurance as an Estate Planning Tool*, 23 LOY. L. REV. 59, 69 (1977) (noting that the French Civil Code viewed life insurance

as a form of gambling). Should the subject of a wager matter? Given that the subject of the wager may well implicate different public policy concerns than those against gambling itself, should we treat all gambling in the same manner? Do some forms of gambling have socially redeeming qualities?

6. Is the motive for a transaction relevant to whether a transaction should be characterized as "gambling?"

7. Recall the question from the notes following the *Green* case involving horse racing. In *Green*, one game that is occurring is the horse race itself, with horses and jockeys as participants. Simultaneously, another game is occurring between bettors in the pari-mutuel system. In *Grigsby*, one could argue that Dr. Grigsby was playing a game of chance, but that simultaneously the decedent Burchard was not. Indeed, can Burchard win a prize?

8. When a person buys life insurance, is that person engaging in gaming, or more conceptually the opposite of gaming? In its most natural form as pure entertainment, gambling is considered to be risk-seeking behavior. A patron in a casino is very much purchasing risk. Insurance, however, is classic risk avoidance or mitigation. If the three elements that generally define gambling are generally met when a person pays an insurance premium, is gambling adequately defined?

9. In the next excerpt, the author argues that American policy has long sought to discourage gambling in other commercial contexts as well.

## LYNN A. STOUT, WHY THE LAW HATES SPECULATORS: REGULATION AND PRIVATE ORDERING IN THE MARKET FOR OTC DERIVATIVES

Duke L.J. 701, 712-718, 724-735 (1999)

### I. ANTISPECULATION RULES IN AMERICAN LAW

To some observers, the claim that the law discourages speculation at first may seem implausible. Speculative trading appears to be the order of the day on stock exchanges like the New York Stock Exchange, and on commodities futures exchanges like the Chicago Board of Trade, not to mention the burgeoning derivatives market. How then can the law be hostile to speculators?

The answer lies in recognizing that speculators' presence in such highly visible but limited arenas obscures their relative absence elsewhere. In theory, there is no need for speculators to limit themselves to trading corporate securities and those relatively few commodities contracts officially listed for trading on an organized futures exchange. They also could wager on the future prices of plastic surgery, narrow ties, Manhattan condos, popular television shows, and law school graduates. In practice, speculation in such goods and services is rare. The reason can be traced to a network of obscure but important legal doctrines that severely limit speculators' role in most markets.

One of the most fundamental of these doctrines is the common law requirement that speculators who want to wager on prices through futures and options agreements have to make and accept delivery of the goods and services they trade. Although few contemporary legal scholars seem aware of this rule, it persists in a variety of modern forms, most notably in insurance law and the Commodity Exchange Act. Its net effect is to confine speculation primarily to regulated commodities futures exchanges, which are exempt from the general rule, and to the corporate securities market, where delivery is relatively easy and inexpensive. Even in these markets, moreover, speculators who seek short-term profits must run an obstacle course of margin requirements, position limits, short sales restrictions, capital gains rules, and other technical regulations that have both the purpose and the effect of deterring speculative trading. The arcana of modern tax, securities, and commodities law provide a second important curb on speculation.

The net result is a legal system that works with surprising consistency to channel our nation's economic energy toward the actual production and distribution of goods and services, and away from the pursuit of short-term trading profits. In illustration, the discussion below considers some important examples of antispeculation rules drawn from both statutes and common law. These rules suggest a pattern of legal antipathy toward speculators that springs from the longstanding belief that speculation wreaks economic harm because it is nonproductive, distorts market prices, and impoverishes speculators themselves.

### A. THE COMMON LAW RULE AGAINST DIFFERENCE CONTRACTS

One of the earliest and most important examples of antispeculation law can be found in the common law doctrine that shall be referred to below as "the rule against difference contracts." Difference contracts were close cousins to futures (contracts for the sale of goods for future delivery) and options (agreements granting one party the right but not the obligation to buy or sell at a specified price at or before some predetermined future date). In a difference contract, however, the contracting parties would agree to perform not by actually delivering the good that was the subject of the contract, but by paying the difference between the contract price and the market price at the time of performance. Thus a "seller" who didn't own wheat and a "buyer" who didn't want wheat might have entered a difference contract for one ton of wheat at a contract price of $1,000 per ton, to be settled in six months. If at the end of six months the market price for wheat had risen to $1,200 per ton, the seller would pay the buyer $200. If the price had dropped to $900 per ton, the buyer would pay the seller $100. In either case, no wheat would actually change hands.

The common law regarded difference contracts as legally unenforceable on grounds of public policy. As the United States Supreme Court described the rule in the 1884 case of *Irwin v. Williar*:

> The generally accepted doctrine in this country is . . . that a contract for the sale of goods to be delivered at a future day is valid, even though the seller has not the goods, nor any other means of getting them than to go into the market and buy them; but such a contract is only valid when the parties really intend and agree that the goods are to be delivered by the seller and the price to be paid by the buyer; and, if under guise of such a contract, the real intent be merely to speculate in the rise or fall of prices, and the goods are not to be delivered, but one party is to pay to the other the difference between the contract price and the market price of the goods at the date fixed for executing the contract, then the whole transaction constitutes nothing more than a wager, and is null and void.

This rule against "settling differences" offers a variety of useful insights into antispeculation law. First, it suggests a perceived link between speculation and gambling[.] Common law courts regarded speculation as a type of wagering rather than a useful form of economic commerce. Thus difference contracts, like private wagers, were declared legally unenforceable.

A second striking aspect of the rule is the strategy it employed to discourage speculation. In effect, the rule forced speculators who wanted their contracts to be enforceable to trade in the underlying "spot market," making and accepting delivery of the goods they bought and sold. The rule thus imposed a "tax" on speculators by requiring them to incur expenses that they could have avoided if difference agreements had been enforceable. For example, spot market speculators would incur substantial transportation expenses trading in commodities that were bulky (wheat), obstinate (livestock), or difficult to transfer securely (gold bullion). Requiring delivery also forced speculators to bear the costs and risks of "carrying" goods—storing, protecting, maintaining, even feeding and watering them—during the period between purchase and sale. Finally, the rule reduced speculators' liquidity by tying up their wealth in inventory. For some forms of property, these transaction costs would be relatively small: baseball cards and corporate stocks could each be spot traded relatively cheaply. In most markets, however, delivery greatly increased the cost of taking a speculative position. The rule against difference contracts thus raised a significant hurdle to speculation in most goods and services.

A third remarkable feature of the rule against difference contracts is that it was explicitly grounded in public policy. Some cases phrased this policy in moral terms, describing difference contracts as "tainted and poisoned" and "the source of great injury to morals." Other cases, however, justified the rule as necessary to temper speculation's supposedly pernicious economic consequences. In other words, speculation was thought to harm not just morals, but markets.

Concern for speculation's economic effects was reflected in three curious charges courts lodged against speculators in difference contract cases. The first was that speculators were nonproductive. Thus judges refused to enforce difference contracts on the grounds that speculation "promote[d] no legitimate trade" and "discourage[d] the disposition to engage in steady business or labor. . . ." This argument seems to have been based on a perception that speculators' profits came out of the pockets of the unfortunates who traded with them, so that speculators were social parasites who fed on others' labor while themselves contributing nothing to the community.

A second economic concern mentioned in difference contract cases arose from speculators' supposedly harmful effects on market prices. Speculators were associated with market instability and especially the puzzling phenomenon of price bubbles. Thus judges condemned speculators because their trading "agitate[d] the markets" and "derang[ed] prices to the detriment of the community."

A third apprehension judges voiced in difference contracts cases related to speculation's supposedly deleterious effects on speculators themselves. By offering an easy way to bet on market prices, difference agreements were thought to tempt people into accepting unreasonable risks. The sad result, according to some cases, was to "fill the cities with . . . bankrupt victims" of speculative fever, along with their impoverished dependents. . . .

While generally refusing to enforce contracts of sale not intended to be settled by delivery, common law courts applied an exception in cases where one party to a difference contract could demonstrate that the contract served a legitimate hedging function. Such a party would have to show that at the time she entered the contract, she held an economic interest that would be damaged by the happening of the very same event that would allow her to profit under the contract. Thus, for example, a plaintiff seeking to enforce a difference agreement that allowed her to profit if wheat prices fell might demonstrate that she held a wheat inventory, the value of which would be damaged by a price decline. Because such a contract would offset a preexisting source of loss rather than creating an opportunity for gain, courts recharacterized these types of contracts as enforceable "indemnity" agreements.

The indemnity exception to the rule against difference contracts suggests that judges recognized that difference agreements could be used for insurance as well as for gambling. At the same time, the fact that the indemnity exception was an exception implies a judicial perception that many difference contracts didn't insure against a preexisting risk. In other words, risk hedging was perceived as the exception—not the rule—in difference contract trading.

The notion that some difference contracts served a useful hedging function while others did not also underlays the second important exception to the rule against difference contracts: the exception for exchange-traded futures. To finance theorists, any contract of sale for future delivery is a "future." In legal terminology, however, the word "future" is sometimes interpreted more narrowly to apply only to the highly standardized contracts for future delivery that are traded in "pits" on organized commodities exchanges such as the Chicago Board of Trade. Traders who buy exchange-traded futures are technically entitled to demand delivery. As a practical matter, however, most exchange-traded futures are settled through an "offset" process in which one party to the contract extinguishes her obligation by reentering the pit and purchasing a second, offsetting contract. Thus a trader obligated to sell 100 bushels of wheat on May 1 might offset her obligation by purchasing a contract to buy 100 bushels on May 1, absorbing the price difference as profit or loss.

In economic substance, an offset futures contract looks very much like a difference agreement. Courts nevertheless adopted very differing attitudes toward the two types of transactions. As Justice Holmes explained in the 1905 case *Board of Trade of Chicago v. Christie Grain & Stock Co.*:

> There is no doubt that the large part of those [futures] contracts is made for serious business purposes. Hedging, for instance, as it is called, is a means by which collectors and exporters of grain or other products, and manufacturers who make contracts in advance for the sale of their goods, secure themselves against the fluctuations

of the market by counter contracts for the purchase or sale, as the case may be, of an equal quantity of the product, or of the material of manufacture. . . . It seems to us an extraordinary and unlikely proposition that the dealings which give its character to the great market for future sales in this country are to be regarded as mere wagers. . . . A set-off is in legal effect a delivery. We speak only of the contracts made in the pits, because in them the members are principals.

As this language suggests, courts perceived organized futures markets as serving primarily the bona fide insurance needs of commodities suppliers and consumers, rather than the passions of speculators. . . . It also laid the foundation for the primary legal regime governing "difference contract" trading today: the Commodity Exchange Act of 1936 [(CEA)]. . . .

### C. ANTISPECULATION RULES IN INSURANCE LAW: THE DOCTRINES OF INDEMNITY AND INSURABLE INTEREST

The common law rule against difference contracts and the CEA both deter speculation in a similar fashion: by requiring speculators outside a regulated futures exchange to incur the costs associated with spot market delivery. This strategy, it turns out, is mirrored in insurance law. Two doctrines that lie at the heart of insurance—the requirement of insurable interest and the indemnity principle—have both evolved, in part, to prevent speculators from using insurance for speculation.

There are several different tests for determining whether a policyholder has an "insurable interest." As a general rule, however, courts refuse to enforce an insurance policy unless the policyholder can demonstrate that she would suffer some significant economic detriment if the insured property is destroyed. Thus, the owner of an automobile has an insurable interest in her car, and her bank also may be able to purchase a policy if it financed the purchase and holds a collateral interest in the vehicle. Neither the owner nor the bank, however, can purchase a policy on some third party's vehicle.

Even for policyholders who hold insurable interests, recovery will be limited by a second antispeculation rule: the indemnity principle. Under the indemnity rules, a policyholder cannot recover any amount exceeding the economic value of her interest in the insured property. An automobile owner whose car is destroyed can recover the fair market value of the vehicle, but cannot recover three times that amount even if she has purchased and paid for three policies. Similarly, her bank can recover only the amount of its unpaid loan.

The doctrines of indemnity and insurable interest arose in the earliest days of insurance law and persist, often in statutory form, to this day. Both reflect an axiom of insurance so fundamental that it goes to the very meaning of the word: insurance policies are to compensate for losses suffered—not to generate profits. Two evils are thought to flow from using insurance policies for gain. The first is "moral hazard," a picturesque phrase referring to the fear that insurance might tempt policyholders into not protecting adequately against losses, or even destroying insured property for profit. The second fundamental concern underlying the indemnity and insurable interest requirements, however, is the fear that speculators otherwise would use insurance policies to wager on the future.

Both early and modern insurance cases frequently cite the antispeculation function of the indemnity and insurable interest rules, as does academic commentary dating well into the mid-twentieth century. More recently, however, scholars have shown a curious reluctance to credit the traditional antispeculation rationale, instead emphasizing moral hazard as the rules' underlying foundation. . . .

Another aspect of the indemnity and insurable interest rules that highlights their antispeculation origins is the fact that neither rule is waivable. Suppose a homeowner wants to violate the indemnity principle by taking out a policy that would pay three times her home's value in the event of its destruction. The insurance company could insist on a variety of terms (such as exclusions for arson) to protect itself against moral hazard. Moreover, to the extent moral hazard could not be eliminated entirely, the company could charge a higher premium. If no third parties are harmed, why not let the company sell the policy?

As in the case of the rule against difference agreements, the doctrines of indemnity and insurable interest are curiously unyielding legal barriers to contract—even contracts entered by legally competent and mutually consenting parties. This inflexibility seems unjustified if moral hazard is the law's primary concern. Nonwaivability makes sense, however, if the insurable interest and indemnity rules are intended to protect society from the detrimental effects of speculation, as well as to protect insurance companies from their policyholders' misbehavior.

### D. THE SECURITIES EXCHANGE ACT OF 1934

The rule against difference contracts, the CEA's ban on off-exchange futures, and the insurance requirements of indemnity and insurable interest all force individuals who wish to wager on market prices to incur the transportation, carrying, and liquidity costs associated with doing business in the spot market. This makes speculative trading in most goods and services far more difficult and expensive. However, there is one spot market where transportation, carrying, and liquidity costs are inherently negligible: the market for corporate securities.

Corporate stocks and bonds are cheap to transport and almost costless to store. Because lenders readily accept them as collateral, buyers often can borrow the money needed to buy them, avoiding much sacrifice of liquidity. As a result, the spot market for corporate securities offers a safe haven for speculators driven from other spot markets by high transaction costs. It is far easier to bet on petroleum prices by buying stock in Exxon than by hoarding fuel oil.

Not surprisingly, securities markets have long been associated with speculation. This association, moreover, has long troubled lawmakers. Although movements to curb stock market speculation date back at least to the beginning of the twentieth century, it was not until the market crash of 1929 and the ensuing Great Depression that Congress decided to take action. The result was the Securities Exchange Act of 1934 (SEA).

The SEA is not usually thought of as an antispeculation law. Nevertheless, curbing stock speculation was one of Congress's primary goals in passing that statute. Rampant speculation was believed to be a root cause of both the 1929 market crash and the hardtimes that followed. Section 2 of the SEA accordingly describes the need for regulation as follows:

> [T]ransactions in securities as commonly conducted upon securities exchanges and over-the-counter markets are affected with a national public interest. . . . Frequently the prices of securities on such exchanges and markets are susceptible to . . . excessive speculation, resulting in sudden and unreasonable fluctuations in the prices of securities. . . . National emergencies . . . are precipitated, intensified, and prolonged by . . . sudden and unreasonable fluctuations of securities prices and by excessive speculation. . . .

Like judges in difference contract cases, the 1934 Congress associated speculation with specific economic harms. Thus the House Reports accompanying the SEA condemned stock speculation as a nonproductive activity that drained credit and other valuable resources away from "other more desirable uses of commerce and industry." A second familiar concern highlighted in the legislative history was the fear that speculation produced "wide fluctuations in the price of securities, which ultimately imperiled the holdings of bona fide investors of every type."

Dedicated to curbing stock speculation in principle, in practice Congress found it difficult to design policies that would rein in speculators without also discouraging "legitimate" stock transactions. One strategy eventually adopted to attack speculative excess was to impose "margin requirements" limiting investors' ability to borrow to buy stocks. . . . A second provision of the SEA designed to curb speculation places restrictions on "short selling"—that is, selling borrowed stock. The 1934 Congress believed that short selling encouraged speculation, and concern about "shorting" played a central role in the hearings surrounding the SEA's passage.

Whether the SEA's margin requirements and short sales restrictions are effective or not, however, they are compelling evidence that the 1934 Congress believed both that speculators are endemic in the spot market for securities, and that they work much mischief there. . . .

These observations highlight a curious phenomenon: many contemporary scholars and policymakers appear to have forgotten the SEA's antispeculation goals. Instead, conventional wisdom now views the SEA as first and foremost a disclosure statute. Thus the Supreme Court has opined that "the fundamental purpose of the 1934 Act [is] 'to substitute a philosophy of full disclosure for the philosophy of caveat emptor,'" while academics have asserted that the dominating principle of federal securities regulation "is that anyone willing to disclose the right things can sell or buy whatever he wants at whatever price the market will sustain." . . .

Concern for excessive stock speculation nevertheless seems to have largely disappeared from the agendas of modern securities scholars and policymakers.

### E. SUMMARY: THE PREVALENCE OF ANTISPECULATION LAW

"Antispeculation law" generally is not taught as a subject in the modern legal curriculum. Perhaps it ought to be, for hostility towards speculators appears to be a fundamental characteristic of American law. The rule against difference contracts, the CEA, the doctrines of indemnity and insurable interest, and the SEA's margin requirements and short sales restrictions each play important roles in deterring speculative trading. They are, however, only a few of the many legal doctrines that work to rein in speculators. . . . The Internal Revenue Code also deters speculation by limiting preferential capital gains treatment of income earned from the sale of assets to those held for some minimum period (under current law, one year). This discourages speculation in . . . markets for fine art, real estate, and other tangible assets. Although modern observers often attribute the holding period requirement to concerns over inflation, income averaging, and "lock in" effects, legislative history indicates that Congress adopted the requirement to reward long-term "investment" while discouraging short-term "speculation."

Throughout most of the nineteenth and twentieth centuries, American judges and legislators appear to have followed a policy of actively and deliberately discouraging speculative transactions. Recent years have seen a curious development, however. Lawmakers' long-standing belief that speculation is harmful seems to be eroding. Although antispeculation rules remain a staple of American law, contemporary observers seem increasingly reluctant to subscribe to the notion that deterring speculation should be a goal of public policy. . . .

What explains this modern skepticism towards antispeculation laws? The answer may lie in economic theory's growing influence on legal thinking. Judges and legislators traditionally condemned speculators as nonproductive parasites whose trading destabilizes market prices and often brings financial ruin to speculators themselves. Contemporary economic theory, however, describes speculators in far more flattering terms. [Modern theorists now seem to believe] that speculators serve the economic goal of allocative efficiency.

### NOTES

1.  In this lengthy and enlightening excerpt, Professor Stout demonstrates that U.S. policy has long been hostile toward gambling in commodities, insurance, and the stock market. What are the reasons for the hostility? Are there valid reasons to oppose speculative activity? Many modern economic theorists believe that speculation is valuable because it provides an important source of liquidity in markets and therefore promotes transactional efficiency. Professor Stout is dubious.

2.  Professor Stout observes that the longstanding antipathy toward speculation has been diminishing. For policymakers, speculation is no longer a chief target for market regulation. Perhaps the same cultural changes in the attitude toward speculation in the commercial context help to explain the tremendous growth in the gambling industry. But if casino gambling is gaining widespread acceptance as a direct form of speculation, is there any longer a basis for limiting speculation in securities or commodities markets?

3.  We can answer these questions in a satisfactory manner only if we have a clear understanding of the potential harms of gambling. The next chapter explores the real and perceived harms associated with gambling.

# CHAPTER
# 2

## The Social Harms of Gaming/Gambling

While legalized gambling has grown rapidly in the United States, some state jurisdictions continue to prohibit all forms. While some state jurisdictions are more permissive than others, most states have adopted a highly restrictive legal and regulatory structure. What makes gambling so controversial? What are the harms of gambling and what are the "evils" that gambling regulation or prohibition are attempting to address? On what basis can some states authorize gambling while other states prohibit it? Do the "evils" vary according to the state? If not, what produces these divergent approaches to the same activity?

Some view "gaming" as a harmless form of entertainment, and others view "gambling" as a dangerous activity with significant negative social consequences. The purpose of this chapter is to consider the common objections to gambling and to catalogue those concerns and the broader social ills that they represent. In the cases in this chapter, the courts suggest various analogues, such as tobacco or liquor. Are either of these useful in determining how to regulate gambling?

While different concerns resonate with different observers, it is crucial to identify the particular "evil" or social ill that gambling represents in order to determine how best to address those concerns. The broader question is whether such concerns justify absolute prohibition, or whether the concerns can be addressed through some form of regulation.

As you consider the various objections to gambling, consider whether a strict regulatory regime or an outright ban would be more effective in addressing these objections. Consider also the arguments in favor of legalized gambling. Are there legitimate justifications that offset the widely noted harms?

# A. COMPULSIVE GAMBLING AND THE PUBLIC HEALTH

One of the most common objections to gambling involves the significant public health problem known as "compulsive" or "pathological" gambling. It is also perhaps the most tangible social problem related to gaming.

## STATE v. LAFFERTY

### 456 A.2d 272 (Conn. 1982)

PER CURIAM

The defendant was charged by information with two counts of larceny in the first degree for allegedly embezzling approximately $309,000 from his employer. At trial, the defendant presented evidence that at the time of the commission of the crimes with which he was charged he was unable to conform his conduct to the requirements of the law as the result of a mental defect known as pathological or compulsive gambling. On the basis of the psychiatric testimony presented, the trial court found the defendant not guilty by reason of insanity[.] Thereafter, the defendant was ordered committed to a state mental hospital under General Statutes §53a-47(a)(1) to determine whether "his release [from custody] would constitute a danger to himself or others." General Statutes §53a-47(a)(3). At a subsequent hearing under §53a-47(a)(4), the trial court heard the testimony of Hans Lang-hammer, a staff psychiatrist at Norwich State Hospital called by the state, and Marvin Steinberg, a psychologist called by the defendant. At the conclusion of the hearing, the trial court in an oral decision found that the defendant did not constitute a danger to himself or others, and it ordered his release.

The state . . . appealed to this court claiming that the trial court erred by interpreting the phrase "a danger to himself or others" in §53a-47(a)(4) to mean only a physical danger, and not a danger to property.[2] The state argues that the trial court found the defendant to

---

2. Sec. 53a-47 ACQUITTAL ON GROUNDS OF MENTAL DISEASE OR DEFECT; CONFINEMENT AND EXAMINATION; RELEASE. (a) . . . (1) When any person charged with an offense is acquitted on the grounds of mental disease or defect, the court shall order such person to be temporarily confined in any of the state hospitals for mental illness for a reasonable time, not to exceed ninety days, for an examination to determine his mental condition, except that, if the court can determine, on the basis of the evidence already before it, that such person is not mentally ill to the extent that his release would constitute a danger to himself or others, the court

be a danger to property and that such a danger is included within the meaning of "a danger to himself and others" in the statute. The defendant responds that the court found only that the defendant was "possibly" a danger to property, but that even if he were so, he was nonetheless properly released because the statute is limited to physical danger.

In its oral decision, the court stated: "[A]s this court understands the testimony, I believe Dr. Lang-hammer was very precise in this: he indicated that there was no danger as far as physical harm was concerned. There was a danger as far as property was concerned possibly by the defendant's action in this matter." It is unclear whether the trial court was merely recapitulating the psychiatrist's testimony or whether it was making a finding of fact. Also, the use of the word "possibly" regarding danger to property adds to the ambiguity of the court's oral decision. Whether the defendant was a danger to property is a question of fact which must be determined before we may properly review the claims made in this appeal. It is the function of the trial court, not this court, to find facts. It is therefore necessary for us to remand this case for a further articulation of the trial court's decision on whether the defendant was a danger to property.

[Remanded.]

### NOTES

1.  What likely is the social ill associated with compulsive gambling? Is it any greater than a mere threat to property? Is it relevant that this broader issue arose in a criminal case?
2.  Now, consider the formal psychological description of the diagnosis reprinted from the leading manual for diagnosing mental disorders.

---

may order his immediate release, either unconditionally or conditionally pursuant to subdivision (2) of subsection (e). (2) The person to be examined shall be informed that, in addition to the examination provided for in subdivision (1), he has a right to be examined during such confinement by a psychiatrist of his own choice. (3) Within sixty days of the confinement pursuant to subdivision (1), the superintendent of such hospital and the retained psychiatrist, if any, shall file reports with the court setting forth their findings and conclusions as to whether such person is mentally ill to the extent that his release would constitute a danger to himself or others. Copies of such reports shall be delivered to the state's attorney or prosecutor and to counsel for such person. (4) Upon receipt of such reports, the court shall promptly schedule a hearing. If the court determines that the preponderance of the evidence at the hearing establishes that such person is mentally ill to the extent that his release would constitute a danger to himself or others, the court shall confine such person in a suitable hospital or other treatment facility. . . .

## DIAGNOSTIC AND STATISTICAL MANUAL OF MENTAL DISORDERS (FOURTH EDITION)

### Text Revision (DSM-IV TR) 312.31 Pathological Gambling

DIAGNOSTIC CRITERIA FOR 312.31 PATHOLOGICAL GAMBLING

A. Persistent and recurrent maladaptive gambling behavior as indicated by five (or more) of the following:

(1)   is preoccupied with gambling (e.g., preoccupied with reliving past gambling experiences, handicapping or planning the next venture, or thinking of ways to get money with which to gamble)

(2)   needs to gamble with increasing amounts of money in order to achieve the desired excitement

(3)   has repeated unsuccessful efforts to control, cut back, or stop gambling

(4)   is restless or irritable when attempting to cut down or stop gambling

(5)   gambles as a way of escaping from problems or of relieving a dysphoric mood (e.g., feelings of helplessness, guilt, anxiety, depression)

(6)   after losing money gambling, often returns another day to get even ("chasing" one's losses)

(7)   lies to family members, therapist, or others to conceal the extent of involvement with gambling

(8)   has committed illegal acts such as forgery, fraud, theft, or embezzlement to finance gambling

(9)   has jeopardized or lost a significant relationship, job, or educational or career opportunity because of gambling

(10)  relies on others to provide money to relieve a desperate financial situation caused by gambling

B. The gambling behavior is not better accounted for by a Manic Episode.

DIAGNOSTIC FEATURES

The individual may be preoccupied with gambling (e.g., reliving past gambling experiences, planning the next gambling venture, or thinking of ways to get money with which to gamble) (Criterion A1). Most individuals with Pathological Gambling say that they are seeking "action" (an aroused, euphoric state) or excitement even more than money. Increasingly larger bets, or greater risks, may be needed to continue to produce the desired level of excitement (Criterion A2).

Individuals with Pathological Gambling often continue to gamble despite repeated efforts to control, cut back, or stop the behavior (Criterion A3). There may be restlessness or irritability when attempting to cut down or stop gambling (Criterion A4). The individual may gamble as a way of escaping from problems or to relieve a dysphoric mood (e.g., feelings of helplessness, guilt, anxiety, depression) (Criterion A5). A pattern of "chasing" one's losses may develop, with an urgent need to keep gambling (often with larger bets or the taking of greater risks) to undo a loss or series of losses. The individual may abandon his or her gambling strategy and try to win back losses all at once. Although all gamblers may chase for short periods, it is the long-term chase that is more characteristic of individuals with Pathological Gambling (Criterion A6). The individual may lie to family members, therapists, or others to conceal the extent of involvement with gambling (Criterion A7). When the individual's borrowing resources are strained, the person may resort to antisocial behavior (e.g., forgery, fraud, theft, or embezzlement) to obtain money (Criterion A8). The individual may have jeopardized or lost a significant relationship, job, or educational or career opportunity because of gambling (Criterion A9). The individual may also engage in "bailout" behavior, turning to family or others for help with a desperate financial situation that was caused by gambling (Criterion A10).

### ASSOCIATED FEATURES AND DISORDERS

Associated descriptive features and mental disorders. Distortions in thinking (e.g., denial, superstitions, overconfidence, or a sense of power and control) may be present in individuals with Pathological Gambling. Many individuals with Pathological Gambling believe that money is both the cause of and solution to all their problems. Individuals with Pathological Gambling are frequently highly competitive, energetic, restless, and easily bored. They may be overly concerned with the approval of others and may be generous to the point of extravagance. When not gambling, they may be workaholics or "binge" workers who wait until they are up against deadlines before really working hard. They may be prone to developing general medical conditions that are associated with stress (e.g., hypertension, peptic ulcer disease, migraine). Individuals seeking treatment for Pathological Gambling have relatively high rates of suicidal ideation and suicide attempts. Studies of men with Pathological Gambling suggest that a history of inattentive and hyperactive symptoms in childhood may be a risk factor for development of Pathological Gambling later in life. Increased rates of Mood Disorders, Attention-Deficit/Hyperactivity Disorder, Substance Abuse or Dependence, other Impulse-Control Disorders, and Antisocial, Narcissistic, and Borderline Personality Disorders have been reported in individuals with Pathological Gambling.

Associated laboratory findings. There are no laboratory findings that are diagnostic of Pathological Gambling. However, a variety of laboratory findings have been reported to be abnormal in males with Pathological Gambling compared with control subjects. These include measures of neurotransmitters and their metabolites in cerebrospinal fluid and urine, and response to neuroendocrine challenges, implicating abnormalities in a variety of neurotransmitter systems, including the serotonin, norepinephrine, and dopamine systems. Abnormalities in platelet monoamine oxidase activity have also been reported in males with Pathological Gambling. Individuals with Pathological Gambling may display high levels of impulsivity on neuropsychological tests.

### SPECIFIC CULTURE AND GENDER FEATURES

There are cultural variations in the prevalence and type of gambling activities (e.g., pai go, cockfights, horse racing, the stock market). Approximately one-third of individuals with Pathological Gambling are females, but in different geographic areas and cultures, gender ratio can vary considerably. Females with the disorder are more apt to be depressed and to gamble as an escape. Females are underrepresented in treatment programs for gambling and represent only 2%-4% of the population of Gamblers Anonymous. This may be a function of the greater stigma attached to female gamblers.

### PREVALENCE

The prevalence of Pathological Gambling is influenced by both the availability of gambling and the duration of availability such that with the increasing availability of legalized gambling, there is an increase in the prevalence of Pathological Gambling. Community studies estimate the lifetime prevalence of Pathological Gambling to range from 0.4% to 3.4% in adults, although prevalence rates in some areas (e.g., Puerto Rico, Australia) have been reported to be as high as 7%. Higher prevalence rates, ranging from 2.8% to 8%, have been reported in adolescents and college students. The prevalence of Pathological Gambling may be increased in treatment-seeking individuals with a Substance Use Disorder.

### COURSE

Pathological Gambling typically begins in early adolescence in males and later in life in females. Although a few individuals are "hooked" with their very first bet, for most the course is more insidious. There may be years of social gambling followed by an abrupt onset that may be precipitated by greater exposure to gambling or by a stressor. The gambling pattern may be regular or episodic, and the course of the disorder is typically chronic. There is generally a progression in the frequency of gambling, the amount wagered, and the preoccupation with gambling and obtaining money with which to gamble. The urge to gamble and gambling activity generally increase during periods of stress or depression.

### FAMILIAL PATTERN

Pathological Gambling and Alcohol Dependence are both more common among the parents of individuals with Pathological Gambling than among the general population.

### DIFFERENTIAL DIAGNOSIS

Pathological Gambling must be distinguished from social gambling and professional gambling. Social gambling typically occurs with friends or colleagues and lasts for a limited period of time, with predetermined acceptable losses. In professional gambling, risks are limited and discipline is central. Some individuals can experience problems associated with their gambling (e.g., short-term chasing behavior and loss of control) that do not meet the full criteria for Pathological Gambling.

Loss of judgment and excessive gambling may occur during a Manic Episode. An additional diagnosis of Pathological Gambling should only be given if the gambling behavior is not better accounted for by the Manic Episode (e.g., a history of maladaptive gambling behavior at times other than during a Manic Episode). Alternatively, an individual with Pathological Gambling may exhibit behavior during a gambling binge that resembles a Manic Episode. However, once the individual is away from the gambling, these manic-like features dissipate. Problems with gambling may occur in individuals with Antisocial Personality Disorder; if criteria are met for both disorders, both can be diagnosed.

## NOTES

Is the diagnostic information in the DSM-IV likely to describe a wide range of people? Is a diagnosis of compulsive gambling likely to be useful for a court analyzing whether to hold a gambler legally responsible for his losses?

## UNITED STATES v. LIBUTTI

### 1994 U.S. Dist. LEXIS 19916 (D. N.J.)

SIMANDLE, District Judge:

[The defendant Robert LiButti was convicted by a jury of tax evasion and bank fraud. He sought a downward departure under the United States Sentencing Guidelines, among other reasons, for his compulsive gambling disorder which caused him to suffer from significantly reduced mental capacity contributing to his commission of the tax offenses. He also sought a downward departure on the basis that the Government knowingly permitted him to gamble away hundreds of thousands of dollars instead of seizing the funds and negotiating a compromise of his unpaid multi-million-dollar tax liability.]

\* \* \*

Defendant argues that under the policy statement in §5K2.13, extraordinary factors are present and justify a downward departure due to defendant's alleged diminished mental capacity caused by a pathological gambling disorder. . . . It is undisputed that Mr. LiButti was an intensive casino gambler who lost millions of dollars during the period of 1986 to 1989 when he committed his tax offenses. . . . [All four experts who testified for the defendant and the government agreed] that he manifests the diagnostic criteria for pathological gambling under DSM-III-R, Code 312.31.

Under §5K2.13, for this non-violent offense an individual "suffering from significantly reduced mental capacity" may warrant a lower sentence "to reflect the extent to which reduced mental capacity contributed to the commission of the offense." Such a reduction then is appropriate "provided that the defendant's criminal history does not indicate a need for incarceration to protect the public."

Compulsive gambling has been rejected as a basis for departure under the Sentencing Guidelines in [numerous cases. Another] court observed:

> §5K2.13 must be interpreted in light of the fact that, with the decreased relevance of deterrence and desert, incapacitation becomes the primary rationale for incarcerating those whose crimes were committed as a result of "significantly reduced mental capacity."

Conceptually, it is conceivable that pathological gambling can satisfy the requirements for a diminished capacity departure in an appropriate case. Pathological gambling has become more widely recognized as a mental disorder, that is, a disorder of the logical thinking processes

in persons who are consumed with the thought of little else than
gambling, if the defendant becomes unable to absorb information
in the usual way and to exercise the power of reason. For example,
if compulsive gambling was so all-consuming an obsession that the
individual lacked ability to understand his taxpaying obligations,
such a diminished capacity could be found to have contributed to
his or her diminished willfulness in failing in pay taxes. Short of
this degree of mental impairment, compulsive gambling may create
a special need for money and a special drain on resources, in much
the same way as a drug addiction preoccupies the addict's financial life
undermining his financial capacity and creating the need for money
resulting in non-payment of taxes. No one would suggest that the
need for money justifies commission of a crime nor that it dilutes
the actor's criminal intent. Such an individual resorts to nonpayment
of taxes "not because of any inability to understand his situation, but
because he need[s] money." [*United States v.*] *Hamilton*, 949 F.2d at
193. Mr. LiButti's situation falls into this latter category; he knew if he
evaded payment of millions in taxes, he'd have more money to spend
on himself, including but hardly limited to gambling.

To qualify for a departure for diminished capacity, of course, a
defendant is not required to prove a complete defense, i.e., that his
intent to commit the crime has been negated entirely, for one could
not be convicted of a specific intent crime if that were the case. One
commentator has pointed this out:

> Compulsive gambling certainly reduces a defendant's mental capacity;
> that it does not preclude a defendant from understanding his circum-
> stances or from exercising the power of reason renders it an incomplete
> defense. This, of course, does not preclude it from providing the basis
> for downward departure under section 5K2.13.

Lawrence S. Lustberg, *Sentencing The Sick: Compulsive Gambling
as the Basis for a Downward Departure under the Federal Sentencing
Guidelines*, 2 Seton Hall J. Sports L. 51, 69-70 (1992). It is not at all
clear, however, that Mr. Lustberg is correct when he writes, "Defendants suffering from this disease lack control over their behavior,
including their criminal actions." Such loss of control is not one of
the diagnostic criteria, nor has any expert witness in this case opined
that persons with this disorder usually cannot control their criminal
actions. Plenty of pathological gamblers nonetheless manage to pay
taxes. There is nothing inconsistent about it. Some may tend to plan
on paying their taxes when they have satisfied other priorities by big
winnings, yet these choices are the product of conscious decisions, as
Dr. Greenfield has testified in this case.

The task, then, is to demonstrate whether in the given case the pathological gambler defendant has demonstrated that his mental capacity was "significantly reduced" in a manner contributing to the commission of the tax offenses here. As a factual basis for this departure, defendant asserts the following facts:

> (i) Mr. LiButti suffers from a severe form of compulsive gambling disorder; (ii) that disorder manifested itself to an unprecedented degree—reported losses of approximately $15 million at Trump Plaza—between 1986 and 1989, the critical period during which he allegedly committed the tax offenses; (iii) he never possessed, at a single moment, sufficient monies to pay his tax deficiencies in full; (iv) his compulsive gambling disorder as manifested tended to preclude him from using his available monies to make partial payments against those deficiencies by instead tending to compel him to gamble such monies in an effort to win sufficient monies to pay those deficiencies in full; and (v) his manifestation of those tendencies was so extraordinary that they compelled him to gamble as much as $500,000 at one time.

Additionally, Dr. Cancro has expressed his opinion that Mr. LiButti's compulsive gambling disorder impaired his judgment to an extent sufficient to constitute diminished capacity. The "impairment of judgment" that Dr. Cancro speaks about concerns the compulsive and addictive behavior of continuing to gamble, rather than the decision to not pay taxes.

Testimony of some friends and family members at trial, who wanted the jury to believe that Mr. LiButti would discuss his tax situation and his intention to pay his tax bills while literally sitting at the gaming tables, was incredible. The jury obviously rejected it and so does this court. Even if LiButti may have uttered such a remark, it served to demonstrate that he was at all times aware that he was obligated to pay taxes, was failing to do so, and was not intending to do anything about it.

Mr. LiButti also failed to explain how he could have such large sums of cash available to him and yet never make even a quarterly estimated payment or a partial payment toward his indebtedness for the 1970, 1971, 1987 and 1988 tax liabilities. This was argued as a manifestation of the partial payment aversion that compulsive gamblers are said to have (although again not part of the DSM III-R criteria for this disorder, above). Such compulsive gamblers, the thesis goes, don't repay part of a debt if they only had part of the funds needed; instead, they gamble the part payment hoping to turn it into the full payment. This theory was fully explained in expert testimony at trial to the jury. It was not accepted; indeed, the proofs at trial were to the contrary.

Mr. LiButti had plenty of installment obligations, for his many car loans and for mortgage payments on his . . . mansions. For considerable periods of time he provided the funds to make the monthly payments. To everyone but the I.R.S.

Despite Mr. LiButti's enormous gambling losses, however, he at all relevant times had sufficient funds and assets to live in a luxurious lifestyle for himself and his family befitting his economic status as a millionaire. He was chauffeured in his luxury automobiles, sometimes buying a new Mercedes every month because he was quite taken with brand new cars. He was the true owner of his residences in mansions worth $1-2 million at all relevant times. He selected the finishing touches to furnish his homes—the antiques, the chandeliers, the oriental rugs, the marble, the wine cellar and cases of fine wines. He concealed his ownership of the Kentucky Derby horse Groovy. He made the important decisions for his own multimillion dollar business (Buck Chance Stable) and for his daughter's business (Lion Crest Stables) both run from his same office. All these multimillion-dollar personal financial decisions resulted in earning and spending money on himself and his family and choosing not to pay his taxes, but choosing instead to evade the payment of them.

Mr. Arseneault, in his closing statement to the jury, argued frankly to the jury that Mr. LiButti's lifestyle was "piggish," in his words, but that living in an opulent manner was not a crime. That's correct, but the "piggishness" was the product of an extremely crafty mind, fully aware of his tax obligations and scheming to evade them, while managing to both gamble millions and consume millions more himself. This anti-tax pro-LiButti mindset was not in any part the consequence of his pathological gambling disorder.

His intent to evade payment was manifested as early as 1984, which was a year before LiButti began his gambling sprees in Atlantic City. Defendant LiButti vowed that the IRS would "never collect a penny" of the taxes due and owing, and he urged IRS to accept a trivial fraction of his multi-million dollar tax liability in settlement of his Tax Court case concerning his unpaid 1970 and 1971 assessments, which later formed part of his conviction on Count 1 herein for evasions of payment. That vow, like his bitterness from his 1977 conviction for filing a false return (which failed to disclose sizeable racehorse interests held by a nominee although resulting in a business loss to him), had nothing to do with pathological gambling and everything to do with his belief that he could forever structure his personal wealth to evade his duty to pay taxes.

I find that his capacity to conform his conduct to the law was not diminished by his compulsive gambling. It would be a miscarriage of justice to recognize Mr. LiButti's compulsive gambling as an excuse to avoid the full consequences of his own criminal decisions, and the motion for downward departure under the policy statement of §5K2.13 will be denied.

The defendant [also] seeks a departure under §5K2.0 arguing that the government "acted unconstitutionally, vindictively and outrageously by, among other actions, knowingly permitting Mr. LiButti to gamble away hundreds of thousands of dollars instead of seizing those funds and refusing to negotiate an offer in compromise with him." . . .

The policy statement in §5K2.0 generally recognizes that grounds for departure may exist if the court finds "that there exists an aggravating or mitigating circumstances of a kind, or to a degree, not adequately taken into consideration by the Sentencing Commission in formulating the guidelines that should result in a sentence different from that describe."

The defendant argues that the IRS agents witnessed him on several occasions gambling away hundreds of thousands of dollars without seizing the funds to satisfy tax liabilities, and this is said to amount to a governmental manipulation of the charges against him resulting in a greater tax owed than if the IRS had seized some of the money on these occasions, or if it would have settled for a fractional amount, referring by analogy to the holdings in *United States v. Lieberman*, 971 F.2d 989, 999 & n.10 (3d Cir. 1992) (affirming downward departure based on government's manipulation of indictment charges), and in *United States v. Monaco*, 23 F.3d 793, 799 (3d Cir. 1994) (downward departure permissible if loss table overstates true loss due to actions of a third party beyond defendant's control).

There is no evidence to support defendant's contention that governmental misconduct has led to an overstating of the amount of tax loss. The government acted reasonably in refusing to entertain overtures by Mr. LiButti's attorney (Mr. Wishnia) for an overall settlement amounting to pennies on the dollar, when LiButti was earning millions annually and had the clear ability to make full payment. Further, even in the statements to the IRS of Mr. LiButti's projected annual income at that time, there was a dramatic understatement on behalf of defendant. LiButti's taxable income for 1987 turned out to be $3,166,101, and his taxable income for 1988 was $782,000. He castigates the IRS now for not accepting his paltry efforts toward settlement during those years. In fact, the IRS would have been derelict if it had done so. Similarly, this defendant should not be heard to complain that the IRS was not more aggressive in placing a lien upon his casino account each time he showed up to gamble; there is no evidence that the IRS's sluggishness in that regard was intentional, and the agents who occasionally observed LiButti did not have a collection mission foremost in mind as they gathered information. Where is the evidence that the defendant, who now says he was denied the opportunity to negotiate a compromise settlement on his terms, ever sent a check to the IRS to even begin reducing his enormous liabilities at any time after the first assessment (July 11, 1986)?

In seeking to blame the agents, and claiming to be the victim of governmental manipulation and abuse, this defendant is just repeating the sad, tired refrain that has been stuck like an old phonograph needle, "It ain't my fault, they done me wrong." It is the defendant, Robert LiButti, who has manipulated the truth and cast a broad net of blame while accepting none himself. His position is utterly unsupported in reality. His motion for departure on this ground is denied.

## NOTES

1.   Did the *LiButti* court take seriously the unanimous medical diagnosis of four different doctors, including two for the prosecution, that Libutti suffered from pathological gambling disorder? If not, is it because the court disagreed with the diagnosis of the illness or the legitimacy of the illness? Did the judge reach a reasoned decision?
2.   Can *LiButti* be reconciled with *Lafferty*?

## MARK MERRILL v. TRUMP INDIANA, INC.,
### 320 F.3d 729 (7th Cir. 2003)

EVANS, Circuit Judge.

Mark Merrill robbed banks in December 1998 and January 1999 and for that activity he was convicted and is now serving time at a federal prison in Florida. But this is not a criminal case dealing with the robberies: it's a civil suit, under our diversity jurisdiction, alleging that a riverboat casino didn't do what it was supposed to do to prevent Merrill from gambling. His substantial gambling losses fueled a need for money, and although his complaint doesn't come right out and say it, Merrill's present predicament can be traced to his need for cash to cover his gambling tab.

Trump Indiana operates a riverboat casino on the shore of Lake Michigan in Gary, Indiana. We recently noted some of the political machinations that led to the licensing of the casino in the mid-1990's. *See Mays v. Trump Indiana, Inc.*, 255 F.3d 351 (7th Cir. 2001). Mr. Merrill, by his own admission, is a compulsive gambler. Like East and West, this is a twain that should never meet. But it did.

According to the third version of Merrill's complaint, which seeks over $6 million in damages, he entered a clinic for compulsive gamblers in Peoria, Illinois, in 1996. The clinic soon became his "guardian/custodian/trustee in all matters pertaining to the recognition and treatment of the symptoms and underlying causes of his addictive and compulsive behaviors . . . ." Acting in that capacity, Merrill alleged that his rehab counselor at the clinic contacted the casino in 1996 and formed with it an oral contract to keep Merrill off its premises. The consideration for this contract, it is alleged, was that the clinic would "publicize to the community" the casino's support of programs to help compulsive gamblers get over their addictions. Discovery in the case, particularly a deposition given by the rehab counselor, however, disclosed that no oral contract was created. But it is undisputed that Merrill himself, in 1996, wrote to the casino asking that he be evicted from it if he ever showed up to gamble. And Merrill's name does appear on the casino's "eviction list."

In 1998, Merrill relapsed and returned to gambling at the casino. And now, as we said, he's serving federal time for bank robbery.

Merrill's complaint alleged causes of action for fraud, constructive fraud, strict liability, breach of contract, intentional and reckless disregard for others' safety (willful and wanton misconduct), negligence, and breach of the implied covenant of good faith and fair dealing. The district court dismissed the constructive fraud and strict liability claims on a Rule 12(b)(6) motion and, a year later, granted summary judgment for Trump on all other counts. The court concluded that Trump never promised to honor Merrill's self-exclusion request and so no contract existed between Trump and Merrill. The court further found that, because Trump owed no statutory or contractual duty to Merrill, it did not act negligently or engage in willful and wanton misconduct.

On appeal, Merrill does not contest the district court's finding that he and Trump did not have a contract. He challenges only the grant of summary judgment on his tort claims. Merrill argues that the court erred in holding that Trump had neither violated a duty of care nor engaged in willful and wanton misconduct when it allowed Merrill to gamble in its casino.

In Indiana, the existence of a tort duty is a question of law. Thus, we review de novo whether Trump owed a duty to Merrill. We resolve the issues in this case as we believe Indiana courts would resolve them.

A defendant is not liable for negligence unless it owes a duty of care to an injured plaintiff. *Webb v. Jarvis*, 575 N.E.2d 992, 995 (Ind. 1991). Merrill argues that Indiana statutory provisions and administrative regulations impose a duty on Trump to exclude gamblers who ask to be placed on the casino's eviction list. The Indiana Gaming Commission is empowered by statute to eject or exclude individuals who "call into question the honesty and integrity of the gambling operations." Ind. Code §4-33-4-7 (2002). But it is not clear that Merrill's conduct while in the casino put the "honesty and integrity" of Trump's operations in question. Moreover, the statute addresses exclusion by the gaming commission, not the casinos.

Indiana regulations do require casinos to maintain an eviction list, including individuals who request to be excluded, and to prohibit entry to those on the list: "Each riverboat licensee shall maintain a list of evicted persons. . . . At minimum, the eviction criteria shall include . . . [a] person [who] requests that his or her own name be placed on the riverboat licensee's eviction list." Ind. Admin. Code tit. 68, r. 6-2-1 §1(c)(5) (2002). But this is a recent amendment, implemented in 2000. In 1998, when Merrill's relapse occurred, no statute or regulation explicitly obligated Indiana casinos to honor self-eviction requests.

Even if the amended regulation applied, however, it is by no means certain that the regulation would sustain a cause of action against Trump. Trump is required by regulation to maintain an exclusion log and to add to that list individuals who request to be put on it. But Trump's obligation to follow regulations promulgated by the Indiana Gaming Commission does not automatically translate into a duty of care owed to compulsive gamblers. At most, the rules impose upon Trump a duty to the state through the gaming commission, not to a self-requesting evictee.

If Trump violates regulations, it must answer to the gaming commission—the current rules provide for administrative and disciplinary hearings, as well as sanctions against casinos, including fines and rescindment of licenses. Ind. Admin. Code tit. 68, r. 13-1-1 et seq. But neither the regulations nor the statute expressly creates a private cause of action against nonconforming casinos. When a statute is silent regarding the imposition of civil liability, the Indiana Supreme Court looks to legislative intent to determine whether a private cause of action exists. *Vaughn v. Daniels Co.*, 777 N.E.2d 1110, 1134 (Ind. 2002). As the district court noted, the statutory provisions and administrative rules surrounding gambling are voluminous, and although the legislature was silent regarding civil liability, it specifically created administrative penalties to be enforced through the gaming commission. Given the extent of gambling regulation in Indiana, we conclude that the Indiana Supreme Court would not conclude that the legislature intended to create a private cause of action. *See Hakimoglu v. Trump Taj Mahal*, 70 F.3d 291, 293-94 (3d Cir.

1995) (where state intensely regulated casinos without creating cause of action, casino was not liable to plaintiff who suffered extensive gambling losses while intoxicated).

But Merrill also argues that, even in the absence of a statutory duty, Trump owed him a duty of care under common law. We can find no Indiana case addressing the extent of the duty owed by casinos to their patrons. Indeed, it appears that no court has addressed the specific issue whether casinos can be sued in tort when they fail to evict a gambler who requests his own exclusion.

Courts elsewhere that have addressed the liability of casinos to injured plaintiffs have imposed on casinos no higher duty to their patrons than any on other business. *Lundy v. Adamar of N.J., Inc.*, 34 F.3d 1173, 1180-81 (3d Cir. 1994) (casino had duty to summon aid and take reasonable first aid measures); *Marmer v. Queen of New Orleans at the Hilton, J.V.*, 787 So. 2d 1115, 1120 (La. Ct. App. 2001) (casino has duty to protect patrons from foreseeable criminal acts); *Saucier v. Players Lake Charles*, 751 So. 2d 312, 319 (La. Ct. App. 1999) (casino has duty to take reasonable care of patrons' safety); *Joynt v. Cal. Hotel & Casino*, 108 Nev. 539, 835 P.2d 799, 801 (Nev. 1992) (casino has duty to maintain reasonably safe premises). Under Indiana law, a business owes its invitees a duty to take reasonable care for their safety. *Ellis v. Luxbury Hotels, Inc.*, 716 N.E.2d 359, 360 (Ind. 1999). Merrill never alleged in district court that Trump had not taken reasonable care for his safety or that he ever felt unsafe on the premises.

The closest analogy to Merrill's situation is that of a tavern's liability to exercise reasonable care to protect its patrons. In Indiana, a tavern proprietor serving alcohol can be held liable, under certain conditions, if an intoxicated patron injures another patron or a third party. *E.g., Paragon Family Restaurant v. Bartolini*, 769 N.E.2d 609, 614 (Ind. Ct. App. 2002); *Fast Eddie's v. Hall*, 688 N.E.2d 1270, 1272 (Ind. Ct. App. 1997). But a patron who drives while intoxicated, causing his own injuries, cannot recover from the tavern that served him alcohol. *Davis v. Stinson*, 508 N.E.2d 65, 68 (Ind. App. 1987). Essentially, Merrill thinks that the casino should be held responsible for the destructive effects of his 1998 relapse into gambling. But Indiana law does not protect a drunk driver from the effects of his own conduct, and we assume that the Indiana Supreme Court would take a similar approach with compulsive gamblers.

Merrill's last argument is that the court erred in granting Trump summary judgment on his willful and wanton misconduct claim. In Indiana, a defendant engages in willful and wanton misconduct when it consciously acts or refuses to act knowing, or with reckless disregard to the probability, that injury will result to the plaintiff from its conduct or from its failure to take steps to avoid an impending danger. *Witham v. Norfolk and W. Ry. Co.*, 561 N.E.2d 484, 486 (Ind. 1990); *Conder v. Hull Lift Truck*, Inc., 435 N.E.2d 10, 21 (Ind. 1982). The defendant must know that injury is probable or likely, as opposed to possible. *Conder*, 435 N.E.2d at 21. Under this standard, we cannot conclude that the district court erred in concluding that Merrill raised no issue of material fact that could lead a jury to find that Trump engaged in willful and wanton misconduct. For these reasons, the judgment of the district court is AFFIRMED.

## NOTES

1. In a Ninth Circuit opinion, the court opened its opinion this way: "John William Forrester . . . is a gambling addict and recovering alcoholic. In May 1991, he and his wife of one month moved to Las Vegas to seek a fresh start." *United States v. Forrester*, 19 F.3d 482, 483 (9th Cir. 1994). In *Forrester*, the court went on to describe the tragic story of a man who gambled and lost $13,000 of his wife's money, which represented the family's entire nest egg. In desperation, Forrester robbed a bank, but he was immediately remorseful and soon turned himself in, eventually pleading guilty. Thus did gambling impact the life of a 42-year old man who had no history of prior criminal conduct.

2. What explains the ironic and cynical tone used by federal circuit court judges in *Merrill* and *Forrester*? What does the tone suggest about the judge's view of the defendant's plight and compulsive gambling in general?

3. *Merrill* likens the question it faced to so-called tavern-owner liability in which the drunk driver is not able to sue the bar that sold him liquor for his own injuries caused by an accident attributable to his own drunk driving. What the court fails to mention because it is not necessary to the decision is that third parties injured in such accidents sometimes *can* recover from the bar that contributed to the drunk driver's intoxication. If a teller or a patron had been injured in Merrill's bank robbery attempt, would they have a cause of action against the casino? Would Forrester's wife have a claim against the casino for his loss of her half of the nest egg?

4. How useful is *Merrill*'s analogy to tavern owners and, by extension, abuse of alcohol. What are the similarities in alcohol abuse and compulsive gambling? What are the differences?

5. Like much of tort law, these cases present the question of who ought to bear the social costs of harmful side effects of an industry.

Should tort law be used to answer this question by allocating liability to casinos? How might we compare or contrast the duty of a casino to gamblers with the duty of tobacco companies to its consumers? If lawsuits against tobacco companies brought by people who suffered ill health effects as a result of smoking cigarettes prevailed in favor of the plaintiffs, why should not the same result occur in cases against casinos brought by people who suffered the ill effects of compulsive gambling? On the other hand, can it be determined that casinos have engaged in the same kind of wrongdoing alleged of tobacco companies?

6. One mechanism for regulating tobacco is through disclosure requirements on tobacco products. Would disclosure requirements be an effective way to address problems with compulsive gambling in the casino environment?

7. *Merrill* describes Indiana's sophisticated regulatory regime for compulsive gambling which includes an exclusion list and a mechanism for voluntary exclusion. What is the best way to insure that casinos meet their obligations under these rules?

8. The topic of Internet gaming will be discussed in great detail in a later chapter. However, David Carruthers, the CEO of BetOn-Sports, PLC, an online casino, argues that it is easier to regulate compulsive gamblers who engage in Internet gaming than it is to regulate compulsive gamblers who engage in casino gambling: "I run a multi-billion-dollar public company listed on the London Stock Exchange, and we operate with the highest standards of practice to protect consumers, restrict minor access and protect the vulnerable. My company has controls in place that restrict access by minors and would cut off gambling from customers who exhibit excessive compulsive behavior. Online gambling is the most transparent form of gambling there is—every transaction is logged and every transaction is available for scrutiny. I, and my peers at other major online operators, want regulation of our industry." *See Should Internet Gambling Be Banned?* WALL ST. J. ONLINE NEWS ROUNDUP (April 4, 2006). Is close scrutiny of Internet gaming a useful way to address compulsive gambling?

## ALEXANDRA BERZON, THE GAMBLER WHO BLEW $127 MILLION

### Wall St. J., Dec. 5, 2009

During a year-long gambling binge at the Caesars Palace and Rio casinos in 2007, Terrance Watanabe managed to lose nearly $127 million. The run is believed to be one of the biggest losing streaks by an individual in Las Vegas history. It devoured much of Mr. Watanabe's personal fortune, he says, which he built up over more than two decades running his family's party-favor import business in Omaha, Neb. It also benefitted the two casinos' parent company, Harrah's Entertainment Inc., which derived about 5.6% of its Las Vegas gambling revenue from Mr. Watanabe that year.

Terrance Watanabe, 52, is believed to have the biggest losing streak in Las Vegas history, losing $127 million dollars in one year. Today, Mr. Watanabe and Harrah's are fighting over another issue: whether the casino company bears some of the responsibility for his losses.

In a civil suit filed in Clark County District Court last month, Mr. Watanabe, 52 years old, says casino staff routinely plied him with liquor and pain medication as part of a systematic plan to keep him gambling. Nevada's Gaming Control Board has opened a separate investigation into whether Harrah's violated gambling regulations, based on allegations made by Mr. Watanabe.

In April, the Clark County District Attorney's office charged Mr. Watanabe with four felony counts in district court for intent to defraud and steal from Harrah's, stemming from $14.7 million that the casino says it extended to him as credit, and that he lost. Although Mr. Watanabe has paid nearly $112 million to Harrah's, he has refused to pay the rest. He denies the charges, alleging that the casino reneged on promises to give him cash back on some losses, and encouraged him to gamble while intoxicated. If convicted, Mr. Watanabe faces up to 28 years in prison.

Jan Jones, Harrah's senior vice president for communications and government relations, says Mr. Watanabe's civil suit and his defense against the criminal charges are attempts to get out of paying a debt and to avoid accepting responsibility for his own actions. "Mr. Watanabe is a criminal defendant who faces imprisonment," Ms. Jones says. "All of his statements need to be seen in that light."

Several former and current Harrah's employees say their managers told them to let Mr. Watanabe continue betting while he was visibly intoxicated, even though casino rules and state law stipulate that anyone who is clearly drunk shouldn't be allowed to gamble. These employees say they were afraid they would be fired if they did anything to discourage Mr. Watanabe from gambling at the casinos.

Ms. Jones says company policy is to ask intoxicated gamblers to refrain from gambling. She says Harrah's has conducted an internal investigation into how its staff treated Mr. Watanabe but declined to release details because of the ongoing litigation. Mr. Watanabe declined to be interviewed for this article. His lawyer, Pierce O'Donnell, says Harrah's "preyed" on Mr. Watanabe's condition. But he says his client also acknowledges that he "drank to excess." Mr. Watanabe "takes full responsibility for his condition at the time. . . . He's not saying the devil made me do it."

LURING THE "WHALES"

Mr. Watanabe's situation illustrates the often-uneasy relationships casinos have with their biggest clients, also known as "whales." Casinos vie to lure these high rollers by doling out luxury suites, use of private jets, and a cadre of personal handlers to fulfill every flight of fancy, from wire transfers to fishing trips to Alaska.

Analysts say competition for this group has become especially fierce because the portion of revenue from big-spending clients appears to be increasing amid a downturn in overall gambling. Part of that analysis is based on revenue from baccarat, a high-stakes game favored by high rollers. Baccarat play on the Las Vegas Strip grew to 14.7% of gambling revenue in the last 12 months from 13% during the same period in 2007, according to state gaming regulators. Revenue from all gambling on the Strip over the same period has declined 19.1%.

But casino operators often struggle to manage high rollers. Some are compulsive gamblers whose losses—and lives—can quickly spiral out of control. In some instances, gamblers have tried to turn the blame around on casinos in civil suits. Such attempts are rarely, if ever, successful, experts say.

In 1993, former Philadelphia Eagles owner Leonard Tose failed to convince a jury in a civil suit against Hollywood Casino Corp. that employees of the casino had gotten him so drunk that he didn't know what he was doing when he gambled away millions in Atlantic City, N.J. As a result, he had to pay the casino $1.23 million in gambling debt. He died in 2003.

Nevada treats unpaid gambling debt as a criminal matter handled by the District Attorney's bad-checks unit. Most defendants agree to pay the debt through a payment plan before charges are filed, with around 10% tacked on to fund the D.A. unit. Clark County, which encompasses Las Vegas, prosecutes roughly 200 cases involving gambling debts a month, says Bernie Zadrowski, who runs the bad-checks unit.

Just as in civil cases, people with alleged unpaid debts sometimes try to get out of criminal charges by claiming that casinos had a hand in keeping them intoxicated. Although Mr. Zadrowski declined to comment specifically on Mr. Watanabe's case, he says this kind of defense never works in criminal court: "Uniformly, the rule is nobody made you drunk."

State regulators have the authority to fine casinos for letting people gamble who are visibly intoxicated, but such fines haven't been levied, says Brian Duffrin, executive secretary to the Nevada Gaming Control Board and the Nevada Gaming Commissions.

Still, casinos will sometimes bar gamblers who are behaving erratically or whom they suspect won't pay their debts. "It almost becomes a cost-benefit decision," says Glenn Christenson, a former Station Casinos executive who is chairman of the National Center for Responsible Gaming, an industry-funded addiction organization.

Mr. Watanabe says in court documents that he was barred from the Wynn casino in 2007 because of compulsive drinking and gambling. A Wynn spokeswoman declined to comment on the matter.

Harrah's Caesars and Rio casinos continued to put out the welcome mat. As part of the criminal case against Mr. Watanabe, Wilson Ning, a Harrah's marketing executive, testified before a grand jury in April that he didn't see Mr. Watanabe intoxicated at Caesars or Rio casinos, according to Mr. Zadrowski, the chief deputy district attorney who runs the bad-checks unit.

In 2007, Mr. Watanabe's prodigality became almost as legendary as his gambling. According to court documents, Mr. Watanabe says he regularly handed out to Caesars employees bundles of $100 bills that could total as much as $20,000.

Al Deleon and Kristian Kunder, two of Mr. Watanabe's personal handlers at Caesars, say he had thousands of Tiffany gift boxes filled with $50 gift cards or $100 gift coins that he would hand out to bartenders, nightclub operators, security guards and others. They say he once told a security guard to go to a supermarket and buy every cut of steak, and then proceeded to hand them out to employees.

### THE TRINKET EMPIRE

A native of Omaha, Neb., Mr. Watanabe built his fortune on plastic trinkets, the kind given away at carnivals and church fund-raisers: batons filled with tinsel, magic wands that light up, plastic spider rings that cost $1 for a bag of more than 100. His father, Harry Watanabe, founded the import business, Oriental Trading Co., in 1932, after immigrating to the U.S. from Japan. As children, Mr. Watanabe and his younger sister and brother worked with their father after school. His mother, Fern, a Nebraska native, was a secretary there. When Terrance Watanabe was 15, his father asked him if he wanted to take over the business, as is Japanese tradition for the first-born son, says his sister, Pam Watanabe-Gerdes. By the time he was 20, he was chief executive.

Some who knew Mr. Watanabe in Omaha describe him as guarded and shy. But he was also savvy at both marketing and selecting merchandise, says Bob Thomas, a chief operating officer at the company.

It was those skills that helped Mr. Watanabe grow a modest toy business into a catalog empire that raked in $300 million in revenue by the time of its sale in 2000, Mr. Thomas says. The job was all-consuming, say former associates. He traveled for long stretches of time examining merchandise in Asia. He never married. His sister and others who know him say they don't believe he ever had a significant romantic relationship. "That was his life, that company," Mr. Thomas says. "It engulfed him."

In 1995, Mr. Watanabe bought an 18,000-square-foot mansion on four acres for $1.8 million, according to RealQuest. A major Omaha philanthropist, he gave millions to AIDS services, according to his foundation's records. He also donated nearly $500,000 to political causes, mostly to the Democratic National Party. In 2000, Mr. Watanabe sold his company to Brentwood Assoc. of Los Angeles for an undisclosed sum. Oriental Trading has since been acquired by the Carlyle Group.

After the sale, Mr. Watanabe said his plan was to throw himself into his philanthropic work and have more fun. "If it's not fun, it's not worth doing," Mr. Watanabe told his hometown newspaper, the Omaha World-Herald, in 2000. Donations from his foundation grew, but he soon became restless. Several business ideas, including opening a restaurant, went nowhere. "He didn't know what to do with his time," says his sister.

### BETTING THE HOUSE

He found an answer at a Harrah's casino in Council Bluffs, Iowa, across the river from Omaha. He started gambling there in 2003, according to documents filed in Mr. Watanabe's civil suit. He became one of the casino's top customers, says Gabe Sullivan, a former Harrah's host who attended to Mr. Watanabe there.

Once he began traveling to Las Vegas frequently in 2005, Mr. Watanabe's gambling and drinking intensified, according to his civil suit. In 2006, Mr. Watanabe resided primarily at Wynn Resorts' Wynn Las Vegas casino. But, he says, his heavy betting drew the attention of Chief Executive Steve Wynn. After meeting with him in June 2007, Mr. Wynn concluded that he was a compulsive gambler and alcoholic, and barred him from the casino, according to a letter to the Nevada Gaming Control Board drafted by Mr. Watanabe's attorney, Pierce O'Donnell. Ms. Jones, the Harrah's vice president, says, "It was not our understanding that he was kicked out of Wynn because of problem gambling."

The casino operator offered him lucrative terms to gamble at its casinos, according to Mr. Watanabe's letter to the Control Board and copies of emails sent from Harrah's to Mr. Watanabe's assistant that were included in the court filings. In a series of emails signed by Mr. Ning, the Harrah's marketing executive, the casino company laid out the terms that it was willing to offer him, which included "a special formula just for Mr. Watanabe." Mr. Ning specified such offers as tickets to the Rolling Stones, $12,500 a month for airfare and $500,000 in credit at the gift stores. Harrah's also offered 15% cash back on table losses greater than $500,000, special high-limit games and other incentives. Mr. Watanabe alleges that Harrah's later rolled those terms back. Mr. Ning didn't respond to requests for comment. Ms. Jones declined to comment on whether the company rolled back any incentives, but says "the practice of offering incentives and discounts to significant players is not unusual."

Harrah's Total Rewards Player's Club system, a loyalty program similar to that of other big casinos, created a special rank for Mr. Watanabe, "chairman," according to the filing and several employees. Before Mr. Watanabe, the most exclusive rank was "Seven Star." Mr. Watanabe resided for free in a three-bedroom suite at Caesars, had access to his favorite bartender, drank a special brand of vodka, Jewel of Russia, and was constantly surrounded by attendants to serve his every need, such as a seven-course meal from the casino's Bradley Ogden restaurant delivered to him while he was gambling, according to the court filing and employee accounts. Ms. Jones says Mr. Watanabe was treated just like any other high-end gambler: "When his requests were appropriate we met them."

### LOSING $5 MILLION IN A DAY

One reason Mr. Watanabe was seen as so valuable to Harrah's, say Messrs. Deleon and Kunder, two of his handlers, is that he gravitated toward games with low odds, including roulette and slots. "He was considered a 'house' player because slots and roulette are house games—they have terrible odds for the player," says Mr. Kunder. "And the way he played blackjack, he made it a house game. He made such bad decisions on the blackjack table."

Ms. Jones disputes this interpretation. "I don't put a lot of credibility" in that, she says. Several employees say Mr. Watanabe would stay at the tables for up to 24 hours, sometimes losing as much as $5 million in a single binge. He was allowed to play three blackjack hands simultaneously with a $50,000 limit for each hand. At one point, the casino raised his credit to $17 million, according to court documents. Ms. Jones says for high rollers, the company will often extend credit.

When Mr. Sullivan, the Iowa casino host, visited Mr. Watanabe in Las Vegas during the height of his binge in 2007, he says, Mr. Watanabe appeared incoherent and had trouble remembering details of conversations. Other employees recall Mr. Watanabe stumbling around and dozing off at casino tables, some of which were located next to a nightclub blaring loud music. Mr. Kunder and Mr. Deleon say they both voiced concerns to managers that Mr. Watanabe was too intoxicated, and were told not to get involved. "Nobody wanted to be the one to cut him off," Mr. Kunder says. "We were afraid of what upper management would do if he left because of our actions."

Mr. Kunder left Harrah's in the summer of 2008 to work at nightclubs. He has since moved to Chicago and works at a cell-phone company. Mr. Deleon left the casino in March 2009 to do similar work at Red Rock casino, owned by Station Casinos. Mr. Sullivan left Harrah's in March 2008 when his contract wasn't renewed by Harrah's. Ms. Jones says the departures were not related to Mr. Watanabe, but declined to further discuss the situations of individual employees.

### LOOKING THE OTHER WAY

Mr. Watanabe alleges that during this period Harrah's not only didn't make him leave when he was drunk, but it plied him with alcohol and prescription drugs to encourage him to stay and gamble. Several Caesars employees say there was no policy to keep Mr. Watanabe drugged or drunk. But, they say, staff knew the company wanted to keep one of the Strip's most lucrative customers, and so looked the other way. A picture of him was hung in employee back rooms, they say.

Ms. Jones says there was nothing inappropriate or unusual about fulfilling the reasonable requests of a good customer. "We're in the gambling business," she says. "We had no reason to believe that Terry Watanabe was anything other than a big player with huge resources who made an adult decision to bet the money he did. Are we going to provide an environment that keeps him very happy? Of course we are."

Regarding Harrah's alcohol policy, Ms. Jones says, the company tells its employees to ask people who are clearly intoxicated to refrain from gambling, as required under state regulations. Employees attend a responsible-gaming class every year where they learn how and when to tell gamblers to leave the casino. The company has a phone number that employees can call to anonymously report unethical or improper behavior by other employees. There are no reports that anyone called the number regarding Mr. Watanabe, Ms. Jones says. In its marketing materials, Harrah's reports its record as an early advocate and funder of organizations that help gambling addicts. Among other measures, it honors requests from addicts that they be barred from all casinos run by the company.

In September 2007, Mr. Watanabe fell in his room and hurt his back. He says his handlers—including Mr. Kunder and Mr. Deleon—supplied him doses of the prescription pain medication Lortab without a doctor's prescription, his court filing says. Mr. Kunder says he gave Mr. Watanabe prescription pain medication from his personal supply a single time on the day after the fall upon Mr. Watanabe's request. Mr. Deleon says he never gave Mr. Watanabe drugs. Ms. Jones said that if employees ever provided Mr. Watanabe drugs, it would be against company policy.

Mr. Watanabe's sister says she and her brother and sister-in-law weren't aware of how much money he was losing until a 2007 Thanksgiving visit, when he opened up to her about the depth of his losses. "It was embarrassing for him," she says. Two weeks later, she says, she returned to Las Vegas and brought him home. Mr. Watanabe was back in Las Vegas gambling for a period in 2008. But he entered a residential treatment facility that year and hasn't entered a casino since, Ms. Watanabe-Gerdes says.

In July 2008, Mr. Watanabe sold his Omaha mansion for $2.66 million to a developer, according to Douglas County records. He now lives near San Francisco. Next summer, Mr. Watanabe is due to stand trial on the felony charges stemming from his debts. In May, he pled not guilty.

*NOTE*

Where is the line between a compulsive gambler and a "really good customer"? Is that line easy to identify?

## B. IMMORALITY

An often heard objection to gambling is that it is "immoral." Although perceptions of morality vary depending on cultural and personal traits, at least some of these objections derive from deep-seated religious values. These views give rise to a difference in conception about illegal gambling. Criminal law has long drawn a distinction between offenses that are *malum in se* and those that are *malum prohibitum*. To some, illegal gambling appears to be *malum in se*, but to others, illegal gambling is merely *malum prohibitum*.

## DON FEENEY, BEYOND THE ODDS: IS GAMBLING IMMORAL?*

http://www.miph.org/gambling/bto/jun99/1.html (June 1999)

It seems like an uncomplicated question, and one for which most people would undoubtedly venture an opinion. Certainly, if you gamble, you have no problem with its morality, and if you don't gamble, maybe you do. Simple enough.

Or is it? The history of the world's cultures and religions reveals a consistent lack of consensus on gambling from time to time and place to place. For the early Jews, the casting of dice or lots was used to determine God's will when serious decisions could not be made. Gambling for entertainment, therefore, was trifling with sacred ritual. Early Islamic writers rarely, if ever, mentioned gambling among the many major and minor sins they condemned. Later theologians, however, denounced gambling as encouraging the notion that fate, rather than divine will, determined man's affairs. In some Asian cultures gambling on sports is considered immoral but gambling on other human activities is not. Many people are surprised to learn that the Bible contains no prohibition on gambling, resulting in Christian theologians being sharply divided on the subject. Medieval philosophers like Aquinaus stressed that divine providence and luck were not incompatible, but later theologians sharply disagreed. Calvin in 1559 wrote "Who likewise does not leave lots to the blindness of fortune? Yet the Lord leaves them not, but claims the disposal of them to himself." A century and a half later, the Puritan cleric Cotton Mather argued that since not all wagers were returned as prizes, gambling for civic purposes constituted theft. But at the same time, every Christian denomination in colonial America (except the Quakers) operated lotteries.

Surprisingly, compulsive gambling has played at best a minor part in this debate. Moral objections to gambling have focused on its perceived incompatibility with God's role in man's affairs and its alleged subversion of the work ethic. Gambling also struggles with its image as a lower-class activity (there is a long history in England of distinctions between the games favored by the wealthy and those played by the poor). Other critics condemn it, along with other leisure activities, as a waste of time that could be devoted to a higher purpose.

With this as background, it should come as no surprise that Minnesotans' attitudes towards the morality of gambling are

---

* At the time this essay was published, Feeney was the Research Director of the Minnesota State Lottery.

ambivalent. In a recent survey, 15 percent of the state's adults strongly agreed with the statement "I am opposed to gambling for moral or religious reasons." Another 9 percent "agreed somewhat" with the statement, meaning that almost one in four Minnesotans express some moral misgivings.

Yet many of these people gamble. More than half (56 percent) of those in strong agreement with the statement reported gambling in the previous year, as did 79 percent of those expressing mild agreement. What accounts for this seeming inconsistency? It's tempting to blame hypocrisy or our willingness (as it has been said) to confess our neighbor's sins.

But I think, instead, that it's recognition of the complexity of the issue. It may be that to some gambling is acceptable when it is done to benefit charity, as with the purchase of a raffle ticket or pulltab, but not when it is done at a for-profit facility such as a Las Vegas casino. It may be acceptable as casual entertainment, like buying a lottery ticket at a convenience store, but not as the focus of an evening's entertainment. Or it may be that gambling with restraint is acceptable, but gambling in excess is immoral, with "restraint" often defined as what you do and "excess" what your neighbor does.

It is this ambiguity that has made policy decisions so difficult. (Only 12 percent of the state's adults strongly agree that all gambling should be outlawed.) No single form of gambling is either universally accepted or universally despised, and there are few people who either condemn all or accept all. We have both gambled and opposed gambling for thousands of years without reaching a consensus, and we should not expect one anytime soon. Most of us are stuck somewhere in the vast, ambiguous, constantly shifting middle ground. Like art, we don't know much about it, but we know what we like.

*NOTES*

1. This author sidesteps the hypocrisy question reflected in the fact that many people who believe that gambling is immoral nevertheless gamble. What does the widespread gap between words and actions signal about the strength of morality as a basis for regulation or criminalization of gambling activity?
2. In January of 2002, Léger Marketing conducted a public opinion poll in Canada. A total of 1,519 Canadian adults were surveyed, with a margin of error at 2.6 percentage points. The pollsters

suggested different activities and asked whether the action was immoral or not. The following percentage of adult Canadians consider these activities to be immoral:

Shoplifting 89.3%
Infidelity: 80.8%
Hard-core drug use: 79.2%
Tax evasion: 77%
Prostitution: 68.4%
Alcohol abuse: 66.1%
Suicide: 61.8%
Working "under the table": 52.8%
Taking soft drugs, like marijuana: 47.5%
Abortion: 41.8%
Gambling: 41.4%
Swearing: 40.2%
Homosexuality: 32.1%
Physician assisted suicide: 31.3%
Pre-marital sex: 27.3%
Atheism: 26.2%
Divorce: 22.3%

*Theft Worse than Infidelity: Poll*, Toronto Star, Feb. 18, 2002, Page A3. Some of these activities are legal and others are illegal. Many might be considered victimless offenses, at least when viewed narrowly. Should immorality track the law more closely than it does?

3.   One common perspective that has appeared occasionally is that gambling is destructive of traditional religious values reflected in the so-called "Protestant work ethic." Consider whether this is a compelling explanation for opposition to gambling as it is amplified in the next excerpt.

### STEPHANIE MARTZ, LEGALIZED GAMBLING AND PUBLIC CORRUPTION: REMOVING THE INCENTIVE TO ACT CORRUPTLY
#### 13 J.L. & Pol. 453 (1997)

#### THE U.S.'S AMBIVALENT RELATIONSHIP WITH GAMBLING AND THE INHERENT DIFFICULTIES IN REGULATING THE INDUSTRY

Gambling, like prostitution, abortion, and homosexuality, is a consensual act that some consider to work deleterious affects on the individual participants in the act and on society as a whole. We have criminalized such acts for reasons that are justified, but not entirely explained, by normative theories of government action. Professor Gilbert Geis, reviewing Western views of gambling, traces our hostility towards gambling as both avocation and vocation—or, today, our suspicion of gambling that exists outside special conditions (the church bingo, the casino night fund-raiser)—to the Puritan ethic, "a set of postulates about human existence which maintain that man should prosper and enjoy the good (i.e., conspicuous consumption) only by means of his own efforts, and not through sheer intervention of chance or providence." This ethic contrasts sharply with the equally strong human tendency to equate success at the craps table with "a general sign of favor from otherwise inscrutable gods," and a view of luck as the capricious factor in, and handy rationalization of, individual success (e.g., "I work just as hard as she does, she's more successful because she's lucky"). Gambling and its mystical element of luck thus embody two irreconcilable explanations for success and failure, undermining our orderly explanations of outcomes, but consoling us when these orderly explanations fail.

---

### UNITED METHODIST CHURCH, STATEMENTS ON GAMBLING
**Book of Resolutions 2004, Gambling**

When asked which commandment is first of all, Jesus answered, "Hear, O Israel: the Lord our God, the Lord is one; you shall love the Lord your God with all your heart, and with all your soul, and with all your mind, and with all your strength" (Mark 12:29-30). Gambling feeds on human greed and invited persons to place their trust in possessions rather than in God. It represents a form of idolatry that contradicts the first commandment. Jesus continued: "the second is this, "You shall love your neighbor as yourself" (Mark 12:31). In relating with compassion to our sisters and brothers, we are called to resist those practices and systems that exploit them and leave them impoverished and demeaned. The apostle Paul wrote in 1 Timothy 6:9-10a: "People who want to get rich fall into temptation and a trap and into many foolish and harmful desires that plunge men into ruin and destruction. For the love of money is a root of all kinds of evil."

Gambling, as a means of acquiring material gain by chance and at the neighbor's expense, is a menace to personal character and social morality. Gambling fosters greed and stimulates the fatalistic faith in chance. Organized and commercial gambling is a threat to business, breeds crime and poverty, and is destructive to the interests of good government. It encourages the belief that work is unimportant, that money can solve all our problems, and that greed is the norm for achievement. It serves as a "regressive tax" on those with lower income. In summary, gambling is bad economics; gambling is bad public policy; and gambling does not improve the quality of life.

The United Methodist Church opposes gambling in any form. Gambling is a menace to society, deadly to the best interests of moral, social, economic, and spiritual life, and destructive of good government. As an act of faith and concern, Christians should abstain from gambling and should strive to minister to those victimized by the practice. Where gambling has become addictive, the Church will encourage such individuals to receive therapeutic assistance so that the individual's energies may be redirected into positive and constructive ends. The Church should promote standards and personal lifestyles that would make unnecessary and undesirable the resort to commercial gambling—including public lotteries—as a recreation, as an escape, or as a means of producing public revenue or funds for support of charities or government. In practice, this means that United Methodist churches should not raise funds through methods such as raffles, lotteries, or drawings for door prizes or through games of chance such as bingo. (From the 2004 United Methodist Church Book of Resolutions, Gambling and ¶163G of the 2004 Book of Discipline.)

### NOTES

1.  The policy statement above, from a large Protestant church denomination, shows concerns far broader than the so-called "Protestant work ethic." What other values animate the church's position on gambling? This church is against gambling, but why?
2.  Is the church's position too broad? The pursuit of money and profit and, indeed, the concept of greed is present in other industries as well. Doubtless, some of those pursuits also have disastrous consequences. Is the church justified in singling out gambling for special scrutiny?
3.  "According to Rev. Stephen J. Sidorak, Jr., executive director of the Christian Conference of Connecticut, church-sponsored gambling and commercial gambling are qualitatively different because charity gambling meets social needs, whereas commercial gambling benefits only a few." REX M. ROGERS, GAMBLING: DON'T BET ON IT 109 (2005). Do you agree with Reverend Sidorak's statement? Is gambling qualititatively different when offered by a church or a charity?

4.  Should church policy statements ever be considered relevant in the interpretation of gambling laws? The next case is a reprise of the chapter one question, "what is gambling?" Consider how morality and "church policy" contributes to the answer to the question for at least one judge.

## CREACH v. STATE

### Supreme Court of Florida
### 131 Fla. 111, 179 So. 149 (1938)

TERRELL, Justice.

Plaintiffs in error were tried and convicted in the criminal court of record for Hillsborough county on an information charging them with keeping and operating a gambling house[.] ... The question of whether or not defendants were guilty of the charge lodged against them turns on that of whether or not they owned or operated a room or house in which gaming or gambling was carried on. The statutes of this state do not attempt to define gambling, or to point out all games and devices that constitute gambling. This court did, however, venture a definition of the term in *McBride v. State*, 39 Fla. 442, 22 So. 711, 712, as follows:

> "Gaming is an agreement between two or more to risk money on a contest of chance of any kind, where one must be loser and the other gainer." A most apt definition of "gambling," adopted by Anderson in his Law Dictionary, is by Judge Thompson, in Brua's Appeal, 55 Pa. 294, text 298, as follows: "Anything which induces men to risk their money or property without any other hope of return than to get for nothing any given amount from another is gambling, and demoralizing to the community, no matter by what name it may be called. It is the same whether the promise be to pay on the color of a card, or the fleetness of a horse, and the same numerals indicate how much is lost and won in either case, and the losing party has received just as much for the money parted with in the one case as in the other, viz. nothing at all."

To constitute gambling, it is immaterial by what name it is called if the elements of gambling are present and it is condemned by statute in nothing more than the use of the generic term. It is charged here that plaintiffs in error kept a house in which "Bingo" was played. ... A fair epitome of the evidence with reference to the manner of playing and the apparatus used in the conduct of "Bingo" shows that the management of the house offers a prize to the winner which is announced before the beginning of each game. Each player pays an entrance fee of 10 cents which entitles him to participate in the game. On entering the game he selects a card containing twenty-four different numbers ranging from 1 to 75, arranged in rows of five across the card up and down and diagonally; the center being blank and the numbers on each card being arranged differently. Neither the management nor its employees participate in the game. . . . As each ball is thrown in the box and lands in a slot, the management calls out the number of that particular slot and all players having the corresponding number on their card place a bean over that number. The first player who has five numbers covered by beans in a row, either horizontally, perpendicularly, or diagonally from the corners, is the winner. When this occurs, the player calls "Bingo." He is checked by the management, and, if found true, he is declared the winner and the corresponding prize awarded him.

All the games are run strictly on schedule, but the prizes vary. There are three $5 games, then a $10 game, then four $5 games, then a $15 game, and then a $10 game, when the schedule is completed and a new one is begun. The prizes are not in cash, but orders for merchandise upon Tampa merchants selected by the winner. The schedule of prizes and games are run at regular intervals regardless of the number of players and entrance fees paid.

The management has a bank account from which all prizes, general operating expenses of the establishment, including license fees and overhead costs, are paid. All entrance fees go into this account, but the amount or value of the prize offered is always in the bank account before any entrance fees are paid and the prize is in no sense determined by the number of such fees paid. It is shown that both the hope of winning a prize and amusement induce the playing. It is also shown that the prospect of winning depends to some extent on the skill in selecting the cards and in throwing the balls.

Does such a state of facts about which there is no dispute constitute gaming or gambling as defined by the law of this State? Plaintiffs in error contend that this question must be answered in the negative, that the facts show nothing more than a contest for a "purse, prize, or premium" as distinguished from a "stake, bet, or wager" which is essential to constitute gambling, that a contest for a "purse, prize, or premium" is not gambling, but is essentially a game of skill because of the element of skill involved in the result.

It is quite true that we [have] defined a "purse, prize, or premium" as something of value offered for the winner of a contest, but for which the one offering it does not compete and stands no chance to recover any part of it. We also [have] held that a "purse, prize, or premium" was different from a "stake, bet, or wager" as to which each party interested has a chance to win and takes the risk of losing the whole or some material part of it.

We do not understand, however, that the question of gambling or one's guilt who is charged with operating a gambling house is concluded by the question of whether the thing contested for was a "purse, prize, or premium" or a "stake, bet or wager."

Chance actuated by the hope of getting something for nothing is the controlling element in gambling. Any agreement or inducement by which one person risks his money or other thing of value with no prospect of return except to get for nothing the money or goods of another is gambling. If the contest for a "purse, prize, or premium" or a "stake, bet or wager" has this element in it, it is gambling, regardless of the name by which it is called, the implements employed to accomplish the act, or the manner in which it is conducted. AFFIRMED.

BUFORD, J. (concurring specially).

We know that it is somewhat difficult in this day and time of liberal-mindedness for the average well-informed individual to become reconciled to the thought and holding that a comparatively harmless game, such as is involved in this case, is denounced as gambling. The game known as "Bingo" has become very popular among all classes of people, and is played in the most exclusive and reputable places.

An article appearing in the issue of January 1, 1938, of Literary Digest, reads in part:

> A sign in front of a New York church reads: "Bingo every Thursday night in the Holy Spirit Room." On a rural Arkansas church a poster proclaims: "Bingo party every week—Everybody welcome." Encircled in neon lights another outside a Chicago suburban church announces: "Don't miss Bingo Friday. Handsome prizes." Attracted by such extra-spiritual heralds, thousands of Americans sit down in church weekly to try their luck in this national craze. In some localities the Tuesday or Thursday game at the corner church-house overshadows all other events. A survey made by the Literary Digest shows that the playing of Bingo is spreading rapidly throughout the United States. Neighborhood merchants have begun to complain of competition. Movie exhibitors are protesting.
>
> Some church leaders take a definite stand against the game. Last week religious editors and others admitted freely that discussion of the moral issue had reached controversial proportions. Phillip Yarrow, chairman of the civic relations commission of the Chicago Church Federation, expresses this opinion to the Literary Digest: "The commission has repeatedly pleaded with churches to stop petty gambling as a means of raising money. Churches a few years ago would have been horrified at the mere suggestion of such methods as playing

bunco, beano, or bingo, and raffling quilts or other articles. The argument of some church officials is that, if wealthy churches can raise money by bridge, why should not the smaller one play beano? We say the kingdom of God cannot be established by shooting craps."

Typical of church sentiment in favor of bingo is this view of the Rev. H. A. Velte, of Milwaukee's St. Boniface Church, despite Archbishop Stritch's ban: "How absurd to think that it is wrong when parents and their children sit down to a game that costs them a little 35 cents for the sake of a thrill that comes to them when seeing themselves or their friends win a prize. Of course, this innocent game can be carried to extremes."

The Rev. Francis Talbot, S. J., editor of America, sends this comment to the Literary Digest: "I cannot grow frenzied with the puritanic precisionists who rate the bourgeois pastime of bingo as a major sin. Rather am I frenzied at those pulpiteers who remain silent on such major ills as godless schools, loose faith, easy divorce, and shout down wrath on a little shell game that ruins neither piety nor morals, character nor families. Played under proper auspices with petty stakes, the worst harm that bingo causes is a sore throat. Church bingo parties are a healthy substitute for gossip teas, lovesick movies, and liberal-minded lecturers. All life is a gamble but nobody gambles life away at a bingo fest. Let us concentrate on the stock market and politics."

Beano and bingo, with their allure, swift turnover, and simplicity of operation—placing beans or corn on five squares in a straight line and shout "Beano" or "Bingo"! had a way of stimulating gambling instincts. The International Reform Federation (Washington, D. C.) investigated. Its law enforcement director, Henry N. Pringle, said he found that practically all churches had gone in for bingo and such games, with professional promoters running many of them. He added: "The percentage which churches will get out of the intake varies with the value of the prizes. In some cases trinkets worth only a few cents constitute prizes; in others cash prizes are given. The churches probably get 50 percent of the take."

In December, 1936, Bishop Edmund F. Gibbons, of Albany, in an archiepiscopal letter, forbade the playing of bingo in church buildings and the renting of church property for bingo game, and forbade Catholics in his diocese to play even on non-church property, on the ground that bingo tended to undermine morals. Archbishop Stritch of Milwaukee took the stand that sometimes such games were sinful or the places in which they were played tended to encourage sin. Archbishop John J. Glennon of St. Louis, writing to the churches of his diocese last month said: "Gambling devices and games promoted ostensibly for the benefit of churches, schools, institutions or societies are unworthy of our Catholic people, inducing the gambling habit."

In New York the Federal Council of the Churches of Christ in America and the Greater New York Federation of Churches condemned bingo, but they reported that playing in churches in their group had not yet reached an issue stage. In Chicago Bishop Ernest

Lynn Waldorf, head of the Methodist Episcopal Church there, told the Literary Digest: "We deprecate the use of gambling devices and practices of any kind to raise church finances."

So we see that there is much conflict of opinion between the best of people as to the moral status of the game. Operating a gambling house is a statutory offense and is defined very clearly by the language used in [the statute].

Playing the game "Bingo" as described in the record does not come within the definition of gambling . . . because while each player pays a small fee for the privilege of participating in the game he parts with that when he pays it and it goes to the house. The prize is no loss to the house and its purpose is to stimulate the interest of the public in the game just as "Bank Nite" is used to stimulate patronage of picture shows. The players may be presumed to get the value of the fee in the pleasure and recreation afforded by participating in the game. So it appears that a case is not made wherein one or more parties lose and one or more win, because of the lack of the element of loss.

We are not called upon to determine in this case whether or not the players in the game of "Bingo" are gambling, but only whether or not the defendants were guilty of operating a place where a game was conducted in which the winner was awarded a prize of something of value.

# C.   ECONOMIC CONCERNS

Opponents raise a number of economic concerns about gambling. For some of them, gambling preys on the poor. For others, it preys on a wider segment of the economy by starving other forms of entertainment.

## 1.   Poverty

Lawful forms of gambling, and in particular state-run lotteries, have been hailed as a voluntary form of taxation, a tax on the willing. Given the odds of winning the lottery, the more apt description might be a tax "on the gullible" or "on the ignorant." Not surprisingly, those who play the lottery tend not only to be less educated, but also less wealthy. Thus, if likened to taxation, the lottery is a highly regressive form of taxation. It has been criticized for this and other reasons.

## RONALD J. RYCHLACK, LOTTERIES, REVENUES AND SOCIAL COSTS: A HISTORICAL EXAMINATION OF STATE-SPONSORED GAMBLING

34 B. C. L. Rev. 11, 72-74 (1992)

### PROBLEMS OF POVERTY

Because lotteries hold out the promise of quick riches, they are particularly appealing to those in dire economic straits. "The dream of financial security offered by lotteries and illegal numbers finds a special place in the subculture of poverty and despair that pervades the inner cities of our society."

In general, persons in lower income groups have the most incentive to purchase lottery tickets. Leading routine lives for lack of money, they derive comparatively more benefit from the lottery's excitement and potential profits than do the affluent. Indeed, a "Massachusetts study showed that four out of five who could least afford to gamble purchased lottery tickets." Recent newspaper reports suggest that most lottery players are poor and middle-income persons. The Task Force on Legalized Gambling concluded that "legalization of gambling will produce relatively small amounts of revenue and will raise it from the wrong people in the wrong way." Although contrary evidence exists, it appears that many of those who play the lottery are those who can least afford it. As such, it is not surprising to find that poor people tend to spend a disproportionate amount of their income purchasing lottery tickets.

Recent studies indicate that lotteries are marketed more heavily in poor neighborhoods than elsewhere. The Delaware Council on Gambling Problems conducted a study in 1979 and found that there were no lottery machines in the highest income area of New Castle County; one machine for every 17,774 people in the upper-middle income areas; one machine for every 5,032 people in the lower-middle to middle working income areas; and one machine for every 1,981 persons in the poorest income areas. Similar distributions have recently been noted elsewhere. These numbers indicate that marketing efforts are not actively trying to offset the general regressive nature of the lottery.

Rather than trying to combat the regressive nature of lotteries, lottery promotions have exploited this feature by targeting relatively poorer lottery players. Lottery advertisers often time their advertisements to come out on days when people have disposable income readily available, such as days when Social Security checks are released. Radio advertisements are concentrated on stations with formats that are popular with working class individuals. Billboards that are seen throughout the inner city do not exist in neighboring suburbs.

Not long ago the Illinois Lottery had a campaign featuring billboards with the slogan, "How to go from ____ Street to Easy Street—Play the Illinois State Lottery." The blank was filled in with the street where the billboard was located. When one such billboard was placed in a section of Chicago where residents have little disposable income, community leaders were justifiably upset.

A society that is truly interested in breaking the cycle of poverty would normally be expected to promote the traditional virtues of education, hard work, thrift and savings. Lottery promotions send the opposite message. In some cases, the contradiction is especially apparent. A recent television advertising campaign compared the Illinois lottery to an investment. The scene was a job site, and various workers were discussing their investments. One character mentioned stocks; another suggested bonds. Then one began extolling the virtues of a high-risk, low investment, short-term venture with the possibility of a large return—a lottery ticket. This is hardly the type of economic advice that the state should be providing. The promise of great riches may provide a fantasy for those who can afford it, but the lottery is a poor vehicle to rely upon for financial security. Yet, too often lotteries are seen as a type of investment. It is particularly offensive for the state to promote such a viewpoint. The impact of a lottery on the poorer segments of society must be considered by lawmakers when they discuss lotteries.

### NOTES

1. Professor Rychlack mentions one troubling advertisement by the Illinois Lottery. Another advertisement for the Illinois Lottery featured a man playing the lottery who scoffed at a man putting his money in the bank, suggesting that the "the lottery is the only way an ordinary person can get rich." Is such marketing appropriate for a government agency?

2. On the other hand, what is the proper role of a public commercial entity? If the obligation of any commercial entity is to maximize revenues to its stockholders, then we should expect—and perhaps even desire—for a public entity to use aggressive marketing techniques to maximize revenue to the "stockholders," that is, the public, at least if such techniques are effective in increasing sales and therefore revenues.

# CHARLES T. CLOTFELTER, DO LOTTERIES HURT THE POOR? WELL, YES AND NO

## A Summary of Expert Testimony to the House Select Committee on a State Lottery on April 19, 2000

### WHO PLAYS LOTTERIES?

As a result of many household surveys over the years, including the national survey completed by the National Opinion Research Organization (NORO) in 1999 for the National Gambling Impact Study Commission, we know several general facts about the pattern of lottery play in the United States. About 60 percent of adults in lottery states play at least once a year. In terms of amount of money bet, men play more than women, and those in middle age play more than the youngest or the oldest adults. The bulk of attention in policy discussions has concerned the relationship between lottery purchases and income. Most of the studies that I have seen . . . yield the following conclusion: average sales do not vary systematically by income. That is, taking averages over all adults, both players and nonplayers, those in lower income brackets tend to spend roughly the same number of dollars a year as those in middle and upper income brackets. Some studies show that the amount increases somewhat with income, while other studies indicate that the amount declines with income. But in virtually every case we have examined, one conclusion is constant: lower-income individuals spend a higher percentage of their income than those in middle and upper income brackets. This fact does not by itself make lotteries a good thing or a bad thing. It only means that lotteries tend to have a particular pattern of consumption, which is unlike, for example, the pattern of expenditures for brie or Chablis, commodities the expenditures for which tend to increase as a percentage of income in upper income brackets. Instead, the relationship of lottery purchases to income looks more like those of chicken wings or barbeque, items for which lower income households tend to spend a larger share of their income than those who are more affluent.

\* \* \*

### DO LOTTERIES "PREY" UPON THE POOR?

. . . Like those who sell other consumer products, state lotteries do engage in what is called "target marketing," that is, pitching their message to likely players. So in one sense it is true that the poor are "the lottery's targets," [citation omitted]. But it would not be rational for them to go after the poor exclusively. The primary goal of state lotteries is to maximize their net revenues, so they are simply doing what any business wishing to sell, for example, more chicken wings or barbeque would do. This means aiming their advertising and other marketing differently than if they were trying to sell a product whose sales were more highly concentrated in middle or upper income brackets.

### SIX PROPOSITIONS ABOUT A STATE LOTTERY

Given its pattern of consumption, what then can be said about lotteries as an activity of government? Let me suggest six propositions.

1.  While some people will surely suffer, most of those who play a lottery will be made better off simply by its legalization. Most people who play lottery games do not win, but that does not make the activity of playing any more "wasteful" or irrational than, say, playing video games, eating candy bars, or attending a hockey game. They play because they evidently get something out of it. This could explain why most opinion polls show that a majority of citizens would like to have a state lottery.
2.  Among those who would be worse off would be "problem gamblers," some of whom will have serious financial problems as a result, and those who find the existence of a lottery and its advertising to be offensive. Make no mistake about it: there will be some social costs associated with a state lottery. This is the reason some states require funds to be set aside for programs dealing with gambling addiction, or why some states place limits on the amount or nature of advertising.
3.  By taking a high profit rate from the sale of lottery tickets, the state would be placing a very high "implicit tax" on lottery purchases. For each dollar bet, the average state lottery pays 55 cents in prizes, spends 12 cents on retailer commissions and other operating costs, which leaves 33 cents for the state. [This is] an "implicit tax" because it has exactly the same effect as a tax on lottery expenditures. If it were an excise tax, it would amount to a 50% tax on the cost of operating the lottery (67 cents), making it much higher than the excise taxes we place on alcohol or tobacco products.
4.  Since lower income people spend more in proportion to their incomes than those with middle and upper incomes, they will tend to benefit more from playing a North Carolina lottery. Although no one can be certain how large the benefits of playing are, economists are inclined to look at people's own behavior and assume that those who play the most will get the most enjoyment out of it. To be sure, this approach applies to consumers who are not addicted and who have a pretty good idea of the odds and the prize structure.

5.  The implicit tax contained in lottery finance is regressive. Just as a regressive tax is defined as one whose percentage of income is highest for those at low incomes levels, the implicit tax in lotteries, no matter what the rate, is regressive. By placing a high implicit tax on lottery purchases, a state in effect makes its revenue structure more regressive than it would be if the implicit tax on lotteries were in line with other tax rates. Thus the same lower income people who benefit from the lottery's legalization could benefit even more if the implicit tax on the lottery were in line with taxes on other taxed products, such as alcohol and tobacco.

6.  Through heavy marketing of lottery products, states compound this burden on lower income citizens and increase the social cost to problem gamblers and those who find state sponsored gambling distasteful.

## 2.   *Impact on the Economy*

### JOHN WARREN KINDT, LEGALIZED GAMBLING ACTIVITIES: THE ISSUES INVOLVING MARKET SATURATION

#### 15 N. Ill. U.L. Rev. 271, 271-278 (1995)

In his classic book entitled *Economics,* Nobel Prize laureate Paul Samuelson summarized the economics involved in gambling activities as follows:

> There is a substantial economic case to be made against gambling. First, it involves simply sterile transfers of money or goods between individuals, creating no new money or goods. Although it creates no output, gambling does nevertheless absorb time and resources. When pursued beyond the limits of recreation, where the main purpose after all is to "kill" time, gambling subtracts from the national income. The second economic disadvantage of gambling is the fact that it tends to promote inequality and instability of incomes.

Furthermore, Professor Samuelson observed that "[j]ust as Malthus saw the law of diminishing returns as underlying his theory of population, so is the 'law of diminishing marginal utility' used by many economists to condemn professional gambling."

The concern of the legalized gambling interests over "market saturation" is largely a non-issue. From the governmental perspective, focusing on this issue misdirects the economic debate, because fears of market saturation are predicated upon the unwarranted assumption that legalized gambling operations constitute regional economic development—which they do not. In reality, legalized gambling operations consist primarily of a transfer of wealth from the many to the few—accompanied by the creation of new socio-economic negatives. . . . [T]he inherently parasitic manner in which legalized gambling activities must apparently collect consumer dollars to survive is frequently described as "cannibalism" of the pre-existing economy—including the pre-existing tourist industry. According to the skeptics of legalized gambling activities, this industry-specific phenomenon means that in comparison with most other industries, legalized gambling activities must *a fortiori* not only grow as rapidly as possible, but also grow as expansively as possible. . . .

The basic principle at work in most legalized gambling scenarios is that "when local people substitute spending on gambling for their other expenditures, this induced impact has a negative multiplier effect of decreasing spending on other forms of recreation and businesses in the area." The gambling interests argue that the dollars they take in are "entertainment dollars" or "recreational dollars." This observation is valid with regard to approximately 35% of the "gambling dollar," but it is invalid with regard to the remaining 65%. Opponents of legalized gambling argue that there are also differences because the entertainment dollars spent on a movie, for example, largely generate more movies, and recreation dollars spent on a speedboat, for example, largely generate orders for more speedboats. Accordingly, while most entertainment or recreational dollars contribute to a positive multiplier effect, legalized gambling dollars result in a negative multiplier effect. This negative impact apparently occurs, in part, because approximately two-thirds of the gambling dollars are not recreationally-oriented, but are spent by a compulsive market segment reacting to an addictive activity—probable or possible pathological gambling—as delimited by the American Psychiatric Association. Opponents also note that gambling dollars spent in a legalized gambling facility are usually reinvested in more gambling facilities—which just intensifies the socioeconomic negatives associated with gambling activities and "reduces the national income" even further.

Notably, gambling "winnings" to one gambler do not come from the gambling parlor but from the pockets of other gamblers. Since dollar winnings (and not entertainment enjoyments) constitute the rationale for many gamblers to gamble, the gamblers in this category are not provided entertainment per se when they gamble. Furthermore, skeptics question whether a person who earns $30,000 per year really experiences $3,000 worth of "entertainment" when that $3,000 is lost in one night. . . .

Once again, the net result according to Professor Jack Van Der Slik, who echoed the sentiments of much of the academic community, was that state-sanctioned "gambling produces no product, no new wealth, and so it makes no genuine contribution to economic development." Similarly, in 1989 Professor William Thompson cautioned that Illinois riverboat gambling would "not be a catalyst for general economic development." Of course, if the focus is only on a localized gambling area, such as Las Vegas, instead of the proper perspective on the overall region Las Vegas is draining, there can be the illusion of an overall positive economic impact.

Most insidious to traditional businesses and to the rest of the economy, practically all of the dollars flowing into gambling organizations are "reinvested" in more and newer and "harder" forms (i.e., "more thrilling" forms) of gambling, as well as their associated cluster services. This process tends continually to intensify the large socioeconomic negatives (as well as the local positives) associated with legalized gambling activities. In other words, the truism "gambling begets gambling" appears accurate, and the gambling dollars are almost exclusively kept "in-house" despite the protestations of the gambling supporters to the contrary.

The drain on economies is real, but obviously, the bigger the economy of the anticipated gambling market, the longer this draining can occur without being noticed by the public. In fact, it could transpire over a course of years if the market was big enough and unsaturated by competition from other gambling interests.

### NOTES

Are Kindt's economic arguments legitimate? Are they compelling? Is gambling materially different than other forms of entertainment? How so, or why not?

## D.  CRIME AND CORRUPTION

Gambling has often been associated with both crime and corruption. The relevant question in this discussion, perhaps, is whether gambling *causes* or *facilitates* crime or corruption. It is useful to think of the kind of crime that might bear some relation to gambling.

Prohibitory approaches to gambling have one kind of effect, legalized gambling another. During Prohibition, liquor distribution became strongly connected with "organized" crime. Since the end of Prohibition, of course, organized crime related to alcohol dwindled, and alcohol and liquor is now much more closely associated with violent crime. Organized crime is an expected outcome with a prohibitory approach toward gambling. Legalized gambling also may draw the criminal element. The following excerpts survey some of the crime risks related to legal gambling, such as loan-sharking, public corruption, embezzlement, and money laundering.

## 1. Loan Sharking

### SHANNON KARI, CITY OF RICHMOND PLAYS DOWN CASINO-CRIME ALLEGATIONS

**Globe British Columbia (Aug. 16, 2006) at B1**

The City of Richmond is playing down reports of alleged illegal activity, including loan sharking, related to gambling at the River Rock Casino Resort. "Our relationship with the casino is very positive," Bill McNulty, acting mayor and Richmond city councillor, said yesterday. "We have a very safe city." Mr. McNulty was responding to comments made this weekend by [Royal Canadian Mounted Police] Superintendent Ward Clapham to a local newspaper. The senior officer suggested there is an increase in organized crime in Richmond connected to gambling that has taxed police resources. The RCMP have set up a working group, including the Great Canadian Gaming Corp., which operates the casino, and the British Columbia Lottery Corp. The police force is considering the creation of a four-officer squad dedicated to illegal gambling activity.

Supt. Clapham said yesterday there have been three kidnappings this year in Richmond involving extortion that are connected to gambling. Speaking at a news conference, he declined to provide more details about the connections. A 40-year old woman, Rong Lilly Li, suspected of being involved in loan shark activity, disappeared outside the River Rock Casino nearly three months ago and is still missing. More than 30 people have been barred from the casino in the past year, because they have been suspected of engaging in loan sharking. "It is a small group of people involved in loan sharking, with willing victims," Supt. Clapham stressed. The general public is in no danger, the officer added. Richmond City Council will decide in October whether police will be provided with additional resources. "As long as we stay proactive, it should not be a problem," said Richmond councillor Rob Howard, who is also the chairman of the city's community safety committee. "I know the casino is on top of this, big time."

Howard Blank, a spokesman for Great Canadian Gaming, said, "Our security and surveillance personnel in the casino are specially trained to look for any alleged criminal activity." He explained that any relevant information is passed on and enforcement is the responsibility of the provincial lottery corporation and police.

*NOTES*

Are casino security and surveillance personnel likely to be able to identify loan sharking? Is it likely to happen in the casino itself? What is the casino's incentive to interdict illegal borrowing to prevent people from borrowing to spend money in the casino?

## 2.  *Public Corruption*

### STEPHANIE MARTZ, LEGALIZED GAMBLING AND PUBLIC CORRUPTION: REMOVING THE INCENTIVE TO ACT CORRUPTLY, OR TEACHING AN OLD DOG NEW TRICKS
#### 13 J.L. & Pol. 453, 453-455, 462-465 (1997)

Five men pay Indianapolis cops to tip them off about raids planned on their "pea-shake" house, an illegal neighborhood gambling joint where patrons buy numbers they hope will match the numbers on peas shaken out of a milk bottle, winning up to $1000. Across the border in Illinois, Primadonna Resorts, a Nevada gambling company, offers two of the state's biggest political insiders $20 million to help them win a casino license, allegedly violating a state law that prohibits lobbyists from working on contingency fees and raising grave concerns at the Illinois Gaming Board about possible influence-buying. The first story illustrates the type of corruption that traditionally has accompanied illegal gambling businesses. The second story has become a new template for corruption, generally occurring in states that legalize gambling through the lucrative sponsoring of monopolies or oligopolies in which only one or a few companies may operate casinos, riverboat sites or flashy video lottery terminals. . . .

The burgeoning corruption problem that has accompanied legalized gambling springs from the tense relationship between the two talismanic goals of legalized gambling: raising revenue and controlling crime. These public policy aims often find themselves at odds with one another, and sometimes have proven completely incompatible. . . .

Interestingly, one of the chief reasons for the prevalence of gambling-related corruption in local law enforcement agencies begins with society's ambivalence towards gambling. Even while citizens decry legalization, they put less pressure on police and prosecutors to enforce existing anti-gambling laws because of the practice's essentially consensual and victimless nature. An articulation of this phenomenon came recently during closing arguments in a rural Ohio gambling ring case. The defense lawyer for an alleged gambling proprietor charged under the state's racketeering laws told jurors that his client ran a successful numbers business not because he bribed local police officers but because those officers had more important things to do than enforce gambling laws. A 1971 San Francisco Crime Commission report went so far as to say that police officers in San Francisco often failed to investigate alleged illegal gambling operations because an "immeasurable cost [of active enforcement] is the loss of respect for law when it tries to illegalize what the people largely desire." Through "refusing to enforce broadly drawn [anti-gambling] laws to the letter," the Commission asserted that the police save[d] themselves—and the rest of the legal system—from public ridicule." Yet such an argument may prove too much. One doubts whether the San Francisco Crime Commission would countenance police officers who tacitly agreed not to enforce narcotics laws, even in neighborhoods where the people seemed "largely to desire" an active drug trade. Thus, not only a lack of communal outrage, but also a lack of resources helps to explain the kind of limited, controlled enforcement often practiced by scarcely staffed and poorly funded law enforcement agencies.

Selective enforcement encourages the notion that police are at best disregarding their duty and at worst more vulnerable to corrupt practices. However, this apathy towards enforcing anti-gambling laws still fails to explain fully why police take money not to enforce these laws; it merely underscores the lack of incentive to enforce them. A better explanation for the presence of bribery is that a temporal pattern of violations, like those associated with gambling or prostitution, makes it easy to structure efficient payments with few transaction costs. And even if a community decides it doesn't care about whether anti-gambling laws are enforced locally, its members might care about the corruption of law enforcement officials. Corruption begets corruption, as the Knapp Commission noted in its 1972 report on extensive corruption in the New York Police Department. The Commission found that gambling-related corruption rarely exists in a vacuum; it is accompanied by payoffs from the same people for narcotics offenses and other crimes.

Legalizing gambling will not eradicate this corruption, but instead will shift its focus from local law enforcement to state-level legislators and bureaucrats. Payoffs and gifts normally (although not exclusively) slipped into the pockets of corrupt police officers will decline, replaced by campaign contributions and promises of future benefits to licensing officials and other regulators. Whether legal or illegal, these practices still serve to undermine the public's faith in its elected officials. The important public policy point is that states need to be particularly concerned about gambling-related corruption because legalizing gambling allies the government with a seemingly corrupt industry. Ensuing scandals send the message that government endorses and even colludes in corrupt practices.

## 3.  Money Laundering

### CASINO VULNERABILITIES

**2007 U.S. Money Laundering Threat Assesment**
**U.S. Departments of Homeland Security and Justice—Joint Report**

Law enforcement and media reports indicate that criminals typically launder money through casinos by exchanging illicit cash for casino chips and then either:

- Holding the chips for a period of time and later cashing them in for a casino check or having the casino wire the money elsewhere;
- Using the chips as currency to purchase narcotics, with the drug dealer later cashing in the chips; or,
- Using the chips to gamble in hopes of generating certifiable winnings.

Criminals also use casinos to launder counterfeit money as well as large currency notes that would be conspicuous and difficult to use elsewhere, and which may be marked by undercover law enforcement officers. Suspicious activities at casinos often involve customers structuring transactions to avoid recordkeeping or reporting thresholds, using agents to cash-out multiple transactions for an anonymous individual, providing false documents or identifying information, or layering transactions to disguise their source.

The IRS-Criminal Investigation division reports the following case examples of casinos used for money laundering:

Criminals laundered money through video poker games by feeding illicit proceeds into the machines (one, five, and ten dollar bills) and then either after playing briefly or not at all, they pressed the "cash out" button which generated a receipt that was redeemed for a casino check.

A major cocaine and heroin dealer played the $100 slot machines in Las Vegas and Atlantic City, wagering hundreds of thousands of dollars, in order to receive a casino check for his eventual winnings and an IRS Form W-2G to legitimize the income. The drug dealer also purchased Pennsylvania lottery tickets from winners, paying them more than the winning payout in order to receive a state check and an IRS Form W-2. The individual eventually invested the laundered money in rental properties.

While criminals will often structure their transactions to avoid financial institutions' filing CTRs [cash transaction reports, required by the Department of the Treasury], money launderers using casinos have the opposite strategy. In one case, a number of people purchased chips with illicit cash in amounts below the CTR threshold, but then passed the chips to one individual who cashed out, receiving a casino check and triggering the filing of a CTR that gave the appearance of further authenticating the transaction. Over a twelve-month period, one individual was named in casino CTRs reporting $1.1 million paid out, but was not named in a single CTR for cash taken in.

In one case, a money launderer purchased casino rewards cards from legitimate patrons. The cards increase in value with each casino visit and with each gambling session. The cards were purchased with illicit cash and were then traded in for gold coins at a casino store. An employee at the store was an accomplice in the laundering scheme.

A constant threat at casinos is insiders taking advantage of their position either to steal or assist others with money laundering. [U.S. Immigrations and Customs Enforcement or "ICE"] recently charged six people, including a tribal leader, with attempting to steal $900,000 from a Native American casino. Among the charges are conspiracy, theft, and money laundering.

### REGULATION AND PUBLIC POLICY

Casinos in the United States are subject to a decentralized regulatory structure and are primarily regulated by the states and by tribal regulatory authorities. Under the [Bank Secrecy Act of 1970 ("BSA")] and its implementing regulations, a gaming operation is defined as a financial institution subject to the requirements of the BSA if it has annual gaming revenue of more than $1,000,000 and is licensed as a gaming establishment under state or local law and authorized to do business in the United States, or is an Indian gaming operation conducted under or pursuant to the Indian Gaming Regulatory Act (IGRA).

State-licensed gambling casinos were generally made subject to the recordkeeping and currency reporting requirements of the BSA by regulation in 1985. Casinos authorized to do business under the IGRA were made subject to the BSA in 1996. Card clubs became subject to the BSA in 1998.

Casinos in Nevada, with gross annual gaming revenues of $10,000,000 or more and "table games statistical win" of $2 million or more, currently are, under a special agreement with the Department of the Treasury, subject to Nevada Gaming Commission Regulation 6A. The Nevada Gaming Commission's regulation, like the BSA, stipulates currency reporting and recordkeeping requirements.

All casinos (including those in Nevada) and card clubs, with gross annual gaming revenue in excess of $1,000,000, are required to file casino CTRs to report each currency transaction involving cash-in or cash-out of more than $10,000 in a "gaming day" with a customer. Under the BSA, multiple currency transactions conducted by or on behalf of the same customer on the same gaming day are considered to be one transaction for CTR purposes.

*NOTES*

1. "The particular vulnerability of gaming is that casino gaming involves large sums of cash changing hands in millions of transactions each day by thousands of people across the country. In an age in which transactions in most other areas of commerce are dominated by less fungible and more secure financial instruments, such as credit cards, debit cards and checks, casinos still predominantly operate with cash. The cash intensive nature of the gaming industry makes it particularly attractive—and particularly vulnerable—to crime and corruption." Kevin K. Washburn, Testimony before the Resources Committee, United States House of Representatives, Oversight Hearing on the NIGC Minimum Internal Control Standards, May 11, 2006.

2. One of the analogues to the casino business is the banking business. Both industries are primarily, or at least substantially, cash-oriented businesses. Regulatory efforts have moved more and more toward treating casinos like banks, through the filing of cash transaction reports (CTRs) requirements and suspicious activity reports (SARs). What are the potential limits on the effectiveness of such disclosure requirements?

3. Two of the principal federal bans on money laundering are found in 18 U.S.C. §§1956 and 1957. Section 1956 contains four different money laundering crimes, including: a "sting" provision, which applies to undercover operations used to determine if an individual is involved in or is willing to engage in money laundering; a conspiracy provision; and, a provision prohibiting the transportation of money in or out of the United States with illegal intent. Section

1957 prohibits many ostensibly innocent financial transactions if the person involved in the transaction knows that the property was previously acquired through criminal activity

## 4.  Fraud

There is some evidence to suggest that people who seek to earn money through gambling may be especially vulnerable to fraud. The general notion is that the same type of improper mental reasoning that causes someone to wager when the odds are sharply unfavorable may also lack the ability to exercise sufficient scrutiny to avoid fraud. To paraphrase a common saying, there is a fraud victim born every minute. To illustrate the nexus to gambling, please revisit three-card monte.[1]

### PEOPLE v. SMITH

**New York City Criminal Court**
**402 N.Y.S.2d 310 (1978)**

IRVING LANG, J.

In France it is an "escroquerie." In Belgium it is "un jeu essentielle-ment d'adresse." In England Lord Alverstone of the King's Bench called it "sleight of hand and nothing more." The Canadian court followed England, but the Canadian Parliament outlawed it. American cases are in conflict. Scarne scorns it and Leff ignores it. There are no New York cases on it, but hundreds were arrested for it in New York City in 1977. It is "three-card monte" and the question to be resolved by this court, previously undecided in this State, is whether it is a known confidence game under New York's fraudulent accosting statute.

The defendant is charged with fraudulent accosting (Penal Law, §165.30). The complaint states that "defendant accosted unknown passersby and engaged in conduct of a kind commonly performed in perpetration of a known confidence game, to wit: three-card

---

1. The statute which the defendant is accused of violating reads as follows: "165.30 Fraudulent Accosting. 1. A person is guilty of fraudulent accosting when he accosts a person in a public place with intent to defraud him of money or other property by means of a trick, swindle or confidence game. 2. A person who, either at the time he accosts another in a public place or at some subsequent time or at some other place, makes statements to him or engages in conduct with respect to him of a kind commonly made or performed in the perpetration of a known type of confidence game, is presumed to intend to defraud such person of money or other property. Fraudulent accosting is a class A misdemeanor."

monte. Deponent further observed defendant receive a sum of [cash] as a wager from another individual. Deponent . . . observed defendant is in possession of . . . three playing cards."

Defendant contends that the complaint fails to allege facts showing an intent to defraud, an essential element of the crime, and therefore should be dismissed. The People maintain, however, that under subdivision 2 of section 165.30 of the Penal Law, defendant's conduct is "of a kind commonly . . . performed in the perpetration of a known type of confidence game" and therefore is presumptively fraudulent, validating the complaint.

Thus, if three-card monte is a "known confidence game" under New York law, the complaint survives the challenge. If not, it must be dismissed.

Webster's Seventh New Collegiate Dictionary (1963) defines three-card monte as follows: "a gambling game in which the dealer shows three cards and then shuffles and throws them face down before anyone who wishes to pick out a particular card." Hence it is a variation of the old "shell game" (thimblerig) with cards substituted for cups, under one of which (purportedly but most often not) is a pea.

The skilled monte dealer verifies the adage that the hand is quicker than the eye and provides practical proof of Heisenberg's uncertainty principle. The odds are clearly two to one against the player, but some dealers are so good at this trompe l'oeil that they induce the bettor to specifically pick a wrong card rather than guess one out of three, thus increasing the odds against the bettor.[1]

But it was not merely concern for the player against the monte dealer's legerdemain that caused men like John Scarne to call it "the most popular con game of the old West . . . it is a swindle, not a game" (Scarne, Complete Guide to Gambling, pp. 520-524).

Not content to have the odds two to one in their favor, history and practice reveal a number of swindles and hustles in order to insure the operator's success. "[T]he manipulator of the game frequently became so skilled in his sleight-of-hand performances that the 'court-card' would be held in the palm of his hand, or slipped up his sleeve, without being noticed by the 'victim,' so that any card the victim picked up from the table was certain not to be the court-card, with the result that he was sure to lose." (*State v. Terry*, 141 Kan. 922, 924.)

---

1. Dean Michael Sovern of Columbia Law School suggests that the odds can be reduced to even money if the player rejects what he believes is the court card and selects one of the other two, a proposition logically compelling but psychologically difficult.

Again, the use of confederates or "shills" was and probably is the most frequent form of ripping off the bettor. The shill's participation might range from convincing the player that the dealer is unskilled to pretending to have made a "winning" bet previous to the player (thus causing the dealer to graciously declare a misdeal) to getting the player to believe that the shill has bent the court card and therefore has a sure thing. (For a demonstration of the last variation see Scarne, supra, and The Flim-Flam Man, starring George C. Scott.)

It is, of course, these variations on the basic theme that have caused divergent views of three-card monte in courts throughout the world.

While this State has no reported cases on the character of three-card monte, the game has had a lengthy association with the law in the rest of the western world. The earliest reported cases interpreting the oldest statute are from France, where "bonneteau" (three-card trick) has been declared an "escroquerie" (swindle) since 1881 (C. PÉN. §405; [1882] S. Jur. II, 52 [Cour d'Appel, Paris].)

Reaffirming this position, the highest French court has said that "The game consists in shuffling three cards in such a manner as to give the players the illusion of almost certain gain to be had, but which can be realized only at the will of the dealer and not, as is falsely claimed, by chance. By this means, the dealer nourishes the hope of impossible gain" ([1958] Bull. Crim., No. 1027).

Opposed to the French view are those of the Belgian and British courts. Belgium, under virtually the same generally worded false pretenses statute (C Pen, §496), considers three-card monte "primarily a game of skill" ("un jeu essentiellement d'adresse"). [1885] Pasic III, 224 [Cour d'Appel, Bruxelles]). However, the conviction was upheld because an abuse of confidence was found in arranging for confederates to win in order to build false hopes among the real players.

England is much less equivocal in declaring "three-card trick" a game of skill. In the leading case of *Rex v. Governor of Brixton Prison* (3 K.B. 568) the King's Bench refused to authorize an extradition to Norway in a monte caper. As Lord Alverstone, C.J., asserted (p. 570): "What is known as the three card trick is a game in which one player backs his ability to indicate the position of a particular card, and the other player by sleight of hand and quickness of movement in manipulating the cards in such a way as to deceive the eye induces the former to indicate the wrong card. That in my opinion . . . is sleight of hand and nothing more". Indeed, the English court went further than its Belgian counterpart in holding that (p. 570) "fraudulent conduct whereby the prosecutor is induced to play and which is preliminary to the playing itself is not sufficient to constitute an offense" thereby ruling that any ruse undertaken to lure a player into the game was irrelevant.

Moving further westward, in Canada, Rex v. Rosen (61 DLR 500) followed the English case, while citing the Belgian position (supra) and distinguishing French cases based on the differences in the underlying statutes. However, the Canadian Parliament took care of the Canadian court by specifically outlawing three-card monte (11-12 Geo 5, ch 25, §7 [1921]).

The Canadian statute was preceded in the United States by the actions of several States outlawing three-card monte as an evil in itself. (Illinois [Ill Rev Stat, 1874, p. 348, div 1, §100]; Missouri [1874 Mo Stat, p 50, §1]; Kansas [1876 Kans Stat, ch 81, §1]; Minnesota [1877 Minn Stat, ch 130, esp §4]; California [1877 Cal Stat, p. 8]; Montana [1887 Mont Comp Stat, §208]; the District of Columbia [31 Stat 1331, ch 854, §867, 1901], and Arizona [1913 Ariz Sess L, §533])—all made the obtaining of property by playing three-card monte subject to heavy penalties, even in the absence of fraud. Typical is the following: "Whoever shall deal, play or practice, the confidence game or the game called top and bottom swindle, three-card monte, bunko, or any similar play, game or practice, or practice any confidence trick not mentioned in this section, shall be deemed guilty of a felony" (Ariz. Rev Code, §4791 [1928]). No doubt these statutes, except in the District of Columbia, were the result of the widespread operation of three-card monte men throughout the developing American West (Nash, Hustlers and Con Men, pp. 22-24).

Consequently, all of the American cases considering the character of three-card monte have, until recent times, been grounded in statutes which left no room for deciding whether or not it was a confidence game or swindle but declared it and barred it as one. Thus, in State v. Terry (141 Kan 922, supra) the Supreme Court of Kansas upheld the dismissal of a complaint holding that "[f]ive-card stud poker is not 'any such game, play, or practice' as 'the confidence game or swindle known as three-card monte,' the dealing, playing or practicing of which is made a felony by R. S. 21-930."

Two relatively recent cases discuss three-card monte under general statutes and come to different conclusions. Metcalf v. State (205 Tenn 598) reversed a conviction and United States v. Edwards (516 F2d. 913) affirmed a conviction. Significantly the fact patterns are distinguishable.

In Metcalf, the defendants were convicted of larceny by trick in " 'playing a game named Three Card Monte' " (p. 599). The victims were soldiers at Fort Campbell, Kentucky, who were met at the entrance gate of the post on pay day by the defendants, who on pretense of giving them a ride took the soldiers for a financial ride in monte. Finding (p. 602) that the soldiers "did have a chance to win" the Supreme Court of Tennessee reversed the conviction and stated (p. 603):

In the absence of statute, the fact situation in this case is inconsistent with the generally accepted definition of larceny. These soldiers necessarily knew that the manner in which the dealer was dealing these cards was for the purpose of confusing them. . . . But they thought they saw where it was put, and based on that thought selected that card, voluntarily surrendering the money placed on the bet if their selection proved erroneous. Judging from the many cases annotated in 8A Words and Phrases, under the title, Confidence Game . . . it appears that a number of states have brought the situation described in the instant case within the definition of larceny by statute. But this State has no such statute.

On the other hand, in United States v. Edwards (supra) the Eighth Circuit affirmed a conviction under a fraudulent interstate travel statute where the victim had been taken for $15,000 in monte against a claim that there had been no evidence of cheating. Rationally, the Circuit Court concluded that an intent to defraud could be inferred from the fact that one of the defendants, Edwards, had actually selected the supposed court card on behalf of the victim.

Our findings thus far indicate a split in foreign authority, some jurisdictions holding three-card monte a game of skill and others a confidence game, some per se and others explicitly by statute. The logical question now is "What is a confidence game under New York law?"

This court has found no New York cases or statutes interpreting the general term "confidence game" but it has a fairly universally accepted meaning. A "confidence game" is a term of art involving the taking of money by fraud from a victim by means of trick or deception after the victim's confidence has first been secured through some false representation or deception (*State v. Carr*, 112 Ariz. 453). It is the obtaining of money or property by means of some trick, device or swindling operation in which advantage is taken of the confidence which the victim reposes in the swindler (Black's Law Dictionary [3d ed. 1933]). The elements of the crime of "confidence game" are (1) an intentional false representation to the victim as to some present fact, (2) knowing it to be false, (3) with intent that the victim rely on the representation, (4) the representation being made to obtain the victim's confidence and thereafter his money and property, (5) which confidence is then abused by defendant (*United States v. Brown*, 309 A2d 256, 257 [DC APP]).

While every confidence game necessarily involves false pretenses or ruses, not every false pretense constitutes a confidence game (*Clark v. State*, 53 Ariz. 416). The gist of the crime is the obtaining of the confidence of the victim by some false representation or device

(People v. Friedlander, 328 Ill 35; People v Epstein, 338 Ill 631). Within this framework there are such classic confidence games as the Spanish Prisoner, the Magic Wallet, the Pigeon Drop, Sir Francis Drake's Will, and the Pyramid (Ponzi) Scheme. (See Nash, supra, and Leff, Swindling and Selling, The Story of Legal and Illegal Con Games.).

All of these schemes prey on the credulity and/or greed of the victim. Thus, in the Gypsy Swindle, the confidence man (or woman) convinces the mark that he can exorcise the evil spirits which are tormenting him, generally by burning the victim's money. In a magic-wallet-big-store con, the mark "finds" a wallet, returns it to the "owner," and refuses a reward. The grateful owner places a bet on a race on behalf of the victim, "wins" and turns over hundreds of dollars to the victim. The owner convinces the victim that he is in on a "fix" wherein transmission of race results are delayed to a bookmaking parlor so that a bet on the winner can be made after the race is run. The victim is taken to the betting establishment, bets thousands of dollars on the sure thing and then—"The Sting."

There are "long cons" (Spanish Prisoner, big store) and "short cons" (Pigeon Drop, handkerchief switch). Nash considers three-card monte a short con while Leff does not even mention monte in his chapter on short cons or anywhere else (see Nash and Leff, supra). But whether it is a long or a short con, one salient factor is manifest. The essence of the classic confidence game is that the victim views the confidence man as a protagonist, someone on his side. The monte player, on the other hand, always views the monte dealer as an antagonist, someone to beat.

Viewed in this context, there is no real distinction between *Metcalf* and *Edwards*. In *Metcalf*, no classic confidence game took place. It was merely a straight monte operator's victory. In Edwards, however, a confidence game swindle occurred, the confederate who picked the wrong card playing the role of the confidence man. What has emerged, therefore, in American jurisprudence are two forms of confidence games: the classic confidence game involving a more or less elaborate plot to gain the confidence of the victim as a prelude to a swindle and carnival hustle swindles such as the shell game, three-card monte, two-card faro box, brace wheeled roulette and loaded dice which have been denominated as confidence games by statute.

This dichotomy is clearly illustrated in the case of *State v. Hale* (134 Mont. 131). In *Hale*, the Montana Supreme Court upheld a conviction for operating a game called "Morocco" under a statute penalizing every person who uses or deals with or wins any money by any game commonly known as a confidence game or bunco. The defendant claimed on appeal that since no evidence was adduced to show any confidence reposed by the victim in the operator, the conviction should be reversed. The court held, however, that two different statutes were involved.

Under section 94-1806 of the Revised Code of Montana of 1947, entitled "Confidence games," Montana made punishable the obtaining or attempting to obtain property, by "artifice, device . . . or pretence, commonly called confidence games or bunco" (State v. Hale, supra, p. 137). The court held (pp. 137-138) that "The confidence games described in section 94-1806 are those whereby an elaborate scheme is developed to play upon the credulity or sympathy or some other trait of the victim . . . under this type of a statute it is essential to a conviction that it be proved that the victim reposed confidence in the accused."

Nevertheless, the court pointed out that the defendant was not convicted under this classic confidence game statute. Rather the defendant was charged with violating section 94-2406 of the Revised Code of Montana of 1947 entitled "Brace and Bunco games prohibited." The statute provides that "'Every person who uses or deals with or wins any money . . . with loaded dice or with marked cards, or by any game commonly known as a confidence game or bunco, is punishable' . . . Emphasis supplied."

The court held that it was obvious that section 94-2406 is directed to "an entirely different form of confidence game. . . . Such games . . . bilk the victim of his wager by manipulation . . . [o]f the same ilk are the old shell game, three-card monte or other sleight of hand or manipulated games which effect the same result, all accompanied by fast work, fast count and, buncombe talk by the operator." Montana has two statutes to cover the two types of confidence games discussed above.

Does the New York fraudulent accosting statute cover either or both of these situations? It is evident that the New York statute encompasses only the classic confidence game. The language of subdivision 2 of section 165.30 of the Penal Law creating a presumption of intent to defraud, clearly alludes to the plot type of con game. So does the memorandum accompanying what became chapter 640 of the Laws of 1952 which gave its purpose: "The bill is designed to aid the police in stamping out an ever-increasing number of swindle rackets which include 'pocketbook [pigeon] drops', 'handkerchief switches' and other confidence games. There are many variations of these swindles" (NY Legis Ann, 1952, pp. 36, 37). The examples given in the legislative memorandum to the fraudulent accosting bill are manifestly of the classic confidence game genre and do not include the carnival type swindle. See *Pender v. United States* (310 A2d. 252 [DC App]) holding that "pigeon drop" is not within the three-card monte statute.

In sum, merely alleging the operating of three-card monte does not state a crime under the statute. Palming the court card would constitute a swindle under the statute but that would have to be alleged. The "bent card" ploy would indeed be a classic confidence game, the shill actually becoming the con man. That, too, would have to be alleged. In the instant case no facts are alleged which would justify the complaint. The defendant's motion is granted and the complaint is dismissed.

Lest this opinion be viewed as the emancipation proclamation for the monte sharpie plying his skills on Broadway to an unwary public, his conduct would in my view be a clear violation of subdivision 2 of section 240.35 of the Penal Law—loitering for the purpose of gambling.

## NOTES

Judge Lang suggests that three-card monte is not a game of chance. Indeed, he seems to suggest that the game of skill vs. game of chance distinction is irrelevant here. He suggests that sometimes it is not a game at all, but rather a swindle. If so, then is his recommendation to prosecute under the loitering statute sound? Is the three-card monte dealer engaging in gambling or fraud? Are they the same?

## 5. *Embezzlement and Other Property Offenses*

Inevitably, many of the people who gamble do so with other people's money. Embezzlement relevant to gambling comes in at least two important varieties. First, numerous reported decisions reflect the actions of employees embezzling from their employers to finance their own gambling expenditures. Second, some casino employees are not above reaching into the till at the casino itself.

### CITIBANK v. TRUMP TAJ MAHAL

**U.S. District Court—Southern District of New York**
**1996 WL 640860 (S.D.N.Y.)**

ROBERT P. PATTERSON, Jr., District Judge.

. . . Plaintiff's claims arise out of a series of embezzlements of approximately $2.5 million between April 1988 and April 1993 by Yota Kalikas, an operations manager at a Citibank branch. In March

1993, during a routine random audit of cash equivalents received at [Trump Taj Mahal Associates ("TRUMP")], Agent Thomas Havey of the New Jersey Division of Gaming Enforcement ("DGE") discovered that Kalikas was the authorized signatory of two official Citibank checks dated February 26, 1993, totaling $100,000, and that she presented these two checks to TRUMP in payment of or as credit toward gambling debts. Upon a review of Kalikas' TRUMP credit application, Havey confirmed Kalikas' employment at Citibank, and noticed that Kalikas' signature on the credit application matched the authorized signature on the Citibank official checks. Havey then contacted Citibank's Investigation and Potential Loss Department and spoke with Citibank investigator John Rogan, who informed Havey that it would be "irregular" under Citibank policy for a Citibank employee to be listed both as remitter and authorized signatory of an official check. As a result of Havey's finding, the DGE investigated Kalikas' activity at the TRUMP to determine whether any TRUMP employee had knowledge of Kalikas' embezzlement. Neither the DGE nor the New Jersey Casino Control Commission filed charges or took any other action against TRUMP regarding Kalikas' play there.

In this diversity action, Citibank seeks to recover nine cashier's checks each in the amount of $50,000, one cashier's check in the amount of $75,000, and one cashier's check for $40,000, all drawn on Citibank to the order of TRUMP and signed by Kalikas as the issuing officer, with either her name or her initials as remitter. Two of the checks also bore Kalikas' endorsement and her driver's license number on the reverse side. All the checks were presented to and accepted by TRUMP on weekends between October 1992 and March 1993. Citibank honored all eleven cashier's checks which totaled $565,000.

Citibank asserts that TRUMP had knowledge that the cashier's checks were on their face so irregular as to call into question their validity, that TRUMP failed to verify the checks adequately, which amounted to bad faith, and that TRUMP breached its duty to Citibank by accepting the checks without verifying them adequately. Citibank also asserts that TRUMP failed to verify Kalikas' creditworthiness in May 1990 when it granted her a $5,000 credit line to engage in gambling which was increased in increments until it reached $50,000 in August 1992.

It is not in dispute that Kalikas came to the casinos on Friday evenings or on weekends, outside of banking hours, so that the sufficiency of the funds in the pertinent Citibank account could only be verified on the following business day. It is also not in dispute that cashiers at TRUMP accepted the checks and when banking hours resumed they verified that each of Kalikas' cashier's checks would be honored by Citibank by calling a 1-800 telephone number listed on the back of the check to determine if there were sufficient funds in the account to pay the check. It is also undisputed that TRUMP did not call the bank to confirm that Kalikas, the bank officer who authorized the checks, had the right to present the check for her own use.

According to David Walker, TRUMP's casino shift manager from 1992-1993, TRUMP's "rules, policies and practices" called for verification of cashier's checks by placing a telephone call to the issuing bank to determine whether funds were available for every cashier's check received; if the check, like these checks, was not presented during banking hours, the check would be verified "by other means," and the call would be placed to the issuing bank when banking hours resumed. As stated by Walker, under TRUMP policy "other means" included a visual inspection of the check or a comparison of the check with previously verified checks from the same institution and/or the same patron.

While Kalikas used some of the checks to pay off her credit line, she used others to make "front money deposits" for vouchers against which she could draw chips at the blackjack table. TRUMP also had internal regulations governing front money deposits, which required TRUMP's cashiers to have the customer sign a Customer Deposit Form in the presence of a casino cage cashier simultaneously with each front money deposit, and required the cashiers to maintain a computerized record of those customers using front money deposits. The cashiers were required to examine a computerized facsimile of the customer's signature and other personal signature identification.

Defendant [TRUMP] moves for summary judgment asserting that the checks in question were negotiable instruments, and TRUMP was a holder in due course under N.Y.U.C.C. §3-302(1). Plaintiff does not dispute that the checks were negotiable instruments, but claims TRUMP was not a holder in due course because the evidence does not show that TRUMP accepted the bad checks in good faith. Plaintiff's cross-motion is based on the evidence adduced of TRUMP's negligence and its position that TRUMP is not a holder in due course. Defendant counters that under New Jersey law there is no common law right of private action for negligence against casinos. The holder in due course issue is dispositive of both motions for summary judgment because holder in due course status precludes liability for common law negligence.

### DISCUSSION

A holder in due course is one who is (1) a holder (2) of a negotiable instrument (3) who took it for value (4) in good faith, and (5) without notice of any defense or claim to it on the part of another. Payment or acceptance of any instrument is final in favor of a holder in due course.

There is no question that TRUMP is a holder who took the notes for value. TRUMP either used the checks to reduce Kalikas' debt to TRUMP or to provide her with gambling chips. Plaintiff contends, however, that TRUMP is not a holder in due course because it had notice that the cashier's checks were irregular and did not take the checks in good faith.

The holder's initial burden on the issues of notice and good faith, in response to a defense that a check is facially irregular, is " 'a slight one' that may be satisfied by [its] affidavit disclaiming any knowledge of the maker's defense when the notes were negotiated. . . . [T]he holder will be entitled to summary judgment based on such an affidavit unless the maker proffers evidence of facts that, if accepted, would establish the holder's notice of a valid defense. *A.I. Trade Finance, Inc. v. Laminaciones de Lesaca, S.A.*, 41 F.3d 830, 836-37 (2d Cir. 1994). Generally, the issue of whether a holder of a negotiable instrument gave value for the checks in good faith is a subjective one that requires proof of what the holder actually knew, not speculation as to what it had reason to know or what would have aroused suspicion of a reasonable person in the holder's circumstances. Bad faith under the U.C.C., "represents more than a failure to observe reasonable commercial standards. . . . [T]he circumstances of which the holder is aware must be such that the failure to inquire signals a desire to evade knowledge because of a belief or fear that the inquiry would reveal a defense." *Scarsdale Nat. Bank & Trust Co. v. Toronto-Dominion Bank*, 533 F. Supp. 378, 386 (S.D.N.Y. 1982). In order to deny defendant holder in due course status, plaintiff must show defendant had actual notice of irregularity, not just the opportunity to have noticed it.

Plaintiff need not, however, show "actual notice" to defeat a motion for summary judgment; plaintiff need only show there is a genuine issue of fact from which a reasonable jury could infer notice and bad faith. Gross carelessness may also be sufficient to refute a claim to holder in due course status. "[G]ross carelessness . . . or willful ignorance . . . may constitute evidence of bad faith." *Chartered Bank v. American Trust Co.*, 263 N.Y.S.2d 53, 56 (N.Y. 1965) (citations omitted).

New Jersey statutory law governing casinos, and the case law interpreting it, sheds further light on the requirements of good faith for transactions involving cash equivalents at gambling casinos. There is no dispute that TRUMP was aware of the special requirements for the acceptance of negotiable instruments by casinos under New Jersey law, which provides that,

[p]rior to the acceptance of any cash equivalent from a patron, the general cashier shall determine the validity of such cash equivalent by performing the necessary verification for each type of cash equivalent and such other procedures as may be required by the issuer of such cash equivalent. N.J. Admin. Code tit. 19, §45-1.25(e) 1.

According to the Casino Control Commission, "[t]he phrase 'necessary verification' in this regulation has been construed to require whatever action is 'reasonable under the circumstances.' " (citation omitted). "[C]asinos and their employees are obliged to exercise reasonable care in the conduct of their business, and thereby assure that they are neither conduits for nor victims of criminal enterprise. . . ."

TRUMP argues that its phone call to the bank on the first business day subsequent to acceptance should be sufficient to satisfy this standard. A jury could regard this verification procedure, however, as only designed to ensure that sufficient funds were available for payment of the check, and not designed to help ascertain whether TRUMP was being used as a "conduit for criminal enterprise" by the check's presenter. A trier of fact could find that TRUMP had knowledge, based on its own records, that Kalikas was a heavy and habitual gambler, and that, as compulsive gamblers often resort to crime in order to obtain money to continue gambling, TRUMP's practices deliberately avoided inquiry into the customer's right to present the cash equivalent.

TRUMP's internal regulations, relating to the front money vouchers, could be regarded by the trier of fact as designed to verify the customer's identity and gambling history for Trump Taj Mahal's internal use, and not designed to ensure that the presenter of a cashier's check placed on deposit has a legitimate right to use the cash equivalent in question. The law, as interpreted by the Casino Control Commission, the agency with the responsibility for its administration, places a responsibility on casinos to do more than merely to protect themselves by ensuring that the funds presented are available, but rather to also protect the public through policies that take reasonable care to prevent gamblers from using cash equivalents which do not belong to them. In *State v. Resorts International*, the Commission strongly criticized the failure of the defendant casinos' managements to promulgate appropriate oversight procedures, concluding that,

[T]he responsibility lies with the [casinos] who devised procedures which failed to suggest, much less require, the exercise of sound judgment. . . .[T]he casinos should have advised their cashiers that expanded verification procedures would be applicable to situations in which . . . transactions are on their face unique, unusual or suspicious.

TRUMP claims that on each occasion that Kalikas presented a faulty check the cashiers did not notice that the signature of the bank officer who authorized the cashier's check was identical with that on Kalikas' customer deposit form and the computerized facsimile signature the cashiers were often required to examine; that the cashiers had no obligation to notice the similarities of the signatures; that plaintiff has presented no evidence that the cashiers did notice the similarities; and that plaintiff has thus failed to establish notice under N.Y.U.C.C. §3-301. Joyce Clegg ("Clegg"), one of the cashiers whose signature appeared on customer deposit slips and redemption vouchers relating to the cashier's checks Kalikas presented on December 19, 1992 and February 27, 1993, testified that she had no recollection of the transactions involving Kalikas. She also added she did not notice the authorized signature was similar to Kalikas' signature, but if she had, she would have called it to the attention of her supervisor. A trier of fact could determine that such testimony, far from exonerating TRUMP, merely shows that the procedures adopted by TRUMP did not meet its duty to train its cashiers to exercise reasonable care in scrutinizing the instrument before honoring a cash equivalent.

The facts here permit Citibank to attempt to persuade a jury that TRUMP has not implemented internal procedures designed to elicit the "sound judgment" of its cashiers, and ensure that the cashiers are trained to inspect closely and scrutinize effectively the instruments that are presented to them. If such heightened procedures, required by the 1985 decision in *Resorts Int'l*, had been in place, it could be found that TRUMP's cashiers would have noticed, like Agent Havey, the suspicious fact that the signature of the bank's issuing officer, on the face of the check, was the same as the signature presented on the patron's identification; and that they would also have noticed, in turn, that the patron's identification had the same name as that of the check remitter, printed on the face of the check. A reasonable juror could determine that TRUMP's failure to institute appropriate training and oversight procedures, that would ensure adequate verification and careful scrutiny, constituted a deliberate avoidance of the casino's responsibility to ensure that it was not used as a criminal conduit by gamblers, and amounted to bad faith. Summary judgment is thus inappropriate on the issue of whether TRUMP is a holder in due course.

For all the reasons stated above, defendant's motion for summary judgment is denied. Plaintiff's cross-motion for summary judgment is also denied.

*NOTES*

1. This case was a black eye for "the industry." But which industry? Who should have borne primary responsibility for preventing such a crime from happening? Note that both the banking industry and the gaming industry have strong "internal controls" and, for that matter "external controls," which are rules designed to prevent loss. One method for answering the question as to who is responsible is to ask the question, "who is the least cost avoider?" That is, which entity, the bank or the casino, is best suited or best located to catch the problem? One might conclude that the least cost avoider is Citibank who somehow allowed its employee to steal $2.5 million over the course of five years. Citibank clearly has the greatest financial interest in preventing this kind of offense. The casino is more compromised on that question; its interests are conflicted. Legal liability rules can, of course, change the incentive structure by insuring that the casino also has a strong incentive to prevent it from facilitating embezzlement.

2. While the bank may be, in some ways, best suited to have prevented this offense, could embezzlement of this magnitude have happened as easily without the willing, though perhaps innocent, cooperation of casinos? Where else would someone be willing to find a commercial enterprise willing to cash checks of such magnitude without engaging in greater due diligence? If casinos create easier opportunities to engage in embezzlement, is there a strong argument that the social costs of embezzlement should be borne by the gaming industry?

3. The embezzlement offense in *Citibank* was uncovered apparently not by the victim, but by gaming regulators. What enables them to be so effective in ferreting out wrongdoing? This is a question to which this text will return later.

# CHAPTER
# 3

---

# Private Law and the Prohibition of Gambling

Very few American jurisdictions prohibit gambling altogether, but most jurisdictions prohibit certain forms of gambling. Even in jurisdictions that have adopted the most permissive stance toward regulated gambling, illegal and unregulated gambling is nevertheless prohibited. Indeed, unregulated gambling is sometimes prohibited aggressively, particularly in gaming-permissive states because such gaming siphons revenues away from a carefully regulated, and taxed, industry.

Efforts at prohibition have long been fraught with peril and, thus, strategies for enforcement of gambling prohibitions take different legal forms. State and federal (and sometimes tribal) criminal and regulatory laws, generally characterized collectively as "public law," are relevant in enforcing the prohibition, but less direct efforts, through the regulation of private intercourse, is relevant as well. Private law covers the regulation and enforcement of consensual legal relationships between, for example, individuals or between corporations. In a society highly involved in commerce, private law strategies are sometimes more effective in regulating behavior.

The principal private law subject in the law school curriculum is, of course, the law of contracts. It is particularly relevant in the law of gambling. Every bet is, in essence, a contract, and thus, contract law is perhaps the best place to begin the thorny problem of how to enforce a gambling prohibition, or partial prohibition. This chapter examines efforts at regulating private agreements indirectly through private actions in courts, or the denial of the same.

# A.  CONTRACT LAW APPROACHES TO PROHIBITIONS ON ILLEGAL GAMBLING

One of the early efforts to ban gambling was the Statute of Queen Anne, enacted in England in 1710. Gambling was thought to have undesirable effects in England because it threatened a particular kind of social instability: wealthy noblemen who gambled excessively were in danger of losing their assets to mere commoners. Queen Anne's solution to this problem was to allow losers to litigate to recover their losses from winners, but to make gambling contracts unenforceable in the courts. By denying the enforcement of gambling contracts in the courts, Queen Anne made gambling activity more unpredictable and thus less profitable for winners.

The rule of the unenforceability of gambling debts made its way into American laws in two ways. First, it was deemed to be the common law of England and several American jurisdictions have "reception" statutes providing that absent other guidance, the courts of the state should follow England's common law as of 1776. Second, many states have enacted laws similar to the Statute of Queen Anne.

The Statute of Queen Anne rule can arise in at least three different contexts. First, it can arise in actions between individuals, often friends, who make purely private wagers. When one fails to pay, the other may wish to bring a legal action. Second, the rule may arise in a more ambiguous quasi-commercial context, in which a player makes a claim against an entity or organization that is engaged in gambling activity not simply as a mere participant but seeking to profit by offering gambling to others. Since it is sometimes unclear whether or not such activity is authorized by law, this type of activity sometimes occurs in a gray area of the law. Third, the rule arises in the context of legalized commercial gambling. Since each context presents slightly different issues, they will be treated separately.

## 1.  Private Gambling Agreements

### DICKERSON v. DENO

**Supreme Court of Alabama**
**770 So. 2d 63 (Ala. 2000)**

MADDOX, Justice.

The parties to these proceedings dispute whether the holder of a winning Florida lottery ticket must share the winnings with others because of an alleged prior oral agreement they all had made to share the winnings if any one of them was a winner. The trial court held that the one had to share the winnings with the others. The resolution of that question raises at least two legal questions:

> (1) Given the evidence presented, did the trial judge err in finding that the holder of the winning lottery ticket had orally agreed to share any winnings equally with four other persons?

> (2) Assuming, arguendo, that the proof was sufficient to establish an oral agreement, was the agreement unenforceable on the basis that it was a contract made in Alabama and was "founded . . . on a gambling consideration," as that term is used in Ala. Code 1975, §8-1-150?

The facts are basically undisputed. The plaintiffs—Sandra Deno, Angie Tisdale, Matthew Adams, and Jackie Fairley—and the defendant Tonda Dickerson were all employees at the Waffle House restaurant in Grand Bay, Alabama. Edward Seward, who is not a party to this action, was a regular customer of the Waffle House. On several occasions Seward would travel to Florida and purchase lottery tickets and upon his return would give the tickets to various friends and family members, including the employees of the Waffle House. Seward did not expect to share any potential lottery winnings based on the tickets he gave away, but he claimed that he was promised a new truck by the employees of the Waffle House if one of the tickets he distributed there was a winning ticket. Several employees of the Waffle House received lottery tickets from Seward during the several weeks that he gave out the tickets.

A drawing for the Florida lottery was scheduled for Saturday night, March 6, 1999. During the week before that drawing, Seward traveled to Florida and purchased several lottery tickets. He placed each individual ticket in a separate envelope and wrote the name of the intended recipient on the outside of the envelope. On March 6, 1999, before the lottery drawing, Seward presented the plaintiffs Deno, Tisdale, and Adams each with an envelope containing one lottery ticket. The drawing was held as scheduled. The numbers on the lottery tickets held by Deno, Tisdale, and Adams did not match the numbers drawn in the March 6 drawing.

On March 7, 1999, after the March 6 drawing had already been concluded and the winning numbers had been determined, Seward presented a ticket to the plaintiff Fairley, who had never previously received a ticket from Seward; he also on that date presented the defendant Dickerson with a ticket. Each of those tickets was for the March 6 drawing, and each was presented in a separate envelope. Upon opening her envelope, Fairley determined that the numbers on her ticket did not match the winning numbers. Subsequently,

Dickerson opened her envelope and determined that the numbers on her ticket matched the winning numbers drawn in the lottery the night before. The ticket won a prize of approximately $5 million.

Shortly thereafter, on March 18, 1999, the plaintiffs sued Dickerson, alleging that they and Dickerson had orally contracted with each other that if any one of them should win, then the winner would share any lottery winnings with the other ticket recipients. The plaintiffs asked the court to issue a preliminary injunction enjoining distribution of the winnings until a declaration of their rights could be made, and on March 19, 1999, the trial court ordered all parties to refrain from any further efforts or attempts to collect any funds from the State of Florida Department of Lottery that were, or might be, the subject of a dispute between the parties. This order remained in effect throughout the trial of the case. The plaintiffs sought to have the alleged oral agreement specifically performed, and they also asked the trial court to declare that a constructive trust had been created by the parties. . . . Following the trial, the advisory jury returned a verdict for the plaintiffs, and the trial court entered a final judgment in the plaintiffs' favor. It issued a written order holding that there was an oral contract and that each party was entitled to 20% of the proceeds of Dickerson's Florida lottery ticket.

Dickerson argues on appeal that the alleged oral agreement testified to by the plaintiffs was unenforceable because, she says, it lacked the necessary elements of a valid and enforceable contract. She also argues that, assuming, arguendo, that the alleged oral agreement did have all the elements ordinarily necessary for a contract, it was void as a gambling contract, because, she argues, it was an agreement made in Alabama and §8-1-150 specifically provides that "all contracts founded in whole or in part on a gambling consideration are void."

Dickerson argues at some length that the plaintiffs failed to prove that the parties made an oral agreement. However, we conclude that the parties presented sufficient evidence to support a finding that the parties did orally agree that if any one of them should win the lottery, then they all would divide the proceeds. But, assuming they entered into such an agreement, was that agreement void and unenforceable as a "contract[] founded . . . on a gambling consideration"? See Ala. Code 1975, §8-1-150. We now address the parties' arguments on that question.

The plaintiffs concede that §8-1-150 seeks to prohibit the enforcement of any payment for actual wagering or gambling, or on games of chance, but they argue that the oral agreement in this case is not void, because, they contend, "an agreement to share proceeds from a legal winning lottery ticket is simply not a wager between the parties to the agreement in the State of Alabama." They cite several cases they contend support their argument that the oral agreement made in this case was not founded on a gambling consideration. They first cite *Talley v. Mathis*, 265 Ga. 179, 453 S.E.2d 704 (1995), as being a "strikingly similar case." In that case, the complaint alleged that two friends, both residents of Georgia, had agreed to jointly purchase tickets from the State of Kentucky lottery and to share the proceeds if they won. Mathis made the same argument in that case that Dickerson makes here: that the alleged agreement was against the public policy of the State where it was made and therefore was unenforceable. The Georgia Supreme Court, as the plaintiffs correctly argue, not only held that the alleged agreement would not violate Georgia public policy but stated that "the public policy of this state would be violated if appellant were denied the opportunity to seek to enforce the alleged agreement against appellees."

We agree with Dickerson that the facts in this case show that there was no agreement to jointly purchase or to jointly hold the lottery tickets. Each lottery ticket was purchased by Seward in Florida and was presented by him to one or the other of the parties, separately. The alleged oral contract in this case was an exchange of promises to share winnings from the parties' individually owned lottery tickets upon the happening of the uncertain event that the numbers drawn in the Florida lottery matched the numbers on one of the tickets held by the five individuals. Consequently, the agreement between the parties was nothing more than an attempt by each of the five lottery-ticket holders to increase his or her odds of winning some portion of the Florida lottery. Stated differently, the agreement, according to the plaintiffs' own evidence, was that Dickerson would pay the plaintiffs a sum of money upon the happening of an uncertain event over which no party had control, that is, upon Dickerson's ticket winning the Florida lottery. Consequently, we conclude that the agreement at issue here was "founded . . . on a gambling consideration," within the meaning of that phrase in §8-1-150 and that it was, therefore, void.

The judgment of the trial court is due to be reversed and a judgment rendered for the defendant Dickerson.

JOHNSTONE, Justice (dissenting).

I respectfully dissent. The substance of the agreement among the parties is that each agreed that the lottery ticket held by him or her was jointly owned by all the parties. The consideration to each of the parties for his or her agreement in this regard consists of the mutual agreements to the same effect made by all of the other parties. That is, each party received the acknowledgment of each other party that such other's ticket was jointly owned by all the parties. The consideration consisted not of the uncertain event (the lottery) or the possible winnings from the lottery but rather of the mutual agreements among the parties. Likewise, none of the parties agreed to pay money upon the happening of the uncertain event; but, rather each agreed to acknowledge the joint ownership of his or her ticket by all the parties regardless of the happening of the uncertain event.

Thus the agreement, or contract, at issue is not "founded in whole or in part on a gambling consideration" as outlawed by §8-1-150, Ala. Code 1975. Accordingly, the judgment of the trial court should be affirmed.

## NOTES

1.  The law that makes a "contract founded upon a gambling consideration" void and unenforceable is a common version of the Statute of Queen Anne adopted in many states. Does application of the Statute of Queen Anne serve a useful purpose in *Dickerson*? If so, what purpose?

2.  *Dickerson* provides evidence of problems related to the prohibition of gambling in a jurisdiction when a neighboring jurisdiction not only allows gambling, but encourages it. More on this subject later.

3.  Consider this history: "The appellant [cites] the early English Statutes entitled "An Act against deceitful, disorderly and excessive gaming," 16 Charles 2, Ch. 7 (1664), and "An Act for the better preventing of excessive and deceitful gaming," 9 Anne, Ch. 14 (1710). It is contended that these Acts are still in force in Maryland, and that the procedural limitations set forth in these Statutes must be read into the Maryland Statute upon which the plaintiff relies. In England the first of these was repealed by 8 and 9 Vict., Ch. 109 (1845) and the second modified by 55 and 56 Vict., Ch. 9 (1892) so as to prevent recovery by a loser after payment. For discussion of these and subsequent English Statutes, see *Williston, Contracts*, Rev. Ed., Sec. 1679, and *Pollock, Contracts*, 11th Ed., p. 297 *et seq.* Wagers were legal at common law (*Williston, Contracts*, Rev. Ed., Sec. 1667), but by the Statutes of Charles and Anne certain forms of wagering were made illegal, and recovery by a winner was denied. 2 *Alexander's British Statutes*, 2d Ed., p. 648. The Statute of Charles provided that the loser "by any Fraud, Shift, Cousenage, Circumvention, Deceit, or unlawful Device, or

ill Practice whatsoever," might recover treble damages, one moiety thereof for the Crown, by suit within 6 months "next after such play," or suit might be brought by any other person within one year after the six months expired. Another provision denied recovery to any winner in excess of one hundred pounds. The Statute of Anne provided in Section 1 that all notes or other securities given for money lost by gaming, or for repaying money knowingly loaned or advanced for gaming or betting, should be void. Section 2 provided that any person "who shall, at any time or sitting, by playing at Cards, Dice, Tables or other Game or Games whatsoever, or by betting on the Sides or Hands of such as do play," lose "in the whole, the Sum or Value of ten Pounds, and shall pay or deliver the same," shall be "at Liberty, within three months then next, to sue for and recover the Money or Goods so lost . . . from the respective Winner or Winners thereof, with Costs of Suit, by Action of Debt Founded on this Act." If the loser did not sue, any other person could sue for treble damages, one moiety for the suitor, and one moiety for the poor of the parish. Section 3 provided for discovery; Section 4, that repayment should acquit of further punishment; Section 5, that winning by fraud above ten pounds should be punished as perjury, with recovery of five times the amount won; and Section 8 provided penalties and imprisonment for assault on account of money won at play." *LaFontaine v. Wilson*, 45 A.2d 729 (Md. App. 1946).

4.  To review principles from Chapter 1, consider at what point in the narrative the plaintiffs in *Dickerson* began engaging in "gambling." Were they gambling?

### PEARSALL v. ALEXANDER
**572 A.2d 113 (D.C. 1990)**

NEWMAN, Associate Judge.

In what must be a common development wherever there are state-sponsored lotteries, this is the story of two friends who split the price of a ticket only to have the ticket win and split their friendship.

**I**

Harold Pearsall and Joe Alexander were friends for over twenty-five years. About twice a week they would get together after work, when Alexander would meet Pearsall at the Takoma Metro station in his car.

The pair would then proceed to a liquor store, where they would purchase what the two liked to refer to as a "package"—a half-pint of vodka, orange juice, two cups, and two lottery tickets—before repairing to Alexander's home. There they would "scratch" the lottery tickets, drink screwdrivers, and watch television. On occasion these lottery tickets would yield modest rewards of two or three dollars, which the pair would then "plow back" into the purchase of additional lottery tickets. According to Pearsall, the two had been sharing D.C. Lottery tickets in this fashion since the Lottery began.

On the evening of December 16, 1982, Pearsall and Alexander visited the liquor store twice, buying their normal "package" on each occasion. The first package was purchased when the pair stopped at the liquor store on the way to Alexander's home from the Metro station. Pearsall went into the store alone, and when he returned to the car, he said to Alexander, in reference to the tickets, "Are you in on it?" Alexander said "Yes." When Pearsall asked Alexander for his half of the purchase price of the tickets, Alexander replied that he had no money. When they reached Alexander's home, Alexander, expressing his anxiety that Pearsall might lose the tickets, demanded that Pearsall produce them, snatched them from Pearsall's hand, and "scratched" them, only to find that both were worthless.

At about 8:00 P.M. that same evening, Alexander, who apparently had come by some funds of his own, returned to the liquor store and bought a second "package." This time Pearsall, who had been offended by Alexander's conduct earlier in taking both tickets, snatched the two tickets from Alexander and announced that he would be the one to "scratch" them. Intending only to bring what he regarded as Alexander's childish behavior to Alexander's attention, Pearsall immediately relented and gave over one of the tickets to Alexander. Each man then "scratched" one of the tickets. Pearsall's ticket proved worthless; Alexander's was a $20,000 winner.

Alexander became very excited about the ticket and began calling friends to announce the good news. Fearing that Alexander might lose the ticket, Pearsall told Alexander to sign his name on the back of the ticket. Subsequently, Alexander cashed in the ticket and received the winnings; but, when Pearsall asked for his share, Alexander refused to give Pearsall anything.

Pearsall brought suit against Alexander, claiming breach of an agreement to share the proceeds of the winning ticket. Alexander denied that there was any agreement between the two to share the winnings of the ticket and further claimed, inter alia, that any such agreement was unenforceable because it was not in writing and contravened public policy.

The trial court dismissed Pearsall's complaint on the public policy grounds raised by Alexander, finding that the enforcement of contracts arising from gaming transactions is barred by the Statute of Anne, as enacted in D.C. Code §16-1701, even when such contracts concern legalized gambling. Citing Hamilton v. Blankenship, 190 A.2d 904 (D.C. 1963), for this latter proposition, the trial court went on to determine that §16-1701 applies to bets placed legally within the District pursuant to D.C. Code §2-2501 to 2537, which authorizes the D.C. Lottery. The court did not reach the issue of whether such an agreement must be in writing pursuant to the Statute of Frauds, as enacted in D.C. Code §28:1-206 (1981).

## II

The Statute of Anne, as enacted in the District of Columbia, provides, in relevant part, as follows:

> §16-1701. Invalidity of gaming contracts.
> (a) A thing in action, judgment, mortgage, or other security or conveyance made and executed by a person in which any part of the consideration is for money or other valuable thing won by playing at any game whatsoever, or by betting on the sides or hands of persons who play, or for the reimbursement or payment of any money knowingly lent or advanced for the purpose, or lent or advanced at the time and place of play or bet, to a person so playing or betting or who, during the play, so plays or bets, is void except as provided by subsection (b) of this section.

Thus, the statute invalidates only those contracts in which one party agrees either to (1) pay something to another as the result of losing a game or bet, or (2) repay money knowingly advanced or lent for the purpose of gambling.

Pearsall's cause of action does not involve either of these types of transactions. First, he is not suing Alexander to recover a gambling debt owed by Alexander. Pearsall and Alexander did not wager against one another on the outcome of the D.C. Lottery or any other event, and they did not play against one another at cards, dice, or any other game. Second, Pearsall is not suing to recover money loaned to Alexander for the purpose of gambling. Rather Pearsall and Alexander entered into an agreement to share the winnings of a jointly-purchased lottery ticket, and it is this agreement, and not any gaming contract, that forms the basis of Pearsall's cause of action. Moreover, the Pearsall-Alexander agreement is not based upon the type of consideration described in §16-1701, i.e., money or valuables won at gambling or knowingly loaned for the purpose of gambling. Rather, each man gave as consideration for the agreement his promise to share the proceeds of the ticket he "scratched." Such consideration does not derive from one man having bested the other in a game of chance. Nor does it derive from any sort of loan.

Therefore, the agreement that forms the basis of Pearsall's cause of action is not a gaming contract as defined in §16-1701, and the trial court erred in applying the statute in this case.

In addition to concluding that the Pearsall-Alexander agreement does not offend the letter of §16-1701, we are equally convinced that it gives no offense to the statute's spirit. The public policy behind §16-1701, and similar statutes, is to deny use of judicial process to those who would undermine laws meant to prevent gambling by using the courts to collect on gambling debts. That policy cannot be vindicated here, where the gambling involved, betting on the D.C. Lottery, is legal under the laws of this jurisdiction . . . and is encouraged by the authorities responsible for promoting such gambling in the jurisdiction.

Stated differently, denying Pearsall recovery is not going to discourage illegal gambling in this instance, because the gambling involved, betting on the D.C. Lottery, is not illegal. Nor does it make sense to say that denying Pearsall recovery will serve the public policy interest of discouraging gambling in general, whether legal or illegal, when the District is spending money to encourage people like Pearsall and Alexander to gamble on the Lottery in order to serve the public policy behind the Lottery.

We note that other jurisdictions faced with public policy challenges to agreements to share the proceeds of winning lottery tickets have reached the same result we reach today. Although these decisions concerned actions brought in jurisdictions where lotteries were illegal by residents of those jurisdictions seeking to recover a share of the proceeds from winning tickets purchased in jurisdictions where lotteries were legal, and therefore turned on conflict-of-law analyses, the public policy concerns at stake were similar to those before us in this case. Thus, we find persuasive the reasoning set forth by the Supreme Court of Indiana in *Kaszuba v. Zientara,* supra, 506 N.E.2d at 2-3, in which the court said: [t]here is no benefit to the citizens of this State in prohibiting an agreement of this nature. It will not shelter them from lotteries conducted in sister states. It will not deter people from purchasing lottery tickets in Illinois, Ohio or Michigan. Finding the agreement between Zientara and Kaszuba illegal and unenforceable as against public policy, rather than being of benefit to Indiana residents, would instead reward people who convert the property of others to their own use.

We further note that the force of this reasoning is only increased where, as in this situation, the gambling at issue is legal in the court's own jurisdiction. If a jurisdiction surrounded by states with legalized lotteries cannot expect to deter its citizens from betting on such lotteries by prohibiting agreements of this kind, then surely a jurisdiction with its own legalized lottery cannot expect, and more to the point should not be about the business of trying, to deter its citizens from betting on its own lottery by prohibiting such agreements either.

News accounts and personal observations reveal that it is common practice for friends, relatives, and coworkers to pool their resources and purchase large blocks of tickets on those occasions when various state lotteries present exceptionally large prizes. The approach taken by the trial court would make such arrangements perilous indeed, by permitting the unscrupulous holders of winning tickets to renege on their agreement and keep the winnings for themselves. We agree with the Supreme Court of Indiana that such an approach would only reward those who convert the property of others, without conferring any benefit on the citizens of the District.

## III

The record supports the trial court's finding that an agreement existed between Pearsall and Alexander to share equally in the proceeds of the winning ticket at issue.

The conduct of the two men on the evening of December 16, 1982, when the ticket was purchased, clearly demonstrates a meeting of the minds. After purchasing the first pair of tickets, Pearsall asked Alexander if he was "in on it." Not only did Alexander give his verbal assent, but later, when the two reached Alexander's home, Alexander, who had contributed nothing to the purchase price of the tickets, snatched both tickets from Pearsall and anxiously "scratched" them. It is evident from this that Alexander considered himself "in on" an agreement to share in the fortunes of the tickets purchased by his friend. It is equally clear that in giving over tickets he had purchased, Pearsall gave his assent to the agreement he had proposed earlier in the car. Moreover, this conduct took place within the context of a long-standing pattern of similar conduct, analogous to a "course of conduct" as described in the Uniform Commercial Code,[5] which

---

5. U.C.C. §1-205(1), adopted in the District of Columbia as D.C. Code §28:1-205(1) (1981), provides that "[a] course of dealing is a sequence of previous conduct between the parties to a particular transaction which is fairly to be regarded as establishing a common basis of understanding for interpreting their expressions and other conduct."

included their practice of "plowing back" small returns from winning tickets into the purchase of additional tickets.

It is also clear to us that, by exchanging mutual promises to share in the proceeds of winning tickets, adequate consideration was given by both parties. An exchange of promises is consideration, so long as it is bargained-for. Restatement (Second) Contracts, §75 (1932). Moreover, consideration may consist of detriment to the promisee. *Clay v. Chesapeake & Potomac Tel. Co.*, 87 U.S. App. D.C., 284 F.8d 995 (1950). The giving over of one-half of the proceeds of a winning ticket would be a detriment to either man. Therefore, Pearsall's promise to share, as expressed in his question to Alexander, "Are you in it?" induced a detriment in Alexander. Likewise, Alexander's promise to share, as contained in his assent, induced a detriment in Pearsall.

Finally, we find no merit in Alexander's contention that the agreement is unenforceable under [the D.C. statute of frauds].

This statute, which applies only to the sale of personal property "beyond" $5000, is inapplicable on its face. The Pearsall-Alexander agreement does not involve the sale of personal property. There was no agreement between the parties for the holder of a winning ticket to "sell" half of his winnings, as personal property, to the other. This was simply an agreement to share the proceeds of a jointly-purchased ticket; no buying or selling as between the parties was contemplated or required.

In conclusion, we find that there was a valid, enforceable agreement between Pearsall and Alexander to share in the proceeds of the $20,000 ticket purchased by Alexander on the evening of December 16, 1982. Therefore, we reverse and remand with instructions to enter judgment in favor of the appellant.

*NOTES*

1. Can *Dickerson* and *Pearsall* both be correct? How can they be reconciled?
2. Is the District of Columbia's Statute of Queen Anne provision drafted narrowly or broadly? Should that make a difference in how it is interpreted? Does the court interpret it correctly?
3. Consider the following commentary, wherein the author argues that agreements to share in lottery winnings should be unenforceable as "social engagements":

> Most lottery pooling agreements are in essence social engagements and therefore should be unenforceable. The parties involved in these agreements are simply agreeing to participate in a social

activity together: the playing of a game. However, for some reason, courts have not hesitated to elevate the social activity of playing the lottery to commercial transaction status.

For illustrative purposes, consider Pearsall v. Alexander, in which a winning lottery ticket worth $20,000 ended a twenty-five year friendship. Harold Pearsall and Joe Alexander routinely met twice a week after work and jointly purchased a "package," which consisted of orange juice, a half-pint of vodka, two cups, and two lottery tickets. They would then return to Alexander's home, where they would scratch off the tickets, drink screwdrivers, and watch television.

The men did not follow this routine exactly on the day the winning ticket was purchased. On that day, Alexander claimed not to have money for tickets, so Pearsall bought the "package" with his own money. Pearsall asked Alexander if he was "in on it," however, and Alexander said he was. Alexander scratched off both tickets, but they proved to be worthless. Alexander, after coming into some money, returned to the store later that evening and bought another "package," this time entirely with his own funds. Pearsall grabbed one of the tickets and scratched it, but it was not a winner. Alexander scratched the other ticket and found that it was a $20,000 winner. Alexander subsequently cashed in the ticket and refused to give Pearsall any of the prize.

The appellate court, in its reversal of the lower court's dismissal of the case, determined that "an agreement existed between Pearsall and Alexander to share equally in the proceeds of the winning ticket at issue." The court based its conclusion on the fact that each party let the other scratch tickets that were purchased with only one party's funds and on its finding that they had a "long-standing pattern of similar conduct." These facts produced "mutual promises to share in the proceeds," and these mutual promises were "adequate consideration" to sustain a contract.

The court stretched to find a contract in this case. Because there was no actual pooling of funds to buy the ticket, the court instead found consideration by stating that the pattern of conduct suggested mutual promises. However, Alexander and Pearsall were simply agreeing to engage in a social endeavor. Consider, for example, if Alexander had bought a "package," but had refused to share the vodka with his friend even though there was a promise to do so and a return promise to help drink it. A court of law probably would not have enforced that "contract" because the promise to share the vodka, like a promise to go on a date, was simply a promise to engage in a social activity.

Why is an agreement to engage in the social activity of playing the lottery any different? The answer might be that courts believe that when people actually pool their funds to buy tickets, the expectation becomes that the agreement is enforceable. But that may not realistically reflect the expectations of such parties, and it is instead likely that the large amounts of money involved when tickets turn out to be winners have swayed the courts toward enforcement even though the parties have no such expectation.

> Matthew J. Gries, Note, *Judicial Enforcement of Agreements to Share Winning Lottery Tickets*, 44 DUKE L.J. 1000, 1012-1014 (1995).

Do you agree?

4. Both *Dickerson* and *Pearsall* demonstrate that it is difficult to contain legal gaming and its effects. Legal gambling gives rise to additional intercourse, whether considered commercial or social, between individuals. Should these ancillary products or "side effects" of lawful commercial gambling activity be subject to the Statute of Queen Anne?

5. *Pearsall* suggests, though it does not explicitly hold, that the policies animating the Statute of Queen Anne are not implicated in the context of legal commercial gambling. Ponder this question as you read the next few cases dealing with commercial forms of gambling.

## 2. *Charitable Gaming in Prohibitive Jurisdictions*

### WILLIAMS v. WEBER MESA DITCH EXTENSION CO.

**Supreme Court of Wyoming**
**572 P.2d 412 (1977)**

RAPER, Justice.

. . . Defendant-appellee, a nonprofit corporation, conducted a raffle, the prize being a 40-acre tract of land in Carbon County, Wyoming. Printed tickets were sold at $5.00 each or three for $10.00. Each ticket had printed on its face that the drawing would be held May 1, 1976.

The plaintiff purchased a ticket prior to the scheduled drawing. On May 1, 1976, his name was drawn and he was notified of his lucky win. On May 6, 1976, the defendant received several more ticket stubs which had been delayed in the mails. Plaintiff's ticket stub, along with all others, was returned to the hopper and a new raffle held on the latter date. As a result, a new winner, not plaintiff, was announced and notified that a conveyance of the land would be forthcoming.

Plaintiff sued defendant for specific performance. The district court denied relief and gave judgment generally in favor of the defendant [the trial judge having resolved to leave the parties where he found them on what he held to be a gambling contract].

Gambling contracts are statutorily declared void and of no effect by §16-2, W.S.1957, as follows:

> All contracts, promises, agreements, conveyances, securities, and notes, made, given, granted, executed, drawn, or entered into, where the whole or any part of the consideration thereof shall be for any money, property, or other valuable thing won by any gaming, or by playing cards or any gambling device or game of chance, or by betting on the side or hands of any person gaming, or for the reimbursing or paying any money or property knowingly lent or advanced at the time and place of such play, to any person or persons so gaming or betting, shall be utterly void and of no effect. No assignment of any bill, bond, note, or other evidence of indebtedness where the whole or any part of the consideration for such assignment shall arise out of any gaming transaction, shall in any manner offset the defense of the person or persons making, entering into, executing, or giving such instrument so assigned, or the remedies of any person interested therein.

However, on the criminal side, raffles by charitable and non-profit corporations are not declared criminal conduct, as an exception contained in §6-213, W.S.1957, 1975 Cum. Supp., in language as follows:

> If any person shall in this state open, set on foot, carry on, or promote, make or draw publicly or privately, any lottery, or scheme of chance, of any kind or description, by whatever name, style, or title the same may be known; or if any person shall by such ways and means, expose or set for sale any house, or houses, mine or mining property, lands or real estate, or any goods or chattels, cash or written or printed evidence of debt, or certificates of claims, or any thing or things of value whatever, every person so offending shall be deemed guilty of a misdemeanor, and upon conviction, fined in any sum not exceeding one thousand dollars, and be imprisoned in the county jail for a period not exceeding three months. But *nothing in this section shall be construed as applying to games of chance known as raffles or bingo conducted by charitable or non-profit organizations and the tickets of such raffles or bingo shall be sold only in this state.* [Emphasis added.]

Webster defines "raffle" as "a lottery in which each participant buys a ticket for an article put up as a prize with the winner being determined by a random drawing." Webster declares "chance" to be a synonym for "random." "Raffle" and "lottery" are synonymous. *State [of] West Virginia v. Hudson*, 1946, 128 W. Va. 655, 37 S.E.2d 553, 559, 163 A.L.R. 1265. The simplest form of a lottery is the raffle, a game of chance. *United States v. Baker*, 3 Cir. 1966, 364 F.2d 107, 111, cert. denied 385 U.S. 986, 87 S. Ct. 596, 17 L. Ed. 2d 448. The three elements of a lottery are consideration, chance and prize. *Morrow v. State,* Alaska, 1973, 511 P.2d 127; *State v. Nelson,* 1972, 210 Kan. 439, 502 P.2d 841, 846; Cudd v. Aschenbrenner, 1962, 233 Or. 272, 377 P.2d 150, 153. A raffle as a lottery is a game of chance. Section 6-213. The authority for all these propositions is so enormous, for further citations, see West's Words and Phrases "Raffle" and "Lottery." See also 6A Corbin on Contracts, §1487, pp. 653-654. There is no question but [that] defendant conducted a game of chance and plaintiff participated.

The rule is well settled that even though gambling may be allowed and carried on without any criminal violation of the law or criminal responsibility, a gambling debt is unenforceable, even in absence of a statute. [Citations omitted]. Courts refuse to lend their aid in enforcing a gaming contract pursuant to the policy announced by the legislature of the State of Wyoming. Section 16-2. The basis for such statutes, as declared in the authorities cited, is that wagers are against human welfare, considered to be of a higher interest, and are not to be encouraged. We hold the gaming contract to be void. AFFIRMED

### NOTES

1. The legal effect of buying a raffle ticket is to enter a contract. By statute, Wyoming law forbade the enforcement of a gambling contract in *Weber.* Is this a fruitful approach to enforcing a gambling prohibition? If so, what is the social ill that the prohibition is designed to prevent?
2. Is there a gambling prohibition in Wyoming? What is the policy of Wyoming with regard to gambling opportunities offered by charitable organizations? Is Wyoming law internally consistent?
3. What if the charity in *Weber* had refused to award the prize to the other "winner" as well and thereby dramatically increased the value of this fundraising effort? Different result?

## HARRIS v. ECONOMIC OPPORTUNITY COMMISSION OF NASSAU COUNTY

### 575 N.Y.S.2d 672 (NY App. 1991)

MILLER, Justice.

The question before us on this appeal, while seemingly innocuous at first blush, severely impacts upon a fundraising practice widely utilized by charitable organizations. Simply stated, we are called upon to determine whether a charitable organization may interpose the defense of illegality to defeat the claim by the winner of a raffle who was denied his winning prize.

* * *

The facts underlying this appeal are not in substantial dispute. The defendant Economic Opportunity Commission of Nassau County, Inc. (hereinafter the EOC) is a charitable organization which provides various services to needy citizens in Nassau County. Among those services is the Martin Luther King Scholarship Fund, a privately-funded endeavor which provides educational aid for qualified area students. In 1986 the EOC conducted a charitable raffle to raise money for this scholarship fund.

The plaintiff Ray Harris, vice president of the appellant corporation B.W. Harris, Inc., operated a pharmacy in West Hempstead. In May 1986 a man whom Mr. Harris recognized as a customer entered the pharmacy to sell raffle tickets on behalf of the EOC to raise money for the Martin Luther King Scholarship Fund. Mr. Harris, recognizing an opportunity to enhance the good will of his business, purchased five raffle tickets at a cost of $2 each. Rather than write out his name and address on each of the tickets, Mr. Harris used a rubber stamp identifying the corporation as the purchaser of the tickets. The seller of the tickets left the store, thanking Mr. Harris for his "contribution". The prize being raffled was a 1986 Chevrolet Camaro.

At the very time Mr. Harris purchased the raffle tickets, he was negotiating the sale of the corporation's pharmacy. After concluding those negotiations, he began a vacation. During his absence, on June 7, 1986, the EOC held its drawing. One of the tickets purchased by Mr. Harris on behalf of the corporation was selected as the winner of the automobile.

The one area in which the factual allegations of the parties were in significant dispute concerned the time frame in which Mr. Harris allegedly claimed his prize. It is conceded by all that the drawing on the raffle occurred on June 7, 1986. Mr. Harris testified that he was on vacation at that time, but he returned during the second week of June and was informed by the pharmacist who had purchased the business that EOC representatives had visited the pharmacy to inform him of his good fortune. Mr. Harris claimed that he called the EOC on June 8 or 9, 1986, to claim his prize. He claimed he was given a "run-around" until he finally spoke with the Chief Executive Officer of the EOC John Kearse, who asked him to come to the EOC offices for a meeting the following Saturday. At that meeting, which Mr. Harris estimated occurred on June 11, 1986, Mr. Kearse reportedly told him that the EOC had attempted to award his prize, but, because of his absence following the drawing, the prize had been withdrawn. In lieu thereof, Mr. Kearse reportedly offered a letter to Mr. Harris which would entitle him to a tax deduction for the value of the car. Mr. Harris rejected this offer.

In stark contrast, John Kearse testified that following the raffle drawing on June 7, he and another EOC representative visited the pharmacy on June 10, 1986, to award the car. On that date they met Craig Niederberger, the pharmacist who had purchased the business, and Mr. Niederberger informed them that Mr. Harris was unavailable and that his whereabouts were unknown. Mr. Kearse left his business card with Mr. Niederberger and the latter agreed to convey the good news to Mr. Harris. Mr. Kearse further testified that he did not hear from Mr. Harris until some time in early August 1986. By that time, however, to take advantage of a limited refund offer, the EOC had returned the car to the dealer from which it was purchased. The refund that was obtained was added to the scholarship fund.

The only documentary evidence concerning the actual sequence of events was a letter from Mr. Kearse dated June 17, 1986, memorializing his June 10, 1986, visit to the pharmacy. Mr. Kearse testified that at the time he sent this letter, the car was still available for delivery. Mr. Harris, however, insinuated that the letter was written after the return of the car in June 1986 in anticipation of litigation. Curiously, no documentation was presented as to when the car was returned to the dealer, information presumably available to the defendant.

In any event, this action was commenced on or about August 26, 1986, and was tried in the District Court of Nassau County, First District. Rejecting the defendant's argument that the raffle of the car was an illegal lottery, the court submitted the case to the jury, which returned a verdict in the plaintiffs' favor in the amount of $15,000. On appeal to the Appellate Term, however, the award to Ray Harris was stricken, and the award to the appellant was reduced to $20 representing twice the cost of the wager, on the ground that the raffle was illegal and hence void

\* \* \*

As a logical starting point for our discussion, N.Y. Constitution, article I, §9 provides in pertinent part:

> no lottery or the sale of lottery tickets, pool-selling, bookmaking, or any other kind of gambling [except as otherwise provided herein] shall hereafter be authorized or allowed within this state; and the legislature shall pass appropriate laws to prevent offenses against any of the provisions of this section.

The exceptions to the foregoing authorize State-operated lotteries, pari-mutuel wagering on horse races, and certain specified games of chance, which, inter alia, under the auspices of local governments, are run by charitable organizations and which, unless otherwise provided by law, offer individual prizes which do not exceed $250 and aggregate prizes which do not exceed $1,000 (N.Y. Const. art. I, §9(2)). It is uncontroverted that the raffle of a new automobile in the case at bar does not fall within the above constitutional exceptions to the prohibitions against illegal gambling.

Among the "appropriate laws" enacted by the Legislature in furtherance of the constitutional prohibition against gambling is Penal Law article 225, which supplies the definitions of proscribed gambling activities. Penal Law §225.00(2) provides:

> [a] person engages in gambling when he stakes or risks something of value upon the outcome of a contest of chance or a future contingent event not under his control or influence, upon an agreement or understanding that he will receive something of value in the event of a certain outcome.

It has been held that three elements cause an event to constitute an unlawful game of chance, or lottery, to wit, consideration, chance, and a prize. [Citations omitted.] Furthermore, Penal Law §225.00(10) defines a lottery as:

> an unlawful gambling scheme in which (a) the players pay or agree to pay something of value for chances, represented and differentiated by numbers or by combinations of numbers or by some other media, one or more of which chances are to be designated the winning ones; and (b) the winning chances are to be determined by a drawing or by some other method based upon the element of chance; and (c) the holders of the winning chances are to receive something of value.

"Unlawful" means anything "not specifically authorized by law" (Penal Law §225.00(12)). Clearly, the instant raffle in which a "contribution" of $10 purchased five chances to win an automobile constitutes a lottery proscribed by the Penal Law.

Throughout the course of this action, the appellant has taken the position that Mr. Harris did not wager $10 on five chances to win a car, but rather that he made a donation or charitable contribution in this amount to the EOC in return for which he was permitted to enter a raffle, run by a benevolent organization, seeking to raise funds for a worthy cause. Characterization of the EOC's motivations aside, the appellant asserts that a mere "donation" having been made, the entry in the raffle was incidental thereto and no illegal wager was made for consideration. The appellant thus seeks to bring this case within what it claims is the rule of *Johnson v. New York Daily News*, 97 A.D.2d 458, 467 N.Y.S.2d 665, aff'd. 61 N.Y.2d 839, 473 N.Y.S.2d 975, 462 N.E.2d 152, which, it asserts, stands for the proposition that a contest winner may sue to recover the value of the winning prize. The appellant's reliance thereon, however, is misplaced, as the facts of that case have no application to the matter presently before us.

The issue before the court in the Johnson case was not whether the contest was illegal. In *Johnson*, the issue to be decided was whether or not the plaintiff, who had entered a newspaper promotional contest by submitting the name of her 14-year-old grandson, had violated contest rules which, inter alia, provided that the contest was open to persons 18 years of age and older. The court held that the contest rule had been violated, and that the Daily News was not obligated to award the prize to the plaintiff. The issue of the legality or illegality of the contest was not raised before the court in that case and thus the opinion therein provides no authority for the plaintiffs' present argument, as "'opinions must be read in the setting of the particular cases and as the product of preoccupation with their special facts.'" [Citations omitted.]

Moreover, as Appellate Term correctly noted, *Johnson* is factually distinguishable, as the rules governing the contest in that case expressly provided that no purchase was necessary to enter and that manually reproduced game cards could be submitted to the Daily News in lieu of official game cards available in copies of the newspaper. Indeed, copies of the newspaper were available at libraries and no rule prohibited contestants from entering the contest by utilizing the game form in a borrowed or discarded copy of the newspaper. Thus, there is plainly no merit to the appellant's unsubstantiated allegation that consideration in the form of a purchase of the newspaper was necessary to enter that contest. More significantly, the record before us is devoid of any evidence to suggest that the EOC would have permitted entrants to join its fundraising raffle without paying for their tickets. Thus, there being no consideration necessary to enter the Daily News contest, the game therein was not an illegal lottery and the rule of that case has no application to this case. In juxtaposition, the facts of this case lead to the inescapable conclusion that the appellant purchased chances, for valuable consideration, to participate in a contest which, pursuant to Penal Law §225.00(10), constituted an illegal lottery.

Having determined that the raffle in this case constitutes an unlawful gambling scheme, we note that General Obligations Law §5-417 provides:

> All contracts, agreements and securities given, made or executed, for or
> on account of any raffle, or distribution of money, goods or things in

action, for the payment of any money, or other valuable thing, in consideration of a chance in such raffle or distribution, or for the delivery of any money, goods or things in action, so raffled for, or agreed to be distributed as aforesaid, shall be utterly void.

It is clear, pursuant to the plain meaning of this statute, that the parties agreed to participate in an unlawful raffle and that that agreement is void and unenforceable. "All contracts and dealings in respect to lotteries, and tickets in lotteries, being illegal, no right of action can accrue to a party, by reason of such contracts and dealings" (citing cases). AFFIRMED.

## NOTES

1. Is *caveat emptor* an appropriate legal standard for protecting the innocent citizen from the dangers of illegal gambling? Is there an alternative that might be more effective?
2. Taken together, could *Harris* and perhaps especially *Williams* be interpreted to protect fraud performed for charitable purposes? Can the law reach this behavior?
3. It is difficult to find reported decisions by bettors against, for example, unregulated bookies for the enforcement of illegal sports bets. Can you guess why this might be so?

## WEBB v. FULCHIRE

**Supreme Court of North Carolina**
**25 N.C. (3 Ired.) 485 (1843)**

RUFFIN, C. J.

It is not denied that the law gives no action to a party to an illegal contract, either to enforce it directly, or to recover back money paid on it after its execution. Nor is it doubted, that money, fairly lost at play at a forbidden game and paid, cannot be recovered back in an action for money had and received. But it is perfectly certain, that money, won by cheating at any kind of game, whether allowed or forbidden, and paid by the loser without a knowledge of the fraud, may be recovered. A wager won by such undue means is not won in the view of the law, and, therefore, the money is paid without consideration and by mistake, and may be recovered back. That, we think, was plainly this case.

The bet was, that the plaintiff could not tell, which of the three cups covered the ball. Well, the case states that the defendant put the ball under a particular one of the cups, and, then, that the plaintiff selected that cup, as the one under which the ball was. Thus we must understand the case, because it states as a fact, that the defendant "placed the ball under one of the cups," and that the plaintiff "pointed to the cup," that is, the one under which he had seen the ball put, as being that which still covered it.

We are not told how this matter was managed, nor do we pretend to know the secret. But it is indubitable, that the ball was, by deceit, not put under the cup, as the defendant had made the plaintiff believe, and under which belief he had drawn him into the wager; or that, after it was so placed, it was privily and artfully removed either before or at the time the cup was raised. If the former be the truth of the case, there was a false practice and gross deception upon the very point, that induced the laying of the wager, namely, that the ball was actually put under the cup. For, clearly, the words and acts of the defendant amount to a representation, that such was the fact; and indeed the case states it as the fact. Hence, and because we cannot suppose the vision of the plaintiff to have been so alluded, we rather presume the truth to be, that the ball was actually placed where the defendant pretended to place it, that is to say, under the particular cup which the plaintiff designated as covering it. Then the case states that the defendant raised that cup, and the ball was not there: a physical impossibility, unless it had been removed by some contrivance and slight of hand by the defendant. Unquestionably it was affected by some such means; for presently we find the defendant in possession of the ball, ready for a repetition of the bet and the same artifice.

Such a transaction cannot for a moment be regarded as a wager, depending on a future and uncertain event; but it was only a pretended wager, to be determined by a contingency in shew only, but in fact by a trick in jugglery by one of the parties, practiced upon the unknowing and unsuspecting simplicity and credulity of the other. Surely, the art-less fool, who seems to have been alike bereft of his senses and his money, is not to be deemed a partaker in the same crime, *in pari delicto*, with the juggling knave, who gulled and fleeced him. The whole was a downright and undeniable cheat; and the plaintiff parted with his money under the mistaken belief, that it had been fairly won from him, and, therefore, may recover it back. The judgment of nonsuit is reversed, and judgment for the plaintiff according to the verdict.

*NOTES*

1.  Is the general rule in *Webb* different than the rule in *Harris*?
2.  How would this court characterize the social ills related to gambling?

3. How does *Webb* evade the principle that "the law gives no action to a party to an illegal gambling contract"? In finding that the patron, or perhaps the "mark," or "artless fool" in the terms of the court, was not *in pari dilecto* with the operator of the shell game, *Webb* opens the courts to the cheated gambler, but only to recover restitution. Jurisdictions vary widely on this point. In jurisdictions that decline to enforce gambling contracts, should courts nevertheless be available to the gambling loser to seek restitution for amounts paid under the illegal gambling contract? Or, on the other hand, does the most rigid application of *caveat emptor* provide the more effective policy approach?

## 3. Statutes of Queen Anne and Legalized Gambling

The policies embodied in the statute of Queen Anne seem largely prohibitory in effect. They discourage gambling by insuring that a winner cannot enforce the contract and is entirely subject to the good will of the person on the losing side of the transaction. Should a law with such prohibitive intentions have any role in the context of gambling in a jurisdiction that has legalized gambling?

### CORBIN v. O'KEEFE
#### 484 P.2d 565 (Nev. 1971)

Kenneth W. Corbin seeks to recover $20,000 on a winning bet of $100 at 200-to-1 odds that the Boston Red Sox would win the American Baseball League pennant in 1967. Corbin placed the bet at the Jockey Turf Club in March 1967. When he attempted to collect on the bet in the fall of 1967 the club's proprietors rebuffed his attempts on the basis that the bet had been taken by an employee who failed to record it and who kept the money, so the club never received the bet.

Corbin and his attorneys subsequently sought aid of the Nevada Gaming Control Board but were denied relief. Thereafter, Corbin commenced this civil action seeking to enforce the bet in the Second Judicial District Court. The court granted the respondents' motion to dismiss on the basis that gambling debts are not collectible through the courts.

It is clear from the complaint and record in this case that what is presented is a court action for recovery of a gambling debt. Corbin makes recurring references to the asserted arbitrariness of the Gaming Control Board in denying his claim, but he is not seeking review of the administrative procedures followed. Therefore, we need not address such questions as the asserted arbitrariness, exhaustion of administrative remedies and, indeed, the very reviewability of administrative procedures in this area.

[The court then cited *Weisbrod v. Fremont Hotel. Inc.*, 326 P.2d 1104 (Nev. 1958), in which Weisbrod contended that the Queen Anne provision should be held to apply only against the proprietors of gambling establishments and should not be held to apply against the patrons of such establishments since the rule exists for the protection of the patrons. The court held "so long as such practices remain lawful, however, the rule must be held to apply equally to all lawful gambling transactions. It must, then, cut both ways. If money won at gambling is not recoverable through resort to the courts it is not because of who has won it but because of the nature of the transaction itself. This is not to say that the state provides no adequate protection to the gambling patron. It must be recognized that the state has an interest in seeing that its licensees honestly and honorably respect their gambling obligations. Repudiation of such obligations would most certainly be regarded as reflecting upon the suitability of one to hold a state license. . . . No licensee is likely to place his license in jeopardy through refusal to pay a gambling debt found to be properly due."]

This court has refused to aid in the collection of gambling debts for nearly a century and we will not depart from those cases. AFFIRMED.

*NOTES*

1.  What is the purpose of the Statute of Queen Anne in Nevada? Is Nevada's use of the statute in *Corbin* in accord with the statute in other states?
2.  *Corbin*, and the *Weisbrod* case cited therein, foreshadows the central role of gaming regulators, such as Nevada's Gaming Control Board and Gaming Commission, in legalized gambling jurisdictions. Are administrative remedies as useful as judicial remedies?
3.  The principle in *Corbin* has been legislatively overruled in Nevada:

> Nevada legalized gambling in 1931, but it did not legalize the enforcement of gambling debts until 1983. . . . Today, Nevada enforces gambling debts when credit instruments, such as markers or checks, are cashed at a casino. The Nevada legislature made this change for two reasons. First, the gaming collection rate, generally about ninety-five percent, had "dipped below 90% for the first time in history." Second, Nevada lost a major case regarding taxation of gaming debts "removing [the] benefit of having gaming debts remain unenforceable." The Ninth Circuit ruled that unpaid

casino receivables should be treated and taxed as income, even though the debts were legally unenforceable. Under recent laws, a casino may enforce gambling debts by immediately filing suit on any enforceable credit instrument and the underlying debt. While regulations for the issuing of credit to a patron are stringent, failure to follow the regulations does not invalidate the credit instrument. Rather, such violations result in disciplinary action by the Gaming Control Board. An example of a credit instrument is a marker signed by the patron, which may be undated and issued to a non-affiliated company "so that the patron does not have to expose his gaming to his banker or spouse." The casinos have an additional weapon to use against patrons who refuse to pay their debts: the unpaid markers may be handed over to the district attorney for possible criminal prosecution. One Illinois debtor, who owed fifty thousand dollars in markers, pled guilty after being extradited to Nevada and "agreed to make restitution." Another gambler from Texas escaped prosecution only by filing bankruptcy.

Joseph Kelly, *Caught in the Intersection Between Public Policy and Practicality: A Survey of the Legal Treatment of Gambling-Related Obligations in the United States*, 5 CHAP. L. REV. 87 (2002).

## WISCONSIN v. GONNELLY
### 496 N.W.2d 671 (Wisc. App. 1992)

SNYDER, J.

[The State charged Gonnelly with three counts of uttering a worthless check.] Between November 9 and 21, 1990, Gonnelly cashed three checks at Geneva Lakes Kennel Club (GLKC) worth a total of $ 23,700. The checks were returned for nonsufficient funds (NSF). Gonnelly moved to dismiss the complaint on the grounds that the checks were gaming contracts void under [Wisconsin's Statute of Anne law]. For purposes of the motion, the parties stipulated that Gonnelly cashed the checks to obtain money to bet on the dog races at GLKC and, in fact, bet the money he received on the dog races. They also stipulated that GLKC cashed Gonnelly's checks to provide him with money to bet on the dog races at GLKC and knew that Gonnelly was going to bet the money on the dog races at GLKC. The trial court granted the motion, concluding that the checks were void under §895.055. The state appeals.

We begin with the gaming contract statute. Section 895.055 provides:

Gaming contracts void. *All promises*, agreements, notes, bills, bonds, or other contracts, mortgages, conveyances or other securities, *where the whole or any part of the consideration of such promise*, agreement, note, bill, bond, mortgage, conveyance or other security *shall be for money* or other valuable thing whatsoever won or lost, laid or staked, or *betted at* or upon any game of any kind or under any name whatsoever, or by any means, *or upon any race,* fight, sport or pastime, or any wager, or for the repayment of money or other thing of value, lent or advanced at the time and for the purpose, of any game, play, bet or wager, or of being laid, staked, betted or wagered thereon *shall be absolutely void;* provided, however, that contracts of insurance made in good faith for the security or indemnity of the party insured shall be lawful and valid. [Emphasis added.]

The state asserts that the checks are not gaming contracts, and that a gaming contract arose only later when Gonnelly actually placed a bet. It contends that although both parties may have contemplated that Gonnelly would use the proceeds for gambling purposes, that was simply their understanding, not a requirement. Nothing written on the checks indicates that they were cashed only upon the condition that the money received in exchange would be used to place bets.

The state also points out that the checks necessarily could not have contained any other promise or obligation such as one to use the proceeds to gamble at the track. In support, it looks to ch. 403, Stats., which provides that a check is a negotiable instrument and a negotiable instrument must contain an unconditional promise or order to pay a sum certain in money and no other promise or obligation.

These arguments fail. Taking the state's Chapter 403 argument first, we reject it because it presumes that the check is not void in the first instance. As will be explained later in the opinion, there is a difference between "worthless" and "void" checks. Chapter 403 may apply to "worthless" checks but it does not apply to "void" ones.

We also reject the state's argument that the checks had to contain, as consideration, some condition that the money be used to gamble. Section 895.055 requires no such written condition. Rather, it requires only that "the whole or any part of the consideration" be for "money . . . won or lost, laid or staked, or betted at or upon . . . any race . . . for the repayment of money," such as the races at GLKC. *Id.* The parties established this by stipulation.

Finally, we reject the state's argument that the checks are not themselves gaming contracts. The Minnesota Court of Appeals recently had occasion to address a similar question to that posed here. *State v. Stevens,* 459 N.W.2d 513 (Minn. Ct. App. 1990). Like Wisconsin, Minnesota endorses certain forms of gambling yet also has a statute voiding gaming contracts. *See* Minn. Stat. sec. 541.21 (Supp. 1989). In *Stevens,* the defendant wrote checks to purchase $465 worth of legal "pull-tabs." When the checks were returned NSF, the state charged him with theft by check. The trial court granted the defendant's motion to dismiss. The court of appeals affirmed, concluding that the gaming contract statute applied to Stevens's checks. The state's attempt to distinguish *Stevens* from the case here is to no avail. It notes that in *Stevens* the checks were exchanged directly for the pull-tabs; here, Gonnelly exchanged the checks for cash and then placed wagers. The state argues that if instead of gambling with the cash received from the checks Gonnelly had taken it and spent it elsewhere, GLKC would have had no recourse against him.

The trial court found *Stevens* persuasive and so do we. We agree with Gonnelly that the distinction the state draws is insignificant. Permitting the placing of wagers by check would be inefficient and time-consuming. On-track betting is not conducive to such a set-up. By contrast, purchasing pull-tabs by check does not pose such time and administrative obstacles. Moreover, the parties' stipulation satisfies us that both GLKC and Gonnelly contemplated that the money would be used for gambling and that, in fact, it was.

Undaunted, the state argues that by legalizing various gambling activities, Wisconsin has impliedly repealed its long-held legislative ban on the collection of certain gambling debts such as those incurred in parimutuel wagering. The state concedes that the implied repeal of statutes is disfavored. *Pattermann v. City of Whitewater*, 145 N.W.2d 705, 708 (Wisc. 1966). Indeed, a strong public policy exists which favors the continuing validity of a statute except where the legislature has acted explicitly to repeal it. *State v. Christensen*, 110 Wis. 2d 538, 546, 329 N.W.2d 382, 385-86 (1983). The rule against implied repeal especially applies where the earlier statute is of long standing and has been stringently followed, unless it is so manifestly inconsistent and repugnant to the later statute that the two cannot reasonably stand together. The earlier statute also may be set aside where the legislative intent to repeal by implication clearly appears.

The statute's history reveals that the legislature considered addressing this problem and rejected that avenue. A proposed amendment to sec. 895.055, Stats., would have added this sentence: "This section does not apply to wagers permitted under ch. 562." Chapter 562 permits, among other things, pari-mutuel wagering at dog tracks. The proposed amendment did not pass. That it was considered and rejected deflates the state's argument of implied repeal. It is not for this court to do what the legislature has chosen not to do.

It is the conclusion of this court that the legalization of gambling in a limited and regulated manner, while constituting a change to some degree in this state's ancient and deep-rooted public policy prohibiting gambling, has had no effect on the long-established policy of this state condemning gambling on credit and prohibiting the enforcement of any claimed obligation relating thereto.

Finally, the state argues that not to hold Gonnelly responsible will result in his unjust enrichment. . . . We make no comment as to whether the result dictated here is a desirable one. Our task is simply to ascertain the legislative intent of the statutes. If another result is deemed wiser, it is for the people—through the legislature—and not for this court to fashion one. Order affirmed.

## NOTES

1. At the end of the opinion, the court refuses to comment on whether the outcome of the case is a desirable one. Do you think that the judge has an opinion? Is this court motivated solely by the principle of judicial restraint, or is it something else?
2. *Is* this outcome desirable? Is it sensible to legalize gambling and then hold that a gambling debt is uncollectible as an illegal debt? Is there a way to read all the relevant statutes in harmony? Or does the law require the court to reach this result?

## NGUYEN v. NEVADA
### 14 P.3d 515 (Nev. 2000)

MAUPIN, J.

Tuan Ngoc Nguyen is a resident of the state of Texas. In December of 1995, he secured gambling credit through the issuance of markers from several licensed Las Vegas gaming establishments. Each followed standard industry procedures with respect to the extension of credit to Nguyen. These procedures are described immediately below.

In general, patrons apply for casino credit by completing a standard form setting forth the name of the applicant, his or her address, the name of the applicant's bank, and the bank account number. Casino personnel approve the applications pending verification of the basic bank information, including the average balance of the applicant's account.

An applicant may receive all or a portion of the credited amount at a gaming table in the form of a "marker." The marker is an instrument, usually dated, bearing the following information: the name of the player; the name, location, and account number of the player's bank; and the instruction "Pay to the Order of" the casino for a specific value in United States dollars. The marker also contains a stipulation whereby the payor represents that the amount drawn by the marker is on deposit in the referenced financial institution, and that he guarantees payment. The player and a casino representative sign the marker. The player then exchanges the marker for gaming tokens or "chips," which may be exchanged for currency with the casino cashier.

When a patron has concluded play, he either pays the full amount of the marker he has obtained or leaves the casino with the marker outstanding. If the marker remains outstanding, casino personnel attempt to notify the patron and, after a specified period of time, submit the marker to the patron's bank for collection.[1] Should the bank account contain insufficient funds, the casino will again attempt contact with the patron. If payment is not forthcoming, the gaming establishment has the option to refer the customer for possible criminal prosecution.

On December 9, 1995, Harrah's Las Vegas issued a marker to Nguyen in the amount of $5,000. On December 10, 1995, he obtained markers for $5,000 from the Luxor Hotel and Casino and $2,500 from the Excalibur Hotel Casino. Nguyen signed each marker and departed the state without paying the debt incurred.

Each establishment sent notice to Nguyen that his obligation remained outstanding. Later, each establishment sent its marker to Nguyen's bank, the Texas First National Bank, for payment. The bank returned all of the markers with the notation, "Account Closed." Casino representatives unsuccessfully sought to personally contact Nguyen. Thereafter, these matters were referred for prosecution and

---

1. A representative of Harrah's described the casino's practice of deferring deposit of the marker:

Q: What is the date on that check?
A: On the marker? 12/9 of '95.
Q: And on the back, does it indicate when that check was deposited to Harrah's account?
A: January 11th of '96.
Q: That is more than 30 days?
A: Yes it is.
Q: [The cashiers] don't deposit [the markers] when they get them?
A: Everybody has a different disposition date, 30 days, 90 days.
Q: What is the disposition date [for Harrah's]?
A: Thirty days.
Q: What does it mean?
A: If a customer has a 30-day disposition date, they have 30 days from the time they sign the marker to send us a check, and after those 30 days, we usually allow seven days for them to put a check in the mail.

    The practice of allowing a customer to pay gaming debts with a second check is a matter of courtesy and convenience to the customer.

the Clark County District Attorney charged Nguyen in three criminal complaints with violations of NRS 205.130.

Nguyen entered into a plea agreement with the State, pursuant to which he pleaded guilty in connection with the Harrah's Las Vegas marker to one count of drawing and passing a check without sufficient funds in the drawee bank and with intent to defraud. The plea agreement included a provision reserving Nguyen's right to appeal two issues: (1) whether NRS 205.130(1) applies to casino markers and (2) whether he was selectively prosecuted in violation of his right to equal protection under the Federal Constitution. The district court accepted the guilty plea and entered a judgment of conviction accordingly.

The primary question before us is whether the term "check or draft," as used in NRS 205.130(1), the Nevada criminal statute prohibiting the drawing or passage of "bad" checks, applies to gaming credit instruments commonly known as "markers."

The Nevada bad check statute prohibits a person from drawing or passing "a check or draft" to obtain "credit extended by any licensed gaming establishment," drawn on a bank "when the person has insufficient money, property or credit with the drawee of the instrument to pay it in full upon its presentation." Although the statute does not explicitly define the term "check or draft," we construe this undefined term in accordance with its ordinary and plain meaning.

A "draft" is "[a] written order by the first party, called the drawer, instructing a second party, called the drawee (such as a bank), to pay money to a third party, called the payee." Black's Law Dictionary 493 (6th ed. 1990). The Uniform Commercial Code [which has been adopted in Nevada] defines "draft" as an "order," a "written instruction to pay money signed by the person giving the instruction." U.C.C. §3-103(a)(6); U.C.C. §3-104(e). A "check" is an instrument drawn upon a bank and payable on demand, signed by the drawer, containing an instruction to pay a certain amount to another party.

We believe the language of this statute is abundantly clear and unmistakable. By its terms, NRS 205.130 applies to instruments that are drawn upon a bank, payable on demand, signed by the payor, and which instruct the bank to pay a certain amount to the payee.

Given the foregoing analysis, we conclude that the markers at issue in the instant case fall within the purview of the bad check statute. The markers provided a mechanism for payment of a specific sum of money from the Texas National Bank to the order of these gaming establishments. Nguyen signed the instruments, which stated no time or date of payment—they were payable on demand, thus "subjecting

the [drawer] payor to a repayment obligation at the will of the payee."
[Citation omitted.] We therefore hold that these markers were
"checks" within the meaning of NRS 205.130(1).

Nguyen contends that the markers are better characterized as credit
instruments outside the scope of NRS 205.130. According to Nguyen,
the practice of delaying payment of a marker renders the instrument a
loan document, whereby the signer agrees to pay the debt before an
agreed-upon but unwritten disposition date. We disagree. Whether an
obligee chooses to cash a check immediately or at a later date does not
alter the character of the instrument. Further, there is no evidence that
Nguyen and the casinos understood the marker to effect a contract for
a loan.

We turn now to Nguyen's contention that his conduct did not
evidence sufficient criminal intent. The statute provides that, in
order to be convicted for passing bad checks, a person must act "with
an intent to defraud." NRS 205.130(1). Also, in a criminal action for
issuing a check or draft against insufficient or no funds with intent to
defraud, that intent and the knowledge that the drawer has insufficient money, property or credit with the drawee [bank] is presumed to
exist if . . . payment of the instrument is refused by the drawee when it
is presented in the usual course of business, unless within [five] days
after receiving notice of this fact from the drawee or the holder, the
drawer pays the holder of the instrument the full amount due plus any
handling charges. NRS 205.132.

We conclude that Nguyen's intent to defraud was circumstantially
demonstrated by his failure to pay the full amount due within the
statutory period, and by the return of the instruments from his
bank with the notation "Account Closed." Thus, evidence such as that
present in this case is sufficient to raise a jury question on the issue of
guilt or innocence under NRS 205.130. Accordingly, we hold that
Nguyen was properly convicted under NRS 205.130(1).

## NOTES

1.  As *Nguyen* reflects, the extension of credit in gambling establish-
    ments is an integral, though still controversial, fact of life in some
    gambling jurisdictions. Does credit in this context pose different
    problems than credit generally poses?
2.  The court swiftly and surely resolves the question of whether
    a marker is more like a check or a loan. Is its conclusion com-
    pelling? What are the ramifications of treating markers like
    checks?

## IN RE BAUM

### U.S. Bankruptcy Court—Northern District of Ohio
### 386 B. R. 649 (2008)

KENDIG, Bankruptcy Judge.

This matter is before the Court on the Motion to Dismiss Case for Abuse filed by the U.S. Trustee ("UST") on September 10, 2007. . . .

Debtor began to gamble online in June or July of 2006, at first for personal entertainment (i.e., with no money involved), then for increasing monetary stakes, financing the transactions with payments from credit cards, which the online gambling sites accepted. The spiral continued for three or four months, during which online gambling began to consume Debtor's life: she would visit gambling sites in the morning before going to work, at lunch (coming home from work), and at home in the evenings. Although all of the gambling was online, it came to a point at which Debtor realized it was materially affecting her life, financially and non-financially.

In November of 2006, Debtor ceased gambling and began seeing a counselor. At some point during treatment, she canceled her home internet service and now checks her e-mails only at work. However, by the time she began seeing her counselor, she had already amassed substantial balances on the credit cards she had dedicated to gambling. . . . Debtor stated on the record that her gambling losses during this comparably short period of time totaled approximately $40,000.00. At this time, she also began speaking with a family friend who was also an attorney—albeit not a bankruptcy attorney—about the bills she had accumulated. For some months thereafter, until approximately January 2007, she investigated approximately five debt consolidation services, but found that even the consolidated loan payments that would have been offered would have been approximately $500 a month, beyond her means, so she never signed up for any such service. . . . In February of 2007, she contacted her current counsel and shortly thereafter filed her Chapter 7 petition.

On September 10, 2007, the UST filed a motion to dismiss the case for abuse of Chapter 7. [T]he UST argued that Debtor's attempt to discharge her obligations to her creditors via Chapter 7 amounted to either bad faith or a dishonest relationship with her creditors, either of which would warrant dismissal for abuse under 11 U.S.C. §707(b). UST cites as evidence the fact that this case was not filed as the result of sudden illness, calamity, disability, or unemployment. Debtor's gambling debts were the decisive factor that pushed her to seek bankruptcy protection. UST argues that Debtor incurred debts knowing they were beyond her ability to repay, intent on keeping the winnings if she won while foisting the losses off on her creditors if she lost. Debtor argues that she did in fact intend to pay back her creditors at the time she incurred her debts, and even attempted to do so when the bills arrived and were much steeper than anticipated; her efforts simply failed. Therefore, she argues, her filing was not in bad faith and her relationship with her creditors was not dishonest.

The Code provides that the court may dismiss an individual's case under Chapter 7 if the debtor's debts are primarily consumer debts and the court finds that the granting of relief would be an abuse of the provisions of Chapter 7. 11 U.S.C. §707(b)(1). [O]ne factor that the Code explicitly directs a bankruptcy court to consider in determining if relief would nonetheless be an abuse of Chapter 7 is whether the debtor filed her petition in bad faith. 11 U.S.C. §707(b)(3)(A). [In the case of *In re Zick*, 931 F.2d 1124, 1128 (6th Cir. 1991), the Sixth Circuit offered the following factors to identify bad faith:

(a)   frivolous purpose, absent any economic reality;
(b)   lack of an honest and genuine desire to use the statutory process to effect a plan of reorganization;
(c)   use of a bankruptcy as a device to further some sinister or unworthy purpose;
(d)   abuse of the judicial process to delay creditors or escape the day of reckoning in another court;
(e)   lack of real debt, creditors, assets in an ongoing business;
(f)   lack of reasonable probability of successful reorganization.]

... *Zick* makes clear ... that while bankruptcy courts may face few constraints regarding what factors they may consider as evidence of bad faith, they should nevertheless be cautious in concluding that it is in fact present, and that dismissal is therefore warranted. ... The standard is thus a flexible one, but a high one.

UST argues in its brief that this case was filed in bad faith because this case was not prompted by "sudden illness, calamity, disability, or unemployment." In addition, UST argues, Debtor recklessly gambled with other people's money, taking the risk that she would lose, and would therefore have to pay back the debts so incurred. UST argues that "[Debtor] now indicates that her creditors should bare [sic] the brunt of her bad choices, while she enjoys the benefits of a 'fresh start' reserved for honest but unfortunate debtors."

However, the facts as presented at trial do not support a finding of bad faith. Indeed, most of the facts that UST alleges in its brief would not be sufficient to support such a finding even were all proven true. Debtor conceded at trial that her case was not a result of sudden illness, calamity, disability, or unemployment. She did incur gambling debts which she could not reasonably afford to repay. She is now trying to obtain shelter from those creditors via a Chapter 7 discharge. Even given these facts, however, there is still insufficient evidence to support a finding of bad faith on Debtor's part. As such, Debtor's ability to repay her debts is only relevant insofar as it bears indirectly on the actual material fact in issue: whether Debtor intended to repay her debts. The Sixth Circuit has held that "the representation made by the cardholder in a credit card transaction is not that he has an ability to repay the debt; it is that he has an intention to repay." *Rembert v. AT & T Universal Card Svcs., Inc. (In re Rembert)*, 141 F.3d 277 (6th Cir. 1998) (internal citation omitted). . . . [T]he Sixth Circuit elaborated thus:

> the focus should not be on whether the debtor was hopelessly insolvent at the time he made the credit card charges. A person on the verge of bankruptcy may have been brought to that point by a series of unwise financial choices, such as spending beyond his means, and if ability to repay were the focus of the fraud inquiry, too often would there be an unfounded judgment of non-dischargeability of credit card debt. Rather, the express focus must be solely on whether the debtor maliciously and in bad faith incurred credit card debt with the intention of petitioning for bankruptcy and avoiding the debt. Rembert at 281 (citation omitted).

[Here,] Debtor intended to pay the credit card debts she was accruing. She was extraordinarily careless in allowing them to accumulate to such sums in such a short period of time, but nothing presented in the parties' briefs or at the hearing suggests that she was deliberately incurring debts with the intention of using Chapter 7 to escape them. This point is undergirded by Debtor's testimony of an epiphany when she realized what she had done. The testimony was believable, but more importantly, the fact that Debtor's conduct immediately changed is profound evidence of Debtor's state of mind before and after this moment. The changed conduct undergirds the existence of an epiphany, leading one to an inescapable conclusion: the testimony is true. The Court can also discern no other facts on this record tending to suggest "concealed or misrepresented assets and/or sources of income, and excessive and continued expenditures, lavish lifestyle, and intention to avoid a large single debt based on conduct akin to fraud, misconduct, or gross negligence." See *Zick*, 931 F.2d at 1129.

A fool, but an honest fool, Debtor remains.[1]

---

1. See J.R.R. Tolkien, The Two Towers 579 (Houghton Mifflin 2003) (1954) ("A fool, but an honest fool, you remain, Peregrin Took.")

The Code also provides, separately, that a bankruptcy court may dismiss a Chapter 7 case if "the totality of the circumstances . . . of the debtor's financial situation demonstrates abuse." 11 U.S.C §707(b)(3)(B). . . . UST appropriately cites *In re Krohn*, 886 F.2d 123 (6th Cir. 1989), for the proposition that "[t]he goals of bankruptcy are to provide an honest debtor with a fresh start and to provide an equitable distribution to creditors." Id. at 127-28. UST also cites a contrast between this honest debtor and an archetypical dishonest debtor's case, a case in which "there is no evidence of an unforeseen calamity, be it economic and/or medical, whereby the debtor is involuntarily forced to seek chapter 7 relief. On the contrary, the evidence indicates that the debtor is merely using the chapter 7 provisions to gain relief from past excesses." *In re Krohn*, 78 B.R. 829, 833 (Bankr. N.D. Ohio 1987).

[Notwithstanding this factor, the] other factors listed in Krohn are in Debtor's favor here. She did not engage in profligate eve-of-bankruptcy purchases. She ceased gambling at some point in November of 2006 and did not file for bankruptcy until May 21, 2007. The other consumer debts listed on her schedules are unremarkable. Many of the largest sums appear to be the result of double counting both the claims of the credit card companies and the claims of collection agencies. (She does have one large student loan obligation, $44,752.83.) Likewise, there has been no evidence that she was less than candid in completing her schedules or any other component of her petition. . . . There are additional circumstances that speak to Debtor's honesty in this case: beginning in November of 2006, Debtor began seeing a counselor, began speaking with a non-bankruptcy attorney about her finances, and made good faith efforts at getting her debts under control via a consolidation plan. There is no evidence that, at the time she incurred the debts, she had no intention of repaying her creditors. In fact, there is every indication that she looked for ways to repay them for months after incurring them.

UST cites authority from bankruptcy courts in other circuits holding that gambling losses are to be viewed as "an excess similar to other excesses associated with living beyond one's means." *In re Vianese*, 192 B.R. 61, 71 (Bankr. N.D.N.Y. 1996). . . . However, if this alone were sufficient to indicate such dishonesty with one's creditors as to warrant a dismissal for abuse, a staggering number of Chapter 7 cases would have to be dismissed as abusive. Therefore, while Debtor's accrual of debt was excessive, and this factor therefore tends in UST's favor, it is simply outweighed by other factors showing that Debtor intended to repay her debt, took steps attempting to make that intention a reality, and only filed for bankruptcy as a last resort, after non-bankruptcy alternatives failed her.

[Are the gambling debts enforceable?] The Court raises this issue sua sponte; neither party briefed it and no factfinding on it was developed through discovery or trial. Nevertheless, the Court feels compelled to address the issue because it raises threshold questions. . . . The Court is not convinced that the gambling debts at issue in this case were valid in the first place. Void or unenforceable debts cannot legally form the basis of a motion to dismiss for abuse of Chapter 7.

Gambling debts have long been unenforceable under Ohio law and, since October 13, 2006, online credit card payments to persons engaged in the business of betting or wagering have been illegal under federal law. Contracts in support of gambling debts are void under Ohio Rev. Code §3763.01, which provides:

> All promises, agreements, notes, bills, bonds, or other contracts, mortgages, or other securities, when the whole or part of the consideration thereof is for money or other valuable thing won or lost, laid, staked, or betted at or upon a game of any kind, or upon a horse race or cockfights, sport or pastime, or on a wager, or for the repayment of money lent or advanced at the time of a game, play, or wager, for the purpose of being laid, betted, staked, or wagered, are void. Ohio Rev. Code §3763.01(A).

There is then an exception in Ohio Rev. Code §3763.01(B), which provides, inter alia, that the voiding provision shall not apply to games of chance not subject to criminal penalties under Ohio Rev. Code §2915.02.

[Ohio law provides] that no person shall "establish, promote, or operate or knowingly engage in conduct that facilitates any game of chance conducted for profit or any scheme of chance," Ohio Rev. Code §2915.02(A)(2). [It] classifies gambling as a first degree misdemeanor for a first offense and a fifth degree felony for subsequent offenses. Ohio Rev. Code §2915.02(F). The section does not prohibit gambling expressly permitted by law, Ohio Rev. Code §2915.02(C), and contains a broad exception for many forms of gambling for the benefit of charitable organizations. Ohio Rev. Code §2915.02(D). This latter exception is clearly inapplicable here; Ms. Baum was not gambling at charity functions. The Court cannot establish that any of the gambling sites at which Ms. Baum incurred the debts underlying the UST's motion to dismiss qualify as gambling "expressly permitted by law," and the Court has found nothing in Ohio statutes to indicate such express permission for any online gambling site. . . . [W]hile the state of the evidence on this point is considerably less than the Court might desire, based on the record as constructed, those debts in Debtor's petition flowing from gambling losses, particularly those incurred via electronic credit card payments after October 13, 2006, are unenforceable under Ohio (and, after October 13, 2006, federal) law.

### NOTES

What motivated the bankruptcy judge in *Baum* to rule in the debtor's favor? What would be the ramifications if other bankruptcy courts adopted similar approaches to the discharge of gambling debts and to their enforceability? Could such an approach help to alleviate the harmful effects of compulsive gambling? Or could it exacerbate them?

## B.   CONFLICTS OF LAW APPROACHES TO PROHIBITIONS ON ILLEGAL GAMBLING

In an era of expanding gambling, some of the most pressing problems stem from the fact that gambling remains controversial in many jurisdictions. Conflicts inevitably arise in a system that allows broad freedom to travel from a restrictive jurisdiction to a permissive jurisdiction. This section examines how courts have resolved the public policy conflicts that arise in such circumstances.

In choice of law cases involving contracts, the Restatement (Second) of Conflicts counsels that a court should apply the law of the state which "has the most significant relationship to the transaction and the parties" and that, in determining significance, the court should look to factors such as the place of contracting, the place of negotiation, the place of performance, the location of the subject matter, and the domicile, residence and nationality of the parties. Restatement (Second) of Conflicts, §188. The same treatise also counsels that a court should consider the relevant policies of the forum and other interested states, and the protection of justified expectations. Id. at §6.

### RAHMANI V. RESORTS INTERNATIONAL HOTEL, INC.

**U.S. District Court—Eastern District of Virginia**
**20 F. Supp. 2d 932 (1998)**

T. S. Ellis, III, Judge.

In this unusual diversity case, a Virginia plaintiff hopes to use her home state's laws against gambling to help her recover from New

Jersey casinos the large gambling losses she incurred there. Plaintiff Najia Rahmani alleges that defendants Boardwalk Regency Corporation ("Boardwalk") and Resorts International Hotel, Inc. ("Resorts") induced her to travel to New Jersey and squander her money in their casinos. She further alleges that her acceptance of such inducements created a contract between the parties, but that these contracts were void as a matter of Virginia law. She therefore seeks restitution of all monies she has lost gambling in defendants' New Jersey casinos over the past thirteen years. For the reasons that follow, plaintiff's effort fails; the law sensibly affords no remedy in these circumstances.

Rahmani is a Virginia citizen, while defendants Resorts and Boardwalk are New Jersey corporations that own and operate gambling casinos. Rahmani's first experience with casino gambling occurred in 1984 when she visited Resorts. During that visit, Resorts employees noticed that Rahmani lost a considerable sum of money, and that she appeared to be a wealthy woman. As a result of these observations, Resorts repeatedly contacted Rahmani in Virginia over the course of the next thirteen years and induced her to return to Atlantic City to gamble. Boardwalk became aware of Rahmani's gambling habits in 1990, and it, too, began to encourage her to visit Atlantic City. Specifically, Resorts and Boardwalk called Rahmani and sent her letters, promising that if she agreed to come to the casino to gamble, Resorts or Boardwalk would send limousines to transport her and her friends and family to New Jersey, where she would be provided free hotel accommodations, meals and entertainment. These solicitations, which continued through November 1997, largely succeeded, for according to Rahmani, soon after her introduction to casino gambling in 1984, she became addicted to the activity, i.e., she became a compulsive gambler. She claims that both Resorts and Boardwalk knew or should have known of her condition, but nonetheless continued to induce her to travel to Atlantic City to gamble. Over approximately a thirteen-year period, Rahmani claims to have lost over $3.8 million while gambling at Resorts and Caesars.

Rahmani filed suit on February 11, 1998, arguing that her agreements with Resorts and Boardwalk were void under Virginia law and seeking rescission of the contracts and restitution of the money she gambled and lost at the casinos over the thirteen-year period.

As this is a diversity case, Virginia's choice-of-law rules govern. In this regard, Virginia adheres to the traditional First Restatement rule for contracts cases, namely that the laws of the place of contracting govern the validity of a contract. Under the traditional First Restatement rule, the place of contracting is determined by the location of the last act necessary to complete the contract. The threshold inquiry, therefore, is where the last act necessary to complete the contracts occurred, and thus where the contracts between Rahmani and the defendants were formed.

To determine where the last act necessary to complete the contracts occurred, it is important to identify with some precision just what the contracts were. In this regard, Rahmani alleges that the contracts consisted of the defendants' promise of limousines and free accommodations (the offer) and her agreement to travel to Atlantic City to enjoy these amenities and gamble (the acceptance). Accordingly, under Rahmani's theory, the last act necessary to form the contracts, namely Rahmani's acceptance of the offers, occurred in Virginia. Thus, Rahmani argues, Virginia law should apply.

Boardwalk and Resorts counter by arguing that common sense suggests that the contracts were formed not in Virginia, but in New Jersey when Rahmani placed her bets at the casino gambling table. Resorts attacks Rahmani's characterization of the contracts on the ground that such contracts could not have been enforced under Virginia law for they would lack the mutuality required for formation of a valid contract in Virginia.[2] Thus, if after arriving in Atlantic City and enjoying Resorts' hospitality, Rahmani had decided not to gamble, Resorts would not have been able to enforce such a contract under Virginia law. Both defendants argue that the only contracts between the casinos and Rahmani arose when Rahmani placed her bets at the casino gambling tables in New Jersey, and thus New Jersey law governs.

Although not free from doubt, the argument for application of New Jersey law is more persuasive. No mutually enforceable obligations were created until Rahmani placed a bet at a New Jersey gambling table.

Given that New Jersey law governs, Rahmani's claims for rescission and restitution plainly fail. In New Jersey, "casino gambling has been legal . . . since 1977, and the casino industry is purely a creature of statute." *Hakimoglu v. Trump Taj Mahal Assoc.*, 876 F. Supp. 625, 633 (D.N.J. 1994), *aff'd* 70 F.3d 291 (3d Cir. 1995). New Jersey's casino industry is governed exclusively by New Jersey's Casino Control Act, N.J.S.A. §§5:12-1 to -210 (1997) ("CCA"), which provides a "regulatory scheme [that] is both comprehensive and minutely elaborate." *Knight v. City of Margate*, 86 N.J. 374, 431 A.2d 833 (N.J. 1981); *Hakimoglu*, 876 F. Supp. at 631. The Casino Control Commission establishes the rules governing the operation of casinos, including

---

2. *See, e.g., Piland Corporation v. REA Construction Co.*, 672 F. Supp. 244, 247-48 (E.D. Va. 1987) ("In Virginia, and generally, the rule of contract law is that there must be absolute mutuality of engagement so that each party is bound and has the right to hold the other party to the agreement.")

setting the odds for each game, odds that always favor the casino. More importantly, the CCA specifically "permits casinos to offer free food, lodging, transportation and other inducements to potential customers" as part of "junkets" that casinos may offer to their patrons. *See Tose v. Greate Bay Hotel & Casino Inc.*, 819 F. Supp. 1312, 1319 n. 11 (D.N.J. 1993) (describing a junket as the provision of "complimentary transportation, food, lodging and entertainment based on [a] person's propensity to gamble").

Under New Jersey law, therefore, the casino gambling contracts are valid. Not only does the CCA legalize casino gambling generally, it specifically recognizes and authorizes the very activity Rahmani complains of, namely the practice of offering junkets to people with a propensity to gamble for the purpose of encouraging them to travel to New Jersey to do so. *See* N.J.S.A. 5:12-29 and 5:12-102 (defining junkets and setting forth conditions for junkets). Accordingly, under New Jersey law, the contracts are valid and enforceable, and thus Rahmani cannot sue for their rescission or for restitution.

Given the closeness of the choice of law issue, it is worth noting that Rahmani fares no better under Virginia law. To begin with, it is readily apparent that Virginia affords Rahmani no contract remedies. If, as Rahmani asserts, the last act necessary to the contract occurred in Virginia, the contract created, putting aside the absence of mutuality, would be deemed a gambling contract under Virginia law. Such a contract, of course, is void under Virginia law;[3] it is "a complete nullity, one that has no legal force or binding effect." *Kennedy v. Annandale Boys Club Inc.*, 221 Va. 504. Further, "it is one which never had any legal existence or effect, and one which cannot in any manner have life breathed into it."

As gambling contracts are illegal or immoral contracts in Virginia, "[Virginia] law simply leaves the litigants in the plight in which they have seen fit to place themselves without undertaking to balance benefits or burdens." *Phillip Levy & Co. v. Davis*, 115 Va. 814, 80 S.E. 791, 792 (Va. 1914). Given that the contracts defined by Rahmani are a nullity under Virginia law, it follows that she cannot sue for rescission or restitution,[4] under Virginia law, she is simply left "in the plight in which [she has] seen fit to place [herself]."

---

3. "All wagers, conveyances, assurances, and all contracts and securities whereof the whole or any part of the consideration be money or other valuable thing won, laid, or bet, at any game, horse race, sport or pastime . . . shall be utterly void." Va. Code §11-14.

4. It is well settled principle that Virginia courts will not enforce a contract validly formed in another state if that contract would offend the public policy of Virginia; thus, a gambling contract that would be valid in the state where it was formed will not be enforced in Virginia. *See Hughes*, 465 S.E.2d at 827-28; *Resorts Int'l Hotel, Inc.*, 569

Nor does Virginia law afford Rahmani any statutory remedies for the losses she incurred at casino gambling tables in New Jersey. To be sure, Virginia's statutes reflect an unambiguous hostility to gambling. Thus, §11-15 of the Virginia Code provides for the return of gambling losses sought within the three-month statutory limit. But §11-15 cannot be applied to gambling losses that occur lawfully outside Virginia. A state cannot invalidate the lawful statutes of another state or penalize activity that lawfully occurs in another state. Put another way, the Virginia General Assembly has no power to invalidate lawful gambling taking place wholly outside of Virginia. *See, e.g., Edgar v. MITE Corp.*, 457 U.S. 624, 642-43 (1982) (noting that the Commerce Clause precludes application of state statutes to commerce taking place wholly outside of the state's borders). Were this not so, absurd results would follow. If this statute could provide a basis for relief from a gaming contract entered into and fully performed in another state, then it would wreak havoc on the established–and legal–gambling industries across the country. Any gambling loser from Virginia could simply invoke §11-15 and thereby absolve herself of any losses she suffered in Atlantic City, Las Vegas, or any other city where gambling is legal. Indeed, were §11-15 to permit this, it would have the perverse effect of encouraging Virginians to gamble, albeit out-of-state. Therefore, even under Virginia law, Rahmani has neither a common law contractual basis nor a statutory basis for her claims for the return of her gambling losses. [Complaint dismissed.]

## NOTES

1.  Is this case as easy as the court makes it appear? Presumably, Virginia's Statute of Queen Anne is designed to express and enforce a public policy against gambling. Is Virginia most concerned with gambling in Virginia, or by Virginians? New Jersey's comprehensive gaming laws authorize licensed casinos to engage in junketeering. In other words, New Jersey allows its casinos to send limousines to Virginia, a state in which gambling is illegal, to entice wealthy Virginia citizens to the casinos to gamble. Does the New Jersey practice violate Virginia public policy? Does the *Rahmani* court's approach serve to advance or frustrate Virginia public policy?

---

F. Supp. at 26; *Coghill v. Boardwalk Regency Corp.*, 240 Va. 230, 233, 396 S.E.2d 838, 839 (Va. 1990). But this principle cannot be extended to support the proposition that Virginia would apply a foreign state's laws to recognize the validity of a contract legally formed in another state, thus providing a basis for suit, but would then apply its own law to undo that contract.

2.  Is Rahmani the natural result of a federalist system that encourages each state to make its own policies regarding gambling and allows freedom to travel? Or does it constitute exploitation by one state in using another state's public policy choices against it? Is there any solution in a federalist system? Does it create a "race to the bottom?" Or is it a "race toward freedom?"

3.  Where was the contract formed? Is the court correct that there is not one contract but thousands of contracts between Resorts and Rahmani corresponding to each individual bet? Is this empty formalism? Is the limousine ride and the hotel room a gift or is it consideration for an explicit or implicit agreement to gamble in an Atlantic City casino?

4.  In *McCurry v. Keith*, the trial court found that McCurry sustained losses of $8,560 at the Keiths' video poker business. During that same period of time, however, McCurry won $5,000 at the same establishment. South Carolina statute provided that: "Any person who shall at any time or sitting, by playing at cards, dice table or any other game whatsoever or by betting on the sides or hands of such as do play at any of the games aforesaid, lose to any person or persons so playing or betting, in the whole, the sum or value of fifty dollars and shall pay or deliver such sum or value or any part thereof shall be at liberty, within three months then next ensuing, to sue for and recover the money or goods so lost and paid or delivered or any part thereof from the respective winner or winners thereof, with costs of suit, by action to be prosecuted in any court of competent jurisdiction." . . . Pursuant to this rule, the appeals court upheld the trial court decision to allow McCurry to recover for his losses. However, both courts awarded McCurry only $3,560, offsetting his losses by his wins despite his arguments that he should have been awarded the entire sum of his losses. See 481 S.E.2d 166 (S.C. 1997).

5.  If gambling is harmful, as Virginia laws suggest, which state bears the weight of the harm involved in the gambling in this case? Is that question relevant to the analysis?

## CONNECTICUT NATIONAL BANK OF HARTFORD v. KOMMIT

**Massachusetts Court of Appeals**
**577 N.E.2d 639 (Mass. App. 1991)**

PERRETTA, J.

It is the law of Massachusetts, Connecticut, and New Jersey that a contract to pay money knowingly lent for gambling is void. New Jersey, however, has an exception to this rule, its so-called Casino Control Act. That statute, essentially, provides that a loan made for casino gambling in Atlantic City is legal and enforceable. *See Gottlob v. Lopez*, 205 N.J. Super. 417 (1985). The Kommits are Massachusetts residents who hold a Mastercharge card pursuant to a credit agreement with the Connecticut National Bank of Hartford (bank). The bank brought this action in Massachusetts seeking payment of $5,500 borrowed by the Kommits with the use of their card. The Kommits refused to pay because, as appears from Richard Kommit's affidavit filed in opposition to the bank's motion for summary judgment, he borrowed the money for gambling. It seems that, "on diverse dates" while at a casino in Atlantic City, Richard Kommit used his Mastercharge card to withdraw a total of $5,500 from an automatic teller machine. That machine was located in the "pit," the gambling area, of the casino. He claims that the machine was intended "to advance funds expressly for the purpose of gambling." Denying none of these facts, the bank argued that the debt is enforceable under New Jersey law. The Kommits relied upon Massachusetts law.

*The choice of law.* There are three States which have an interest in this action: Massachusetts, where the Kommits reside, Connecticut, the bank's principal place of business, and New Jersey, where the money was withdrawn and used to gamble. The bank argues that, because Richard obtained the money in New Jersey for a purpose there legal, the substantive law of that forum controls under Massachusetts choice-of-law rules.

In *Dicker* [*v. Klein*, 360 Mass. 735 (1972)], the plaintiff sought to recover on a debt incurred in the Bahama Islands for purposes of casino gambling. Applying the *lex loci* rule, the court looked to the law of the Bahama Islands. As the debt was void under the substantive law of that forum, the court refused to enforce it. From this conclusion, the bank reasons that had the debt been valid under the law of the Bahama Islands, it would have been enforceable in Massachusetts.

We do not view *Dicker* as dispositive for two reasons. In the first instance, Massachusetts has abandoned the *lex loci* rule, see *Choate, Hall & Stewart v. SCA Servs., Inc.*, 378 Mass. 535, 540-541 (1979), and we now "determine the choice-of-law question by assessing various choice-influencing considerations." *Bushkin Assocs. v. Raytheon Co.*, 393 Mass. 622, 631 (1985). Additionally, the question whether Massachusetts would enforce a debt legal where incurred but void under our substantive law was not present in *Dicker v. Klein*, because, as there noted, 360 Mass. at 737, the law of the Bahama Islands was "in accord with our own public policy." But see Restatement (Second) of Conflict of Laws §90 (1969) ("No action will be entertained on a foreign cause of action the enforcement of which is contrary to the strong public policy of the forum").

Turning to the "various choice-influencing considerations" discussed with Restatement (Second) of Conflict of Laws §6, in Bushkin *Assocs. v. Raytheon Co.*, 393 Mass. at 634, we consider the fact that this type of debt has been considered so offensive to the public policy of the bank's principal place of business that Connecticut refused to enforce a gambling contract notwithstanding its validity in the State where the debt was incurred. More recently, in *Casanova Club v. Bisharat*, 189 Conn. 591, 598 (1983), the Connecticut Supreme Court held that, although its Legislature had legalized some forms of gambling, gambling on credit remains a forbidden "vice" under Conn. Gen. Stat. §§52-553 and 52-554 (1960 & Supp. 1990).

Although the bank may have thought itself in compliance with the laws of New Jersey, and even though Richard may have known that his debt would be void under the law of Connecticut, we must also consider the facts that the bank expressly intended Connecticut law to control the use of its credit cards and that the Kommits accepted that condition. The bank's form credit contract conspicuously states: "This agreement and the use of your account is governed by Connecticut Law."

This clause, if enforced, favors the bank, which cannot control the use to which a person puts borrowed money obtained against a line of credit to which there is ready access from almost anywhere. It would be commercially unreasonable to have each incident of use of a bank's credit cards controlled by the law of the forum of the specific transaction. See Restatement (Second) of Conflict of Laws §6(2)(g) and comment j, stressing that choice-of-law rules should lead to "desirable results."

Had this action been brought in New Jersey, that forum, under its choice-of-law rules, would have applied Connecticut law. Although the transaction occurred in New Jersey, that State would have looked to the law chosen by the parties in the credit card agreement and to the strong public policy of Connecticut. *Cf. Winer Motors, Inc. v. Jaguar Rover Triumph, Inc.*, 208 N.J. Super. 666, 672 (1986) ("We will reject even the parties' choice of New Jersey local law in order to preserve the fundamental public policy of the franchisee's home state [Connecticut] where its statutes afford greater protection"). See also Restatement (Second) of Conflict of Laws §6 comment d ("Probably the most important function of choice-of-law rules is to make the interstate and international systems work well. Choice-of-law rules, among other things, should seek to further harmonious relations between states and to facilitate commercial intercourse between them. In formulating rules of choice of law, a state should have regard for the needs and policies of other states and of the community of states").

There is no reason for us not to honor the parties' choice of Connecticut law, especially in view of the fact that Connecticut (and Massachusetts) still provide the bank with ample protection: the debt is void only if the bank knew or should have known that the money was borrowed for gambling.

*The material fact.* In opposing summary judgment, the Kommits filed an affidavit from Richard claiming that the bank, by allowing ready access to credit from the automatic teller machine in the center of the casino's gambling area, knew or should have known that the borrowed money would be used to gamble. Although the bank would have no burden on the issue of its knowledge at trial, it was incumbent upon the bank to show that proof of its knowledge was unlikely to be produced at trial.

We think that the bank's alleged and unrefuted deliberate allowance of access to credit from the machine in the gambling area of the casino is a circumstance from which the essential element of the Kommits' defense to the action, knowledge, could (but need not) be inferred. It makes no difference that at the time of the motion the Kommits did not cite Connecticut law. The point of the matter is that, if the judge decided the motion on the basis of *Dicker v. Klein*, 360 Mass. 735 (1972), and the substantive law of New Jersey, he was in error, and there is a question of fact open under the law of Connecticut. Judgment reversed.

### NOTES

The facts do not indicate whether Kommit won or lost at the casino after playing with the $5500 he withdrew from the ATM. Should it matter whether he won or lost? Would it comport with the intent of Connecticut law to find in favor of Kommit if he had won money while gambling with his withdrawal?

# CHAPTER
## 4

---

# Federalism and Direct Enforcement
# of Gambling Prohibitions

In a society that strongly values individual liberty, prohibiting gambling presents a challenge. Indeed, curtailing any voluntary commercial activity between consenting adults is difficult. Consider for example the liquor prohibition of the early twentieth century or the ongoing "war on drugs." Private law approaches to enforcement, such as Queen Anne's provisions prohibiting the enforcement of gambling contracts, which are necessarily indirect, cannot be fully effective because they rely on the participants' need and willingness to utilize the judicial system. If participants voluntarily pay their gambling debts, then such provisions will be largely ineffective. As a result, regulators seeking to enforce an absolute prohibition have often sought more direct action. The most direct and aggressive manner for addressing gambling is criminal or civil enforcement. Criminalizing persistent consensual commercial behavior, however, may have unintended consequences. It may not stop the behavior but simply drive it underground, or toward other state or national jurisdictions.

A threshold question in a federalist system is which order of government should handle routine enforcement of a gambling prohibition. The Constitution is generally interpreted as leaving the question of the legality of gambling to the will of individual states. And indeed states have adopted widely divergent positions toward gambling. Nevada, for example, has broadly legalized gambling and made such activity the centerpiece of the state's economic development model. In contrast, the neighboring state of Utah maintains one of the strictest prohibitions of gambling in the entire United States. Utah law prohibits even charitable bingo.

Since the Constitution does not explicitly delegate to Congress the power to regulate gambling, an obvious question is, "What is the proper role of the federal government in this context?"

Given the lack of a specific enumeration of the power to regulate gambling, and the divergent state approaches toward the subject, one possible role to be served by federal actors is to assist each state in maintaining the integrity of its geographic boundaries and its particular policy approach toward gambling activity. The federal criminal code contains numerous provisions addressing illegal gambling and most of them are, more or less, consistent with this role. But despite an apparently circumscribed role, federal law enforcement officials have had a key role in addressing illegal gambling for more than a century and have often done so aggressively. Most recently, this role has manifested in the federal government's initiatives against Internet gambling.

Thus, before addressing other issues related to prohibition, this chapter will begin with a discussion of the role of federal institutions in enforcing prohibitions on gambling. It will then consider some of the key federal anti-gambling statutes, which have been among the primary tools for enforcing a prohibition, and the issues that have arisen under them. Finally, it will take up the subject of Internet gambling, which has gained steady federal attention and enforcement efforts since the late 1990s.

While dealing with the general question of how to enforce gambling prohibitions, almost all of the cases throughout this chapter present underlying questions about the proper role of the federal government in setting social policy in an area in which states have adopted widely divergent stances.

## A.   FEDERALISM AND THE ROLE OF THE FEDERAL GOVERNMENT

The Constitution does not delegate to Congress the power to regulate gambling. However, Congress has used certain enumerated powers, including the Commerce Clause, to enact federal laws that, in some cases authorize, and in others restrict, gambling activity. A state, meanwhile, maintains police powers within its own jurisdiction.

The existence of overlapping federal and state powers to regulate the same subject has resulted in conflicts. Some of the key tests have involved gambling prohibitions. Conflicts arose with regard to lotteries, which were popular, but also controversial, in the colonial and early federal period. Some states used them as revenue opportunities, while others sought to outlaw them. An early test of the scope of federal power arose in *Cohens v. Virginia*, 19 U.S. 264 (1821). That case arose when Virginia prosecuted the defendants for unlawfully selling lottery tickets for the District of Columbia lottery. The case presented two questions. The first concerned the scope of the federal judicial power to review a state conviction. Chief Justice Marshall, writing for the Court, used the case to establish the authority of the federal courts to review state convictions for constitutionality.

The second question nominally presented in *Cohens v. Virginia* was about federal legislative power, namely, whether by legalizing a lottery in the District of Columbia, Congress could pre-empt state gambling laws in Virginia. The defendant argued that his sale of lottery tickets for a lottery authorized by Congress could not be the subject of interference by Virginia, even for sales in Virginia. Here, Chief Justice Marshall sidestepped the issue by ruling that Congress, in the lottery ordinance, had not intended to authorize the sale of lottery tickets outside the District of Columbia.

Perhaps the most famous conflict over state and federal power, however, played out in the Lottery Case, *Champion v. Ames*, which is excerpted below. While some students may be familiar with *Champion v. Ames* from introductory constitutional law courses, the case is also worth studying for its lessons about the respective roles of states and the federal government in the particular context of gaming.

By the late 1800s, most American states had outlawed lotteries, often by including an outright ban in their state constitutions. In the last decades of the Nineteenth Century, Congress began flexing its regulatory muscles within the national economy, enacting the Interstate Commerce Act of 1887 and the Sherman Antitrust Act of 1890. It also made its presence known in the gaming sphere. Congress first prohibited, in 1890, the shipment of lottery tickets or advertisements in the U.S. mail. Then, in 1895, Congress enacted a far broader law, making it a felony to carry a lottery ticket from one state to another, through the mails, or otherwise.

In an early test of federal power, defendant Champion was convicted in federal court of violating the federal lottery statute. He challenged the statute as unconstitutional.

## CHAMPION v. AMES ("THE LOTTERY CASE")
### 188 U.S. 321 (1903)

HARLAN, J.

The appellant insists that the carrying of lottery tickets from one State to another State by an express company engaged in carrying freight and packages from State to State, although such tickets may be contained in a box or package, does not constitute, and cannot by any act of Congress be legally made to constitute, commerce among the States within the meaning of the clause of the Constitution of the United States providing that Congress shall have power "to regulate commerce with foreign nations, and among the several States, and with the Indian tribes;" consequently, that Congress cannot make it an offence to cause such tickets to be carried from one State to another.

The Government insists that express companies when engaged, for hire, in the business of transportation from one State to another, are instrumentalities of commerce among the States; that the carrying of lottery tickets from one State to another is commerce which Congress may regulate; and that as a means of executing the power to regulate interstate commerce Congress may make it an offence against the United States to cause lottery tickets to be carried from one State to another.

The questions presented by these opposing contentions are of great moment, and are entitled to receive, as they have received, the most careful consideration. What is the import of the word "commerce" as used in the Constitution? It is not defined by that instrument. Undoubtedly, the carrying from one State to another by independent carriers of things or commodities that are ordinary subjects of traffic, and which have in themselves a recognized value in money, constitutes interstate commerce. But does not commerce among the several States include something more? Does not the carrying from one State to another, by independent carriers, of lottery tickets that entitle the holder to the payment of a certain amount of money therein specified also constitute commerce among the States?

[P]ower to regulate commerce among the several States is vested in Congress as absolutely as it would be in a single government, having in its constitution the same restrictions on the exercise of the power as are found in the Constitution of the United States; that such power is plenary, complete in itself, and may be exerted by Congress to its utmost extent, subject only to such limitations as the Constitution imposes upon the exercise of the powers granted by it; and that in determining the character of the regulations to be adopted Congress has a large discretion which is not to be controlled by the courts, simply because, in their opinion, such regulations may not be the best or most effective that could be employed.

It was said in argument that lottery tickets are not of any real or substantial value in themselves, and therefore are not subjects of commerce. . . . We are of opinion that lottery tickets are subjects of traffic and therefore are subjects of commerce, and the regulation of the carriage of such tickets from State to State, at least by independent carriers, is a regulation of commerce among the several States.

But it is said that the statute in question does not regulate the carrying of lottery tickets from State to State, but by punishing those who cause them to be so carried Congress in effect prohibits such carrying; that in respect of the carrying from one State to another of articles or things that are, in fact, or according to usage in business, the subjects of commerce, the authority given Congress was not to prohibit, but only to regulate. . . .

It is to be remarked that the Constitution does not define what is to be deemed a legitimate regulation of interstate commerce[.] While our Government must be acknowledged by all to be one of enumerated powers, *McCulloch v. Maryland,* 4 Wheat. 316, 405, 407, the Constitution does not attempt to set forth all the means by which such powers may be carried into execution. It leaves to Congress a large discretion as to the means that may be employed in executing a given power. The sound construction of the Constitution, this court has said, "must allow to the national legislature that discretion, with respect to the means by which the powers it confers are to be carried into execution, which will enable that body to perform the high duties assigned to it, in the manner most beneficial to the people. Let the end be legitimate, let it be within the scope of the Constitution, and all means which are appropriate, which are plainly adapted to that end, which are not prohibited, but consist with the letter and spirit of the Constitution, are constitutional." 4 Wheat. 421.

[I]f lottery traffic, carried on through interstate commerce, is a matter of which Congress may take cognizance and over which its power may be exerted, can it be possible that it must tolerate the traffic, and simply regulate the manner in which it may be carried on? Or may not Congress, for the protection of the people of all the States, and under the power to regulate interstate commerce, devise such means, within the scope of the Constitution, and not prohibited by it, as will drive that traffic out of commerce among the States? . . .

[T]he suppression of nuisances injurious to public health or morality is among the most important duties of Government[. Indeed], this court [has] said: "Experience has shown that the common forms of gambling are comparatively innocuous when placed in contrast with the widespread pestilence of lotteries. The former are confined to a few persons and places, but the latter infests the whole community; it enters every dwelling; it reaches every class; it preys upon the hard earnings of the poor; it plunders the ignorant and simple." In other cases we have adjudged that authority given by legislative enactment to carry on a lottery, although based upon a consideration in money, was not protected by the contract clause of the Constitution; this, for the reason that no State may bargain away its power to protect the public morals, nor excuse its failure to perform a public duty by saying that it had agreed, by legislative enactment, not to do so.

If a State, when considering legislation for the suppression of lotteries within its own limits, may properly take into view the evils that inhere in the raising of money, in that mode, why may not Congress, invested with the Power to regulate commerce among the several States, provide that such commerce shall not be polluted by the carrying of lottery tickets from one State to another?

[W]hat clause can be cited which, in any degree, countenances the suggestion that one may, of right, carry or cause to be carried from one State to another that which will harm the public morals? We cannot think of any clause of that instrument that could possibly be invoked by those who assert their right to send lottery tickets from State to State except the one providing that no person shall be deprived of his liberty without due process of law. We have said that the liberty protected by the Constitution embraces the right to be free in the enjoyment of one's faculties; "to be free to use them in all lawful ways; to live and work where he will; to earn his livelihood by any lawful calling; to pursue any livelihood or avocation, and for that purpose to enter into all contracts that may be proper." *Allgeyer v. Louisiana*, 165 U.S. 578, 589. But surely it will not be said to be a part of any one's liberty, as recognized by the supreme law of the land, that he shall be allowed to introduce into commerce among the States an element that will be confessedly injurious to the public morals. . . .

As a State may, for the purpose of guarding the morals of its own people, forbid all sales of lottery tickets within its limits, so Congress, for the purpose of guarding the people of the United States against the "widespread pestilence of lotteries" and to protect the commerce which concerns all the States, may prohibit the carrying of lottery tickets from one State to another. In legislating upon the subject of the traffic in lottery tickets, as carried on through interstate commerce, Congress only supplemented the action of those States— perhaps all of them—which, for the protection of the public morals, prohibit the drawing of lotteries, as well as the sale or circulation of lottery tickets, within their respective limits. . . . We should hesitate long before adjudging that an evil of such appalling character, carried on through interstate commerce, cannot be met and crushed by the only power competent to that end. We say competent to that end, because Congress alone has the power to occupy, by legislation, the whole field of interstate commerce. . . .

If the carrying of lottery tickets from one State to another be interstate commerce, and if Congress is of opinion that an effective regulation for the suppression of lotteries, carried on through such commerce, is to make it a criminal offence to cause lottery tickets to be carried from one State to another, we know of no authority in the courts to hold that the means thus devised are not appropriate and necessary to protect the country at large against a species of interstate commerce which, although in general use and somewhat favored in both national and state legislation in the early history of the country, has grown into disrepute and has become offensive to the entire people of the Nation. It is a kind of traffic which no one can be entitled to pursue as of right.

It is said, however, that if, in order to suppress lotteries carried on through interstate commerce, Congress may exclude lottery tickets from such commerce, that principle leads necessarily to the conclusion that Congress may arbitrarily exclude from commerce among the States any article, commodity or thing, of whatever kind or nature, or however useful or valuable, which it may choose, no matter with what motive, to declare shall not be carried from one State to another. It will be time enough to consider the constitutionality of such legislation when we must do so. . . . But, as often said, the possible abuse of a power is not an argument against its existence. There is probably no governmental power that may not be exerted to the injury of the public. If what is done by Congress is manifestly in excess of the powers granted to it, then upon the courts will rest the duty of adjudging that its action is neither legal nor binding upon the people. But if what Congress does is within the limits of its power, and is simply unwise or injurious, the remedy is that suggested by Chief Justice Marshall in *Gibbons v. Ogden,* when he said: "The wisdom and the discretion of Congress, their identity with the people, and the influence which their constituents possess at elections, are, in this, as in many other instances, as that, for example, of declaring war, the sole restraints on which they have relied, to secure them from its abuse. They are the restraints on which the people must often rely solely, in all representative governments." . . . The judgment is AFFIRMED.

Mr. Chief Justice FULLER, joined by Mr. Justice BREWER, Mr. Justice SHIRAS and Mr. Justice PECKHAM, dissenting.

Although the [statute] is inartfully drawn, I accept the contention of the Government that it makes it an offence (1) to bring lottery matter from abroad into the United States; (2) to cause such matter to be deposited in or carried by the mails of the United States; (3) to cause such matter to be carried from one State to another in the United States; and further, to cause any advertisement of a lottery or similar enterprise to be brought into the United States, or be deposited or carried by the mails, or transferred from one State to another. . . . That the purpose of Congress in this enactment was the suppression of lotteries cannot reasonably be denied. That purpose is avowed in the title of the act, and is its natural and reasonable effect, and by that its validity must be tested.

The power of the State to impose restraints and burdens on persons and property in conservation and promotion of the public health, good order and prosperity is a power originally and always belonging to the States, not surrendered by them to the General Government nor directly restrained by the Constitution of the United States, and essentially exclusive, and the suppression of lotteries as a harmful business falls within this power, commonly called of police.

It is urged, however, that because Congress is empowered to regulate commerce between the several States, it, therefore, may suppress lotteries by prohibiting the carriage of lottery matter. Congress may indeed make all laws necessary and proper for carrying the powers granted to it into execution, and doubtless an act prohibiting the carriage of lottery matter would be necessary and proper to the execution of a power to suppress lotteries; but that power belongs to the States and not to Congress. To hold that Congress has general police power would be to hold that it may accomplish objects not entrusted to the General Government, and to defeat the operation of the Tenth Amendment, declaring that: "The powers not delegated to the United States by the Constitution, nor prohibited by it to the States, are reserved to the States respectively, or to the people."

The ground on which acts forbidding the transmission of lottery matter by the mails was [previously] sustained, was that the power vested in Congress to establish post offices and post roads embraced the regulation of the entire postal system of the country, and that under that power Congress might designate what might be carried in the mails and what excluded. . . . But . . . this act cannot be brought within the power to regulate commerce among the several States, unless lottery tickets are articles of commerce, and, therefore, when carried across state lines, of interstate commerce; or unless the power to regulate interstate commerce includes the absolute and exclusive power to prohibit the transportation of anything or anybody from one State to another. . . .

[C]ould Congress compel a State to admit lottery matter within it, contrary to its own laws? In *Alexander v. State*, 86 Georgia, 246, it was held that a state statute prohibiting the business of buying and selling what are commonly known as "futures," was not protected by the commerce clause of the Constitution, as the business was gambling, and that clause protected interstate commerce but did not protect interstate gambling. . . .

If a lottery ticket is not an article of commerce, how can it become so when placed in an envelope or box or other covering, and transported by an express company? To say that the mere carrying of an article which is not an article of commerce in and of itself nevertheless becomes such the moment it is to be transported from one State to another, is to transform a non-commercial article into a commercial one simply because it is transported. I cannot conceive that any such result can properly follow.

It would be to say that everything is an article of commerce the moment it is taken to be transported from place to place, and of interstate commerce if from State to State. An invitation to dine, or to take a drive, or a note of introduction, all become articles of commerce under the ruling in this case, by being deposited with an express company for transportation. This in effect breaks down all the differences between that which is, and that which is not, an article of commerce, and the necessary consequence is to take from the States all jurisdiction over the subject so far as interstate communication is concerned. It is a long step in the direction of wiping out all traces of state lines, and the creation of a centralized Government.

Does the grant to Congress of the power to regulate interstate commerce impart the absolute power to prohibit it? It will not do to say—a suggestion which has heretofore been made in this case—that state laws have been found to be ineffective for the suppression of lotteries, and therefore Congress should interfere. The scope of the commerce clause of the Constitution cannot be enlarged because of present views of public interest. . . .

The power to prohibit the transportation of diseased animals and infected goods over railroads or on steamboats is an entirely different thing, for they would be in themselves injurious to the transaction of interstate commerce, and, moreover, are essentially commercial in their nature. And the exclusion of diseased persons rests on different ground, for nobody would pretend that persons could be kept off the trains because they were going from one State to another to engage in the lottery business. However enticing that business may be, we do not understand these pieces of paper themselves can communicate bad principles by contact.

I regard this decision as inconsistent with the views of the framers of the Constitution, and of Marshall, its great expounder. Our form of government may remain notwithstanding legislation or decision, but, as long ago observed, it is with governments, as with religions, the form may survive the substance of the faith.

*NOTES*

1. *Champion v. Ames* represents an early, expansive view of Congressional power under the Commerce Clause. Though, it was a controversial 5-4 decision, it was precedent for the constitutionality of a host of other statutes enacted under the Commerce Clause, including federal food and drug laws, and an early federal criminal vice statute, the Mann Act, which prohibited the transportation of women across state lines for immoral purposes.

2. The dissent seems to argue that, since lottery tickets are illegal in some states, a lottery ticket would not be a lawful item of commerce in such a state. Therefore, it is not subject to congressional regulation under the Commerce Clause. Is this argument compelling? If the dissent had prevailed, what would have been the ramifications? Would the federal government have a broad role in law enforcement today? Consider, for example, the federal role in addressing illegal narcotics.

3. The dissent argues that the majority's opinion constitutes "a long step in the direction of wiping out all traces of state lines, and the creation of a centralized Government." True? Has this ensued?

4. Since *Champion v. Ames* was decided, the majority's expansive approach to federal power has been widely accepted, though interest in limited federal government and concern for the prerogatives of states has never vanished entirely. In the 1990s, the Supreme Court seemed to take a greater interest in issues of federalism, *see United States v. Lopez,* 514 U.S. 549 (1995) (discussed in *United States v. Wall,* infra). As *Cohens v. Virginia* and *Champion v. Ames* foreshadow, the issue of the scope of federal authority has come up repeatedly in the context of gambling. As you read the cases that follow, try to determine what role the federal government should play as to gambling, particularly in light of the fact that states have had such divergent views on the subject.

## UNITED STATES v. WALL
### 92 F.3d 1444 (6th Cir. 1996)

SILER, Circuit Judge.

Defendants Nathan and Donald Wall appeal the district court's denial of their motion to dismiss the information charging them with operating an illegal gambling business. They entered conditional pleas of guilty to a violation of 18 U.S.C. §1955. Defendants . . . attack the constitutionality of §1955. For reasons stated hereafter, we affirm the district court.

Section 1955 of Title 18 of the United States Code criminalizes illegal gambling operations of a certain size. [Section 1955 is reproduced below at page 212—ED.] Defendants contend that §1955 is void as a prohibited exercise of congressional power.

This century has seen the aggrandizement of power by the legislative branch of our government heretofore unknown. Nonetheless, the power of Congress is by no means absolute: it may exercise only those powers enumerated in the Constitution. *McCulloch v. Maryland*, 17 U.S. (4 Wheat.) 316, 4 L. Ed. 579 (1819). Expressly delegated to Congress is the ability "to regulate Commerce with foreign Nations, and among the several States, and with the Indian Tribes." The interpretation of this seemingly innocuous clause has a storied history in Supreme Court jurisprudence that is well-documented elsewhere.

Action by Congress pursuant to the Commerce Clause must be examined by the courts to verify that the legislative body acted within its Constitutional authority. This court has examined and upheld the constitutionality of 18 U.S.C. §1955. Other circuits have similarly upheld §1955 as an appropriate exercise of Congress's power. To this court's knowledge, no other court has found §1955 to be constitutionally infirm.

Before April 1995, a discussion on the constitutional viability of §1955 would have terminated at this point. This statute would have been summarily upheld as a valid exercise of congressional power under the Commerce Clause. For the first time in over fifty years, however, the Supreme Court invalidated a federal statute because Congress had exceeded its authority under the Commerce Clause. *United States v. Lopez*, 131 L. Ed. 2d 626, 115 S. Ct. 1624, 1634 (1995). Thus, this court must renew its examination of §1955.

In *Lopez*, the Supreme Court invalidated the Gun-Free School Zones Act. 18 U.S.C. §922(q). Canvassing past Commerce Clause decisions, the Court identified three categories of activities that Congress may regulate under its commerce power: (1) "the use of the channels of interstate commerce"; (2) "the instrumentalities of interstate commerce, or persons or things in interstate commerce, even though the threat may come only from intrastate activities"; and (3) "those activities having a substantial relation to interstate commerce, i.e., those activities that substantially affect interstate commerce." *Lopez*, 115 S. Ct. at 1629-30 (citation omitted). The Court concluded that §922(q), classified in the third category, failed to substantially affect interstate commerce.

In *Lopez*, the Court distinguished §922(q) from other regulatory statutes. First, it emphasized the non-commercial nature of the statute:

> Section 922(q) is a criminal statute that by its terms has nothing to do with "commerce" or any sort of economic enterprise, however broadly one might define those terms. Section 922(q) is not an essential part of a larger regulation of economic activity, in which the regulatory scheme could be undercut unless the intrastate activity were regulated. It cannot, therefore, be sustained under our cases upholding regulations of activities that arise out of or are connected with a commercial transaction, which viewed in the aggregate, substantially affects interstate commerce.

*Lopez*, 115 S. Ct. at 1630-31 (footnote omitted). On its face, §922(q) did not regulate commercial activity; it did not regulate commercial actors. The statute was therefore non-commercial.

The second distinction hailed by the Court was that §922(q) "contains no jurisdictional element which would ensure, through case-by-case inquiry, that the firearm possession in question affects interstate commerce." *Lopez*, 115 S. Ct. at 1631. The Court emphasized that "neither the statute nor its legislative history contains express congressional findings regarding the effects upon interstate commerce of gun possession in a school zone." Id. at 1631. In sum, "unlike the earlier cases to come before the Court here neither the actors nor their conduct have a commercial character, and neither the purposes nor the design of the statute have an evident commercial nexus." *Lopez*, 115 S. Ct. at 1640 (Kennedy, J., concurring).

Significantly, the Court rejected two arguments that would justify the lack of congressional findings. First, §922(q) represented a "sharp break" with prior firearm regulation. The "importation of previous findings ... [would therefore be] especially inappropriate." *Lopez*, 115 S. Ct. at 1632. Second, and more important, the Court was unwilling to construct a tenuous argument that possession of a firearm in a school zone results in violent crime, which affects interstate commerce through increasing insurance costs and decreasing educational opportunities. Id. at 1632. Were this argument successful, the Court reasoned, "it is difficult to perceive any limitation on federal power, even in areas such as criminal law enforcement or education where States historically have been sovereign." Id. at 1632.

The potential reach of *Lopez* has been debated. The Supreme Court itself conceded that *Lopez* would result in legal uncertainty. Criminal defendants across the country have exploited this uncertainty, citing *Lopez* in hopes that the statutes underlying their convictions will similarly be invalidated. Most courts have resisted urgings to extend *Lopez* beyond §922(q).

The question thus becomes if and how *Lopez* will apply to 18 U.S.C. §1955. This court will apply the *Lopez* framework to organize this discussion. Like §922(q), §1955 must be classified under the third category. Thus, to be sustained, §1955 must regulate activities that substantially affect interstate commerce. To make this determination, this court will conduct a *Lopez* analysis: Is §1955 commercial in nature? Is the statute otherwise connected to interstate commerce?

First, this court must determine whether §1955 is commercially related—whether the statute regulates part of an economic enterprise. On one hand, §1955 resembles §922(q). Both are criminal statutes of general application. Ostensibly, the purpose of both statutes is not to regulate commercial intercourse; rather, Congress's primary intent was to deter and punish criminal behavior. See, e.g., *Mussari*, 894 F. Supp. at 1363-64 (interpreting statute that punished non-payment of child support as criminal in nature rather than commercial).

On the other hand, §1955 has a stronger link to commerce than does §922(q). On its face, the statute has a commercial aspect. It does not prohibit gambling per se; rather, it punishes those who "conduct[] . . . an illegal gambling business." 18 U.S.C. §1955(a). To sustain a conviction, Congress required federal prosecutors to demonstrate that a certain amount of commercial activity took place—the business had to "remain[] in substantially continuous operation for a period in excess of thirty days or have a gross revenue of $2,000 in any single day." Id. §1955(b)(1)(iii). Gambling itself, in its multiple forms, is a commercial activity. See, e.g., *Pic-A-State PA*, 76 F.3d at 1301 (affirming that lottery tickets are "subjects of commerce" and that it was "beyond dispute that state lotteries affect interstate commerce"). By its terms, §1955 is commercial in nature and is not favorably compared to possession of a gun in a school zone, which clearly does not involve commercial activity.

Next, this court must analyze the purpose and design of §1955 to determine whether it affects interstate commerce. Like §922(q), §1955 "contains no jurisdictional element which would ensure, through case-by-case inquiry," that the gambling operation in question affects interstate commerce. *Lopez*, 115 S. Ct. at 1631. The prosecutor need not prove and the jury need not find that the accused or his instrumentalities crossed any state lines or affected interstate commerce. There is nothing in the statute that "might limit its reach to a discrete set of [gambling operations] that additionally have an explicit connection with or effect on interstate commerce." *Lopez*, 115 S. Ct. at 1631.

Unlike §922(q), however, §1955 contains reams of legislative historical information to guide the courts. Enacting the Organized Crime Control Act of 1970, "Congress passed [§1955] in an attempt to attack sophisticated, large-scale illegal gambling operations which Congress thought to be a major source of income for organized crime." *United States v. King*, 834 F.2d 109, 112 (6th Cir. 1987)[.] Congress determined that "organized crime posed a major threat to American society and that illegal gambling operations provided organized crime with its greatest source of revenue." *United States v. Sacco*, 491 F.2d 995, 999 (9th Cir. 1974) (en banc). Congress specifically found that "illegal gambling involves widespread use of, and has an effect upon, interstate commerce and the facilities of interstate commerce." H.R. Rep. No. 91-1549, 91st Cong., 2d Sess. (1970)[.]

The Supreme Court cited *Perez v. United States*, 402 U.S. 146 (1971), as an example of appropriate congressional regulation. *Lopez*, 115 S. Ct. at 1630. Perez upheld 18 U.S.C. §891, which outlawed extortionate credit practices. Like §1955, §891 was a criminal statute that punished commercial activity. Section 891 primarily regulated intrastate activity and did not contain any jurisdictional interstate element. However, attached to it were extensive legislative findings and history that analyzed the burden that extortionate credit practices placed on interstate commerce. *Perez*, 402 U.S. at 155-57. Under these circumstances, the Supreme Court confirmed that §891 "substantially affected interstate commerce" and was therefore properly enacted.

*Lopez* casts a shadow on regulation that is tenuously related to interstate commerce. *Lopez*, however, does not mandate that §1955 be invalidated. Until the Supreme Court provides a clearer signal or cogent framework to handle this type of legislation, this court is content to heed the concurrence of two Justices that the history of Commerce Clause jurisprudence still "counsels great restraint." *Lopez*, 115 S. Ct. at 1634 (Kennedy, J. concurring). Section 1955, in language, purpose, and legislative history, better resembles commercial regulation than does §922(q). Section 1955 compares favorably to the statute analyzed in *Perez*. As a result, we affirm that 18 U.S.C. §1955 is a proper exercise of congressional power under the United States Constitution.

*NOTES*

1.  Given the relative danger of lottery tickets (*Champion v. Ames*) and guns (*Lopez*), do these cases present meaningful boundaries on the role of the federal government? Or does the analysis in these

cases represent empty formalism? What role ought the federal government serve in such matters?

2.  As explained in the opinion, section 1955 is limited to fairly extensive gambling operations. Are the "magnitude" elements of section 1955, which require a certain amount of gambling activity to trigger an offense, designed to insure federal jurisdiction? Or do they have a different purpose?

3.  The next case, *Casino Ventures v. Stewart*, addresses the preemptive effect of federal gambling regulatory laws. To understand the case, it is useful to have an understanding of the broader context, including especially the Johnson Act.

Congress enacted the Johnson Act in 1950 "to support the policy of those States which outlaw slot machines and similar gambling devices, by prohibiting use of the channels of interstate or foreign commerce for the shipment of such machines or devices into such States." Since the Johnson Act was concerned primarily with the threat of proliferation of slot machines, it prohibited the transport of any gambling device "to any place in a state." 15 U.S.C. §1172(a). After the Johnson Act, a state that wished slot machines to be legal would need to enact a statute that explicitly authorized their use.

## CASINO VENTURES v. STEWART
### 183 F.3d 307 (4th Cir. 1999)

WILKINSON, Chief Judge:

Casino Ventures plans to offer gambling cruises from a port in South Carolina. Fearing prosecution, it brought suit seeking a declaration that state gambling laws prohibiting such cruises had been preempted by the Johnson Act, 15 U.S.C. §1175. The district court found the state laws were preempted. We reverse, holding that the Act does not preempt state regulatory authority over gambling. Thus South Carolina authorities remain free to enforce state criminal prohibitions against illicit gambling cruise activity.

### I.

Casino Ventures seeks to operate a "day cruise" or "cruise to nowhere" business from a dock in South Carolina. The business would entail short cruises on ships that depart from and return to the same port in South Carolina without making any intervening stops.

Once the ship is outside of the state's territorial waters, Casino Ventures would offer gambling to its passengers.

Casino Ventures fears that its cruise business will violate South Carolina criminal laws restricting gambling. State statutes have long prohibited the possession and use of certain gambling devices within South Carolina territory. In particular, Casino Ventures alleges that its business operations may violate South Carolina's ban on lotteries, its ban on unlawful games and betting, and its ban on the possession and use of gaming tables and machines.

To allay this fear of criminal prosecution, Casino Ventures brought suit against Robert M. Stewart, Chief of the State Law Enforcement Division, and Charles M. Condon, Attorney General of South Carolina. Casino Ventures sought a declaration that South Carolina's gambling laws are preempted by federal law and an order enjoining the enforcement of those state laws. Specifically, it asserted that the 1992 amendments to the Johnson Act created a federal right to operate a gambling cruise to nowhere.

The 1992 amendments altered the Johnson Act's general ban on maritime gambling. Prior to the amendments, it was "unlawful to manufacture, recondition, repair, sell, transport, possess, or use any gambling device . . . within the special maritime" jurisdiction of the United States. 15 U.S.C.A. §1175 (1990). The Justice Department, however, interpreted this prohibition not "to apply to foreign-flag vessels entering the United States." H.R. Rep. No. 102-357 (1991). The effect was that American flag vessels were restricted from offering gambling to their passengers while foreign flag vessels were free to do so. This put American flag vessels at a competitive disadvantage in the lucrative leisure cruise industry.

Congress reacted to the disparity by amending the Johnson Act to make clear that it applied to vessels "documented under the laws of a foreign country." 15 U.S.C. §1175(a). Additionally, Congress crafted exceptions to the Johnson Act's blanket restrictions related to gambling devices. First, section 1175 no longer restricts the transport and possession of gambling devices on vessels, provided that those devices are not used while the vessel is within the boundaries of a state or possession of the United States. Second, section 1175 no longer prohibits the repair and use of gambling devices outside of those boundaries, unless the ship is on a cruise to nowhere and the state in which that cruise "begins and ends has enacted a statute the terms of which prohibit that repair or use on that voyage."

After examining these amendments, the district court granted Casino Ventures' request for a declaratory judgment. First, the court held that the 1992 amendments created a federal right to operate day cruises, thereby preempting conflicting state laws. Second, the court noted that under section 1175 a state could defeat preemption if it "has enacted a statute the terms of which prohibit that repair or use" on cruises to nowhere. But it found that South Carolina's existing laws restricting gambling did not meet this statutory requirement because they were not passed after the 1992 amendments took effect. Thus, the district court declared that Casino Ventures could lawfully operate a cruise to nowhere business in South Carolina. Stewart and Condon appeal. Because we hold that the district court's initial finding of federal preemption was erroneous, we reverse.

## II.

Although the Constitution plainly permits federal law to supplant state authority, "consideration under the Supremacy Clause starts with the basic assumption that Congress did not intend to displace state law." *Maryland v. Louisiana,* 451 U.S. 725, 746 (1981). This presumption is at its zenith when federal law impinges upon core state police powers. States have long possessed primary responsibility in our federal system to protect the health, welfare, safety, and morals of their citizens. The Supreme Court has indicated "that when a State's exercise of its police power is challenged under the Supremacy Clause, 'we start with the assumption that the historic police powers of the States were not to be superseded by the Federal Act unless that was the clear and manifest purpose of Congress.' " This "approach is consistent with both federalism concerns and the historic primacy of state regulation of matters of health and safety." *Medtronic, Inc. v. Lohr,* 518 U.S. 470, 485 (1996).

The state laws at issue in this case restrict gambling within South Carolina. Because such restrictions are aimed at promoting the welfare, safety, and morals of South Carolinians, they represent a well-recognized exercise of state police power. For this reason, respect for state prerogatives dictates a cautious preemption analysis—one which is reluctant to imply a broad ouster of state authority.

## III.

Neither party contends that Congress has expressly preempted the state laws at issue here. Instead, Casino Ventures argues that state laws banning the use and possession of gambling devices on vessels have been impliedly preempted by federal law. Casino Ventures asserts that the 1992 amendments to the Johnson Act worked an implicit preemption of state laws, such as South Carolina's, that prohibit gambling voyages to nowhere.

We disagree. "The purpose of Congress is the ultimate touchstone" in a preemption case. *Retail Clerks v. Schermerhorn*, 375 U.S. 96, 103 (1963). That being so, state law is preempted "if federal law so thoroughly occupies a legislative field as to make reasonable the inference that Congress left no room for the States to supplement it." *Cipollone v. Liggett Group, Inc.*, 505 U.S. 504, 516, (1992). Additionally, courts imply preemption if state law "actually conflicts with federal law, that is, when it is impossible to comply with both state and federal law, or where the state law stands as an obstacle to the accomplishment of the full purposes and objectives of Congress." *Silkwood v. Kerr-McGee Corp.*, 464 U.S. 238, 248 (1984).

**A.**

There is no basis for finding federal field preemption of South Carolina's restrictions on gambling. Maritime matters and gambling are not fields subject to exclusive federal control. To the contrary, federal law in these fields respects both our system of dual sovereignty and the important regulatory interests of the states.

As a general matter, "Maritime law is not a monistic system. The State and Federal Governments jointly exert regulatory powers today as they have played joint roles in the development of maritime law throughout our history." *Romero v. International Terminal Operating Co.*, 358 U.S. 354, 374 (1959).

This is also true of the regulation of gambling. Indeed, Congress has explicitly recognized the preeminent state interests in controlling gambling and has sought to extend, not curb, state police power in this field. Congress has done so by delegating to the states significant authority to shape applicable federal law. For example, it is a federal crime "to transport any gambling device to any place in a State." 15 U.S.C. §1172(a). But such activity is not a federal crime if a state so chooses: each state may change the content of this federal law simply by "enacting a law providing for the exemption of such State from the provisions of this section." Id. Similarly, it is a federal crime for a person engaged in the business of betting to knowingly use wire communications to transmit bets interstate. 18 U.S.C. §1084(a). But Congress has decided not to make that conduct illegal if both the transmitter and receiver of such information are located in states that have legalized such betting. Id. §1084(b). In each case, Congress has acted in aid, not in derogation, of state regulatory authority.

Likewise, the combined field of maritime gambling leaves room for state regulation. In fact, Congress initially enacted the Johnson Act "to support the policy of those States which outlaw slot machines and similar gambling devices, by prohibiting use of the channels of interstate or foreign commerce for the shipment of such machines or devices into such States." H.R. Rep. No. 81-2769 (1950). In that supporting role, Congress expressly did not apply 15 U.S.C. §1175 to state territorial waters. By its terms, section 1175 applies only to vessels "within the special maritime and territorial jurisdiction of the United States as defined in section 7 of Title 18." 15 U.S.C. §1175(a). The special maritime jurisdiction of the United States specifically excludes waters subject to the control of state authorities. 18 U.S.C. §7(1) (special maritime jurisdiction includes the high seas and "any other waters within the admiralty and maritime jurisdiction of the United States and out of the jurisdiction of any particular State").

Additionally, by enacting section 1175 Congress extended the reach of state police power beyond state territorial waters: that provision permits states to change the content of federal law with respect to cruises to nowhere. Although the 1992 amendments to the Johnson Act generally permit the use of gambling devices on the high seas, they permit states to reverse course and opt to have cruising to nowhere remain a federal crime. 15 U.S.C. §1175(a)-(b). Cruises to nowhere remain a federal crime if a state "has enacted a statute the terms of which prohibit" the use of gambling devices on such cruises.

Section 1175—which expressly withdraws federal regulation from state territorial waters and permits states to determine the content of federal law outside of those waters—recognizes the vital state regulatory interests in gambling controls. From this we cannot conclude that maritime gambling is a field "in which the federal interest is so dominant that the federal system will be assumed to preclude enforcement of state laws on the same subject." *Hillsborough County v. Automated Med. Labs., Inc.*, 471 U.S. 707, 713 (1985). The criminal regulation of gambling, even gambling taking place within the admiralty and maritime jurisdiction of the United States, is simply not a field over which Congress has sought exclusive regulatory authority and the displacement of state law.

### B.

Nor do we find that South Carolina's laws conflict with the federal statute at issue here. As noted, the plain language, structure, and purpose of section 1175 is completely at odds with preemption. That federal enactment does not even apply to South Carolina's territorial waters—it leaves regulation of those waters to the state. 15 U.S.C. §1175(a); 18 U.S.C. §7(1). This alone leads to the conclusion that state and federal laws are not in conflict. But the statute goes even further. It criminalizes gambling cruises to nowhere outside of a state's territorial waters if a state enacts a law banning them. 15 U.S.C. §1175(b)(2). By permitting states to adjust the contours of federal law, section 1175 augments state authority. In fact, the entire theme of this statute is one of cooperative federalism and respect for dominant state interests. Nothing leads to the conclusion that federal law has supplanted South Carolina's regulatory authority over gambling. . . .

Finally, allowing states to make their own regulatory choices about gambling does not interfere with the purpose of the 1992 amendments. Before the amendments, foreign flag ships were permitted to offer gambling on the high seas while American vessels were forbidden from doing so. By amending the Johnson Act, Congress sought to place all vessels on equal footing. Congress never suggested that it was legislating to remedy an inefficient patchwork of varied state laws. Instead, the amendments sought only to put an end to the discriminatory treatment of United States flag vessels under federal law.

The committee reports and floor statements speak only to this purpose. H.R. Rep. No. 102-357 (1991) ("The clear intent and purpose of this amendment to the Johnson Act is to allow those activities on U.S.-flag vessels to the same extent that they are currently allowed on foreign-flag vessels."); 138 Cong. Rec. H71 (daily ed. Jan. 28, 1992) (statement of Rep. Davis) (same); id. at H70 (statement of Rep. Jones) (The law "will enable our U.S. vessels to operate on a level playing field with foreign flag cruise ships with respect to gambling."). And Congress explicitly recognized that state laws regulating gambling would continue to operate. 138 Cong. Rec. H72 (daily ed. Jan. 28, 1992) (statement of Rep. Lent) ("This bill preserves the right of a coastal State to enact legislation that prohibits gambling on a vessel that operates from a port of that State even if the vessel sails from that port out into international waters and then returns to the same port."). Representative Lent made it clear that federal law was not ousting the authority of states to prohibit and regulate gambling. He noted that "The committee was aware that a number of coastal States do not want gambling on vessels in their waters and this legislation retains the right of States to continue to prohibit gambling." Id.

For all of these reasons, we join those courts that have rejected the argument that 15 U.S.C. §1175 preempts state laws prohibiting gambling and gambling devices. The lifting of federal restrictions on gambling outside state territorial waters does not preempt state gambling prohibitions within those waters. States remain free to regulate gambling within their territorial waters.

## IV.

Casino Ventures suggests that in amending the Johnson Act, Congress prohibited states from exercising their core police powers to ban gambling and gaming devices. We do not agree. States have long regulated in this area. And state primacy here has only been reinforced by congressional enactments, including the one before us, which grant states significant control over the substance of federal criminal laws dealing with gambling. Far from expressing the required "clear and manifest" purpose to displace state authority, Congress has voiced a desire to retain and defer to state choices in this area. Implying preemption here would defeat, not advance, these federal objectives. For this reason, the judgment of the district court is hereby REVERSED.

*NOTES*

1. As noted above, Congress enacted the Johnson Act in 1950 "to support the policy of those States which outlaw slot machines and similar gambling devices, by prohibiting use of the channels of interstate or foreign commerce for the shipment of such machines or devices into such States." Though support for state policies was the ostensible purpose, the Johnson Act created a presumption that slot machines were illegal in every state. Thus, after the Johnson Act, a state that wished to legalize slot machines would need to enact a statute that explicitly authorized their use. Since activity is normally lawful in the absence of a state statute prohibiting it, the Johnson Act had the effect of reversing the legal status quo in states in which there was no existing legal prohibition of slot machines.

2. The 1992 amendment to the Johnson Act authorized "cruises to nowhere" in the United States. For this limited purpose, it also reversed the approach discussed in Note 1 above. The Johnson Act now required a state that desires exemption from the general provisions of the statute to prohibit explicitly the use of gambling on a sea vessel. In the absence of such a state statute, such gaming is now presumably authorized under the 1992 amendments. In other words, the Johnson Act treats the default position of "no statute" differently in the two circumstances. Is this sound policy? Is a statute the best way to express state public policy authorizing gaming? Is it the only way?

3. The district court's opinion would have required the affirmative enactment of a state statute after the 1992 amendments. California,

Hawaii, and New York enacted legislation specifically outlawing and/or regulating such gambling. Is the district court's approach unsound?

4.  The court in *Casino Ventures* suggests that the federal government is neutral as to any value judgment about slot machine gambling, and is merely operating in this instance as an instrument to "augment state authority." Would you agree?

5.  Ultimately, *Casino Ventures* was a case about preemption of state authority. According to a leading constitutional source, "problems arise when the federal legislation does not clearly impose its intended impact on state laws. In those situations, the claim is nevertheless often made that congressional action 'preempts' state authority regarding the same subject matter. The Courts preemption rulings often turn on a determination of congressional intent in the setting of the particular text, history and purposes of the federal legislation involved." KATHLEEN M. SULLIVAN & GERALD GUNTHER, CONSTITUTIONAL LAW 324 (2004). Did the court reach the correct decision in *Casino Ventures*?

6.  Preemption addresses federal legislative power. Similar issues arise with regard to federal judicial power around issues of abstention, as the next case demonstrates.

## JOHNSON v. COLLINS ENTERTAINMENT CO.
### 199 F.3d 710 (4th Cir. 1999)

WILKINSON, Chief Judge

Plaintiffs are habitual gamblers who have sued South Carolina video poker operators as part of an effort to kick their habits. They requested an injunction to prevent the video poker operators from paying out more than $125 daily to a customer at one location. Plaintiffs also sought damages based on alleged violations of the payout limit and other statutes. The district court granted the injunction based on its interpretation of state law and ruled in plaintiffs' favor on a question of state unfair competition law. In doing so, however, the district court improperly interfered with a state regulatory scheme whose design is at the heart of the state's police power. The district court should instead have abstained under the doctrine of *Burford v. Sun Oil Co.*, 319 U.S. 315 (1943). We therefore vacate the injunction and remand this case with directions to dismiss or remand to state court all claims for equitable relief and to stay proceedings on claims for damages pending the resolution by the state courts of disputed questions of state law. We do so in the belief that the resolution of the volatile questions surrounding video poker must be committed above all to the legislative, judicial, and regulatory processes of South Carolina.

I

Video poker has arguably been the most hotly contested issue in South Carolina in recent years. For nearly two centuries, South Carolina law prohibited gambling. This ban did not extend, however, to "coin operated nonpayout machines with a free play feature" so long as the machines did not disburse "money or property" to a player. A 1986 amendment to this provision simply deleted the words "or property."

In 1991, the South Carolina Supreme Court interpreted the amended provision as authorizing cash payouts to players of video gaming machines so long as the money was dispensed by a person and not by a machine. See *State v. Blackmon*, 304 S.C. 270, 403 S.E.2d 660 (S.C. 1991). The ruling encouraged the exponential growth of the video poker industry and the intense debates that have accompanied it. As of March 1999, there were nearly 34,000 reported video poker machines in the state. Over $2.5 billion was deposited into these machines in 1998.

South Carolina has employed a variety of legislative, administrative, and judicial mechanisms to regulate this multi-billion dollar business. These mechanisms constitute an interdependent state network aimed at the comprehensive regulation of video poker.

The South Carolina General Assembly has been engaged in extensive efforts to regulate the video poker industry. For example, in 1993 the legislature enacted the Video Game Machines Act (VGMA), S.C. Code Ann. §§12-21-2770 et seq., to impose licensing requirements and a wide range of other restrictions on the industry. The statute requires detailed quarterly reports on the location, use, and profitability of each video poker machine. See S.C. Code Ann. §12-21-2776(B). The statute also limits the number of machines at a single place or premises to five, see S.C. Code Ann. §12-21-2804(A), and forbids businesses that provide cash payouts for video poker from operating within three hundred feet of municipal schools, playgrounds, and places of worship, see S.C. Code Ann. §12-21-2793. Other provisions deal with everything from the mechanical requirements of machines, see S.C. Code Ann. §12-21-2774, to the permissible hours of machine operation, see S.C. Code Ann. §12-21-2804(E). The statute also prescribes various remedies for violations of its terms. The General Assembly has revisited the problems of video poker regulation frequently since 1993, balancing the revenue gained from licensing and taxation of video poker against the social costs of gambling addiction.

State administrative agencies have also been involved with the regulation of video poker. The South Carolina Department of Revenue (DOR) and State Law Enforcement Division (SLED) share responsibility for enforcement of the state's gaming laws. The DOR and SLED have enforced these laws, inter alia, by conducting on-premise inspections and levying fines against video poker operators for infractions. The General Assembly has also vested the Department of Revenue with the authority to promulgate regulations governing video poker machines and operators.

In 1993, the legislature created the Administrative Law Judge (ALJ) Division, which deals in part with the issues arising from regulation of the video poker industry. Most importantly, the ALJ Division has appellate jurisdiction over DOR license denials and revocations. The ALJ Division hears scores of cases each year involving the interpretation and enforcement of gaming laws.

Finally, the state judiciary has also been an active partner with the legislative and executive branches in forging the landscape of video poker regulation. The state courts are intimately involved in this scheme through the adjudication of private actions and the review of administrative decisions.

## II

The procedural history of this case also underscores its state law nature. Plaintiffs Joan Johnson, et al., claim to be habitual gamblers who have lost money on video poker. Defendants Collins Entertainment Co., et al., comprise a substantial segment of the video poker industry in South Carolina. Plaintiffs filed suit against defendants in state court alleging numerous statutory and common law violations and seeking both injunctive relief and damages.

Plaintiffs claimed that they became addicted to video poker because defendants were offering cash payouts in excess of the maximum amount allowed under South Carolina law. The parties offered competing interpretations of the $125 per customer per day per location limit imposed by S.C. Code Ann. §12-21-2791. Plaintiffs contended that the statute imposes an absolute $125 cap on payouts. Defendants argued that it merely prohibits them from paying out more than $125 above the amount deposited by a player into the machines. Defendants also offered the interpretation that this provision authorizes successive daily payouts of up to $125 for winnings accumulated in one day.

Plaintiffs further claimed that the offering of illegal cash prizes constituted both a "special inducement" to play video poker in violation of S.C. Code Ann. §12-21-2804(B) and an unfair trade practice in violation of the South Carolina Unfair Trade Practices Act (SCUTPA), S.C. Code Ann. §§39-5-10 et seq. (Law. Co-op. 1976). Plaintiffs also asserted federal claims under the Racketeer Influenced Corrupt Organizations (RICO) Act, 18 U.S.C. §§1961-1968 (1994 & Supp. III 1997), based on the alleged underlying state law violations. Defendants have contested all of these claims.

Plaintiffs also raised a number of other claims not directly involved in this appeal but which accentuate the intensely state character of this litigation. For example, plaintiffs sought a declaration that video poker violated the state constitution's prohibition of lotteries. This question was ultimately certified to the Supreme Court of South Carolina, which ruled that video poker was not unconstitutional. See *Johnson v. Collins Entertainment Co.*, 508 S.E.2d 575 (S.C. 1998).

Defendants removed this case to federal court on the basis of the federal RICO claims. In December 1997, plaintiffs moved for a preliminary injunction to prevent defendants from exceeding the $125 daily payout limit. In response, defendants moved to enjoin plaintiffs from entering their premises. The district court denied defendants' request for an injunction in July 1998 and later denied defendants' motion for abstention. Defendants filed this interlocutory appeal, challenging the denial of their motion for an injunction. They also asserted that the district court should abstain from exercising its jurisdiction in this case on the grounds that the case involved difficult questions of state law and that federal judicial involvement would constitute an unwarranted interference with a state regulatory program.

In the meantime, the Attorney General of South Carolina, who had intervened in this action, withdrew from the case except as to the question of whether video poker violates the state constitution's lottery ban. In doing so, he indicated that it was his practice to defer to the DOR on "primarily regulatory" questions of statutory interpretation, including the meaning of the $125 payout limit. The Attorney General further noted that the payout limit statute was ambiguous and susceptible to at least three different interpretations.

Plaintiffs eventually abandoned their pursuit of a preliminary injunction. In February 1999, they instead requested a permanent injunction enforcing an absolute $125 payout limit against eight defendants. Plaintiffs also moved for partial summary judgment on the interpretation of the payout limit and the questions of whether defendants' offering of illegal jackpots constituted special inducements, unfair trade practices, and RICO violations.

In April 1999, the district court entered partial summary judgment for plaintiffs on the interpretation of the $125 payout limit and found that defendants' activities constituted unfair trade practices as a matter of South Carolina law. The district court rendered no decision on the special inducement issue and plaintiffs' RICO claims, instead keeping these matters under advisement.

The district court, citing its "inherent equitable power," also granted the permanent injunction sought by plaintiffs. In doing so, the district court did not claim that any statute expressly authorized it to grant such relief. As part of its injunctive order, the district court imposed on defendants an extensive set of requirements as an "enforcement mechanism." For example, the district court mandated that defendants post a designated "clarifying sign" on each video poker machine. The district court also required defendants to maintain detailed, signed logs containing personal information about each recipient of a video poker payout. The district court imposed numerous other requirements on the eight targeted defendants as well.

Defendants appealed these rulings on the grounds that the district court lacked the authority to issue the injunction, abused its discretion in enjoining defendants, and erred in finding unfair trade practices as a matter of law. Defendants again claimed that the district court should have abstained from entertaining the merits of the action. All appeals were consolidated. Defendants also petitioned this court for a stay of the district court's injunction. We granted the stay because of the serious federalism concerns raised by this case. We now address the issues raised on appeal.

## III

At the heart of the parties' contentions in this case is the doctrine of abstention. Although that doctrine has many different forks and prongs, its central idea has always been one of simple comity. Notwithstanding the overlapping obligations of state and federal courts with regard to both state and federal law, the federal judiciary has always maintained some modicum of respect for state public policies in areas of paramount state concern.

Federal courts should thus "exercise their discretionary power with proper regard for the rightful independence of state governments in carrying out their domestic policy." *Burford*, 319 U.S. at 318. And the federal judiciary should accordingly abstain from deciding cases (1) that present "difficult questions of state law bearing on policy problems of substantial public import whose importance transcends the result in the case then at bar" or (2) whose adjudication in a federal forum "would be disruptive of state efforts to establish a coherent policy with respect to a matter of substantial public concern." *New Orleans Pub. Serv., Inc. v. Council of New Orleans*, 491 U.S. 350, 361 (1989).

The Supreme Court has admonished the federal courts to respect the efforts of state governments to ensure uniform treatment of essentially local problems. Principles of federalism and comity require no less. Basic abstention doctrine requires federal courts to avoid interference with a state's administration of its own affairs. Though "abstention from the exercise of federal jurisdiction is the exception, not the rule," *Colorado River Water Conservation Dist. v. United States*, 424 U.S. 800, 813 (1976), its importance in our system of dual sovereignty cannot be underestimated. It safeguards our federal system from the "delay, misunderstanding of local law, and needless conflict with a state policy" that inevitably results from federal judicial intrusions into areas of core state prerogative.

Plaintiffs contend that abstention is improper in this case. They argue that the district court's actions pose no risk of federal-state friction and do not interfere with state regulation of the video poker industry. Plaintiffs claim that the district court instead properly entertained the merits of this action. We disagree. The exercise of federal equitable discretion in this case supplanted the legislative, administrative, and judicial processes of South Carolina and sought to arbitrate matters of state law and regulatory policy that are best left to resolution by state bodies.

**A**

It is important to note at the outset that the district court ventured into an area where state authority has long been preeminent. The regulation of gambling enterprises lies at the heart of the state's police power. Formulations of that power underscore the state's paramount interest in the health, welfare, safety, and morals of its citizens. The regulation of lotteries, betting, poker, and other games of chance touch all of the above aspects of the quality of life of state citizens. The question of how best to regulate gambling activity is also one to which different states can arrive at different answers based on their different experiences.

State gaming policies reflect a delicate trade-off between the economic boon of increased tax revenue and enhanced employment on the one hand and the risk of moral rot, human exploitation, and political corruption on the other. Put another way, the question is whether the maximization of individual freedom and choice works a wholesale diminution in general social well-being. Each side of this scale embodies the classic subject matter of state prerogative.

In fact, the parties' claims in this case illustrate the high stakes of even the most finely calibrated gaming policy decisions. Plaintiffs on the one hand argue that the conduct of video poker operators warrants strong sanctions for causing the economic and emotional ruin of the lives of many South Carolinians. Defendants on the other hand argue that unfavorable interpretations of state statutes may destroy their businesses and put hundreds of other South Carolinians out of work. The search for proper balance in this police power function is a task presumptively committed to the democratically accountable institutions of a state.

**B**

Given that state policy concerns are paramount, the district court contravened *Burford* principles by attempting to answer disputed questions of state gaming law that so powerfully impact the welfare of South Carolina citizens. Issues of state law and state public policy have dominated this action from day one. Most notably, the parties have contested the meaning of the $125 payout limit in S.C. Code Ann. §12-21-2791. When the district court interpreted this provision, it was necessarily trying to predict how the South Carolina Supreme Court would decide the question. But because this question involved a most basic problem of South Carolina public policy, the state court system should have been permitted the first opportunity to resolve it. . . .

Our conclusion that the district court should have refrained from deciding the state law issues in this case is not altered by plaintiffs' assertion of federal RICO claims. In *Pomponio v. Fauquier County Bd. of Supervisors*, 21 F.3d 1319 (4th Cir. 1994) (en banc), we held that abstention was appropriate where federal constitutional claims asserted by a real estate developer against a county boiled down to questions of state land use law. The developer had alleged that the misconduct of county officials in rejecting his subdivision plan constituted violations of federal due process and equal protection guarantees. But the dispute was essentially about "whether the zoning ordinance was incorrectly construed." We thus observed that "the federal claims [were] really state law claims" because local zoning laws and decisions were the bases of the federal claims.

Plaintiffs' claims depend ultimately on alleged violations of state law for their predicate acts. An examination of their complaint reveals the state law essence of the RICO litigation. Plaintiffs assert that defendants deployed video poker machines that "violate the Constitution, laws and public policies of the State of South Carolina." The complaint then lists a number of state statutes that defendants allegedly violated, including the payout limit and the prohibition of special inducements. . . .

The existence of each of these federal law violations, however, turns on underlying questions of state law. As plaintiffs' complaint shows, their entire theory of liability rests on the premise that defendants have violated statutory provisions governing gambling activity, such as the $125 payout limit. There can be no "false, fraudulent, or illegal" conduct unless plaintiffs first prove the underlying state law violations. Indeed, plaintiffs allege state law fraud claims that depend on asserted violations of several of the same underlying statutes as their federal RICO claims. And as we have noted, the interpretation and application of these statutes is a matter properly left in state hands.

Of course, federal courts decide questions of state law in innumerable contexts. Abstention remains the exception and the exercise of congressionally mandated jurisdiction remains the rule.

C

It is not only the predominance of state law issues affecting state public policy that counsels caution on the part of federal courts. The district court also overreached when it effectively commandeered South Carolina's enforcement efforts in this area of state prerogative. Federal equitable intervention risks the disruption of state efforts to establish a coherent policy with respect to video poker and threatens the creation of a patchwork of inconsistent enforcement efforts.

A variety of state actors have been involved in crafting and implementing the state regulatory scheme at issue. Enforcement decisions rest with state agencies and dispute resolutions rest with state judicial and quasi-judicial officers. As noted in section I, supra, the Department of Revenue and the State Law Enforcement Division have been invested by statute with the authority to enforce state gaming laws. See S.C. Code Ann. §§12-21-10, 23-3-15. The legislature has also specifically charged the DOR with the task of promulgating regulations governing video poker. See S.C. Code Ann. §12-21-2798. The ALJ Division has jurisdiction over many disputes arising from enforcement of video gaming laws, including protests of DOR determinations. See S.C. Code Ann. §§12-60-1320. And the state court system hears cases involving all aspects of video poker brought by both private litigants and state agencies. Each of these institutions must contend with the statutory ambiguities and terms of art, the delicate policy dilemmas, and the resource allocation decisions that pervade this state regulatory program.

In granting the injunction, the district court effectively established parallel federal and state oversight of the South Carolina video poker industry. . . . Though doubtless guided by the best of intentions, the trial court strayed beyond its proper role. Whether even to permit video poker in the first place is a quintessential state decision. And it is certainly for the state regulatory system—and ultimately for the people of South Carolina—to decide how best to implement their state gaming policy and to remedy any violations. Federal equitable forays into such state enforcement schemes risk the creation of confusing, duplicative directions that cause friction and impermissibly transfer power from democratically accountable state officials to life-tenured federal judges. Federalism does not countenance one cook too many stirring the state brew.

A state's interest in maintaining uniform regulation in an area of core state concern has long been a factor counseling abstention. Federal intrusions into state regulatory affairs may lead to "contradictory adjudications by the state and federal courts." . . . VACATED AND REMANDED.

## *NOTES*

1. What laws were the plaintiffs suing to enforce? Would the federal court's willingness to hear the action have undermined state policy decisions in this case? Or would it have furthered them? The court was working to give existing state laws effect in *Casino Ventures*. Why not here? Wouldn't the federal court's enforcement of the statute "augment state authority" as the Johnson Act did in *Casino Ventures*? Can the non-preemption finding in *Casino Ventures* be justified in the same way as the abstention holding in *Johnson*?

2. Now compare *Johnson v. Collins Entertainment* to the *Casino Ventures* case through a different lens. *Casino Ventures* looked at the federal statutes at issue and held that they did not preempt state gambling laws. Preemption is thought to work only in one direction. The Constitution's Supremacy Clause means that federal law can preempt state law. State law, however, can never preempt federal law. In *Johnson*, the federal court seems to be ruling that the existence of a comprehensive state statutory and regulatory scheme has occupied the field and preempted a federal cause of action. Is such a holding sound?

3. The Supreme Court has found *Burford* abstention appropriate only in two cases in its entire history. Both cases involved the actions of public utility commissions in which federal court review of a "complex [local] regulatory scheme" would "disrupt the State's attempt to ensure uniformity in the treatment of an essentially local problem." *New Orleans Pub. Serv., Inc. v. New Orleans City Council*, 491 U.S. 350, 362-64 (1989).

4.  In section III.B of *Johnson*, the court suggested that the federal court should abstain because the matters at issue were fundamentally state law questions. Many federal criminal gambling statutes address conduct only if it is illegal under state law in the state in which the action arose. See, for example, the Johnson Act discussed in *Casino Ventures*. If state law is ambiguous as alleged in *Johnson*, should the federal courts abstain from hearing such federal prosecutions on the same basis?
5.  When the appellate court says that the trial court was guided by "the best of intentions," to what intentions do you think the appeals court was referring? Also, why did the state Attorney General withdraw from the case? Couldn't such an official serve a key role in guiding a federal court as to how to be respectful of state public policy?
6.  What is the appropriate order of government to deal with the problems presented in this case? Is compulsive gambling a national issue or a state issue? Can this case be reconciled with *Champion v. Ames*?

### NOTE ON THE PROFESSIONAL & AMATEUR SPORTS PROTECTION ACT OF 1992

One federal statute takes a decidedly interventionist approach to gambling. In 1992, Congress enacted a law called the Professional and Amateur Sports Protection Act, codified at 28 U.S.C. §§3701-04. PASPA makes it unlawful for state governments to operate or authorize "a lottery, sweepstakes, or other betting, gambling, or wagering scheme" based on "competitive games in which amateur or professional athletes participate, or are intended to participate, or on one or more performances of such athletes in such games." In PASPA, Congress grandfathered jurisdictions in which sports betting was already occurring. PASPA is thus fairly unique in that it privileges certain states against others, raising even more curious federalism concerns. PASPA can be enforced by the Attorney General or an affected sports organization, through an injunction in federal court.

Led by Senator Charles Grassley, several Senators opposed the bill. In a Senate Committee Report on the bill, the minority views of the Committee were expressed as follows:

> The majority attempts to argue that this legislation is warranted because "sports gambling is a national problem" and because the "moral erosion it produces cannot be limited geographically." But these arguments can be made with respect to any form of wagering and many

other State revenue raising programs. Thus, this legislation would set the dangerous precedent that the Federal Government can prohibit any State revenue raising program, under the guise of "interstate commerce," at the behest of any special interest. Moreover, the legitimate concerns regarding sports wagering can be addressed to States which are fully capable of and even better equipped to consider such matters.

The majority also attempts to establish that this legislation is consistent with existing Federal law. Nothing could be further from the truth. The Federal Government has never sought to regulate purely intrastate wagering activities. Indeed, this is how the State of Nevada, which would be exempted from this legislation, has created a lawful $1.8 billion State-licensed sports wagering industry. This legislation would prohibit purely intrastate activities. The Federal Government also has never authorized private parties to enforce such restrictions against the States. This legislation would do so. . . .

Perhaps even more troubling, this legislation would blatantly discriminate between the States. Under S. 474, Nevada, Oregon, and Delaware would be grandfathered. Thus, these three States would be granted a Federal monopoly on lawful sports wagering to the exclusion of the other 47 States.

See S. Rep. No. 102-248, 102nd Cong., 1st Sess. 1991, 1992 U.S.C.C.A.N. 3553.

## NOTES

1.  Senator Grassley's view that PASPA burdens the ability of a state to raise revenue from such activity is certainly true. Is the burden justified? Is PASPA constitutional?
2.  In a passage not reproduced here, Senator Grassley quotes the Department of Justice as finding it "particularly troubling" that the law "would permit enforcement of its provisions by sports leagues." Why is this "particularly troubling"?
3.  Next, consider a judicial opinion that addresses the benefits and burdens of an anti-gambling policy somewhat more directly.

## GREATER NEW ORLEANS BROADCASTING ASS'N v. UNITED STATES

### 527 U.S. 173 (1999)

Justice Stevens delivered the opinion of the Court.

Federal law prohibits some, but by no means all, broadcast advertising of lotteries and casino gambling. In *United States v. Edge Broadcasting Co.*, 509 U.S. 418 (1993), we upheld the constitutionality of 18

U.S.C. §1304 as applied to broadcast advertising of Virginia's lottery by a radio station located in North Carolina, where no such lottery was authorized. Today we hold that §1304 may not be applied to advertisements of private casino gambling that are broadcast by radio or television stations located in Louisiana, where such gambling is legal.

I

Through most of the 19th and the first half of the 20th centuries, Congress adhered to a policy that not only discouraged the operation of lotteries and similar schemes, but forbade the dissemination of information concerning such enterprises by use of the mails, even when the lottery in question was chartered by a state legislature. Consistent with this Court's earlier view that commercial advertising was unprotected by the First Amendment, see *Valentine v. Chrestensen*, 316 U.S. 52, 54 (1942), we found that the notion that "lotteries . . . are supposed to have a demoralizing influence upon the people" provided sufficient justification for excluding circulars concerning such enterprises from the federal postal system, *Ex parte Jackson*, 96 U.S. 727, 736-737 (1878). We likewise deferred to congressional judgment in upholding the similar exclusion for newspapers that contained either lottery advertisements or prize lists. . . .

Congress extended its restrictions on lottery-related information to broadcasting as communications technology made that practice both possible and profitable. It enacted the statute at issue in this case as §316 of the Communications Act of 1934, 48 Stat. 1088. Now codified at 18 U.S.C. §1304 ("Broadcasting lottery information"), the statute prohibits radio and television broadcasting, by any station for which a license is required, of [any advertisement for a "lottery, gift enterprise or similar scheme," offering prizes based on chance]. . . .

Responding to the growing popularity of state-run lotteries, in 1975 Congress enacted the provision that gave rise to our decision in Edge, 509 U.S., at 422-423[.] With subsequent modifications, that amendment now exempts advertisements of state-conducted lotteries from the nationwide postal restrictions in §§1301 and 1302, and from the broadcast restriction in §1304, when "broadcast by a radio or television station licensed to a location in . . . a State which conducts such a lottery." The §1304 broadcast restriction remained in place, however, for stations licensed in States that do not conduct lotteries. In *Edge*, we held that this remaining restriction on broadcasts from nonlottery States, such as North Carolina, supported the "laws against gambling" in those jurisdictions and properly advanced the "congressional policy of balancing the interests of lottery and nonlottery States." 509 U.S., at 428.

In 1988, Congress enacted two additional statutes that significantly curtailed the coverage of §1304. First, the Indian Gaming Regulatory Act (IGRA), 102 Stat. 2467, 25 U.S.C. §2701 et seq., authorized Native American tribes to conduct various forms of gambling—including casino gambling—pursuant to tribal-state compacts if the State permits such gambling "for any purpose by any person, organization, or entity." The IGRA also exempted "any gaming conducted by an Indian tribe pursuant to" the Act from both the postal and transportation restrictions in 18 U.S.C. §§1301-1302, and the broadcast restriction in §1304. Second, the Charity Games Advertising Clarification Act of 1988, 18 U.S.C. §1307(a)(2), extended the exemption from §§1301-1304 for state-run lotteries to include any other lottery, gift enterprise, or similar scheme—not prohibited by the law of the State in which it operates—when conducted by [non-profits, government agencies, or as ancillary activities to commercial organizations]. . . .

Thus, unlike the uniform federal antigambling policy that prevailed in 1934 when 18 U.S.C. §1304 was enacted, federal statutes now accommodate both progambling and antigambling segments of the national polity.

## II

Petitioners . . . operate FCC-licensed radio and television stations in the New Orleans metropolitan area. But for the threat of sanctions pursuant to §1304 and the FCC's companion regulation, petitioners would broadcast promotional advertisements for gaming available at private, for-profit casinos that are lawful and regulated in both Louisiana and neighboring Mississippi. According to an FCC official, however, "[u]nder appropriate conditions, some broadcast signals from Louisiana broadcasting stations may be heard in neighboring states including Texas and Arkansas," where private casino gambling is unlawful. [Petitioners challenge §1304 on First Amendment grounds.]

## III

In a number of cases involving restrictions on speech that is "commercial" in nature, we have employed *Central Hudson*'s four-part test to resolve First Amendment challenges:

> "At the outset, we must determine whether the expression is protected by the First Amendment. For commercial speech to come within that

provision, it at least must concern lawful activity and not be misleading. Next, we ask whether the asserted governmental interest is substantial. If both inquiries yield positive answers, we must determine whether the regulation directly advances the governmental interest asserted, and whether it is not more extensive than is necessary to serve that interest." 447 U.S., at 566.

In this analysis, the Government bears the burden of identifying a substantial interest and justifying the challenged restriction. The four parts of the *Central Hudson* test are not entirely discrete. All are important and, to a certain extent, interrelated: Each raises a relevant question that may not be dispositive to the First Amendment inquiry, but the answer to which may inform a judgment concerning the other three. . . .


## IV


All parties to this case agree that the messages petitioners wish to broadcast constitute commercial speech, and that these broadcasts would satisfy the first part of the *Central Hudson* test: Their content is not misleading and concerns lawful activities, i.e., private casino gambling in Louisiana and Mississippi. As well, the proposed commercial messages would convey information . . . about an activity that is the subject of intense public debate in many communities. In addition, petitioners' broadcasts presumably would disseminate accurate information as to the operation of market competitors, such as pay-out ratios, which can benefit listeners by informing their consumption choices and fostering price competition. . . .

The second part of the *Central Hudson* test asks whether the asserted governmental interest served by the speech restriction is substantial. The Solicitor General identifies two such interests: (1) reducing the social costs associated with "gambling" or "casino gambling," and (2) assisting States that "restrict gambling" or "prohibit casino gambling" within their own borders. Underlying Congress' statutory scheme, the Solicitor General contends, is the judgment that gambling contributes to corruption and organized crime; underwrites bribery, narcotics trafficking, and other illegal conduct; imposes a regressive tax on the poor; and "offers a false but sometimes irresistible hope of financial advancement." With respect to casino gambling, the Solicitor General states that many of the associated social costs stem from "pathological" or "compulsive" gambling by approximately 3 million Americans, whose behavior is primarily associated with "continuous play" games, such as slot machines. He also observes that compulsive gambling has grown along with the expansion of legalized gambling nationwide, leading to billions of dollars in economic costs; injury and loss to these gamblers as well as their families, communities, and government; and street, white-collar, and organized crime.

We can accept the characterization of these two interests as "substantial," but that conclusion is by no means self-evident. No one seriously doubts that the Federal Government may assert a legitimate and substantial interest in alleviating the societal ills recited above, or in assisting like-minded States to do the same. But in the judgment of both the Congress and many state legislatures, the social costs that support the suppression of gambling are offset, and sometimes outweighed, by countervailing policy considerations, primarily in the form of economic benefits. . . . That Congress has generally exempted state-run lotteries and casinos from federal gambling legislation reflects a decision to defer to, and even promote, differing gambling policies in different States. . . . Whatever its character in 1934 when §1304 was adopted, the federal policy of discouraging gambling in general, and casino gambling in particular, is now decidedly equivocal.

Of course, it is not our function to weigh the policy arguments on either side of the nationwide debate over whether and to what extent casino and other forms of gambling should be legalized. . . . But we cannot ignore Congress' unwillingness to adopt a single national policy that consistently endorses either interest asserted by the Solicitor General. Even though the Government has identified substantial interests, when we consider both their quality and the information sought to be suppressed, the crosscurrents in the scope and application of §1304 become more difficult for the Government to defend.

## V

The third part of the *Central Hudson* test asks whether the speech restriction directly and materially advances the asserted governmental interest. . . . The fourth part of the test complements the direct-advancement inquiry of the third, asking whether the speech restriction is not more extensive than necessary to serve the interests that support it. The Government . . . must demonstrate narrow tailoring of the challenged regulation to the asserted interest—"a fit that is not necessarily perfect, but reasonable; that represents not necessarily the single best disposition but one whose scope is in proportion to the interest served." . . .

As applied to petitioners' case, §1304 cannot satisfy these standards. With regard to the first asserted interest—alleviating the social costs of casino gambling by limiting demand—the Government contends that its broadcasting restrictions directly advance that interest because "promotional" broadcast advertising concerning casino gambling increases demand for such gambling, which in turn increases the amount of casino gambling that produces those social costs. Additionally, the Government believes that compulsive gamblers are especially susceptible to the pervasiveness and potency of broadcast advertising. Assuming the accuracy of this causal chain, it does not necessarily follow that the Government's speech ban has directly and materially furthered the asserted interest. While it is no doubt fair to assume that more advertising would have some impact on overall demand for gambling, it is also reasonable to assume that much of that advertising would merely channel gamblers to one casino rather than another. More important, any measure of the effectiveness of the Government's attempt to minimize the social costs of gambling cannot ignore Congress' simultaneous encouragement of tribal casino gambling, which may well be growing at a rate exceeding any increase in gambling or compulsive gambling that private casino advertising could produce. . . .

We need not resolve the question whether any lack of evidence in the record fails to satisfy the standard of proof under *Central Hudson*, however, because the flaw in the Government's case is more fundamental: The operation of §1304 and its attendant regulatory regime is so pierced by exemptions and inconsistencies that the Government cannot hope to exonerate it. Under current law, a broadcaster may not carry advertising about privately operated commercial casino gambling, regardless of the location of the station or the casino. On the other hand, advertisements for tribal casino gambling authorized by state compacts—whether operated by the tribe or by a private party pursuant to a management contract—are subject to no such broadcast ban, even if the broadcaster is located in, or broadcasts to, a jurisdiction with the strictest of antigambling policies. . . .

Even putting aside the broadcast exemptions for arguably distinguishable sorts of gambling that might also give rise to social costs about which the Federal Government is concerned—such as state lotteries and pari-mutuel betting on horse and dog races—the Government presents no convincing reason for pegging its speech ban to the identity of the owners or operators of the advertised casinos. The Government cites revenue needs of States and tribes that conduct casino gambling, and notes that net revenues generated by the tribal casinos are dedicated to the welfare of the tribes and their members. Yet the Government admits that tribal casinos offer precisely the same types of gambling as private casinos. Further, the Solicitor General does not maintain that government-operated casino gaming is any different, that States cannot derive revenue from taxing private casinos, or that any one class of casino operators is likely to advertise in a meaningfully distinct manner from the others. The Government's suggestion that Indian casinos are too isolated to warrant attention is belied by a quick review of tribal geography and the Government's own evidence regarding the financial success of tribal gaming. If distance were determinative, Las Vegas might have remained a relatively small community, or simply disappeared like a desert mirage.

Ironically, the most significant difference identified by the Government between tribal and other classes of casino gambling is that the former is "heavily regulated." If such direct regulation provides a basis for believing that the social costs of gambling in tribal casinos are sufficiently mitigated to make their advertising tolerable, one would have thought that Congress might have at least experimented with comparable regulation before abridging the speech rights of federally unregulated casinos. . . . There surely are practical and nonspeech-related forms of regulation—including a prohibition or supervision of gambling on credit; limitations on the use of cash machines on casino premises; controls on admissions; pot or betting limits; location restrictions; and licensing requirements—that could more directly and effectively alleviate some of the social costs of casino gambling. . . .

It is well settled that the First Amendment mandates closer scrutiny of government restrictions on speech than of its regulation of commerce alone. And to the extent that the purpose and operation of federal law distinguishes among information about tribal, governmental, and private casinos based on the identity of their owners or operators, the Government presents no sound reason why such lines bear any meaningful relationship to the particular interest asserted: minimizing casino gambling and its social costs by way of a (partial) broadcast ban.

## VI

Accordingly, respondents cannot overcome the presumption that the speaker and the audience, not the Government, should be left to assess the value of accurate and non-misleading information about lawful conduct. Had the Federal Government adopted a more coherent policy, or accommodated the rights of speakers in States that have legalized the underlying conduct, this might be a different case. But [this broadcast prohibition] violates the First Amendment.

Justice THOMAS, concurring in the judgment.

I continue to adhere to my view that "[i]n cases such as this, in which the government's asserted interest is to keep legal users of a product or service ignorant in order to manipulate their choices in the marketplace," the *Central Hudson* test should not be applied because "such an 'interest' is per se illegitimate and can no more justify regulation of 'commercial speech' than it can justify regulation of 'noncommercial' speech." Accordingly, I concur only in the judgment.

*NOTES*

1. *Greater New Orleans Broadcasting* and *Champion v. Ames* address different legal questions entirely, but both cases are much more willing to discuss the important value judgments associated with gambling than the two intervening opinions by Judge Wilkinson. Does the federal government have a proper role in making such value judgments? What is the federal interest in this context? Is it appropriate for the federal government to have an interest in this subject matter that is independent and different than that of states?

2. The Supreme Court seems to hold that gambling is legitimate conduct and, as such, can be the subject of protected speech. Did the federal government overreach in attempting to enforce its regulations in this context? What federal interest(s) may have motivated the government?

## B. THE FEDERAL ROLE IN CONTEXT

During the last 120 years, the federal government has enacted numerous criminal statutes designed to curb gambling. This section examines some of those statutes. First, however, it describes a rare, unsuccessful effort by the federal government to prohibit gambling under the guise of taxation and regulation.

### MARCHETTI v. UNITED STATES
#### 390 U.S. 39 (1968)

Mr. Justice HARLAN delivered the opinion of the Court.

Petitioner was convicted in the United States District Court for the District of Connecticut under two indictments which charged violations of the federal wagering tax statutes. The first indictment averred that petitioner and others conspired to evade payment of the anuual occupational tax imposed by 26 U.S.C. §4411. The second indictment consisted of two counts: the first alleged a willful failure to pay the occupational tax, and the second a willful failure to register, as required by 26 U.S.C. §4412, before engaging in the business of accepting wagers. . . .

The issue before us is not whether the United States may tax activities which a State or Congress has declared unlawful. The Court has repeatedly indicated that the unlawfulness of an activity does not prevent its taxation, and nothing that follows is intended to limit or diminish the vitality of those cases. The issue is instead whether the methods employed by Congress in the federal wagering tax statutes are, in this situation, consistent with the limitations created by the privilege against self-incrimination guaranteed by the Fifth Amendment.

We must for this purpose first examine the implications of these statutory provisions. . . . Wagering and its ancillary activities are very widely prohibited under both federal and state law. [In addition to federal laws, the] laws of every State, except Nevada, include broad prohibitions against gambling, wagering, and associated activities. . . . By any standard, in Connecticut and throughout the United States, wagering is "an area permeated with criminal statutes," and those engaged in wagering are a group "inherently suspect of criminal activities." [Moreover, information] obtained as a consequence of the federal wagering tax laws is readily available to assist the efforts of state and federal authorities to enforce these penalties.

In these circumstances, it can scarcely be denied that the obligations to register and to pay the occupational tax created for petitioner "real and appreciable," and not merely "imaginary and unsubstantial," hazards of self-incrimination. Petitioner was confronted by a comprehensive system of federal and state prohibitions against wagering activities; he was required, on pain of criminal prosecution, to provide information which he might reasonably suppose would be available to prosecuting authorities, and which would surely prove a significant "link in a chain" of evidence tending to establish his guilt. . . .

The Court held in *Lewis* [*v. United States*, 348 U.S. 419 (1955)] that the registration and occupational tax requirements do not infringe the constitutional privilege because they do not compel self-incrimination, but merely impose on the gambler the initial choice of whether he wishes at the cost of his constitutional privilege, to commence wagering activities. The Court reasoned that even if the required disclosures might prove incriminating, the gambler need not register or pay the occupational tax if only he elects to cease, or never to begin, gambling. There is, the Court said, "no constitutional right to gamble."

We find this reasoning no longer persuasive. The question is not whether petitioner holds a "right" to violate state law, but whether, having done so, he may be compelled to give evidence against himself. . . . We cannot agree that the constitutional privilege is meaningfully waived merely because those "inherently suspect of criminal activities" have been commanded either to cease wagering or to provide information incriminating to themselves, and have ultimately elected to do neither.

[W]e can only conclude, under the wagering tax system as presently written, that petitioner properly asserted the privilege against self-incrimination, and that his assertion should have provided a complete defense to this prosecution. This defense should have reached both the substantive counts for failure to register and to pay the occupational tax, and the count for conspiracy to evade payment of the tax. We emphasize that we do not hold that these wagering tax provisions are as such constitutionally impermissible; we hold only that those who properly assert the constitutional privilege as to these provisions may not be criminally punished for failure to comply with their requirements. [REVERSED.]

### NOTES

It was, of course, a tax statute that successfully enabled the federal government to prosecute Al Capone. *See United States v. Capone*, 93 F.2d 840 (7th Cir. 1937). In that case, the court held that the failure to file a return is "distinct and separate" from the underlying claim of a willful evasion of tax. Is *Capone* still good law after *Marchetti*?

## 1.   The Federal Prohibition of Illegal Gambling Businesses

One statute that has figured prominently in gambling prosecutions is Section 1955 of the federal criminal code, discussed obliquely in *United States v. Wall*, previously. Section 1955 was enacted as part of the Organized Crime Control Act of 1970. That statute, which also produced the Racketeer Influenced and Corrupt Organizations (RICO) provisions (18 U.S.C. §§1961-68), devoted one title exclusively to gambling in an effort to curb the use of gambling as a key source of revenue for organized crime.

## UNITED STATES v. BOX

### 530 F.2d 1258 (5th Cir. 1976)

GOLDBERG, Circuit Judge.

Henry Floyd "Red" Box was convicted by a jury of violating 18 U.S.C. §1955, the federal antigambling statute.* On appeal, Box argues that the evidence was insufficient to support this verdict. We agree and therefore reverse the conviction.

Federal agents conducted an extensive investigation of several bookmaking operations in the Shreveport-Bossier City area during the 1973 football season, culminating in simultaneous raids on the last day of the season. A one-count indictment filed on April 25, 1974, charged appellant Box and ten other persons with the operation of an illegal gambling business in violation of 18 U.S.C. §1955. The indictment named three unindicted principals as having been involved in the same illegal gambling business. One of the defendants was granted a continuance and severance, due to the death of his counsel. Six others entered pleas of nolo contendere or guilty prior to trial. Trial of the four remaining defendants began on September 30, 1974. The guilty plea of one of these was accepted on October 4, 1974. Later the same day the jury returned a verdict of guilty as to Box and the other two. Only Box has appealed.

Our review of the evidence and application of the law in this case require an understanding of the general nature of a bookmaking

---

* 18 U.S.C. §1955 provides in part as follows:

(a) Whoever conducts, finances, manages, supervises, directs, or owns all or part of an illegal gambling business shall be fined not more than $20,000 or imprisoned not more than five years, or both.
(b) As used in this section—
(1) "illegal gambling business" means a gambling business which—
(i) is a violation of the law of a State or political subdivision in which it is conducted;
(ii) involves five or more persons who conduct, finance, manage, supervise, direct, or own all or part of such business; and
(iii) has been or remains in substantially continuous operation for a period in excess of thirty days or has a gross revenue of $2,000 in any single day.
(2) "gambling" includes but is not limited to pool-selling, bookmaking, maintaining slot machines, roulette wheels or dice tables, and conducting lotteries, policy, bolita or numbers games, or selling chances therein.

The relevant state law, Louisiana Revised Statutes, §14:90, provides as follows: Gambling is the intentional conducting, or directly assisting in the conducting, as a business, of any game, contest, lottery, or contrivance whereby a person risks the loss of anything of value in order to realize a profit. Whoever commits the crime of gambling shall be fined not more than five hundred dollars, or imprisoned for not more than six months, or both.

operation, and so we preface our consideration of the issues here with a very brief summary on that subject.

## The Nature of a Bookmaking Operation

This section might be subtitled, "How to Succeed in Gambling Without Really Gambling," because a successful bookmaker makes his profit not from winning bets, but rather from collecting a certain percentage of the amount bet that losing bettors are required to pay for the privilege of betting. This percentage, 10% in the Shreveport area, is called "juice" or "viggerish," and its effect is to require a bettor to risk $110 in an attempt to win $100. So that betting odds can remain even on each game, a bookmaker normally has a "line" on each game on which he is taking bets, one team will be favored by a certain number of points, called the "point spread."

In an ideal situation, a bookmaker would have bets from bettors exactly balanced on each contest, so that no matter which team "wins" (read: beats the point spread), the bookmaker is assured a definite percentage of the amount bet. That is, he would collect 110% of the amount he would be required to pay. With a multitude of bets each week, this ideal of perfectly balanced books cannot be achieved. When the bets placed with a bookmaker on a certain contest become very unbalanced on one side, however, there are certain measures the bookmaker might take to lessen the incumbent risk.[4] He can refuse to take further bets on that side, hoping enough bets will be placed on the other side to effect some rough balance. Alternatively, he can adjust his "line" on the contest, thus making the underbet side more attractive.[5]

Another common solution to the bookmaker's problem of grossly unbalanced bets on a game is the "lay off" bet. By this device, a book-maker whose customers had bet $10,000 on Dallas +6 and only $6000 on Pittsburg -6 would himself seek to make a $4000 bet on Dallas +6 with another individual. This bet would have the effect of "laying off" $4000 of the $10,000 the bookmaker's customers had bet on Dallas,

---

4. The ever-present possibility that the individual in the adjacent booth of the restaurant is Agent Beinner, see infra, prevents this risk minimizing enterprise from becoming tediously dull.

5. The adjustment of line is apparently disfavored as a solution, because it may result in two local bookmakers offering a significantly different point spread on an event. This would offer local bettors an opportunity for a "middle"—two bets placed on different teams with two bookmakers which together could not lose more than 10% of one of the bets, and, if the actual point difference were in the middle, might both be won. Avoiding possibilities for "middles" is one reason for the constant exchange of line information among bookmakers.

leaving the bookmaker in the net position of having $6000 bet with him on each side. Normally, the bookmaker would look to another bookmaker to make this bet, and would be required to give up the same favorable 11 to 10 odds which he had received from the Dallas bettors. Indeed, several cases dealing with §1955 have *in dicta* defined a lay off bet as a "bet between bookmakers." It seems clear, however, that the individual accepting a lay off bet from a book-maker need not be another bookmaker. That individual could be part of a professional "lay off" operation, an organization dealing only with bookmakers rather than with retail customers, and having sufficient capital so that risk-taking at 11 to 10 odds posed little problem. On the other hand, the individual could be a mere bettor who wanted to bet $4000 on Dallas +6, but was told by his book-maker that no more such bets were being taken and was invited by the bookmaker to accept instead a wager in which the bettor received 11 to 10 odds for agreeing to bet on Pittsburgh. The point of all this is that a "lay off" bet should be defined solely in relation to the occupation and the purpose of the person making the bet—the occupation and motives of the person accepting the bet are irrelevant to the definition.

We do not warrant the foregoing as constituting all the structural information a lay person (as distinct from a lay off person) would need to organize his or her own business, but we think it sufficient for our purposes, and we turn now to the case before us.

### THE EVIDENCE RELATING TO BOX

During this five day trial, twenty-one witnesses testified and several kilograms of evidence were introduced. The testimony of the only four witnesses who had any knowledge concerning Box may be sum-marized as follows:

F.B.I. Agent Beinner testified that Lombardino, a bookmaker, vis-ited the Guys & Dolls Billiard Parlor, an establishment owned by Box, on three separate Tuesdays during the 1973 football season. Beinner believed Tuesday to be "payoff day" in the bookmaking operations he had been investigating. Beinner had obtained and executed search warrants on the homes or places of business of eight of the defen-dants, but had been unsuccessful in his attempt to obtain a warrant on the home and place of business of Box. Beinner's principal informant, whose information was the basis for the search warrant affidavit, described the other defendants who were named in the affidavit as "bookmakers" and described Box only as a "bettor." It was through the testimony of Agent Beinner that the government introduced the telephone toll records, discussed below.

Messina, a bookmaker who had been granted immunity by the government in return for his testimony, testified that he himself had never "laid off" bets to Box, but that he had personal knowledge that Cook had done so. Cook, a bookmaker also given immunity, testified that he had occasionally "laid off" bets with Box and with several of the other defendants. Cook explained that when he lost such a bet to Box or one of the others, he would pay the winner an extra 10% in excess of the amount bet. Cook testified that Box, as a customer, also placed bets with Cook in which Cook received this 10% advantage. Cook did not consider Box a bookmaker and knew of no one who did. He related that Box had been free to take or reject bets offered by Cook, and he described Box only as a bettor.

Stewart, a bookmaker, testified that Box was one of his customers, i.e., a bettor. No one asked Stewart the direct question, "Is Box a bookmaker?", but the prosecutor asked that question of Stewart concerning every other defendant remaining on trial when Stewart testified, and received an affirmative answer in each case. Stewart testified that Box placed bets with him, and that he (Stewart) placed bets for Box with other bookmakers. It was through Stewart that the betting slip testimony was introduced. Stewart testified that he made bets with two other bookmakers in which he gave the others 11 to 10 odds—some of these were "lay off" bets, and some were bets Stewart made because he liked the team. Stewart did not testify that he ever made such bets with Box.

The two items of documentary evidence which related to Box were as follows:

The Telephone Toll Records. No wiretaps or pen registers were used in this case, but the Government introduced at trial several long distance telephone records, including those of the telephone at Box's house and the telephone at Guys & Dolls, Box's establishment. These records showed that during the period of the investigation (autumn, 1973), 20 calls were made from Box's home and 223 calls were made from Guys & Dolls to one Price, a Baton Rouge bookmaker.

The Betting Slips. The simultaneous raids conducted on the last day of the 1973 football season yielded, inter alia, large numbers of betting slips which had been used in the Stewart operation. Most of these slips were marked in a similar simple manner, e.g., G.B. +14 $200 (translated, the bettor had wagered $200 that the score of Green Bay plus fourteen points would be greater than that of Green Bay's opponent). In the lower right hand corner a name, a set of initials, or a number would appear, indicating the individual making the bet. Finally, an indication of the result was added, e.g., "+200" (the bettor won), or "-220" (the bettor lost and was required to pay the additional 10%).

A smaller number of these slips were marked in a second, distinct, fashion, e.g., G.B. +14 $330/300. On these, the results would be recorded as +330 or -300. The testimony of Stewart on this point was quite confused, but it could be inferred that the slips marked in this second fashion represented bets in which he was giving 11 to 10 odds to the person with whom he was betting. Of the five individuals whose names or initials appeared on Stewart's slips marked in this second fashion, four were clearly bookmakers. The fifth was Box. The seized slips represented about $230,000 of Stewart bets and approximately $3800 of this amount was comprised of slips labeled "Box" and marked "330/300", " 550/500", or the like.

### Was Box a Bookmaker?

In reviewing the evidence upon which the jury based its verdict of guilty, we of course examine the evidence in the light most favorable to the government. When the conviction is based upon circumstantial evidence, our question becomes whether the jury could reasonably conclude that the evidence excluded all reasonable hypotheses of innocence.

If we were to find that the jury could reasonably conclude that Box was a bookmaker (engaged in a business with the other defendants), our analytical task would be at an end, for the statute in express terms covers bookmakers. Even viewing the evidence most favorably to the Government, however, we are convinced that the jury could not reasonably reach such a conclusion. This evidence must be regarded as consistent with the hypothesis that Box was not a bookmaker.

The only direct testimony on this matter clearly categorizes Box as a bettor rather than a bookmaker. Of course, the jury might not have credited this testimony, although we note that Cook and Stewart had no hesitation in labeling the other defendants as "bookmakers." The fact remains that there is no evidence in this record upon which an opposite conclusion, i.e., that Box was a bookmaker, could be based. Bookmakers have customers. The names of over 150 bettors were seized during the raids, numerous bettors were interviewed by the FBI, and bettors who were customers of each of the other defendants on trial testified, but no evidence was introduced relating to any "customers" Box might have.

The testimony of Cook and the betting slips of Stewart indicate that Box on occasion accepted "lay off" bets from two bookmakers.

The Government argues that since a lay off bet must be defined as a bet between two bookmakers, Box was a bookmaker simply because he accepted lay off bets. As explained above, we reject the premise of this argument—a lay off bet is one placed by a bookmaker, but the individual accepting the bet need not be a bookmaker.

An additional characteristic of a bookmaker is that she distributes a "line." There is no testimony that Box ever distributed a line, either to customers or to bookmakers. Finally, we note the calls made from Box's telephones to Price. Assuming the jury could conclude that Box himself made all 223 calls to Price from the Guys & Dolls phone, it cannot be said that this number of calls in that direction is inconsistent with the hypothesis that Box was merely a heavy bettor, placing bets with Price.

### §1955 AND NONBOOKMAKERS

Having established that Box cannot be labeled a bookmaker, we have not yet shown him to be within an unassailable hypothesis of innocence, because §1955 clearly was meant to proscribe some bookmaking-related activities of individuals who were not themselves bookmakers. The legislative history indicates that §1955

> applies generally to persons who participate in the ownership, management, or conduct of an illegal gambling business. The term "conducts" refers both to high level bosses and street level employees. See H.R. Rep. No. 1549, 91st Cong., 2d Sess. (1970).

This reflects an intent to reach employees of large bookmaking operations, and that intent has been followed in cases affirming §1955 convictions of runners, telephone clerks, salesmen, and watchmen. On the other hand, individuals who are only bettors or customers of bookmakers clearly are not within the scope of the statute. The case before us cannot be fit easily into either of these two categories. No evidence supports the theory that Box was an employee of other bookmakers; yet, Box's acceptance of lay off bets arguably makes him more important to the operation of a bookmaking business than would be a mere customer. Our question, then, is in what circumstances can an individual who accepted lay off bets from bookmakers be convicted under §1955? The language of the statute does not resolve this, so we turn again to the legislative history.

Clearly, the dominant concern motivating Congress to enact §1955 was that large-scale gambling operations in this country have been closely intertwined with large-scale organized crime, and indeed may have provided the bulk of the capital needed to finance the operations of organized crime. The target of the statute was large-scale gambling operations—local "mom and pop" bookmaking operations were to be left to state law. In this connection, the requirements of dollar volume ($2000 gross on any day) or duration (30 days or more), and number of participants (5), were drafted into the legislation. These requirements are such that relative small-fry can conceivably be ensnared in the statutory strictures, but apparently Congress was of the opinion that the size of gambling operations was often much larger than could be proved, and that law enforcement officials needed some flexibility in order effectively to combat the large scale operations.

There are indications in the legislative history of a concern that one way in which large-scale organized crime profited from bookmaking operations was to act as a regular market for lay off bets from local bookmakers. Remarks of supporters of the bill demonstrate that the Congress was aware of the general function of lay off betting. For example, Senator McClellan stated: . . . (describing a lottery operation) The gambler thus seldom gambles. In addition he hedges his bet by a complicated layoff system. . . . (A bookmaker) has at least the virtue of exploiting primarily those who can afford it. Yet he seldom gambles either. He gives track odds or less without track expenses, pays no taxes, is invariably better capitalized or "lays off" a certain percentage of his bets with other gamblers. . . .

Nothing in the legislative history, however, deals with the question of whether the recipient of a lay off bet, on that basis alone, should be convicted under the statute.[22]

The phenomenon of lay off betting has been a factor in a large number of cases which have construed §1955. In almost every case, the question has been whether the exchange of lay off bets, usually in addition to the exchange of line information, could be enough to link two separate bookmaking operations into one business for the purposes of meeting the §1955 jurisdictional requirement of five participants in one business. The answer has in every case been affirmative—the regular direct exchange of lay off bets and line information can connect otherwise independent gambling operations, which alone would be illegal under state but not federal law (because less than five participants were involved), into one business. Further, the case law supported by legislative history establishes that an individual who

---

22. The silence of the statute and the legislative history on this matter can be contrasted with §1831(a)(2) of President Nixon's proposed Revised Criminal Code, not accepted by Congress, under which one who received a lay off bet would be in violation of an express statutory provision. *See* 13 Crim. L. Rep. 3015 (1973).

is in the business of providing a regular market for a large volume of lay off bets should also be considered to be part of the gambling operation he services. Finally, it seems clear that, at least in this circuit, a professional gambler who accepts bets in the nature of lay off bets and, additionally, provides line information to the same bookmaking operation can be convicted as part of that operation under §1955.

The cases establish, then, that one who accepts lay off bets can be convicted if any of the following factors is also present: evidence that the individual provided a regular market for a high volume of such bets, or held himself out to be available for such bets whenever bookmakers needed to make them; evidence that the individual performed any other substantial service for the bookmaker's operation, as, for example, in the supply of line information; or evidence that the individual was conducting his own illegal gambling operation and was regularly exchanging lay off bets with the other bookmakers. Our review of the legislative history, and our adherence to the doctrine that statutes mandating penal sanctions are to be strictly construed, convinces us that one of the listed factors, or other evidence that the defendant was an integral part of the bookmaking business, is necessary before an individual who accepts lay off bets can be convicted under the statute. Evidence establishing only that a person received occasional lay off bets from bookmakers cannot be considered inconsistent with the possibility that the individual was for all practical purposes only a bettor.

In these circumstances, we do not feel that the cases finding "lay off bettors" within the scope of §1955 are dispositive. If *dicta* in these cases can be read to indicate that a "lay off bettor," as the recipient of a lay off bet, is on that basis alone a part of an illegal gambling operation, we reject such *dicta* as being based on an erroneous assumption regarding the nature of lay off betting. We stress again that the recipient of a lay off bet need not be a bookmaker, but rather might be any individual willing to accept a single bet. Section 1955 was directed at the professionals— the persons who avoided gambling themselves, but profited from the gambling of others. Although a heavy bettor might be a crucial source of revenue for a bookmaking operation, the statute was meant to exclude bettors. Gambling becomes a federal case only when a person is charged with more than betting, and evidence that a person accepted lay off bets, without more, is insufficient to expel that person from §1955's sanctuary of bettordom.

The question remaining, then, is whether the evidence relating to Box, viewed most favorably to the Government, could sustain a jury finding that one of the additional factors noted above was present in this case. Such a jury finding would in effect be a conclusion that the evidence was inconsistent with any hypothesis of innocence.

In reaching this conclusion, of course, the jury is limited to evidence in the record and supportable inferences therefrom. If a conclusion that all hypotheses of innocence have been excluded by the evidence could be reached only as a result of speculation or assumptions about matters not in evidence, then the jury verdict must be overturned.

The evidence against Box shows that he accepted lay off bets of undetermined amounts from Cook on a number of occasions, and that in one week he may have accepted $3800 in lay off bets from Stewart. These are the only two pieces of evidence which distinguish Box in any way from the "mere bettor" so clearly excluded from the statute's scope. We do not find any reasonable basis in the evidence upon which the jury could conclude that Box was an integral part of these bookmaking operations. While the volume of bets with Stewart was substantial, no evidence indicates that Box regularly accepted lay off bets from Stewart. There is no evidence on amounts from Cook, and while Cook's testimony could support a conclusion that Box accepted lay off bets on several occasions, that testimony flatly contradicts any suggestion that Box held himself out to be a regular market for such bets upon which local bookmakers could depend. As we have already noted, no evidence supports the suggestion that Box was himself a bookmaker, or that he provided line or other gambling information to bookmakers.

Box may have gambled with the gamblers, but he has not been shown to be a gaming entrepreneur. Nothing indicates that he solicited the lay off bets that he accepted. Box was a customer of bookmakers and was perhaps a bargain-seeking bettor, but the record does not permit him to be cast in a role as a necessary or integral part of a gambling operation. The testimony of admitted bookmakers, the multiplicity of phone calls and the shower of betting slips suggest only that Box bet with continuity and in magnitude, and on occasion received a discount when the professionals with whom he dealt needed to lay off a bet. We conclude, then, that the jury could not reasonably find the evidence inconsistent with the hypothesis that Box was simply a heavy bettor who on occasion received favorable odds in bets with bookmakers.[32] For purposes of §1955, this hypothesis is one of innocence. . . .

---

32. Perhaps Box was a valued customer who was occasionally given a "right of first refusal" when his bookmakers needed to make a lay off bet. Alternatively, the bookmakers may have on occasion turned to Box when other bookmakers had bets unbalanced in the same direction on a certain event, and thus were unwilling to accept lay off bets. In any event, no evidence could support an inference that Box ever placed lay off bets himself—indeed, the evidence indicates that if Box were to place lay off bets, he would simply be negating the only 11 to 10 action he received. . . . Nothing in the evidence contradicts the proposition that Box was an inveterate gambler.

The conviction of Box is reversed, the sentence is vacated, and the case is remanded to the district court for entry of a judgment of acquittal.

## NOTES

1.  Section 1955 requires the involvement of least five people and a minimum handle of $2000 a day or, alternatively, that the gaming venture have been in continuous operation for at least a month. The court offers an explanation for these requirements, but are they also jurisdictional? If the statute was enacted pursuant to the Commerce Clause, would the statute be constitutional without them?

2.  Presumably, smaller gambling operations must be prosecuted, if at all, by the states. What if the state refuses to prosecute such cases, and for all intents and purposes, the state law against gambling is a dead letter? What is the appropriate role of federal authorities in such a case?

## UNITED STATES v. HAMMOND, A/K/A "BIG JOHN"
### 821 F.2d 473 (8th Cir. 1987)

LAY, Chief Judge.

John William Hammond was convicted of one count of conducting a gambling business involving five or more persons in violation of 18 U.S.C. §1955 and of four counts of aiding and abetting in the use of interstate facilities for transmitting wagering information under 18 U.S.C. §1084. Hammond was sentenced by the district court to three years imprisonment for violation of §1955, [and] for two years on each of the aiding and abetting counts, all sentences to be served concurrently. He was also fined a total of $30,000. Hammond now appeals challenging the sufficiency of the evidence as to each count. We affirm his convictions.

Between August, 1983, and January, 1984, Hammond ran an illegal bookmaking operation in St. Paul, Minnesota. In an attempt to avoid detection, Hammond hired at least three individuals to communicate with bettors over the telephone. One such employee was James Rebeck, whose job it was to receive telephone calls from bettors wishing to place wagers. Rebeck would record the names of the bettors, usually code names, and possibly their telephone numbers or location, on rice paper; he never actually recorded bets. The reason

Rebeck used rice paper is that it can be quickly and easily destroyed by immersion in water. Periodically, Rebeck would receive telephone calls from either Hammond or one of two other employees, Steven Chiarella or William Klabunder, and give the caller the information provided by the bettors.

Chiarella and Klabunder each had lists, supplied by Hammond, of the code names used by Hammond's clients and the telephone numbers where they could be reached. Chiarella and Klabunder would record the names given to Rebeck, then call the bettors and record the respective wagers, also using water-soluble rice paper. Occasionally, they made long-distance telephone calls to take wagers. Every fifteen minutes or so an unknown caller, but in all probability Hammond himself, would call Chiarella and Klabunder and ask them to communicate the bets they had taken. Once communicated, Chiarella and Klabunder destroyed the tally sheets.

The main issue in this case was whether a fifth person, in addition to Hammond, Rebeck, Chiarella, and Klabunder, participated in Hammond's gambling operation to such an extent that he or she would be a person who "conducts" part of an illegal gambling business within the contemplation of 18 U.S.C. §1955. The primary target of the government's case was Sandra Crawford, Hammond's friend for the previous ten years. In August, 1983, Crawford agreed to allow Rebeck to use the telephone at her residence for the purpose of taking incoming telephone calls from bettors. Although Hammond did not tell Crawford the reason he needed the use of her phone, she testified that "he didn't have to." She knew that it was in connection with his gambling business. Crawford was paid fifty dollars every two weeks or every month for the use of her telephone.

Hammond supplied Crawford with a quantity of rice paper which Crawford made available for Rebeck's use. Crawford was often present when Rebeck took calls from bettors and observed him making notes. She occasionally answered the telephone herself and recorded the information given her, later relaying it to persons calling and requesting the names. Crawford also occasionally forwarded the call to Rebeck's residence when he could not make it to her house or when she did not wish to be disturbed.

Hammond contends that this court should adopt the interpretation of the word "conducts," as used in 18 U.S.C. §1955, that has been adopted by the Tenth Circuit. In *United States v. Boss*, 671 F.2d 396 (10th Cir. 1982), the Tenth Circuit held that waitresses who served drinks to dance hall customers, who were gambling in an illegal dice room at the hall, did not fall within the purview of section 1955's prohibition against one who "conducts" a gambling operation. The court held that section 1955 contemplates that participants in an illegal gambling operation must perform duties "necessary" to the operation of the gambling business. The waitresses, who did nothing more than serve drinks to the gamblers, were not "necessary" to the business within the meaning of the act. *See also United States v. Morris*, 612 F.2d 483 (10th Cir. 1979) (person who allowed principals in a bookmaking operation to use her apartment and who received telephone messages for the principals was not a conductor of the business since her actions were merely helpful to the operation of the enterprise).

The Tenth Circuit's approach has not been adopted in the clear majority of the circuits. In *United States v. Bennett*, 563 F.2d 879 (8th Cir.), *cert. denied*, 434 U.S. 924, 54 L. Ed. 2d 282, 98 S. Ct. 403 (1977), in approval of the majority position, this court stated that section 1955 includes anyone who participates in a gambling business other than a customer or bettor. The scope of section 1955 is quite broad; all levels of personnel involved in the operation of a gambling business, not just those on the management level, are to be considered in determining whether five or more persons conduct such business within the meaning of section 1955. Accordingly, we hold that the trial court's denial of Hammond's requested jury instructions incorporating the Tenth Circuit's view of section 1955 was proper.[1]

Hammond further argues that he was convicted on insufficient evidence because even under the view of section 1955 as expressed in *Bennett*, Crawford and the other individuals involved were, at most, passive or inactive participants who may have been convicted for aiding and abetting Hammond, but not as participants. The evidence does not support this argument. Crawford clearly had more than a passive role. Not only did she knowingly permit her telephone to be used in the operation of Hammond's gambling enterprise, she was paid for that service. Crawford also supplied Rebeck with the water-soluble rice paper used to record bettors and, on occasion, actually recorded bettor's names herself. The fact that she was compensated

---

1. The trial court instructed the jury:

The term "conduct" as it is used in connection with the gambling business means to perform any act, function or duty which is necessary to or helpful in the ordinary operation of the business. A person may be found to conduct a gambling business even though he is a mere servant or employee having no part in the management or control of the business and no share in the profits. A mere bettor or customer of a gambling business cannot properly be said to conduct the business.

for her inconvenience helps bring her within the purview of section 1955. AFFIRMED.

BRIGHT, Senior Circuit Judge, concurring in the result.

While I concur in the result, I write separately to state my view that persons who do not directly participate in gambling operations should not be counted as persons "involved" in the "conduct" of such business within the purview of 18 U.S.C. §1955(b).

Thus, neither cocktail waitresses nor passive lessors of the betting place who do not partake in the gaming process should be counted in the determination of whether or not a defendant "conducts, finances, manages, supervises, directs, or owns all or part of an illegal gambling business," 18 U.S.C. §1955(a), as has been determined by the Tenth Circuit in *United States v. Boss*, 671 F.2d 396 (1982) and *United States v. Morris*, 612 F.2d 483 (1979). We need not disapprove of the results reached in the Tenth Circuit's decisions in order to affirm here. Crawford on occasion participated directly in the gambling operation and the evidence entitled the jury to conclude that Hammond's gambling activity included at least five persons.

### NOTES

1. Why do you think that the majority refused to amend its opinion to account for Judge Bright's concern?
2. Would the *Hammond* court have affirmed the conviction of Red Box? Why or why not?

## 2.   *The Federal Wire Act (18 U.S.C. §1084)*

One of the most important statutes related to the federal government's efforts to curb unlawful gambling is the federal Wire Act, 18 U.S.C. §1084. It has served a central role in many of the government's gambling enforcement efforts. It provides as follows:

(a) Whoever being engaged in the business of betting or wagering knowingly uses a wire communication facility for the transmission in interstate or foreign commerce of bets or wagers or information assisting in the placing of bets or wagers on any sporting event or contest, or for the transmission of a wire communication which entitles the recipient to receive money or credit as a result of bets or wagers, or for information assisting in the placing of bets or wagers, shall be fined under this title or imprisoned not more than two years, or both.

(b)   Nothing in this section shall be construed to prevent the transmission in interstate or foreign commerce of information for use in news reporting of sporting events or contests, or for the transmission of information assisting in the placing of bets or wagers on a sporting event or contest from a State or foreign country where betting on that sporting event or contest is legal into a State or foreign country in which such betting is legal.

In Section A, the Wire Act prohibits the use of "a wire communication facility for the transmission in interstate or foreign commerce of bets or wagers" related to "any sporting event or contest." Some commentators believe that this means that the Wire Act applies only to sports betting. (This issue will be taken up in greater detail in another section of this chapter below).

In Section B, the Wire Act specifically excludes from its coverage communications "from a State or foreign country where [such betting] is legal in to a State or foreign country in which such betting is legal." This seems to create a circumscribed role for the federal government. However, it does not resolve all of the subtle issues that arise by virtue of the fact that the activity covered is prohibited in some jurisdictions and permitted in others. Consider the following cases.

## LESLY COHEN v. UNITED STATES
### 378 F.2d 751 (9th Cir. 1967)

Browning, Circuit Judge.

Appellant was convicted on two counts of an indictment charging knowing utilization of interstate telephone facilities for the transmission of wagers and wagering information in violation of 18 U.S.C. §1084(a).

The first count alleged that during the period September 16, 1962, to December 15, 1962, appellant knowingly used interstate telephone facilities to transmit information from Las Vegas, Nevada, to San Francisco, California, for the purpose of assisting in placement of a wager on a San Francisco Forty-Niner's football game. A bill of particulars specified that this count involved a number of telephone calls between appellant and two bettors, Raymond Syufy and Adolph Schuman. The second count, as amplified by the bill of particulars, alleged a telephone call by Syufy to appellant on September 25, 1962, placing a wager on the Sonny Liston-Floyd Patterson heavyweight boxing match.

\* \* \*

The court instructed the jury that there was a rebuttable presumption that appellant knew what the law forbade.[2] Appellant objected because "it was a new law and enacted so closely to the time of the alleged offense."

The threshold question is whether knowledge of the statutory prohibition is an element of the offense under 18 U.S.C. §1084. If it is not, the instruction would be harmless even if wrong. Whether knowledge of illegality is an ingredient of a statutory offense depends upon the legislative intent. *United States v. Balint*, 258 U.S. 250, 251-252 (1922).

Congress knew that betting on sporting events was lawful in Nevada, and anticipated that it would continue to be. Congress also contemplated that interstate telephone facilities would continue to be used for the transmission into Nevada of information useful in gambling.[3] In Nevada, apparently, the conduct prohibited by section 1084(a) would be a neutral act, free of culpability unless the actor were aware of the statutory prohibition. Yet a violation of section 1084(a) is punishable as a felony, subject to two years' imprisonment and a fine of ten thousand dollars.

If knowledge of illegality is an element of the section 1084(a) offense, those innocent of intentional wrongdoing are afforded a defense. And if at the same time a rebuttable presumption of such knowledge is recognized, the requirement of knowledge will not substantially impede accomplishment of the statute's purpose to discourage professional interstate gambling.[4] In contrast with the occasional or social bettor, the professional gambler will find it difficult to go

---

2. The court said:

It is not necessary for the prosecution to prove knowledge of the accused if the particular act or failure to act is in violation of the law. Unless and until outweighed by evidence in the case to the contrary, the presumption is that every person knows what the law forbids and what the law requires to be done. However, evidence that the accused acted or failed to act because of ignorance of the law is to be considered by the jury in determining whether or not the accused acted or failed to act with a specific intent as charged. (R. 547-548)

3. Subsection (b) of 18 U.S.C. §1084, which exempts from the statute the transmission of information on a sporting event from a state where betting on that event is legal to a state in which such betting is legal was adopted with Nevada specifically in mind. H.R. 967, 1961 U.S. Code Cong. & Admin.News, 87th Cong., 1st Sess. 1961, 2631, 2632-2633.

4. As the government states, "Section 1084 was not designed to be applicable to isolated acts of wagering by individuals not engaged in the business of wagering." "The legislative history of Section 1084 clearly indicates that the purpose of the legislation was to curb the activities of the professional gambler."

forward with evidence of ignorance of the law pertaining directly to his business, and even more difficult to prevail on that issue with the fact finder.

We hold, therefore, that Congress intended knowledge of the statutory prohibition to be an element of the offense under section 1084(a), and that the district court properly instructed the jury that there is a rebuttable presumption that the accused in fact had knowledge of the law. *Edwards v. United States*, 334 F.2d 360, 366-368 (5th Cir. 1964).

## UNITED STATES v. BLAIR
### 54 F.3d 639 (10th Cir. 1995)

BRORBY, Circuit Judge.

The defendant, Albert John Blair Jr., brings this appeal challenging the district court's acceptance of his guilty plea and calculation of sentence. We have jurisdiction pursuant to 28 U.S.C. 1291, and affirm.

The relevant facts are essentially undisputed. Mr. Blair accepted wagers on professional and college basketball games from residents of the Northern District of Oklahoma over the phone via a toll-free number he had established. At the time, Mr. Blair was residing in the Dominican Republic. As part of his gambling operation, Mr. Blair employed a number of people who answered the phones, who used his information and capital, who paid a percentage of the profits from their own customers to him, and whose losses he covered. Mary J. Meyer played an active role in the enterprise. She would take and collect bets and place and lay off bets with other bookmakers for Mr. Blair.

[The Defendant pleaded guilty to knowingly using a wire communication facility for the transmission of bets or wagers, contrary to 18 U.S.C. §1084 and knowingly and willfully conspiring to commit the offense of illegal gambling against the United States, contrary to 18 U.S.C. §§1084 (the Wire Act), 1955 (the statute prohibiting illegal gambling businesses), and 371 (the general federal conspiracy statute).]

Mr. Blair brings this appeal arguing the district court erred in accepting his guilty pleas as no factual basis was established showing he was guilty of the crimes charged[.] His argument is premised on the contention that 18 U.S.C. §§1084 and 371 are "specific intent" crimes and, further, that a specific intent crime requires a showing the defendant was cognizant of the illegality of his actions. In short, Mr. Blair argues ignorance of the law is a defense to specific intent crimes generally and to the crimes he pled guilty to specifically. We are not persuaded.

Section 1084 provides, in pertinent part:

> (a) Whoever being engaged in the business of betting or wagering knowingly uses a wire communication facility for the transmission in interstate or foreign commerce of bets or wagers . . . which entitles the recipient to receive money or credit as a result of bets or wagers . . . shall be fined not more than $10,000 or imprisoned not more than two years, or both.

The term "knowledge" as used in the criminal law has long had a very distinct and definite meaning. It specifies that the mens rea needed to establish the crime be that of general intent. E.g., *United States v. Bailey*, 444 U.S. 394, 405 (1980) (the term knowledge corresponds with the concept of general intent). Because 1084 proscribes the knowing use of wire communication facilities to take bets, the plain language of the statute clearly evinces Congress's judgment that general intent is the mens rea needed to establish a violation of 1084.

In arguing to the contrary, Mr. Blair relies exclusively on *Cohen v. United States*, 378 F.2d 751, 756-57 (9th Cir.), cert. denied, 389 U.S. 897 (1967). While the court in *Cohen* did not conclude that 1084 was a specific intent crime, the court did hold that "Congress intended knowledge of the statutory prohibition to be an element of the offense under section 1084(a)." Id. at 757. We do not find the analysis of *Cohen* compelling and thus, decline to adopt it.

First, the *Cohen* case contains no discussion of the plain meaning of 1084 or the clearly established import of the term "knowledge." The language of the statute is, in our judgment, dispositive on the question of the mens rea needed to establish the crime. Second, we disagree with the *Cohen* court's conclusion Congress intended the statute to require knowledge of the statutory prohibition to support a conviction for its violation. The court reached this conclusion simply by observing that wagering is legal in the state of Nevada and thus, were the court to read the statute as requiring knowledge of its prohibition, "those innocent of intentional wrongdoing are afforded a defense." While this undoubtedly is true, Congress nowhere manifested its intent to provide such a defense. Our duty is to apply the law as written, not rewrite it as we see fit. We decline to adopt the rule laid out in *Cohen*, and hold that the mens rea required to establish a violation of 1084 is that of general intent. Accordingly, we reject Mr. Blair's allegation that reversible error was committed in accepting his plea to count one because no factual basis existed to establish he acted with specific intent.

The judgment of the district court is, therefore, AFFIRMED.

*NOTES*

1. In *Lesly Cohen*, the defendant argued that he ought not be held
   criminally culpable, absent proof of his awareness of illegality, for
   engaging in behavior that is, at worst, *malum prohibitum*. Is this a
   compelling argument? Does his residence in Las Vegas, Nevada,
   have any bearing on the question? Professors Murphy and O'Hara
   dissect the decision of the 9th Circuit's decision in *Cohen* as follows: "Given that gambling is legal in Nevada, some individuals
   might have no reason to believe their acts were culpable.
   The court placed the burden of proof regarding knowledge on
   the defendant, in an effort to separate occasional or social bettors
   from others. According to the court, 'the professional gambler
   will find it difficult to go forward with evidence of ignorance
   of the law pertaining directly to his business and even more difficult to prevail on that issue with the fact finder.'" Richard S.
   Murphy & Erin A. O'Hara, *Mistake of Federal Criminal Law:
   A Study of Coalitions and Costly Information*, 5 SUP. CT. ECON. REV.
   217, 264-65 n.117 (1997). What is the legal basis for this distinction? Is it jurisdictional?
2. The circuit split represented by *Cohen* and *Blair* remains unre-
   solved. Murphy and O'Hara argue that the practical reason for
   the split lies in "the fact that gambling is generally illegal in all of
   the states in the Tenth Circuit but not in Nevada, where the
   events at issue in *Cohen* took place." *See* Barbara E. Armacost,
   *Qualified Immunity: Ignorance Excused*, 51 VAND. L. REV. 581
   (1998). Does the federal legal regime allow for different interpretations of federal law in different regions of the country? Is
   that consistent with general notions of fairness and equal protection? Could Congress possibly have intended such a result? Is
   the split a problematic discrepancy, or a workable solution to a
   difficult problem?
3. While some sort of mens rea requirement is a bedrock requirement of almost every criminal action, the mens rea requirement
   found in *Cohen*, knowledge of illegality, is a rare requirement
   found to exist in few federal statutes. The law generally presumes
   that citizens know the law and "ignorance of the law is no excuse."
   For mere regulatory offenses, courts and legislatures often dispense with any mens rea requirement and allow strict liability to
   govern. But since illegal gambling is subject to criminal laws,
   which are more strictly construed than regulatory laws, and lawful
   gambling is governed by regulatory laws, the law is in some ways
   more protective of the illegal gambling entrepreneur than the

licensed gambling operator engaged in a lawful and regulated business.

4. With regard to criminal law, this case presents an interesting question. But what about other relevant interests: are there federalism issues presented by the question? How would Judge Wilkinson rule in this case?

5. Is the federal government merely a passive referee with the job of protecting the boundaries of states so that they are free to make their own value judgments? Or is the United States taking a more aggressive role in these cases? As a matter of enforcement discretion, how aggressive should the federal government be in addressing conduct that is so ambiguous that it is legal in some U.S. jurisdictions and illegal in others?

## UNITED STATES v. JAY COHEN
### 260 F.3d 68 (2d Cir. 2001)

KEENAN, District Judge.

In 1996, the Defendant, Jay Cohen ("Cohen") was young, bright, and enjoyed a lucrative position at Group One, a San Francisco firm that traded in options and derivatives. That was not all to last, for by 1996 the Internet revolution was in the speed lane. Inspired by the new technology and its potential, Cohen decided to pursue the dream of owning his own e-business. By year's end he had left his job at Group One, moved to the Caribbean island of Antigua, and had become a bookmaker.

Cohen, as President, and his partners, all American citizens, dubbed their new venture the World Sports Exchange ("WSE"). WSE's sole business involved bookmaking on American sports events, and was purportedly patterned after New York's Off-Track Betting Corporation.[5] WSE targeted customers in the United States, advertising its business throughout America by radio, newspaper, and television. Its advertisements invited customers to bet with WSE either by toll-free telephone or by Internet.

WSE operated an "account-wagering" system. It required that its new customers first open an account with WSE and wire at least $300 into that account in Antigua. A customer seeking to bet would then contact WSE either by telephone or Internet to request a particular bet. WSE would issue an immediate, automatic acceptance and

---

5. We note, however, that the Off-Track Betting Corporation's business is limited to taking bets on horseracing, not other sporting events.

confirmation of that bet, and would maintain the bet from that customer's account.

In one fifteen-month period, WSE collected approximately $5.3 million in funds wired from customers in the United States. In addition, WSE would typically retain a "vig" or commission of 10% on each bet. Cohen boasted that in its first year of operation, WSE had already attracted nearly 1,600 customers. By November 1998, WSE had received 60,000 phone calls from customers in the United States, including over 6,100 from New York.

In the course of an FBI investigation of offshore bookmakers, FBI agents in New York contacted WSE by telephone and Internet numerous times between October 1997 and March 1998 to open accounts and place bets. Cohen was arrested in March 1998 under an eight-count indictment charging him with conspiracy and substantive offenses in violation of 18 U.S.C. §1084 ("§1084").... In the conspiracy count (Count One) and in five of the seven substantive counts (Counts Three through Six, and Eight), Cohen was charged with violating all three prohibitive clauses of §1084(a) ((1) transmission in interstate or foreign commerce of bets or wagers, (2) transmission of a wire communication which entitles the recipient to receive money or credit as a result of bets or wagers, (3) information assisting in the placement of bets or wagers). In two counts, Counts Two and Seven, he was charged only with transmitting "information assisting in the placing of bets or wagers."

Cohen was convicted on all eight counts. The jury found in special interrogatories that Cohen had violated all three prohibitive clauses of §1084(a) with respect to the five counts in which those violations were charged. Judge Griesa sentenced Cohen on August 10, 2000 to a term of twenty-one months' imprisonment. He has remained on bail pending the outcome of this appeal.

### DISCUSSION

On appeal, Cohen asks this Court to consider [several] issues[, including]: (1) whether the Government was required to prove a "corrupt motive" in connection with the conspiracy in this case; (2) whether the district court properly instructed the jury to disregard the safe-harbor provision contained in §1084(b); (3) whether Cohen "knowingly" violated §1084; [and] (4) whether the rule of lenity requires a reversal of Cohen's convictions[.] We will address those issues in that order.

## I. CORRUPT MOTIVE

Cohen appeals his conspiracy conviction on the grounds that the district court instructed the jury to disregard his alleged good-faith belief about the legality of his conduct. He argues that *People v. Powell*, 63 N.Y. 88 (1875), requires proof of a corrupt motive for any conspiracy to commit an offense that is *malum prohibitum*, rather than *malum in se*. We disagree, and we hold that whatever remains of *Powell* does not apply to this case.

In 1875, the New York Court of Appeals ruled in *Powell* that a conspiracy to commit an offense that was "innocent in itself" required evidence of a "corrupt" or "evil purpose." The *Powell* defendants were commissioners of charities for Kings County and had been convicted of conspiring to violate state law by purchasing supplies without first advertising for proposals and awarding a contract to the lowest bidder.

The *Powell* Court upheld an appellate court's reversal of the trial court, which had ruled that ignorance of the law was no defense to conspiracy. In doing so, the Court concluded that a conspiracy offense, by nature, required some form of corrupt motive, even if its underlying substantive offense required only an intent to commit the prohibited act. The Court stated that "persons who agree to do an act innocent in itself, in good faith and without the use of criminal means, are not converted into conspirators [] because it turns out that the contemplated act was prohibited by statute."

The *Powell* doctrine was echoed in federal cases from the first half of the last century, but many circuits have since, in effect, moved away from the doctrine. *Compare*, e.g., *Landen v. United States*, 299 F. 75 (6th Cir. 1924) (applying *Powell* to drug wholesalers' conspiracy to sell intoxicating liquor for nonbeverage purposes without the necessary permit), with *United States v. Blair*, 54 F.3d 639 (10th Cir. 1995) (involving, as does this case, offshore bookmaking in violation of §1084); *United States v. Murray*, 928 F.2d 1242 (1st Cir. 1991) (involving an illegal gambling business in violation of 18 U.S.C. §1955); *United States v. Thomas*, 887 F.2d 1341 (9th Cir. 1989) (involving trafficking in wildlife that the defendant should have known was taken in violation of state law).

Although this Court has long expressed its discontent with the *Powell* doctrine, we have done so in dicta in cases involving conspiracies to commit acts that were not "innocent in themselves." See, e.g., *United States v. Mack*, 112 F.2d 290, 292 (2d Cir. 1940). In *Mack*, Judge Learned Hand criticized the *Powell* doctrine as "anomalous" and questioned "why more proof should be necessary than that the parties had in contemplation all the elements of the crime they are charged with conspiracy to commit." He nevertheless found " 'corrupt motive' in abundance" in connection with the defendant's conspiracy to employ unregistered alien prostitutes.

The American Law Institute has expressly rejected *Powell* in its commentary to the Model Penal Code. The Institute noted that the "melodramatic and sinister view of conspiracy" upon which *Powell* was premised is no longer valid. It further observed that *Powell* now has "little resolving power in particular cases" and instead "serves mainly to divert attention from clear analysis of the mens rea requirements of conspiracy." See Model Penal Code §5.03 note on subsec. 1 & cmt. 2(c)(iii) (1985).

In the Institute's view, the Powell doctrine was essentially "a judicial endeavor to import fair mens rea requirements into statutes creating regulatory offenses that do not rest on traditional concepts of personal fault and culpability." See id. The Institute itself disagreed with that policy, however, concluding that it was a function better left to the statutes themselves.

In *United States v. Feola*, 420 U.S. 671 (1975), the Supreme Court, in another context, rejected the notion that a federal conspiracy conviction required proof of scienter. We conclude that the *Powell* doctrine does not apply to a conspiracy to violate 18 U.S.C. §1084.

## II. THE SAFE HARBOR PROVISION

Cohen appeals the district court for instructing the jury to disregard the safe-harbor provision contained in §1084(b). That subsection provides a safe harbor for transmissions that occur under both of the following two conditions: (1) betting is legal in both the place of origin and the destination of the transmission; and (2) the transmission is limited to mere information that assists in the placing of bets, as opposed to including the bets themselves. See §1084(b).

The district court ruled as a matter of law that the safe-harbor provision did not apply because neither of the two conditions existed in the case of WSE's transmissions. Cohen disputes that ruling and argues that both conditions did, in fact, exist. He argues that betting is not only legal in Antigua, it is also "legal" in New York for the purposes of §1084. He also argues that all of WSE's transmissions were limited to mere information assisting in the placing of bets. We agree with the district court's rulings on both issues.

### A. *"Legal" Betting*

[Cohen argued that New York law only prohibits engaging in the business of gambling in New York and no New York law criminalized mere betting.] There can be no dispute that betting is illegal in

New York. New York has expressly prohibited betting in both its Constitution, see N.Y. Const. art. I, §9 ("no . . . bookmaking, or any other kind of gambling [with certain exceptions pertaining to lotteries and horse racing] shall hereafter be authorized or allowed within this state"), and its General Obligations Law, see N.Y. Gen. Oblig. L. §5-401 ("all wagers, bets or stakes, made to depend on any race, or upon any gaming by lot or chance, or upon any lot, chance, casualty, or unknown or contingent event whatever, shall be unlawful") [.]

Nevertheless, Cohen argues that Congress intended for the safe-harbor provision in §1084(b) to exclude only those transmissions sent to or from jurisdictions in which betting was a crime. Cohen concludes that because the placing of bets is not a crime in New York, it is "legal" for the purposes of §1084(b).

By its plain terms, the safe-harbor provision requires that betting be "legal," i.e., permitted by law, in both jurisdictions. See §1084(b); see also Black's Law Dictionary 902 (7th ed. 1999); Webster's 3d New Int'l Dictionary 1290 (1993). The plain meaning of a statute "should be conclusive, except in the rare cases in which the literal application of a statute will produce a result demonstrably at odds with the intentions of its drafters." *United States v. Ron Pair Enters., Inc.,* 489 U.S. 235, 242 (1989). This is not the rare case.

Although, as Cohen notes, the First Circuit has stated that Congress "did not intend [for §1084] to criminalize acts that neither the affected states nor Congress itself deemed criminal in nature," it did not do so in the context of a §1084 prosecution. See *Sterling Suffolk Racecourse Ltd. P'ship v. Burrillville Racing Ass'n,* 989 F.2d 1266, 1273 (1st Cir. 1993). Instead, that case involved a private bid for an injunction under RICO (18 U.S.C. §1961 et seq.) and the Interstate Horse-racing Act (15 U.S.C. §§3001-07) ("IHA"). It does not stand for the proposition that §1084 permits betting that is illegal as long as it is not criminal.

In *Sterling,* the defendant was an OTB office in Rhode Island that accepted bets on horse races from distant tracks and broadcasted the races. The office typically obtained the various consents required under the IHA, i.e., from the host track, the host racing commission, and its own racing commission. However, it would often neglect to secure the consent of the plaintiff, a live horse-racing track located within the statutory sixty-mile radius from the OTB office. The plaintiff sought an injunction against the OTB office under RICO, alleging that it was engaged in a pattern of racketeering activity by violating §1084 through its noncompliance with the IHA.

The *Sterling* court affirmed the district court's denial of the RICO injunction. It noted first that because the OTB office's business was legitimate under all applicable state laws, it fell under the safe-harbor provision in §1084(b). Furthermore, the court held that in enacting the IHA, Congress had only created a private right of action for damages on the part of certain parties; it did not intend for any Government enforcement of the IHA. Consequently, the plaintiff could not use the IHA together with §1084 to transform an otherwise legal OTB business into a criminal racketeering enterprise. Id.

Neither *Sterling* nor the legislative history behind §1084 demonstrates that Congress intended for §1084(b) to mean anything other than what it says. Betting is illegal in New York, and thus the safe-harbor provision in §1084(b) cannot not apply in Cohen's case as a matter of law. As a result, the district court was not in error when it instructed the jury to disregard that provision.

### B.   *Transmission of a Bet, Per Se*

Cohen appeals the district court's instructions to the jury regarding what constitutes a bet per se. Cohen argues that under WSE's account-wagering system, the transmissions between WSE and its customers contained only information that enabled WSE itself to place bets entirely from customer accounts located in Antigua. He argues that this fact was precluded by the district court's instructions. We find no error in those instructions.

Judge Griesa repeatedly charged the jury as follows:

> If there was a telephone call or an internet transmission between New York and [WSE] in Antigua, and if a person in New York said or signaled that he or she wanted to place a specified bet, and if a person on an internet device or a telephone said or signaled that the bet was accepted, this was the transmission of a bet within the meaning of Section 1084. Congress clearly did not intend to have this statute be made inapplicable because the party in a foreign gambling business deemed or construed the transmission as only starting with an employee in an internet mechanism located on the premises in the foreign country.

Jury instructions are not improper simply because they resemble the conduct alleged to have occurred in a given case; nor were they improper in this case. It was the Government's burden in this case to prove that someone in New York signaled an offer to place a particular bet and that someone at WSE signaled an acceptance of that offer. The jury concluded that the Government had carried that burden.

Most of the cases that Cohen cites in support of the proposition that WSE did not transmit any bets involved problems pertaining either to proof of the acceptance of transmitted bets, or to proof of the locus of a betting business for taxation purposes. No such problems existed in this case.

This case was never about taxation, and there can be no dispute regarding WSE's acceptance of customers' bet requests. For example, a March 18, 1998 conversation between Spencer Hanson, a WSE employee, and a New York-based undercover FBI agent occurred as follows:

> Agent:   Can I place a bet right now?
> Hanson:   You can place a bet right now.
> Agent:   Alright, can you give me the line on the um Penn State/ Georgia Tech game, it's the NIT Third Round game tonight.
> Hanson:   Its [sic] Georgia Tech minus 7 1/2, total is 147.
> Agent:   Georgia Tech minus 7 1/2, umm I wanna take Georgia Tech. Can I take 'em for 50?
> Hanson:   Sure.

WSE could only book the bets that its customers requested and authorized it to book. By making those requests and having them accepted, WSE's customers were placing bets. So long as the customers' accounts were in good standing, WSE accepted those bets as a matter of course.

Moreover, the issue is immaterial in light of the fact that betting is illegal in New York. Section 1084(a) prohibits the transmission of information assisting in the placing of bets as well as the transmission of bets themselves. This issue, therefore, pertains only to the applicability of §1084(b)'s safe-harbor provision. As we have noted, that safe harbor excludes not only the transmission of bets, but also the transmission of betting information to or from a jurisdiction in which betting is illegal. As a result, that provision is inapplicable here even if WSE had only ever transmitted betting information.

### III. COHEN'S MENS REA

Cohen appeals the district court's instruction to the jury regarding the requisite mens rea under §1084. Section 1084 prohibits the "knowing" transmission of bets or information assisting in the placing of bets. See §1084(a). The district court instructed the jurors that to convict, they needed only to find that Cohen "knew that the deeds described in the statute as being prohibited were being done," and that a misinterpretation of the law, like ignorance of the law, was no excuse.

Cohen argues that he lacked the requisite mens rea because (1) he did not "knowingly" transmit bets, and (2) he did not transmit information assisting in the placing of bets or wagers to or from a jurisdiction in which he "knew" betting was illegal. He contends that in giving its jury charge, the district court improperly instructed the jury to disregard that argument.

The district court was correct; it mattered only that Cohen knowingly committed the deeds forbidden by §1084, not that he intended to violate the statute. Cohen's own interpretation regarding what constituted a bet was irrelevant to the issue of his mens rea under §1084.

In any event, Cohen is culpable under §1084(a) by admitting that he knowingly transmitted information assisting in the placing of bets. His beliefs regarding the legality of betting in New York are immaterial. The legality of betting in a relevant jurisdiction pertains only to §1084(b)'s safe-harbor provision. As we have already discussed, that safe-harbor provision, as a matter of law, does not apply in this case.

### IV. RULE OF LENITY

Cohen argues that the rule of lenity, a concept grounded in due process, requires a reversal of his convictions. According to Cohen, §1084 is too unclear to provide fair warning of what conduct it prohibits. In particular, he contends that the statute does not provide fair warning with respect to (1) whether the phrase "bet or wager" includes account wagering, (2) whether "transmission" includes the receiving of information as well as the sending of it, and (3) whether betting must be legal or merely non-criminal in a particular jurisdiction in order to be considered "legal" in that jurisdiction. None of these contentions has any merit.

The rule of lenity applies where there exists a "grievous ambiguity" in a statute, see *Huddleston v. United States*, 415 U.S. 814, 831 (1974), such that "after seizing everything from which aid can be derived, [a court] can make no more than a guess as to what Congress intended." *Reno v. Koray*, 515 U.S. 50, 65 (1995). The rule exists to prevent courts from "applying a novel construction of a criminal statute to conduct that neither the statute nor any prior judicial decision has fairly disclosed to be within its scope." *United States v. Lanier*, 520 U.S. 259, 266-67 (1997).

We need not guess whether the provisions of §1084 apply to Cohen's conduct because it is clear that they do. First, account-wagering is wagering nonetheless; a customer requests a particular bet with WSE by telephone or internet and WSE accepts that bet. WSE's requirement that its customers maintain fully-funded accounts does not obscure that fact.

Second, Cohen established two forms of wire facilities, internet and telephone, which he marketed to the public for the express purpose of transmitting bets and betting information. Cohen subsequently received such transmissions from customers, and, in turn, sent such transmissions back to those customers in various forms, including in the form of acceptances and confirmations. No matter what spin he puts on "transmission," his conduct violated the statute.

Third, it is clear to lawyer and layman alike that an act must be permitted by law in order for it to be legal. It is also clear that betting is not permitted under New York law. Where a state's statute declares an act to be "unlawful," that act is not "legal," see §1084(b). The safe-harbor provision is unambiguous, and is not applicable in Cohen's case. . . . AFFIRMED.

## NOTES

1. Cohen was sentenced to 21 months in federal prison. Ironically, he served that sentence in Nellis Federal Prison Camp which sits adjacent to the gambling capital of the United States—Las Vegas, Nevada. *See* Ed Koch, *Net Gaming Operator Freed from Prison*, LAS VEGAS SUN (March 23, 2004).

2. The court in *Cohen* was confident that the Federal Wire Act made Jay Cohen's behavior illegal. Elsewhere, however, the Wire Act musters considerable ambiguity as it relates to some forms of internet gambling. *See* Ronnie D. Crisco, Jr. *Follow the Leaders: A Constructive Examination of Existing Regulatory Tools That Could Be Applied to Internet Gambling* 5 N.C. J.L. & TECH. 155, 157 (Fall 2003). "As the statutory language suggests, the Wire Act has been interpreted to apply only to sports wagering. This reading, however, is not universal; at least one state court has construed the Wire Act to prohibit virtual casino gambling sites as well. The Fifth Circuit Court of Appeals, on the other hand, announced in *In re MasterCard International, Inc.*, that the scope of the Wire Act excludes virtual casinos by the plain language of the statute. Exactly how the Wire Act should be read in light of technological advances not contemplated by its drafters is still open for debate."

3. The practical effects of the ambiguity discussed in the note above may be significant. Prudent, publicly-traded companies are likely to stay away from an activity that is possibly unlawful, even if there is a strong legal argument otherwise. However, others may be willing to take a risk. What are the practical ramifications of the disparity in the risk appetites between publicly-traded and privately-held enterprises?

4. Cohen makes an argument that has come up in varied forms in numerous other cases. Cohen's activity was legal where he conducted it, and his customers' behavior was not necessarily illegal,

or at least not criminal, where they engaged in behavior. In *United States v. Gotti*, 459 F.3d 296, 340-41 (2d Cir. 2006), the court faced a similar argument in the context of §1955, which was discussed previously. In *Gotti*, §1955 and other federal statutes were used to indict members of the Gambino crime family. On appeal, one of the defendants asserted that the alleged bookmaking business was not a violation of New York law (and therefore did not satisfy the requirements of §1955) "because Pelican Sports was located offshore in Costa Rica, its actions were legal there, and no bets were received or accepted in New York." The court held that the government had introduced "evidence sufficient to conclude that the defendants, who were New York-based, had been operating a local branch of the business, essentially managing a stable of clients who placed their bets from New York. When bets are placed from New York, the gambling activity is illegal under New York law, regardless of whether the activity is legal in the location to which the bets were transmitted. . . . It is irrelevant that Internet gambling is legal in Antigua. The act of entering the bet and transmitting the information from New York via the Internet is adequate to constitute gambling activity within New York State. New York Penal Law §225.00(4) further provides that '[a] person "advances gambling activity" when, acting other than as a player, he engages in conduct which materially aids any form of gambling activity,' which the defendants here did. Thus, the defendants violated New York law by organizing a bookmaking operation through which bettors made their bets from New York." Because of the local activities that were established in *Gotti*, the court had sufficient evidence to sustain the conviction. What if the defendant had not operated the business from New York, and never visited that state? That is a question posed often in the Internet gaming context.

5. Looking back at the Wire Act (§1084) and the prohibition on illegal gambling businesses (§1955), do these statutes reach the patron, the illegal bettor? Note that other statutes used in gambling prosecutions, such as the Travel Act, 18 U.S.C. §1952, are constructed similarly. Would prosecutions of individual bettors be more fruitful? Wouldn't prohibitory strategies work better if the individual patron was targeted as well?

6. Did the *Cohen* court rule correctly on the rule of lenity? By now, it must be clear to the casual student of gambling law that American policies toward gambling are incoherent and often uncertain. In *McNally v. United States*, 483 U.S. 350, 360 (1987), the Supreme Court applied the rule of lenity to the federal mail fraud statute, holding: "We believe that Congress' intent in passing the mail

fraud statute was to prevent the use of the mails in furtherance of such schemes. The Court has often stated that when there are two rational readings of a criminal statute, one harsher than the other, we are to choose the harsher only when Congress has spoken in clear and definite language. As the Court said in a mail fraud case years ago: 'There are no constructive offenses; and before one can be punished, it must be shown that his case is plainly within the statute.' Rather than construe the statute in a manner that leaves its outer boundaries ambiguous and involves the Federal Government in setting standards of disclosure and good government for local and state officials, we read §1341 as limited in scope to the protection of property rights. If Congress desires to go further, it must do more than it has."

7.  Note that the rule of lenity is applied more often in cases in which an offense is *malum prohibitum* than *malum in se. See* WILLIAM N. ESKRIDGE, JR., PHILIP P. FRICKEY, ELIZABETH GARRETT, CASES AND MATERIALS ON LEGISLATION: STATUTES AND THE CREATION OF PUBLIC POLICY 852-53 (3d ed. 2001). Are gambling offenses *malum prohibitum* or *malum in se?*

# C.  THE PROHIBITION OF INTERNET GAMING

The Internet has posed a host of new challenges to gambling prohibition. The federal government has met these challenges in an ambivalent manner. The next case presents a federal statute, RICO, that arguably creates a private cause of action that can be used to address illegal gambling operations.

## IN RE MASTERCARD INTERNATIONAL INC.

### 132 F. Supp. 2d 468 (E.D. La. 2001)

STANWOOD R. DUVAL, JR., Judge.

This multidistrict litigation arises from allegations that MasterCard International, Visa International and several banks that issue MasterCard and Visa credit cards have interacted with a number of Internet casinos in a manner that violates United States law. . . . Presently before the Court are Rule 12(b)(6) motions to dismiss for failure to state a claim upon which relief can be granted . . . limited to defendants' liability under federal law, namely the Racketeer Influenced and Corrupt Organizations Act ("RICO"), found at 18 U.S.C. §1961 et seq. . . .

Larry Thompson ("Thompson) and Lawrence Bradley ("Bradley") (together referred to as "plaintiffs") filed class action complaints on behalf of themselves and others similarly situated against certain credit card companies and issuing banks for those entities alleged illegal involvement with the internet gambling industry. Named as defendants by Thompson are MasterCard International, Inc. ("MasterCard"), Fleet Bank and Fleet Credit Card Services ("Fleet") [and by] Bradley are Visa International Service Association ("Visa") and Travelers Bank USA Corp ("Travelers").[6]

Plaintiffs' class action complaints allege that defendants have violated several federal and state laws with respect to defendants' involvement with internet casinos. Plaintiffs argue that defendants' actions constitute a pattern of racketeering activity in violation of the Racketeer Influenced and Corrupt Organizations Act, found at 18 U.S.C. §§1961-1968.

As the internet breaks down the geographic and temporal walls that once restricted the flow of information and commerce, plaintiffs argue that several illegitimate businesses have used the medium to further their illegal industries. Plaintiffs allege that "numerous sites have been created to offer the opportunity to engage in illegal gambling on the internet. Many of these sites operate from outside the borders of the United States, but through use of the Internet and interstate telephone lines they can be accessed easily from any computer in the United States with Internet access." Those gambling sites "allow persons with credit card accounts to gamble using their credit cards." The credit cards are used to purchase credits which the bettor may then use, or not use, as he pleases. According to the complaints, the process entails one of two methods. An individual may "call and verbally authorize a deposit from his or her credit card whereby chips or gambling credit are made available for gambling, or the individual may download his credit card information to the site or may be required to access a web-site embedded in the gambling site which allows the electronic deposit of credit card funds for "chips" or gambling credit." It is the plaintiffs' contention that "whether the gambling is characterized as chips, credits, points, or in other ways, the end result is the same: a charge for gambling losses is submitted on the credit card, and the player is gambling with real money electronically

6. Since the arguments asserted by the various defendants are substantially similar, for ease of reference the Court shall refer to MasterCard International, Inc., Fleet Bank, Fleet Credit Card Services, Visa International and Travelers Bank as "defendants." When referring solely to MasterCard International Inc. and Visa International Service Association the Court shall use the term "credit card companies." When referring to Fleet Bank, Fleet Credit Card Services and Travelers Bank, the Court shall designate those parties the "issuing banks."

withdrawn from the credit card and paid to the casino to be billed later by the issuer of the credit card."

Each respective credit card company, Visa and MasterCard, "is responsible for the operation and upgrading of its computer payment system. This consumer financial transaction processing system provides authorization, transaction processing, and settlement services for approximately [millions] of merchants worldwide." Each credit card company processes every charge submitted by the millions of merchants, including Internet casinos, and is aware of the allegedly illegal nature of the gambling debt.

Bradley states that he "placed internet gambling wagers" on approximately nineteen different days using seven different internet casino websites. Although he pleads that he wagered a total of $16,445, he was charged $7,048 by Visa and Travelers.[7] On the billing statements, the various transactions were characterized as purchases as opposed to cash advances. As Bradley accessed each of the seven different casino websites he was instructed to enter his billing information, including his street address, billing state and country and for each dollar he deposited he received a "gambling credit" whose only purpose was to act as gambling tender. The Visa logo was visible on each website as a means of encouraging plaintiff to use his Visa card to place bets.

Thompson "placed wagers" through two different web sites on approximately 13 different days. Thompson pleads that he wagered a total of $1520 and was charged $1510 by MasterCard and Fleet. As with Bradley, the various transactions were characterized as purchases rather than cash advances on the billing statements. Thompson also states that as he accessed each website he was instructed to enter his billing information, including his billing state and country and that for each dollar he deposited he received a "gambling credit" whose only purpose was to act as gambling tender. In his case, the Master-Card logo was visible on each website as a means of encouraging plaintiff to use his MasterCard to place bets.

Each plaintiff admits that all internet casinos accept forms of payment other than credit cards. However, all other forms of payment required a waiting period for that particular form of payment to clear before a bettor could place a wager. Bradley and Thompson each contend that the casinos' acceptance of their respective credit cards was the most immediate method by which plaintiffs could purchase credits and that "but for" the casinos' acceptance of the plaintiffs credit cards, neither would have placed bets with the internet casinos.

---

7. Plaintiff does not explain the discrepancy but presumably this indicates that Bradley was not always unsuccessful.

Plaintiffs allege that the Internet casinos and the defendants have engaged in "a worldwide gambling enterprise" through the transmissions and facilitation of internet casino gambling, sports betting[8] and the collection of gambling debt. Through an association with the internet casinos, plaintiffs claim that the defendants "directed, guided, conducted, or participated, directly or indirectly, in the conduct of an enterprise through a pattern of racketeering activity and/or collection of unlawful debt" as defined by RICO, 18 U.S.C. §1961 et seq.

In support of these accusations, plaintiffs contend that the defendants' services support "the internet casinos . . . in foreign countries where their presence may be legal" but that they also "actively directed, participated in and aided and abetted [the casinos] book making activities in the United States where they are not legal." Thompson supports this accusation by alleging that employees of MasterCard attended an on-line gaming seminar and gave an impromptu presentation explaining MasterCard's role in the internet gambling system. Bradley supports his claim by alleging that Visa had detailed procedures in place to handle internet gambling transactions. It is plaintiffs' contention that the credit card companies know the exact nature of each transaction processed through their international payment system and continue to allow internet gamblers to use their credit cards when defendants knew that internet gambling debts were allegedly illegal. Plaintiffs do not allege that the defendants received or transmitted any bets or that they have an ownership interest in the online casinos.

Plaintiffs bring their suits under 18 U.S.C. §1964(c) arguing that the defendants have violated 18 U.S.C. §1962(c) as well as state law. . . . "It is the purpose of [RICO] to seek the eradication of organized crime in the United States by strengthening the legal tools in the evidence-gathering process, by establishing new penal prohibitions, and by providing enhanced sanctions and new remedies to deal with the unlawful activities of those engaged in organized crime." Organized Crime Control Act of 1970, Pub. L. No. 91-452, 84 Stat. 922, 923. "Congress enacted . . . RICO . . . for the purpose of seeking the eradication of organized crime in the United States." *Beck v. Pupris*, 529 U.S. 494, 496 (2000). To simplify the statute as it applies to the case before this Court, RICO has eight sections, four of which apply directly to the action sub judice. [Section] 1962(a)-(d) sets forth the four activities prohibited by the statute. "Subsections (a), (b), and (c) were designed to work together to deal with the three different ways in

---

8. The Court notes that neither plaintiff alleges that he placed wagers on sporting events.

which organized crime infiltrates and corrupts legitimate organizations." David B. Smith & Terrance G. Reed, *Civil RICO*, §5.02, p. 5-2 (Matthew Bender & Co. 2000). Subsection (d) is an inchoate offense, prohibiting conspiracy to violate sections (a), (b), or (c).

Pertinent to this case is §1962(c) which provides that "it shall be unlawful for any person employed by or associated with any enterprise engaged in, or the activities of which effect, interstate or foreign commerce, to conduct or participate, directly or indirectly, in the conduct of such enterprise's affairs through a pattern of racketeering activity or collection of unlawful debt." §1962(c). The United States Court of Appeals for the Fifth Circuit has simplified section 1962(c) to mean that "a person who is employed by or associated with an enterprise cannot conduct the affairs of the enterprise through a pattern of racketeering activity." Section 1963 imposes criminal penalties upon those who violate section 1962. A civil remedy is provided under section 1964, which states that "any person injured in his business or property by reason of a violation of section 1962 of this chapter may sue therefor in any appropriate United States district court and shall recover threefold the damages he sustains and the cost of the suit, including a reasonable attorney's fee. . . ." 18 U.S.C. §1964(c).

Common elements are present in all four RICO subsections. [A]ny RICO claim necessitates "(1) a person who engages in (2) a pattern of racketeering activity, (3) connected to the acquisition, establishment, conduct or control of an enterprise." Once those fundamental prerequisites are satisfied, the court "may then continue to the substantive requirements of each respective subsection." In this case, plaintiffs allege an association in fact enterprise in violation of §1962(c) and as such, they must also plead that the association in fact enterprise (1) has an existence separate and apart from the pattern of racketeering, (2) is an ongoing organization and (3) functions as a continuing unit as shown by a hierarchal or consensual decision making structure.

The Court will resolve this dispute in a cartesian manner. The Court's substantive RICO analysis will first address those elements common to all RICO claims: the existence of a RICO person, a pattern of racketeering activity, and the existence of an enterprise. Next, the Court will address those requirements discrete to alleged violations of 18 U.S.C. §1962(c), including whether that section encompasses aiding and abetting liability. Finally, the Court will discuss standing. Although standing is generally a threshold question, in this case it is more appropriately analyzed last because RICO standing is dependant upon first finding a violation of section 1962, and then determining whether that violation caused plaintiffs' injuries.

## IV. Elements Common to All RICO Claims

### A. RICO Person

A RICO person is ... "any individual or entity capable of holding a legal or beneficial interest in property." Recognizing that the statute provides a very broad definition, the United States Court of Appeals for the Fifth Circuit has added a gloss to that definition, requiring that "the RICO person must be one that either poses or has posed a continuous threat of engaging in the acts of racketeering." The panel in *Crowe* expounded upon the requirement by stating that "the continuous threat requirement may not be satisfied if no more is pled than that the person has engaged in a limited number of predicate racketeering acts."

Plaintiffs alleged that the defendants have engaged in the predicate acts for at least a year and that they continue to engage in the same course of conduct. Taking those facts as true for the purposes of these motions, the Court finds that plaintiffs have adequately alleged the existence of RICO persons.

### B. Pattern of Racketeering Activity

Plaintiffs [in a RICO action] must identify and prove a pattern of racketeering activity, defined as two "predicate acts" of racketeering activity within a 10 year period. Therefore, "in order to make out a RICO claim, [plaintiffs] first must show that the [defendants] committed the predicate acts enumerated by RICO." In other words, "[a] pattern of racketeering activity requires two or more predicate acts and a demonstration that the racketeering predicates are related and amount to or pose a threat of continued criminal activity."

The RICO statute proscribes categories that constitute racketeering activity. The first category consists of certain generically enumerated state law offenses that are "chargeable under State law and punishable by imprisonment for more than one year." 18 U.S.C. §1961(1)(A). The second group of offenses includes specific offenses indictable under the federal criminal code, found at Title 18 of the United States Code. 18 U.S.C. §1961(1)(B). The third group entails certain labor related acts indictable under the Title 29 of the United States Code. 18 U.S.C. §1961(1)(C). The final category consists of offenses involving securities fraud and narcotics transactions. 18 U.S.C. §1961(1)(D).

In this case, plaintiffs' allegations ... are that the defendants violated gambling laws that are chargeable under state law and punishable by imprisonment of more than one year. In plaintiff Thompson's case, he alleges violations of Kan. Stat. Ann. §§60-1704, 21-4302, 21-4304 and 21-3104. In plaintiff Bradley's case, he alleges violations of N.H. Rev. Stat. Ann. §§491:22, 338:1, 338:2 and 338:4. As to their claims under §1961(1)(B), plaintiffs claim violations of 18 U.S.C. §1084(a) ("The Wire Act"); 18 U.S.C. §1952 ("The Travel Act"); 18 U.S.C. §1955 (Prohibition of Illegal Gambling Business); 18 U.S.C. §1957 (Engaging in Monetary Transactions in Property Derived from Specified Unlawful Activity); and 18 U.S.C. §1960 (Prohibition of Illegal Money Transmitting Business). There are currently no federal statutes addressing Internet gambling.

It is the defendants' argument that both plaintiffs failed to sufficiently allege a violation of any predicate act listed in the complaint. As such they argue that plaintiffs cannot satisfy a RICO prerequisite and that plaintiffs' case should be dismissed accordingly. Plaintiffs' response is that internet gambling violates the several federal and state statutes as alleged in the complaint. Thus, in order to establish that plaintiffs' have established a crucial RICO prerequisite, the Court turns to the alleged underlying offenses.

## 1.   *State Law Claims*

### a.   **New Hampshire Claims**

Plaintiff Bradley alleges several violations of New Hampshire state law. However, all four statutes cited by plaintiff are civil statutes. Logically, then, a violation of the civil statutes cited by plaintiff are not "chargeable under state law and punishable by imprisonment of more than one year", and thus do not qualify as a predicate act to establish a pattern of racketeering activity[.]

### b.   **Kansas Claims**

Plaintiff Thompson has alleged violations of Kansas Statutes Annotated 60-1704, 21-4302, 21-4304, and 21-3104. Of the four statutes, three are insufficient on their face to qualify as a predicate act under RICO, which as stated above requires an act "chargeable under state law and punishable by imprisonment of more than one year." Section 21-3104 is not a substantive criminal statute and merely sets forth the geographic reach of Kansas' substantive criminal law. Section 60-1704 is a procedural statute dealing with civil declaratory judgements. Gambling activity is the subject matter of section 21-4303, but only imposes class B nonperson misdemeanor penalties. Kan. Stat. Ann. 21-4303(b). Under Kansas law, a class B nonperson misdemeanor carries a penalty that "shall not exceed six months." Kan. Stat. Ann. 21-4502(1)(b). As the misdemeanor penalty falls short of the "more than one year" requirement under 18 U.S.C. §1961(1)(A), an alleged violation of Kan. Stat. Ann. 21-4502 cannot be a predicate act under RICO.

However, the Kansas Criminal Code does establish a felony offense for commercial gambling under Kan. Stat. Ann. §21-4304. The law establishes four activities as felony offenses, namely (1) operating or receiving all or part of the earnings of a gambling place, (2) receiving, recording or forwarding bets, (3) becoming a custodian of anything of value bet or offered to be bet, (4) conducting a lottery, or (5) setting up for use or collecting the proceeds of any gambling device. Kan. Stat. Ann. 21-4304. Although there are no cases applying the statute to internet gambling, plaintiff cites an opinion issued by the Kansas Attorney General, purporting to deal with the factual scenario before this Court, to support his claims.

Keeping in mind that the Kansas Supreme Court has stated that "an attorney general's opinion is neither conclusive nor binding on us", and that such an opinion is merely "persuasive authority," the Court addresses plaintiff's argument. The Kansas Attorney General addressed the issue of "legality of gambling over the internet." Kan. Atty. Gen. Op. No. 96-31, 1996 WL 156795 (3/25/96). The attorney general opined that "placing, receiving or forwarding a bet, or conducting a lottery, over the telephone or the internet is illegal." It also stated that "if a bet is placed or a lottery entered into via a computer located in the state of Kansas . . . [then] the crime may be prosecuted in this state." Id.

The Court must consider this opinion and the statutory language upon which it is based, remembering that "Kansas courts are required to strictly construe penal statutes in favor of the accused." The relevant statute, Kan. Stat. Ann. 21-4304, makes five commercial gambling activities felony offenses. The only activity remotely applicable to the instant case is section (e), which makes it a felony to "set[] up for use or collect[] the proceeds of any gambling device." Kan. Stat. Ann. 21-4304(e). As applied to the complaint, plaintiff makes no allegation that either the credit card company or issuing bank collected the proceeds of a gambling device. What plaintiff does state is that he purchased credits using his credit card before he gambled. It is a temporal impossibility for the defendants to have completed their transaction with the plaintiff before he gambled and to then be prosecuted for collecting the proceeds of a gambling device, which can only take place after some form of gambling is completed. This analysis is in accord with the Attorney General's opinion, which clearly does not address the conduct alleged against the credit card companies or banks in this case. Indeed, the activities encompassed by the opinion are those of the bettors, the plaintiff here, and the internet casinos, who have not been made a party to this suit. Thus, Thompson has failed to allege that the defendants violated Kansas law.

As the Court is satisfied that plaintiffs have failed, as a matter of law, to state a cause of action against any defendant for violation of state law, the Court turns to the applicable federal statutes.

### 2.   *The Wire Act*

... The Wire Act, found at 18 U.S.C. §1084 provides in pertinent part as follows,

> (a) Whoever being engaged in the business of betting or wagering knowingly uses a wire communication facility for the transmission in interstate or foreign commerce of bets or wagers or information assisting in the placing of bets or wagers on any *sporting event or contest*, or for the transmission of a wire communication which entitles the recipient to receive money or credit as a result of bets or wagers, or for information assisting in the placing of bets or wagers, shall be fined under his title or imprisoned. . . .

(emphasis added). Section (b) of the statute carves out an exception to the rule, instructing that the Wire Act shall not "be construed to prevent the transmission in interstate or foreign commerce of information for use in news reporting of *sporting events or contests*" from a state or country where betting on the sporting event or contest is legal to another state or country where "such betting is legal." 18 U.S.C. §1084(b) (emphasis added).

The defendants argue that plaintiffs' failure to allege sports gambling is a fatal defect with respect to their Wire Act claims, while plaintiffs strenuously argue that the Wire Act does not require sporting events or contests to be the object of gambling. However, a plain reading of the statutory language clearly requires that the object of the gambling be a sporting event or contest. Both the rule and the exception to the rule expressly qualify the nature of the gambling activity as that related to a "sporting event or contest." See 18 U.S.C. §§1084 (a) & (b).

As the plain language of the statute and case law interpreting the statute are clear, there is no need to look to the legislative history of the Act as argued by plaintiffs. See *In re Abbott Laboratories*, 51 F.3d 524, 528 (5th Cir. 1995). However, even a summary glance at the recent legislative history of internet gambling legislation reinforces the Court's determination that internet gambling on a game of chance is not prohibited conduct under 18 U.S.C. §1084. Recent legislative attempts have sought to amend the Wire Act to encompass "contest[s] of chance or a future contingent event not under the control or influence of [the bettor]" while exempting from the reach of the statute data transmitted "for use in the new reporting of any activity, event or contest upon which bets or wagers are based." See S. 474, 105th Congress (1997). Similar legislation was introduced the 106th Congress in the form of the "Internet Gambling Prohibition Act of 1999." See S. 692, 106th Congress (1999). That act sought to amend Title 18 to prohibit the use of the internet to place a bet or wager upon "a contest of others, a sporting event, or a game of chance...". Id. As to the legislative intent at the time the Wire Act was enacted, the House Judiciary Committed Chairman explained that "this particular bill involves the transmission of wagers or bets and layoffs on horse racing and other sporting events." See 107 Cong. Rec. 16533 (Aug. 21, 1961). Comparing the face of the Wire Act and the history surrounding its enactment with the recently proposed legislation, it becomes more certain that the Wire Act's prohibition of gambling activities is restricted to the types of events enumerated in the statute, sporting events or contests. Plaintiffs' argument flies in the face of the clear wording of the Wire Act and is more appropriately directed to the legislative branch than this Court.

. . . Plaintiffs fail to allege the identity of the games that they played, i.e. games of chance or sports related games. Pleading such matters is critical when their right to relief hinges upon the determination of whether Internet casino gambling is legal. That being said, the Court cannot simply assume that plaintiffs bet on sporting events or contests when they make no such allegation in their otherwise extremely thorough complaints.

The sole reference to "sports betting" is a conclusory allegation that the alleged enterprise engaged in sports betting. However, nowhere does either plaintiff allege personal participation in sports gambling. Such an allegation is not enough to survive a motion to dismiss where there is no claim that plaintiffs themselves, or the defendants they have sued, participated in sports gambling. Since plaintiffs have failed to allege that they engaged in sports gambling, and internet gambling in connection with activities other than sports betting is not illegal under federal law, plaintiffs have no cause of action against the credit card companies or the banks under the Wire Act.[9] . . .

---

9. Since plaintiffs have not alleged a substantive violation of the Wire Act, the Court need not consider the issue of whether the credit card companies or issuing banks are "engaged in the business of betting or wagering', a condition to Wire Act liability. The Court does note that according to the Fifth Circuit Pattern Criminal Jury Instructions, the first finding necessary to impose liability is that "the defendant was in the business of betting or wagering. By this I mean the defendants was prepared on a regular basis to accept bets placed by others—that is, the defendant was a bookie." Pattern Jury Instructions (Criminal Cases)—Fifth Circuit §2.50 (West 1990).

## 5.  *Collection of Unlawful Debt*

A stated above, section 1962(c) also makes it unlawful "for any person through a pattern of racketeering activity or through a collection of unlawful debt to acquire or maintain, directly or indirectly, any interest in or control of any enterprise which is engaged in, or the activities of which affect, interstate or foreign commerce." 18 U.S.C. §1962 (c). The language clearly indicates that in formulating RICO, Congress created an alternative means to trigger the statute aside from engaging in a pattern of racketeering activity—that is, collection of an unlawful debt. Therefore, in most cases, discussion of the alleged collection of an unlawful debt would be most appropriately positioned as an alternative, separate section apart from the averments concerning the pattern of racketeering activity. However, because the factual bases for each allegation is the same, the Court will discuss the allegation in this section of the opinion.

Although "relatively few RICO prosecutions and even fewer civil RICO cases have charged collection of an unlawful debt instead of a pattern of racketeering activity," plaintiffs in this case have done so. Section 1961 defines two categories of unlawful debt. The first category of unlawful debt is debt incurred or contracted in a gambling activity illegal under state or federal law, or those debts unenforceable under federal or state usury law. 18 U.S.C. §1961(6)(A). The second category are those debts incurred in connection with the business of gambling in violation of federal or state law or the business of lending money or a thing of value at usurious rates, where those rates are at least double the enforceable rates. 18 U.S.C. §1961(6)(B).

Neither plaintiff has alleged usury, and the Court has already decided that defendants' activities have not violated state or federal law. Accordingly, plaintiffs fail to allege the collection of unlawful debt as defined in 18 U.S.C. §1961(6)(A) or (B).

In the final analysis, plaintiffs are unable to allege that Visa, MasterCard, Travelers or Fleet engaged in a pattern of racketeering activity as defined by 18 U.S.C. §1961. As such, plaintiffs have failed to satisfy a necessary prerequisite to the RICO action. Accordingly, their RICO claims must be dismissed.

Simply put, the Court finds that RICO, no matter how liberally construed, is not intended to provide a remedy to this class of plaintiff. The remedial portion of the statute was intended to provide a remedy for victims of racketeering activity as described in section 1962. Plaintiffs in these cases are not victims[. T]hey are independent actors who made a knowing and voluntary choice to engage in a course of conduct. Litigation over their own actions arose only when the result of those actions became a debt that they did not wish to pay. At this point in time, Internet casino gambling is not a violation of federal law. To the extent that plaintiffs' unsuccessful venture in a legal activity turned out to be less than profitable, they have no remedy at law.

The Court is mindful that motions to dismiss should be rarely granted. However, in this case, plaintiffs fail to plead several elements necessary to sustain a RICO claim as a matter of law, including failure to allege any racketeering activity, the existence of an enterprise, the requisite level of conduct or control, and standing. The defects in plaintiffs' complaints appear insurmountable. With such a legally flawed cause of action, the Court must dismiss plaintiffs' RICO claims without leave to amend.

## *NOTES*

Is the result surprising? Is it possible that the plaintiffs might have been able to amend their pleadings to state a cause of action? The case was affirmed on appeal. *In re MasterCard Intern. Inc.*, 313 F.3d 257 (5th Cir. 2002).

## SHOULD ONLINE GAMBLING BE BANNED?

### Wall Street Journal Online News Roundup, April 4, 2006

Internet gambling is booming as Americans continue to wager billions of dollars on online sports books, Web casinos and virtual poker rooms even though the U.S. Department of Justice considers such activities illegal.

Several U.S. lawmakers are trying to crack down on the industry by clarifying existing U.S. laws and making it easier to go after offenders. One of those measures, the Unlawful Internet Gambling Enforcement Act, seeks to curb online gambling by trying to cut off the money supply: the bill would outlaw the use of credit cards, checks or money transfers to settle wagers. The bill is sponsored by Rep. Jim Leach (R-Iowa).

The Wall Street Journal Online asked Rep. Leach and David Carruthers, chief executive of BetOnSports PLC, an online sports book and casino based in Costa Rica, to debate whether Internet gambling should be banned in the U.S. Their exchange, carried out over e-mail, is below.

**Rep. Leach writes:** Casino gambling, as it is practiced in all Western democracies, has been allowed to exist only with comprehensive regulation. Internet gambling lacks such oversight.

Offshore Internet gambling sites, which target the U.S. market and accept bets from Americans, operate in direct violation of U.S. law. This is not theoretical or subject to interpretation. When a site solicits and accepts wagers on sporting events and games of chance, these online casinos violate the Wire Act and the Professional and Amateur Sports Protection Act.

Gambling is one field where the efficiencies of the Internet are counterproductive for society. When consumers deal with an offshore entity, they give their personal financial information to unknown individuals, who, by definition, are engaged in criminal activity. Internet casinos introduce a gaming room in homes, offices and school dormitories with bettors who abdicate the comprehensive protections afforded by U.S. law.

Offshore Internet gambling sites sweep dollars out of the U.S. into largely unknown, often criminal hands. The potential threat of identity theft and fraud is high for the individual bettor just as the risk posed to our national security from terror and criminal organizations that control such sites or used them for money laundering purposes is real.

Internet gambling's characteristics are unique: Online players can gamble 24 hours a day from home; children may play without sufficient age verification; and betting with a credit card can undercut a player's perception of the value of cash, leading to gambling addiction, bankruptcy and crime.

The illegal Internet gambling business is booming and the consequences of this unfettered illegal activity are profound. Americans will send nearly $6 billion to unregulated, offshore online casinos this year, nearly half of the $12 billion bet world-wide on Internet gambling. These sites evade rigorous U.S.-based regulations that control gaming by minors, problem gamblers, and ensure the integrity of the games.

But Internet gambling is more than a theoretical issue of technology confronting law. Society is the family writ large, and it is the American family that is jeopardized by the lure of Internet gambling.

Problem gambling can lead to serious psychological and physical as well as financial harm. Individuals who become "hooked" frequently lose their jobs, homes and marriage and sometimes even contemplate suicide. Internet gambling is not alone in causing such consequences, but it facilitates and accentuates the challenges posed by problem gambling.

The problem with the current circumstance is that enforcement tools are so inadequate. What the Unlawful Internet Gambling Enforcement Act (H.R. 4411) basically does is make it illegal to use a bank instrument such as a credit card or money transfer or check to settle an Internet wager. No approach to squelching Internet gaming will ever prove perfectly effective, but one that constrains the payment system has the highest chance of achieving credible results.

H.R. 4411 focuses on the gambling business, not the gambler. It puts the principal enforcement burden on financial intermediaries such as banks. The law stays generally static on what is illegal; but enforcement is upgraded by making it more difficult for an Internet casino to operate.

**Mr. Carruthers responds:** It may surprise Rep. Leach to know that I share his concerns about problem gambling and underage gambling. That is why I would like our business to be regulated by the U.S. government.

I run a multi-billion-dollar public company listed on the London Stock Exchange, and we operate with the highest standards of practice to protect consumers, restrict minor access and protect the vulnerable. My company has controls in place that restrict access by minors and would cut off gambling from customers who exhibit excessive compulsive behavior. Online gambling is the most transparent form of gambling there is—every transaction is logged and every transaction is available for scrutiny. I, and my peers at other major online operators, want regulation of our industry. Regulation would standardize and strengthen our best practices and in addition provide taxable revenues to the U.S. government.

It is inconsistent to have comprehensive regulation of land-based casino gambling and to not have the same oversight of the Internet-gambling industry. This is what we seek. Precedents for regulation of our industry exist. Online gambling is regulated in 64 countries, including the United Kingdom. Gambling is a source of entertainment for millions of people around the world and has been for centuries. Online, millions of people enjoy it every day. We are asking to be regulated. Prohibiting online gambling would be catastrophic. Prohibiting the industry would have the exact opposite effect to what the congressman seeks. Prohibition would not stop online gambling, it would send it underground and leave the vulnerable unprotected.

While Rep. Leach maintains that online gambling is illegal in the U.S., the legal issues are not clear. Rep. Leach is relying on an outdated, irrelevant law that is inapplicable and unenforceable for online gambling. That is why we are looking for clear standards, regulations and licensing for what is an everyday entertainment medium enjoyed by millions.

**Rep. Leach:** Mr. Carruthers is correct that there is some imprecision in the Wire Act, which dates back to 1961. But there is little imprecision in the Professional and Amateur Sports Protection Act of 1993, which stipulates that it is "unlawful for a person to sponsor, operate, or advertise . . . any gambling scheme . . . based on games in which amateur or professional athletes participate."

When he calls for "regulation of our industry," he is really suggesting that gambling companies should be allowed to do legally what they are currently doing illegally. He is also suggesting not only that the law of the U.S. (the above two referenced statutes) but similar laws that currently exist in all 50 states be overturned.

He suggests that prohibition would not stop online gambling, but "send it underground and leave the vulnerable unprotected." This is the case today. The vulnerable are unprotected because companies that tap the American market violate our law and its protections. No amount of regulation can address Web-based gaming's particular intrusiveness and harm to the American home.

Internet gambling regulation cannot work like traditional casino-based regulation. Brick-and-mortar casinos have the means to keep kids and problem gamblers away. But not an Internet casino. The anonymity the Internet provides a gambler is unique and novel. Regulation over the Internet would not have the effect of protecting underage or problem gamblers nor would it eliminate the money laundering problem or deal as comprehensively with the integrity of games. Even if one concedes that a regulatory regime could attempt to address each of these things, the Internet is so pervasive and borderless that one country's regulations are woefully insufficient. Ultimately the result of regulating Internet gambling will be extending an industry which adds few advantages to the economy and many disadvantages to society.

It is no accident that supporters of the legislation I have introduced range from every major sporting organization—the NFL, MLB, NHL, NBA, NCAA—to the American Bankers Association to the Christian Coalition to the Episcopal, Presbyterian, Methodist, Baptist and Lutheran churches, to 48 of the 50 state attorneys general.

**Mr. Carruthers:** Gambling on the Internet is entertainment and a personal choice. Why is the congressman trying to tell Americans what they can and cannot do in the privacy of their own homes? Isn't he supposed to represent his constituents? According to the Wall Street Journal's own poll on online gambling last month, 85% of those polled believe Congress should not ban online gambling.

The fact that a small number of people gamble more than they should is not reason to prohibit the entertainment for every adult. [The poll Mr. Carruthers refers to was an informal online survey of WSJ.com readers' opinions, and not a scientific sampling.—ED.]

Thinking that one can ban a form of entertainment on the Internet is ludicrous. The Internet gives people access to the world and is a communications tool. Ultimately, it is the individual in his or her own privacy who should be in control of their access to the Internet—not any government.

There is no other institution that has more interest in preserving the integrity of sports than the online gambling industry. Had the online gambling industry been in existence and been regulated, Pete Rose's gambling problem, for example, would have been brought to the attention of authorities immediately. My company currently maintains controls to protect the interest of our customers. We utilize specific customer tracking controls that help customers assess and limit their own behavior, but also allow us to set limits for deposits and indicate a cooling off period for customers who may need it. We train our customer relations employees to recognize excess or irregular behavior and address it immediately. Regulation would standardize these best practices throughout the industry. American consumers would then know which companies are licensed and which are not.

I would like to invite Rep. Leach and any of his colleagues to see our operations first-hand in Costa Rica. This way, he can see directly the controls and practices we have in place. We have found that once people are educated about our business, they are willing to work with us to address those social concerns that we all care about.

**Rep. Leach:** Entertainment is multi-dimensional, but gambling online is not the same as bowling. No home, no office, no college dormitory should be a casino.

American law varies by state but generally makes no moral judgments on the wisdom of gambling. The legislation I have introduced does not extend existing prohibitions on gambling; it only provides an enforcement mechanism for laws on the books. In a country of laws, upholding the law is fundamental.

In addition to protecting the rule of law, it is also fundamental for a society to protect the security of its citizens. Here, it is relevant to note the testimony before Congress of Dennis Lormel, then chief of the FBI's Financial Crimes Section:

> "The Internet gambling and online capabilities have become a haven
> for money laundering activities. We believe there is a huge potential for
> offshore sites being utilized to launder money, and there are examples

of pending cases, particularly in our organized crime program, involving enterprises using these types of services as conduits for money laundering."

Likewise, in a formal report, the U.S. Department of State expressed a similar concern:

"The Internet gambling operations are, in essence, the functional equivalent of wholly unregulated offshore banks with the bettor accounts serving as bank accounts for account holders who are, in the virtual world, virtually anonymous. For these reasons, Internet gambling operations are vulnerable to be used, not only for money laundering, but also criminal activities ranging from terrorist financing to tax evasion."

Mr. Carruthers's invitation to visit the gambling operations of BetOn-Sports in Costa Rica may seem a generous gesture. But for a congressman to accept it would be ethically dubious, if not illegal.

**Mr. Carruthers:** I take offense to the congressman's unsubstantiated allegations about this industry and money laundering. He talks about money laundering but doesn't have any specific facts to back it up. There have been absolutely no convictions of online gambling's association with money laundering. And, as a CEO of a multi-billion-dollar public company, it is clear that I follow very specific transparent reporting practices and governance procedures to run this company. I have fiduciary responsibility to my shareholders and ethical responsibilities to my customers.

The congressman's refusal to educate himself about the realities of our industry are disturbing. Has he asked his constituents what they think about this kind of government invasion of their privacy and whether they want the government to ban online gambling? If he won't fund a poll to ask his constituents, then I will. The fact is millions of Americans are now gambling online everyday. They are enjoying this form of entertainment and doing it responsibly.

And if the congressman does not want to accept my invitation to visit our operations and see our effort first-hand, I suggest then that we get together in Washington. I would like to meet him and tell him first hand all that we are doing to protect American citizens. How could one possibly think of legislative action without knowing all the information?

**Mr. Carruthers adds:** The fact is Americans account for 45% of the consumers who bet online. Overall, Americans wagered nearly $6 billion dollars online in 2005, compared to $1.5 billion dollars in 2001. This is a thriving, legitimate and successful business that will not go away.

Trying to prohibit the online gaming industry is a futile exercise and waste of resources. The constantly evolving structure of the Internet will make prohibition increasingly difficult, if not impossible. Time could be much better spent establishing regulations to prevent underage gambling and protecting the vulnerable members of society from excessive and compulsive behavior. These controls currently exist and the best operators use them. Regulation and licensing would help standardize best practice across the board and allow the customer to differentiate the good operator from any bad operator.

There is a lot of hypocrisy in the effort to ban online gaming. Some forms of online gaming are permitted—state lotteries and horse racing, for example. Regulation would bring clarity to efforts clouded with hypocrisy. Regulation and licensing would set standards that demand businesses operate in the best interests of their customers, or they would not be licensed in the U.S.

The issue is: What are the most viable and effective ways to regulate a business that not only exists, but is growing? We have begun the process by working with the International Institute for Conflict Prevention and Resolution to spearhead the creation of an independent advisory council to bring together individuals from both sides of the argument in hopes of creating operating standards that could be acceptable to everyone. Not only would regulation strengthen companies that wish to operate responsibly, licensing our companies would also bring billions of dollars of tax revenues to state and local budgets.

*NOTES*

A mere two months after this exchange, Carruthers and his company, BetOnSports, PLC, were charged by the U.S. Department of Justice under RICO, the Wire Act, and other statutes, in an indictment that included a claim for forfeiture of up to $4.5 billion dollars. Shortly thereafter, he was arrested and prosecuted.

### RYAN D. HAMMER, DOES INTERNET GAMBLING STRENGTHEN THE U.S. ECONOMY? DON'T BET ON IT
#### 54 Fed. Comm. L.J. 103-22 (Dec. 2001)

Commercial gambling in the United States is a mammoth industry. In the past few decades, the United States developed from a country with few gambling options to one permitting some form of legalized gambling in every state except Utah and Hawaii. A series of incremental decisions by local and state governments paved the way for tremendous growth in the gambling industry. Presently, a new wave of technology affects this industry. Legislators and regulators must deal with the phenomenon of Internet gambling—once dubbed "the crack cocaine of gambling."

The advent of the Internet introduced an entirely new medium for individuals to participate in gambling activities. Unlike traditional land-based casinos, the action at online casinos is perpetual and available to anyone with Internet access. Many online gambling sites operate from locations such as Antigua and Belize, unsupervised by U.S. government regulators. Perhaps the most frightening aspect of Internet gambling is the rampaging growth of the young industry. The Internet gambling explosion poses serious concerns to society.

This Note asserts that Internet gambling must be curbed to lessen its negative impact on the American economy. Many state and local governments are dependent on tax revenues associated with traditional forms of gambling. Internet gambling not only deprives the economy of these valuable tax revenues, but also costs the economy valuable jobs and assorted fees associated with traditional gambling. In order to lessen its negative impact on the economy, Internet gambling must be more judiciously regulated in the United States.

### III. Negative Economic Consequences of Internet Gambling

The recent explosion of Internet gambling poses serious concerns to the U.S. economy. With the U.S. economy slowing significantly after a decade of expansion, the impact of Internet gambling will be detrimental. One effect will be the reduction in tax revenues collected by state and federal governments from legalized gambling operations. The gambling industry in America represents a significant source of tax revenues to the various jurisdictions in which gambling operates. A second area that will be affected by the Internet gambling phenomenon is the consumer credit card industry. Thirdly, Internet gambling harms families, leads to crime, and increases addiction. Although difficult to quantify, these areas of concern will negatively impair the economy.

#### A. Reduction in Tax Revenue

Legal gambling operations in the United States pay millions of dollars in taxes annually to local and federal governments. Without question, these taxes contribute to the overall revenues in the vast majority of states with legalized gambling. "State and local governments in Iowa collected more than $197 million in taxes and fees from Iowa casinos and racetracks [in 2000]." The Casino Queen Riverboat in East St. Louis generates between $10 million and $12 million annually in tax revenues for the city. In addition, the riverboat casino created more than 1,200 full-time jobs. "Gaming revenues have enabled the city to make dramatic strides in its quality of life." The willingness of states to legalize certain forms of gambling, such as lotteries, often hinges on revenue shortfalls of their treasuries. During the 1980s, sixteen of the twenty-two states with the greatest increase in unemployment created lotteries. It is always easier for politicians to support a lottery or a casino riverboat than to propose a tax increase on their constituents.

When Americans participate in Internet gambling, however, no state budget receives a windfall of revenues. The money gambled by Americans on the Internet is done so with companies that pay no taxes in the United States. With over $2 billion gambled on the Internet in 2000, the amount of tax revenues that the United States loses is staggering. Included in this loss of revenues are secondary items purchased when one attends a gambling facility, such as food, souvenirs, and clothing.

An investigation of tax revenue lost to Internet gambling can be optimally displayed by looking at a specific state. For example, [consider] the effect Internet gambling has on a riverboat casino in Illinois. Gambling riverboats in Illinois are subject to the Illinois Riverboat Gambling Act. This law imposes an annual graduated wagering tax on adjusted gross receipts from gambling. Adjusted gross receipts are defined as "gross receipts less winnings paid to wagerers." The graduated tax rate for each riverboat is as follows: up to $25 million—15%; $25 million to $50 million—20%; $50 million to $75 million—25%; $75 million to $100 million—30%; in excess of $100 million—35%. Of the projected $2.2 billion gambled on the Internet in 2000, assume that $50 million is done so by Illinois residents. Assuming that Internet gambling did not exist and that Illinois residents would have spent the remaining $50 million gambling legally, $50 million less is gambled in Illinois as a result of Internet gambling. Now examine a large riverboat casino in the suburbs of Chicago. If this riverboat handles 10% of the dollars gambled in Illinois annually, then the riverboat alone will lose $5 million in revenues to Internet gambling in a year. With the large riverboat being taxed at 35% for adjusted receipts over $100 million, the riverboat by itself will pay $1.75 million less in annual graduated wagering taxes.

The proceeds of the graduated wagering tax in Illinois are to be disbursed as follows: 25% is delegated to the local government where the home dock is located, a small portion goes to the Illinois Gaming Board for expenses, and the remainder goes to the state education assistance fund. This wagering tax does not take into consideration admission taxes and excise taxes on food and beverages. The Illinois Riverboat Gambling Act requires that licensees pay a two dollar admission tax for each person admitted to a gaming cruise. Of this admission tax, the host county or municipality receives one dollar. If one million people board Illinois riverboats in a year, then $1 million in tax revenues are being provided to local municipalities as a result of legalized gambling.

While any gambler desires to win money, the depression of losing can be somewhat alleviated when the money is being reinvested to improve the economy. This is the case when people lose money in regulated gambling environments. For example, when an individual buys a lottery ticket at a convenience store, a portion of the cost of that ticket will be used to improve education or to build better roads. When an individual plays an online lottery, the proceeds are not reinvested to improve any government projects. Legal gambling operations are permitted to function in the United States when they comply with strict regulations such as accounting procedures. No such procedures exist in the world of Internet gambling, which deprives the United States of millions of dollars annually in tax revenues.

### B. CONSUMER CREDIT CARD INDUSTRY

Internet gambling places banks and credit card companies in a precarious position. On the one hand, these institutions can profit greatly by offering credit to individuals to gamble online. Credit card charges for Internet gambling are often posted as cash advances, which carry higher interest rates than ordinary purchases. The cash advance rate for most credit cards exceeds 20%. The downside to credit card companies stems from the processing of Internet gambling transactions. Numerous lawsuits are filed by individuals who have lost money gambling online and who refuse to pay their gambling debts. These lawsuits could leave banks unable to collect debts from individuals who partake in Internet gambling.

As a result of the uncertainty surrounding the litigation of Internet gambling issues, many credit card issuers prohibit transactions from Internet gambling sites. Among the credit card companies that [have] ceased allowing Internet gambling transactions is Delaware-based MBNA. According to a company spokesman, it "began prohibiting transactions from Internet gambling sites . . . 'when it became apparent how the bank's cards were being used.' " It is expected that other credit card companies will adopt a similar stance to that of MBNA, as the risk of the number of individuals failing to pay their Internet gambling debts increases.

The biggest losers with respect to the use of credit cards in Internet gambling transactions are those who do not gamble online. Regardless of how the litigation evolves in cases of Internet gamblers against credit card companies, the ordinary American loses. If Internet gamblers are successful in having their debts alleviated, non-Internet gamblers will ultimately pay the economic price for their fellow Americans' victory. This price will come in the form of higher fees, charges, and interest rates passed on to all American credit card holders. Because the number of those in the non-Internet gambling community far outweighs the number of those who gamble online, a vast majority of Americans will experience the negative effects of credit card use in Internet gambling transactions.

Even if credit card companies are successful in litigation against Internet gamblers, Americans will still feel negative effects. Victories for credit card companies would provide credibility to the Internet gambling industry and encourage more people to participate. The result of this certification of the Internet gambling industry would cause more and more people to accumulate large Internet gambling debts. When the factor of gambling addiction is added, inevitably many individuals would assume debts unrecoverable to credit card companies. Once again, higher interest rates and fees will be passed on to non-Internet gamblers as a result of the use of credit cards in Internet gambling transactions.

#### C. MISCELLANEOUS COSTS TO SOCIETY

The societal concerns that led to the intense regulation of traditional forms of gambling do not disappear when dealing with Internet gambling. As Internet gambling invades American households, society is "left to deal with the crime, bankruptcy, and gambling disorders that may result." Among the many problems exacerbated by Internet gambling are gambling addiction and gambling by minors. Pathological gambling negatively affects not only the gambler, but also the gambler's family and friends, and society at large. Societal costs of pathological gambling includes the expenditure of unemployment benefits, physical and mental health problems, theft, embezzlement, bankruptcy, suicide, domestic violence, and child abuse and neglect.

Experts predict that "the number of compulsive gamblers could soon quadruple from 5 million to 20 million addicts nationwide."

The primary reason for this anticipated increase in compulsive gambling is the Internet. With the accessibility of the Internet, gamblers do not have to travel to casinos or contact their local bookie to place a bet. Internet gambling is more addictive than other forms of gambling because it combines high-speed, instant gratification with the anonymity of gambling from home. The temptations that lead to compulsive gambling are as close as one's computer.

Despite the severe impact that pathological gambling has on Americans, minimal research exists on the topic. The research performed on pathological gambling has often been half-hearted. An addiction specialist before the House Committee on Banking and Finance offered the following testimony on pathological gambling:

> Our research indicated that we have a growing number of problem and pathological gamblers in America.
>
> We are just beginning to address this problem and calculate its costs. The casino industry is supporting limited research, but, sadly, it has been difficult to get this matter on the radar screen of the major federal funders of research on addictive behaviors. . . . In this environment, are we really ready for a potentially exponential increase in gambling activity? The answer should be obvious.
>
> Compulsive gamblers are responsible for an estimated fifteen percent of the dollars lost in gambling. Beyond this monetary figure, how can society quantify a divorce caused by a gambling addiction or a gambling-induced suicide?

Another troubling aspect of Internet gambling is the potential access to minors. Many minors are adept at playing games online and are especially vulnerable to Internet gambling. Whereas state legislation allows casinos to forbid gambling by minors, "Internet gambling eludes these safeguards." The development of Internet gambling sites has made wagering even more accessible to minors. In a majority of gambling studies, high school- and college-aged individuals possessed the highest problem rates. Gambling as a phenomenon among minors is two to four times more common than among adults. The continued development of Internet gambling enhances this problem.

Internet gambling sites employ different approaches to prevent minors from participating. The majority of Internet gambling sites utilize credit card information to screen minors because credit is not extended to those under the age of majority. Sites that rely on credit card information, however, alert their company to the possibility that minors will steal credit card information from adults. To prevent this problem, the most sophisticated Internet gambling sites employ credit reporting databases to match credit cards and taxpayer identification numbers to verify the true identities of users. While the number of sites using the matching system is in the minority, this heightened security is a step in the right direction to limit Internet gambling. Regardless, the dangerous combination of minors and gambling is enhanced by the accessibility of Internet gambling sites.

## TOM BELL, INTERNET GAMBLING: POPULAR, INEXORABLE, AND (EVENTUALLY) LEGAL
### Policy Analysis No. 336 for Cato Institute 12 (1999)

### THE INEVITABLE FAILURE OF PROHIBITION

Several factors will frustrate attempts to prohibit Internet gambling. This section discusses three of them:

#### INTERNET TECHNOLOGY RENDERS PROHIBITION FUTILE

The very architecture of the Internet renders gambling prohibition futile. Even the Department of Justice admits that traditional attacks on interstate gambling "may not be technically feasible or appropriate with regard to Internet transmissions." In contrast to telephone communications, which typically travel over circuit-switched networks, Internet communications use packet switching. Each Internet message gets broken into discrete packets, which travel over various and unpredictable routes until received and reassembled at the message's destination. In other words, sending a message over the Internet is a bit like writing a letter, chopping it up, and mailing each piece separately to the same address. The recipient can piece it together, but anyone snooping on your correspondence has a tougher go of it.

Understanding Internet communications as akin to the postal system clarifies why prohibition of Internet gambling will not work. Imagine telling the U.S. Postal Service that it must henceforth crack down on all letters conveying information used in illegal gambling. It would rightly object that it already has its hands full just delivering the mail and that it lacks the equipment and personnel to snoop through every letter. Furthermore, it cannot always tell which messages relate to illegal activities. People use "bet" and "wager" in everyday conversations, whereas gamblers often speak in code. Finally, customers of the mail service would strongly object to having the Postal Service paw through their correspondence.

Prohibitionists could not expect the Postal Service to simply stop delivering mail to and from certain addresses associated with illegal gambling. The Postal Service would again object to the burdens of implementing such a program, and citizens would again object to law enforcement officials' spying on private correspondence. More important, trying to cut off mail to certain addresses would utterly fail to stop gambling: gamblers would rely on post office boxes—which they could change at a moment's notice—and drop off outgoing correspondence with no return address. All of those considerations apply with equal or greater force to Internet gambling. The high volume of traffic alone ensures that Internet service providers would find it impossible to discriminate between illicit gaming information and other Internet traffic. It is easier to encrypt messages, to change addresses, and to send and receive messages anonymously over the Internet than through the postal system. The inherently private nature of the Internet would also stymie prohibitionists. In contrast to the quasi-public and monolithic postal system, the Internet relies on thousands of separate and wholly private service providers to carry out its deliveries. All of them would stridently object to the burdens of enforcing a ban on Internet traffic. More than a few would simply refuse to cooperate.

Does that sound like a pessimistic account? To the contrary, it merely describes the current situation. As technological innovation continues to drive the development of Internet communications, law enforcement officials will fall further and further behind the tricks used by illegal gamblers.

Given the technological constraints, prohibiting Internet gambling plainly will not work as intended. As an unintended side effect, however, prohibition would sorely compromise the cost, efficiency, and security of Internet communications. In criticizing recent legislative proposals to outlaw the consumption of Internet gambling services, the Department of Justice observed that "this would likely require the backbone provider to filter messages by examining the content of traffic flowing across its network in a way that may have serious economic and societal consequences for Internet usage generally." We would never accept the cost—in money, time, or privacy—of authorizing the post office to open every letter in a futile crusade against gambling. Internet users will hardly allow their network to suffer a similar fate. Given the inevitable failure of technical fixes, legalizing Internet gambling offers the only viable solution.

### INTERNET GAMBLING CAN ESCAPE DOMESTIC PROHIBITIONS

Outlawing Internet gaming services domestically will simply push the business overseas. Federal law enforcement agents admit that they cannot stop overseas gaming operations. "International Internet gambling? We can't do anything about it," Department of Justice spokesman John Russell said. "That's the bottom line." Even Kyl has confessed that "this would be a very difficult kind of activity to regulate because we don't have jurisdiction over the people abroad who are doing it."

Both practical and legal considerations ensure that no domestic ban on Internet gambling will have an international reach. Because the Internet provides instant access to overseas sites, to be effective, any domestic prohibition on gaming services will have to cover the entire planet. American law enforcement agents can—and recently did—arrest local citizens accused of running Internet gambling businesses, but smart operators will quickly learn to set up abroad and stay there.

Gaming services can find ample shelter overseas. A growing number of countries, including Australia, New Zealand, Antigua, and Costa Rica, have decided to legalize and license Internet gaming services. Principles of international law, which protect each country's sovereignty, bar the United States from extraditing its citizens merely for violating domestic anti-gambling laws. Furthermore, the Sixth Amendment of the Constitution's Bill of Rights, because it guarantees criminal defendants the right to confront their accusers, prohibits the prosecution of those who remain overseas while operating Internet gambling sites. Law enforcement officials in the United States can therefore neither arrest nor sentence anyone who offers Internet gambling services from a safe harbor abroad.

Even if through international negotiations U.S. authorities managed to export a domestic ban on Internet gambling, that sort of foreign trade carries too high a price. As the Department of Justice observed in its critique of the Kyl bill, "If we request that foreign countries investigate, on our behalf, conduct that is legal in the foreign state, we must be prepared to receive and act upon foreign requests for assistance when the conduct complained of is legal, or even constitutionally protected, in the United States." That threat looms all too large, given that most foreign states regulate speech in ways forbidden by the First Amendment.

### POLITICAL DEMAND FOR INTERNET GAMBLING

As discussed above, consumers have already demonstrated a huge demand for Internet gambling. Soon, though, the prohibitionists will have more than angry voters to worry about. Law enforcement agents have seized the media spotlight by telling scary stories and demanding new powers to crush Internet gambling. As the futility of prohibition becomes more and more evident, however, cooler heads in state revenue departments will begin to see Internet gambling as a huge new cash cow. Prohibition merely ensures that Internet gamblers will ship their money to places like Antigua, New Zealand, and Australia. State governors and legislatures will soon demand a share of that bounty. The same political forces that have led to the widespread legalization of lottery, casino, and riverboat gambling will eventually favor the legalization of Internet gambling.

Indeed, the trend toward the legalization of Internet gambling has already started. When he introduced his bill banning Internet gambling, Senator Kyl proclaimed, "Gambling erodes values of hard work, sacrifice, and personal responsibility." He nonetheless amended his bill to ensure that the incumbent gambling industry would remain free to exploit the Internet (even while would-be competitors remained shut out). Kyl's generosity attracted the attention of the Department of Justice, which noted that "the numerous exceptions for pari-mutuel wagering would expand the scope of permissible parimutuel activities beyond what is currently permitted by existing law." As Internet gambling grows and spreads both in its officially sanctioned legal forms and in its unstoppable illegal ones, so too will the power of its lobbyists to wear down prohibitionists.

Notwithstanding lawmakers' apocalyptic tales to the contrary, legalized Internet gambling will come as no great shock. Representative Goodlatte defended his bill to prohibit Internet gambling with the claim that existing laws "have been turned on their head" by the Internet because "no longer do people have to leave the comfort of their homes" to access casinos. In fact, however, nine states already allow their citizens to access professional gaming services at home via telecommunications devices. Far from revolutionizing American culture, legalized Internet gambling will merely extend current social and technological trends.

#### THE BENEFITS OF INTERNET GAMBLING

For the reasons set forth above, attempts to prohibit Internet gambling will inevitably fail and give way to legalization. Futility, however, hardly suffices to bar bad public policy. It thus bears noting that the legalization of Internet gambling offers a number of benefits.

Internet gambling will encourage the private sector to develop network capacity and commerce. Just as real-world casinos have competed to build innovative and appealing environments, so too will Internet gaming services compete to offer the flashiest graphics and most sophisticated user interfaces. That competition will result in broader bandwidth and better software for all sorts of Internet applications.

Critics of real-world casinos fault them for luring consumers into windowless caverns far from the real world, with money traps at every turn and free-flowing booze. Some gambling analysts even claim that casinos, tracks, and other real-world sites rely on giving gamblers a place to socialize, creating little communities that console losers and—for a price—administer to the lonely. Regardless of the validity of such criticisms, they certainly do not apply to Internet gambling. To the contrary, consumers who log on from home computers will find it impossible to escape yelling kids, barking dogs, and all the other distractions of the real world. Internet gambling thus offers a more wholesome environment than its real-world counterpart.

Gamblers deserve all the benefits that other consumers of entertainment services enjoy—including the benefits of a competitive marketplace. By giving consumers cheap and easy access to a variety of gaming opportunities, the Internet will bring competition to an industry that has too long enjoyed the shelter of highly restrictive licensing practices. Freeing the gambling market will help to ensure that only the most honest and generous casinos succeed in drawing bettors' business.

Gamblers also deserve the same legal protections that other consumers enjoy. Prohibition will not cut off access to Internet gambling; it will, however, cut off access to the courts. Internet gamblers, like other consumers, will undoubtedly suffer fraud, breach of contract, and other legal wrongs from time to time. Prohibition ensures that Internet gamblers, like people involved in the drug trade, will have no recourse to legal remedies. Prohibiting Internet gambling will not make it inaccessible, whereas legalizing it will put the benefits of increased competition within the rule of law.

### ON THE REGULATION OF INTERNET GAMBLING

For the reasons set forth above, we should both recognize and celebrate that legalization will trump the prohibition of Internet gambling. But regulators will no doubt remain worried. What role will they have in the brave new world of Internet gambling? Playing off that worry, proponents of a ban on Internet gambling have argued that, if prohibition will not work, then neither will any scheme of regulation. Such an argument fundamentally misunderstands a basic principle of governance: if they offer greater benefits than burdens, regulations can succeed even where prohibition fails.

The comparative advantage of limited regulation over prohibition explains why people do not illegally shoot craps in Las Vegas alleys.

In the case of Internet gambling, the benefits of winning an official stamp of approval might convince an online casino to submit to regulation, even if that same casino could easily flout a total ban on its business. Exactly how much regulation will the Internet gambling industry tolerate? In all likelihood, not very much; for the reasons set forth above, providers and consumers of Internet gambling services will find it relatively easy to escape unduly burdensome regulations.

It may well turn out that Internet gambling tolerates only such simple and general rules as those that common law stipulates for property, contracts, and torts. That would still constitute regulation of a sort. Those basic principles already suffice to make regular many other types of commerce, after all, and would probably suffice for the rest were commerce more free. Politicians and bureaucrats might not regard it as "regulation" to treat Internet gambling as an ordinary business, but their preferred solution—detailed and particular rules enforced by specialized administrative bodies— would arguably do more to make Internet gambling subject to rent seeking and industry capture than it would to make it regular. At any rate, such statist "irregulation" has little chance of affecting Internet gambling.

### THE RIGHT TO GAMBLE, ONLINE AND OFF

Friends of liberty argue convincingly that the right to peaceably dispose of one's property includes the right to gamble. Although utterly sound in philosophical terms, such an argument will almost certainly fail to affect public policy. Lawmakers typically care more about practices than principles. They will thus comfortably ban Internet gambling on the assumption that history has demonstrated the legitimacy of prohibiting, or at least heavily regulating, games of chance.

Of course, history alone could never defeat the moral argument for the right to gamble. Somewhat surprisingly, however, history does not even support lawmakers who would infringe on that right. Gambling in fact played a major role in the personal and political lives of the Founders of the United States. The infamous Stamp Act, which triggered the shot at Concord "heard round the world," infuriated colonists by taxing playing cards and dice. Thomas Jefferson, while drafting the Declaration of Independence, relaxed by gambling on backgammon, cards, and bingo. Jefferson later declared the lottery preferable to conventional means of raising government revenue on grounds that it is "a tax laid on the willing only."

Benjamin Franklin—using his era's most advanced technology— printed a good portion of the colonies' playing cards. George

Washington regularly bet on horses, gambled in card games, and bought lottery tickets. Washington also managed public lotteries, as did Franklin and John Hancock. Lotteries even helped to pay for the first home of the U.S. Congress, as well as for public buildings throughout the new U.S. capital.

Clearly, the Founders embraced gambling as part of their inalienable right to "the Pursuit of Happiness." The historical record should give pause even to lawmakers willing to ignore the moral argument against interfering with the right to gamble. How could any modern politician justify stripping the American people of rights that the Founders fought for, won, and exercised? Certainly, the advent of Internet gambling is no excuse for ignoring honorable historical precedents.

*NOTES*

Alcohol prohibition in the United States led to an increase in organized crime; and the subsequent repeal of Prohibition led to a decrease in organized crime. Is it possible that stricter regulations on legal gaming will produce greater activity by organized crime in the gaming industry? By definition, illegal gambling is organized crime because it takes at least two people cooperating to engage in an illegal gambling transaction. For more on Prohibition, see generally Mark Thornton, Alcohol Prohibition Was a Failure, CATO Institute Policy Analysis (1991) available at http://www.cato.org/pubs/pas/pa-157.html.

## ANTHONY N. CABOT & LOUIS V. CSOKA, THE GAMES PEOPLE PLAY: IS IT TIME FOR A NEW LEGAL APPROACH TO PRIZE GAMES?

### 4 Nev. L.J. 197, 243-46 (2004)

The position taken by the United States Department of Justice and some members of Congress is that most Internet gambling is, or should be, unlawful. Nevertheless, any actions taken by members of our government may be rendered meaningless by virtue of the Internet's characteristics. By its very nature, the Internet is global in reach. Therefore, the efforts and policy of the United States must be considered in light of international developments. This is one of the most difficult issues concerning the ways in which United States policy can successfully implement a communications medium that defies national boundaries.

Since the dawn of modern history, mankind has existed under a system whereby the government has physical control over a geographic area and its inhabitants. Indeed, according to one authority, "[u]nder International law, a state is an entity that has a defined territory and a permanent population, under the control of its own government. . . ." Modern technology, however, has gradually eroded government control by facilitating inter-jurisdictional transactions. The creation of a national mail system spurred the development of mail fraud, as well as the advent of the first national lottery. More recently, the dawn of electronic bank transfers made the movement of money received from illegal transactions more difficult to track. The Internet also significantly raises the stakes. We now live in a human community that exists without traditional notions of territory. Therefore, the question for each government is whether to extend its monopoly to a boundless territory, or to control the Internet only within its own territorial boundaries.

For many countries, this proposition is easily answered. So long as government controls access to the Internet, it can also control the content that its citizens view. While this approach may be acceptable in some regions of the world, it is unacceptable in most Western cultures, such as the United States, Canada, Western Europe, and Australia. The most daunting option is for a country to maintain traditional governmental controls over its citizens while relinquishing control of the Internet infrastructure.

Without government control over Internet access, citizens can buy virtually anything over the Internet from a business that does not exist anywhere but in "cyberspace." For example, consider the online gaming industry. Where is the sports book located? Is it really in Antigua where it is licensed? Or is it next door, but routed through a surrogate server in Antigua? Moreover, how long does it take to move the Internet sports book between countries? These questions illustrate that the physical location of the Internet business is increasingly irrelevant. These questions also point to a greater issue: without having physical control over the business, the government lacks the ability to control or tax gambling activity.

The basic struggle concerns whether government can control the Internet or whether the Internet will control the government. This issue goes beyond gambling to include issues such as bank fraud, consumer fraud, theft of intellectual property, copyright infringement, and child pornography, and may need to be addressed via international treaty.

In particular, even assuming that operating a gambling site on the Internet is illegal, under national or international law, governments must have a vehicle to enforce the particular law at issue. Prior to creation of the Internet, enforcement was accomplished more easily. For example, the sheriff could simply locate the alleged perpetrator within his jurisdiction, arrest him, and bring him before the magistrate. The Internet world is much different. Mobility allows the alleged perpetrator to be in another state or halfway around the world. Jurisdictional battles often overshadow questions of guilt or innocence.

---

## THE UNLAWFUL INTERNET GAMBLING ENFORCEMENT ACT OF 2006

In 2006, Congress attempted an indirect approach to enforcement of a ban on Internet gaming when it enacted the Unlawful Internet Gambling Enforcement Act of 2006 (UIGEA). The statute's operative provisions are as follows:

**31 U.S.C. §5361**. Congressional findings and purpose
   (a) Findings. Congress finds the following:
      (1) Internet gambling is primarily funded through personal use of payment system instruments, credit cards, and wire transfers.
      (2) The National Gambling Impact Study Commission in 1999 recommended the passage of legislation to prohibit wire transfers to Internet gambling sites or the banks which represent such sites.
      (3) Internet gambling is a growing cause of debt collection problems for insured depository institutions and the consumer credit industry.
      (4) New mechanisms for enforcing gambling laws on the Internet are necessary because traditional law enforcement mechanisms are often inadequate for enforcing gambling prohibitions or regulations on the Internet, especially where such gambling crosses State or national borders.
   (b) Rule of construction.—No provision of this subchapter shall be construed as altering, limiting, or extending any Federal or State law or Tribal-State compact prohibiting, permitting, or regulating gambling within the United States.

* * *

**31 U.S.C. §5363**. Prohibition on acceptance of any financial instrument for unlawful Internet gambling
   No person engaged in the business of betting or wagering may knowingly accept, in connection with the participation of another person in unlawful Internet gambling—
      (1) credit, or the proceeds of credit, extended to or on behalf of such other person (including credit extended through the use of a credit card);

(2) an electronic fund transfer, or funds transmitted by or through a money transmitting business, or the proceeds of an electronic fund transfer or money transmitting service, from or on behalf of such other person;

(3) any check, draft, or similar instrument which is drawn by or on behalf of such other person and is drawn on or payable at or through any financial institution; or

(4) the proceeds of any other form of financial transaction, as the Secretary and the Board of Governors of the Federal Reserve System may jointly prescribe by regulation, which involves a financial institution as a payor or financial intermediary on behalf of or for the benefit of such other person.

## NOTES

1. The UIGEA has been highly controversial. It appears to have been successful in driving publicly traded Internet gaming companies out of the U.S. market (and, indeed, into bankruptcy).
2. For critical views of the statute, consider the following works: I. Nelson Rose, *Viewpoint: The Unlawful Internet Gambling Act of 2006 Analyzed*, 10 GAMING L. REV. 537 (2006); SARA BAASE, A GIFT OF FIRE: SOCIAL, LEGAL, AND ETHICAL ISSUES FOR COMPUTING AND THE INTERNET 294 (2007).

# CHAPTER
# 5

---

# The Challenge of Limiting Gambling in a Permissive Legal Environment

While Chapters 3 and 4 explored many of the difficulties in maintaining a gambling prohibition, particularly in the context of a nation with numerous political subdivisions that have independent approaches toward gambling, Chapter 5 begins the discussion of legalized gambling and its regulation and control. Section A further addresses the problems posed by our free trade policies in the context of Internet (and international) gaming, that is, gaming offered from jurisdictions outside the United States. Section B, which is an introduction to Indian gaming, demonstrates problems that plague attempts to limit gambling when gambling is not entirely prohibited. Section C explores geographical and other limitations on gambling. It explores some of the unintended consequences of these limitations and encourages consideration of the efficacy of such limitations.

## A. INTERNET GAMING, FREE TRADE, AND PRESSURES ON STATE CONTROL

The impacts to individual U.S. states by Indian gaming are mirrored by impacts of Internet gaming on the U.S. state itself. In March of 2003, Antigua, backed by the European Union, Mexico, Canada, and Taiwan, brought a case against the United States before the World Trade Organization (WTO), an international body supported in part by the United States. Antigua claimed that the United States discriminated against foreign Internet betting operations by, among other things, prohibiting foreign corporations from providing Internet betting on horse racing to Americans, but allowing certain American firms to provide such betting under the U.S. Interstate Horseracing Act, at least in states where horse betting is legal.

Antigua's complaint claimed violations of the General Agreement on Trade in Services (GATS), namely violations of the "market access" and "national treatment" provisions of GATS. The market access provisions provide generally that each member country must provide terms of access to services and service suppliers from any other country that do not unduly restrict such access. The national treatment provisions likewise require member countries to accord treatment to foreign services and service providers that is "no less favourable" than that it accords to its own like services and service suppliers.

The United States responded by explaining its concerns about the "explosive growth in remote supply of gambling over the past decade." It explained:

> This dramatic increase, whatever its origin, has raised serious regulatory and law enforcement concerns in the United States, where authorities throughout U.S. history have consistently imposed tight regulation on gambling and the remote supply of gambling. Gambling has been one of the staple activities of organized crime syndicates. Law enforcement authorities in North America have seen evidence that organized crime plays a growing part in remote supply of gambling, including Internet gambling. In 1999, the Racketeering Records Analysis Unit of the Federal Bureau of Investigation provided an analysis to the Senate Committee on the Judiciary confirming that "organized crime groups are 'heavily involved' in offshore gambling." On April 29, 2003, Deputy Assistant Attorney General John Malcolm testified at a Congressional hearing that the "Department of Justice is concerned about the potential involvement of organized crime in Internet gambling. . . . We have now seen evidence that organized crime is moving into Internet gambling." (*See* World Trade Organization, *United States—Measures Affecting the Cross-Border Supply of Gambling and Betting Services; Report of the Panel,* WT/DS285/R (10 November 2004).)

The United States asserted an exemption to the WTO's principles of free trade by invoking the general exception to GATS for measures "necessary to protect public morals or to maintain public order." *See* GATS Article XIV(a).

## JEREMY C. MARWELL, TRADE AND MORALITY: THE WTO PUBLIC MORALS EXCEPTION AFTER GAMBLING

### 81 N.Y.U. L. Rev. 802 (May 2006)

In October 2004, Antigua and Barbuda (Antigua) brought a complaint against the United States, alleging that certain U.S. federal and state laws constituted a ban on the cross-border provision of Internet gambling services. In response to the Antiguan claims, the United States invoked the "public morals" clause of the General Agreement on Trade in Services (GATS). This clause, found in substantially similar form in the General Agreement on Tariffs and Trade (GATT), is one of several general exceptions to the WTO norm of trade liberalization. Other exceptions apply to measures protecting human, animal, and plant life and health, and exhaustible natural resources. These provisions allow states to enact trade-restrictive regulatory measures to serve legitimate public policy goals, despite general obligations of trade liberalization under the WTO.

Although [*Antigua v. United States*] is the first WTO dispute to feature the public morals clause, the emergence of a coherent doctrine governing trade-morality disputes could have substantial implications for the WTO and international law more generally. Some commentators have viewed the public morals clause as a vehicle for incorporating human rights, women's rights, and labor standards into the WTO and giving practical effect to these norms through the WTO's economic sanctions. However, a broad public morals exception could potentially serve as a shelter for protectionism, vitiating the relatively robust doctrines that now govern environmental and human health regulations and undermining the WTO's substantial progress toward trade liberalization.

[*Antigua v. United States* raised serious questions about how the WTO should determine the substantive content of the term "public morals," and how a WTO Member State's interest in protecting morality should be weighed against the desire for increased trade liberalization.]

The holdings in [*Antigua v. United States*] only partially resolved these questions. On the former, gambling was found to constitute a legitimate issue of public morality, based primarily on evidence that many countries in addition to the United States held this view. On the latter, a multi-factor balancing test from existing WTO jurisprudence was invoked to weigh the interest of the United States in controlling online gambling against the interests of other WTO Member States in trade liberalization. . . .

The WTO is a treaty-based trade regime with 148 Member States currently representing some ninety-five percent (by value) of all international trade. The WTO contains a number of core agreements, including GATT, GATS, and side agreements on other matters, including sanitary and phytosanitary measures and technical barriers to trade.

The "public morals" clause, which appears in both GATT and GATS, is structured as one of several general exceptions to the basic obligation of trade liberalization contained in those agreements. The GATS public morals clause provides, in pertinent part:

> Subject to the requirement that such measures are not applied in a manner which would constitute a means of arbitrary or unjustifiable discrimination between countries where like conditions prevail, or a disguised restriction on trade in services, nothing in this Agreement shall be construed to prevent the adoption or enforcement by any Member of measures:
>     (a) necessary to protect public morals. . . .

Under the structure of GATT and GATS, the general exceptions clauses are invoked as a defense by a respondent Member State after a prima facie showing by a complaining state that the respondent State violated a trade obligation. As such, the Appellate Body has described the general exceptions clause as striking a balance between the right of a Member State to regulate in the enumerated areas (e.g., public morals, health, environment) and the obligation not to interfere with the free flow of goods and services.

Several trends suggest that the public morals exception will play an increasingly important role in international trade relationships within and outside of the WTO. Most importantly, the increased heterogeneity of the WTO, combined with the growing economic importance of foreign trade to Member States, may increase the frequency of trade-morality disputes. In contrast to the twenty-three members of the original 1947 GATT, the modern WTO consists of 148 member states, more than half of which are developing countries, and which represent a diverse variety of religious, cultural, ethnic, and social backgrounds. Expanded membership will bring more countries into contact (and potential conflict), and trading partners with diverse socioeconomic compositions as well as differing cultural and religious views may have more frequent trade-morality conflicts than a more homogenous grouping. . . .

[One] reason to expect increased use of the public morals exception is the emergence of technologies that have begun to blur the line between environment, health, and morality. For instance, since 1998, the European Union (EU) has maintained a ban on beef treated with growth hormones despite an Appellate Body ruling that this measure violates the SPS Agreement. The EU has refused to change its regime—thus inflicting upon itself reciprocal trade sanctions by the United States—due to strong consumer opposition to the use of such hormones. This opposition stems, at least in part, from a desire to preserve traditional European methods of farming and food production against the spread of large-scale commercial farming techniques, interests which could conceivably be cast as matters of public morality. Similarly, an ongoing dispute over regulation of agricultural biotechnology has raised concerns about health and environmental risks as well as religious and ethical considerations.

### The [Antigua v. United States] Dispute

In March 2003, Antigua and Barbuda brought a complaint before the WTO Dispute Settlement Body alleging that numerous U.S. state and federal laws prohibited the cross-border provision of Internet gambling services in violation of U.S. obligations under GATS. The laws found by the Panel to be in question included the federal Wire Act, the Travel Act, the Illegal Gambling Business Act, as well as state gambling laws in Colorado, Louisiana, Massachusetts, Minnesota, New Jersey, New York, South Dakota, and Utah.

In response, the United States gave several reasons why the state and federal laws, even if found to violate GATS concessions, could be justified under the public morals clause of Article XIV. First, the remote supply of gambling services is particularly vulnerable to exploitation by organized crime due to low set-up costs, ease of provision, and geographic flexibility. Protecting American society against the "destructive influence" of organized crime on persons and property was a matter of public morality. Second, the Internet could introduce gambling into inappropriate settings, such as homes and schools, where it would not be subject to traditional, in-person controls. Internet gambling would facilitate gambling by children and have detrimental effects on compulsive gamblers by allowing anonymous, twenty-four-hour access.

The Panel's analysis began with a textual definition of public morals: "standards of right and wrong conduct maintained by or on behalf of a community or nation." To determine whether gambling fell within this definition, the Panel looked to a variety of international practices: the domestic regulations of other states, regional practice such as rulings of the European Court of Justice, and historical evidence of broad international agreement about gambling and morality at the League of Nations. Based on this evidence, the Panel concluded that gambling was an issue of public morality that could be encompassed by the GATS public morals clause.

The Panel then addressed whether the particular U.S. measures at stake (as distinguished from gambling generally) were directed at protecting public morals. For this analysis, the Panel looked to the legislative history of the federal Wire Act and the Illegal Gambling Business Act, testimony by the U.S. Attorney General about the implementation of the Travel Act, and decisions of U.S. federal courts, ultimately concluding that the U.S. measures were designed to protect public morals within the meaning of GATS Article XIV(a).

The Panel then addressed whether the U.S. measures were "necessary" to protect public morals per GATS Article XIV(a). The Panel applied a multi-factor balancing test developed in prior GATT jurisprudence that considers the vitality of the interests to be protected, the extent to which the measure contributes to the stated goal, and the measure's overall effect on trade. The exact mechanics of this balancing test are somewhat opaque. The Panel acknowledged that the interests the United States sought to preserve (control of organized crime, protection of children and compulsive gamblers) were extremely important, and that the measures made a substantial contribution to the stated goal, but, noting that they also had a "significant restrictive trade impact," judged the balance of these conflicting factors to lie against the United States.

On appeal, the WTO Appellate Body overturned the Panel's ruling that the U.S. measures were not "necessary," but it ultimately ruled against the United States on the ground that the U.S. laws had not been shown not to discriminate against foreign gambling service providers. In particular, the Interstate Horseracing Act potentially exempted U.S. (but not foreign) companies supplying remote gambling services (e.g., off-track and pari-mutuel betting) from the laws in question. In reaching this conclusion, the Appellate Body affirmed the Panel's ruling that the U.S. measures fell within the scope of XIV(a), leaving undisturbed both its definition of "public morals" and its evidentiary approach to determining whether gambling could be considered an issue of public morals. . . .

[One] doctrinal question raised by the [*Antigua v. United States*] dispute [is] whether gambling is a matter of "public morals" for the purpose of GATS Article XIV(a). Although the legal doctrine is likely to be driven by underlying policy factors (i.e., political beliefs about the appropriate balance between regulatory autonomy and trade), any solution must fit within the bounds of the treaty text as informed by well-settled principles of treaty interpretation.

The difficulty of defining "public morals" is evident from both policy and textual perspectives. Amongst 148 WTO Member States, "public morals" could mean anything from religious views on drinking alcohol or eating certain foods to cultural attitudes toward pornography, free expression, human rights, labor norms, women's rights, or general cultural judgments about education or social welfare. What one society defines as public morals may have little relevance for another, at least outside a certain core of religious or cultural traditions.

The problem of deciding whether a given measure falls within the scope of an enumerated exception is not unique to public morals. The Appellate Body has previously determined, for instance, whether sea turtles are an "exhaustible natural resource[]" per GATT Article XX(g) and whether the risk of mesothelioma from asbestos inhalation is a threat to "human health" per GATT Article XX(b). The most significant contrast between public morals and natural resources or health is the existence or absence of internationally accepted objective evidence as to the nature of the exception itself. In a dispute over U.S. restrictions on the import of shrimp harvested in a way that endangered sea turtles, the Appellate Body interpreted "exhaustible natural resources" in GATT Article XX(g) in light of strong scientific evidence that living natural resources could be exhaustible and a broad international consensus that this threat was significant for sea turtles. Similarly, in a dispute over a French public health prohibition on the import of asbestos and asbestos-containing products, the Appellate Body referred to internationally accredited scientific findings—such as reports by the World Health Organization—on the carcinogenic nature of asbestos fibers in concluding that asbestos was a threat to "human life or health."

By contrast, it is far more difficult to draw substantive boundaries around the term "public morals" based on commonly accepted objective evidence. Measures related to a core of near-universal human moral values can probably be identified, such as prohibitions on murder, genocide, slavery, and torture, though the precise content of such norms and even the extent of consensus on such issues is probably debatable. Beyond this core, there is at best a tenuous consensus on issues such as trade in pornography, gambling, alcohol, and illegal drugs, which many commentators would perhaps readily agree fall within the public morals exception. . . .

The [*Antigua v. United States*] decision can be understood as using historic and contemporary state practice to limit, for policy reasons, a treaty text of potentially broad scope. Conceivably, any law passed by a representative government prohibiting any behavior could be considered a social judgment about right and wrong, thus falling within a broad textual definition of public morals. But an approach under which the exception would effectively swallow the rule of trade liberalization would conflict with the explicit object and purpose of GATS and GATT. . . .

Taken to an extreme, the [*Antigua v. United States*] doctrine might be read as implying that states cannot unilaterally define public morals. There is empirical evidence that Members' views of what constitute "public morals" regulations are currently broader than such a definition would allow. A review of recent WTO Trade Policy Reviews—regular declarations by WTO Member States about their domestic trade policies—reveals that products currently subject to morality-based import restrictions include alcohol, pornographic or obscene materials, child pornography, gambling equipment or games of chance, hate propaganda, illegal drugs, lottery tickets, non-kosher meat products, posters depicting crime or violence, stolen goods, treasonous or seditious materials, counterfeit money, automobile radar detectors, and video tapes and laser discs.

Although this list is relatively broad, and although the data set is likely underinclusive, several features stand out. First, a relatively small range of products and services (e.g., pornography, gambling equipment, illegal drugs) are subject to moral trade restrictions in multiple countries. Second, and more importantly, morality-driven trade restrictions in certain countries (e.g., on non-kosher meat products, video tapes, automobile radar detectors) may not reflect shared international practice. Applied literally, the [*Antigua v. United States*] standard may exclude from the scope of the public morals exception some of the[se] measures[.]

A superior alternative would be to permit a country to define public morals unilaterally but to require evidence from that country supporting its claim that a particular issue has moral significance. First, such a solution charts a middle course between the moral minority and unrestrained unilateralism problems outlined above. Second, judging a regulation based solely on domestic evidence is more respectful of state sovereignty than conditioning such review on the views of an international tribunal or practices of other countries. The [*Antigua v. United States*] Panel explicitly recognized that "Members should be given some scope to define and apply for themselves the concept[] of 'public morals' ... in their respective territories, according to their own systems and scales of values." ...

In the context of public morals, a [WTO Dispute Settlement] Panel's task would be to assess the evidence presented by a regulating party about the existence of a morality-related interest. This determination would turn on the content and credibility of documentary and other evidence as to whether a particular group held the moral belief asserted as the basis for regulation. In addition to evidence presented before it, a Panel has authority to seek information "from any relevant source," including experts and "any individual or body which it deems appropriate"—such as, for instance, religious or civil society organizations, public opinion firms, local government officials, and individual citizens. ...

This approach provides several advantages over the [*Antigua v. United States*] result: It gives meaning to the public morals clause while preserving the essential core of national sovereignty implicated by issues of moral regulation, offers a predictable and transparent legal standard, and provides a more stable, enduring decision rule for future "hard cases" likely looming on the trade-morality horizon.

*NOTES*

1. *Antigua v. United States* raises a difficult question about the definition of "morals" and how to determine which arguments about morality are legitimate and honestly held and which, in contrast, are masking a trade-discriminatory purpose. A strong subtext in the case was whether the United States could claim, in good faith, that American jurisdictions have a moral opposition to gaming. If such moral opposition exists, is there a moral distinction between, for example, state-run lotteries and casinos, or between horse-racing and Internet gaming? If not, then many jurisdictions have "compromised their morals" when it was profitable to do so. Indeed, as we have seen, numerous American laws authorize gaming in large or small ways.

2. *Antigua*, like *California v. Cabazon* which follows, reflects the principle that some gambling may lead inexorably to more gambling. A jurisdiction that authorizes some limited form of gaming may have difficulty keeping the genie in the bottle. In legalizing some kinds of gaming, the jurisdiction loses the moral authority, and thus in the *Antigua* case the *legal* authority to maintain a broader prohibition on gaming.

3. The phenomenon also crosses jurisdictions. As we have seen in numerous other contexts, legalized gambling in one jurisdiction exerts enormous economic pressure on the neighboring jurisdictions. Policymakers in non-gaming jurisdictions face the difficult choice between legalizing gambling or passively watching as millions of dollars are exported to the other jurisdiction. This dynamic produces an effect that is sometimes described by gambling opponents as a "race to the bottom." Is there any way to prevent this result? Can a jurisdiction effectively limit gaming within its borders?

4. Antigua maintains that the United States has not complied with the WTO decision. Consider the potential consequences should the United States fail to comply. Antigua's (American) attorney has said that Antigua would seek compensatory trade sanctions

against the United States. Antigua was awarded $21 million per year in damages for the horseracing trade restriction alone, but the United States has largely ignored the judgment. Antigua may ask the WTO to lift U.S. patent and copyright protections in Antigua, allowing Antiguan companies to manufacture U.S. products, such as music and movies. If the implication of these actions is that the United States is protecting its own gaming vendors from competition abroad, the irony is that the cost of American protectionism may be borne by a competing entertainment industry; it is recording artists and the motion picture industry that would pay if Antigua is successful in obtaining trade sanctions.

5.  The United States has long been one of the major forces behind principles of free trade and the establishment of the WTO. If the United States fails to abide by this WTO ruling, what other consequences might result?

# B.  INDIAN GAMING: MORE PRESSURES ON STATE CONTROL OF GAMING

## CALIFORNIA v. CABAZON BAND OF MISSION INDIANS
### 480 U.S. 202 (1987)

Justice WHITE delivered the opinion of the Court.

The Cabazon and Morongo Bands of Mission Indians, federally recognized Indian Tribes, occupy reservations in Riverside County, California. Each Band, pursuant to an ordinance approved by the Secretary of the Interior, conducts bingo games on its reservation. The Cabazon Band has also opened a card club at which draw poker and other card games are played. The games are open to the public and are played predominantly by non-Indians coming onto the reservations. The games are a major source of employment for tribal members, and the profits are the Tribes' sole source of income. The State of California seeks to apply to the two Tribes Cal. Penal Code Ann. §326.5 (West Supp. 1987). That statute does not entirely prohibit the playing of bingo but permits it when the games are operated and staffed by members of designated charitable organizations who may not be paid for their services. Profits must be kept in special accounts and used only for charitable purposes; prizes may not exceed $250 per game. Asserting that the bingo games on the two reservations violated each of these restrictions, California insisted that the Tribes comply with state law. Riverside County also sought to apply its local Ordinance No. 558, regulating bingo, as well as its Ordinance No. 331, prohibiting the playing of draw poker and the other card games.

The Tribes sued the county in Federal District Court seeking a declaratory judgment that the county had no authority to apply its ordinances inside the reservations and an injunction against their enforcement. The State intervened, the facts were stipulated, and the District Court granted the Tribes' motion for summary judgment, holding that neither the State nor the county had any authority to enforce its gambling laws within the reservations. The Court of Appeals for the Ninth Circuit affirmed, 783 F.2d 900 (1986), the State and the county appealed, and we postponed jurisdiction to the hearing on the merits. 476 U.S. 1168.

The Court has consistently recognized that Indian tribes retain "attributes of sovereignty over both their members and their territory," *United States v. Mazurie*, 419 U.S. 544, 557 (1975), and that "tribal sovereignty is dependent on, and subordinate to, only the Federal Government, not the States," *Washington v. Confederated Tribes of Colville Indian Reservation*, 447 U.S. 134, 154 (1980). It is clear, however, that state laws may be applied to tribal Indians on their reservations if Congress has expressly so provided. Here, the State insists that Congress has twice given its express consent: first in Pub. L. 280 in 1953, 67 Stat. 588, as amended, 18 U. S. C. §1162, 28 U. S. C. §1360 (1982 ed. and Supp. III), and second in the Organized Crime Control Act in 1970, 84 Stat. 937, 18 U. S. C. §1955. We disagree in both respects.

In Pub. L. 280, Congress expressly granted six States, including California, jurisdiction over specified areas of Indian country within the States and provided for the assumption of jurisdiction by other States. In §2, California was granted broad criminal jurisdiction over offenses committed by or against Indians within all Indian country within the State. Section 4's grant of civil jurisdiction was more limited. In *Bryan v. Itasca County*, 426 U.S. 373 (1976), we interpreted §4 to grant States jurisdiction over private civil litigation involving reservation Indians in state court, but not to grant general civil regulatory authority. *Id.*, at 385, 388-390. We held, therefore, that Minnesota could not apply its personal property tax within the reservation. Congress' primary concern in enacting Pub. L. 280 was combating lawlessness on reservations. *Id.*, at 379-380. The Act plainly was not intended to effect total assimilation of Indian tribes into mainstream American society. *Id.*, at 387. We recognized that a grant to States of general civil regulatory power over Indian reservations would result in the destruction of tribal institutions and values. Accordingly, when a State seeks to enforce a law within an Indian reservation under the authority of Pub. L. 280, it must be determined whether the law is criminal in nature, and thus fully applicable to the reservation under §2, or civil in nature, and applicable only as it may be relevant to private civil litigation in state court.

The Minnesota personal property tax at issue in *Bryan* was unquestionably civil in nature. The California bingo statute is not so easily categorized. California law permits bingo games to be conducted only by charitable and other specified organizations, and then only by their members who may not receive any wage or profit for doing so; prizes are limited and receipts are to be segregated and used only for charitable purposes. Violation of any of these provisions is a misdemeanor. California insists that these are criminal laws which Pub. L. 280 permits it to enforce on the reservations.

Following its earlier decision in *Barona Group of Capitan Grande Band of Mission Indians, San Diego County, Cal. v. Duffy*, 694 F.2d 1185 (1982), cert. denied, 461 U.S. 929 (1983), which also involved the applicability of §326.5 of the California Penal Code to Indian reservations, the Court of Appeals rejected this submission. 783 F.2d, at 901-903. In *Barona*, applying what it thought to be the civil/criminal dichotomy drawn in *Bryan v. Itasca County*, the Court of Appeals drew a distinction between state "criminal/prohibitory" laws and state "civil/regulatory" laws: if the intent of a state law is generally to prohibit certain conduct, it falls within Pub. L. 280's grant of criminal jurisdiction, but if the state law generally permits the conduct at issue, subject to regulation, it must be classified as civil/regulatory and Pub. L. 280 does not authorize its enforcement on an Indian reservation. The shorthand test is whether the conduct at issue violates the State's public policy. Inquiring into the nature of §326.5, the Court of Appeals held that it was regulatory rather than prohibitory. This was the analysis employed, with similar results, by the Court of Appeals for the Fifth Circuit in *Seminole Tribe of Florida v. Butterworth*, 658 F.2d 310 (1981), cert. denied, 455 U.S. 1020 (1982), which the Ninth Circuit found persuasive.

We are persuaded that the prohibitory/regulatory distinction is consistent with *Bryan*'s construction of Pub. L. 280. It is not a bright-line rule, however; and as the Ninth Circuit itself observed, an argument of some weight may be made that the bingo statute is prohibitory rather than regulatory. But in the present case, the court reexamined the state law and reaffirmed its holding in *Barona*, and we are reluctant to disagree with that court's view of the nature and intent of the state law at issue here.

There is surely a fair basis for its conclusion. California does not prohibit all forms of gambling. California itself operates a state lottery, Cal. Govt. Code Ann. §8880 *et seq.* (West Supp. 1987), and daily encourages its citizens to participate in this state-run gambling. California also permits pari-mutuel horserace betting. Cal. Bus. & Prof. Code Ann. §§19400-19667 (West 1964 and Supp. 1987). Although certain enumerated gambling games are prohibited under Cal. Penal Code Ann. §330 (West Supp. 1987), games not enumerated, including the card games played in the Cabazon card club, are permissible. The Tribes assert that more than 400 card rooms similar to the Cabazon card club flourish in California, and the State does not dispute this fact. Brief for Appellees 47-48. Also, as the Court of Appeals noted, bingo is legally sponsored by many different organizations and is widely played in California. There is no effort to forbid the playing of bingo by any member of the public over the age of 18. Indeed, the permitted bingo games *must* be open to the general public. Nor is there any limit on the number of games which eligible organizations may operate, the receipts which they may obtain from the games, the number of games which a participant may play, or the amount of money which a participant may spend, either per game or in total. In light of the fact that California permits a substantial amount of gambling activity, including bingo, and actually promotes gambling through its state lottery, we must conclude that California regulates rather than prohibits gambling in general and bingo in particular.

California argues, however, that high stakes, *unregulated* bingo, the conduct which attracts organized crime, is a misdemeanor in California and may be prohibited on Indian reservations. But that an otherwise regulatory law is enforceable by criminal as well as civil means does not necessarily convert it into a criminal law within the meaning of Pub. L. 280. Otherwise, the distinction between §2 and §4 of that law could easily be avoided and total assimilation permitted. This view, adopted here and by the Fifth Circuit in the *Butterworth* case, we find persuasive. Accordingly, we conclude that Pub. L. 280 does not authorize California to enforce Cal. Penal Code Ann. §326.5 (West Supp. 1987) within the Cabazon and Morongo Reservations.

California and Riverside County also argue that [Section 1955—the Illegal Gambling Businesses provision of] the Organized Crime Control Act authorizes the application of their gambling laws to the tribal bingo enterprises. [Section 1955] makes certain violations of state and local gambling laws violations of federal law. The Court of Appeals rejected appellants' argument, relying on its earlier decisions[.] The court explained that whether a tribal activity is "a violation of the law of a state" within the meaning of [Section 1955] depends on whether it violates the "public policy" of the State, the same test for application of state law under Pub. L. 280, and similarly concluded that bingo is not contrary to the public policy of California.

The Court of Appeals for the Sixth Circuit has rejected this view. Since the [Section 1955] standard is simply whether the gambling business is being operated in "violation of the law of a State," there is no basis for the regulatory/prohibitory distinction that it agreed is suitable in construing and applying Pub. L. 280. And because enforcement of [Section 1955] is an exercise of federal rather than state authority, there is no danger of state encroachment on Indian tribal sovereignty. Ibid. This latter observation exposes the flaw in appellants' reliance on [Section 1955]. That enactment is indeed a federal law that, among other things, defines certain federal crimes over which the district courts have exclusive jurisdiction. There is nothing in [Section 1955] indicating that the States are to have any part in enforcing federal criminal laws or are authorized to make arrests on Indian reservations that in the absence of [Section 1955] they could not effect. We are not informed of any federal efforts to employ [Section 1955] to prosecute the playing of bingo on Indian reservations, although there are more than 100 such enterprises currently in operation, many of which have been in existence for several years, for the most part with the encouragement of the Federal Government. Whether or not, then, the Sixth Circuit is right and the Ninth Circuit wrong about the coverage of [Section 1955], a matter that we do not decide, there is no warrant for California to make arrests on reservations and thus, through [Section 1955], enforce its gambling laws against Indian tribes.

## II

Because the state and county laws at issue here are imposed directly on the Tribes that operate the games, and are not expressly permitted by Congress, the Tribes argue that the judgment below should be affirmed without more. They rely on the statement in *McClanahan v. Arizona State Tax Comm'n*, 411 U.S. 164, 170-171 (1973), that " '[state] laws generally are not applicable to tribal Indians on an Indian reservation except where Congress has expressly provided that State laws shall apply' " (quoting United States Dept. of the Interior, Federal Indian Law 845 (1958)). Our cases, however, have not established an inflexible *per se* rule precluding state jurisdiction over tribes and tribal members in the absence of express congressional consent. "[Under] certain circumstances a State may validly assert authority over the activities of nonmembers on a reservation, and . . . in exceptional circumstances a State may assert jurisdiction over the on-reservation activities of tribal members." *New Mexico v. Mescalero Apache Tribe*, 462 U.S. 324, 331-332 (1983) (footnotes omitted). Both *Moe v. Confederated Salish and Kootenai Tribes*, 425 U.S. 463 (1976), and *Washington v. Confederated Tribes of Colville Indian Reservation*, 447 U.S. 134 (1980), are illustrative. In those decisions we held that, in the absence of express congressional permission, a State could require tribal smokeshops on Indian reservations to collect state sales tax from their non-Indian customers. Both cases involved nonmembers entering and purchasing tobacco products on the reservations involved. The State's interest in assuring the collection of sales taxes from non-Indians enjoying the off-reservation services of the State was sufficient to warrant the minimal burden imposed on the tribal smokeshop operators.

This case also involves a state burden on tribal Indians in the context of their dealings with non-Indians since the question is whether the State may prevent the Tribes from making available high stakes bingo games to non-Indians coming from outside the reservations. Decision in this case turns on whether state authority is pre-empted by the operation of federal law; and "[state] jurisdiction is pre-empted . . . if it interferes or is incompatible with federal and tribal interests reflected in federal law, unless the state interests at stake are sufficient to justify the assertion of state authority." *Mescalero*, 462 U.S., at 333, 334. The inquiry is to proceed in light of traditional notions of Indian sovereignty and the congressional goal of Indian self-government, including its "overriding goal" of encouraging tribal self-sufficiency and economic development. *Id.*, at 334-335.

These policies and actions, which demonstrate the Government's approval and active promotion of tribal bingo enterprises, are of particular relevance in this case. The Cabazon and Morongo Reservations contain no natural resources which can be exploited. The tribal games at present provide the sole source of revenues for the operation of the tribal governments and the provision of tribal services. They are also the major sources of employment on the reservations. Self-determination and economic development are not within reach if the Tribes cannot raise revenues and provide employment for their members. The Tribes' interests obviously parallel the federal interests.

California seeks to diminish the weight of these seemingly important tribal interests by asserting that the Tribes are merely marketing an exemption from state gambling laws. In *Washington v. Confederated Tribes of Colville Indian Reservation*, 447 U.S., at 155, we held that the State could tax cigarettes sold by tribal smokeshops to non-Indians, even though it would eliminate their competitive advantage and substantially reduce revenues used to provide tribal services, because the Tribes had no right "to market an exemption from state taxation to persons who would normally do their business elsewhere." We stated that "[it] is painfully apparent that the value marketed by the smokeshops to persons coming from outside is not generated on the reservations by activities in which the Tribes have a significant interest." *Ibid.* Here, however, the Tribes are not merely importing a product onto the reservations for immediate resale to non-Indians. They have built modern facilities which provide recreational opportunities and ancillary services to their patrons, who do not simply drive onto the reservations, make purchases and depart, but spend extended periods of time there enjoying the services the Tribes provide. The Tribes have a strong incentive to provide comfortable, clean, and attractive facilities and well-run games in order to increase attendance at the games. The tribal bingo enterprises are similar to the resort complex, featuring hunting and fishing, that the Mescalero Apache Tribe operates on its reservation through the "concerted and sustained" management of reservation land and wildlife resources. *New Mexico v. Mescalero Apache Tribe,* 462 U.S., at 341. The Mescalero project generates funds for essential tribal services and provides employment for tribal members. We there rejected the notion that the Tribe is merely marketing an exemption from state hunting and fishing regulations and concluded that New Mexico could not regulate on-reservation fishing and hunting by non-Indians. *Ibid.* Similarly, the Cabazon and Morongo Bands are generating value on the reservations through activities in which they have a substantial interest.

The State also relies on *Rice v. Rehner,* 463 U.S. 713 (1983), in which we held that California could require a tribal member and a federally licensed Indian trader operating a general store on a reservation to obtain a state license in order to sell liquor for off-premises consumption. But our decision there rested on the grounds that Congress had never recognized any sovereign tribal interest in regulating liquor traffic and that Congress, historically, had plainly anticipated that the States would exercise concurrent authority to regulate the use and distribution of liquor on Indian reservations. There is no such traditional federal view governing the outcome of this case, since, as we have explained, the current federal policy is to promote precisely what California seeks to prevent.

The sole interest asserted by the State to justify the imposition of its bingo laws on the Tribes is in preventing the infiltration of the tribal games by organized crime. To the extent that the State seeks to prevent any and all bingo games from being played on tribal lands while permitting regulated, off-reservation games, this asserted interest is irrelevant and the state and county laws are pre-empted. See n. 3, *supra.* Even to the extent that the State and county seek to regulate short of prohibition, the laws are pre-empted. The State insists that the high stakes offered at tribal games are attractive to organized crime, whereas the controlled games authorized under California law are not. This is surely a legitimate concern, but we are unconvinced that it is sufficient to escape the pre-emptive force of federal and tribal interests apparent in this case. California does not allege any present criminal involvement in the Cabazon and Morongo enterprises, and the Ninth Circuit discerned none. 783 F.2d, at 904. An official of the Department of Justice has expressed some concern about tribal bingo operations, but far from any action being taken evidencing this concern—and surely the Federal Government has the authority to forbid Indian gambling enterprises—the prevailing federal policy continues to support these tribal enterprises, including those of the Tribes involved in this case.

We conclude that the State's interest in preventing the infiltration of the tribal bingo enterprises by organized crime does not justify state regulation of the tribal bingo enterprises in light of the compelling federal and tribal interests supporting them. State regulation would impermissibly infringe on tribal government, and this conclusion applies equally to the county's attempted regulation of the Cabazon card club. We therefore affirm the judgment of the Court of Appeals and remand the case for further proceedings consistent with this opinion.

*It is so ordered.*

Justice STEVENS, with whom Justice O'CONNOR and Justice SCALIA join, dissenting.

Unless and until Congress exempts Indian-managed gambling from state law and subjects it to federal supervision, I believe that a State may enforce its laws prohibiting high-stakes gambling on Indian reservations within its borders. Congress has not pre-empted California's prohibition against high-stakes bingo games and the Secretary of the Interior plainly has no authority to do so. While gambling provides needed employment and income for Indian tribes, these benefits do not, in my opinion, justify tribal operation of currently unlawful commercial activities. Accepting the majority's reasoning would require exemptions for cockfighting, tattoo parlors, nude dancing, houses of prostitution, and other illegal but profitable enterprises. As the law now stands, I believe tribal entrepreneurs, like others who might derive profits from catering to non-Indian customers, must obey applicable state laws.

In my opinion the plain language of Pub. L. 280, 67 Stat. 588, as amended, 18 U. S. C. §1162, 28 U. S. C. §1360 (1982 ed. and Supp. III), authorizes California to enforce its prohibition against commercial gambling on Indian reservations. The State prohibits bingo games that are not operated by members of designated charitable organizations or which offer prizes in excess of $250 per game. Cal. Penal Code Ann. §326.5 (West Supp. 1987). In §2 of Pub. L. 280, Congress expressly provided that the criminal laws of the State of California "shall have the same force and effect within such Indian country as they have elsewhere within the State." 18 U. S. C. §1162(a). Moreover, it provided in §4(a) that the civil laws of California "that are of general application to private persons or private property shall have the same force and effect within such Indian country as they have elsewhere within the State." 28 U. S. C. §1360(a) (1982 ed., Supp. III).

Our more recent cases have made it clear . . . that commercial transactions between Indians and non-Indians—even when conducted on a reservation—do not enjoy any blanket immunity from state regulation. In *Rice v. Rehner*, 463 U.S. 713 (1983), respondent, a federally licensed Indian trader, was a tribal member operating a general store on an Indian reservation. We held that the State could require Rehner to obtain a state license to sell liquor for off-premises consumption. The Court attempts to distinguish *Rice v. Rehner* as resting on the absence of a sovereign tribal interest in the regulation of liquor traffic to the exclusion of the States. But as a necessary step on our way to deciding that the State could regulate all tribal liquor sales in Indian country, we recognized the State's authority over transactions, whether they be liquor sales or gambling, between Indians and non-Indians. . . .

Today the Court seems prepared to acknowledge that an Indian tribe's commercial transactions with non-Indians may violate "the State's public policy." . . . The Court reasons, however, that the operation of high-stakes bingo games does not run afoul of California's public policy because the State permits some forms of gambling and, specifically, some forms of bingo. I find this approach to "public policy" curious, to say the least. The State's policy concerning gambling is to authorize certain specific gambling activities that comply with carefully defined regulation and that provide revenues either for the State itself or for certain charitable purposes, and to prohibit all unregulated commercial lotteries that are operated for private profit. To argue that the tribal bingo games comply with the public policy of California because the State permits some other gambling is tantamount to arguing that driving over 60 miles an hour is consistent with public policy because the State allows driving at speeds of up to 55 miles an hour.

In my view, Congress has permitted the State to apply its prohibitions against commercial gambling to Indian tribes. Even if Congress had not done so, however, the State has the authority to assert jurisdiction over appellees' gambling activities. We recognized this authority in *Washington v. Confederated Tribes, supra*; the Court's attempt to distinguish the reasoning of our decision in that case is unpersuasive. In *Washington v. Confederated Tribes*, the Tribes contended that the State had no power to tax on-reservation sales of cigarettes to non-Indians. The argument that we rejected there has a familiar ring:

"The Tribes contend that their involvement in the operation and taxation of cigarette marketing on the reservation ousts the State from any power to exact its sales and cigarette taxes from nonmembers purchasing cigarettes at tribal smokeshops. The primary argument is economic. It is asserted that smokeshop cigarette sales generate substantial revenues for the Tribes which they expend for essential governmental services, including programs to combat severe poverty and underdevelopment at the reservations. Most cigarette purchasers are outsiders attracted onto the reservations by the bargain prices the smokeshops charge by virtue of their claimed exemption from state taxation. If the State is permitted to impose its taxes, the Tribes will no longer enjoy any competitive advantage vis-a-vis businesses in surrounding areas." *Id.*, at 154.

In *Confederated Tribes*, the tribal smokeshops offered their customers the same products, services, and facilities that other tobacconists offered to their customers. Although the smokeshops were more modest than the bingo palaces involved in this case, presumably they were equally the product of tribal labor and tribal capital. What made them successful, however, was the value of the exemption that was offered to non-Indians "who would normally do their business elsewhere." *Id.*, at 155.

Similarly, it is painfully obvious that the value of the Tribe's asserted exemption from California's gambling laws is the primary attraction to customers who would normally do their gambling elsewhere. The Cabazon Band of Mission Indians has no tradition or special expertise in the operation of large bingo parlors. See Declaration of William J. Wallace, para. 2, App. 153, 171. Indeed, the entire membership of the Cabazon Tribe—it has only 25 enrolled members—is barely adequate to operate a bingo game that is patronized by hundreds of non-Indians nightly. How this small and formerly impoverished Band of Indians could have attracted the investment capital for its enterprise without benefit of the claimed exemption is certainly a mystery to me.

Presumably the State has determined that its interest in generating revenues for the public fisc and for certain charities outweighs the benefits from a total prohibition against publicly sponsored games of chance. Whatever revenues the Tribes receive from their unregulated bingo games drain funds from the state-approved recipients of lottery revenues—just as the tax-free cigarette sales in the *Confederated Tribes* case diminished the receipts that the tax collector would otherwise have received.

Moreover, I am unwilling to dismiss as readily as the Court does the State's concern that these unregulated high-stakes bingo games may attract organized criminal infiltration. Indeed, California regulates charitable bingo, horseracing, and its own lottery. The State of California requires that charitable bingo games may only be operated and staffed by members of designated charitable organizations, and that proceeds from the games may only be used for charitable purposes. Cal. Penal Code Ann. §326.5 (West Supp. 1987). These requirements for staffing and for dispersal of profits provide bulwarks against criminal activity; neither safeguard exists for bingo games on Indian reservations. In my judgment, unless Congress authorizes and regulates these commercial gambling ventures catering to non-Indians, the State has a legitimate law enforcement interest in proscribing them.

Appellants and the Secretary of the Interior may well be correct, in the abstract, that gambling facilities are a sensible way to generate revenues that are badly needed by reservation Indians. But the decision to adopt, to reject, or to define the precise contours of such a course of action, and thereby to set aside the substantial public policy concerns of a sovereign State, should be made by the Congress of the United States. It should not be made by this Court, by the temporary occupant of the Office of the Secretary of the Interior, or by non-Indian entrepreneurs who are experts in gambling management but not necessarily dedicated to serving the future well-being of Indian tribes. I respectfully dissent.

*NOTES*

1.  *Cabazon* briefly served as the legal foundation of the Indian gaming industry, but it was not the case that originally provided that foundation. Indeed, by the time *Cabazon* was decided, Indian gaming was already a rapidly growing industry, producing millions of dollars in revenues. For background on the Supreme Court case that laid the legal cornerstone for the industry, see Kevin K.

Washburn, *The Legacy of Bryan v. Itasca County: How a $147 County Tax Notice Helped Bring Tribes $200 Billion in Indian Gaming Revenues*, 92 MINN. L. REV. 919 (2008).

2.  In *Cabazon*, the State of California sought to regulate the tribe's ability to offer high stakes bingo. What were California's motives in seeking to prohibit such tribal gaming? Is the majority convincing when it denies that tribes are exploiting an exception to state laws?

3.  After *Cabazon*, what avenue was available to California to prohibit Indian gaming?

4.  Shortly after *Cabazon* was decided, Congress enacted the Indian Gaming Regulatory Act of 1988, codified at 25 U.S.C. §§2701-2721. Relevant provisions of that Act are described below.

## KEVIN K. WASHBURN, RECURRING PROBLEMS IN INDIAN GAMING

### 1 Wyo. L. Rev. 427, 428-30, 440-44 (2000)

Following the *Cabazon* decision, Indian tribes increased development of Indian gaming establishments. Meanwhile, states went to Congress, seeking a legislative limitation to the tribal power recognized in the *Cabazon* decision. Congress responded by enacting the Indian Gaming Regulatory Act of 1988 (IGRA). In IGRA, Congress provided that tribes have the unilateral authority to conduct bingo and similar games such as "pull-tabs" games (which are defined as "Class II" games in the Act) on Indian lands, if such games are not prohibited in the state in which the tribe is situated.

In contrast to Class II gaming, Congress realized that states were likely to have more serious and more legitimate public policy concerns related to more expansive casino-type gaming which is defined as "Class III" gaming in IGRA. Accordingly, Congress stopped short of giving tribes the unilateral power to conduct full casino-style Class III gaming. Congress limited Class III gaming to those states that already allow some measure of Class III gaming and gave states a voice in tribal decisions to conduct such gaming.

As for Class III gaming, Congress adopted the criminal-prohibitory versus civil-regulatory distinction set forth in the *Cabazon* decision. IGRA allows tribes to offer Class III gaming if a state permits Class III gaming for any purpose by any person, organization or entity. In other words, if a state allows a limited class of organizations such as charitable groups to offer low-stakes gambling on a limited number of occasions each year, a tribe may offer such gambling activities.

The theory is that state public policy toward such activity is merely regulatory rather than prohibitory. On the other hand, IGRA forbids a tribe from conducting Class III gaming if the state has adopted a "no-Class III-gaming-and-no-exceptions" approach.

Congress imposed one other major requirement for Class III gaming. IGRA provides that tribes may engage in Class III casino-style gaming only if they first negotiate "compacts" with states. Through the compacting process, Congress empowered states to negotiate with tribes to address seven areas of legitimate state concerns related to public safety and regulation of gaming. Each of the seven subjects are directly related to the operation of gaming establishments.[9] Since the enactment of IGRA, twenty-four states have entered compacts with Indian tribes involving some level of Class III, casino-style gaming.

Through the compacting process, Congress offered states the right to negotiate with tribes regarding specific state interests that might be affected by Indian casinos. With this right came a responsibility. Congress imposed upon states the responsibility of engaging in good faith negotiations. [Yet, w]hile IGRA gives states the right and responsibility to negotiate with tribes to protect the limited interests set forth in IGRA, including the collection of fees from tribes related to the costs of any state regulation, IGRA explicitly disclaims any state authority to impose taxes on Indian gaming revenues. Despite IGRA's specific and narrow provision as to how Indian tribes may use gaming revenues and despite the prohibition on taxation, many states and tribes have negotiated compacts in which tribes agree to share a portion of gaming revenues with state and/or local governments. While some tribes have agreed to such terms reluctantly or under protest, other tribes have willingly accepted such terms as a cost of doing business.

IGRA's prohibition on state taxation of Indian gaming revenues has required the Secretary of the Interior to be creative in finding ways to approve compacts that contain revenue sharing provisions. The Secretary has generally taken the position that such compacts are lawful only if the tribe obtains separate consideration for revenue sharing.

---

9. The subjects that Congress allows states and tribes to address in compacts are: (1) the application of state or tribal laws and regulations regarding the licensing and regulation of Indian gaming; (2) the allocation of jurisdiction necessary to make those laws and regulations enforceable; (3) the collection of fees by the states for their costs in regulating the gaming; (4) taxation by the tribe in comparable amounts to amounts that the state may assess for comparable regulatory activities; (5) remedies for breach of contract; (6) standards for the operation, maintenance and licensing of gaming facilities; and, (7) any other subjects directly related to the operation of Indian gaming. 25 U.S.C. §2710(d)(3)(A).

One example of such consideration is an exclusivity agreement giving tribes a monopoly over gaming. Absent such consideration, the Secretary has taken the position that the sharing of revenue works like a tax.

Doctrinally, it is difficult to reconcile revenue sharing arrangements with Congress's intentions in IGRA. It is apparent from the language and structure of IGRA that Congress recognized a tribe's unmitigated right to engage in Class III gaming in a state that allows any such gaming. The compacting process was not intended to give states an avenue to obstruct this right, but rather to give states an opportunity to address legitimate public policy concerns related to the tribes' exercise of the right. In other words, the compacting process was intended to give states a voice in Indian gaming to address legitimate concerns, not to give states an opportunity to demand a cut of the profits.

As a political matter, revenue-sharing agreements have served a useful role in encouraging states to sign compacts. [A portion of IGRA that allowed tribes to sue states for failing to negotiate was struck down as unconstitutional by the Supreme Court in *Seminole Tribe v. Florida*, 517 U.S. 44 (1996). Thus, w]here tribes once had a stick to force states to negotiate, tribes are now forced to offer carrots. Indeed, in states where opposition to gaming is high, revenue sharing provides an incentive for state officials to sign compacts. Absent revenue sharing, it is difficult to determine what incentive a state official might have to sign a compact.

Opposition to tribal casinos frequently arises in county and local governments, many of which provide services, such as road maintenance and traffic control, that are highly impacted by large scale Indian gaming facilities. While tribes remain outside the domain of county planners, some tribes have embraced local governments by promising to help rejuvenate local economies and by agreeing to provide payments in lieu of taxes to local governments.

### The Scope of Gaming Allowed Under IGRA

One of the prime areas of controversy has been the scope of gaming allowed under IGRA. According to the language of IGRA, an Indian tribe may engage in Class III gaming on Indian lands if such activities are "are located in a state that permits such gaming for any purpose by any person, organization or entity." This language is the subject of great disagreement as to whether it requires states and tribes to negotiate over particular types of games.

On the one hand, the language can plainly be interpreted to indicate that if a state allows any Class III gaming activities, IGRA requires states to negotiate with tribes generally about Class III games and does not necessarily limit the negotiations to the particular Class III games that are offered under state law. Under this reading, the language constitutes an adoption of the criminal-prohibitory versus civil-regulatory distinction set forth in Cabazon.

In Connecticut, for example, a state statute allowed charities and religious organizations to conduct "Las Vegas night" fund raisers. In seeking to limit the scope of compact negotiations, state officials initially argued that "the limited authorization" of some casino-style games by non-profit organizations "does not amount to a general allowance of" casino-style gaming. The state argued that Indian tribes could conduct such games, but only "in accordance with, and by acceptance of," the state legal and regulatory apparatus with the inherent limitations on such gaming.

In *Mashantucket Pequot Tribe v. Connecticut*, the Second Circuit disagreed with the state's argument. It read IGRA to require a determination whether, as a matter of criminal law and public policy, the state prohibits Class III gaming. It found the state's "Las Vegas nights" law dispositive on this issue because the statute demonstrated that the state had adopted a regulatory rather than prohibitory policy toward gambling in general. The court rejected the state's argument that existing state law should control the extent of play of the subject games. It held that the extent to which such games could be offered by tribes was a proper subject for compact negotiation.

At least in some circumstances, it seems clear that it is possible to divide the broad range of Class III gaming into portions that the state prohibits and portions that do not violate state policy. For example, if a state prohibits gambling on cock-fighting, it is doubtful that any court would hold the state liable for failing to negotiate in good faith regarding that activity. On the other hand, what if the state bans seven-card poker but allows five card poker, or bans single-deck blackjack, but allows blackjack that is dealt out of a six-deck shoe? In such circumstances, it seems that the proper approach is a negotiation process in which the state can explain its concerns about the particular evil that accompanies a particular game.

Another vexing problem is the interpretation of the word "permits." Recall that IGRA requires negotiation over Class III gaming activities "in a state that permits such gaming." What types of state action must a state take to "permit" such gaming? What if a state has a century-old law on the books that prohibits gambling, but the law is never enforced against charities that regularly violate this law in an open manner?

In such circumstances, the issue of the scope of gaming can lead to a philosophical discussion as to who sets state policy toward gambling. Is it the legislature that sets such policy? Or, is it the prosecutor who makes the discretionary decision as to whether or not to prosecute violations? What if the legislature enacted the law a century earlier and it has never been prosecuted? What if the only criminal gambling law on the books was held unlawful by the state supreme court for a technical deficiency and the legislature never reenacted a proper law? What if the only reported case involving the law held that the law was unconstitutional as applied but did not reach the question of whether the law was unconstitutional as written?

The broader evaluation allowed under a criminal-prohibitory versus civil regulatory distinction may be helpful in providing a framework here in this area. It may be easier to determine a state's "gestalt" toward gambling by looking at a wider variety of state action.

## RUMSEY INDIAN RANCHERIA OF
## WINTUN INDIANS v. WILSON

**64 F.3d 1250 (9th Cir. 1994), as Amended
on Denial of Rehearing (1996)**

O'SCANNLAIN, Circuit Judge:

We decide whether certain gaming activities are permitted under California law and thus subject to tribal-state negotiation under the Indian Gaming Regulatory Act.

Numerous federally recognized Indian tribes currently engage in various gaming activities on tribal lands in California. Desiring to engage in additional activities (the "Proposed Gaming Activities"), several tribes asked the State of California (the "State") to negotiate a compact permitting the operation of certain stand-alone electronic gaming devices[1] and live banking and percentage card games.[2] The State refused to negotiate with the tribes, asserting that the Proposed Gaming Activities were illegal under California law.

The State and seven tribes subsequently entered into a stipulation to seek judicial determination of whether the State was obligated to negotiate with the tribes. These tribes filed a complaint for declaratory

---

1. Included among these electronic games are electronic pull tab machines, video poker devices, video bingo devices, video lotto devices, and video keno devices. The parties agree that California allows these games to be played in non-electronic formats.

2. A card game is "banked" if a gaming operator participates in the game with the players and acts as a house bank, paying all winners and retaining all other players' losses. Sullivan v. Fox, 189 Cal. App. 3d 673, 679, 235 Cal. Rptr. 5 (1987). A card game is a "percentage" game if the gaming operator has no interest in the outcome of a game but takes a percentage of all amounts wagered or won.

judgment with the district court under the Indian Gaming Regulatory Act ("IGRA"), 25 U.S.C. §§ 2701-2721. Since the State agreed not to "plead the Eleventh Amendment to the United States Constitution as a jurisdictional bar to the instant action," the Supreme Court's decision in *Seminole Tribe v. Florida*, 517 U.S. 44 (1996) (holding that §2710(d)(7) of IGRA "cannot grant jurisdiction over a State that does not consent to be sued") has no effect on our jurisdiction over this appeal. The district court awarded summary judgment to the Tribes, finding that, except for banking and percentage card games using traditional casino game themes, the Proposed Gaming Activities were a proper subject of negotiation. The State timely appealed, and the Tribes filed a cross-appeal.

Enacted in 1988 as means of "promoting tribal economic development, self-sufficiency, and strong tribal governments," IGRA creates a framework for Indian tribes to conduct gaming activities on tribal lands. IGRA divides gaming into three classes. " 'Class I' consists of social games for minimal prizes and traditional Indian games; 'Class II' includes Bingo and similar games of chance such as pull tabs and lotto; 'Class III' includes all games not included in Classes I or II." The parties agree that the Proposed Gaming Activities are Class III games.

A tribe seeking to operate Class III gaming activities on tribal lands generally may do so only under a compact. . . . In the instant case, the State opted not to negotiate over the Proposed Gaming Activities. . . . The State contends that IGRA does not obligate it to negotiate with the Tribes over the Proposed Gaming Activities. IGRA provides that "Class III gaming activities shall be lawful on Indian lands only if such activities are . . . located in a State that permits such gaming for any purpose by any person, organization, or entity. . . ." 25 U.S.C. §2710(d)(1)(B). Consequently, where a state does not "permit" gaming activities sought by a tribe, the tribe has no right to engage in these activities, and the state thus has no duty to negotiate with respect to them.

The parties disagree as to whether California "permits" the Proposed Gaming Activities. The State's argument is straightforward: the Proposed Gaming Activities are illegal. California law prohibits the operation of a banked or percentage card game as a misdemeanor offense. Cal. Penal Code §330 (Deering 1993). In addition, according to the State, the stand-alone electronic gaming machines sought by the Tribes are electronic "slot machines." California law prohibits the operation of slot machines as a misdemeanor offense, Cal. Penal Code §§330a, 330b, and a California appellate court has indicated that electronic machines of the sort requested by the Tribes fall within the scope of this prohibition.

The Tribes offer a broader reading of IGRA, claiming that a state "permits" a specific gaming activity if it "regulates" the activity in general rather than prohibiting it entirely as a matter of public policy. Under this approach, a specific illegal gaming activity is "regulated," rather than "prohibited," if the state allows the operation of similar gaming activities. The Tribes observe that video lottery terminals, pari-mutuel horse racing, and nonbanked, nonpercentage card gaming are legal in California. Because the Tribes view these activities as functionally similar to the Proposed Gaming Activities, they conclude that California regulates, and thus permits, these activities.

The Tribes cite to the Supreme Court's pre-IGRA decision, *California v. Cabazon Band of Mission Indians*, in support of their view. In *Cabazon*, the State of California objected to an Indian tribe's operation of bingo games on tribal land. The State argued that the tribe's bingo games violated a penal statute imposing prize limits and limiting bingo operators to unpaid members of charities. When the State sought to enforce its penal statute against the tribe, the tribe brought a declaratory judgment action. The district court awarded summary judgment to the tribe, and this court affirmed.

The Supreme Court held that summary judgment properly was granted. At the time, gaming on tribal lands fell under Public L. 280. . . . Congress enacted IGRA in response to *Cabazon*. The Tribes assert that IGRA codified *Cabazon*'s "criminal/regulatory" test. Under this approach, which was adopted by the district court in this case, a court must determine whether a gaming activity, even if illegal, violates a state's public policy. If it does, then the activity is "criminally" prohibited. If it does not, then the activity is merely "regulated" and, thus, "permitted" for the purpose of applying IGRA.

We reject this reading of IGRA. In interpreting IGRA, we use our traditional tools of statutory construction. "Interpretation of a statute must begin with the statute's language." "The plain meaning of legislation should be conclusive, except in the rare cases in which the literal application of a statute will produce a result demonstrably at odds with the intention of its drafters." In most cases, "if we find the statutory language unambiguous, then we will not resort to legislative history" to guide our review. Finally, although statutes benefitting Native Americans generally are construed liberally in their favor, we will not rely on this factor to contradict the plain language of a statute.

Section 2710(d)(1)(b) is unambiguous. In *United States v. Launder*, 743 F.2d 686 (9th Cir. 1984), we adopted a dictionary definition of the term "permit" as meaning " '[t]o suffer, allow, consent, let; to give leave or license; to acquiesce, by failure to prevent, or to expressly assent or agree to the doing of an act.' " (quoting from Black's Law

Dictionary). Clearly, California does not allow banked or percentage card gaming. With the possible exception of video lottery terminals, electronic gaming machines fitting the description of "slot machines" are prohibited.

The fact that California allows games that share some characteristics with banked and percentage card gaming—in the form of (1) banked and percentage games other than card games and (2) nonbanked, nonpercentage card games—is not evidence that the State permits the Proposed Gaming Activities. Nor is it significant that the state lottery, if not technically a slot machine, is functionally similar to one. . . .

IGRA does not require a state to negotiate over one form of Class III gaming activity simply because it has legalized another, albeit similar form of gaming. Instead, the statute says only that, if a state allows a gaming activity "for any purpose by any person, organization, or entity," then it also must allow Indian tribes to engage in that same activity. In other words, a state need only allow Indian tribes to operate games that others can operate, but need not give tribes what others cannot have.

Because we find the plain meaning of the word "permit" to be unambiguous, we need not look to IGRA's legislative history. However, a brief examination helps to clarify why the word has different meanings with respect to Class II and Class III gaming.

The primary source of IGRA's legislative history, the Senate Report accompanying its passage, does not describe the circumstances in which a state "permits" a gaming activity in the context of Class III gaming. The only relevant passages occur in the Senate Report's discussion of Class II gaming:

> [T]he Committee anticipates that Federal courts will rely on the distinction between State criminal laws which prohibit certain activities and civil laws of a State which impose a regulatory scheme upon those activities to determine whether class II games are allowed in certain States. This distinction has been discussed by the Federal courts many times, most recently and notably by the Supreme Court in Cabazon.

S. Rep. No. 446, 100th Cong., 2d Sess., reprinted in 1988 U.S.C.C.A.N. 3071, 3076. The Senate Report continues:

> The phrase "for any purpose by any person, organization or entity" makes no distinction between State laws that allow class II gaming for charitable, commercial, or governmental purposes, or the nature of the entity conducting the gaming. If such gaming is not criminally prohibited by the State in which tribes are located, then tribes, as governments, are free to engage in such gaming.

Id. at 3082.

The Tribes point to those statements as evidence that Congress intended that *Cabazon*'s "criminal/regulatory" test govern for the purposes of determining whether a Class II gaming activity is permitted on Indian lands. The Tribes then observe that IGRA's Class II gaming provisions contain the same language used for Class III gaming: "An Indian tribe may engage in . . . Class II gaming on Indian lands . . . if . . . such Indian gaming is located within a State that permits such gaming for any purpose by any person, organization or entity. . . ." 25 U.S.C. §2710(b)(1)(A). Relying upon the maxim that identical language in a statute should be interpreted to have the same meaning, the Tribes infer that the Senate Report establishes the applicability of the *Cabazon* test to Class III gaming.

However, that inference is incorrect. "Identical words appearing more than once in the same act, and even in the same section, may be construed differently if it appears they were used in different places with different intent." *Vanscoter v. Sullivan*, 920 F.2d 1441, 1448 (9th Cir. 1990). Such is the case for Class III gaming. The Senate Report repeatedly links the *Cabazon* test to Class II gaming while remaining silent as to Class III gaming—a fact that itself suggests that Class II and [Class] III provisions should be treated differently. Further, Congress envisioned different roles for Class II and Class III gaming. It intended that tribes have "maximum flexibility to utilize [Class II] games such as bingo and lotto for tribal economic development," S. Rep. No. 466, 1988 U.S.C.C.A.N. at 3079, and indicated that Class II gaming would be conducted largely free of state regulatory laws. Id. at 3079, 3082. Congress was less ebullient about tribes' use of Class III gaming, however, and indicated that Class III gaming would be more subject to state regulatory schemes. Id. at 3083-84. Even if we found it necessary to rely upon IGRA's legislative history, it supports the plain meaning of the term "permit" with regard to IGRA's Class III provisions.[6]

With the possible exception of slot machines in the form of video lottery terminals, California has no obligation to negotiate with the

---

6. The Tribes cite to *Mashantucket Pequot Tribe v. Connecticut*, 913 F.2d 1024 (2d Cir. 1990), cert. denied, 499 U.S. 975 (1991). . . . It concluded that, because Connecticut permitted the games of chance to be operated by some persons in the state, the state had to negotiate over those games with the Tribes. While we disagree, for the reasons expressed above, with the Mashantucket court's use of the Class II legislative history to interpret IGRA's Class III provisions, we believe that the court nevertheless reached the correct result. As we have explained, IGRA's text plainly requires a state to negotiate with a tribe over a gaming activity in which the state allows others to engage, and no resort to legislative history is necessary to support this conclusion. Because Connecticut allowed charities to operate games of chance, it had to negotiate with the tribe over these games.

Tribes on the Proposed Gaming Activities, and the trial court judgment is reversed to that extent. We affirm the district court's judgment that the State need not negotiate over banked or percentage card games with traditional casino themes. We remand to the district court to consider the limited question of whether California permits the operation of slot machines in the form of the state lottery or otherwise.

WALLACE, Chief Judge, concurring.

I concur with parts . . . of this opinion. However, I concur only in the result . . . because the discussion of the legislative history of the Indian Gaming Regulatory Act (Act) is unnecessary. Having concluded that the plain language of the Act controls this case, our opinion should end. The discussion of the Act's legislative history gives the impression that the Act is not as clear as we say, and that some additional reason is required before we hold as we do. "Where we are not prepared to be governed by what the legislative history says—to take, as it were, the bad with the good—we should not look to the legislative history at all. This text is eminently clear, and we should leave it at that." *United States v. Taylor*, 487 U.S. 326, 345 (1988) (Scalia, J., concurring).

\* \* \*

Following the issuance of the opinion in this case, the appellants sought rehearing and rehearing en banc. The court declined to grant rehearing en banc.

CANBY, Circuit Judge, joined by PREGERSON, REINHARDT, and HAWKINS, Circuit Judges, dissenting from the denial of rehearing en banc:

This is a case of major significance in the administration of the Indian Gaming Regulatory Act ("IGRA") and it has been decided incorrectly, in a manner that conflicts with the Second Circuit's interpretation of the same statutory language. The result is to frustrate the scheme of state-tribal negotiation that Congress established in IGRA. We should have granted rehearing en banc to prevent the near-nullification of IGRA in a circuit that encompasses a great portion of the nation's Indian country. Our failure to do so may close the only route open to many tribes to escape a century of poverty.

*Rumsey* holds that California, which permits several varieties of Class III gambling, has no duty under IGRA to negotiate with the tribes over the tribes' ability to conduct any game that is illegal under California law. This ruling effectively frustrates IGRA's entire plan governing Class III Indian gaming. The primary purpose of IGRA, as set forth in the Act, is "to provide a statutory basis for the operation of gaming by Indian tribes as a means of promoting tribal economic development, self-sufficiency, and strong tribal governments." 25 U.S.C. §2702(1). IGRA's otherwise drastic extension of state gaming law to Indian country (to be enforced only by the federal government) was modified by IGRA's process by which the states and tribes could arrive at compacts specifying what games might be allowed and who might have jurisdiction to enforce gaming laws. See 25 U.S.C. §2710(d)(3); 18 U.S.C. §1166(c)(2) (exempting Class III gaming conducted pursuant to a tribal-state compact from the application of state gaming laws extended into Indian country by §1166(a)). The whole idea was to foster these compacts. That goal is defeated if the details of the state's regulatory schemes, allowing some games and prohibiting others, apply if the state does nothing. Thus the Second Circuit, in arriving at a conclusion precisely opposite to that of *Rumsey*, stated:

> Under the State's approach, . . . even where a state does not prohibit class III gaming as a matter of criminal law and public policy, an Indian tribe could nonetheless conduct such gaming only in accord with, and by acceptance of, the entire state corpus of laws and regulations governing such gaming. The compact process that Congress established as the centerpiece of the IGRA's regulation of class III gaming would thus become a dead letter; there would be nothing to negotiate, and no meaningful compact would be possible.

*Mashantucket Pequot Tribe v. Connecticut*, 913 F.2d 1024, 1030-31 (2d Cir. 1990).

The Second Circuit's fears of turning IGRA's compact process into a dead letter are well-founded. It is well to keep in mind that the issue here is not whether California must allow every game the tribes want to conduct; it is merely whether California has a duty to negotiate with the tribes to determine what games should be conducted, on what scale, and who has jurisdiction to enforce gaming laws. In passing IGRA, Congress knew that states and tribes both had important interests at stake. If a state has a genuine prohibitory public policy against all Class III gaming, as some states do, it can rest on that policy and not entertain the possibility of Indian Class III gaming within its borders. States like California that have no such wholesale public policy against Class III gaming must, under IGRA, reach an accommodation between their interests and the strong interests of the tribes in conducting such gaming. IGRA's method of reaching such an accommodation is by negotiation between the two affected groups. IGRA imposes on the states a duty to negotiate compacts in good faith. That duty is enforceable in federal court with the aid, if necessary, of a court appointed mediator to arrive at a compact and the Secretary of the Interior to dictate a compact if the parties do not accept the mediator's ruling. But under *Rumsey*, this whole process is nipped in the bud if the tribe seeks to operate games that state law, criminal or regulatory, happens to prohibit. The state has no duty to begin negotiations, even though under IGRA a compact may permit the tribe to operate games that state law otherwise prohibits. 18 U.S.C. §1166(c)(2). The State thus has no incentive to negotiate, and there is no system to require negotiation. IGRA is rendered toothless.

Such a nullifying interpretation of IGRA might be understandable if it were required by the plain words of the statute, but it is not. *Rumsey* defeats the congressional plan for Class III gaming by a manifestly flawed interpretation of the statutory language. In deciding that California had no duty to negotiate with the plaintiff tribes, the *Rumsey* opinion asked and answered the wrong question. IGRA provides:

> Class III gaming activities shall be lawful on Indian lands only if such activities are—
>
> . . .
>
>     (B) located in a State that *permits such gaming* for any purpose by any person, organization, or entity. . . .

25 U.S.C. §2710(d)(1)(B) (emphasis added). Thus the state must negotiate with a tribe if the state "permits such gaming." The *Rumsey* opinion regards the key question as being whether the word "permits" is ambiguous; it holds that the word is not ambiguous, so the State need not bargain. But the proper question is not what Congress meant by "permits," but what Congress meant by "such gaming." Did it mean the particular game or games in issue, or did it mean the entire category of Class III gaming? The structure of IGRA makes clear that Congress was dealing categorically, and that a state's duty to bargain is not to be determined game-by-game. The time to argue over particular games is during the negotiation process.

The only natural reading of section 2710(d)(1)(B) is that, when Congress says "Class III gaming activities shall be lawful . . . if located in a State that permits such gaming," then "such gaming" refers back to the category of "Class III gaming," which is the next prior use of the word "gaming." *Rumsey* interprets the statutory language as if it said: "A Class III game shall be lawful . . . if located in a State that permits that game." But that is not what Congress said, and it is not a natural reading of the statutory language. The plain language cuts directly against *Rumsey*; Congress allows a tribe to conduct Class III gaming activities (pursuant to a compact) if the State allows Class III gaming by anyone.

Furthermore, Class II gaming is governed by virtually identical language in section 2710(b)(1)(A). A tribe may conduct and regulate "Class

II gaming . . . if such Indian gaming is located within a State that permits such gaming for any purpose by any person, organization or entity. . . ." 25 U.S.C. §2710(b)(1)(A) (emphasis added). We have held that the state cannot allow or disallow Class II Indian gaming game-by-game. *Sycuan Band of Mission Indians v. Miller*, 54 F.3d 535 (9th Cir. 1995) (amended opinion). Our decision in *Sycuan Band* followed the reasoning of the Supreme Court in [*Cabazon*,] the seminal Indian gaming case that ultimately led to the passage of IGRA. In deciding for purposes of Public Law 280 whether California's prohibition of high-stakes bingo could be enforced against the Band, the Supreme Court noted that "[t]he shorthand test is whether the conduct at issue violates the State's public policy." After reviewing California's treatment of gambling, the Court stated:

> In light of the fact that California permits a substantial amount of gambling activity, including bingo, and actually promotes gambling through its state lottery, we must conclude that California regulates rather than prohibits *gambling in general* and bingo in particular.

Id. at 211 (emphasis added). Thus, *Cabazon* ascertained California's public policy at a level of generality far above that of the individual game in issue, and concluded that the Band could conduct high-stakes bingo even though California made that activity a misdemeanor. We applied a similarly broad and categorical approach to Class II gaming in *Sycuan Band*.

The *Rumsey* opinion refuses to apply the reasoning of *Cabazon* and *Sycuan Band*, and instead holds that a class-wide, categorical approach is precluded by the "unambiguous" plain words of section 2710(d)(1)(B), even though identical words in section 2710(b)(1)(A) require a contrary result for Class II gaming. The majority in *Rumsey* justifies its interpretation by referring to the Senate Committee Report on IGRA, which approves the approach of *Cabazon* for Class II gaming but says nothing about *Cabazon*'s applicability to Class III gaming. See Sen. Rep. No. 100-446, 1988 U.S.C.C.A.N. 3071, 3076. But we should not read a congressional negative into a committee report's failure to mention *Cabazon* in regard to Class III gaming. *Cabazon* dealt with games that IGRA placed in Class II, and that is explanation enough why the discussion of *Cabazon* in the Committee's report arose only in connection with Class II gaming. The fact remains that Congress wrote provisions of essentially identical wording and structure to govern both Class II and Class III gaming. We should give them both the same categorical meaning.

*Rumsey* has thus misconstrued IGRA's Class III gaming provisions, and has done so in a manner that defeats Congress's intention and causes great economic harm to numerous tribes. With all respect to the Rumsey panel, we dissent from the denial of rehearing en banc.

## NOTES

1.  Though it may not have been fully apparent at the time, hundreds of millions of dollars were at stake in *Rumsey*. *Rumsey* produced a stalemate between tribes and the State of California. No tribal-state gaming compacts were signed for several years. But since tribes possess sovereign immunity from lawsuits by states, the stalemate put the state in a bind. The only way for a state to obtain a waiver of sovereign immunity from the tribe is to sign a tribal-state compact. As a result, even without tribal-state gaming compacts, tribes engaged in Class III or quasi-Class III gaming. Arguably, one result of *Rumsey* and the state's refusal to negotiate was that the rule of law suffered. When the United States finally took enforcement action (tribal sovereign immunity is not a bar to an action by the United States), tribes became much more interested in entering tribal-state gaming compacts.
2.  When tribes were ready to sign compacts in California, however, they did not go directly to the Governor's office to negotiate. They first engaged a higher authority. See the excerpt that follows.

## KEVIN K. WASHBURN, FEDERAL LAW, STATE POLICY, AND INDIAN GAMING
### 4 Nev. L.J. 285, 296-98 (2003-04)

For two centuries, Indian tribes had a nearly exclusive relationship with the United States and no relationship with state governments. This relationship began even before the United States came into existence and became part of the federalist structure of our government. Indian tribes counted on the federal government to protect them from the rapacious settlers that sought to overrun Indian lands, as well as the state governments that sanctioned such activity. Tribes rarely consulted with state governments or engaged them on a government-to-government basis. . . .

But where the federal government once refereed cross-border issues between states and tribes with little direct dialogue between the groups, the states and the tribes are now carrying on active dialogue directly with one another and, for the most part, are bypassing the federal government. Even where one side or the other has sought federal intervention in Indian gaming issues, the federal intervention has worked primarily as a catalyst for state-tribal negotiations.

One of the most vivid examples was the compacting process in Arizona. In 1992, a team of FBI agents and U.S. Marshals were deployed to seize gaming devices at an Indian casino run by the Fort McDowell Apache Tribe in Arizona. The tribe refused to surrender the gaming devices and actively obstructed the federal agents. During the ensuing standoff, the Governor of Arizona flew in by helicopter, met with the tribes, requested a "cooling off" period and, ultimately, reached gaming compacts with the tribe.

A similar situation arose in California, when then-Governor Pete Wilson of California refused to negotiate with Indian tribes in the 1990s[. T]he tribes continued gaming without compacts, [but] threats and the filing of a complaint for forfeiture of gaming machines filed by the United States Department of Justice motivated the tribes to seek a compact that would resolve the dispute.

[In both Arizona and California, tribes ultimately forced the hands of state policymakers by engineering expensive ballot initiatives that forced state officials to bend to the will of voters who wanted to patronize casinos.] Tribes thus bypassed state officials and went straight to the voters to demand tribal-state gaming compacts. This ultimately succeeded. Once the state realized that it was foregoing revenues by not having a compact with a revenue sharing provision, it moved to obtain new compacts with broad revenue sharing provisions.

In both Arizona and California, tribes deftly outmaneuvered state governmental leadership by working at the grassroots level. These tribes successfully convinced state citizens to support Indian gaming directly by approving statewide voter initiatives. In several states, tribal governments then succeeded in making Indian gaming indispensable to state governments through "revenue sharing" agreements that provide substantial funding to state governments and give state appropriators a vested interest in continued Indian gaming.

The result of this activity, prompted by IGRA, has been a paradigm shift in Indian policy in the United States. In light of aggressive state political activities, the federal-tribal relationship has given way to a state-tribal relationship that has had far greater economic importance to Indian tribes. . . . [T]he gaming compacts that tribes have entered with states might, in any other context, be called treaties.

Thus, Indian gaming has transformed the nature of Indian policy in the United States from an exclusively federal issue to an important issue of state politics. From the tribal government perspective, the good news is that tribes have proven very effective at the state level. Tribal organization and financial resources have made them powerful forces within state politics. On the other hand, tribal governments are subject to state political power to a far greater extent than in the past.

## C. GEOGRAPHICAL AND MARKET LIMITATIONS ON GAMING

Because of the ambivalent attitudes of citizens toward gambling, every state that has legalized gambling has nevertheless adopted substantial regulatory limitations on the activity. Most have done so in ways far more robust than traditional forms of regulations, such as municipal zoning ordinances, although these may also apply.

One manner in which gambling is limited is by imposing geographic limitations on where gambling may occur. Another manner to limit the extent of casino gambling is to limit the number of licenses available for casino facilities or to impose substantial requirements on casino scope. This section will introduce some of those approaches and take up the effectiveness of such approaches, as well as some of the unintended consequences of such approaches.

### 1. *Temporal/Geographic Limitations on Growth in Indian Gaming*

Federal law limits Indian gaming in (at least) two ways relevant to this discussion. First, Indian tribes can conduct gaming only on "Indian lands" which is defined fairly narrowly. Unless the land is within an Indian reservation, the land must, for example, generally be land that is held in trust for the tribe by the federal government.

Second, Section 20 of the Indian Gaming Regulatory Act prohibits tribes from offering gaming on any lands taken into trust after the effective date of that Act (October 17, 1988). There are, however, numerous exceptions to Section 20. Consider Section 20, which is set forth below, and think about whether it constitutes a sensible exercise of federal policymaking.

### Section 20 of the Indian Gaming Regulatory Act, 25 U.S.C. §2719, addressing gaming on lands acquired after October 17, 1988

(a) Prohibition on lands acquired in trust by Secretary

Except as provided in subsection (b) of this section, gaming regulated by this chapter shall not be conducted on lands acquired by the

Secretary in trust for the benefit of an Indian tribe after October 17, 1988, unless: (1) such lands are located within or contiguous to the boundaries of the reservation of the Indian tribe on October 17, 1988; or (2) the Indian tribe has no reservation on October 17, 1988, and—

(A) such lands are located in Oklahoma and—
(i) are within the boundaries of the Indian tribe's former reservation, as defined by the Secretary, or
(ii) are contiguous to other land held in trust or restricted status by the United States for the Indian tribe in Oklahoma; or
(B) such lands are located in a State other than Oklahoma and are within the Indian tribe's last recognized reservation within the State or States within which such Indian tribe is presently located.

(b) Exceptions

(1) Subsection (a) of this section will not apply when—
(A) the Secretary, after consultation with the Indian tribe and appropriate State and local officials, including officials of other nearby Indian tribes, determines that a gaming establishment on newly acquired lands would be in the best interest of the Indian tribe and its members, and would not be detrimental to the surrounding community, but only if the Governor of the State in which the gaming activity is to be conducted concurs in the Secretary's determination; or
(B) lands are taken into trust as part of—
(i) a settlement of a land claim,
(ii) the initial reservation of an Indian tribe acknowledged by the Secretary under the Federal acknowledgment process, or
(iii) the restoration of lands for an Indian tribe that is restored to Federal recognition.
(2) Subsection (a) of this section shall not apply to—
(A) any lands involved in the trust petition of the St. Croix Chippewa Indians of Wisconsin that is the subject of the action filed in the United States District Court for the District of Columbia entitled St. Croix Chippewa Indians of Wisconsin v. United States, Civ. No. 86-2278, or
(B) the interests of the Miccosukee Tribe of Indians of Florida in approximately 25 contiguous acres of land, more or less, in Dade County, Florida, located within one mile of the intersection of State Road Numbered 27 (also known as Krome Avenue) and the Tamiami Trail.
(3) Upon request of the governing body of the Miccosukee Tribe of Indians of Florida, the Secretary shall, notwithstanding any other

provision of law, accept the transfer by such Tribe to the Secretary of the interests of such Tribe in the lands described in paragraph (2)(B) and the Secretary shall declare that such interests are held in trust by the Secretary for the benefit of such Tribe and that such interests are part of the reservation of such Tribe under sections 465 and 467 of this title, subject to any encumbrances and rights that are held at the time of such transfer by any person or entity other than such Tribe. The Secretary shall publish in the Federal Register the legal description of any lands that are declared held in trust by the Secretary under this paragraph.

(c) Authority of Secretary not affected. Nothing in this section shall affect or diminish the authority and responsibility of the Secretary to take land into trust.

## NOTES AND QUESTIONS

1.  Consider just a few of the myriad questions that might arise under Section 20: Are lands across a state highway right of way from an Indian reservation sufficiently "contiguous" to the boundraries of an Indian reservation to come within the exception in Section 20(a)(1)? If not, if a tribe locates the casino's parking lot on those lands, is it in violation of IGRA? What is the difference between the "initial reservation" exception and the "governor concurrence" exception in 25 U.S.C. §2719? Could land placed into trust satisfy both the "initial reservation" exception and the "restored lands" exception? Could a tribe be "restored," but the land at issue not be "restored lands" for purposes of 25 U.S.C. §2719? Does 25 U.S.C. §2719(b)(1)(B)(i) require that the land claim that be settled with the United States?
2.  What are "Indian lands" for purposes of IGRA? See 25 U.S.C. §2703(4).

## CITY OF ROSEVILLE v. NORTON
### 348 F.3d 1020 (D.C. Cir. 2003)

Rogers, Circuit Judge:

This appeal involves the intersection of two statutes concerning Indian tribes. The Indian Gaming Regulatory Act, 25 U.S.C. §§2701-2721 ("IGRA"), prescribes the conditions under which Indian tribes may engage in commercial gaming on their reservations. The Auburn Indian Restoration Act, 25 U.S.C. §§1300l-1300l-7 (2003) ("AIRA"), restored the Auburn Indian Band located near Sacramento, California to federal recognition as an Indian Tribe and authorized the creation of a new reservation on its behalf. The cities of Roseville and Rocklin, both located near land approved by the Secretary of the Interior as part of the Tribe's new reservation, and Citizens for Safer Communities, a local nonprofit organization (hereafter "the Cities"), challenge the district court's interpretation of section 20 of IGRA. . . .

The Auburn Indian Band is a small tribe, numbering somewhere around 247 members, most of whom live near the village of Auburn in central California, not far from Sacramento. The Auburn Band currently has no reservation; in fact, the Auburn Tribe had no federally recognized existence between 1967 and 1994. The Band appears to have been formed when several surviving families of the Maidu and Meiwok Tribes, both devastated by the settlement policies of the nineteenth century, grouped into a small community that survived much of the depredation that came with the settlement of California. In 1917, the federal government provided the Auburn Tribe with a small 20-acre reservation, which was expanded to 40 acres in 1953, known as the Auburn "Rancheria." As part of then-prevailing policies on Indian assimilation, however, Congress withdrew the Auburn Tribe's recognition and terminated its reservation in 1967, distributing most of the Rancheria land in fee to individual holders, pursuant to the terms of the Rancheria Act, Pub. L. No. 85-671 (1958). The policy of attempting to assimilate Indians by terminating federal trust responsibilities has since been repudiated by the President and Congress, and many tribes terminated as part of those policies have now been restored to federal recognition.

Congress restored the Auburn Band's rights as a federally recognized tribe in 1994 and authorized the Secretary of the Interior to take land into trust to serve as the Auburn Tribe's reservation. See AIRA, Pub. L. No. 103-434 tit. II (1994), 25 U.S.C. §§1300Ill-1300Il-7 (2003). AIRA directs the Secretary to accept lands located on the Tribe's former reservation into trust, but also authorizes the Secretary to accept other unencumbered lands located elsewhere in Placer County. AIRA also references the Secretary's authority, pursuant to the Indian Reorganization Act, 25 U.S.C. §461 et seq., to take additional land into trust within the tribe's "service area," which includes several neighboring counties. Under AIRA, all land taken into trust pursuant to its terms "shall be part of the Tribe's reservation." Id. §1300l-2(c).

Rather than apply to the Secretary to re-establish their reservation on the Rancheria, most of which land was unavailable because held in fee by individual Indians or non-Indians, the Auburn Tribe applied for three separate parcels of land: one for residential and community use, one for commercial use as a gaming casino, and a third, containing a church within the boundaries of the old reservation, for community use. The Tribe submitted a revised application in 2000, however, to request only the gaming site, reserving the other two sites for later applications. The gaming site consists of 49.21 acres located in an unincorporated portion of Placer County, California, and photographs of the area indicate that the land is flat, barren, and virtually uninhabited. The parties disagree over how far the land is from the Auburn Tribe's Rancheria, but viewing the record most favorably to the Cities, see *Browning v. Clinton*, 292 F.3d 235, 242 (D.C. Cir. 2002), it is at least clear that the land is neither on nor close to the Tribe's former reservation, and is possibly as far as 40 miles away. What is clear, however, is that the land is close to the Cities.

In response to the Bureau of Indian Affairs' notice and request for comments, the Cities opposed the Auburn Tribe's application, arguing that the casino would increase crime in their communities and interfere with planned residential developments nearby, as well as with the family-oriented nature of the area. Moreover, they argued that because the proposed gaming was to take place on land acquired after the IGRA's effective date of October 17, 1988, the Secretary was not authorized to permit gaming on the land unless she made a threshold determination under IGRA §20(b)(1)(A), 25 U.S.C. §2719(b)(1)(A), that the proposed gaming activity "would not be detrimental to the surrounding communities" and obtained the concurrence of the Governor. The Bureau, relying on opinions of two Associate Solicitors of the Interior Department, took the position that the land was exempt from the threshold no-community-detriment finding normally applicable under IGRA §20(b)(1)(A) to Indian lands acquired after 1988 because AIRA brought the Auburn Tribe's land within IGRA's exception for a "restoration of lands" to a restored tribe under §20(b)(1)(B)(iii). The Cities' objections based on local community detriment were therefore not legally relevant, as IGRA does not require a no-community-detriment finding on lands that are part of a "restoration of lands" before the Secretary can authorize gaming. . . .

Section 20(a) creates a prohibition: gaming is not permitted on Indian land taken into trust by the Secretary after IGRA's effective date, October 17, 1988, unless the land borders an existing reservation or is within the last recognized reservation of a tribe that was landless at the time IGRA was enacted (unless the tribe is in Oklahoma, in which case lands bordering its former reservation are exempted as well). This prohibition is subject to two exceptions in §20(b). The first, §20(b)(1)(A), allows the Secretary of the Interior to override

§20(a) and permit gaming on a newly acquired parcel when, "after consultation with the Indian tribe and appropriate State and local officials" the Secretary "determines that a gaming establishment . . . would be in the best interest of the Indian tribe and its members, and would not be detrimental to the surrounding community, but only if the Governor of the State . . . concurs. . . ." The second, §20(b)(1)(B), exempts lands taken into trust as part of the "settlement of a land claim," "the initial reservation of an Indian tribe acknowledged by the Secretary," or the "restoration of lands for an Indian tribe that is restored to federal recognition." The IGRA does not define a "restoration of lands."

On appeal, the Cities contend that the district court erred as a matter of law in holding, contrary to the plain meaning of IGRA §20(b)(1)(A), that the Secretary was not required to make a threshold determination that the use of the Auburn Tribe's land for gaming would not be detrimental to the surrounding communities and to obtain the Governor's concurrence. . . . [T]he Cities' appeal presents a single question of statutory interpretation. They contend that the Secretary violated IGRA because the Auburn Tribe's acquisition of the 49.21 acres cannot be a "restoration of lands" under IGRA §20(b)(1)(B)(iii) as the Tribe never owned those acres in the past as part of its former reservation, the Rancheria, and the tract of land is too different from the Rancheria to be a "restoration" of it. IGRA §20(b)(1)(A) therefore forbids gaming on the land absent a finding by the Secretary, concurred in by the Governor, that gaming will not have a detrimental effect on the local community—a finding the Secretary did not make pursuant to §20(b)(1)(A). The Cities maintain that the "restoration of lands" exception can bear only one meaning, namely, that lands must be either identical or almost identical to those previously owned in order to be a "restoration," and that that reading is necessitated by the IGRA's overall policy of limiting the expansion of Indian gaming. . . .

[W]e turn to the merits of the Cities' contentions, examining the text of the statutory exception, its context within IGRA, and IGRA's structure and purposes to determine the intent of Congress in enacting the "restoration of land" exception. All parties urge plain meaning constructions of the exception, albeit with different nuances. The Cities, citing Webster's Dictionary, urge the narrowest construction of the word "restoration" as " bring[ing] back to an original state," in light of their view that IGRA is designed to restrict gambling on Indian reservations and to protect surrounding communities. The Secretary and the Tribe, also referring us to the dictionary, urge an interpretation of the word "restoration" that encompasses the concept of " restitution." The Tribe also points to this meaning of the word in ancient times as encompassing a broader concept of compensation. The Book of Exodus, for instance, at Chapter 22, Verse 1, requires that someone guilty of killing or selling another's stock must "restore five oxen for an ox, and four sheep for a sheep."

No circuit court of appeals has yet had occasion to address the scope of IGRA's "restoration of lands" exception under §20(b)(1)(B)(iii), and district courts have assumed that lands are "restored" when included in a tribe's restoration act. . . . Because the Auburn Tribe's land is located in Placer County, which was a designated area in the AIRA, and thus became, by operation of law, the Tribe's reservation, see 25 U.S.C. §1300l-2(c), the court has no occasion to decide whether land obtained by a tribe other than through the tribe's restoration act is the "restoration of lands" for IGRA purposes, nor whether "restored" tribes include those whose termination or recognition has not been the result of congressional action. Instead, the court must decide the ancillary question presented by the Cities' appeal of whether lands identified in a tribe's restoration act as its reservation must meet the additional qualification of prior tribal ownership before the land can be considered a "restoration of lands for an Indian tribe that is restored to federal recognition."

All parties contend that the plain meaning of §20(b)(1)(B)(iii) controls. The Cities point to the dictionary definition of the word "restore," and contend that the plain meaning of the term "restoration of lands" cannot encompass lands over which a tribe did not exert prior ownership, or which are dissimilar from those the tribe previously owned. Because to "restore" something means to "bring [it] back to an original state," they maintain that the only lands that can be "restored" to the Auburn Tribe are those on its prior reservation, the Rancheria, or lands sufficiently similar in nature that they can be said to bring the reservation back to its "original" state. Other land acquired pursuant to AIRA, such as the 49 acres that the Secretary has agreed to take into trust, are simply "lands acquired by the Secretary in trust for the benefit of an Indian Tribe after October 17, 1988" for which the Auburn Tribe, like any other tribe that acquires new land, must meet the requirements of IGRA §20(b)(1)(A) before the land can be used for commercial gaming. The Cities maintain that the narrow reading of the word "restore" is supported by IGRA's general ban on Indian gaming because if a "restoration" of lands is allowed to encompass lands to which a tribe does not demonstrate a prior connection, such as prior ownership, the exception will swallow the rule. However, the Secretary and the Tribe respond with dictionary definitions of their own, contending that "restoration" encompasses the concept of "restitution," such that it can be a "restoration" to give the Auburn Tribe lands to make restitution for past wrongs. They point out that this meaning of the word, even if less common in everyday parlance, is also included in the dictionary, fits far better with the structure of IGRA and the remedial purposes of AIRA, and is supported by AIRA's provision that all lands taken into trust pursuant to the act "shall be part of the Tribe's reservation." 25 U.S.C. §1300l-2(c).

There is much to commend the interpretation of the Secretary and the Auburn Tribe regarding the scope of the "restoration of lands" exception. . . . But, for the reasons advanced by the Cities, a narrower construction of the exception is not without a measure of plausibility. In sum, neither side can prevail by quoting the dictionary.

We turn, therefore, to context, for the court is to "consider not only the bare meaning of the word but also its placement and purpose in the statutory scheme," *Bailey v. United States*, 516 U.S. 137, 145 (1995). The force of the Cities' interpretation fades upon closer analysis, particularly in light of the general environment in which IGRA was enacted, its structure and general purpose. Even assuming that the Cities' definition of " restore" as to "bring back to an original state" is the more common meaning of the word, the statutory context makes broader readings of §20(b)(1)(B)(iii) more plausible. That a "restoration of lands" could easily encompass new lands given to a restored tribe to re-establish its land base and compensate it for historical wrongs is evident here, where much of the Auburn Tribe's Rancheria is, as a practical matter, unavailable to it. Further, even under the Cities' definition of "restore" as to "bring back to an original state," there would appear to be no reason to limit the "original state" to 1967, rather than the earlier period before the Tribe was granted only a 40-acre reservation. Section 20(b)(1)(B)(iii) refers to the restoration of "lands," not the restoration of a "reservation." The Maidu and Meiwok Tribes from which the Auburn Tribe descended once occupied much of central California. For the Cities to now argue that the 49 acres are a windfall, as if the Tribe's ancestors had never possessed any more, is ahistorical. Given the history of Indian tribes' confinement to reservations, it is not reasonable to suppose that Congress intended "restoration" to be strictly limited to land constituting a tribe's reservation immediately before federal recognition was terminated.

The Cities' interpretation is also difficult to reconcile with IGRA's other provisions. Limiting a "restoration of lands" to the return of lands on a tribe's prior reservation practically reads the "restoration of lands" provision out of existence. As one of the exemptions under

§20(b), the "restoration of lands" in §20(b)(1)(B)(iii), unless it is surplusage, must exempt some land that would otherwise fall within the gaming prohibition of §20(a). But §20(a)(2)(B) explicitly excludes the "last recognized reservation" of a tribe that "has no reservation on October 17, 1988" from §20(a)'s prohibition. Under the Cities' plain meaning interpretation whereby the only lands that can be part of a "restoration" are those in a tribe's former reservation, the exception would be virtually bereft of meaning because gaming on such lands is not prohibited in the first place. If the Auburn Tribe had reacquired some of the land on its former reservation, the Rancheria, it would have no need to look to the "restoration of lands" exception in §20(b)(1)(B)(iii) in order to use the land for commercial gaming because §20(a)(2)(B) would have excluded its Rancheria from §20(a)'s ban on gaming. . . . It is generally presumed that Congress does not intend to enact surplusage. The difficulty of reassembling a former reservation as a result of the passage of substantial periods of time between the loss of federal recognition and its restoration is illustrated by the experience of the Auburn Tribe: its Rancheria is largely held in fee by individuals and unavailable as a practical matter more than a quarter of a century later. To be given meaningful effect, then, a "restoration of lands" would seem to encompass more than only the return of a tribe's former reservation.

[T]he Cities' view that the Secretary violated IGRA by failing to make a factual determination that the accepted tract of land was substantially identical to the old Rancheria depends on their view that the 49.21 acres cannot meet this standard because is too geographically distant, considerably more valuable, and to be put to commercial rather than residential use. But to the extent the Cities rely on the notion that the Auburn Tribe's new land cannot be a "restoration" because it is not being used residentially, like the old Rancheria was, their argument is nonsensical. The point of the "restoration of lands" exception is that such lands may be used for commercial gaming; it would make no sense if a tribe's use of land for gaming could defeat the land's eligibility for gaming. Moreover, these considerations undermine the Cities' plain meaning interpretation by admitting that a "restoration of lands" to a tribe can include different lands than those on its former reservation, as occurred here.

Essentially, the Cities maintain that the "restoration of lands" exception cannot be read in a manner that would allow the Auburn Tribe to put together a new reservation that an "established" tribe would not be permitted to acquire, namely, a gaming parcel separate from its residential and community areas. This explains the Cities' reasoning that a broad reading of the exception would swallow the rule. Because the Tribe would not have been permitted to acquire the 49 acres for gaming if its federal recognition had never been terminated, its "restoration" should not allow it greater rights than it otherwise would have enjoyed as a chronologically continuous tribe. This approach is problematic for several reasons. Had the Auburn Tribe never been terminated, it would have had opportunities for development in the intervening years, including the possible acquisition of new land prior to the effective date of IGRA. A "restoration of lands" compensates the Tribe not only for what it lost by the act of termination, but also for opportunities lost in the interim.

The Cities also point to *Sac and Fox Nation v. Norton*, 240 F.3d 1250 (10th Cir. 2001), although their reliance is largely misplaced. In that case, a tribe had acquired land in downtown Kansas City, Missouri, that was located more than two hundred miles from the tribe's principal reservation. The tribe sought permission to use the land for gaming under §20(a)(1), which exempts land bordering a tribe's "reservation" from §20(a)'s ban. The Tenth Circuit rejected the Secretary's position that a "reservation" could include land held in trust for an Indian tribe by the federal government for non-residential purposes, reasoning that such a broad reading of the word "reservation" would undermine the anti-gaming-expansion policies of §20(a). Id. 1264-67. By contrast, the Auburn Tribe's 49.21 acres are part of the Tribe's reservation by operation of law, under AIRA, 25 U.S.C. §1300l-2(c), regardless of whether the land falls within IGRA's "restoration of lands" exception in §20(b)(1)(B)(iii). To the extent, however, that the Tenth Circuit interpreted "reservation" in light of §20's general limit of gaming on lands acquired by tribes after 1988, the decision in *Sac and Fox Nation* is consistent with the Cities' view that the "restoration of lands" exception be similarly narrowly construed.

The approach of the Tenth Circuit in *Sac and Fox Nation* is not persuasive here. First, Congress rebuked the decision almost immediately, enacting legislation stating that the authority to determine whether land is a "reservation" was delegated to the Secretary as of the effective date of IGRA. See Pub. L. No. 107-63, §134 (2001). Second, the Cities point to nothing to indicate that Congress contemplated that the Auburn Tribe's reservation would be composed of only one parcel of land. Had the Tribe acquired one tract of land for residential and gaming purposes, the Cities would not want the land considered a "restoration of lands" if the land was not part of the former Rancheria, even if it bordered on the Rancheria. Had the Tribe been able to reacquire the Rancheria, used it solely for gaming, and then acquired, pursuant to the land-acquisition provision in the Indian Reorganization Act, 25 U.S.C. §465, other land in a different county for residential use, the reacquired Rancheria would be a "restoration of lands" under the Cities' interpretation even though the resulting reservation would conflict with the no-off-reservation-gaming policy of §20(a).

[T]he IGRA exceptions in §20(b)(2) as well as AIRA itself all embody policies counseling for a broader reading [of restoration]. The general purpose of IGRA is "promoting tribal economic development" and "self-sufficiency." 25 U.S.C. §2702(1). A reading allowing the Auburn Tribe to participate in that economic base furthers this purpose of IGRA while a reading that confines "restoration of lands" to the old reservation, the Rancheria, (most of which is now in the hands of homeowners, many non-Indian, and hence unavailable for development) would likely deny the Tribe this opportunity. . . .

Furthermore, the fact that IGRA §20(b)(1)(B)(ii) provides a parallel exception for the "initial reservation of an Indian Tribe acknowledged by the Secretary" supports the broad reading of the "restoration of lands" exception. Acknowledged tribes, which may or may not have been formally recognized by the federal government at some point in the past, are those that gain recognition by administrative, rather than Congressional, action, see generally 25 C.F.R. pt. 83. The parallel placement of the two exceptions in the statute, as well as the analogous situation in which restored and acknowledged tribes find themselves, imply that these exceptions should be treated similarly. Yet it would be anomalous for Congress to confine restored tribes to whatever of their pre-termination reservation is available while simultaneously allowing acknowledged tribes to conduct gaming anywhere on their initial reservation. A far more sensible reading is that the "restoration of lands" is to a restored tribe what the "initial reservation" is to an acknowledged tribe: the lands the Secretary takes into trust to re-establish the tribe's economic viability. . . .

The Cities' real policy objection is that the 49 acres ultimately selected by the Secretary is not an appropriate site for gaming. Although they disagree with the Secretary's determination in weighing the relevant factors in 25 C.F.R. §§151.10-151.11, the Cities do not contend on appeal that the Secretary failed to engage in the requisite balancing or acted arbitrarily or capriciously in applying those factors.

Finally, were there any remaining doubt that Congress intended IGRA's "restoration of lands" exception to be read broadly, to encompass more than a tribe's former reservation as of the date of the termination of its federal recognition, [the] Indian Canon of statutory construction would resolve any doubt. The Supreme Court has on numerous occasions noted that ambiguities in federal statutes are to be read liberally in favor of the Indians. See generally *County of Yakima v. Confederated Tribes & Bands of Yakima Indian Nation*, 502 U.S. 251, 269 (1992); *Montana v. Blackfeet Tribe*, 471 U.S. 759, 766 (1985). IGRA is designed to promote the economic viability of Indian Tribes, and AIRA focuses on ensuring the same for the Auburn Tribe. In this context, the Indian canon requires the court to resolve any doubt in favor of the tribe.

To the extent the Cities contend the canon is inappropriately applied to laws disfavoring Indians, pointing to IGRA §20(a), the Cities continue to overlook the role that IGRA's exceptions in §20(b)(1)(B) play in the statutory scheme, namely to confer a benefit onto tribes that were landless when IGRA was enacted. Moreover, the Cities' suggestion that the Indian canon is no longer relevant because it is predicated upon the weakness of, and special trust responsibilities of the federal government for, American Indians, conditions no longer true in an age when tribes have "increasing political clout and sophistication," ignores that the Supreme Court has applied the canon even when the federal government is not a party, e.g., *Blackfeet Tribe*, 471 U.S. 759. Hence, even assuming that the purpose behind the canon is more apposite to the interpretation of Indian treaties forced upon tribes then lacking legal sophistication than to third-party suits involving federal statutes, its applicability to ambiguous statutes purporting to benefit Indians is settled.

Accordingly, we hold, as the Secretary has concluded, in light of IGRA's language, structure, and purpose, that the Auburn Tribe's land qualifies as the "restoration of lands" under IGRA §20(b)(1)(B)(iii) even though the land is not located on the Tribe's former reservation as of the time the Auburn Tribe lost federal recognition and is being put to a different use than the lands on the former reservation, the Rancheria. Hence, the Secretary did not violate IGRA by failing to make a no-detriment finding under §20(b)(1)(A). Affirmed.

## NOTES

As this case demonstrates, Section 20 of IGRA bars gaming on lands acquired by Indian tribes after IGRA's enactment in 1988, but Section 20 is rife with exceptions to its general prohibition. The Cities argued not that the land could not be taken into trust for the tribe for gaming, but only that the Secretary of the Interior should have used a different process and therefore engaged a different exception. What was the basis for this argument and how does it differ? How, if at all, might the use of the other exception have changed the outcome?

## 2. Other Common Methods of Geographically Limiting Gambling

### WILLIAM R. EADINGTON, THE ECONOMICS OF CASINO GAMBLING

13 Journal of Economic Perspectives 173-92 (Summer 1999)

In the early 1960s, commercial gaming in the United States was at low ebb. . . . The only major forms of gambling were bingo and horse racing. . . . [Casino gaming existed only in Las Vegas and the industry there was widely viewed by the Department of Justice as a haven for organized crime, and by the media as corrupt. It was a "pariah" industry with high profits, but] no access to mainstream sources of financial capital in the debt or equity markets and therefore had to rely on creative and sometimes questionable sources of financing in order to expand. . . .

The legal climate for American casinos began to shift in the 1970s. In 1969, Nevada passed the Corporate Gaming Act, permitting publicly traded corporations to hold gambling licenses for the first time. Within a few years, corporations with established reputations in other industries—such as Hilton, MGM, Holiday Inn, and Ramada—had entered the casino industry in Nevada.

In 1976, New Jersey's voters authorized casino gaming in Atlantic City, making it the second state with legal casinos. By the mid-1980s, the number of casinos operating in Atlantic City increased to twelve, and the volume of business—as measured by gaming winnings by operators—briefly eclipsed that of Las Vegas. By calendar year 1998, however, Las Vegas had regained the lead with gaming revenues of $5.5 billion compared to Atlantic City's $4 billion.

New Jersey took a different approach than Nevada to shaping its casino industry. Casino operations in Atlantic City had to be built to specific size and space allocation criteria, which limited potential investors to those organizations that could raise the requisite financial capital, and indicated from the outset that the industry would develop as an oligopoly. In contrast, Nevada has had few barriers to entry into its casino industry. Nonetheless, economies of scale and scope pushed the major Nevada casino markets in Las Vegas and Reno toward oligopolistic status as well, even though the state's major tourism areas continue to have large numbers of far less significant smaller casinos. In fiscal 1998, for example, Las Vegas had 78 unrestricted casino licenses, generating total revenues of $9.1 billion, gaming revenues of $4.9 billion and net income before federal income tax of $860 million. However, the largest 21 Las Vegas Strip casinos accounted for 73 percent of these total revenues, 69 percent of gaming revenues, and 98 percent of profits.

A number of serious efforts were made to legalize casinos in other states between 1978 and 1988, including in Florida, New York, Colorado, Minnesota, Ohio, Pennsylvania, and Massachusetts, among others. Some of these efforts used the initiative or referendum process, while others tried legislative action, but all the campaigns fell short. However, beginning in late 1988, three events set the stage for the rapid expansion of casinos and casino-style gaming. In October of that year, Congress passed the Indian Gaming Regulatory Act that defined the relationship of states to tribes in regulating Indian gaming within their borders. In November, South Dakota voters authorized limited stakes gambling in the declining former mining town of Deadwood, South Dakota. Finally, in March 1989, the Iowa legislature authorized limited stakes casino gaming on riverboats on that state's waterways.

Over the next decade, casinos spread rapidly in response to these catalysts. Small stakes casinos were authorized by initiative in three rural mining communities in the mountains of Colorado in 1990. Riverboat casinos were legalized in the states of Illinois, Mississippi, Louisiana, Missouri and Indiana between 1990 and 1993. Indian casinos opened in over 20 states between 1990 and 1997. The cities of New Orleans (in 1992) and Detroit (in 1996) authorized land-based urban casinos; the resulting New Orleans monopoly casino went bankrupt in 1995 but was scheduled to re-open in 1999, and the three permitted Detroit casinos had not yet opened by mid-1999.

Commercial gaming also expanded in the 1980s and 1990s with the legalization of slot machines or other electronic gaming devices outside of casinos. Race tracks in Iowa, Delaware, Rhode Island, West Virginia, New Mexico and Louisiana commenced operations of electronic gaming at their facilities in the 1990s. Video poker machines appeared in bars and taverns or arcades in Montana, Louisiana and South Carolina. Under the guise of the state lottery, video lottery terminals—typically video poker machines without coin output—were introduced in Oregon and South Dakota. Race tracks and other businesses in various other states lobbied for permission to offer slot machines on their premises as well.

A number of factors contributed to the spread of casinos and casino-style gaming in the 1990s. The general apprehension about casino gaming that had dominated public attitudes in the United States gave way to greater public acceptance of gambling as a form of recreational activity, with corresponding changes in legal restrictions on gambling. As the ownership structure shifted to publicly traded corporations, the historic stigma that had long linked casino gaming to organized crime diminished considerably. There was also a strong cross-border effect in the legalization process. When residents of one state where casinos were prohibited would travel to another state to partake in casino gaming, this export of spending, jobs and tax revenues encouraged states that were adjacent to those with permitted casinos to consider legalization. This was particularly the case with the various riverboat gaming jurisdictions.[4]

The expansion of casino gaming in the United States has close parallels in other countries. Casinos had been prohibited in the United Kingdom until the 1968 Gaming Act provided a new legal basis for them. Casinos in Australia were illegal until 1972, when enabling legislation at the state level authorized a single casino in Tasmania. In Canada, charitable casinos first appeared in western provinces in the late 1970s, when temporary casinos allowing small stakes betting to raise money for nonprofit enterprises were permitted at the annual summer exhibitions such as the Calgary Stampede and Edmonton's Klondike Days. Over time, the charitable casinos became less temporary, constraining regulations were relaxed, and regulatory authorities were established at the provincial level, thus paving the way for more substantial Canadian casinos in the 1990s.[5] . . .

Nevada possesses a respected regulatory structure that oversees the most laissez faire casino industry in the world. Providing commercial gambling services in Nevada requires a license from the State Gaming Control Board. The fundamental requirements for licensing in Nevada are meeting probity standards and access to legitimate financial capital. An unrestricted gaming license permits the licensee to operate any number of gaming devices and table games, though local ordinances can constrain location and size, and require certain amenities. Altogether, there were over 400 unrestricted gaming licenses in Nevada in 1998, of which about 230 generated annual gaming revenues of $1 million or more. However, economies of scale and scope in Nevada's casino industry have led to a high concentration of revenues,

4. Competition among adjacent states or provinces for one another's citizens as customers (as in the United States, Canada and Australia) can lead to greater amounts of legalization of casinos than would be the case where such legislative decisions were made at a federal or national level (as in the United Kingdom).

5. The cross-border effect was also an influence on the spread of casinos in Canada. The province of Ontario opened government-owned but privately-operated border casinos in Windsor and Niagara Falls in 1994 and 1996 respectively, primarily to cater to U.S. customers from the metropolitan areas of Detroit and Buffalo. The government-owned and -operated Quebec casino at Hull was positioned to draw customers from the neighboring metropolitan area of Ottawa, Ontario. Furthermore, various Canadian provinces permitted video lottery terminals to be widely placed in age-restricted locations such as bars and taverns during the 1990s.

and an even higher concentration of profit, in the hands of the largest gaming companies and operations.

Other states have attempted to limit gambling to particular cities or particular types of operations. New Jersey, for example, mandated a wide variety of size, design and product mix conditions that effectively limited the industry only to large gaming operations in a single city. At the time the enabling legislation was enacted, there was concern in New Jersey that a Nevada-style approach, allowing small and medium-sized operators into the market, would make control difficult and would invite organized crime and other chicanery into the industry.

The approach taken in the mining town casino communities of South Dakota and Colorado effectively limited casino gaming operations to specific districts in the towns and into qualifying—typically historic—structures. Furthermore, South Dakota limited licensees to no more than 30 games or devices each. As a result, the casinos in the four towns of these two states have involved a large number of small- to mid-sized operations, with limited product differentiation. The size and zoning constraints, along with limited maximum wagers, also prevent the kind of evolution of the industry that has characterized Nevada.

The riverboat states have generally chosen legislative models that limit supply below what the market could bear, and encourage regional monopolies or oligopolies. This created significant economic rents and, in some cases (like Louisiana) has led to allegations of corruption in the bidding processes for the allocation of limited gaming licenses.

Mississippi, on the other hand, followed the Nevada model. As a result, it has seen its casino industry evolve in a market-driven fashion that has allowed the industry to develop multidimensional destination resort centers—particularly in Biloxi and Tunica County—that offer a wider variety of non-gaming amenities, such as accommodation, food product, outdoor recreation, and entertainment, than is typical in other riverboat states. [Mississippi legalized casinos in 1990 but restricted them to the waters of the Mississippi River and the Gulf of Mexico. The floating casinos were damaged or destroyed by Hurricane Katrina in August 2005. A month later, the state legislature passed a law permitting the casinos to build up to 800 feet inland. See Miss. Code Ann. §97-33-1.—ED.]

The urban casinos that were authorized in New Orleans and Detroit were an attempt to create exclusive franchises. The philosophy was that such casinos would concentrate positive economic impacts more than competitive alternatives; they would be easier to regulate and control; and it would be easier for state and local governments to extract economic rents for public purposes from such operations. However, New Orleans has had allegations of corruption and a bitterly contested bankruptcy, an experience which provides a cautionary example of what might happen if governments try to extract too much in the way of economic rents. . . .

Much of the casino gaming that was authorized in the United States in the 1990s placed considerable limitations upon the size, type, or number of casino facilities; the terms and conditions under which customers could gamble; and the locations where gambling was allowed to take place. The effect in various jurisdictions, especially in the short term, was to create situations where providers of gambling services—or other economic stakeholders—were able to capture significant amounts of economic rents.

In some cases, the constraints were significant in preventing the market from reaching a competitive equilibrium. For example, in Illinois, the combination of restrictions to no more than ten riverboat gaming licenses and 1,250 "gaming stations" per license resulted in a considerable undersupply of casino gaming product, especially in the Chicago metropolitan area during the first few years of riverboat casino operations. (A gaming station is a place—a slot machine or a seat at a gaming table—where a customer could gamble.) The economic rents captured by the state's riverboat casino operators, especially those operating near Chicago, eventually led the legislature to increase the maximum percentage tax on casino winnings from 20 percent to 35 percent in 1997.

Such constraints can create disadvantageous competitive conditions in comparison to other regional gaming alternatives. For example, Iowa passed restrictive legislation allowing riverboat gaming in 1989, but legislation later passed over the next two years in Illinois and Mississippi was less confining. Soon thereafter, three of the five original Iowa boats left the state for more accommodating new gaming markets in Mississippi. In 1994, new Iowa legislation removed a mandated cruising requirement, as well as limits on wager size and overall losses. As a result, in local markets that bridged the two states, market share going to Iowa's boats jumped from about 30 percent to 70 percent overnight. The pressure then shifted to Illinois to relax its restrictions. This pattern of states leapfrogging each other to reduce their original restrictions on gambling is a common one.

One of the more interesting dimensions of casino gaming legislation is whether there is any linkage between statutory or regulatory constraints and the actual mitigation of perceived or real social impacts. In retrospect, many of the constraints imposed in new jurisdictions have turned out to be more symbolic than real in providing protections against adverse social effects that might be associated with permitted casino gaming.

Rules that mandate that riverboat casinos make actual cruises are a case in point. Supposedly the primary purpose for mandated cruising for riverboat casinos is to provide protections for customers against their own potential excesses by limiting what they can lose on a particular excursion, and to protect communities against the adverse "neighborhood effects" that land-based casinos might bring about. However, there is no evidence that suggests customers will get themselves into more or less difficulty with their gambling with mandated cruising than without, and there is no evidence that suggests mandated cruising alters neighborhood crime in comparison to land-based casinos. However, the Iowa/Illinois experience demonstrates that customer preference is against mandated cruising. Companies involved in operating riverboat casinos have little interest in cruising their boats; by doing so, they increase their costs of operation and the risks of maritime accidents while undermining their customers' preferences. Local governments must provide adequate safety and rescue resources for cruising riverboats in case of accident. Furthermore, cruising adds to problems of land-based traffic congestion and queuing as customers must adhere to the fixed cruising schedules while getting on and off the boats. The only obvious beneficiaries of mandated cruising are those economically linked to maritime operations.

At best, riverboat casino legislation is a means of imposing restrictive zoning on casinos in political jurisdictions and otherwise limiting the popularity and extent of gaming's presence. However, the rules on mandatory cruising have to be considered either economically inefficient or just plain eccentric; one could describe it as regulation by inconvenience. As might be expected, in those states with mandated cruising requirements for riverboat casinos, there has been ongoing political pressure to remove the requirement and thus "rationalize" the riverboat casino industry.

The purported intent of establishing constraints on casino operations is to mitigate some of the social impacts that might be associated with less restrictive gaming, or else to concentrate the positive economic impacts from casino legalization on investment, job creation, and development into certain geographic areas. However, unintended side effects of such constraints include reductions in overall demand for casino gaming from potential customers because of the inconveniences involved; increased economic rents accruing to operators or to the government in the form of excise taxes when artificial barriers to entry limit supply; and dampened incentives for the casino industry to develop more fully non-gaming complementary amenities—such as hotels and entertainment venues—because of lower expected return on investment. Some restrictions, such as prohibitions against a casino granting credit, or forbidding the use of bank debit cards in gaming devices or at gaming tables, undoubtedly lessen the amount of "impulse spending" by some casino customers. However, the impact of such rules on social costs are difficult to measure, as is discussed in the next section.

## NOTES

1. Because of the radical differences in the approaches to regulation in the two jurisdictions, Nevada and New Jersey have come to represent opposing paradigms for the regulation of gaming. Nevada uses a laissez-faire open market approach, allowing any suitable person or entity with sufficient financing to open a casino of whatever scale the owner wishes. While Nevada's gaming regulators have tremendous discretion to deny or revoke a gaming license for misbehavior, the gaming regulatory staff is relatively small in comparison to the size of the industry. One commentator describes Nevada this way: "the 'Nevada model,' seeks to maximize the economic benefits of gaming, and allows the industry to meet market demands with little regulatory involvement, including determining the number, location, and size of gaming facilities. Although business decisions are vested with the industry, integrity and suitability issues are strictly regulated." Cory Aronovitz, *The Regulation of Commercial Gaming*, 5 CHAP. L. REV. 181, 190-91 (2002). In contrast, New Jersey has a far more controlled regulatory environment. "The 'New Jersey model' . . . focuses on the potential negative impacts of gaming, and establishes a comprehensive regulatory framework that strictly governs virtually every aspect of the business." Id. By regulating facilities to require, for example, a minimum number of hotel rooms, New Jersey policymakers had hoped to make Atlantic City a tourist destination. One could say that the legal/regulatory attitude in Las Vegas toward gambling was unmitigated enthusiasm. In Atlantic City, gambling was treated as a necessary evil. Despite the economic success in Nevada, most jurisdictions approach gaming with an attitude much closer to the New Jersey attitude though without the extensive (and expensive) New Jersey regulatory apparatus.

2. As the excerpt of Professor Eadington's work implicitly suggests, the conventional wisdom is that Wall Street ultimately was at least as important as gaming regulation in driving organized crime out

of the casino business in Nevada. As market advantage required each new casino to be bigger and better than the one before, the cost of casino construction skyrocketed, requiring casino developers to seek substantial outside financing. Venture capitalists and other financiers were willing to satisfy the demand for the ever increasing requirements for capital, but were only willing to finance developers that were suitable to be licensed and that would be reasonable credit risks. Presumably, traditional organized crime was unable to compete in such a marketplace. Is this relevant to the market's ability to police the gaming industry?

3.  Professor Eadington has also suggested that

> to legalize casinos but also to restrict the social impacts associated with the presence of casinos . . . jurisdictions will have to constrain artificially the tendency for the casino industry to expand in response to excess profitability. This could be done by limiting the opportunities of a casino to earn excess profits through, for example, restrictions on credit policy or on betting limits, or with strict limitations on the ability of a casino to market its activities. Such limitation is essentially the approach taken by England, where the stated purpose of national policy toward casino gambling is to allow the operation of casinos only to the extent of accommodating the inherent demand for casino activity among the populace, but not to allow casinos to generate new demand through their marketing efforts. Such an approach could prevent a casino industry from becoming a major economic, social, and political force in the jurisdiction where it is located, and thus, it is hoped, avoid many of the negative side effects that have been associated with casinos elsewhere over the years.

William R. Eadington, *The Casino Gaming Industry: A Study of Political Economy*, THE ANNALS OF THE AMERICAN ACADEMY 474, July 1984. Is Professor Eadington correct?

4.  Gaming activities in nearby jurisdictions can have a powerful influence on the actions in a given jurisdiction. "[C]ertain gaming markets in Illinois were at one time at a disadvantage because they were subject to more restrictive gaming regulations than nearby Iowa casinos. Illinois casinos were required to cruise on the water, and were therefore unable to compete with Iowa casinos not subject to the same requirement. Patrons clearly favored the ability to come and go at their leisure from the casinos in Iowa, as opposed to the restricted schedules and gaming cruises required by the Illinois regulations. Cory Aronovitz, *The Regulation of Commercial Gaming*, 5 CHAP. L. REV. 181, 187 (2002).

5.  What purpose do the limitations serve within jurisdictions and what effects do they have on the market? Would they survive a cost-benefit analysis? Who bears the costs of such restrictions?

## 3.  Geographical Limitations on Legalized Gaming in the American System

Geographic limitations on gaming have often produced unintended consequences. In reading the following cases, consider whether the United States has an effective means of regulating gambling activity and its broader effects.

### BOOTEN v. ARGOSY GAMING CO.
#### 848 N.E.2d 141 (Ill. App. 2006)

Justice GOLDENHERSH delivered the opinion of the court.

Plaintiffs, Angela L. Booten and Craig L. Willeford, employees of defendant, Argosy Gaming Company, doing business as the Alton Belle Casino, appeal from orders of the circuit court of Madison County granting a summary judgment in favor of defendant. Booten was employed as a housekeeper on board defendant's gambling boat, the M/V Alton Belle II (Alton Belle). Willeford was employed as a slot attendant on the Alton Belle. They were injured in separate accidents while performing their respective jobs for defendant.

Plaintiffs filed separate cases under the Jones Act (46 U.S.C. §688 (2000)) and the maritime doctrine of unseaworthiness. Defendant moved for a summary judgment in both cases on the issue of seaman status under the Jones Act. The summary judgment motions were heard by the same judge on the same day. The trial court granted a summary judgment in favor of defendant in both cases. The cases were consolidated on appeal.

The facts surrounding each particular accident and the issues of liability and damages are not relevant here. Rather, our focus is on whether the Alton Belle is a "vessel in navigation" pursuant to the Jones Act. Plaintiffs contend the trial court erred in granting summary judgments in favor of defendant because there was a genuine issue of material fact regarding whether the Alton Belle was a "vessel in navigation" pursuant to the Jones Act. . . .

Initially, the Alton Belle operated as a gambling boat that took excursions on the Mississippi River pursuant to the Riverboat Gambling Act (Act). Under the original Act, gambling could only be conducted on licensed "self-propelled excursion boats" during a "gambling excursion." Ill. Rev. Stat. 1991, ch. 120, pars. 2404(d), (e). The Act required excursion boats to leave their docks and cruise on "navigable streams" in order for gambling to be allowed. Ill.Rev.Stat.1991, ch. 120, pars. 2403(c), 2411(a)(1).

The Act was amended, effective June 25, 1999, to allow gambling on a "permanently moored barge", as well as a "self-propelled excursion boat." 230 ILCS 10/4(d) (West Supp. 1999). Accordingly, riverboat gambling in Illinois can now be conducted on a boat, regardless of whether or not the boat takes an excursion. On June 26, 1999, the 1,500-passenger Alton Belle discontinued cruising. According to Dennis Crank, defendant's facility manager, there are no plans for the Alton Belle to resume cruising.

In addition to the 1,500-passenger boat known as the Alton Belle, the present gambling complex consists of a fun barge, the Spirit of America barge, the employee barge, and the patio barge. All five components of the complex float and rise and fall with the level of the river. The boat itself is moored to a dock and is connected to land-based utilities, including electric, telephone, water, and sewer. Before the boat can leave the dock, the utility lines must be disconnected, five boarding ramps must be raised, and cables that hold the boat to the dock must be disconnected. These procedures take approximately 15 minutes; however, Dennis Crank testified that in the case of an emergency, it would only take the crew approximately 5 to 7 minutes to disconnect the mooring cables.

Since June 1999, the Alton Belle has left its mooring for dedrifting approximately five times per year. During this process the boat is spun two or three times to dislodge any accumulated drift materials. The boat then returns to its mooring. Despite no longer cruising, the vessel always has fuel on board and remains fully capable of navigating the river. Defendant has never applied for permanent mooring status.

The Alton Belle is required to comply with all Coast Guard regulations for a passenger vessel. For example, the Coast Guard requires lifesaving equipment to be on board, so that even today the Alton Belle is equipped with 1,500 life jackets, 6 ring buoys, and 6 inflatable rafts. The Alton Belle is inspected every 90 days by the Coast Guard to ensure compliance with regulations. When customers are on board, a full marine crew must also be on board. The Alton Belle employs a senior captain, 3 captains, 4 engineers, 4 mates, and 21 deck hands. The Alton Belle remains a licensed passenger vessel.

Plaintiffs' complaints were premised on the Jones Act. Defendant filed motions for a summary judgment on the basis that the Alton

Belle was not a "vessel in navigation" and that, therefore, neither plaintiff was a seaman, thus barring plaintiffs' claims under the Act. The trial court agreed and entered summary judgments in defendant's favor.

The Jones Act provides that "[a]ny seaman who shall suffer personal injury in the course of his employment may, at his election, maintain an action for damages at law" under the Federal Employers' Liability Act (45 U.S.C. §51 et seq. (2000)). In order for the Jones Act to apply, the structure on which the worker is working must qualify as a "vessel in navigation." Given the highly fact-intensive inquiry necessary to determine a structure's status, the question of whether a structure constitutes a vessel in navigation for purposes of the Jones Act is normally reserved for the jury. It is only appropriate to remove the issue from the jury if there is no genuine issue of material fact and the law supports only one conclusion.

The Jones Act does not define the word "vessel," but numerous cases have considered the question of what constitutes a vessel. Defendant relies on *Howard v. Southern Illinois Riverboat Casino Cruises, Inc.*, 364 F.3d 854 (7th Cir. 2004), which held that the permanently and indefinitely moored dockside casino in issue was not a vessel in navigation for purposes of the Jones Act because it had no transportation function or purpose. In that case, the district court determined the casino was, in fact, permanently moored based upon statements made by defendant's agent that it intended to permanently moor the casino. The Seventh Circuit accepted the district court's finding that the vessel was permanently moored, and the court applied federal summary judgment standards to conclude that despite the vessel's residual capacity for transportation, the vessel was no longer "in navigation" as a matter of law.

We point out, however, that in reaching its conclusion, the *Howard* court discounted the weight of the actions by the defendant which were contrary to its determination. For example, the defendant in *Howard* never relinquished its certificate of inspection from the Coast Guard, nor did it ever apply for permanent mooring status. The Seventh Circuit relied on the self-serving statement by the defendant's agent that it did not intend to cruise the vessel. Moreover, cases decided after *Howard* and the other cases cited above lead us to question whether the Seventh Circuit's holding in *Howard* remains valid.

For example, in the recent case of *Stewart v. Dutra Construction Co.*, 543 U.S. 481 (2005), the Supreme Court considered whether a harbor dredge is a vessel and concluded that it is. *Stewart*, 543 U.S. at 484.

The Stewart Court stated that in order to qualify as a vessel, a ship must be " 'used, or capable of being used, as a means of transportation on water.' " The Stewart Court recognized that "structures may lose their character as vessels if they have been withdrawn from the water for extended periods of time" and that "a watercraft is not 'capable of being used' for maritime transport in any meaningful sense if it has been permanently moored or otherwise rendered practically incapable of transportation or movement", but the Court also stated that a ship does not move in and out of "vessel" status because it is temporarily "at anchor, docked . . . , or berthed for minor repairs." Thus, the Supreme Court specifically declined to adopt any test for vessel status that focuses on either a craft's "primary purpose" or whether the craft is in "actual transit" at the time of an accident. Instead, under *Stewart*, if at the time of the accident a watercraft's use as a means of transportation remains a "practical possibility," rather than "merely a theoretical one," it is a "vessel in navigation."

The dredge at issue in *Stewart* was described as "a massive floating platform from which a clamshell bucket is suspended beneath the water" to remove silt from the ocean floor. The Supreme Court stated: "[The dredge] was not only 'capable of being used' to transport equipment and workers over water—it was used to transport those things. Indeed, it could not have dug the Ted Williams Tunnel had it been unable to traverse the Boston Harbor. . . ." The Stewart Court pointed out "the seeming incongruity of grouping dredges alongside more traditional seafaring vessels under the maritime statutes." Nevertheless, quoting from a Fourth Circuit case more than 100 years old, the Supreme Court observed that although it might be a " 'stretch of the imagination to class the deck hands of a mud dredge in the quiet waters of a Potomac creek with the bold and skillful mariners who breast the angry waves of the Atlantic[,] such and so far-reaching are the principles which underlie the jurisdiction of the courts of admiralty that they adapt themselves to all the new kinds of property and new sets of operatives and new conditions which are brought into existence in the progress of the world.' " *Stewart* is broad and holds that if a ship meets the requirements of jurisdiction, it is a "vessel in navigation" for purposes of the Jones Act.

Relying on *Stewart*, the Eighth Circuit recently determined that a cleaning barge which was originally built for navigation but was later moored to the bed of the Missouri River by spud poles, which are long steel or wood posts placed vertically through the hull of a vessel and embedded into the bed of a waterway to anchor the vessel, was a "vessel" within the meaning of the Jones Act. *Bunch v. Canton Marine Towing Co.*, 419 F.3d 868 (8th Cir. 2005). The Bunch court reasoned that "[a]lthough the cleaning barge was secured in position, strong currents would shift the barge, belying the permanency of its mooring," and that the evidence failed to establish that "the barge had been taken out of service or rendered practically incapable of maritime transportation."

We are aware that the Stewart Court cited with approval *Pavone v. Mississippi Riverboat Amusement Corp.*, 52 F.3d 560 (5th Cir. 1995), which held that a floating casino was not a vessel within the meaning of the Jones Act because it was moored to the shore in a semipermanent or indefinite manner. The casino in *Pavone*, however, is in no way similar to the casino in the instant case. In *Pavone*, the floating casino, the Biloxi Belle, was never used as a seagoing vessel to transport passengers, cargo, or equipment. It lacked a motor and had to be towed to its mooring position, where it was originally used as a restaurant and bar until its conversion to a casino. It was not a vessel because it had "no engine, no captain, no navigational aids, no crew quarters [,] and no lifesaving equipment."

Here, the Alton Belle's ability to cruise is more than a theoretical possibility. It remains a practical possibility, and the Alton Belle actually navigates the river. First, the Alton Belle is required to comply with all Coast Guard regulations pertaining to a passenger vessel and is inspected every 90 days to ensure compliance. Second, the Alton Belle maintains a full maritime crew and is equipped with a motor, fuel, and everything necessary to navigate the Mississippi River on which it is moored. Third, it can be disconnected from its mooring cables within 7 to 15 minutes, depending upon whether there is an urgent need to free the Alton Belle from its mooring. Dennis Crank testified that defendant maintains the quick-disconnect policy in order to be able to get out of harm's way in case of an emergency. Finally, the Alton Belle actually navigates the Mississippi River approximately five times per year when it is released from its mooring and spun around to remove accumulated drift materials.

According to *Stewart*, the term "vessel" refers to "any watercraft practically capable of maritime transportation, regardless of its primary purpose or state of transit at a particular moment." Under the Supreme Court's analysis set forth in *Stewart*, we fail to see how reasonable minds could disagree on whether the Alton Belle is a vessel in navigation for purposes of the Jones Act. The record before us shows that the Alton Belle remains fully capable of maritime transportation. The fact that Dennis Crank testified that the Alton Belle stopped cruising on June 26, 1999, the day after the law changed to allow gambling to occur on either permanently moored barges or self-propelled excursion boats, and has no plans to resume cruising does not alter our finding.

The Alton Belle is clearly capable of maritime transportation as evidenced by its dedrifting expeditions and Dennis Crank's testimony that the Alton Belle can be ready to cruise in approximately five to seven minutes if an emergency situation should arise. Relying on *Stewart*, we find that the Alton Belle is a "vessel in navigation" for purposes of the Jones Act, thereby making plaintiffs seamen. Accordingly, the trial court erred in ruling as a matter of law that the Alton Belle was not a vessel in navigation and in entering summary judgments in favor of defendant. REVERSED.

## NOTES

Though it is perhaps an unexpected result, *Booten* does not appear to be an aberration. A similar case came down the same year on the other side of the river in Iowa. *See Harvey's Casino v. Isenhour*, 713 N.W.2d 247 (Iowa App. 2006) (holding that a riverboat casino was a "vessel in navigation" and that a teller, a slot attendant, and a floor host were among the vessel's "crew" because they contributed to the accomplishment of the riverboat's mission). Was the Jones Act likely enacted to protect housekeepers and slot machine attendants?

### YOUNG v. PLAYERS LAKE CHARLES, L.L.C.
#### 47 F. Supp. 2d 832 (S.D. Tex. 1999)

KENT, District Judge.

On July 28, 1997, [the plaintiffs], all residents of Texas, were traveling west along Interstate Highway 10 in Vinton, Louisiana when their vehicle was struck by a vehicle driven by Third Party Defendant Chris Dewayne West ("West"). West's vehicle was traveling east along I-10, but at the time of the collision, it had crossed over the highway median and was on the westbound side, moving against oncoming traffic. Angelina Rios, Katherine Young, and Seth Young, an eighteen-month-old infant, were killed instantly or died en route to the hospital. A fourth passenger, Joshua Young, was severely injured and has since undergone extensive rehabilitation in Texas. West was also severely injured and remains confined to a nursing home in Texas.

Laboratory tests conducted after the accident determined West's blood alcohol level to be .259, or more than twice the level of per se intoxication in Texas, approximately an hour and a half after the collision. West had undisputedly been drinking for several hours onboard PLAYERS III, Defendants' riverboat casino in Lake Charles, Louisiana, where he had gone to gamble. During the time he gambled, West received eleven "comps" from the casino, at least some of which he used to purchase drinks. West had left the riverboat only a short time before the accident. . . .

Plaintiffs' theory of Defendants' alleged negligence is that Defendants were negligent in serving alcohol to West when Defendants knew or should have known that West was intoxicated and posed a danger to himself and others, including Plaintiffs.

In their Motion for Summary Judgment, Defendants argue that Louisiana law governs this action. If that is the case, Plaintiffs' claims must be dismissed, because Louisiana law completely insulates providers of alcohol from liability for the actions of those to whom they sell or serve alcohol. See La. Rev. Stat. Ann. §9:2800.1 (West 1986). Plaintiffs make two arguments in response. First, they argue that this Court has admiralty jurisdiction over the action and that consequently it must apply the substantive general maritime law. Second, Plaintiffs argue in the alternative that if maritime law does not apply, Texas choice of law provisions require the Court to apply Texas law. Because the Court agrees with Plaintiffs that the general maritime law provides the substantive law in this action, it does not reach either Plaintiffs' second argument, or the dubious wisdom of Louisiana's appalling insulation of casino boats who use free or discounted liquor as the bait to entice gamblers, while ignoring the consequences when those predictably intoxicated gamblers hit the streets in lethal vehicles.

The Court notes that the existence of admiralty jurisdiction over this action is not in dispute at this time. Nonetheless, the Court feels constrained to address that question as a basis for further analysis. To determine whether it has admiralty jurisdiction under 28 U.S.C. §1333, the Court employs a two-pronged test. Under the first prong, the Court determines whether the tort occurred on navigable water or whether injury suffered on land was caused by a vessel on navigable water. See *Jerome B. Grubart, Inc. v. Great Lakes Dredge & Dock Co.*, 513 U.S. 527, 534 (1995). Under the second prong, the Court must consider two issues: (1) whether, based on the "general features of the type of accident involved," the incident has a "potentially disruptive impact on maritime commerce," and (2) whether the general character of the activity giving rise to the incident bears a substantial relationship to traditional maritime activity.

None of the parties dispute that the alleged negligence, the serving of copious amounts of alcohol on the casino boat, occurred on navigable waters. Therefore, the first prong is indisputably satisfied. With respect to the first issue under the second prong, there appears to exist the potential for a disruptive impact on maritime commerce. Reaching this conclusion requires the Court to describe the incident on an "intermediate level of possible generality." See id. at 538-39, (characterizing the general features of a fire aboard a docked pleasure boat as "damage by a vessel in navigable water to an underwater structure"). At an intermediate level of generality, then, this incident can be described as a potentially negligent condition affecting passengers aboard the vessel. It is not difficult to imagine a slightly different scenario from the case at bar in which an intoxicated passenger falls down a stairway or into the water. *See, e.g., Meyer v. Carnival Cruise Lines*, No. 93-2383, 1994 WL 832006, at *1 (N.D. Cal. Dec. 29, 1994) (stating that admiralty jurisdiction existed over an action in which the plaintiff consumed too much alcohol aboard a cruise ship and fell off a stairway). Such an incident could lead to a disruption as rescue crews attempt to locate and save the passenger or search for his body. With respect to the second issue under the nexus prong, there likewise appears to exist a substantial relationship to traditional maritime activity. The PLAYERS III is a mobile riverboat casino fully and presently capable of, and actually, traveling on navigable waters. In this respect, it is similar to cruise and sightseeing vessels that regularly transport passengers over navigable waters. Courts have consistently stated that torts on such vessels satisfy the traditional maritime activity requirement. Thus, the incident forming the basis of this action satisfies all the requirements of admiralty jurisdiction.

Defendants correctly argue that the presence of admiralty jurisdiction by itself does not necessarily answer the question of which substantive law governs this action. Ordinarily, with admiralty jurisdiction comes the application of substantive maritime law. See *East River S.S. Corp. v. Transamerica Delaval, Inc.*, 476 U.S. 858, 864 (1986). However, where there is no existing maritime rule that would govern an action, a court must determine whether it will fashion such a rule or instead apply existing state law. See *Wilburn Boat Co. v. Fireman's Fund Insurance Co.*, 348 U.S. 310, 314 (1955). It is Defendants' argument that there is no existing maritime rule regarding what is essentially dram shop liability and that under *Wilburn*, this Court must apply state law. In support of such argument, Defendants cite *Meyer*, where a United States District Court in California held that no federal maritime dram shop rule existed and that, as a consequence, California's dram shop statute provided the substantive law governing a plaintiff's admiralty claim. See *Meyer v. Carnival Cruise Lines, Inc.*, No. 93-2383, 1994 WL 832006, at *4 (N.D. Cal. Dec. 29, 1994).

This Court recognizes the scholarship of its distinguished brethren in the Northern District of California. However, the existence of an unreported opinion from that district, as compelling as its reasoning might be to some, does not bind or persuade this Court. In fact, there is analogous precedent in the Fifth Circuit that there is a maritime rule concerning dram shop liability.

This very Court has held that a defendant can be held liable at maritime law for providing alcohol without adequate supervision. In *Thier v. Lykes Bros., Inc.*, the plaintiff suffered severe injuries when a car driven by the defendants' chief officer crashed on the way to a dinner. 900 F. Supp. 864, 866 (S.D. Tex. 1995). The driver, who died in the crash, was legally intoxicated. Evidence indicated that his intoxication was the product of a shipboard atmosphere the Court described as a "floating dram shop." Id. at 870. The vessel maintained an extensive liquor supply, which was restocked frequently and made accessible to both passengers and crew. Id. Despite the existence of a policy ostensibly prohibiting the vessel's crew and officers from consuming alcohol aboard the ship or even bringing it onboard, the Court found in a bench trial that the defendants, the owners of the vessel, were negligent in "allowing a party atmosphere to prevail onboard wherein ship's officers frequently had girlfriends and guests onboard together with a regularly stocked store of party supplies including alcoholic beverages." Id. This negligence was the proximate cause of the plaintiff's injury, the Court held. While *Thier* involved a plaintiff who was held to be a Jones Act seaman, that factor was not critical to the Court's ultimate holding. As the Court clearly emphasized, the seaman status of the plaintiff was irrelevant to the finding that the defendants were directly liable for their negligence in "failing to monitor alcohol consumption onboard, fostering a party atmosphere, and failing to prohibit drunk officers from driving." Id. at 879.

Moreover, this Court's opinion in *Thier* was not without antecedents in the Fifth Circuit. In *Reyes v. Vantage S.S. Co., Inc.*, the United States Court of Appeals for the Fifth Circuit addressed the issue of liability for the death of an intoxicated seaman who leaped from his vessel and drowned. 609 F.2d 140, 141-42 (5th Cir. 1980). The court held that the plaintiff could maintain a cause of action for negligent rescue, then remanded the action for a determination of causation, stating that in assessing the plaintiff's contributory negligence the district court below must consider the defendant's role in operating a "floating dram shop" from which crew members obtained intoxicants with no supervision. The court specifically instructed that the district court, in considering causation and the plaintiff's comparative negligence, weigh the "unseaworthiness or negligence [of defendants] with respect to the operation of a floating dram shop."

While *Reyes*, like *Thier*, is a Jones Act case, the Court finds no talismanic significance in that fact with respect to maritime dram shop liability. Neither opinion expressly premised the existence of a duty regarding the serving of alcohol on the status of the injured party. In fact, *Thier* expressly admonished that regardless of whether the Jones Act applied to the plaintiff's claim, the defendants were directly liable for any injuries resulting from their negligence in allowing alcohol to pervade their ship unsupervised. Similarly, the fact that Defendants in this case sold or gave alcohol to gambling patrons rather than provided it as a sort of "perk" to employees does not distinguish this case from those where courts in this Circuit found dram shop liability applying maritime law. Factually, the cases do not appear to be as distinguishable as Defendants would argue. In *Reyes*, for instance, the defendant shipowner sold alcohol to the seamen it employed.

In the present case, moreover, the line between the sale of alcohol and its free provision has been intentionally blurred by Defendants for their own economic gain. Throughout the period he gambled aboard the PLAYERS III, Chris West received numerous "comps," or free vouchers, which he then used to purchase drinks. In fact, the practice of providing such vouchers reflects an intentional attitude that can only encourage excessive drinking for the very purpose of facilitating gambling. While Defendants are nominally in the business of selling alcohol, it is clear that alcohol sales are merely incidental to Defendants' primary purpose—the creation of a party atmosphere in which patrons are encouraged to freely spend their money gambling and then hit the road when they have exhausted their funds, regardless of their physical condition. Defendants are essentially giving alcohol away in express furtherance of that goal, arguably under the smug misconception that Louisiana law insulates them from the predictable and tragic consequences.

Additionally, to the extent that the sale of alcohol differs from the free provision of alcohol, it is a difference without distinction. Defendants appear to imply that the question of dram shop liability for sellers of alcohol is too complex for a court to adequately address, being left instead to legislative process (properly influenced by well funded lobbyists for the gaming industry). Such a position is patently insulting to the judicial system, and, worse, is factually asinine. What complicates the issue of liability for sellers of alcohol is the tapestry of state legislatures that have involved themselves, each thread of which appearing to represent simply a distinct prevailing special interest. That can hardly be blamed on alleged judicial "simplicity." The fact that numerous state legislatures have each promulgated a different rule on the issue of dram shop liability does not mean that the question of seller liability is an inherently complex one. Rather, it simply means that, for various reasons, each legislature has chosen a distinct approach to a single issue. This Court (however simple it might be) views that issue to be well within its limited capabilities. Did Defendants have a duty toward Plaintiffs, did Defendants breach that duty, and was there a causal connection between Defendants' breach and Plaintiffs' injury? According to the fundamental principles of negligence law, which the general maritime law has adopted, plaintiffs are owed a duty of ordinary care. If a defendant fails to exercise ordinary care and the resulting harm was reasonably foreseeable, liability arises. See id. There is nothing inherently complicated about this rule as it relates to dram shop liability.

In sum, the Court concludes that there is an existing maritime rule governing the issue of dram shop liability. Accordingly, there is no need to perform a Wilburn analysis to determine whether the Court must apply state dram shop law. If Louisiana wants to establish shore-side casinos and insulate their liability, that is solely Louisiana's business. But, where navigable ships in Louisiana are going to entice residents of Texas and other states to flock in huge numbers to their casinos to drink too much and return home in a murderous condition, the general maritime law should and does afford the endangered public with a ready and wholly appropriate remedy. Defendant's Motion for Summary Judgment is therefore emphatically DENIED. The Court finds as a matter of law that the general maritime law of the United States governs Plaintiff's claim.

### NOTES

1. Should the question of which rules govern compensation for injured casino employees or the question of whether casinos bear "dram shop liability" in tort be governed by whether or not a casino barge is moored? Is this an arbitrary way to address important questions of public policy?
2. What, if anything, do these cases suggest about the effectiveness of geographic limitations in limiting the social harms that casinos pose? Are such harms related to gambling or alcohol?

# CHAPTER

# 6

# Regulating Lawful Gaming Through Licensure

## INTRODUCTION

In jurisdictions in which gambling is not altogether prohibited, it is carefully regulated. Although regulation serves a variety of purposes, the chief regulatory goals are to prevent corruption and to maintain the integrity of the business enterprise. One of the chief strategies is licensure of individuals. Most jurisdictions require anyone employed by a gaming operation to be licensed. At the lowest levels of the operation, such as custodial staff and cocktail wait staff, employees are often required to have "work cards" that are issued after perfunctory background checks. Employees with greater involvement in the gaming operation, such as managers and pit bosses, or access to large amounts of cash, such as dealers, cashiers in the "cage," or staff in the "count rooms," are subject to more rigorous scrutiny. Finally, because of their level of control over the operation and other employees, people in casino management are often subjected to still more rigorous scrutiny. The investigation for licensure is called, in most jurisdictions, a "suitability" determination.

In addition to licensure of individuals, jurisdictions require commercial entities that engage in gaming to have licenses, and for each gaming operation to have an individual facility license. Licensure requirements also extend to vendors that do business with the gaming industry. Licensure is an effective regulatory strategy for three reasons. First, it creates a gate-keeping role that allows for scrutiny of every license applicant at the application stage. Second, it provides an ongoing regulatory hook and threat (license revocation) to address problems that may arise after initial licensure. Finally, it creates a closed community that is easier to monitor;

licensees risk their own licenses by doing business with unlicensed vendors.

# A.  DUE PROCESS AND LICENSURE OF GAMING INDUSTRY PARTICIPANTS

In many jurisdictions, due process protections in gaming licensure decisions are carefully circumscribed by legislatures and gaming regulators. Gaming regulators have sought broad discretion to regulate the industry, and the courts have largely acquiesced. One approach has been to say that gaming is a not a right, but a privilege, and therefore, that much less process is due. The cases in this chapter showcase the broad scope of regulatory licensing discretion and address the asserted legal basis for such discretion.

The first case in this chapter involves Frank "Lefty" Rosenthal, who was a well-known figure in Las Vegas and a reputed bookmaker. Rosenthal was one of the first licensees to challenge the denial of a gaming license in Nevada. This section begins with some background on this colorful figure and the hearings before the Nevada Gaming Control Board as they considered his license request.

### THE STARDUST AND FRANK LARRY ROSENTHAL
**in Ronald Farrell & Carol Case, The Black Book and the Mob, pp. 78-84 (Univ. of Wisc. Press 1995)**

Frank Rosenthal was the first of the industry figures to come under the suspicion of the [Nevada Gaming Control B]oard. Although he had earlier been approved for [ownership of] 2.84 percent of Circus Circus in 1969, he was called forward for key-employee licensing in 1976 in connection with his managerial duties at the Stardust as director of Nevada operations. In accordance with gaming regulations, the board can discretionarily call forward for investigation anyone who applies for key licensing for casino duties that appears to constitute a certain degree of influence and carry a salary of more than $40,000 annually; this process allows the board considerable latitude to inquire into the background of suspected associates of organized crime. Rosenthal had a record of illegal bookmaking and bribery, and had been investigated by the McClellan committee in 1968. A 1969 report of the Chicago Crime Commission also named him as an affiliate of organized crime. The expressed concern in calling Rosenthal forward was that he might have a role in the operation of the race and sports book at the Stardust. A large part of the board's inquiry also focused on his long-standing friendship with Anthony Spilotro. Having grown up in the same neighborhood in Chicago, Rosenthal had known Spilotro since birth. The offenses which concerned the regulators most were a 1959 Miami arrest for bookmaking and a 1963 conviction for conspiracy to bribe a New York University basketball player in a 1960 national tournament game with West Virginia University. The Miami arrest had been a major subject of inquiry in Rosenthal's investigation by the McClellan committee. In his closing statements, Senator McClellan said, "... the testimony regarding accused fixer, gambler and handicapper, Frank Lefty Rosenthal, provides us a sordid example of the crooked and contemptible operations in which some of these characters engage."

The licensing hearing ... is a show cause process. The burden of proof in establishing suitability rests with the applicant. This was obviously clear to Rosenthal, inasmuch as he took an unusually active and aggressive stance in arguing his case before the regulators. He denied any regular association with Spilotro or any other wrongdoing since his arrival in Las Vegas in 1970. He attributed a large part of his criminal record to police harassment, citing one instance in which he had been arrested three times within 24 hours for failing to register as a felon with the Las Vegas Metropolitan Police Department. He told of how his unwillingness to pay protection money and to serve as an informant for law enforcement resulted in the 1959 raid on his apartment and subsequent arrest for bookmaking. There were beatings by the FBI and threats on his mother's life; she was told, "... if you don't smarten your son up you'll find your head in Chicago and your body in Chicago Heights" (p. 119).

Rosenthal said that he had been framed by his codefendant in the bribery charge. He said two New York detectives had told him that the North Carolina county solicitor had informed his codefendant that if he could "deliver Frank Rosenthal, [he would] have a chance to walk away free." He characterized his codefendant as one who "would have given his mother up to stay away from what he had to face, [given] what had been substantiated, all the admissions of attempted fixing, and all the positive identifications" (pp. 188-189). He maintained that out of ignorance of the law and because he was a Jew in "Baptist Country," he entered a plea of nolo contendere rather than risk the possibility of going to prison (p. 192).

At times the regulators seemed to believe Rosenthal's story, but at other times they shook their heads in dismay at what must have seemed to them to be outlandish fabrication. His account of the 1959 raid on his apartment and arrest for bookmaking exemplifies the kinds of issues and arguments that the regulators faced in assessing the applicant's suitability. These kinds of stories, together with Rosenthal's vociferous and self-confident style, appear to have tried the patience of, if not offended, some of the regulators. . . .

The 1959 arrest for bookmaking [had] occurred on New Year's Eve. A raid was conducted on Rosenthal's apartment by the chief of police and deputy sheriff of North Bay Village, Dade County, Florida, and members of the state attorney general's office. When the police entered the apartment, they found Rosenthal seated on his bed in his pajamas with a phone in one hand and a small black book in the other. The chief described the incident to the McClellan committee:

> The search warrant was read to him by a deputy sheriff from the Metropolitan County Sheriff's Department, at which time I took the telephone from him and I asked the person on the other end who was talking. I said I was Lefty [Rosenthal]. He said, "This is Cincinnati." He said, "You have 10 and 10 on Windy Fleet, and I will take 4 and 4 of it." We later learned that Windy Fleet was a horse running at Tropical Park that afternoon. He came in second. (pp. 100-101).

The chief went on to explain that he took other calls:

> I answered several phone calls dealing with, as I recall, the Florida-Baylor game, the East-West game, one call in particular from an Amos in Indiana. I answered the telephone, and he asked if this was Lefty, and I replied, "Yes." I asked him, "Who is this?" And he said, "This is Amos from Indiana." He wanted to know what we were doing with the East-West game. I asked Mr. Rosenthal what he was doing, and he gave me a point spread. I think it was five and a half points for the East. I gave it to Amos as the West; anyway, I gave him the opposite team. I asked Mr. Rosenthal if he wanted to talk to this particular man in Indiana, and Mr. Rosenthal took the phone, and he said, "Do you know who you are talking to? You are talking to a cop, you stupid s.o.b.; keep on talking." With that, Amos hung up the telephone.

The police said that they found several phones and an elaborate intercom system in the apartment, along with the usual items found in a lay-off betting operation: rundown sheets, baseball cards, and the like. They also indicated that there were two loaded 0.38 revolvers in the nightstand near Rosenthal's phone. Rosenthal denied that the apartment was set up for bookmaking operations and that any bookmaking was taking place at the time of the raid.

## NEVADA v. ROSENTHAL
### 559 P.2d 830 (Nev. 1977)

THOMPSON, J.

[The Nevada Gaming Commission directed Rosenthal to submit an application for a gaming license as a key employee. In his application, he described his duties "to consult with and to recommend to the Chairman; to advise, to administrate, delegate and supervise Corporate standards, procedures and policies." After an investigation by the Nevada Gaming Control Board (described, in part, above), the Nevada Gaming Commission found: "The applicant is a person whose licensing by the State would reflect or tend to reflect discredit upon the State of Nevada" by reason of a North Carolina court finding of guilt for conspiracy to bribe an amateur athlete; testimony of Mickey Bruce in Senate subcommittee hearings that Rosenthal attempted to bribe him to throw the outcome of a 1960 Oregon-Michigan football game; statements by police officers to a Senate subcommittee and to the Florida Racing Commission that Rosenthal admitted he was corrupting public officials in return for protection; and that Rosenthal had been barred from race tracks and pari-mutuel operations in the State of Florida.]

On February 17, 1976, Rosenthal filed a petition for judicial review of the decision of the Commission. He premised his petition upon NRS 463.315, alleging that the decision of the Commission violated constitutional provisions, was in excess of its jurisdiction, made upon unlawful procedures, was unsupported by any evidence, and was arbitrary and capricious and otherwise not in accordance with law. The petition did not assert that the licensing provisions of the Gaming Control Act were unconstitutional for want of standards. The district court, *sua sponte*, declared NRS 463.140 and 463.220 unconstitutional, and nullified the decision of the Gaming Commission.

It is established beyond question that gaming is a matter of privilege conferred by the State rather than a matter of right. The legislature has so declared. "Any license issued pursuant to this chapter shall be deemed to be a revocable privilege and no holder thereof shall be deemed to have acquired any vested rights therein or thereunder." NRS 463.130(2). In 1931 this court wrote: "We think the distinction drawn between a business of the latter character (liquor) and useful trades, occupations, or businesses, is substantial and necessary for the proper exercise of the police power of the state. Gaming as a calling or business is in the same class as the selling of intoxicating liquors in respect to deleterious tendency. The state may regulate or suppress it without interfering with any of those inherent rights of citizenship which it is the object of government to protect and secure." *State ex rel. Grimes v. Board*, 53 Nev. 364, 372, 373, 1 P.2d 570 (1931).

The licensing and control of gaming requires special knowledge and experience. *Nev. Tax Com. v. Hicks*, 73 Nev. 115, 119, 310 P.2d 852 (1957). In *Hicks*, this court observed "the risks to which the public is subjected by the legalizing of this otherwise unlawful activity are met solely by the manner in which licensing and control are carried out. The administrative responsibility is great." Id. at 120.

The legislature has been sensitive to these basic concepts. Members of the Gaming Control Board and Gaming Commission must have special qualifications suited to the important duties with which they are charged. Their powers are comprehensive. Court intrusion is limited. As we noted in *Gaming Control Bd. v. Dist. Ct.*, 82 Nev. 38, 409 P.2d 974 (1966): "Any effort to obstruct the orderly administrative process provided by the Gaming Control Act casts serious doubt upon the ability of Nevada to control the privileged enterprise of gaming. Control does not exist if regulatory procedures are not allowed to operate. Courts owe fidelity to the legislative purpose. . . ." Id. at 40. Indeed, judicial review is confined to a final decision or order of the Commission and then only in specified instances. With these basic principles in mind we turn to consider the issues of this appeal.

In the district court the State and the Gaming Commission moved to dismiss the petition for review for want of jurisdiction. We particularly note that the petition did not challenge the constitutionality of the licensing statutes. Had such challenge been made, a court would have to resolve it. Jurisdiction to decide that issue would exist since the courts are charged with the duty to decide such a question.

The petition for review was presented pursuant to NRS 463.315. That statute provides that "Any person aggrieved by a final decision or order of the commission made after hearing or rehearing by the commission pursuant to NRS 463.312 . . . may obtain a judicial review thereof in the district court. . . ." An examination of NRS 463.312 reveals its application only to disciplinary or other action against a license. It does not contemplate court review of the denial of a gaming license application. The sole responsibility for licensing is vested exclusively in the commission. NRS 463.220(6) so provides. "The commission shall have full and absolute power and authority to deny any application (for a license) for any cause deemed reasonable by such commission . . . ." In *Nev. Tax Com. v. Hicks*, 73 Nev. 115, 121, 310 P.2d 852, 855 (1957), the court wrote: "It is not the province of the courts to decide what shall constitute suitability to engage in gambling in this state." In this regard the law has not changed since *Hicks*.

The legislature carefully has distinguished between persons who have been licensed and those who never have been licensed. In the former case judicial review of disciplinary action is provided; in the latter instance, it is not. This is a reasonable distinction since licensees possess property interests which those who have never been licensed do not have. The district court should have granted the motion to dismiss filed by the State and the Commission. Instead, that court declared the licensing provisions of the Gaming Control Act unconstitutional for want of standards, notwithstanding the absence of an allegation in the petition placing that question in issue. We proceed, therefore, to resolve that question.

The sections declared unconstitutional are NRS 463.140 and 463.220. In discussing this issue we do not decide whether licensing standards for the privilege enterprise of gaming must be expressed legislatively.[1] However, the legislature has expressed standards which have been implemented administratively. When one considers the interrelationship of the statutory standards, *United States v. Polizzi*, 500 F.2d 856 (9th Cir. 1974), and the regulations adopted administratively, any contention that there is an absence of appropriate standards must fail.

The basic standard is stated in NRS 463.130. Gaming shall be licensed and controlled "so as to protect the public health, safety, morals, good order and general welfare of the inhabitants of the State of Nevada, and to preserve the competitive economy and the policies of free competition of the State of Nevada." The statutes which were ruled unconstitutional by the court below simply state that gaming licenses shall be administered "for the protection of the public and in the public interest in accordance with the policy of this state," NRS 463.140, and that the Gaming Commission has full power to deny any application "for any cause deemed reasonable," NRS 463.220.

Administrative regulations have been adopted by the Commission pursuant to legislative authorization. NRS 463.150(1). Relevant to this case is Regulation 3.090. There, it is stated: "1. No license, registration, finding of suitability, or approval shall be granted unless and until the applicant has satisfied the Commission that the applicant: a) Is a person of good character, honesty, and integrity; b) Is a person whose background, reputation, and associations will not result in adverse publicity for the State of Nevada and its gaming industry; and c) Has adequate business competence and experience for the role or position for which application is made." If we were to assume that the

1. *State ex rel. Grimes v. Board*, 53 Nev. 364, 1 P.2d 570 (1931), may be read to mean that uniform rules and standards are not essential to state control of gaming since it is a privileged enterprise subject to total state regulation and suppression.

standards announced in NRS 463.140 and 463.220 are inadequate legislative expressions for the control of licensing in a privileged industry, the implementing regulation would serve to cure the defect since the "gaps" may be filled in administratively. *Dunn v. Tax Commission*, 67 Nev. 173, 216 P.2d 985 (1950).

Persons of ordinary intelligence surely can understand the intent and purpose of the standards expressed in the quoted regulation. We wish, however, explicitly to state that the statutory standards alone are sufficient since "reasonable" action by the Commission is required in the light of the public interest involved. It is entirely appropriate to lodge such wide discretion in the controlling administrative agency when a privileged enterprise is the subject of the legislative scheme. *State ex rel. Grimes v. Board*, 53 Nev. 364, 1 P.2d 570 (1931); *Gragson v. Toco*, 90 Nev. 131, 520 P.2d 616 (1974). We, therefore, find no basis for the ruling below that NRS 463.140 and NRS 463.220 are unconstitutional.

The district court also found that the applicant was denied procedural due process at the hearings before the Board and Commission. For reasons already stated, the court lacked jurisdiction to so rule. Notwithstanding this fact, the record refutes the court finding. The applicant and his two attorneys were present at each hearing. The applicant testified at each hearing and was given the opportunity to explain certain past alleged criminal activities and argue his position. Seventeen witnesses testified on his behalf, and seven letters attesting his good character and reputation were read into the record.

The district court, by ruling Rosenthal's due process had been violated because he had not been notified of the charges against him, misconceived the purpose of the hearings. They were not criminal proceedings in which Rosenthal had charges against him, but merely administrative proceedings wherein Rosenthal had the burden of proving his qualifications to receive a license. Further, the court mistakenly held that Rosenthal was denied his right to cross-examine apparently because the Board and Commission considered certain "hearsay" evidence consisting of the McClellan subcommittee transcript which was taken under oath, judicial papers from North Carolina, and investigative reports by the North Carolina State Bureau of Investigation. However, these hearings need not technically comport with strict rules of evidence, and hearsay can be accepted and considered by the agencies.

The district court ruling was premised upon the federal constitution. Although due process was not denied the applicant, it is worthwhile briefly to consider whether federal constitutional proscriptions are involved at all. As before noted, gaming is a privilege conferred by the state and does not carry with it the rights inherent in useful trades and occupations. We view gaming as a matter reserved to the states within the meaning of the Tenth Amendment to the United States Constitution. Within this context we find no room for federally protected constitutional rights. This distinctively state problem is to be governed, controlled and regulated by the state legislature and, to the extent the legislature decrees, by the Nevada Constitution. It is apparent that if we were to recognize federal protections of this wholly privileged state enterprise, necessary state control would be substantially diminished and federal intrusion invited.

In this opinion we heretofore have noted the distinction drawn by the legislature between persons who have been licensed and those who never have been licensed. Judicial review is provided for disciplinary action against licensees. It is not provided for one who has not been licensed.

With regard to licensees the legislature, in vague fashion, has recognized that a decision of the gaming commission may violate "constitutional provisions." NRS 463.315(11)(a). We use the term "vague" advisedly. The "constitutional provisions" which the legislature had in mind are not designated. This, along with the mandate of NRS 463.130(2) that any license is a revocable privilege without vested rights, makes it difficult to fathom legislative intent.

Our obligation is to construe the mentioned statutory provisions in such manner as to render them compatible with each other. With this principle in mind we interpret NRS 463.315(11)(a) to refer only to the concept of procedural due process which is embraced within Nev. Const. art. 1, §8, no person shall "be deprived of life, liberty, or property without due process of law." Thus construed, the two statutes are compatible. The license which is declared to be a revocable privilege, may not be revoked without procedural due process first being afforded the licensee.

As a gaming employee, Frank Rosenthal was required to hold a valid work permit. NRS 463.335(3). The denial of his application for a gaming license as a key employee may have caused an automatic revocation of his work permit if NRS 463.595 and Regulation 5.011(6) are to be literally applied, thus precluding his right to work in a gaming establishment in any capacity. Revocation of a work permit is subject to judicial review, NRS 463.337(4), although the denial of his application to be licensed is not for reasons already stated.

The hearings before the Board and Commission were focused entirely upon the suitability of Rosenthal to be licensed as a key employee since he did significantly influence policy. His right to work in a capacity other than that of a key employee was not in issue at all. His suitability to work as a gaming employee has never been questioned by the gaming authorities of this state. To this extent, *O'Callaghan v. District Court*, 89 Nev. 33, 505 P.2d 1215 (1973), is in point. There, an employee's right to work as a gaming employee was revoked without prior notice and an opportunity to be heard. We ruled such action improper. It follows that an automatic revocation of an employee's work permit also must fail for want of fairness.

We, therefore, find Regulation 5.011(6) to be inconsistent with the statutes providing for administrative and judicial review of the revocation of a work permit. The regulation cannot stand.

A portion of NRS 463.595 likewise may be read to require automatic revocation of a work permit held by one found unsuitable to be licensed by reason of the oft repeated phrase in the statute "or any other involvement with the gaming activities of a corporate licensee." An employee with a work permit is involved with the gaming activities of a corporate licensee. This portion of the statute does not square with the statutes providing for administrative and judicial review of the revocation of a work permit and cannot stand.

A reasonable distinction exists between the status of one who seeks to acquire a license, and the status of one who possesses a work permit as a gaming employee. The former does not have existing privileges, but is attempting to acquire them. The latter does have an existing privilege, and is entitled to receive notice and a hearing before his privilege to work as a gaming employee can be nullified.

Therefore, we conclude that Frank Rosenthal may continue to enjoy a work permit as a gaming employee. Our conclusion, however, shall not be construed to preclude further action by the gaming authorities to revoke his work permit should they deem such action advisable.

## NOTES

1. Frank Rosenthal's death in October 2008 was widely reported; here is the account from The Miami Herald: "Sports Illustrated once called Frank Larry 'Lefty' Rosenthal—the bookmaker and Vegas casino operator played by Robert De Niro in the film *Casino*—the greatest living sports handicapper. He got his nickname in 1961 after pleading the Fifth Amendment 38 times before a Senate subcommittee investigating organized crime. Among other things, he refused to say whether he was left- or right-handed. . . . Rosenthal died Monday, reportedly of a heart attack, at his apartment in the Fontainebleau's luxury Tresor Tower in Miami Beach. He was 79."

Elinor J. Brecher, *Casino Operator was Known as Country's Top Sports Handicapper,* THE MIAMI HERALD, Oct. 22, 2008.

2. *Rosenthal* holds that gaming license denials are not judicially reviewable. It thus represents a generous grant of deference from a court to an administrative agency. What could justify such deference? Is such deference sensible?

3. *Rosenthal* also asserts a distinction between a person who already has a gaming license and a person who is applying for one. Is this a tenable distinction? On what basis is the recognition of due process rights justified for renewals or revocations, but not for initial denials?

4. In addition to the licensure process, Nevada has a list of persons who must be excluded from casinos. Informally called the "Black Book," the List of Excluded Persons is authorized by Nevada law and was initially directed at people affiliated with organized crime. Casinos in Las Vegas are required to deny not only employment, but also access to the casino, to those on the List. Casinos risk fines or license revocation if they fail to abide by the rule. Rosenthal was subsequently added to the List in 1988. Because of the small number of people on the List, some commentators are skeptical of the effectiveness of the list in maintaining the integrity of the gaming industry and assert that it is merely a regulatory marketing initiative designed to maintain the illusion of regulatory control over the industry and to create the perception of regulatory control and market integrity. *See, e.g.,* RONALD A. FARRELL & CAROL CASE, THE BLACK BOOK AND THE MOB: THE UNTOLD STORY OF THE CONTROL OF NEVADA'S CASINOS (Univ. of Wisc. Press 1995).

5. *Rosenthal* has become a cornerstone of the due process doctrine in gambling licensure decisions nationwide.

## AMERICAN INTERN. GAMING ASS'N v. RIVERBOAT GAMING COM'N

### 838 So. 2d 5 (La. App. 2000)

KUHN, J.

[A riverboat gaming license applicant, AIGA, and it sole shareholder, Alvin Copeland, challenged the state gaming commission's issuance of license to a competitor to operate a riverboat casino on Lake Pontchartrain near New Orleans. Among other things, the applicant claimed a violation of due process rights. The trial court ruled for the gaming commission and the applicant appealed.]

The State urges that Copeland is not entitled to recover because he has not demonstrated a taking of a constitutionally-protected property interest. . . . The Fourteenth Amendment to the United States Constitution provides, in pertinent part, "[n]or shall any State deprive any person of life, liberty or property, without due process of law. . . ." Similarly, Article I, §2 of the Louisiana Constitution provides that no person shall be deprived of life, liberty, or property, except by due process of law. To claim the protections of due process, a claimant must show the existence of some property or liberty interest which has been adversely affected by state action. *Delta Bank & Trust Co. v. Lassiter*, 383 So. 2d 330, 334 (La. 1980). Property interests are not created by the constitution. Rather they are created and their dimensions are defined by existing rules or understandings that stem from an independent source such as state law-rules or understandings that secure certain benefits and that support claims of entitlement to those benefits. *Board of Regents of State Colleges v. Roth*, 408 U.S. 564, 577 (1972). To have a property interest protected by due process, a person must clearly have more than an abstract need or desire for it. He must have a legitimate claim of entitlement to it rather than a unilateral expectation of it. Id.

It is true that a license, once issued, may create a property interest in the holder that is traditionally protected by due process notions. *Bell v. Burson*, 402 U.S. 535, 539 (1971). But our state law affords a license applicant no individual entitlement to a license that he seeks. *Durham v. Louisiana State Racing Com'n*, 458 So. 2d 1292, 1295 (La. 1984). Accepting all of the allegations of the petition as true, we find no due process violation because neither AIGA nor Copeland had a protected property interest in the benefits conferred by a license that they did not actually hold. Absent a protected property interest, AIGA was not entitled to notice and a hearing before the denial of its application. *Board of Regents v. Roth*, 92 S. Ct. at 2710; *Durham v. Louisiana State Racing Com'n*, 458 So. 2d at 1295. Likewise, Copeland's allegation that he was denied substantive due process rights by being arbitrarily denied a license fails due to the lack of a protected property interest. Affirmed.

GONZALES, J., concurring.

As far back as 1892, in a famous opinion by Justice Oliver Wendell Holmes, the second class status of a mere governmental privilege was engrained into our procedural due process concepts in the case of *McAuliffe v. Mayor of New Bedford*, 155 Mass. 216, 29 N.E. 517 (1892). The case involved a police officer that had been fired. The Supreme Court dismissed his complaints, holding that a governmental job was a mere privilege. The following excerpt 2 Kenneth C. Davis and Richard J. Pierce, Jr., Administrative Law Treatise §9.3, at 11-13 (1994) summarizes the evolution of a mere privilege to the status of a constitutionally protected entitlement:

> Before 1970, due process applied only to deprivation of "rights," determined primarily with a reference to the common law. Anything else government provided was a mere "privilege," outside the scope of due process protection. Justice Holmes' opinion in *McAuliffe v. Mayor of New Bedford*, 155 Mass. 216, 29 N.E. 517 (1892), illustrates this approach. The Mayor fired a policeman for expressing views on an issue of public importance contrary to those of the Mayor. The court dismissed the policeman's complaint that the action violated both due process and the First Amendment because a government job is a mere privilege unprotected by the Constitution.
>
> Before 1970, the Court paid little attention to the nature of the decisionmaking procedure required by due process. Typically, the Court held only that due process required a "hearing," without describing the nature of the hearing required. In some cases, the Court's language seemed to imply that due process required an oral evidentiary hearing of the type routinely provided by courts. In *ICC v. Louisville & Nashville Railroad*, 227 U.S. 88, 93 (1913), for instance, the Court specifically referred to "opportunity to cross-examine witnesses." In other cases, however, the Court's language suggested that due process might be satisfied by a "hearing" less formal than the oral evidentiary hearing routinely available in a court. In *Londoner v. Denver*, 210 U.S. 373, 383 (1908), for instance, the Court stated only that "a hearing in its very essence requires that he who is entitled to it shall have the right to support his allegations by argument however brief, and, if need be, by proof, however informal."
>
> The Court abandoned both of these approaches to due process decisionmaking in 1970. It rejected traditional distinction between protected rights and unprotected privileges, holding that at least some statutory entitlements are within the scope of due process protection. At the same time, the Court announced its intention to address explicitly and in detail the issue of how much process is due in each decisionmaking context to which due process applies. The opinions that best explain the Court's transition to its present approach to application of the Due Process Clause are *Goldberg v. Kelly*, 397 U.S. 254 (1970), and *Mathews v. Eldridge*, 424 U.S. 319 (1976).
>
> Goldberg involved a claim by recipients of Aid to Families with Dependent Children (AFDC) that the procedures of the agency charged with responsibility to implement the AFDC program in New York violated the Due Process Clause. The agency provided an opportunity for an oral evidentiary hearing to determine a recipient's continued eligibility for AFDC payments, but that hearing was available only after the payments were discontinued. The agency first decided on the basis of less formal procedures that the recipient was ineligible and terminated benefits based on that initial decision. If the Court had followed its traditional approach to defining property rights, it would have dismissed the complaint of the welfare recipients in a

brief opinion stating that welfare benefits are mere privileges that are entitled to no due process protection. Instead, the Court held that welfare payments are property interests within the scope of the Due Process Clause.

The Court reasoned that AFDC payments "are a matter of statutory entitlement for persons qualified to receive them." 397 U.S. at 262, 90 S. Ct. 1011. It quoted from an article by Professor Reich in which he argued that (1) a high proportion of property in the United States consists of intangible entitlements to continuing benefits, (2) a high proportion of those entitlements flow from government, and (3) the traditional legal approach to property protects the entitlements of the rich but not the poor. Reich, Individual Rights and Social Welfare: The Emerging Legal Issues, 74 Yale L.J. 1245 (1965). See also Reich, The New Property, 73 Yale L.J. 733 (1964). Thus, for instance the Court had long extended due process protection to the governmental benefit of a license to practice law, characterizing that benefit as a "right." *Schware v. Board of Bar Examiners*, 353 U.S. 232 (1957); Ex Parte Garland, 71 U.S. (4 Wall) 333, 379 (1866). Yet, until *Goldberg*, the Court had declined to extend due process protection to benefits like welfare or most forms of government employment. The Court found Reich's thesis persuasive, and used it as the basis for its holding in *Goldberg* that welfare benefits conferred by statute are "property" subject to due process protection. In later cases, the Court stated that it had "fully and finally rejected the wooden distinction between 'rights' and 'privileges.'. . ." *Board of Regents v. Roth*, 408 U.S. 564, 571 (1972).

In the present case, the majority opinion correctly determines that the petition fails to allege a violation of state or federal due process. The opinion is correct when it points out that "[o]ur state law affords a license applicant no individual entitlement to a license that he seeks."

The majority opinion says that "[a]bsent a protected property interest, AIGA was not entitled to notice and a hearing before the denial of its application," citing *Board of Regents of State Colleges v. Roth*, 408 U.S. 564 (1972). The inference I take issue with is the fact that only a vested property right would be entitled to the full protection of due process. Here the claim was neither vested nor a property right[. H]owever a vested privilege when and if it arises, under the gaming statutes should be entitled to the same constitutional protection. The Gaming Board argues, as many have in similar settings, "The Louisiana legislature has clearly and explicitly stated that no property interests are created in conjunction with gaming licenses, contracts and permits," relying on the language of La. R.S. 27:2(B), which states in part that:

> Any license . . . or thing obtained or issued pursuant to the provisions of this Title or any other law relative to the jurisdiction of the board is expressly declared by the legislature to be a pure and absolute revocable

privilege and not a right, property or otherwise, under the constitution of the United States or of the State of Louisiana.

This seems to indicate that because the license is a privilege, it somehow escapes the protection of due process. Apparently, the drafters of the gaming statutes were some twenty years behind in their constitutional law research and were under the impression that Justice Holmes' relegation of mere privilege to a second-class status somehow still controlled federal due process concepts.

I think the cases as cited in Professor Davis' treatise make it clear that a license, once issued, albeit a privilege, cannot be withdrawn by state action without affording the holders of that license the full procedural protection of due process. The majority opinion in its analysis of the due process claim cites [*Roth*], but omits any reference to the rejection of "the wooden distinction between 'rights' and 'privileges.' " The Supreme Court opinion in *Roth* provides an answer for both a property right analysis and a mere privilege analysis when it says: "The Fourteenth Amendment's procedural protection of property is a safeguard of the security of interests that a person has already acquired in specific benefits." *Roth*, 92 S. Ct. at 2708. Although this license by legislative pronouncement is a mere privilege, the protection afforded to that privilege only exists once it has been acquired.

## NOTES

As Judge Gonzales's concurrence explains, the Supreme Court had seemed to jettison the "rights-privileges distinction" even before the *Rosenthal* case was decided. Can the *Rosenthal* approach survive in light of modern notions of due process? If not, is there likely to be a more robust conception of due process in future cases than *Rosenthal* recognized? Consider the next case.

### KRAFT v. JACKA
**872 F.2d 862 (9th Cir. 1989)**

CHOY, Circuit Judge.

[Sydell R. Kraft, the Levin International Corporation, Trans Atlantic Games, Inc., and Trans Atlantic Games of Nevada brought a Section 1983 action against members of the Nevada Gaming Control Board for violating federal constitutional rights under the color of state law. The plaintiffs alleged their civil rights had been violated because they had been deprived of protected property and liberty interests without due process of law. This claim arose from the Board's refusal to extend further licensing to the plaintiffs after expiration of their one-year limited gaming licenses.]

In 1984, plaintiffs applied to the Board for licenses to manufacture, distribute, and operate gaming devices in Nevada. [At a public meeting, the Board expressed concern] that plaintiffs had engaged in the sale and distribution of slot machines within Nevada without a license, had shipped a machine into the state which had been approved in a particular form but had been modified without approval, and apparently had difficulty maintaining control of their machines in Nevada. The Board also was concerned that Howard Levin ("Levin"), who was then president of all the plaintiff corporations, had been associating with a convicted felon. The Board ultimately voted to recommend approval of one-year limited licenses. . . . The Commission considered the recommendation at a public meeting on February 21, 1984[, and] voted three to two to issue licenses in accordance with the Board's recommendation. Each license stated that it was a "limited license to expire on date of Nevada Gaming Commission meeting of February, 1986."

Plaintiffs and Levin subsequently applied for licenses to become effective at the end of the one-year period. The Board considered these applications at a meeting on February 6, 1986. Kraft and Levin attended the meeting. The Board members again raised numerous concerns, including Levin's substantial gambling debts and the possibility that he had used subterfuge to avoid repayment of those debts. Prior to any decision of the Board, plaintiffs requested withdrawal of the LIC and TAG applications and a continuance of the Board's consideration of the TAG-Nevada application. This continuance allowed LIC, TAG, and Levin time to transfer their interests to Kraft so that only Kraft and TAG-Nevada would be under consideration. . . . The Board ultimately voted unanimously to recommend denial of the applications "without prejudice," meaning that the applicants could attempt to cure the deficiencies in their applications and reapply. . . .

Plaintiff Kraft contends that the Board violated her right to free association by denying her application for a license because she would not terminate her personal relationship with Levin.

As a threshold requirement to any due process claim, the plaintiffs must show that they have a protected property or liberty interest. *Board of Regents v. Roth*, 408 U.S. 564, 569-71, 92 S. Ct. 2701 33 L. Ed. 2d 548 (1972). Plaintiffs contend that TAG-Nevada had a property interest in its limited licenses which was protected by due process. Property rights protected by procedural due process "are not created by the Constitution. Rather, they are created and their dimensions are defined by existing rules or understandings that stem from an independent source such as state law-rules or understandings that secure certain

benefits and that support claims of entitlement to those benefits."
*Roth.* Thus, the issue before us is whether state law or any other source
confers upon a limited licensee an expectation of entitlement to
continued licensing that would give rise to a property interest protected by the federal Constitution. "A reasonable expectation of entitlement is determined largely by the language of the statute and the
extent to which the entitlement is couched in mandatory terms." . . .

Plaintiffs . . . assert that they were licensed and in active business at the
time their limited licenses were reviewed and thus the refusal to extend
any further licensing to them was more a revocation of existing licenses
than a denial of new licensing. As holders of existing gaming licenses,
they contend that they had a sufficient property interest to warrant
procedural due process protection upon revocation of the licenses.

We need not decide whether there is a state-created property
interest in an existing gaming license that would be protected by
the federal Constitution. A close look at the statutory scheme governing licensing and the specific purposes behind issuance of a limited
license instead of a permanent license reveals that the decision to
deny further licensing did not operate as a revocation or suspension
of an existing license. Rather, it is clear as a matter of statutory interpretation that plaintiffs stood in the shoes of first time applicants
when they appeared before the Board in 1986. . . .

Under the Nevada Gaming Control Act (the "Act"), gaming is regulated primarily through licensing and control by the Commission
and the Board. The Board has "full and absolute power and authority
to recommend [to the Commission] the denial of any application, the
limitation, conditioning, or restriction of any license . . . [or] the suspension or revocation of any license . . . for any cause deemed reasonable by the board." Nev. Rev. Stat. §463.1405(2). The Commission has
the same broad authority in making final rulings on licensing applications. *Id.* §463.1405(3).

In making a licensing decision, the Board and Commission are
required to consider numerous factors which indicate whether the
applicant is suitable to participate in Nevada gaming.[2] The Board has

---

2. Nev. Rev. Stat. §463.170 provides in part:

2. An application to receive a license or be found suitable shall not be granted
unless the commission is satisfied that the applicant is:
  (a) A person of good character, honesty and integrity;
  (b) A person whose prior activities, criminal record, if any, reputation, habits
and associations do not pose a threat to the public interest of this state or to the
effective regulation and control of gaming . . . ; and
  (c) In all other respects qualified to be licensed or found suitable consistently with the declared policy of the state.

discretion to recommend issuance of a limited license, rather than a permanent license, when there are serious concerns regarding an applicant's suitability. A limited license is issued to allow a licensee to engage in business temporarily, as a testing period. . . .

We conclude that the Nevada legislature could not have intended to confer any entitlement to further licensing on licensees who initially had not been considered suitable enough for the Board to recommend issuance of a permanent license. TAG-Nevada's limited licenses differed from a permanent license in that they were set to expire automatically in February, 1986. . . . The Board was not required to revoke the limited licenses and TAG-Nevada was not automatically entitled to renewal upon payment of fees. TAG-Nevada's position was indistinguishable from that of any other first time applicant. . . .

The plaintiffs [also argue] that they were deprived of a protected liberty interest in reputation without due process of law. Plaintiffs TAG and LIC contend that they were deprived of their liberty interest when the Board, without first giving notice to the two companies, issued an order finding them unsuitable to engage in Nevada gaming. In addition, plaintiffs TAG-Nevada and Kraft contend that they were deprived of their liberty interest when the Board sent out a letter to all Nevada licensees informing the licensees that the application of TAG-Nevada and Kraft had been denied.

An interest in reputation "is, without more, 'neither "liberty" nor "property" guaranteed against state deprivation without due process of law.'" [citations omitted] To implicate constitutional liberty interests, state action must be "sufficiently serious to 'stigmatize' or otherwise burden the individual so that he is not able to take advantage of other . . . opportunities." The statements at issue must involve charges which rise to the level of "moral turpitude"; "charges that do not reach this level of severity do not infringe constitutional liberty interests."

At the February 13, 1986, meeting, the Board . . . issued an order recommending to the Commission that TAG-Nevada's application be denied. That order stated that one reason for recommending denial was that Kraft had proposed to continue her business association with TAG, LIC, and Levin, "all of whom are found to be unsuitable by the Board." Neither TAG nor LIC was represented at

3. A license to operate a gaming establishment shall not be granted unless the applicant has satisfied the commission that:
(a) He has adequate business probity, competence and experience, in gaming or generally; and
(b) The proposed financing of the entire operation is:
(1) Adequate for the nature of the proposed operation; and (2) From a suitable source.

the February 13 meeting because both companies had withdrawn their license applications. Plaintiffs contend that the Board's statement regarding unsuitability "banished" both TAG and LIC from association with gaming in Nevada, and thus stigmatized them sufficiently to impair liberty interests. Since they were not present at the meeting, they contend that this finding of unsuitability violated due process.

Neither TAG nor LIC was directly affected by the Board's statement that they were unsuitable. Because neither company was before the board as an applicant, the statement did not have the effect of a "finding" of unsuitability which would result in denial of a licensing application. The Board was required to consider Kraft's associations, both business and personal, in ruling on TAG-Nevada's licensing application. The Board's statement constituted only a determination that TAG-Nevada should not be allowed to participate in gaming because the company's president, Kraft, had unsuitable associations. TAG and LIC were not "banished" from Nevada gaming by virtue of the Board's statement. [Thus,] the asserted interest in reputation does not rise to the level of a constitutional liberty interest.

After the Commission issued its order denying TAG-Nevada's application for further licensing, the Board sent a letter to all Nevada gaming licensees informing them that TAG-Nevada and Kraft were no longer able to conduct business in the gaming industry. The Board's action did not invade a constitutional liberty interest in reputation. "Unpublicized accusations do not infringe constitutional liberty interests because, by definition, they cannot harm 'good name, reputation, honor or integrity.' . . . When reasons are not given, inferences drawn from [the state action at issue] are simply insufficient to implicate liberty interests." *Bollow*, 650 F.2d at 1101. The Board's letter did not state any reasons for the denial and did not even say that TAG-Nevada or Kraft had been declared unsuitable. An inference of unsuitability could have been drawn from the denial alone. However, as we stated in *Bollow*, a mere inference is not sufficient to implicate a liberty interest in reputation.

Kraft [also] contends that the Board violated her free association rights by basing the denial of TAG-Nevada's application on her personal association with Levin. Kraft and Levin live together as single adults. There are two possible sources of constitutional protection for personal relationships. The First Amendment protects expressive associations that involve the other activities protected by the amendment such as speaking, religious exercise, and petitioning the government. The Fourteenth Amendment protects " 'certain intimate human relationships . . . against undue intrusion by the State because of the role of such relationships in safeguarding the individual freedom that is central to our constitutional scheme.' " [citation omitted] Kraft contends that the Board's denial of her licensing application violated her Fourteenth Amendment right to free association, because the Board's denial was based on its disapproval of her personal relationship with Levin. . . .

The Board granted plaintiffs a continuance of their applications so that LIC, TAG, and Levin could transfer their interests in TAG-Nevada to Kraft. Kraft purchased TAG-Nevada, in exchange for a promissory note, so that only Kraft and TAG-Nevada would be under consideration. At the February 13 Board meeting, the Board expressed serious concerns about the financial stability of TAG-Nevada and the possibility that Levin would continue to participate in the management of the company. In the Board's order recommending denial of TAG-Nevada's application, the Board stated as one reason for the recommendation that "the applicant, SYDELL R. KRAFT, has proposed to continue her *business associa-tion* with TAG, [LIC], and Howard S. Levin, all of whom are found to be unsuitable by the Board, and this association will create or enhance the danger of unsuitable practices, methods and activities in the carrying on of business and financial arrangements incidental to the conduct of gaming by the applicants . . . ." (emphasis added). Business relationships do not fall within the Fourteenth Amendment's protection of intimate associations. If the Board had denied the application solely on the basis of Kraft's business ties with Levin, there clearly would be no constitutional violation.

However, the . . . Board also was concerned that Kraft would continue to have a personal relationship with Levin.[3] In fact, one Board member stated that Kraft "could not have structured this deal to [his] satisfaction . . . because the only way [he] would be willing to look at this favorably would be with conditions that Sydell Kraft *not work for nor be associated with* LIC, TAG, Inc., or Howard Levin." (emphasis added). Another Board member stated that "if [he] were to move forward as one Board member today with a recommendation to approve this transaction, it would be with a condition that [Kraft] sever herself

---

3. The transcript contains the following testimony:

*Member Hillyer:*  Mrs. Kraft, how about your personal relationship with Mr. Levin? . . . Are you still going to be sharing a household?

*Ms. Kraft:*  That is what we are doing today . . . . We have a very close personal relationship. I hope that it continues, but there are no guarantees. . . .

*Member Hillyer:*  So the personal relationship with Mr. Levin as it stands right now is planned to continue status quo; is that correct?

*Ms. Kraft:*  As far as personal relationship, as far as I know from today, yes.

totally from Mr. Levin." Thus, we must decide whether the Board violated Kraft's free association rights when it denied her licensing application.

We have previously stated that the freedom of intimate association is coextensive with the right of privacy. As we noted in *Fleisher* [*v. City of Signal Hill*, 829 F.2d 1491 (9th Cir. 1987)], the Supreme Court has extended the right of privacy to unmarried individuals only in cases involving contraception and abortion. The relationship between Kraft and Levin as cohabitating, single adults may fit within our description of an intimate protected association in *IDK, Inc. v. Clark County*, 836 F.2d at 1193. However, we need not decide whether the relationship between Kraft and Levin is a protected one, because we conclude that the Board's actions did not intrude on Kraft's free association right. Neither the right to privacy nor the right to free association is absolute. In some cases, these rights must give way to compelling governmental interests. *See Fleisher*, 829 F.2d at 1500 (no violation of free association rights when police officer was terminated for having sexual relationship with a minor); *Fugate v. Phoenix Civil Serv. Bd.*, 791 F.2d 736, 741 (9th Cir. 1986) (no violation of right to privacy when police officers were terminated for having sexual relationships with prostitutes).

On the surface, the Board might appear to be violating Kraft's Fourteenth Amendment right by conditioning receipt of a gaming license on the termination of a possibly protected relationship. However, the Board did not deny licensing because it disapproved of the fact that Levin and Kraft were unmarried. The personal relationship between Kraft and Levin was not even the principal reason for the denial. The ... personal relationship would not have been a deciding factor in the decision to deny further licensing if the transfer of control over TAG-Nevada from Levin to Kraft had not looked so much like a mere subterfuge.

In this case, there was a significant governmental interest that justified the intrusion on any free association right Kraft might have. The Nevada Gaming Control Act sets forth the declared public policy of the state that "the continued growth and success of gaming is dependent upon public confidence and trust that licensed gaming is conducted honestly and competitively, that the rights of the creditors of licensees are protected and that gaming is free from criminal and corruptive elements." Nev. Rev. Stat. §463.0129. This public confidence and trust is to be maintained by "strict regulation of all persons, locations, practices, associations and activities related to the operation of licensed gaming establishments and the manufacture or distribution of gambling devices and equipment." *Id.* In considering the qualifications of a licensee, the Board is required to consider whether the licensee's associations will adversely affect the operation of a gaming establishment. Nev. Rev. Stat. §463.170(2)(b).

The Board determined that Levin was unsuitable to be associated with Kraft because he lacked the business probity, competence, and experience to be in control of a gaming operation. The Board was concerned that Levin's personal relationship with Kraft would allow him to continue to exercise substantial control over TAG-Nevada. In addition, the Board was concerned that the transfer of TAG-Nevada stock from Levin to Kraft was a mere subterfuge, because the entire transfer was financed through promissory notes . . . .

Here, the Board was concerned that Kraft's personal relationship with Levin would allow Levin to exert indirect control over TAG-Nevada even though he was not considered suitable to hold a gaming license. This concern is directly related to the state's interest in maintaining public trust and confidence in the gaming industry. The denial of Kraft's application was based in part on her refusal to sever her personal ties with Levin. However, the Board's action was not directed at the personal aspects of the relationship. . . . The district court's order of summary judgment in favor of the Board is AFFIRMED.

### NOTES

1.  What role, if any, might gender have played in this case? Is it possible that the Board, the Commission, or even the court might have ruled differently if Mr. Levin had been the applicant and Ms. Kraft had been the associate with unsavory ties to convicted felons? Under those circumstances, if Ms. Kraft had transferred her interests to Mr. Levin, would the agencies and the court have been as likely to find that Ms. Kraft would have retained the same amount of influence?

2.  Are *Fleisher* and *Fugate* compelling precedents for the notion that the government had a compelling interest to intrude on Ms. Kraft's right to freedom of association in this case?

3.  Consider the following criticism of modern due process analysis: "Government agencies make countless decisions each year whether to grant or revoke benefits, adjudicating interests as varied as business licenses, parole release dates, and welfare payments. The Supreme Court's recognition in 1970 of a duty to review the process by which agencies make these decisions has contributed to a due process 'explosion.' Unwilling to impose the full burden of this review either on themselves or on government

agencies, the courts now self-consciously apply a two-part test: Before they ask what process is due to assure that decisions are minimally rational, courts first ask if a decision requires due process review at all. In answering these questions, the courts have placed great importance on the extent to which the discretion of a decisionmaker is limited by rules or standards. In general, if officials exercise broad discretion to provide or revoke an interest, courts refuse to examine the procedures they follow. Further, if rules only partially confine discretion, some court decisions have cited the remaining discretion as a justification for reduced procedural protection. This . . . approach [is] inverted. Although broad adjudicative discretion often has merit, it also poses a threat of unequal, capricious, even vindictive decisions." Tim Searchinger, *The Procedural Due Process Approach to Administrative Discretion: The Courts' Inverted Analysis*, 95 YALE L.J. 1017 (1986). Casino licensing boards have wide discretion in considering applications. They are frequently criticized for abusing such discretion. Perhaps ironically, under modern conceptions of due process, it is the very fact of wide discretion that shields the licensing boards from scrutiny.

4. While employing a different mode of analysis, the federal court in *Kraft v. Jacka* reached a result similar to that of the state court in *Rosenthal*. Is the rights/privileges distinction really dead?

## IN RE APPLICATION OF MARTIN
### 447 A.2d 129 (N.J. 1982)

PASHMAN, J.

This case involves a classic confrontation between the power of the State to protect the public through regulation of a highly sensitive industry and the right of individuals thus regulated to be free from unreasonable governmental intrusion into their private lives. Appellants are applicants for licenses to become non-supervisory casino employees. They assert that various constitutional and statutory rights have been invaded by the [Casino Control Act's] comprehensive licensing scheme, including the rights of privacy, freedom of association, freedom from unreasonable searches and seizures and the privilege against self-incrimination.

### [BACKGROUND]

The Casino Control Act prohibits persons from working as casino employees in Atlantic City unless they have first obtained a valid casino employee license. N.J.S.A. 5:12-90(a). On April 14, 1978, Martha Stretton submitted an application form to the Casino Control Commission to obtain such a license. She sought employment as a dealer in a casino hotel in Atlantic City. On April 21, 1978, Maria Martin similarly submitted an application form for a casino employee license to work as a casino dealer.

Both Stretton and Martin refused to answer a number of questions on the application form then used by the Commission pursuant to N.J.S.A. 5:12-70(a) and N.J.A.C. 19:41-7.14. In addition, both Martin and Stretton refused to sign a consent to searches, inspections and seizures. They also sought to limit the scope of the release authorization that empowered various institutions to release to the Division or the Commission confidential information concerning the applicants. Finally, they objected to a waiver of liability that purported to relinquish any rights against the State for disclosures of confidential information acquired by the State in the course of the investigation of the applicant other than wilfully unlawful disclosures. With their forms they submitted a list of reasons why they did not respond to the questions.

Joseph Lordi, the Chairman of the Commission, advised Martin and Stretton that he could not accept their applications for filing since they were incomplete. N.J.A.C. 19:41-8.2 and -8.3. He advised them of their right to a hearing if they contested the decision. On May 3, 1978, Martin and Stretton requested an administrative hearing.[2] [Stretton later agreed to answer the questions and was licensed]. . . . After a pre-hearing conference on June 15, 1978, an order was issued on June 16 by the hearing examiner[, indicating] that certain questions on the existing form were not essential and others could be modified. After the pre-hearing order, the hearing examiner granted a request by appellants to enlarge the list of challenged items to 27 out of the 55 questions on the form. . . . The examiner [held] that the challenged questions did not violate the constitutional rights of freedom of association, privacy, freedom from unreasonable searches and seizures, or the privilege against self-incrimination [but recommended] that parts of the forms be revised to eliminate or narrow the scope of certain questions. . . . [On June 1, 1982, the Commission adopted a new form that omitted most of the questions challenged by appellants.] Although most of the questions challenged by appellants have thus been eliminated from use by the Commission, appellants

2. On May 22, 1978, both Martin and Stretton graduated from Resorts International Dealers School after having completed the prescribed course of study as casino dealers specializing in the game of blackjack.

continue to argue that various provisions of the Casino Control Act violate several of their constitutional and statutory rights.

[W]e note that many of appellants' challenges have become moot since the litigation began. With the adoption of the new form, PHDF-2A, on June 1, 1982, most of the challenged questions have been eliminated from use. . . . However, appellants continue to challenge the statutory criteria on which the forms are based. Moreover, they challenge the validity of other provisions which remain on the forms such as the release authorization, the waiver of liability and the notification that searches on the casino premises are permitted by the statute.

## SEARCH AND SEIZURE

Appellants contend that the Casino Control Act violates their constitutional right to be free from unreasonable governmental searches and seizures [by giving] the Division of Gaming Enforcement power to conduct inspections and seizures far beyond constitutional limits. . . .

Appellants challenge four facets of the statute. First, they challenge the constitutionality of the requirement that applicants and licensees consent to inspections, searches and seizures. N.J.S.A. 5:12-80(c). Second, they challenge the statutory authorization of warrantless searches under N.J.S.A. 5:12-79(a)(6). Third, they claim that the statute unconstitutionally allows administrative searches of non-regulated premises. N.J.S.A. 5:12-79(c). Fourth, they challenge the adequacy of the probable cause showing required to obtain an administrative warrant. N.J.S.A. 5:12-79(d)(1).

The first challenge concerns N.J.S.A. 5:12-80(c). That section provides:

> All applicants, licensees, registrants, intermediary companies, and holding companies shall consent to inspections, searches and seizures and the supplying of handwriting exemplars as authorized by this act and regulations promulgated hereunder.

Appellants contend that the statute unconstitutionally coerces applicants and licensees to consent to otherwise unlawful searches and seizures. However, they misconstrue the purpose of the challenged provision, N.J.S.A. 5:12-80(c). Section 79 gives the Division certain powers to conduct searches and seizures. N.J.S.A. 5:12-79. The purpose of Section 80(c) is not to expand the scope of searches otherwise allowable under Section 79. Section 80(c) merely requires applicants and licensees to submit to searches and seizures "as authorized by this act and regulations promulgated [t]hereunder." N.J.S.A. 5:12-80(c). The section merely places a legal duty on applicants and licensees not to resist lawful searches otherwise authorized by Section 79 or regulations promulgated pursuant to it. For this reason, appellants are incorrect in their claim that the statute coerces consent to otherwise unlawful searches. *See State v. Williams*, 417 A.2d 1046 (N.J. 1980). It merely mandates submission to lawful searches.

The Commission has acted in accord with this interpretation of the statute by deleting the challenged portion of the application form that required applicants to sign a "consent to searches, inspections and seizures." Such a requirement may have erroneously created the impression that applicants were being coerced to waive their Fourth Amendment rights. The current form merely informs applicants that licensees are subject to certain warrantless searches while on the licensed casino premises. It properly notifies applicants that once they are licensed, they will be legally required to submit to searches above and beyond those to which they would have been subject had they not been licensed. [N]either the notice on the form nor N.J.S.A. 5:12-80(c) coerces applicants to consent to otherwise unlawful searches.

Second, applicants challenge the statutory authorization of warrantless searches in the casino facility under N.J.S.A. 5:12-79(a)(6). That section provides:

> The division and its employees and agents, upon approval of the director, shall have the authority, without notice and without warrant . . . [t]o inspect the person, and personal effects present in a casino facility licensed under this act, of any holder of a license issued pursuant to this act while that person is present in a licensed casino facility.

The Division is thus empowered by statute to conduct warrantless searches of a licensee or her personal effects while she is in a licensed casino facility. Such searches may occur only with the approval of the director, N.J.S.A. 5:12-79(a), or the owner or operator in charge of the controlled premises, N.J.S.A. 5:12-79(f)(1). The freedom to conduct such searches is limited by constitutional requirements, N.J.S.A. 5:12-79(b). Licensees are obligated to submit to such searches under N.J.S.A. 5:12-80(c).

The United States Supreme Court has stated that the "basic purpose of [the Fourth Amendment] is to safeguard the privacy and security of individuals against arbitrary invasions by governmental officials." *Marshall v. Barlow's, Inc.*, 436 U.S. 307, 312, (1978)[.] The Supreme Court has held that except in certain carefully defined classes of cases the states may not conduct administrative searches of private property without a warrant. An exception has been recognized for "pervasively regulated" businesses, *United States v. Biswell*, 406 U.S. 311, 316, (1972) (firearms), or industries "long subject to close supervision and inspection," *Colonnade Catering Corp. v. United States*, 397 U.S. 72, 77 (1970) (liquor). The United States Supreme Court has decided that

> Certain industries have such a history of government oversight that no reasonable expectation of privacy . . . could exist for a proprietor over the stock of such an enterprise . . . [W]hen an entrepreneur embarks upon such a business, he [or she] has voluntarily chosen to subject himself [or herself] to a full arsenal of governmental regulation. [(citations omitted)]

It cannot be denied that casino gambling in New Jersey is a pervasively regulated industry that is subject to close supervision and inspection. . . . [T]here can be no question that the governing statute clearly authorizes warrantless searches by the Division upon approval of the director. N.J.S.A. 5:12-79(a). . . .

Appellants further argue that the applicable precedents have gone only so far as to authorize warrantless searches of regulated property, but have not authorized warrantless searches of persons on the regulated property. *See, e.g., Marshall v. Barlow's*, 436 U.S. at 313. Nonetheless, the policy considerations behind the exception to the warrant requirement are equally applicable to searches of licensed persons while they are on regulated business premises. The expectation of privacy in such circumstances is limited, particularly where the applicant has been notified prior to licensing that she will be subject to warrantless searches in the casino facility. Moreover, the ability to conduct such searches is necessary to deter many offenses or violations that might otherwise be virtually undetectable.

We therefore uphold the constitutionality of the statutory provisions allowing the Division to conduct warrantless searches of licensees and their personal effects in the casino facility. N.J.S.A. 5:12-79(a)(6).[9]

Appellants' third contention is that the Casino Control Act unconstitutionally permits administrative searches of non-regulated

---

9. We note that such warrantless searches are themselves subject to the independent constitutional requirement of reasonableness. N.J.S.A. 5:12-79(b); *see, e.g., Marshall v. Barlow's*, 436 U.S. at 312. They must be conducted in a manner that furthers the regulatory purposes of the Casino Control Act. We need not address the specific limits of the search and seizure power granted by N.J.S.A. 5:12-79(a)(6), particularly since no search is being challenged as unreasonable. Whether a search has been conducted in an unreasonable manner is a matter to be determined in the light of the circumstances of the particular case.

premises. Essentially, they claim that the language of N.J.S.A. 5:12-79 is so broad that it authorizes searches outside the casino facility, such as searches of a casino employee's home. This is an incorrect reading of the statute. Section 79(a) permits warrantless searches only of

> "premises wherein casino gaming is conducted; or gaming devices or equipment are manufactured, sold, distributed, or serviced; or wherein any records of such activities are prepared or maintained . . ." [N.J.S.A. 5:12-79(a)(1)]

Warrantless searches on any other premises are not authorized. As a practical matter, appellants, who are not involved in the manufacture of gaming equipment or record-keeping, will be subject to warrantless searches only while in a licensed casino facility.

Moreover, the statutory provisions for searches pursuant to administrative warrant, N.J.S.A. 5:12-79(c), (d) & (e), do not empower the Division to search the homes of casino employees. The statute requires the administrative warrant to "be served during normal business hours of the licensee." N.J.S.A. 5:12-79(d)(2). By implication, this provision limits searches pursuant to administrative warrant to the regulated business premises of casino service industries licensed under N.J.S.A. 5:12-92. . . .

Appellants' fourth and final objection to N.J.S.A. 5:12-79 challenges the probable cause showing required to obtain an administrative warrant from a judge under N.J.S.A. 5:12-79(d)(1).

In the criminal context, a warrant may be issued only on a probable cause showing that would lead a reasonable person to believe that a crime has been committed and that evidence of that crime will be found in a particular place. *Henry v. United States*, 361 U.S. 98, 102 (1959). However, the probable cause showing necessary to obtain an administrative warrant is less stringent. Searches pursuant to administrative warrants are conducted to enforce regulatory statutes, rather than to investigate criminal activity. Experience has demonstrated the utility of periodic inspections in promoting compliance with regulatory statutes. *See, e.g., Camara v. Municipal Court*, 387 U.S. at 538. In such cases, probable cause in the criminal sense is not constitutionally required. For purposes of an administrative search, probable cause justifying the issuance of a warrant may be based on "reasonable legislative or administrative standards for conducting an . . . inspection." *Marshall v. Barlow's*, 436 U.S. at 320-21 (holding that OSHA inspections were constitutionally permissible pursuant to administrative warrants based on less than criminal probable cause)[.]

The Casino Control Act provides a reasonable standard for issuance of an administrative warrant. A judge may issue such a warrant only on a probable cause showing of

> a valid public interest in the effective enforcement of the act or regulations sufficient to justify administrative inspection of the area, premises, building or conveyance in the circumstances specified in the application for the warrant. [N.J.S.A. 5:12-79(d)(1)]

This section clearly requires a showing of a valid public interest in enforcement of the act sufficient to justify the judge's issuance of the warrant. Such a requirement meets the constitutional standard for protection against unreasonable searches and seizures.

In sum, we uphold the constitutionality of the challenged statutory provisions at N.J.S.A 5:12-79 and -80(c), as well as the notification on the application form that licensees are subject to certain searches in the casino facility.

### RIGHT OF PRIVACY

Appellants [next] contend that conditioning license application on the disclosure of personal information to the government impermissibly infringes on their constitutional right of privacy. Their claim is two-fold. First, they assert that certain information is so personal that no one should be required to disclose it to the state in order to receive a government benefit. Second, they contend that even though the state may constitutionally require certain disclosures to the government, it may not do so unless it has taken adequate steps to ensure that private information so acquired will not be disclosed to the public.

In *Whalen v. Roe*, the United States Supreme Court recognized that the Constitution grants protection to the "individual interest in avoiding disclosure of personal matters. . . ." 429 U.S. 589, 599-600 (1977). That case involved a challenge to a New York statute requiring pharmacists or physicians who dispense certain drugs to report the name and address of the patient to a central state office. The court upheld the statutory reporting requirements on the grounds that they were rationally related to a legitimate government law enforcement purpose and that the individual interest in non-disclosure was adequately protected by strict statutory procedures safeguarding the information against further disclosure.

The United States Supreme Court further developed the confidentiality strand of privacy law in *Nixon v. Administrator of General Services*, 433 U.S. 425 (1977). The Court decided that the government had the constitutional power to compel former President Nixon to turn over all of his presidential papers, including personal papers, to government archivists under the Presidential Recordings and Material Preservation Act, 44 U.S.C. §2107 note. The Supreme Court held that "any intrusion [on the individual interest in non-disclosure] must be weighed against the public interest in subjecting the Presidential materials of appellant's administration to archival screening." *Id.* at 458. As with *Whalen v. Roe,* the extent of the intrusion on the individual interest was judged in light of the statutory safeguards against disclosure. *Id.* at 458-59. The Supreme Court emphasized that the underlying statute mandated regulations aimed at "preventing undue dissemination of private materials . . .". *Id.* at 458-59.

Several federal courts have since explained that the government has the constitutional power to compel disclosure of private information to the state when the governmental interest in the information outweighs the individual interest in non-disclosure. *Plante v. Gonzalez,* 575 F.2d 1119, 1134 (5th Cir. 1978); *Fadjo v. Coon,* 633 F.2d 1172, 1175-76 (5th Cir. 1981).

This Court has similarly adopted a balancing test to resolve conflicts between governmental needs for information and an individual's right of confidentiality. "The legitimate public interest must be considered . . . in balance with the competing right of privacy on the part of the affected individuals." *Lehrhaupt v. Flynn,* 140 N.J. Super. at 260, 356 A.2d 35. The Appellate Division held and we agree that

> even if the governmental purpose is legitimate and substantial . . . the invasion of the fundamental right of privacy must be minimized by utilizing the narrowest means which can be designed to achieve the public purpose. [*Lehrhaupt v. Flynn,* 356 A.2d 35; *see Kenny v. Byrne,* 365 A.2d 211.]

This requirement accords with the United States Supreme Court concern for adequate safeguards against public disclosure of private information in government hands when such disclosure is unnecessary to achieve the governmental purposes.

In this case there is a substantial government interest in strict regulation of casino gambling. Until 1976 all casino gambling in New Jersey was prohibited by the Constitution[.] At that time, the Constitution was amended to allow the Legislature to authorize casino gambling only in Atlantic City, N.J. Const. (1947), Art. 4, §7, ¶2(D). Since it is generally constitutionally prohibited, there is a great public interest in regulating the gambling that does exist. The Constitution explicitly provides that gambling in Atlantic City "shall be . . . under the regulation and control [of] the State . . ." *Id.*

Moreover, the Legislature has substantial power to regulate non-essential, dangerous and sensitive industries to protect the public safety and welfare. "We see every reason . . . for legalized casino gambling to take its deserved place among these industries." *In re Boardwalk Regency Casino Application*, 180 N.J. Super. at 341, 434 A.2d 1111.

Pursuant to Art. 4, §7, ¶2(D) of the State Constitution, the Legislature authorized casino gambling in Atlantic City in the Casino Control Act, N.J.S.A. 5:12-1 to -152. The act contains extensive, detailed regulation of every aspect of the industry. The Legislature explicitly stated that the public policy of the statute was: first, to ensure public trust in the credibility and integrity of the regulatory process, N.J.S.A. 5:12-1(b)(6); second, to exclude persons with criminal backgrounds and persons "deficient in business probity, ability or experience" from casino operations, N.J.S.A. 5:12-1(b)(7); third, to exercise regulatory and investigatory powers "to the fullest extent consistent with law" to avoid the entry into casino operations of persons whose economic or occupational pursuits violate the criminal or civil public policies of New Jersey, N.J.S.A. 5:12-1(b)(9); and fourth, to prevent persons with "unacceptable backgrounds and records of behavior" from controlling casinos, N.J.S.A. 5:12-1(b)(15). There is obviously a strong public interest in guarding against the danger of infiltration by organized crime. . . .

In comparison with this strong public interest, the incursion on the applicant's privacy interests by the current questions on the application form, PHDF-2A, is minimal. None of the challenged questions on the form is so personal that applicants should be allowed to assert a right of "selective disclosure," as suggested by appellants in this case. They concern predominantly information of public record, such as the applicant's business interests, prior arrests or convictions, participation in civil suits, automobile ownership, marital status, military record, former spouses and driver's license information.

In promulgating the current application form, PHDF-2A, the Commission reduced the amount of the personal information sought. In doing so, it acted in accord with the principle that "even though the governmental purpose be legitimate and substantial, that purpose cannot be pursued by means that broadly stifle fundamental personal liberties when the end can be more narrowly achieved." *Shelton v. Tucker*, 364 U.S. 479, 488, (1960); *Lehrhaupt v. Flynn*, 356 A.2d 35.

The Commission and the Division reviewed the forms in use at the time this litigation began. . . . After their study the Commission amended the forms in use, in light of the agencies' experience, to protect the privacy of applicants while retaining the questions that were deemed reasonably necessary for their investigation. This was altogether proper. By eliminating most of the challenged questions, the Commission and the Division have sought to accommodate the governmental need for disclosure of information by applicants and the individual interest in nondisclosure of personal materials. We conclude that the remaining disclosure requirements, in this context, do not violate applicants' right to privacy.

A different situation is presented by the release authorization, by which the applicant authorizes access by the Commission and the Division to confidential records held by various institutions such as courts, banks, employers, government agencies and educational institutions.[12] The information contained in the records of these institutions is likely to be at least as personal and perhaps more so than the information at issue in *Whalen* and *Nixon*. In light of the extraordinarily broad nature of the release authorization and the potential intimacy of the private information contained in these documents, we hold that in order for the release authorization to pass constitutional muster, the State must undertake adequate precautions to safeguard the material against disclosure to the public once it is in government hands. *See Whalen v. Roe*, 429 U.S. at 593-94, 597-98, 601, 603-04, and 607 (Brennan, J., concurring)[.] We therefore hold that the State has the constitutional power to condition license application on the applicants' signing the release authorization only if it has instituted adequate safeguards against public disclosure of confidential materials it obtains.

Appellants challenge the adequacy of the State's safeguards on four grounds. First, they contend that N.J.S.A. 5:12-74(e) gives the State

---

12.  The Release Authorization on PHDF-2A states:

To All Courts, Probation Departments, Selective Service Boards, Employers, Educational Institutions, Banks, Financial and Other Such Institutions, And All Governmental Agencies-federal, state and local, without exception, both foreign and domestic. I have authorized the New Jersey Casino Control Commission and the New Jersey Division of Gaming Enforcement to conduct a full investigation into my background and activities. Therefore, you are hereby authorized to release any and all information pertaining to me, documentary or otherwise, as requested by any employee or agent of the Division of Gaming Enforcement or the Casino Control Commission, provided that he or she certifies to you that I have an application pending before the Casino Control Commission or that I am presently a licensee, registrant or person required to be qualified under the provisions of the Casino Control Act. This authorization shall supersede and countermand any prior request or authorization to the contrary.

A photostatic copy of this authorization will be considered as effective and valid as the original.

permission to disclose publicly the confidential information in its possession. That section provides in part:

> All information and data pertaining to an applicant's criminal record, family, and background furnished to or obtained by the commission from any source shall be considered confidential and may be withheld in whole or in part, except that any information shall be released upon the lawful order of a court of competent jurisdiction or, with the approval of the Attorney General, to a duly authorized law enforcement agency. [N.J.S.A. 5:12-74(e) (emphasis added)]

Appellants claim that although the statute provides that the information "shall be considered confidential," it gives the Commission the power to release the information since it merely states that the information "may be withheld." They contend that the language implies that the Commission may also choose to release the data to the public.

Contrary to appellants' claim, we find that the section provides clear evidence of a legislative intent to prevent public disclosure of the private materials. Moreover, the report adopted by the Commission interpreted Section 74(e) as mandatory, allowing disclosure only under the circumstances specified in the statute. In light of the constitutional requirements of confidentiality and the absence of any substantial governmental interest in public disclosure of the information, we affirm the Commission's holding that the State must keep the acquired information confidential, subject only to the specific exceptions noted in N.J.S.A. 5:12-74(e) itself.

Appellants' second objection to the safeguards rests on N.J.S.A. 5:12-74(f). That section provides:

> Notice of the contents of any information or data released, except to a duly authorized law enforcement agency pursuant to subsection (d) or (e) of this section, may be given to any applicant or licensee in a manner prescribed by the rules and regulations adopted by the commission. [N.J.S.A. 5:12-74(f) (emphasis added)]

Again, in light of the confidentiality interest, we hold that, under this section, the State must notify any applicant or licensee of any release of information that may occur, other than disclosures to law enforcement agencies. While we have determined that such information shall remain confidential, any failure in the security system that results in unlawful release of the information should be followed by notification to the affected party. If adequate safeguards are instituted to keep the information confidential, such releases will be extremely rare, and the burden on the State minimal.

Third, appellants claim that the waiver of liability removes any incentive for the State to maintain confidentiality. The waiver of liability in the application form is mandated by N.J.S.A. 5:12-80(b) which provides in part:

> All applicants and licensees shall waive liability as to the State of New Jersey, and its instrumentalities and agents, for any damages resulting from any disclosure or publication in any manner, other than a willfully unlawful disclosure or publication, of any material or information acquired during inquiries, investigations or hearings.

We do not agree with appellants that immunity from civil suits gives Commission employees license to violate the confidentiality requirements of N.J.S.A. 5:12-74(e). We have held that the Commission must promulgate regulations to ensure the adequate safeguarding of confidential information if it intends to require applicants to sign the release authorization. We must assume that Commission employees will be conscientious in obeying these regulations, and that the Commission will sanction those employees who neglect their duties. Civil remedies for negligent disclosure are far from the most important means of ensuring that information in the government's control will be kept confidential.

Appellants' fourth and final objection to the record-keeping practices of the Commission and the Division is that they do not in fact use procedures designed to prevent the unauthorized disclosure of the private materials in their possession. We note that no specific allegation of any unauthorized public disclosure has been made. Nonetheless, we agree that applicants and licensees have a statutory right to adequate safeguards specifically designed to prevent the negligent or unauthorized disclosure of confidential information.

On the basis of this record, we find no assurance that the Commissioner and the Division have instituted adequate procedures to prevent disclosure of the confidential information. The agencies involved expressed concern for confidentiality and we have no criticism of their conduct. However, this is not sufficient protection for the applicants' privacy. To guarantee confidentiality, the Commission must promulgate regulations under the Administrative Procedure Act, N.J.S.A. 52:14B-1 to -15, designed to provide such safeguards. The regulations should include guidelines on the storage of information and access to it, including the circumstances under which files may be removed from government offices. They should recognize the practical needs of investigators and employees in using the information, while providing for its secure storage and handling. The regulations should also address the length of time during which the information will be preserved.

We hold that the challenged statutory provisions on which the application forms are based do not violate appellants' rights of privacy.[13] However, we also hold that the Commission may not constitutionally condition license application on signing the release authorization unless it has provided for adequate safeguards to preserve the confidentiality of applicants' records.

### FREEDOM OF ASSOCIATION

The First and Fourteenth Amendments to the Constitution protect the individual interest in freedom of association. The State is substantially limited in the extent to which it may impinge on this legally protected interest. *NAACP v. Alabama*, 357 U.S. 449, 460, (1958). The right of association is a "basic constitutional freedom . . . which, like free speech, lies at the foundation of a free society." *Buckley v. Valeo*, 424 U.S. 1, 25 (1976). The constitutional liberty to freely associate with others extends not merely to associations designed to advance beliefs and ideas, but to political causes as well[.] It also encompasses associational ties designed to further the social, legal and economic benefit of the group's members, *Griswold v. Connecticut*, 381 U.S. 479 (1965), and associations that promote a "way of life[.]"

State action that withholds a privilege from an individual because she has engaged in a protected association infringes on that constitutionally protected interest. The interest is also implicated if the state seeks to compel disclosures by group members that have the effect of deterring protected associational ties. The crucial factor in deciding whether the state action has invaded the interest is whether individuals are likely to be deterred from engaging in constitutionally protected associations. *In the Matter of Application of Stolar*, 401 U.S. 23, 27-28 (1971).

Once it has been determined that a state action may "have the effect of curtailing the freedom to associate [it] is subject to the closest scrutiny." *NAACP v. Alabama*, 357 U.S. at 460-61[.] The interest in free association may be impeded by the state only if it has a conflicting interest sufficient to justify the deterrent effect

---

13. The challenged statutory provisions include: N.J.S.A. 5:12-86 (disqualifying persons who have committed certain crimes); §§89(b), 90(b), 91(b) (requiring the applicant to give certain information about her associates); §80(a) (placing the burden on the applicant to prove her qualifications); §80(b) (waiver of liability); §74(e) & (f) (confidentiality of records).

on the free exercise of the constitutionally protected right. *NAACP v. Alabama*, 357 U.S. at 463. "Such a . . . subordinating interest of the State must be compelling. . . ." *Id.*; *see Baird v. State Bar of Arizona*, 401 U.S. 1, 6-7 (1971). To determine if the invasion of the interest by the state is constitutionally permissible, the Court must balance the state interest against the extent of the deterrent effect on protected associational ties.

Even when the state interest is sufficiently compelling to justify the government limitation on free association, the intrusion must be accomplished in the least restrictive manner possible, *Nixon v. Admin. of General Services*, 433 U.S. at 467. A significant interference by the state in protected associational interests is permitted only if the state can demonstrate both that it possesses a sufficiently important interest and that the means chosen to achieve that interest are "closely drawn to avoid unnecessary abridgment of associational freedoms." *Buckley v. Valeo*, 424 U.S. at 25.

Appellants challenge the constitutionality of conditioning licensing of casino employees on investigation of their associational ties. They claim that various provisions of the Casino Control Act impermissibly infringe on the constitutional right of freedom of association. N.J.S.A. 5:12-89(b)(2) provides in part:

> Each applicant [for a casino license] shall produce such information, documentation and assurances as may be required to establish by clear and convincing evidence the applicant's reputation for good character, honesty and integrity. Such information shall include, without limitation, data pertaining to family, habits, character, criminal and arrest record, business activities, financial affairs, and business, professional and personal associates, covering at least the 10-year period immediately preceding the filing of the application. [*See also* N.J.S.A. 5:12-84(c)]

This requirement is elucidated by the declaration of policy in the statute, N.J.S.A. 5:12-1(b)(7), which provides:

> Legalized casino gaming in New Jersey can attain, maintain and retain integrity, public confidence and trust, and remain compatible with the general public interest only under such a system of control and regulation as insures, so far as practicable, the exclusion from participation therein of persons with known criminal records, habits or associations, and the exclusion or removal from any positions of authority or responsibility within casino gaming operations and establishments of any persons known to be so deficient in business probity, ability or experience, either generally or with specific reference to gaming, as to create or enhance the dangers of unsound, unfair or illegal practices,

methods and activities in the conduct of gaming or the carrying on of the business and financial arrangements incident thereto.

Appellants claim that these provisions invade their rights of freedom of association by allowing unlimited inquiry into an applicant's personal and business associations. They contend that the constitution requires the inquiry to be limited to the associations that are relevant to determining the applicant's fitness for the license. *See Shelton v. Tucker*, 364 U.S. at 488. The challenged provisions give no guidance on the types of associations that are relevant to determining an applicant's "reputation for good character, honesty, and integrity." N.J.S.A. 5:12-84(c)[.] . . .

We first address the scope of the power granted to the State by the statutory licensing scheme. The contested statutory provisions give broad authority to the Commission and the Division to investigate and to compel disclosure by applicants about "business, professional and personal associates." N.J.S.A. 5:12-84(c), -89(b)(2). While the current form contains few questions on the applicant's associates, the broad release authorization has the potential for uncovering comprehensive information on the applicant's associates.

Nonetheless, the scope of the investigation must be rationally related to the purposes for which the information is sought, i.e., determining whether the applicant is qualified for a casino employee license. The governmental purpose in investigating an applicant's associates is to exclude from licensing persons with "known criminal records, habits or associations" or who are "deficient in business probity, ability or experience." N.J.S.A. 5:12-1(b)(7). There can be no question that information held by banks, employers, educational institutions and government agencies on an applicant is potentially useful in determining whether she has criminal associations or is deficient in business ability. *Cf. Shelton v. Tucker*, 364 U.S. at 488 (holding that disclosure of every organization teachers had joined in the previous five years was not rationally related to the State's interest in determining their fitness and competency).

We therefore address the extent to which the exercise of state power just described impinges on freedom of association. The crucial factor in the cases invalidating state statutes has been the likelihood that individuals would be deterred from freely associating with others.

One important factor in determining the deterrent effect of compelled disclosure is the presence or absence of confidentiality. [*See*] *Nixon v. Admin. of General Services*, 433 U.S. at 467-68 (upholding a compelled disclosure partly on the grounds that the statute protected against improper public disclosure). The statute in this case contains a confidentiality provision, N.J.S.A. 5:12-74(e). This provision mitigates the likelihood that the compelled disclosure in the release authorization will deter free association. In light of the substantial governmental interest in gathering information on applicants for casino licenses, we hold that the challenged statutory provisions do not violate the constitutional freedom of association.

While we uphold the constitutional validity of this broad release authorization, we note that the statutory provision that allows the Commission to compel the disclosure of information has been narrowly construed to protect the constitutional right of free association. By omitting most of the challenged questions concerning associates on the application form, the Commission acted properly in seeking to accommodate the interests of the State and the affected applicants. While the statute provides that information supplied on the applicant's associates shall be "without limitation," N.J.S.A. 5:12-84(c) & -89(b)(2), the Constitution requires that the Commission's inquiries be rationally related to determining whether the applicant is qualified for a license. If experience in administering the Casino Control Act persuades the Commissioner that certain disclosures are not reasonably necessary to its investigation of applicants, it has an independent obligation to limit the compelled disclosure under the release authorization. The statute narrowly construed in this fashion constitutes the least intrusive means of achieving a compelling governmental purpose. The Commission has already shown a laudable sensitivity to the legitimate interests of applicants. We are confident that it will continue to exercise its plenary regulatory powers with such considerations in mind.

### PRIVILEGE AGAINST SELF-INCRIMINATION

The Fifth Amendment prohibits the government from forcing persons to disclose information that would tend to incriminate them in future proceedings. The privilege against self-incrimination is applicable to states through the due process clause of the Fourteenth Amendment, *Malloy v. Hogan*, 378 U.S. 1 (1964). It is firmly established as part of the common law of New Jersey and has been incorporated into our Rules of Evidence. [citations omitted].

Appellants question whether the Commission may constitutionally ask self-incriminating questions. The Fifth Amendment does not prohibit the state from asking questions. It merely prohibits the state from compelling or coercing people to answer self-incriminating questions. The privilege is personal in the sense that, when questioned by the state, one has the liberty either to waive the privilege by answering the incriminatory question or to assert the privilege and refuse to incriminate oneself. *State v. Toscano*, 100 A.2d 170 (1953).

No one in this case has personally claimed the privilege by refusing to answer a question on the grounds that it might tend to incriminate her. Appellant Stretton filled out the application form without invoking the privilege, thereby waiving it. *State v. Toscano*, 100 A.2d 170. Martin merely claimed that certain questions on the form might tend to incriminate some applicants. She did not invoke the privilege as to herself and in fact testified that an investigation of her background would reveal no criminal activity. There is no basis for a claim that defendants have compelled appellants to incriminate themselves.

Appellants' Fifth Amendment claims are therefore technically premature since none of the appellants personally claimed the privilege in response to the questions asked in the forms. Nor have any sanctions been imposed for invocation of the privilege. *See Gillhaus Beverage v. Lerner*, 397 A.2d 307 (1979). No one has been denied a license on the basis of a personal assertion of the privilege. We expressly decline to decide whether the Commission could constitutionally deny a license application solely on the grounds that an applicant has invoked the Fifth Amendment privilege in response to one or more questions on the form.

Nevertheless, appellants claim that the application forms violate the Fifth Amendment through an implied threat that invocation of the privilege in response to a question will automatically result in denial of a license. Form PHDF-2A states:

> Pursuant to Section 86(b) of the Casino Control Act, failure to answer any question completely and truthfully will result in denial of your license application.

N.J.S.A. 5:12-86 provides in part:

> The commission shall deny a casino license to any applicant who is disqualified on the basis of any of the following criteria:
>
> a. Failure of the applicant to prove by clear and convincing evidence that the applicant is qualified in accordance with the provisions of this act;
>
> b. Failure of the applicant to provide information, documentation and assurances required by the act or requested by the commission, or failure of the applicant to reveal any fact material to qualification . . . .

In *Gillhaus*, the Director of the Division of Alcoholic Beverage Control sent a questionnaire to all licensed solicitors in the wholesale liquor industry for the purpose of investigating illegal trade practices. 397 A.2d 307. A cover letter stated that failure to return the questionnaire with "complete and accurate answers to all questions" might result in license suspension or revocation. The letter further implied that those who did not reveal unlawful activity in which they were engaged but were later found to be guilty of criminal conduct would be given harsher sanctions than those who disclosed the incriminating information to the agency. The Court held that the agency could not constitutionally coerce the solicitors to waive their Fifth Amendment privileges by threatening them with sanctions for asserting those privileges.

This case is distinguishable from *Gillhaus* on a number of grounds. First, the questionnaire in that case had been sent by the government agency to a limited number of known recipients who were directed to fill it out and return it to the agency. The agency would know exactly who filled out the questionnaire and who did not. The respondents in *Gillhaus* had no real choice since failure to return it would single them out for investigation. In this case, casino license applicants ask the government for the application forms and have the choice of filling out the application or declining to do so. After appellant Stretton decided to fill out the application, she was investigated by the Division and then licensed by the Commission. Since Middlesworth has declined to fill out an application form, she has not been subject to an investigation. See N.J.S.A. 5:12-76(b)(1). Thus the extent of coercion by the government is far less in this case.

Second, the letter sent to the licensees in *Gillhaus* threatened not only suspension or revocation of licenses but implied that criminal sanctions would be imposed for failure to confess to self-incriminating information. The relevant portion of PHDF-2A contains no such threat.

Third, the questions asked in *Gillhaus* were distributed as part of an investigation into illegal activity. They were asked for the purpose of determining the extent of unlawful practices in the liquor business in the State. Since the respondents were already licensed, the State would have had the burden of proving that they were involved in illegal activity to revoke their licenses. Thus, threatening to revoke or suspend licenses for failure to answer all questions completely and truthfully was a means of shifting part of this burden from the State to the regulated individuals. Instead of independently acquiring the information on illegal conduct, the agency sought to coerce the licensees to incriminate themselves by their responses.

In this case, on the other hand, the burden of proof is on the applicants to show by clear and convincing evidence that they are qualified for licenses. Although the denial of a license may, in some circumstances, be just as coercive an economic sanction as revocation of a license, the State has not tried to shift the burden of proving lack of illegal conduct on the applicants. The Commission has merely informed applicants that they will not be issued licenses if they fail to furnish the Commission with information necessary to establish their qualifications.

We conclude that the notification in the casino license application form is included for the benefit of applicants and merely informs them that they have the burden of proving that they are qualified for licenses by answering the questions on the form. It does not unconstitutionally coerce applicants to waive their privilege against self-incrimination. . . .

## CONCLUSION

As elaborated in this opinion, we uphold the constitutionality of the challenged sections of the Casino Control Act and the application forms promulgated under N.J.A.C. 19:41-7.14. . . . While the State has broad power under the statute to protect the public through regulation of casino gambling, such power should be used sensitively and wisely.

## *NOTES*

1. In this lengthy opinion, the New Jersey Supreme Court upholds a law with breath-taking investigatory powers and intrusion into an applicant's personal "space." Should an application for a gaming license work such a forfeiture for the right to privacy? Is the scope of the forfeiture of privacy justified by the importance of the regulatory interests at stake?
2. A gaming attorney may need to advise a client about the risks of a background investigation. Because of the scope of the investigatory powers at issue, a suitability determination exposes the applicant, as well as his family and associates, to intense scrutiny. Background investigations by gaming regulators frequently yield information of interest to law enforcement officials. A routine background investigation of a gaming contractor indirectly impacted the 2008 presidential candidacy of former New York Mayor Rudy Giuliani. In 2006, gaming officials moved to revoke the license of a construction company, Interstate Industrial Corporation, to work at casinos in Atlantic City because of what they contended were its ties to organized crime, an accusation that the

company denied. Among other allegations that developed were that Interstate had paid roughly $200,000 for renovations to an apartment owned by Guliani's police commissioner Bernard Kerik, in Riverdale, New York, apparently in exchange from favors from Kerik in helping to obtain licensure in other governmental processes. *See* William K. Rashbaum, *Kerik Described as Close to Deal on Guilty Plea*, N.Y. TIMES, June 29, 2006.

3.  Public corruption problems can arise when public officials are responsible for licensing or approving private development projects in private industry. In the casino industry, projects often need numerous types of government approval to proceed. Contractors for such projects are subject to intense scrutiny. Kerik's wrongdoing in a matter unrelated to gaming came to light because the construction company that he was advising on another matter also was involved in a casino project.

## ARRINGTON v. LOUISIANA STATE RACING COMM'N
### 482 So. 2d 200 (La. App. 1986)

WARD, Judge.

On March 3, 1983 a racehorse belonging to Bobby Arrington, a Louisiana licensed owner and trainer of quarter-horses, finished second and shared part of the purse in the fifth race at Evangeline Downs. A post-race analysis of the horse's urine sample indicated the presence of methamphetamine, a central nervous system stimulant prohibited by the Louisiana Rules of Racing, L.A.C. 11-6:53.14. At Arrington's request, a split sample of the urine was later analyzed and proved positive for methamphetamine.

Before the results of the split sample test were known, the Board of Stewards of Evangeline Downs issued a rule suspending Arrington's racing privileges. Arrington appealed the Stewards' rule to the Louisiana State Racing Commission which suspended Arrington's owner and trainer license for eighteen months and imposed a five-hundred dollar fine. The ruling of the Commission was affirmed by Orleans Parish Civil District Court, but upon Arrington's Motion for a New Trial, it remanded the case to the Commission for the purpose of hearing evidence on the results of the split sample test.

After the rehearing, the Commission affirmed its original ruling but reduced Arrington's suspension from eighteen to twelve months. The Commission relied upon the absolute insurer rule of the Rules of Racing and the Louisiana Statutes. That rule makes the trainer responsible for the condition of his horse, whether or not the act of doping a horse was the act of another and whether or not the trainer was negligent. This ruling was affirmed by the District Court.

Arrington now appeals, raising three issues which all amount to the same argument: the absolute insurer rule violates the Due Process Clauses of the Louisiana and United States Constitutions by creating an irrebuttable presumption.

This same argument was rejected in *Owens v. Louisiana State Racing Commission*, 466 So. 2d 764 (La. App. 1985). The holding of *Owens*, which involved strikingly similar facts, controls the disposition of this appeal. The absolute insurer rule which makes the trainer responsible for the condition of his horses does not violate Due Process because the rule is reasonably related to the government interests sought to be advanced by the rule—to insure fair, safe races, to protect the wagering public and to preserve the public's confidence in the integrity of the racing industry.

We agree with *Owens*; the strong public interest justifies close regulation of horse racing, an industry especially susceptible to fraud and corruption. Furthermore, strict regulation of the trainer by making him an absolute insurer is reasonable because the trainer is the person best able to guarantee the condition of the horses. *See Berry v. Michigan Racing Commission*, 321 N.W.2d 880 (Mich. App. 1982). "The insurer rule provides maximum protection against illegal drugging; arguably it is the only practical means of reducing such corrupt practices. . . . The insurer rule is a reasonable alternative to either leaving [the public and State] interests unprotected or forbidding legalized racing." (citations omitted).

Furthermore, hearings and rulings of the Racing Commission are not to be equated with criminal trials. The Commission is governed by the Administrative Procedure Act and functions as a civil administrative body, not as a Trial Court in a criminal case. *Pullin v. Louisiana State Racing Commission*, 477 So. 2d 683 (La. 1985). One appearing before the Commission is not entitled to every constitutional right afforded defendants in criminal trials. Hence, it is not necessary to show either knowledge or intent, or even negligence of the trainer.

Moreover, a trainer voluntarily applies for a license, and upon approval by the Commission, he subjects himself to certain terms and conditions such as the absolute insurer rule which might be inappropriate in other situations. *Id.* at 686-87. The relationship between the Commission and trainers, owners, jockeys and others is analogous to a contractual commitment with each party agreeing not to race a horse that has been stimulated by drugs, no matter who administers the drugs. La.R.S. 4:150(A) and (B). If a horse races when stimulated by drugs, the responsible party has breached his commitment, both to others in the sport and to the public that horse racing will be fair, safe and deserving of public confidence. AFFIRMED.

BARRY, Justice, dissenting (BYRNES, J., joins the dissent).

The "absolute insurer rule" of La.R.S. 4:150(A) and LAC 11-6:53.18 violates the due process clause of both the state and federal constitutions in two respects: they create an irrebuttable presumption of guilt and fail to provide standards or impose a duty which can be breached.

LAC 11-6:53.18 provides:

> The trainer and/or assistant trainer shall be responsible for and be the absolute insurer of the condition of the horses he enters regardless of acts of third parties. Trainers and/or assistant trainers are presumed to know the rules of the Commission.

La.R.S. 4:150(A) provides:

> The granting of a license to a trainer shall make him responsible for and be the absolute insurer of the condition of the horses he enters regardless of the acts of third parties.

In striking down a similar statute, the Illinois Supreme Court reasoned:

> In the case at bar there is not even an evidentiary presumption. The licensee is penalized without showing any act or neglect on his part whatsoever. There is no proof that he even knew of the doping of his horse, much less that he actively participated in it. He loses his license solely because of someone else's conduct, of which he had no personal knowledge. It is a fundamental principle of Anglo-Saxon justice that responsibility is personal and that penalties may not be inflicted on one person because of another's acts. *Brennan v. Illinois Racing Board*, 42 247 N.E.2d 881, 883 (Ill. 1969).

The absolute insurer rule creates an irrebuttable presumption of guilt which deprives the trainer of his right to offer evidence to prove his innocence. It is no defense that a trainer exercised due care or that "doping" occurred under circumstances over which he had no control. A statute that does not permit such legitimate defenses fundamentally violates due process.

Unlike *Briley v. Louisiana State Racing Commission*, 410 So. 2d 802 (La. App. 1982), writ denied, 414 So. 2d 375 (La. 1982) and *Owens v. Louisiana State Racing Commission*, 466 So. 2d 764 (La. App. 1985), writ denied, 468 So. 2d 576 (La. 1985), I am not convinced that the absolute insurer rule has a rational basis and is reasonably related to the governmental interest sought to be advanced.

The reason behind the statute and rule is to protect the public from fraud and deceit by inducing the trainer to take the utmost precautions against tampering with a horse. Yet this is no more than he would do under penalty provisions based on traditional principles of fault, since the consequences of failing to take precautions would be the same. The only applications of the statute which would not be equally covered by one based on fault would be situations which the trainer could not have prevented anyway. As a practical matter, numerous violations have been before this court and I find no proof that a penalty-without-fault statute reduces the number of alleged offenses.

Making the trainer an absolute insurer at peril of losing his license regardless of his innocence is arbitrary and unreasonable. *Brennan v. Illinois Racing Board, supra.* I'm certainly aware that the "nature" of horse racing dictates close scrutiny and supervision, but that necessity must stop short of violating basic constitutional rights.

La.R.S. 4:150(A) and LAC 11-6:53.18 also fail to meet due process requirements because they do not provide any standard or impose any duty which can be breached. Neither provision states what condition the trainer insures, or the consequences to the trainer if the unstated condition is or is not present.

A similar rule was struck down by the Idaho Supreme Court in *Schvaneveldt v. Idaho State Horse Racing Commission*, 578 P.2d 673 (Idaho 1978). In that case the court noted:

> Here, the defect lies in Rule 4.36 itself. Rule 4.36 states: "THE TRAINER SHALL BE RESPONSIBLE FOR AND BE THE ABSOLUTE INSURER OF THE CONDITION OF THE HORSES HE ENTERS REGARDLESS OF THE ACTS OF THIRD PARTIES." The rule provides that the trainer is the insurer of the horse's condition, but does not state (1) what condition the trainer insures; or (2) the consequences to the trainer if the unstated condition is or is not present. In short, Rule 4.36 does not establish any standards or impose any duty which can be violated.

Violation of a rule means the transgression of or noncompliance with some duty, obligation or standard. Inasmuch as Rule 4.36 fixes no standards, it cannot be violated and therefore it alone cannot serve as a basis for suspending the licenses of these trainers pursuant to I.C. §54-2509 or Rules 16.03 and 16.06. Louisiana horse racing has another safeguard which is constitutional and adequate to police the "sport". LAC 11-6:53.15 provides:

> When a report is received from the State chemist reflecting in his expert opinion that the chemical analysis of blood, saliva, urine, or other samples taken from a horse indicate[s] the presence of a forbidden narcotic, stimulant, depressant, or analgesic, local anesthetic or drugs of any description, not permitted by LAC 11-6:54, this shall be taken as

prima facie evidence that such has been administered to the horse. Such shall also be taken as prima facie evidence that the owner, and/or trainer, and/or groom has been negligent in handling of the horse.

The above rule creates a presumption of guilt, but a prima facie showing of negligence can be rebutted. The absolute insurer rule is not only unconstitutionally repugnant, it is unnecessary.

## PIGEONS' ROOST, INC. v. COMMONWEALTH
### 10 S.W.3d 133 (Ky. App. 1999)

COMBS, Judge.

Pigeons' Roost, Inc., appeals from an order of the Franklin Circuit Court affirming the Justice Cabinet's revocation of its charitable gaming license following the appellant's violation of KRS 238.550(4). The appellant does not deny that it violated the provisions of KRS 238.550(4), but it maintains that the revocation of its license is unconstitutional.

The appellant, a non-profit corporation, applied for and was first issued a charitable gaming license in 1994. At issue in this case is the appellant's operation of bingo games and sale of "pull-tabs" under a license valid from April 1, 1996, to May 1, 1997. During a standard review of the appellant's operations for the third and fourth quarters of 1996, the Justice Cabinet's Division of Charitable Gaming ("the Division") discovered that the charity had violated the provisions of KRS 238.550(4), the so-called "40% rule." At that time, KRS 238.550(4) required that licensees retain at least forty (40) percent of adjusted gross receipts for a rolling two-quarter period. Based upon records supplied by Pigeons' Roost, the Division noticed that the charity had failed to retain the required 40% of adjusted gross receipts from charitable gaming operations. In fact, Pigeons' Roost had retained no receipts from its operations in the third and fourth quarters. As a result, [gaming regulators revoked Pigeon's Roost's gaming license and the trial court upheld the revocation.]

On appeal, Pigeons' Roost argues that the revocation of its license violated substantive due process rights under the Fourteenth Amendment to the United States Constitution and Sections 2 and 226 of the Kentucky Constitution. The appellant contends that the provisions of KRS 238.550(4) are arbitrary and unreasonable. It emphasizes that other statutes included in the Charitable Gaming Act sufficiently protect the Commonwealth and charitable gaming as intended by the General Assembly. We conclude that the statutory provision under attack in this case is not unconstitutional.

In response to a 1992 amendment of the Kentucky Constitution, the General Assembly passed the Charitable Gaming Act in 1994. The Act set forth a comprehensive scheme for the conduct, oversight, and regulation of charitable gaming. As a part of the comprehensive scheme, KRS 238.550, entitled "Standards for management and accounting of funds—Quarterly reports," was enacted. As a result of amendments effective April 10, 1996, KRS 238.550(4) provided as follows:

> At least forty percent (40%) of the adjusted gross receipts resulting from the conduct of charitable gaming during each two (2) consecutive calendar quarters shall be retained by the charitable organization and used exclusively for purposes consistent with the charitable, religious, educational, literary, civic, fraternal, or patriotic functions or objectives for which the licensed charitable organization received and maintains federal tax-exempt status. . . . No net receipts shall inure to the private benefit or financial gain any individual.

Section 2 of the Kentucky Constitution prohibits the arbitrary exercise of power by state government.[3] In order to pass constitutional muster, a statute must be rationally related to a legitimate state objective. *Lost Mountain Mining v. Fields*, Ky. App., 918 S.W.2d 232 (1996). The same standard applies for alleged due process violations of the Fourteenth Amendment to the United States Constitution. "Substantive due process requires that a statute have a rational relationship to a legitimate legislative goal." *Kentucky Div., Horsemen's Benevolent & Protective Ass'n. Inc. v. Turfway Park Racing Ass'n Inc.*, 832 F. Supp. 1097, 1104 (E.D. Ky. 1993), *reversed on other grounds*, 20 F.3d 1406 (6th Cir.1994).

As was noted in *Louisville Atlantis*,

> [c]haritable gaming is an exception to the constitutional prohibition against lotteries and gift enterprises. Since the state may prohibit gambling entirely, it may clearly put limits on charitable gaming which may not be put on other legitimate enterprises. Keeping charitable gaming from becoming commercial, preventing participation by criminals, and preventing the diversion of funds from legitimate charitable purposes are all legitimate state objectives.

We find no merit in the appellant's constitutional challenge to KRS 238.550(4). The Commonwealth has an express and legitimate

---

3. Section 2 provides that "[a]bsolute and arbitrary power over the lives, liberty and property of freemen exists nowhere in a republic, not even in the largest majority."

interest in insuring that gaming receipts are used for solely charitable purposes and that they are not unwisely or improperly diverted. The requirement that a significant portion of adjusted gross gaming receipts be retained and accounted for by the charity is rationally related to this state objective. The requirement to retain 40% of adjusted gross receipts is not clearly unreasonable.

The appellant's contentions that the "40% rule" is "at war with good common sense"; that state interests are adequately safeguarded by other statutory provisions; and that the statutory requirement fails to provide for those operations which experience a downturn in gross receipts are not issues of judicial but of legislative concern. Again, we find that the statutory requirement is rationally related to the legitimate state interest of insuring that funds raised by charitable gaming actually benefit charitable works. As a result, we conclude that the challenged provision is, in fact, constitutional. AFFIRMED.

### NOTES

1.  What are the effects of the "40%" rule on the "business" of the enterprise? Why might a charity be opposed to such a standard?
2.  On what basis does the court uphold the law? Has the rights/privileges distinction reared its head again?

## B.  PRACTICAL ISSUES IN GAMING LICENSURE

### SIMMS v. NAPOLITANO
### 73 P.3d 631 (Az. App. 2003)

GEMMILL, Judge.

The Governor of Arizona and the Director of the Department of Gaming (collectively the "State") appeal a trial court ruling prohibiting the Arizona Department of Gaming ("Department") from denying an applicant's request to withdraw his application for certification to provide gaming services. Because we conclude that the Department has the implied authority to deny such requests, we reverse.

Jeremy Simms, as a part owner of T.P. Racing, L.L.L.P., submitted an application for certification to the Arizona Department of Gaming to provide off-track betting services to several tribal gaming casinos. After several months of investigation, the Department advised Simms through a "Notice of Intent to Deny State Certification" ("Notice") that it intended to deny the application. The Notice summarized the investigation and expressed the Department's concern that Simms had been involved in questionable business practices, illegal activities, and financial dealings with a person purportedly involved in organized crime. The Notice also informed Simms that he had thirty days to appeal or it would become a "Final Order of the Department."

Simms appealed the Notice, and an administrative hearing was scheduled. Before the hearing occurred, Simms filed in superior court a complaint for special action and a motion for a preliminary injunction. He sought to prevent the Department from denying the license because it lacked authority to do so. The complaint also alleged that the Department "declined to discontinue [its] efforts to deny Simms' license application, even after he has offered to withdraw it." The State filed several motions to dismiss, and the trial court set a hearing.

> Shortly thereafter, the State offered to allow the withdrawal if Simms would agree not to re-apply. No such agreement was reached, however. . . . Simms argued that the Department exceeded its statutory authority over applicants because, in effect, his withdrawal made him a non-applicant and therefore the State had no power to proceed further.

The trial court concluded that the Department did not have the power to deny Simms' request to withdraw his application. The court reasoned that the Department's power derived from the gaming compact rather than from the State's exercise of police power and that the Department, therefore, did not have inherent power to deny such a request. The court commented that the Department's purpose was not only to deny the application but also to impose punitive sanctions that would prevent Simms from applying in Arizona or any other state.

The State's motion for new trial was denied and the trial court entered a final order enjoining the Department from denying or taking any further action on Simms' application.

## DISCUSSION

On appeal, the State reasserts that the Department's right to deny a request to withdraw an application springs from the State's police power, and specifically from the legislative authorization for the Department to certify gaming employees in order to ensure the exclusion of unsuitable persons from Indian gaming. The Department has, according to the State, an implied discretionary right to prevent withdrawal of an application as part of this mission. The State also urges that Simms improperly failed to exhaust all of his administrative remedies prior to seeking judicial relief. Simms, however, maintains that the Department exceeded its authority in continuing to deny the license application of a non-applicant and that the issue of exhausting administrative remedies was waived because it was not raised in the trial court.

To resolve this dispute, we must interpret the scope of the Department's authority under the applicable statutes.

In 1988, Congress enacted the Indian Gaming Regulatory Act ("IGRA"). One of its stated purposes is "to provide a statutory basis for the regulation of gaming by an Indian tribe adequate to shield it from organized crime and other corrupting influences." 25 U.S.C. §2702(2) (2000). Under the IGRA, Indian tribes may conduct certain types of gaming pursuant to a tribal-state compact. The IGRA allows tribes to consent, through a tribal-state compact, to an extension of a state's jurisdiction and laws to gaming activities conducted on tribal lands. Congress has authorized the states to exercise their police power through tribal-state compacts to keep gaming free from criminal elements and to protect the gaming public, while preserving tribal sovereignty.

The State of Arizona, as authorized by the IGRA, has promulgated statutes for regulating Indian gaming and has entered into numerous tribal-state compacts. See Ariz. Rev. Stat. ("A.R.S.") §5-601(D) (Supp. 2000). The statutes, first enacted in 1992, give the Department authority to certify applicants who want to provide gaming services to tribal casinos under the tribal-state compacts.

A foundational issue in this case is whether the Department's powers derive from the negotiated compact or from the State's police power. The trial court agreed with Simms that the Department's powers derived primarily from contractual rights negotiated in the gaming compacts, rather than the State's exercise of police power. See A.R.S. §5-601(D) ("The department of gaming is authorized to carry out the duties and responsibilities of the state gaming agency in compacts executed by the state and Indian tribes . . . ."). The trial court further concluded that these contractual rights did not give the Department any implied or inherent authority to deny a request to withdraw a licence application. Although we acknowledge the logic of such arguments, we disagree and conclude that the Department's authority derives from the State's police power.

By enacting the IGRA, Congress gave the States—with federal oversight, see 25 U.S.C. §2702(3) (2000), and tribal permission—the ability to exercise jurisdiction over gaming activities occurring on tribal lands. Congress intended to allow state regulation while preserving tribal sovereignty. See 25 U.S.C. §§2701, 2702 (2000). And the IGRA expressly authorizes states to engage in licensing under provisions negotiated in the compacts. 25 U.S.C. 2710(d)(3)(C)(i) (2000). Congress decided that the States should administer this regulatory function, rather than have a federal licensing agency. Although the tribal-state compact is the mechanism through which regulation by the State is possible, we conclude that the regulating activities constitute an exercise of state police power and not merely an exercise of a contractual right. *See Dano v. Collins*, 802 P.2d 1021, 1022 (Ariz. App. 1990) ("The police power is an attribute of state sovereignty, and, within the limitation of state and federal constitutions, the state may, in its exercise, enact laws for the promotion of public safety, health, morals, and for the public welfare.").

Having concluded that the Department is exercising its police power when administering the licensing of gaming activities, we turn to whether the Department exceeded its authority by denying Simms' request to withdraw the application for certification. We conclude that the Department did not exceed its authority.

The Department is a creature of statute and like other state agencies, is "created and maintained for the purpose of administering certain of the State's sovereign powers, and must proceed and act according to legislative authority as expressed or necessarily implied." *Allen v. Indus. Comm'n of Ariz.*, 733 P.2d 290, 296 (Ariz. 1987).

Building on the foundation provided by the IGRA, Arizona's statutes give the Department express authority to certify gaming providers with the goal of excluding unsuitable individuals from Indian gaming. See A.R.S. §5-602(A) (Supp. 2000). The Department is to conduct its duties in a manner "consistent with this state's desire to have extensive, thorough and fair regulation of Indian gaming." A.R.S. §5-602(B) (Supp. 2000). Consistent with this mandate, the Department has been given specific authority to receive, for example, criminal background information on all applicants. A.R.S. §5-602(D) (Supp. 2000). The Department, however, is given discretion in determining how it will certify applicants. The statutes, consequently, confer broad authority on the Department to accomplish its statutory goals, and we conclude that the power to deny withdrawal of an application may fairly be implied from the governing statutes. This power is consistent with the overall regulatory aims of the IGRA and the Arizona statutes.

Simms argues that the Department's power to deny a withdrawal is found nowhere in the statutes because after a person withdraws the application, he or she is no longer an "applicant." Simms also points out that the State has met its objective of deterring the unsuitable individual when the application is withdrawn. It is true that an applicant has been temporarily deterred when an application is withdrawn. The State has an interest, however, in proceeding to a final denial in many cases because of the reciprocal information exchange conducted with tribal and other state gaming authorities. For example, under the tribal-state compact between the Fort McDowell Mohave-Apache Indian Community and the State of Arizona, the Department is required to forward any certification denials to the tribal gaming authorities. States also can exchange such information by agreement to hinder unsuitable applicants from shopping around until perchance they slip through the screening process in this or some other jurisdiction. And the Department is authorized under tribal-state compacts to deny certification if it discovers that an applicant has had a license revoked or denied by any state or tribe in the United States. These provisions illustrate the importance of the Department proceeding to a final decision and having a formal denial on record. Allowing an applicant to avoid scrutiny of his or her background in other jurisdictions by simply withdrawing an application in this jurisdiction does not promote the federal policy of the IGRA to prevent corrupting influences in Indian gaming generally or the specific aims of the Arizona statutes to have thorough and fair regulation of gaming and to ward off unsuitable individuals. See A.R.S. §5-602(A), (B) (Supp. 2000).

In reaching our decision, we find *Perry v. Medical Practice Board*, 737 A.2d 900, 904 (Vt. 1999), instructive. The plaintiff in *Perry* applied to the Vermont medical board for a license. He later requested leave to withdraw his application because he was moving out of state. His request was denied. The board then continued its investigation and uncovered some misrepresentations on the plaintiff's application. The plaintiff appealed the board's decision denying his request to withdraw. The Vermont Supreme Court observed that "the Board, as an administrative body, has only such powers as are expressly conferred upon it by the Legislature, together with such incidental powers expressly granted or necessarily implied as are necessary to the full exercise of those granted." The court then found that the board's statutory authority to issue or deny the medical license carried with it the implied discretionary authority to deny a request to withdraw the application.

The court in *Perry* reasoned that a licensee should not be allowed to escape discipline by resigning or allowing the license to expire. Otherwise, the licensee could apply for admission in another jurisdiction, or subsequently reapply in the same jurisdiction, and maintain that he or she has never been disciplined for professional misconduct. This would patently defeat the underlying purposes of the regulatory scheme to protect the public and maintain the integrity of the profession.

The court noted that the underlying purpose of the regulations in *Perry* was for the protection of the public. Moreover, the court reasoned that the regulatory scheme also gave rise to reciprocal duties owed to other licensing jurisdictions in reporting unsuitable applicants. We believe that the same analysis and reasoning is applicable to demonstrate the Department's authority to deny Simms' attempted withdrawal of his application.

Although we recognize that the public safety concerns involved in regulating the medical profession differ from concerns regarding gambling, we also recognize that gambling attracts corruption and therefore requires a strong regulatory presence. *See Chance Mgmt., Inc. v. South Dakota*, 97 F.3d 1107, 1115 (8th Cir. 1996) (Gambling "is generally understood to have a greater tendency to attract criminal infiltration than most other types of business enterprises."). Accordingly, we find *Perry* persuasive in its determination of implied powers and its recognition of reciprocal duties owed to other jurisdictions. Similarly, the Department's express powers coupled with the legislative mandate to protect the public support the conclusion that the Department can refuse to allow an applicant to withdraw his license application, especially when, as here, substantial investigation has already occurred and the proverbial handwriting is on the wall indicating a probable denial.

Our conclusion is further supported by the following features in this case. First, Simms had notice that once he submitted his application, it could be withdrawn only with the Department's permission. In the instructions on page one of the application form, Simms was advised: "You are further advised that an application . . . may not be withdrawn without the permission of the Department of Gaming." Simms' initials appear nearby on the form, indicating that he had read and understood the instructions. Simms argues that this provision is not backed by legal authority but is instead akin to an adhesive contract term. Because we have determined that the Department has the authority to deny withdrawal of an application, however, this provision is an appropriate notification to applicants that the application may not be withdrawn without the Department's permission.

Additionally, the timing of Simms' attempted withdrawal was such that the Department had already conducted a full investigation, expending time and resources, in order to pursue its legislative mandate. Although we are aware that an applicant must pay a substantial fee for the Department's investigation, we are confident that the extensive investigation conducted by the Department Simms' application represented an investment of administrative resources. Allowing an applicant to withdraw his application may create administrative inefficiencies that hinder the Department's effectiveness in meeting its statutory aims and invites the very kind of "license-hopping" that is contrary to the legislative intent and authorization. This court has previously interpreted contracting statutes to enable the Registrar of Contractors to prevent license-hopping by unscrupulous individuals in the contracting business. *See Better Homes Constr. Inc.*, 53 P.3d at 1144. We similarly conclude here that the Department has the power to prevent the withdrawal of an application for gaming certification, when the Department determines in its discretion that the protection of the public is advanced by completing the certification process. [REVERSED AND REMANDED]

### *NOTES*

1.  Should filing a gaming license application be, in essence, an irrevocable act? Should a person be able to withdraw an application without prejudice?
2.  Simms had a long-running dispute with the Arizona gaming authorities. In a memorandum opinion later issued by the Arizona Court of Appeals in *TP Racing, LLLP v. Arizona Department of Gaming,* the court cited "corrupt dealings" by Simms with former California State Senator Alan Robbins and former California Coastal Commissioner Mark Nathanson in the late 1980s. The first instance involved Simms paying Nathanson, at Robbins' suggestion, $10,000 for Nathanson's assistance in achieving a favorable result for Simms in a consumer fraud investigation conducted by the California Attorney General into Simms' auto dealership. The court also cited a $100,000 loan to Nathanson to assist in getting approval from the Coastal Commission for construction of a lap pool at Simms' residence and to defeat a commercial real estate development that would be a potential competitor of Simms. According to the court, Simms was granted immunity in a federal criminal investigation into Nathanson and Robbins in which he admitted to the grand jury that the $100,000 payment was a bribe. The court also cited the participation by Simms in the extortion of a California real estate developer, for the payment of

$250,000 to Nathanson, at Robbins' request, for assistance in defeating the construction of a project that would threaten the value of another development.

## GAGE v. MISSOURI GAMING COMMISSION
### 200 S.W.3d 62 (Mo. App. 2006).

Lisa White HARDWICK, Judge.

Treva Gage and Shari Douglas appeal from the final order of the Missouri Gaming Commission ("Commission"), which revoked their occupational gaming licenses and resulted in the termination of their employment at a casino. Gage and Douglas were employed by the Isle of Capri Casino ("Casino"), a licensed gambling boat located in Boonville, Missouri. Gage was the Casino's manager of management information systems (MIS) and held a "Level I Gaming License." Douglas was employed as the senior MIS support specialist and held a "Level II Gaming License." Both employees had access to the Casino's information technology (IT) room, where computer hardware was located and a surveillance camera recorded the ingress and egress of all persons.

On July 28, 2003, a third employee, Denise Wilson, covered the lens of the surveillance camera in the IT room, purportedly as a prank to see how long it would take the Casino security officers to notice it. Douglas was present when the camera was covered. The camera remained covered for thirty-three minutes. That same day, Douglas telephoned Gage regarding the camera incident and asked what she should do if questioned by security officers. Gage told Douglas to tell security that Gage had been changing her clothes in the IT Room and forgot to uncover the camera when she finished. The purpose of the fabricated story was to protect Douglas from losing her job.

The Casino's surveillance manager and a Missouri Highway Patrol officer began investigating the camera incident on July 29, 2003. Douglas told the investigators that Gage had been changing clothes in the IT room and forgot to uncover the camera. Gage confirmed the story. Four days later, both women admitted the fabrication and told the investigators about the prank.

Following the investigation, the Missouri Gaming Commission issued preliminary disciplinary orders, notifying Gage and Douglas that their gaming licenses were subject to revocation. The orders alleged that the licensees had violated the Missouri gaming laws, Sections 313.800 to 313.850, RSMO 2000, and related regulations by: (1) knowingly making false statements to Commission agents concerning the camera incident; and (2) failing to prevent the incident from occurring or promptly notifying the Commission that such violations had occurred. [After a hearing, the licenses of Gage and Douglas were revoked and Gage and Douglas appealed.]

Gage and Douglas contend the Commission erred in revoking their gaming licenses because the preliminary disciplinary order provided inadequate notice of the specific administrative charges and thereby deprived the licensees of due process and a fair hearing. Similarly, the licensees argue in Point II that the notice was improper because the final revocation decision was based on statutory violations that were not previously alleged. In the preliminary disciplinary order, the Commission notified Gage and Douglas that their licenses were subject to revocation based on an incident in which a surveillance camera in the Casino's IT room was improperly covered with a piece of white paper. The order alleged that both licensees had engaged in the following misconduct:

> During an investigation of this incident, [Gage and Douglas] knowingly made false statements of material fact to Commission agents concerning the incident. [Gage and Douglas] failed to prevent the incident from occurring or promptly notify the Commission that a violation of law or regulations had been committed.

The preliminary order further notified the licensees that their conduct violated Section 313.830.4(15) FN2 and Section 313.812.14(1) of the gaming laws, and 11 CSR 45-4.260(4)(E) and (Q) and 11 CSR 45-10.030 of the gaming regulations. Those laws and regulations allow the revocation of an occupational license if the licensee:

> (1) "[k]nowingly makes a false statement of any material fact to the commission, its agents or employees." Section 313.830.4(15);

> (2) acts in a manner "injurious to the public health, safety, morals, good order and general welfare of the people of the state of Missouri, or that would discredit or tend to discredit the Missouri gaming industry[,]" including failure to comply with the rules and regulations of the Commission or any federal, state, or local laws or regulations or dishonesty in the performance of duties under the Excursion Gaming Boat Regulations. Section 313.812.14(1) and (9); 11 CSR 45-4.260(4)(E) and (Q).

> (3) fails to report violations of law, minimum internal control standards or commission rules; fails to prevent improper or unlawful conduct upon the licensed premises; or fails to report events on the premises they knew or should have known to be illegal. 11 CSR 45-10.030.

The preliminary order did not provide a full text recitation of these laws and regulations. Citing *McCall v. Goldbaum*, 863 S.W.2d 640, 642-43 (Mo. App. 1993), Gage and Douglas contend the preliminary disciplinary order did not satisfy due process notice requirements because it merely summarized the alleged facts and provided abstract citations to statutes and administrative regulations. The licensees assert the notice must "specify" the charge to avoid confusion over how their conduct might have violated the law. *Brixey v. Personnel Advisory Bd.*, 607 S.W.2d 825, 827 (Mo. App. 1980) [.]

In *Brixey*, the court reversed the termination of an employee where the notice of dismissal did not provide specific incidents of misconduct and did not set forth all of the grounds for termination that were ultimately found after a hearing by the Personnel Advisory Board. In *McCall*, the dismissal letter accused an employee of three work-related offenses, only one of which was punishable by dismissal. *McCall*, 863 S.W.2d 640. The Personnel Advisory Board upheld the dismissal based on an infraction that was not referenced in the dismissal letter. The court found *McCall* had not received adequate notice of the dismissal grounds and reversed the Board's decision. In both of these cases, the employee dismissals were approved by the administrative appeal agency on grounds that were not articulated in the preliminary disciplinary notice. The judicial reversals were based on the fact that the employees were essentially found guilty of offenses for which they had never been charged.

Gage and Douglas have failed to show that similar circumstances exist in this case. The preliminary disciplinary order provided detailed factual allegations that the licensees made material false statements during the investigation of the camera incident and failed to prevent the incident from occurring or promptly report it. The order listed specific statutes and regulations that were violated by this misconduct. Following the administrative hearing, the Commission issued a final order that imposed disciplinary action for the same misconduct and violations referenced in the preliminary order. The final order stated:

> [Gage and Douglas] admitted to the agreed-upon-fabrication of a story to hide the truth about disabling the camera . . . [Gage and Douglas] violated the good order of the gaming industry by providing false information to the Commission's investigator. [Gage and Douglas] did not take the responsibility required of a holder of an occupational license to comply with the law. Such acts of dishonesty discredit the gaming industry. [Gage and Douglas] failed to carry their burden to show by clear and convincing evidence that their acts should preclude the Commission from revoking their licenses.

Furthermore, working in a highly regulated industry, [Gage and Douglas] knew or should have known that surveillance cameras serve a very important function. Covering and disabling a surveillance camera provides reasonable grounds to believe that a violation of law may have occurred . . . [Gage and Douglas'] failure to promptly report to the Commission this event of covering a surveillance camera violates the law.

These were the only two violations cited in the final order. Each violation independently provided legal grounds for the revocation. Although the order references other misconduct that could have been charged, such as tampering with a surveillance camera, none of that conduct was cited as grounds for the revocation decision. . . . No due process violation occurred, as the licensees had sufficient notice to prepare a defense to the specific charges of misconduct. Points I and II are denied.

Gage and Douglas [also] contend the Commission lacked statutory authority to regulate matters regarding the Casino's surveillance camera; therefore, they assert the Commission had no jurisdiction to revoke their occupational gaming licenses for camera-related misconduct.

Section 313.805 grants the Commission full supervisory jurisdiction over "all gambling operations" authorized by Missouri law. Gage and Douglas argue that this statutory authority recognizes a distinction between regulated gaming issues and a casino's internal business issues. They further contend that the camera incident in the IT room occurred outside the scope of the gambling operations at the Isle of Capri Casino and, therefore, outside the regulatory sphere of the Commission. For example, they point out that none of the gaming statutes or regulations required the Casino to maintain a surveillance camera in the IT room. Accordingly, the licensees claim that any misconduct related to the camera was an internal business matter between the Casino and its employees, not a licensing issue for the Commission.

We reject this claim because, regardless of whether the Commission had authority to regulate the IT room surveillance camera, it clearly had jurisdiction over the conduct of Gage and Douglas as occupational licensees. Section 313.812.14 provides in relevant part:

A holder of any [gaming] license shall be subject to imposition of penalties, suspension or revocation of such license . . . for any act or failure to act . . . that is injurious to the public health, safety, morals, good order and general welfare of the people of the state of Missouri, or that would discredit or tend to discredit the Missouri gaming industry or the state of Missouri unless the licensee proves by clear and convincing evidence that it is not guilty of such action. The Commission shall take appropriate action against any licensee who violates the law or the rules or regulations of the Commission.

The Commission's disciplinary authority extends to misconduct outside the workplace under certain circumstances, but it specifically applies when a licensee makes false statements to the Commission or its agents. Thus, no matter where the false statements were made or what aspects of the Casino business they related to, the Commission had jurisdiction to revoke the licenses held by Gage and Douglas.

## NOTES

The revocation of a gaming license can have enormous ramifications for future employment in the gaming industry. Any future license application that Gage and Douglas complete will ask whether they have ever applied for, been denied, or lost through revocation a license to work in a gaming facility. For a copy of the application form required of all persons wishing to work in a gaming establishment in Nevada, *see* http://gaming.nv.gov/forms/frm107.pdf. Disclosure of the incident discussed in this case may well prevent either of them from ever working in this industry again. Why might this be? If you were the gaming regulator reviewing a future application from such applicants, what would guide your decision-making process? What pressures would you feel as you considered whether to grant a license? Consider this question in light of the Nevada criteria described below. Consider this question also in light of the *Eicher v. Louisiana State Police*, which follows.

## NEVADA GAMING COMMISSION CRITERIA FOR DENIAL OF CASINO EMPLOYEE LICENSE

**http://gaming.nv.gov/documents/pdf/ger_denial_criteria.pdf**

**Regulation 5.104 Investigation; uniform criteria for objection; objection.**

1. Upon receipt of an application for registration, the board shall review it for completeness.
2. Unless the board, after reviewing an application for registration, suspends the temporary registration of the applicant pursuant to Regulation 5.103, it shall conduct an investigation of the applicant to determine whether he is eligible to be or continue to be registered as a gaming employee.

3.  The board may object to the registration of an applicant within 120 days after receipt of a complete application for registration for any cause deemed reasonable, including any of the specific grounds cited at NRS 463.335(13).

> [Note: Section 335(13) generally provides as follows:
>
> The Board may suspend or object to the registration of an applicant as a gaming employee for any cause deemed reasonable by the Board. The Board may object to or suspend the registration if the applicant has:
>
> (a) Failed to disclose or misstated information or otherwise attempted to mislead the Board with respect to any material fact contained in the application for registration as a gaming employee;
>
> (b) Knowingly failed to comply with the provisions of this chapter or chapter 463B, 464 or 465 of NRS or the regulations of the Commission at a place of previous employment;
>
> (c) Committed, attempted or conspired to commit any crime of moral turpitude, embezzlement or larceny or any violation of any law pertaining to gaming, or any crime which is inimical to the declared policy of this State concerning gaming;
>
> (d) Committed, attempted or conspired to commit a crime which is a felony or gross misdemeanor in this State or an offense in another state or jurisdiction which would be a felony or gross misdemeanor if committed in this State and which relates to the applicant's suitability or qualifications to work as a gaming employee;
>
> (e) Been identified in the published reports of any federal or state legislative or executive body as being a member or associate of organized crime, or as being of notorious and unsavory reputation;
>
> (f) Been placed and remains in the constructive custody of any federal, state or municipal law enforcement authority; or
>
> (g) Had registration as a gaming employee revoked or committed any act which is a ground for the revocation of registration as a gaming employee or would have been a ground for revoking registration as a gaming employee if the applicant had then been registered as a gaming employee.]

4.  An objection to the registration of an applicant shall be entered if the applicant:
    (a) Has committed, attempted or conspired to commit any offense in violation of NRS 465.070 to 465.085, inclusive. [Note: These sections describe gambling offenses, such as misrepresenting the outcome of a game, using counterfeit gaming equipment, etc.]

(b) Has committed, attempted or conspired to commit any offense, within the past 10 years, involving or related to gambling, which is a felony in this state or, if committed in another state, would be a felony in this state.

(c) Has committed, attempted or conspired to commit any offense involving larceny related offenses committed against a gaming establishment within the past 10 years.

5. If the board objects to the registration of an applicant pursuant to this regulation, the board shall notify:

(a) The applicant pursuant to the notice requirement prescribed in NRS 463.335(11) and the right to apply for a hearing pursuant to NRS 463.335(12); and

(b) The applicant's place of employment.

The failure of an applicant to seek review of a determination that he is not eligible for registration as a gaming employee shall be deemed to be an admission that the objection is well founded and such failure precludes administrative or judicial review.

6. If the board does not object to the registration of an applicant pursuant to this regulation, the applicant shall be deemed registered as a gaming employee and is eligible for employment with any non-restricted licensee in the state until such registration expires as prescribed in NRS 463.335(8), is suspended pursuant to NRS 463.3352 or 463.336, or is revoked pursuant to NRS 463.337.

## EICHER v. LOUISIANA STATE POLICE, RIVERBOAT GAMING ENFORCEMENT DIVISION

### 710 So. 2d 799 (La. Ct. App. 1st Cir. 1998)

Parro, J.

The Louisiana State Police, Riverboat Gaming Enforcement Division ("the Division") revoked a temporary permit it had granted to Meredith Eicher ("Ms. Eicher") which allowed her to work as a gaming employee at a riverboat casino. She appealed the revocation through an administrative process that upheld the decision[, but a court] ordered the Division to reinstate Ms. Eicher's permit. The Division appeals this judgment.

I

The facts of this matter are uncontested. In May 1990, in connection with the highly publicized failure of Champion Insurance Company, Ms. Eicher pled guilty to two counts of aiding and abetting mail fraud, a federal felony offense. She was sentenced to pay a fine of $5000, to serve five months imprisonment, and upon release, to be on supervised probation for two years. In May 1991, based on the same occurrences which led to her conviction on the federal charges, she pled guilty in state court to two counts of accessory after the fact to forgery. She was sentenced to one year of imprisonment at hard labor, which was suspended, and she was placed on probation, to be served concurrently with the federal probation under the supervision of the federal probation office. She fulfilled all the conditions of her sentences and in May 1993, her state convictions were set aside and the prosecutions dismissed, pursuant to LSA-C.Cr.P. art. 893(E).

During the summer of 1994, Ms. Eicher participated in six to eight weeks of casino dealer school at the Belle of Baton Rouge casino. She completed the dealer training ranked in the upper quadrant of her class and in August 1994, completed a gaming employee permit application. On the application, she listed all of the federal and state convictions and wrote "expungement/dismissal" in brackets to the right of these offenses. She also listed an Alabama charge of theft and showed this was "never prosecuted—charges formally dismissed." Another set of brackets suggested all three charges "arose out of same offense."

On September 11, 1994, the Louisiana State Police conducted a registration day to review the gaming permit applications and interview prospective casino employees under oath. Because Ms. Eicher's application indicated she had a criminal record, she was directed to a special table to provide additional information. Trooper Adam White, who interviewed her, was familiar with her case because he had been involved in her initial arrest. She offered him copies of both plea agreements, as well as other documents she had brought, which showed the nature and disposition of the federal and state convictions. But Trooper White just took notes concerning their conversation and did not examine her documents or make copies of them. At the conclusion of this process, Ms. Eicher signed a conditional approval agreement and was granted a temporary work permit. The conditional approval agreement acknowledged that the work permit was conditioned upon a personal background investigation by the Louisiana State Police, at the conclusion of which, the work permit application could be rejected.

On the basis of her temporary work permit, Ms. Eicher began working at the Belle of Baton Rouge. Several days after the casino opened, a local television station broadcast a story criticizing the riverboat casino and the Louisiana State Police for allowing Ms. Eicher, a known convicted felon, to work as a craps dealer. After this story aired, two state troopers approached her at work and pulled her temporary work permit because of her felony convictions, pending further investigation. She was later sent a "Notice of Denial," stating her temporary permit was revoked and no permanent license would be issued to her because she had been convicted of a felony offense and because she had made an omission or misstatement of fact on her application.

At Ms. Eicher's request, an administrative hearing was held to consider her appeal of this decision. On the basis of the testimony and documentary evidence presented at that hearing, the hearing officer found she had not misrepresented the facts concerning her criminal record on her application. However, he upheld the denial of her work permit on the basis that her criminal convictions disqualified her for employment in the gaming industry. On appeal to the Louisiana Riverboat Gaming Commission ("the Commission"), the decision was upheld, and Ms. Eicher [sought] judicial review. . . . [The court ultimately] ruled that, under the facts of this case, the Commission and Division should be estopped from revoking Ms. Eicher's work permit. The judgment directed the reinstatement of her permit. The Division and the Commission's successor, the Louisiana Gaming Control Board, filed this suspensive appeal.

## II

In oral reasons for judgment, the district court explained its decision to reverse the initial judgment on the basis of estoppel, stating:

> The thing that really bothers the court about this whole thing is the facts of this case. It's the way the thing was handled at the outset. I don't know why she ever received the temporary permit to begin with. If in fact they had this problem, then why didn't they go review it and decide if they were going to issue licenses to people or not issue licenses to them. Instead they issued the license knowing full well about her situation because they had the same trooper there. . . . I will go ahead and rule. I think that based on the specific facts of this case, . . . the Division should be estopped from revoking the license. . . . I think the key to this thing is that at the time the state had before it the information that it needed. . . . To issue the permit at that point and then come back and yank it later, they should be estopped from doing that.

All of the parties involved in this appeal have acknowledged that the district court's decision to base its judgment on the grounds of estoppel may not have been legally sound, and we agree it was not. Article 1967 of the Louisiana Civil Code states, in pertinent part:

> A party may be obligated by a promise when he knew or should have known that the promise would induce the other party to rely on it to his

detriment and the other party was reasonable in so relying. Recovery may be limited to the expenses incurred or the damages suffered as a result of the promisee's reliance on the promise.

The factual situation before this court simply does not justify application of estoppel, and the district court's reliance on this principle in this case was legal error. Any misunderstanding that occurred in this case concerned the proper application of the law; there was no misrepresentation of fact. Ms. Eicher was aware from the outset that, because of her felony convictions, the law might preclude her employment in the gaming industry. She testified that she telephoned the Division before taking the dealer's classes to explain her situation and find out if she had any chance of being hired, and was told by someone who answered the phone that each application would be considered on its own merits. This does not constitute unequivocal advice from an unusually authoritative source, and any reliance she may have placed on this statement was not justified. Further, when she submitted her application and was approved for a temporary permit, its conditional nature was clearly spelled out in the agreement which she read and signed. Finally, even if the district court was correct in suggesting that the temporary permit should never have been granted, the failure of public officers to correctly enforce statutory provisions should not be permitted to inhibit correct administration of the law or be construed to estop more diligent enforcement. Accordingly, the district court erred in ordering the Division to reinstate Ms. Eicher's work permit on the basis of estoppel.

# III

The hearing officer found Ms. Eicher did not make any misleading statements about her criminal convictions on her application, so the Division's revocation of her temporary work permit on this basis was inappropriate. The record fully supports the factual finding that Ms. Eicher was completely forthcoming with information and documentary evidence concerning her criminal record. Further, based on the entire administrative record, we find no manifest error in this finding.

However, the hearing officer affirmed the Division's decision to revoke Ms. Eicher's temporary work permit and to deny her application for a permanent gaming employee permit because Ms. Eicher had criminal convictions. . . . The Division's decision to revoke Ms. Eicher's license was based on LSA-R.S. 27:76, which provides, in pertinent part:

The division shall not award a license or permit to any person who is disqualified on the basis of any of the following criteria:

> (3) The conviction of or a plea of guilty or nolo contendere by the applicant, or of any person required to be qualified under this Chapter as a condition of a license, for an offense punishable by imprisonment of more than one year.

This statute, which was first enacted and became effective in 1991, stands in apparent contradiction to earlier legislation, found in LSA-R.S. 37:2950, which states, in pertinent part:

> A. Notwithstanding any other provisions of law to the contrary, a person shall not be disqualified, or held ineligible to practice or engage in any trade, occupation, or profession for which a license, permit or certificate is required to be issued by the state of Louisiana or any of its agencies or political subdivisions, solely because of a prior criminal record, except in cases in which the applicant has been convicted of a felony, and such conviction directly relates to the position of employment sought, or to the specific occupation, trade or profession for which the license, permit or certificate is sought.

In subsequent paragraphs, this statute indicates that if an agency decides to prohibit an applicant from engaging in an occupation because of a prior criminal conviction, that decision must be in writing and may be appealed under the provisions of the Administrative Procedure Act. LSA-R.S. 37:2950(B) and (C). A number of agencies are excepted from the provisions of this statute, including "any law enforcement agency," but the Louisiana Gaming Control Board and its predecessor, the Commission, are not specifically named as entities to which the statute is inapplicable. LSA-R.S. 37:2950(D)(1). Ms. Eicher argues that if the legislature had wished, it could have excepted the Louisiana Gaming Control Board from the application of this statute, and its failure to do so requires the court to enforce this statute in favor of Ms. Eicher, rather than enforcing the provisions of LSA-R.S. 27:76(3) against her position.

In reaching his decision reconciling the apparent contradictions in these two statutes, the hearing officer stated:

> [LSA-R.S.] 37:2950 cannot be read to prohibit the division from barring the employment of persons with certain convictions, namely those which are punishable by imprisonment of more than one year. To do so would render ineffective the later expression of the legislature in its clearly stated purpose of imposing strict controls on the legitimate gaming industry. The clear language of [LSA-R.S. 27:76(3)] not only permits, it requires division agents to reject applicants who have such a criminal record.

We agree with the hearing officer's interpretation and application of the two statutes in this case. The legislative branch is presumed to intend to achieve a consistent body of law. When the legislature enacts a statute without mentioning existing statutes on the same subject matter, the later act may, by necessary implication, effect the repeal of the former law. *State v. Piazza*, 596 So. 2d 817, 819 (La. 1992). However, there is a presumption against implied repeal, based on the theory that the legislature envisions the whole body of law when it enacts new legislation. Therefore, the court should give harmonious effect to all acts on a subject when reasonably possible. Id. It is only when two acts are clearly irreconcilable and so inconsistent that the two cannot have concurrent operation, that the presumption against implied repeal falls, and the later statute governs.

The conclusion of the hearing officer in this case gives effect to the later expression of legislative intent in LSA-R.S. 27:76(3), without abrogating the provisions of LSA-R.S. 37:2950. Accordingly, we find no legal error in this interpretation of the law and no abuse of discretion on the part of the Division in its application of this statute to Ms. Eicher.

Our inquiry does not end there, however. As the hearing officer also noted, . . . Article I, Section 20 of our constitution states, in part, that full rights of citizenship shall be restored upon termination of state and federal supervision following conviction for any offense. Additionally, Article IV, Section 5(E)(1) states:

> [A] first offender never previously convicted of a felony shall be pardoned automatically upon completion of his sentence, without a recommendation of the Board of Pardons and without action by the governor. (footnote omitted).

In addition to these constitutional provisions, for first offense non-capital felonies, LSA-C.Cr.P. art. 893(D)(2) provides, in pertinent part:

> Upon motion of the defendant, if the court finds at the conclusion of the probationary period that the probation of the defendant has been satisfactory, the court may set the conviction aside and dismiss the prosecution. The dismissal of the prosecution shall have the same effect as acquittal, except that the conviction may be considered as a first offense and provide the basis for subsequent prosecution of the party as a multiple offender, and further shall be considered as a first offense for purposes of any other law or laws relating to cumulation of offenses.

Ms. Eicher pled guilty to federal and state felony charges and completed her sentences on both. She did not obtain a governor's pardon, but at the conclusion of her probationary period on the state conviction, the court granted her request to set her conviction aside and dismiss the prosecution on the state offense, pursuant to Article 893. Ms. Eicher argues that, because of this dismissal and set aside, her state felony conviction ceased to exist for purposes of the permitting qualification process. Although, short of a presidential pardon, there is no comparable provision which would dismiss or pardon the federal felony conviction, Ms. Eicher contends the constitutional provisions have the effect of restoring to her all state citizenship rights.

The hearing officer considered the relationship of the constitutional provisions and made the following determination:

> The effect of the first offenders (sic) pardon has been the subject of debate, critical review, and more importantly, analysis by the Louisiana Supreme Court. The Court has distinguished the effects of [the] two aforementioned Louisiana Constitutional provisions and held that the effects of an automatic pardon may be limited by the legislature. *See State v. Wiggins*, 432 So. 2d 234 (La. 1983). In *Wiggins* the Court held that certain rights of citizenship may be restricted by the state.

A gaming permit is not a right of citizenship. The legislature specifically provided in [LSA-R.S.] 4:502(B) in pertinent part that a gaming permit is ... "a pure and absolute [revocable] privilege and not a right, property or otherwise, under the constitutions (sic) of the United States or of the state of Louisiana."

We find no error in this analysis of the law. In the *Wiggins* case, the right to keep and bear arms, distinctly guaranteed by the United States and Louisiana Constitutions, was implicated. U.S. Const. amend. II; LSA-Const. art. I, §11. The statute at issue prohibited any person who had been convicted of certain violent crimes from possessing a firearm or carrying a concealed weapon for ten years after completion of his or her sentence, probation, parole, or suspension of sentence. LSA-R.S. 14:95.1. In upholding this statute against a first felony offender who had been automatically pardoned under LSA-Const. art. IV, §5(E)(1), the Louisiana Supreme Court stated, "Surely, the legislature has the authority under its police power to limit the 'rights of citizenship' restored by an automatic pardon...." *Wiggins*, 432 So. 2d at 237. We agree with the hearing officer's determination that if such a right of citizenship can be legislatively limited, even for persons whose convictions are pardoned under the Louisiana Constitution, then certainly a privilege, such as a gaming employee permit, can also be limited by legislation. [AFFIRMED].

*NOTES*

1. Serious social policy conflicts are presented in *Eicher*. Did the court have room to strike the balance between two conflicting policies in any other way?
2. Now, revisit the notes following *Gage* above. After reading *Eicher*, how would you advise a gaming regulator faced with a new gaming license application from Gage and Douglas following their prank at the Isle of Capri casino?

## CHUNG v. SMSC GAMING ENTERPRISES
### 2007 WL 3537 (Minn. App. 2007)

WILLIS, Judge.

By writ of certiorari, pro se relator challenges the decision of the unemployment law judge (ULJ) that relator was discharged for employment misconduct and is therefore disqualified from receiving unemployment benefits. . . .

Pro se relator Michael Chung was employed by SMSC Gaming Enterprises (SMSC) as a player-services representative at a casino from September 23, 2004, to October 5, 2005. SMSC's player-services representatives are required to have valid gaming licenses. This requirement is set forth in the SMSC employment application that Chung completed. And Chung was aware that criminal convictions could affect his gaming license.

On February 8, 2005, a police officer issued Chung a ticket for careless driving and for making an improper lane change, and Chung ultimately pleaded guilty to careless driving, a misdemeanor. In September 2005, the Shakopee Mdewakanton Gaming Commission held a hearing, apparently to address Chung's careless-driving conviction, and voted unanimously to revoke Chung's gaming license. The gaming commission is an entity entirely separate from SMSC, Chung's former employer. On October 5, 2005, SMSC discharged Chung from his employment because he no longer held a valid gaming license. Chung sought unemployment benefits.

An adjudicator from the Department of Employment and Economic Development (DEED) determined that Chung was qualified to receive benefits. Mistakenly believing that Chung's gaming license had been revoked by his employer, the adjudicator determined that Chung was discharged for reasons other than employment misconduct. SMSC sought de novo review of that determination by an unemployment-law judge (ULJ). The ULJ [reversed] DEED's initial determination and [held] that Chung was disqualified from receiving unemployment benefits. The ULJ found that SMSC has "the right to expect that its employees will avoid committing illegal acts that may result in the revocation of a gaming license," and, therefore, "by driving his vehicle in a careless manner that resulted in a misdemeanor conviction, Chung's conduct clearly displayed a serious violation of the standards of behavior that an employer has the right to reasonably expect of its employee." The ULJ concluded that Chung was discharged because of employment misconduct. . . . [upon reconsideration, a] second ULJ affirmed the findings and decision of the first ULJ. The second ULJ found that "Michael Chung knew he was required to maintain a license in order to work for the employer. He did not do that, it being revoked by a separate entity, the Gaming Commission." . . .

Chung makes three arguments on appeal: (1) that the second ULJ improperly based his decision on the "false assumption" that Chung's driver's license had been revoked; (2) that his gaming license was improperly revoked; and (3) that his careless-driving conviction does not constitute employment misconduct.

First, Chung asserts that the second ULJ improperly based his decision on the false assumption that Chung's driver's license had been revoked and that the decision was therefore "factually and legally incorrect." Chung is simply mistaken. The ULJ did not base his decision on such an assumption or even make such an assumption. The language in the second ULJ's decision to which Chung likely refers is: "This is no different than if Michael Chung's job required that he maintain a driver's license and the driver's license was revoked and, therefore, he could no longer legally perform his job." The ULJ was comparing Chung's situation to one in which a driver's license had been revoked, not stating that Chung's driver's license had in fact been revoked. Other than this mistaken assignment of error, Chung disputes no finding of fact by the ULJ.

Second, Chung argues that SMSC improperly revoked his gaming license and that the second ULJ erred when he declared that the evidence that Chung presented regarding the proper grounds for revocation of a gaming license was not "directly applicable." The evidence that Chung presented appears to be an excerpt from a Mystic Lake Casino Hotel Gaming Department handbook setting forth the grounds on which the gaming commission might revoke or deny an employee's gaming license, and the second ULJ was correct when he determined that the quoted language is not directly applicable to the issue of whether Chung was discharged for employment misconduct. Chung mistakenly argues that his former employer violated this standard and unlawfully revoked his gaming license. As the second ULJ noted, the gaming commission, which revoked Chung's gaming license, is an entity separate from SMSC, Chung's former employer. SMSC did not revoke Chung's gaming license, unlawfully or otherwise; it discharged Chung because he no longer held a gaming license.

The appropriateness of the gaming commission's decision to revoke Chung's gaming license was immaterial to SMSC's decision to discharge Chung on the ground that he no longer held a gaming license. And neither the transcript of Chung's hearing before the gaming commission nor an explanation of the commission's basis for its decision to revoke Chung's gaming license was available to the ULJ, or to SMSC for that matter. The only evidence as to what happened at the gaming-commission hearing—and in fact the only evidence that it was indeed a careless-driving conviction that prompted the commission to revoke Chung's gaming license—was Chung's own testimony at the hearing before the first ULJ. Under the Shakopee Mdewakanton Sioux (Dakota) Community Gaming Ordinance, the proper procedure for appealing a decision of the gaming commission is to appeal to the Shakopee Mdewakanton Sioux (Dakota) Community's Tribal Court. There is no evidence that Chung exercised this right of appeal.

Finally, Chung argues that his careless-driving conviction does not meet the definition of employment misconduct. The issue before this court is not whether Chung's careless-driving conviction was employment misconduct but whether Chung's loss of his gaming license was employment misconduct, for that was the basis for SMSC's decision to discharge Chung. DEED and SMSC argue that Chung engaged in employment misconduct when he lost, through his negligent conduct, a gaming license that was required for his employment.

A person who is discharged from employment because of employment misconduct is disqualified from receiving unemployment benefits. Minn. Stat. §268.095, subd. 4 (Supp. 2005). "Employment misconduct" is defined as

> any intentional, negligent, or indifferent conduct, on the job or off the job (1) that displays clearly a serious violation of the standards of behavior the employer has the right to reasonably expect of the employee, or (2) that displays clearly a substantial lack of concern for the employment. . . .

SMSC argues that Chung's conduct was "negligent and/or indifferent" under Minn. Stat. §268.095, subd. 6(a). We agree. Because the record supports the finding that Chung knew that his employment required a gaming license and he knew that a criminal conviction could result in the revocation of his license, Chung's conduct that resulted in a criminal conviction was "negligent" or "indifferent," or both.

To constitute "employment misconduct," Chung's conduct must also display clearly either "a serious violation of the standards of behavior the employer has the right to reasonably expect of the employee" under Minn. Stat. §268.095, subd. 6(a)(1), or "a substantial lack of concern for the employment" under Minn. Stat. §268.095, subd. 6(a)(2). SMSC argues that Chung's conduct satisfies either definition. We agree.

SMSC is required by law to employ as player-services representatives only individuals with gaming licenses. SMSC had the right to reasonably expect Chung to maintain his licensed status. Chung failed to meet that expectation when the gaming commission revoked his license. Failure to meet SMSC's reasonable expectation that its employees maintain a valid gaming license is a "serious violation." Thus, Chung was discharged for "employment misconduct" under Minn. Stat. §268.095, subd. 6(a)(1).

SMSC and DEED argue that Chung's behavior also qualifies as a "substantial lack of concern for the employment" under Minn. Stat. §268.095, subd. 6(a)(2). As did the second ULJ, DEED compares Chung's situation to cases in which an employee's job requires a driver's license, and the employee engages in conduct that leads to the revocation of his driver's license or otherwise affects his ability to drive. SMSC asserts that because Chung knew that he was required to maintain a gaming license to keep his job, his failure to do so demonstrated a substantial lack of concern for his employment.

SMSC relies on *Markel v. City of Circle Pines*, 479 N.W.2d 382, 385 (Minn. 1992) (concluding that the employee's "conduct in driving drunk, thus putting at risk his ability to drive his employer's vehicles due to loss of his driver's license, is misconduct . . . because it showed an intentional and substantial disregard of his duties and obligations to his employer" and noting that this was particularly true when the employee understood the risk he was taking). We agree with SMSC that the present case is more similar to *Markel* than to other caselaw involving minor traffic offenses affecting an employee's ability to drive a motor vehicle required for his employment.

In *Markel*, the employee's license was revoked for a year, and he was unable to secure the right type of limited license for work purposes, which rendered him completely unable to perform his duties and thus constituted a "substantial disregard" of his duties to his employer. 479 N.W.2d at 383, 385. In contrast, this court found no employment misconduct in *Peterson v. Fred Vogt & Co.*, in which the employee's license was revoked for only 90 days, and the employee would have been able to secure a limited license for work purposes if his employer had cooperated. 495 N.W.2d 875, 877, 879 (Minn. App. 1993); *see also Swanson v. Columbia Transit Corp.*, 248 N.W.2d 732, 733 (Minn. 1976) (finding no employment misconduct when a bus driver's three on-duty accidents did not render him unable to perform his duties); *Eddins v. Chippewa Springs Corp.*, 388 N.W.2d 434, 434-36 (Minn. App. 1986) (finding no employment misconduct when an employee's numerous off-duty traffic tickets caused his employer's insurer to refuse coverage but did not result in the loss of the employee's driver's license, so the employee was still able to perform his duties). Here, the revocation of Chung's gaming license renders him completely unable to perform the requirements of his job. . . . AFFIRMED.

## NJ DIVISION OF GAMING ENFORCEMENT v. WIRTZ

### 2007 WL 486740 (N.J. Super. App. Div. 2007)

PER CURIAM.

Applicant David Wirtz, appeals from a final order of the Casino Control Commission (Commission) . . . which denied Wirtz a casino employee license and revoked his casino service employee registration because he had committed disqualifying conduct as defined in N.J.S.A. 5:12-86c(2) and -86g, and he had failed to clearly and convincingly demonstrate his rehabilitation pursuant to N.J.S.A. 5:12-90h, and good character pursuant to N.J.S.A. 5:12-89b(2) and -90b. . . .

Wirtz was employed by Bally's Casino in a position that required both registration and licensure. N.J.S.A. 5:12-7 requires licensure of casino employees who perform statutorily described functions, including those encompassed by Wirtz's job. N.J.S.A. 5:12-86c(1) provides that applicants who have been convicted of enumerated crimes are automatically disqualified from casino licensure. N.J.S.A. 5:12-86c(2) provides an exception to automatic disqualification if the conviction did not occur within the ten-year period preceding license application, but conditions licensure upon presentation by the applicant of clear and convincing evidence that automatic disqualification is not justified. N.J.S.A. 5:12-86g affords additional grounds for disqualification upon evidence of

> [t]he commission by the applicant . . . of any act or acts which would constitute any offense under subsection c. of this section, even if such conduct has not been or may not be prosecuted under the criminal laws of this State or any other jurisdiction or has been prosecuted under the

criminal laws of this State or any other jurisdiction and such prosecution has been terminated in a manner other than with a conviction.

Wirtz has acknowledged the applicability of N.J.S.A. 5:12-86g to his licensure application.

In order for an eligible person who has committed a disqualifying offense to obtain a casino employee license, the applicant must demonstrate rehabilitation, by clear and convincing evidence, under standards set forth in N.J.S.A. 5:12-90h, and good character as required by N.J.S.A. 5:12-90b, which incorporates by reference the good character requirements of N.J.S.A. 5:12-89b(2). A further statutory provision, of relevance to this case, states that an applicant for a casino employee license whose application is denied or whose license is revoked "shall not . . . be employed by a casino licensee in a position that does not require a license until five years have elapsed from the date of the denial or revocation, except that the commission may permit such employment upon good cause shown." N.J.S.A. 5:12-106c.

Registration is separately governed. N.J.S.A. 5:12-91a provides that "[n]o person may commence employment as a casino service employee unless the person has been registered with the commission." N.J.S.A. 5:12-91b permits revocation of registration upon evidence of disqualification under the criteria set forth in the licensing provisions that we have cited. However, N.J.S.A. 5:12-91d provides that registration shall not be revoked if rehabilitation has been demonstrated. Further, N.J.S.A. 5:12-91e allows waiver of relevant disqualification criteria for registration purposes upon a finding that the interests of justice require such action.

On February 7, 1990, more than ten years prior to Wirtz's application for a casino employee license, Wirtz, believing that he would be sexually assaulted by the police, fired a 22-caliber rifle at the police and a social worker who attempted to forcibly enter his room in a boarding house. Two police officers and the social worker were wounded, as was Wirtz. Following treatment for his injuries, Wirtz, who exhibited symptoms of active paranoid schizophrenia, was confined in the Vroom building of the Trenton Psychiatric Hospital.

Wirtz was indicted for attempted murder, aggravated assault, aggravated assault on a police officer, possession of a rifle for an unlawful purpose, and unlawful possession of a weapon. . . . Wirtz was found not guilty by reason of insanity.

After a further psychiatric evaluation, on March 8, 1994, the trial judge found that Wirtz had not been cured of his acute insanity and that he could not be released without posing a danger to the community or himself; and he ordered Wirtz's involuntary civil confinement at Ancora Psychiatric Hospital, subject to the periodic review procedures of *State v. Krol*, 68 N.J. 236, 344 A.2d 289 (1975) and N.J.S.A. 2C:4-8b(3) and -9.

In early 1998, following a *Krol* hearing, the trial judge authorized Wirtz's transfer from the psychiatric hospital facility to a group home located on the hospital's grounds. In 2000, Wirtz was permitted to relocate from the group home to independent living, while remaining under treatment and monitoring. Wirtz purchased a condominium unit in Absecon and, on September 5, 2000, commenced employment at Bally's Casino as a slot marketing representative and, after a promotion, as a slot services host, a position requiring licensure. Wirtz was issued a casino service employee registration on August 31, 2000, and was granted a temporary casino employee license at the request of Bally's on July 6, 2001. Wirtz's residence in Absecon and employment at Bally's were acknowledged at *Krol* hearings in March and September 2001 and in resultant court orders specifying the terms of Wirtz's conditional release.

Wirtz's employment at Bally's continued without incident until May 28, 2002, when he was placed on administrative leave upon notice to Bally's that the Division of Gaming Enforcement (Division) had filed a complaint with the Commission seeking revocation of Wirtz's casino service employee registration and denial of a permanent casino employee license.[1] Wirtz's employment was terminated one month later as the result of the Commission's denial of licensure following Wirtz's failure to attend a scheduled pre-hearing conference. Since that time, Wirtz has been unable to obtain employment. He remains under the court's supervision pursuant to *Krol* and presently lives in the community in rental housing.

Upon Wirtz's application, the licensing matter was reinstated to permit a determination of Wirtz's suitability for licensure. Pursuant to statute, Wirtz was required to demonstrate by clear and convincing evidence rehabilitation pursuant to N.J.S.A. 5:12-90h and good character pursuant to N.J.S.A. 5:12-89b and -90b. . . . Although no evidence was offered by the Division to challenge Wirtz's assertions of good conduct following his release from the group home, the hearing examiner found that the Commission should be afforded the opportunity to determine, through testimony given at a hearing, whether or not Wirtz had affirmatively demonstrated his rehabilitation and good character. . . .

Testimony at the hearing established without contradiction that Wirtz's mental illness is not cured, but is in remission. He has been

---

1. There is no allegation that Wirtz, at any time, failed to disclose his criminal history in response to pertinent inquiry.

advised that psychiatric therapy is no longer necessary, and such therapy has been terminated. However, he continues to be medicated, and sees his treating psychiatrist every three months for monitoring of that medication. Wirtz testified that he has been informed that cessation of medication would result in the re-emergence of the symptoms of his mental illness, and that he would again become a danger to others. He has therefore been fully compliant with the medical regime imposed upon him, which at the time of the hearing consisted in relevant part only of monitoring of his psychiatric medication at three-month intervals. Wirtz testified that he takes his prescribed medication because he does not want to get sick again. There is no evidence of any recurrence of Wirtz's symptoms while he has lived independently, either in the period of his employment by Bally's or in the lengthy, and undoubtedly stressful, period of unemployment that has continued thereafter.

In an initial decision issued after the conclusion of the hearing and filed with the Commission, the hearing examiner stated that he

> found Applicant to be a credible witness. He candidly admitted what he did and seemed to understand the serious nature of his offenses. Although he is not currently employed, Applicant has previously held a full-time job in the casino industry, apparently without incident. His previous supervisor submitted a letter on Applicant's behalf, attesting to Applicant's positive work ethic. In addition, one of Applicant's former neighbors wrote a letter on Applicant's behalf, attesting to Applicant's good character.

Based upon these findings, the hearing examiner recommended that Wirtz be permitted to work in a non-credential hotel position as permitted by N.J.S.A. 5:12-106c. However, the hearing examiner found insufficient evidence of rehabilitation[, noting] that Wirtz's conduct in 1990 was claimed to have arisen from a lack of medical supervision. He then observed:

> The fact of the matter is that Applicant is not currently medically supervised either. There are no routine or surprise tests or visits conducted to verify Applicant is taking his medication as prescribed, which apparently is what prevents Applicant from acting out in such a manner again. Moreover, there was no evidence from Applicant submitted by a psychiatrist that would indicate such testing is not routinely conducted, or necessary, on a person with Applicant's background. Nor was there any evidence or testimony presented explaining what, if any, consequences there would be were Applicant to discontinue taking his medication as prescribed. The "good character" letters submitted on Applicant's behalf by his previous supervisor and neighbor are positive, but neither reference knowledge of Applicant's former conduct, and thus are not relevant for proving Applicant has been rehabilitated.

The hearing examiner concluded on this basis that Wirtz had failed to prove his rehabilitation by clear and convincing evidence as required by N.J.S.A. 5:12-90h, and ruled that he was disqualified from licensure. The hearing examiner found further that the same evidence also compelled the conclusion that Wirtz had not provided clear and convincing evidence of good character, honesty and integrity pursuant to N.J.S.A. 5:12-90b and -89b. The hearing examiner additionally found that Wirtz had not demonstrated good cause to permit him to work in a position that required registration, but not a license, pursuant to the waiver provisions of N.J.S.A. 5:12-91e and the standards set forth in *State v. Galanti*, 94 N.J.A.R.2d (CCC) 1, 4 (1992). He stated: "I believe that the seriousness of Applicant's conduct, combined with the lack of intensive oversight with his medicinal regimen, prevents me from granting a waiver of disqualification at this time." As stated previously, the hearing examiner did, however, find good cause, pursuant to N.J.S.A. 5:12-106c, to permit Wirtz to obtain employment in a non-credential hotel position. However, the hearing examiner conditioned such employment upon "evidence of [Wirtz's] compliance in taking his prescribed medicine every three months, beginning March 1, 2005." Wirtz's application for a casino employee license was thus denied, and his registration was revoked. Reapplication was permitted after a period of five years, or at an earlier date in accordance with N.J.A.C. 19:41-8.9. . . .

### ANALYSIS

Wirtz argues that the Commission failed to give proper deference to the findings of the *Krol* court and, in essence, usurped the court's power to determine whether he posed a danger to himself or others. We disagree, regarding the *Krol* court's determinations to be relevant to, but not dispositive of, the licensure issue and the foundational questions of adequate rehabilitation and good character. The Supreme Court has recognized that "there is a substantial government interest in strict regulation of casino gambling," *In re Martin*, 90 N.J. 295, 319, 447 A.2d 1290 (1982), and has further recognized the Legislature's "substantial power to regulate non-essential, dangerous and sensitive industries" such as gambling "to protect the public safety and welfare."

The declaration of policy with which the Casino Control Act commences provides the rationale for oversight over casino gambling, stating that the goal is to establish public confidence and trust in the credibility and integrity of oversight procedures and of the casino operations themselves. N.J.S.A. 5:12-1b(6); see also N.J.S.A. 5:12-1b(13).

The means for establishing and maintaining the public's confidence is the regulatory process, which is "designed to extend strict State regulation to all persons, locations, practices and associations related to the operation of licensed casino enterprises." N.J.S.A. 5:12-1b(6). The Legislature has also declared that public policy demands "the exclusion from participation therein of persons with known criminal records, habits or associations," N.J.S.A. 5:12-1b(7); it has required licensure in order to perform certain casino operations, N.J.S.A. 5:12-7; and it has stated that participation in casino operations as a licensee "shall be deemed a revocable privilege conditioned upon the proper and continued qualification of the individual licensee," N.J.S.A. 5:12-1b(8). In furtherance of these purposes, the Legislature established the Commission, N.J.S.A. 5:12-50, and charged it with hearing and promptly deciding all license applications and revocation actions. N.J.S.A. 5:12-63a. It placed the burden on the applicant to demonstrate his qualification for licensure by clear and convincing evidence. N.J.S.A. 5:12-80a. No burden is placed on the Division to disprove qualification.

The strictures placed by the licensure provisions of the Casino Control Act upon employment of those who have committed disqualifying acts and the requirement of an affirmative showing of rehabilitation and good character thus differ from *Krol*'s standard that, in order to be released into the community, a person found not guilty by reason of insanity must be determined not to be a danger to himself or others. *Krol,* supra, 344 A.2d 289. In the highly regulated context of casino employment, it is appropriate that the findings of a court conducting periodic evaluations of mental condition pursuant to *Krol* be evidential, not dispositive. Whether Wirtz is "evil" or, as *Krol* properly characterizes the mentally ill, is "sick," 344 A.2d 289, is not the issue, which instead is whether he meets the licensing requirements of the Casino Control Act.

Similarly, we do not regard the burden-shifting requirements of the New Jersey Law Against Discrimination (NJLAD) (see *Jansen v. Food Circus Supermarkets, Inc.,* 110 N.J. 363, 375, 541 A.2d 682 (1988))[2] to be applicable in a casino licensure context. Although discrimination is to be eschewed in any forum, we do not construe the statutory

---

2. *Jansen,* a NJLAD case, holds in the context of future safety concerns posed by an epileptic person employed as a meatcutter, that in order to assert a safety defense, the employer must establish a reasonable probability of substantial harm arising from continued employment. Ibid.; see also N.J.A.C. 13:13-2.8 (requiring that an employer's decision must be based upon an objective standard supported by factual or scientifically validated evidence). We express no opinion as to whether these evidentiary standards are applicable upon remand, but we trust that, if rejected, the legal basis for such rejection will be articulated.

proscriptions of the NJLAD to be directly applicable to the present appeal from a denial of permissive licensure or to the licensure itself.

We have noted that the Casino Control Act makes it clear that a casino employee license constitutes a revocable privilege conditioned upon proper qualification of the applicant and the applicant's "affirmative responsibility" to provide that information required to meet the Act's licensing requirements. N.J.S.A. 5:12-1b(8). The Legislature, in requiring that an applicant, otherwise disqualified by his conduct, demonstrate rehabilitation and good character, may not have focused upon circumstances such as presented here in which otherwise criminal conduct arose from a mental disability. Nonetheless, we perceive no reason to exempt this circumstance from the Casino Control Act's reach. . . . We thus reject Wirtz's arguments based upon the allegedly preclusive effect of findings under *Krol* and the applicability of the NJLAD.

However, a further concern, crucial to this appeal, exists. . . . The Commission, by adopting the reasoning of its hearing examiner, determined that Wirtz had failed to meet his burden of proving rehabilitation and good character because he had not introduced psychiatric testimony prospectively analyzing his future dangerousness and had failed to provide evidence of intensive oversight of his medicinal regimen or of routine or surprise tests or visits gauged to assure compliance with that regimen. However, Wirtz was never notified of the requirement that he produce the evidence of monitoring, prospective compliance, and future prospects for continued remission that the Commission found to be wanting. Indeed, Wirtz may well have been led to believe such evidence was unnecessary as the result of counsel for the Division's argument in opposition to summary judgment that

> the fact that [Wirtz] is no longer a danger to himself or the public, as I stated, is not the threshold for licensure. However, it certainly should be something that should be considered. But we have to be careful about that because he has rights not to be having his licensure determined on the basis of whether or not we could prospectively think he's going to have an incident in the future. We don't . . . assert that.

When, later in the argument, Wirtz's counsel asserted the existence of rehabilitation and sought, in the face of the Division's continued opposition, a specification of what evidence was lacking, no substantive response was given, other than that, in this licensing context, the hearing examiner should be afforded the opportunity to hear testimony directly from Wirtz, and not just his attorney, in order to make a "present character finding." Similarly, no notice of the Commission's evidentiary requirements regarding Wirtz's compliance and prospective condition was provided by the hearing examiner's decision denying summary judgment or by his specification in the prehearing conference memorandum of issues to be addressed at the hearing itself.

The Supreme Court has held in the context of the recommitment of a sexually violent predator following conditional discharge: "Due process requires that the person in question receive a notice that sufficiently defines the issue to permit him or her a fair opportunity to prepare and defend against the accusation." *In re Civil Commitment of E.D.*, 183 N.J. 536, 547, 874 A.2d 1075 (2005). . . . No lesser standard applies in an administrative context. . . . That is precisely the problem in the present case. Wirtz justifiably regarded his proofs of unexceptional conduct for a period of four years and his non-deviant compliance in taking his medications as sufficient to prove his rehabilitation, because the Division had indicated that it sought no more. The imposition of the additional evidentiary requirement of live psychiatric testimony that addressed monitoring of compliance and the likelihood of recurrence of active psychosis, after proofs had been completed, was fundamentally unfair and constituted a denial of due process.

If the Commission seeks to base its decision on scientific evidence relevant to the danger that Wirtz may pose to the public as the result of his conduct in the future, it must articulate the standards to be met, and afford Wirtz a prompt opportunity to meet them. The Commission will then be obliged to make findings and state conclusions regarding Wirtz's present fitness for casino licensure premised both upon his medical history and a fair assessment, based on the record, of his future prospects. Reversed.

## *NOTES*

1.  Do the *Krol* hearing and the gaming licensing hearing really serve different purposes? Will Wirtz be forced to find employment in a different industry? Will it impose unfair costs on that industry? Does the importance of the gaming industry justify allowing it to avoid the social costs of employing the mentally ill?
2.  Does the gaming industry's special need to protect its integrity and the concomitant ability to screen employees now effectively provide a shield from anti-discrimination laws? If Bally's was willing to hire Wirtz, on what basis should gaming regulators second-guess that decision? Could the decision be seen to undermine anti-discrimination law in New Jersey?
3.  Consider the next case, which presents due process questions in the sports environment.

## MOLINAS v. PODOLOFF
### 133 N.Y.S.2d 743 (1954)

Joseph, Justice.

Plaintiff brings this action for a permanent injunction to set aside his suspension as a player in the National Basketball Association, to maintain his rights to be a player member in the association and for other relief. . . . The Zollner Machine Works, Inc., of Fort Wayne, Indiana, was the owner of the club known as Fort Wayne Zollner Pistons, a member of the NBA; it entered into a written contract on the form prescribed by the NBA with the plaintiff to play professional basketball in the said league for its club, whereby the club and the plaintiff became bound by the terms of the said agreement, and the constitution and bylaws of the NBA.

It is undisputed that on January 9, 1954, the police of Fort Wayne, Indiana, conducted an inquiry as to the Zollner Piston Basketball Team, and the plaintiff, by reason of such investigation, in the late evening of that day, or in the early morning of January 10, 1954, signed a written statement of his having wagered on his team. Specifically the plaintiff admitted: "I have been a member of the Zollner Piston Basketball Team since October 1953. After being on the team for approximately a month I called a man in New York by the name of Mr. X, knowing this man for a long period of time I called him on the telephone and asked him if he could place a bet for me. He said that he could and he would tell me the odds on the game either for or against the Pistons. After hearing the odds or points on the game I either placed a bet on the Pistons or else told him that the odds were too great and I did not want to place the bet. Several times I talked to him over the phone and odds or points were not mentioned and I told him that I thought on some occasions that we could win a particular game and I placed a bet. I did this about ten times. At no time was there a pay-off to throw any games made to me by Mr. X. Nor was there any mention of the fact; however, the only reimbursement I received was for my phone calls which I made to him. Also I received approximately $400 for the total times that I have been betting with him. This included the phone bill also." The plaintiff has admitted, and so testified at the trial, that the statement was a voluntary, free and truthful statement of fact.

Maurice Podoloff, President of the NBA, and Mr. Zollner, President of the Fort Wayne Zollner Pistons, arrived at the police station about midnight, and subsequent to being shown plaintiff's statement Mr. Podoloff sent for him. In the conversation that ensued . . . Mr. Podoloff informed the plaintiff that he was 'through' as a player, and Mr. Podoloff indefinitely suspended the plaintiff.

The plaintiff predicates his action upon two contentions: (1) that no notice of hearing and charges were given the plaintiff as provided by the contract and the constitution; (2) there was no authority to indefinitely suspend the plaintiff. . . .

The pertinent provisions of the contract and the constitution of the NBA [provide that any player who bets on the outcome of any NBA game shall be expelled from the NBA by the President after due notice and hearing and the President's decision shall be final, binding, conclusive, and unappealable]. . . .

Assuming, but not conceding, that there was no due notice and hearing, as provided by the contract and the constitution of the NBA, this court finds that elaboration on plaintiff's contentions is rendered unnecessary because of the conclusions reached by this court in the determination of this matter.

Certain amateur and professional sports, and the athletes participating in such sports, have recently occupied the spotlight of unfavorable public attention. The radio and television have been contributing causes for creating industries out of certain sports. America is sport-minded; we admire the accomplishment of our athletes; we are pleased with the success of our favorite teams and we spend a considerable part of our time rooting, but relaxing nevertheless, with our favorite sports. We inherit from the Greeks and Romans a love for stadia and sport competition.

When the breath of scandal hits one sport, it casts suspicion on all other sports. It does irreparable injury to the great majority of the players, destroys the confidence of the public in athletic competition, and lets down the morale of our youth. When the standards of fair play, good sportsmanship and honesty are abandoned, sporting events become the property of the gamblers and racketeers.

Much has happened in basketball to displease the public. Bribing, fixing and wagering, especially when associated with gamblers and racketeers, are matters of serious nature. . . . Courts take cognizance of public interests and public problems; they reflect the spirit of the times and the sentiment and thoughts of the citizens. Laws are promulgated and contracts are made to protect the public and are abreast with the demands, interest and protection of the people. The wagering by player members of NBA and the contract calling for expulsion is an aftermath of the abuses with which we are concerned. To maintain basketball competition in the NBA, to have open competitive sport, the public confidence and attendance, every effort had to be made to eliminate the slightest suspicion that competition was not on an honest, competitive basis. . . .

[I]f there was a triable issue, this court would have relegated the defendant to his contractual obligations and ordered a hearing.

However, the testimony of the plaintiff before the court that the statement was free, voluntary and true eliminates any question as to the plaintiff's admissions. The position of the plaintiff, in reality, seems to be one of asserting that he wagered on games, he breached his contract, he violated the constitution of the NBA and was morally dishonest. Nevertheless, he now requests this court to order the defendant to cross all its t's and dot all its i's, and award damages for defendant's suspension without due notice and hearing. . . .

To adjudge the suspension null and void, to bring about a hearing for this plaintiff, that must unquestionably and inevitably result in his expulsion or suspension, would be a mere futile gesture. . . . There is no doubt that the matter now before this court has evoked a considerable amount of public interest and discussion. While the interest of the public at large in a given case, as an abstract proposition, can never be allowed to influence the court or become determinative, nevertheless, situations arise wherein the decision of the court is made against a background of public interest which is based on public morality. That morality is one which concerns the public desire of honest sport and clean sportsmanship. It necessarily follows, as the day follows the night, that one who has offended against this concept of good morals, and who admits such offense in open court, does not by that very fact, satisfy the equitable maxim, that he who comes into equity must come with clean hands. [Complaint dismissed.]

### NOTES

1. Sports leagues draw a hard line against players participating in betting. In 1989, famous baseball player Pete Rose, a national icon, and then the manager of the Cincinnati Reds ball club, was alleged to have gambled on baseball games in violation of league rules. *See, e.g., Rose v. Giamatti*, 721 F. Supp. 906 (S.D. Ohio 1989). Rose swore that he never bet on his own team's games, but he was given a lifetime ban from baseball. If his claim is true, were his actions a threat to the integrity of the sport? Is a lifetime ban too harsh? What is the justification for such a harsh approach?
2. The role played by the NBA in *Molinas* and Major League Baseball in the Pete Rose case is somewhat akin to the role played by a state gaming commission in a gaming jurisdiction. One major difference, however, is that sports leagues are private, not governmental organizations. What difference, if any, does that make? Would a private organization be as effective as a governmental

agency in performing licensing in the gaming industry? Less effective? More effective?

3.   What are the broad purposes of the regulatory regime in basketball or baseball? Is licensure in the gaming industry designed to serve the same or different purposes than the regime in these sports? If the purpose of regulation in each venue is to "protect the integrity of the industry," is there a reason that we require the public to pay for public regulation of gambling, but we require the private firm to bear the costs of regulation of sport? What justifies this distinction? Why is gambling privileged in this way?

4.   Numerous scandals involving sports and gambling have occurred over the decades, but the relationship between sports and gambling is complicated. Without a doubt, gambling on sports drives a good deal of the interest in sports, and vice versa. Such gambling also creates the opportunity for corruption. As a result, American sports leagues have taken a hard line approach toward gambling, largely taking the position that gambling corrupts the integrity of sport.

5.   If gambling by players and coaches is troubling because it corrupts the integrity of sports, isn't it also troubling because it corrupts the integrity of gaming? Shouldn't the gaming industry be as concerned with athletes and gambling as the sports industry is? The following essay questions whether sports leagues have been too hostile toward sports gambling bookmaking operations and suggests the need for cooperation.

## ADAM HOSMER-HENNER, PREVENTING GAME FIXING: SPORTS AS INFORMATION MARKETS

### 14 Gaming L. Rev. & Econ. 31 (2010)

The threat of game fixing has been a constant worry for professional and amateur sports leagues since the Black Sox scandal of 1919 threatened public confidence in the integrity of baseball. In June 2007, the National Basketball Association was rocked by reports that a referee, Tim Donaghy, was under investigation for unduly influencing the outcome of games and for providing inside information to gamblers. After each scandal, the usual response for the sports leagues is to toughen anti-gambling policies and call on Congress to further prohibit sports gambling. These implorations have succeeded to the extent that Nevada is the only state that currently licenses comprehensive sports books, and policymakers concerned about game fixing have pressed for a total ban on sports betting.

Although gambling receives the majority of blame for game fixing, prohibiting sports betting in Nevada is not only an ineffective way to reduce game fixing but also counterproductive. Gambling does create the incentives to fix games, but less than one percent of sports bets placed by Americans are wagered legally in Nevada. The remainder of bets are placed outside the regulated system, thus, potential game-fixers would not be prevented from betting upon the contests they rig. Worse, prohibiting sports betting in Nevada would eliminate the most effective method of detecting game fixing. Nevada sports books have been instrumental in uncovering game-fixing scandals when irregular betting patterns raised suspicions. Nevada sports books share a mutual interest with law enforcement and the sports leagues in combating game fixing because they are the financial victims of game-fixers. . . .

Game fixing—when players, coaches, or referees influence a sporting contest for the purposes of gambling—is a significant threat to the integrity of sports. The popularity of sporting contests depends upon the uncertainty of the game's outcome and the drama of live competition. Game fixing or the perception thereof reduces the interest of fans who cease believing that the games reflect actual, fair competition and instead believe that the games are staged contests like professional wrestling matches. Whether players throw games to ensure the other team wins or merely reduce effort to affect the game's final margin (point shaving), the viability of professional and amateur sports is jeopardized when the uncertainty of the game's outcome is completely or partially eliminated.

In an extreme example, corruption crippled the Chinese Super League despite soccer's status as one of the most popular sports in China. After a series of game-fixing scandals, the average television audience dropped by 42 percent and average match attendance dropped by 38 percent. In the United States, game fixing is under-detected, entering the public consciousness only when a major scandal is uncovered. The National Collegiate Athletic Association (NCAA) conducted an anonymous survey in 2004 that revealed a startling number of student-athletes who had engaged in game fixing; approximately 2 percent of Division 1 basketball players reported either accepting money to play poorly or knowing someone who had. An econometric analysis of Division I basketball games supported the survey results and estimated that 6 percent of games where one team was heavily favored and 1 percent of all games were tainted by point shaving.

Game fixing is also a threat to the financial viability of sports books. A fixed game allows bettors with knowledge of the fix to wager without risk; every dollar these bettors win is a loss for the sports book.

Additionally, the demand for sports wagering depends upon the perception among bettors that the contest is fair. After the game-fixing scandals in the Chinese Super League, bettors switched to European soccer because it offered a fair game to bet upon. Consequently, both sports leagues and sports books have tremendous incentives to prevent game fixing. . . .

Before game-fixers can be subject to either public or private penalties, their illegal activity must first be detected. One prosecutor explained that the task of detecting and prosecuting of game fixing is "innately difficult . . . because of the individual nature of what the athletes do" and because determining whether an athlete accepted a bribe requires looking into the athlete's head. Analyzing game film for evidence of game fixing is a snipe hunt due to the inherent subjectivity of officiating decisions and the impossibility of determining whether an athlete missed a shot on purpose or was merely having a poor shooting night. . . . The most successful detection technique has not involved traditional law enforcement methods, but has relied upon the statistical expertise of the Nevada sports books. . . .

Relying upon Nevada's sports books to detect game fixing is not a complete solution. Because only one percent of bets are placed in Nevada, there is theoretically only a one percent chance of detecting irregular betting. This percentage could be even smaller as game-fixers have a disincentive to bet in a regulated market like Nevada. Although a greater market share for legal sports books would increase the chance of detection, even a one percent market share can still contribute to the detection of game fixing. First, game-fixing conspiracies are difficult to keep concealed. There is a tremendous temptation to let other individuals in on the fix because it is nearly costless to the game-fixer. Secondary bettors possessing information or rumors of fixed games may end up wagering in Nevada sports books, leading to the discovery of the actual conspiracy. Second, Nevada sports books may function as a secondary market, where bets placed in other markets can be reflected through the use of layoff bets. A layoff bet is one that a bookie or sports book places with another bookie or sports book to reduce the risk of unbalanced betting. This creates an echo effect whereby bets placed in other markets can be reflected in Nevada's lines. The existence and prevalence of layoff betting is controversial as Nevada law prohibits bets placed from out-of-state or on behalf of an out-of-state bettor.

Sports books can help prevent game fixing if they are viewed as allies to work with, not enemies to work against. . . . Nevada sports books have alerted law enforcement to multiple game-fixing conspiracies that may never have been uncovered without the sports books' assistance. Setting up a formal relationship of information sharing and investigative collaboration between law enforcement, sports leagues, and sports books would help to prevent game fixing.

Sports betting itself does not threaten the integrity of sports, it can exist as an independent activity that is completely separate from the games. Harm arises only when sports and gambling become entangled. Maintaining independence between sports and gambling is positive for both sides and can be accomplished through cooperation to eliminate game fixing.

# CHAPTER
# 7

---

# Regulating Fair Play, Cheating, and Gaming Profitability

Casinos and other commercial gaming operations are businesses. Like other businesses, one of their primary purposes is to earn revenues. Indeed, depending on its structure, a casino may even have a duty to maximize shareholder income or value. Even charitable gaming operations, which are not-for-profit operations, are nevertheless usually seeking to earn revenues to assist the organization in achieving its charitable purposes.

Gaming operators generally earn revenues from gaming activities using one or both of two quite different methods. First, a gaming operator can function as a disinterested service provider that merely facilitates gaming among and between other players. Common examples include poker, sports-betting, and pari-mutuel horseracing. In these gaming activities, the gaming operator is not necessarily an active participant in the game. Rather, the gaming operation merely hosts the activity and coordinates the betting between others. In these types of circumstances, the gaming operator makes its money by taxing the activity in some manner by, for example, taking a fee out of the amounts bet. In poker, the house's fee is sometimes called a "rake." In sports-betting, the house fee is called a viggerish or "vig." State lotteries often operate under an analogous structure. In a lottery, the state will often set aside (or tax) a fixed percentage of 30 or 35 percent of the proceeds to be used for another public purpose, with the remainder of the revenue being used for payouts and administrative costs. In none of these circumstances is the operator gambling against the player. The house is simply charging a fee for a neutral service.

The second method used by gaming operators to earn revenue from gaming activity is by actively participating in the gaming itself. A common example is the "house-banked" card game called blackjack. In serving as the "bank," the "house" places its own money at stake. Though players may be sitting at a common table, players are not playing against one another in blackjack; each is playing against the house. Craps and roulette are other common examples.

All things being equal, bets offered to patrons in this gaming context always favor the house. Indeed, the house makes the rules and carefully structures each game in such a way that the laws of chance will favor the house and, in the long run, the house will win. That is to say, the aggregate of all players' losses will exceed all players' winnings, though inevitably some players will win and some will lose. This is how the gaming operation makes money. Indeed, without losers, the casino would quickly go broke.

In some games much more than others, the odds favor the house. The gambling industry brings in billions of dollars in profits each year at the expense of patrons hoping to be among the lucky few who can prevail against unlikely odds, and therefore "beat" the casino.

From the player's perspective, gaming in the "house-banked" context requires us to define the nature of the product that the casino is selling. Is the casino selling some unspecified form of entertainment? Or is it selling the right to use all one's native abilities to obtain a fair chance to win?

From the casino's perspective, on the other hand, the question may be one of freedom to contract. May the casino choose with whom it may do business or must it offer its product to any interested patron?

Some mathematically gifted patrons have found ways to use finely honed skills to increase their advantage over the house in certain games. Sometimes they do so through cooperative efforts with other patrons. Gambling regulators have generally recognized that these individuals are not necessarily cheating when they use innate skills and even when they cooperate with one another, but jurisdictions have adopted different approaches for dealing with such methods, sometimes euphemistically characterized as "advantage play." This chapter explores such approaches

Perhaps the most famous of all such "advantage players" was a man by the name of Ken Uston, who counted cards while playing blackjack and who enjoyed hefty profits as a result of his successes. As casinos began catching on to Uston's methods, they sought to ban him from their operations. Uston challenged their ability to do so both in New Jersey and in Nevada. The cases in section A reflect the challenges by Uston and other advantage players. The cases in section B ask when an activity goes beyond advantage play to become actual cheating and considers the ability of casinos and regulators to define cheating in the gaming context.

## A. THE SAGA OF KEN USTON: ADVANTAGE PLAY AND EXCLUSION FROM GAMING VENUES

### USTON v. RESORTS INTERNATIONAL HOTEL, INC.
#### 445 A.2d 370 (N.J. 1982)

PASHMAN, J.

Since January 30, 1979, appellant Resorts International Hotel, Inc. (Resorts) has excluded respondent, Kenneth Uston, from the blackjack tables in its casino because Uston's strategy increases his chances of winning money. Uston concedes that his strategy of card counting can tilt the odds in his favor under the current blackjack rules promulgated by the Casino Control Commission (Commission). However, Uston contends that Resorts has no common law or statutory right to exclude him because of his strategy for playing blackjack.

### I

Kenneth Uston is a renowned teacher and practitioner of a complex strategy for playing blackjack known as card counting. Card counters keep track of the playing cards as they are dealt and adjust their betting patterns when the odds are in their favor. When used over a period of time, this method allegedly ensures a profitable encounter with the casino.

Uston first played blackjack at Resorts' casino in November 1978. Resorts took no steps to bar Uston at that time, apparently because the Commission's blackjack rules then in operation minimized the advantages of card counting.

On January 5, 1979, however, a new Commission rule took effect that dramatically improved the card counter's odds. The new rule, which remains in effect, restricted the reshuffling of the deck in ways that benefited card counters. Resorts concedes that the Commission could promulgate blackjack rules that virtually eliminate the advantage of card counting. However, such rules would slow the game, diminishing the casino's "take" and, consequently, its profits from blackjack gaming.

By letter dated January 30, 1979, attorneys for Resorts wrote to Commission Chairman Lordi, asking the Commission's position on the legality of summarily removing card counters from its blackjack tables. That same day, Commissioner Lordi responded in writing that no statute or regulation barred Resorts from excluding professional card counters from its casino. Before the day had ended, Resorts terminated Uston's career at its blackjack tables, on the basis that in its opinion he was a professional card counter. Resorts subsequently formulated standards for identification of card counters and adopted a general policy to exclude such players.

The Commission upheld Resorts' decision to exclude Uston. Relying on *Garifine v. Monmouth Park Jockey Club*, 29 N.J. 47 (1959), the Commission held that Resorts enjoys a common law right to exclude anyone it chooses, as long as the exclusion does not violate state and federal civil rights laws. The Appellate Division reversed. . . .

## II

This Court has recognized that "[t]he statutory and administrative controls over casino operations established by the [Casino Control] Act are extraordinarily pervasive and intensive." *Knight v. Margate*, 86 N.J. 374, 380-81 (1981). . . . [T]he act declares as public policy of this State "that the institution of licensed casino establishments in New Jersey be strictly regulated and controlled." N.J.S.A. 5:12-1(13).

At the heart of the Casino Control Act are its provisions for the regulation of licensed casino games. N.J.S.A. 5:12-100 provides: All gaming shall be conducted according to rules promulgated by the commission. All wagers and pay-offs of winning wagers at table games shall be made according to rules promulgated by the commission, which shall establish such minimum wagers and other limitations as may be necessary to assure the vitality of casino operations and fair odds to and maximum participation by casino patrons. . . .

This provision on games and gaming equipment reinforces the general statutory provisions[, providing] in part:

> The Commission shall, without limitation on the powers conferred in the preceding section, include within its regulations the following specific provisions in accordance with the provisions of the act; . . .
>
> f. Defining and limiting the areas of operation, the rules of authorized games, odds, and devices permitted, and the method of operation of such games and devices. . . .

Pursuant to these statutes, the Commission has promulgated exhaustive rules on the playing of blackjack. These rules cover every conceivable aspect of the game, from determining how the cards are to be shuffled and cut, to providing that certain cards shall not be dealt "until the dealer has first announced 'Dealer's Card' which shall be stated by the dealer in a tone of voice calculated to be heard by each person at the table." It is no exaggeration to state that the Commission's regulation of blackjack is more extensive than the entire administrative regulation of many industries.

These exhaustive statutes and regulations make clear that the Commission's control over the rules and conduct of licensed casino games is intended to be comprehensive. The ability of casino operators to determine how the games will be played would undermine this control and subvert the important policy of ensuring the "credibility and integrity of the regulatory process and of casino operations." N.J.S.A. 5:12-1(b). The Commission has promulgated the blackjack rules that give Uston a comparative advantage, and it has sole authority to change those rules. There is no indication that Uston has violated any Commission rule on the playing of blackjack. Put simply, Uston's gaming is "conducted according to rules promulgated by the Commission." Resorts has no right to exclude Uston on grounds that he successfully plays the game under existing rules.

## III

Resorts claimed that it could exclude Uston because it had a common law right to exclude anyone at all for any reason. While we hold that the Casino Control Act precludes Resorts from excluding Uston for the reasons stated, it is important for us to address the asserted common law right for two reasons. First, Resorts' contentions and the Commission's position concerning the common law right are incorrect. Second, the act has not completely divested Resorts of its common law right to exclude.

The right of an amusement place owner to exclude unwanted patrons and the patron's competing right of reasonable access both have deep roots in the common law. See Arterburn, *The Origin and First Test of Public Callings*, 75 U. Pa. L. Rev. 411 (1927); Wyman, *The Law of Public Callings as a Solution of the Trust Problem*, 17 Harv. L. Rev. 156 (1904). In this century, however, courts have disregarded the right of reasonable access in the common law of some jurisdictions at the time the Civil War Amendments and Civil Rights Act of 1866 were passed.

The current majority American rule has for many years disregarded the right of reasonable access, granting to proprietors of amusement places an absolute right arbitrarily to eject or exclude any person consistent with state and federal civil rights laws. . . . In *State v. Shack*, 58 N.J. 297 (1971), the Court held that although an employer of migrant farm workers "may reasonably require" those visiting his employees to identify themselves, "the employer may not deny the worker his privacy or interfere with his opportunity to live with dignity and to enjoy associations customary among our citizens." Id. at 308. The Court reversed the trespass convictions of an attorney and a social services worker who had entered the property to assist farmworkers there.

[*State v. Schmid*, 423 A.2d 615, 629 (N.J. 1980)] recognizes implicitly that when property owners open their premises to the general public in the pursuit of their own property interests, they have no right to exclude people unreasonably. On the contrary, they have a duty not to act in an arbitrary or discriminatory manner toward persons who come on their premises. That duty applies not only to common carriers, *Messenger v. Pennsylvania Railroad Co.*, 37 N.J.L. 531 (E. & A. 1874), innkeepers, owners of gasoline service stations, *Streeter v. Brogan*, 113 N.J. Super. 486 (Ch. Div. 1971), or to private hospitals, *Doe v. Bridgeton Hospital Ass'n, Inc.*, 71 N.J. 478 (1976), but to all property owners who open their premises to the public. Property owners have no legitimate interest in unreasonably excluding particular members of the public when they open their premises for public use.

No party in this appeal questions the right of property owners to exclude from their premises those whose actions "disrupt the regular and essential operations of the [premises]," *State v. Schmid*, 84 N.J. at 566 (quoting Princeton University Regulations on solicitation), or threaten the security of the premises and its occupants, *see State v. Shack*, 58 N.J. at 308. In some circumstances, proprietors have a duty to remove disorderly or otherwise dangerous persons from the premises. *See Holly v. Meyers Hotel and Tavern, Inc.*, 9 N.J. 493, 495 (1952). These common law principles enable the casino to bar from its entire facility, for instance, the disorderly, the intoxicated, and the repetitive petty offender.

Whether a decision to exclude is reasonable must be determined from the facts of each case. Respondent Uston does not threaten the security of any casino occupant. Nor has he disrupted the functioning of any casino operations. Absent a valid contrary rule by the Commission, Uston possesses the usual right of reasonable access to Resorts International's blackjack tables.

## IV

Although the Commission alone has authority to exclude persons based upon their methods of playing licensed casino games, that authority has constitutional and statutory limits. . . . If the Commission decides to consider promulgating a rule banning card counters, it should review the statutory mandates regarding both the public policy of this State and the rules of licensed games. The Casino Control Act commands the Commission to regulate gambling with such "limitations as may be necessary *to assure the vitality of casino operations and fair odds to and maximum participation by casino patrons,*" N.J.S.A. 5:12-100(e) (emphasis added). The Court recognizes that the goals of casino vitality, fair odds to all players and maximum player participation may be in conflict. It is the Commission which must strike the appropriate balance.

The Commission should also consider that the Legislature has declared as public policy of this state that "[c]onfidence in casino gaming operations is eroded to the extent the State of New Jersey does not provide a regulatory framework for casino gaming that permits and promotes stability and continuity in casino gaming operations." N.J.S.A. 5:12-1(14). Moreover, "[a]n integral and essential element of the regulation and control of such casino facilities by the State rests in the public confidence and trust in the credibility and integrity of the regulatory process and of casino operations." N.J.S.A. 5:12-1(6). The exclusion of persons who can play the licensed games to their advantage may diminish public confidence in the fairness of casino gaming. . . . However, the right of the casinos to have the rules drawn so as to allow some reasonable profit must also be recognized in any realistic assessment. The Commission should consider the potentially broad ramifications of excluding card counters before it seeks to promulgate such a rule. Fairness and the integrity of casino gaming are the touchstones.

## V

In sum, absent a valid Commission regulation excluding card counters, respondent Uston will be free to employ his card-counting strategy at Resorts' blackjack tables. There is currently no Commission rule banning Uston, and Resorts has no authority to exclude him for card counting. However, it is not clear whether the Commission would have adopted regulations involving card counters had it known that Resorts could not exclude Uston. The Court therefore continues the temporary order banning Uston from Resorts' blackjack tables for 90 days from the date of this opinion. After that time, respondent is free to play blackjack at Resorts' casino absent a valid Commission rule excluding him.

*NOTES*

1.  The house advantage in blackjack starts at about 8 percent. If a player follows basic blackjack strategy, the house advantage decreases to .5 percent. *See* Henry Tamburin, *House Advantage in Blackjack*, at http://www.casino.com/blackjack/article.asp?id=1848. By counting cards, however, a player can conceivably shift the odds such that he has an advantage over the house, primarily because the player can increase his bet when the odds become more favorable. Card counting was the subject of BRINGING DOWN THE HOUSE: THE INSIDE STORY OF SIX MIT STUDENTS WHO TOOK VEGAS FOR MILLIONS (2002), a book by Ben Mezrich, which was made into a movie, entitled *21*, released in 2008.

2.  After graduating Phi Beta Kappa and magna cum laude from Yale, Ken Uston went on to become a senior vice president at the Pacific Stock Exchange in San Francisco. In an interview, Uston explained his refusal to invest in the stock market:

> "I don't really consider myself a gambler," Uston says. "I'm more a mathematician and scientist. I majored in economics at Yale and finance at Harvard Business School, and it's funny—I used to work at the stock exchange but I wouldn't put a dime in the goddam stock market. No way in the world."
>
> "Why not?" I ask.
>
> "It's a gamble. And that's another irony. When I resigned from the stock exchange, I wrote a letter to the board explaining that, in my opinion, blackjack is a unique business. It's the only one that I know where you can actually assess the mathematical expectations of winning or losing in advance and know what those expectations are. When you open a laundromat or a brokerage house or a magazine, it's a gamble. You don't really know. But when I play blackjack, I know that in ten days I have about a ninety percent chance of doubling our bank and a ten percent chance of being below that figure; and I know that if we keep going forever, we eventually have a niney-five percent chance of doubling. And I can assess one standard deviation, two standard deviations, four, and so fourth[sic]. You can express it exactly mathematically. It's the only business I know of in the world where you can do that. And it's far more assured than the stock market, where you're betting on other people's expectations of a given equity issue six months hence, given fluctuations in the international gold situation and interest rates and other factors, factors way beyond your control. So blackjack is far better business than the market."

Roger Dionne, *Ken Uston—Barefoot Boy in Bungalow Four*, GAMBLING TIMES, available at: http://www.gamblingtimes.com/blackjack/blackjack_9.html.

3. *Uston* holds that a property owner who opens his property to the general public in pursuit of his own business interest has no right to exclude people unreasonably. This holding presumably applies much more broadly than merely to gaming operations. Are there special reasons for application of such a rule to the gaming context? Is there an argument against applying such a rule to a gaming operation?

4. Is this access question a matter that the courts can address better than markets? What are the commercial interests at stake? Do the courts address those interests adequately? Should they?

## CAMPIONE v. ADAMAR OF NEW JERSEY, INC.
### 714 A.2d 299 (N.J. 1998)

POLLOCK, J.

This appeal presents several issues. Campione was a blackjack player and professional card counter who frequented casinos in Atlantic City. The defendants are Adamar of New Jersey, which operates the Trop-World Casino; Michael Imperatrice, a floor supervisor and a member of TropWorld's card counting team; and Patrick Scully, TropWorld's Sergeant of Security.

## I.

The purpose of blackjack is to obtain cards having a higher count than those of the dealer without exceeding a total count of twenty-one. In blackjack, unlike in other games of chance, players' skill can increase the odds in their favor. Card counting is a method of playing blackjack that involves keeping track of the number of "high value" cards. This technique allows a blackjack player to identify a favorable count, which occurs when an unusually high percentage of the cards remaining in the "dealing shoe" are high value cards. At that time, the chances increase that the dealer will "bust," or deal cards that exceed 21 points, thereby permitting the card counter to win. A favorable count occurs infrequently, and almost exclusively after most of the cards have been dealt. Consequently, card counters must maximize their play at such times. To do so, card counters may increase their bet, play two hands at once, or both.

Neither the Casino Control Act, N.J.S.A. 5:12-1 to 142 ("Act"), nor the CCC prohibits card counting. The CCC, however, authorizes casinos to use various "countermeasures" to discourage card counting. For example, CCC regulations give casinos the discretion to shuffle the cards at will, N.J.A.C. 19:47-2.5a, or to lower the betting limit at any time, N.J.A.C. 19:47-8.3c. In addition to issuing its own regulations, the CCC allows, subject to its approval, casinos to adopt "Section 99 internal controls." N.J.S.A. 5:12-99.

To identify card counters, TropWorld employed a "Card Counting Team." After identifying plaintiff as a card counter, TropWorld's team applied countermeasures against him. Although TropWorld admitted to treating card counters differently from other patrons, it asserted that the treatment complied with CCC regulations and its Section 99 internal controls.

Because of the countermeasures applied by TropWorld and other Atlantic City casinos, plaintiff filed a number of "patron complaints" with the CCC. He particularly objected to the casinos' lowering his betting limit and limiting him to one hand, while simultaneously allowing other players to exceed the betting limit and play two hands. In response, the CCC [indicated that his complaints were invalid and/ or that only the courts had authority to adjudicate claims of money damages].

Plaintiff's action against TropWorld arises from two incidents. According to plaintiff, on April 27, 1989, TropWorld allowed other blackjack players, but not him, to play two hands during one deal. When plaintiff put his chips in the betting circle, the casino floor person instructed the dealer to deal past plaintiff. As a result, plaintiff filed a patron complaint with the CCC [which] informed plaintiff that TropWorld's actions did not constitute a violation of the Act or the regulations. . . .

The second incident took place on November 10, 1989, when plaintiff was playing blackjack at a TropWorld table with a minimum bet of $25 and a maximum bet of $1000. When the card count became favorable, plaintiff placed several unsuccessful bets of $300 and $350. The parties disagree over the ensuing facts.

According to plaintiff, after he placed a $350 bet, Imperatrice placed a sign on the table lowering the betting limit to $100. Imperatrice, however, maintained that plaintiff's initial bet was not in the betting circle before he lowered the limit. Otherwise, according to Imperatrice, he would have honored the bet. Imperatrice informed plaintiff that he could not bet more than $100. According to plaintiff, Imperatrice then told the other player at the table that he could wager up to $1000. Without responding, that player left the table.

When Imperatrice pushed plaintiff's $350 bet out of the circle, plaintiff pushed it back. Plaintiff testified that Imperatrice then instructed the dealer to deal, but to pay plaintiff, if he won, based on a $100 bet. The dealer dealt a hand that qualified for a "double down," which entitled plaintiff to double his bet. N.J.A.C. 19:47-2.10.

Plaintiff then placed another $350 in the betting circle and won. Imperatrice instructed the dealer to pay plaintiff $200—for an initial $100 bet and a $100 "double down" bet. Plaintiff claimed that he was entitled to $700—for the initial $350 bet and the $350 "double down" bet.

Plaintiff stated that he then placed his hand on top of the cards, pulled the cards toward him, and advised the dealer that she had not paid him the proper amount of money. Although plaintiff knew he was not permitted to touch the cards, N.J.A.C. 19:47-2.6n, he wanted to preserve the cards as evidence. According to Imperatrice, however, plaintiff grabbed the cards. When Imperatrice informed plaintiff that he had been paid the proper amount, plaintiff asked to see a CCC representative. Imperatrice told plaintiff that to complain he must go to the CCC booth. He also informed plaintiff that if he did not relinquish his cards, Imperatrice would call security.

Shortly thereafter, Imperatrice called David Duffield, a lieutenant of security. Duffield called Scully, who told plaintiff to remove his hands from the cards. Plaintiff refused. Plaintiff's version is that he explained that he had been paid improperly and that he wanted to keep the cards as evidence. Scully, however, testified that he told plaintiff two or three times that if he did not take his hands off the cards and leave the game, Scully would arrest him. According to plaintiff, when he relinquished the cards, Duffield and Scully arrested him.

Scully and Duffield then escorted plaintiff to the CCC booth, where plaintiff sat down on the floor because, as he testified, he felt weak and lightheaded. Detective Ronald Hungridge of the DGE . . . informed plaintiff that he was under arrest. Although Hungridge described plaintiff as "very upset, very boisterous," plaintiff denied cursing or threatening any casino personnel.

Scully signed a complaint in the Atlantic City Municipal Court charging plaintiff with disorderly conduct, N.J.S.A. 2C:33-2(a), "by causing an annoyance and disrupting the game of blackjack by retaining the playing cards and threatening TropWorld Employees." The complaint also charged plaintiff with defiant trespass, N.J.S.A. 2C:18-3, "by remaining in the casino complex after being formally ejected from same." The entire incident took place in less than an hour. Although plaintiff was never handcuffed or physically restrained, he said that he felt "humiliated" by the incident.

In the municipal court plaintiff was acquitted of the criminal charges. The court dismissed the disorderly conduct count on the ground that plaintiff had not caused a public annoyance. It also found plaintiff not guilty of the trespass charge because plaintiff was "legitimately trying to protect his bet." . . .

On February 4, 1991, plaintiff filed [an action seeking] both compensatory and punitive damages, plaintiff alleged malicious prosecution, denial of equal access, discrimination, and breach of implied contract.

Concerning plaintiff's allegations of discrimination, the Law Division recognized that casinos must treat patrons fairly. The court reasoned that the selective enforcement of card counting countermeasures against patrons at the same table constituted discrimination. Hence, "it is discriminatory to allow others at the same table to play two hands, while limiting [plaintiff] to one." The court, however, rejected plaintiff's complaints about TropWorld's right to "shuffle-at-will." Because shuffling the cards affects all players at the table evenly, "it is not discrimination."

The jury returned a $1,519,873.43 verdict in plaintiff's favor: $300,625.87 against TropWorld and Imperatrice on the discrimination claim; $219,034.06 in compensatory damages against TropWorld and Scully for malicious prosecution; and $1,000,213.50 in punitive damages against TropWorld for malicious prosecution. All parties appealed. . . .

## II.

In 1976, the New Jersey Constitution was amended to enable the Legislature to authorize the operation of casinos in Atlantic City. *Bally Mfg. Corp. v. N.J. Casino Comm'n*, 426 A.2d 1000 (N.J.), *appeal dismissed*, 454 U.S. 804 (1981). One year later, the Legislature enacted the Casino Control Act. N.J.S.A. 5:12-1 to 152. The Act legalizes casino gambling and establishes an elaborate framework for regulating the casino industry. *Knight v. City of Margate*, 431 A.2d 833 (N.J. 1981). . . .

The Act's statutory and regulatory controls cover "virtually every facet of casino gambling and its potential impact upon the public." *Knight, supra*, 431 A.2d 833. To administer the statutory scheme, the Act created a two-tiered regulatory system in which the CCC exercises quasi-legislative and quasi-judicial power, N.J.S.A. 5:12-63, and the DGE conducts investigations and prosecutions[.]

In the exercise of its quasi-legislative power, the CCC promulgates regulations controlling the operation of authorized games, odds, and devices. . . . Pursuant to this authority, the CCC has promulgated detailed regulations on blackjack. For example, the blackjack rules detail the procedure for the shuffle, cut, and deal of cards.

The Act also authorizes the CCC in the exercise of its quasi-judicial authority to adjudicate regulatory violations. Thus, the CCC has the responsibility to "receiv[e] complaints from the public relating to the conduct of gaming," and "to conduct all hearings pertaining to civil violations of this act or regulations." In addition, the CCC may conduct investigative hearings concerning the conduct of gaming and gaming operations, the operation and administration of casino control laws, and any other matter within the CCC's jurisdiction.

Proceedings against a licensee must begin with a written complaint that includes "a statement setting forth . . . the charges and the acts or omissions supporting such charges." On filing the complaint with the CCC, a copy is served on the casino. Within fifteen days, the casino may notify the CCC of any defenses and request a hearing. Should the CCC find evidence of a violation of the Act or of its regulations, the CCC must refer the matter to the DGE for investigation and prosecution. The DGE or "any person aggrieved by a final decision or order of the commission made after hearing or rehearing by the commission . . . may obtain judicial review thereof by an appeal to the Superior Court."

The Act authorizes the CCC to implement various administrative remedies, including the power to grant, deny, or restrict any license or application. Further, the Act permits the CCC to impose a penalty on any casino licensee "for any cause deemed reasonable." Such penalties may include "restitution of any moneys or property unlawfully obtained or retained by a licensee or registrant."

The DGE, the law enforcement agency responsible for enforcing the provisions of the Act, assists the CCC with its quasi-judicial role. After the CCC refers to it evidence of violations of the Act or its regulations, the DGE has the responsibility to "investigate violations of this act and regulations," and to "initiate, prosecute and defend" before the CCC all proceedings for violations of the act or any regulations or appeals therefrom.

In *Uston v. Resorts Int'l Hotel, Inc.*, 445 A.2d 370 (N.J. 1982), this Court addressed the right of a casino to exclude patrons solely because they were card counters. . . . Although we declined to decide whether the Act empowered the CCC to exclude card counters, we gave the CCC ninety days to adopt regulations permitting countermeasures. Although the CCC declined to authorize the exclusion of card counters, it adopted specific countermeasures. According to the CCC, the countermeasures, as opposed to exclusion, "would result in one player segment having the opportunity to play blackjack who has thus far been excluded from enjoying this game." Nevertheless, the CCC intended these countermeasures to minimize the perceived threat of card counters to the statistical advantage that casinos need to remain profitable.

The countermeasures promulgated by the CCC in 1982 included: (1) the "Bart Carter Shuffle," which is a special shuffling procedure, (2) the continuous shuffling shoe, (3) shuffling-at-will, which allows casinos to shuffle after any round of play, and (4) increasing the number of decks from which the cards are dealt. . . . During the pendency of this action, the CCC adopted two additional regulations that authorize card-counting countermeasures. One regulation [adopted in 1991] states that a casino, on posting a notice, "may at any time change the permissible minimum or maximum wager at a game table. . . ." A 1993 regulation permits a casino to offer "different maximum wagers" at the same or different gaming tables.

At the time of the incidents that provide the basis for this action, TropWorld had adopted Section 99 internal controls. Those internal controls recognized that TropWorld had the discretion to shuffle at will, to permit a player to make more than one wager at a table, and to permit known "high limit players" to exceed the table's betting limit. Plaintiff claims that TropWorld discriminated against him by applying the CCC regulations and its Section 99 internal controls selectively against him, but not against other players seated at the same table.

## IV.

### A.

The Appellate Division held that the CCC has exclusive jurisdiction over plaintiff's common-law discrimination and contract claims. Both the CCC and DGE contend, however, that the CCC does not provide a forum for patron complaints seeking money damages. Instead, the two agencies assert that common law claims belong in Superior Court. . . .

If the Legislature vests an administrative agency with exclusive primary jurisdiction, that agency may be the only forum in which a party initially may seek relief. When, however, the Legislature has not vested such jurisdiction in an agency, a plaintiff may still seek relief in the courts. Generally, courts decline to grant relief when an adequate administrative remedy exists. If an adequate administrative remedy is available, a party ordinarily must exhaust that remedy before seeking relief in the courts. . . .

[We] hold that plaintiff did not enjoy an adequate administrative remedy to vindicate his damage claim against TropWorld. His only recourse was in the Law Division. We agree with the CCC and the DGE that the Legislature did not intend the CCC to be a court of claims for actions arising under the Act. The Act, for example, does not authorize private litigants to initiate claims for money damages before the CCC. If the Legislature intends that the CCC may award damages in private matters, it should so state explicitly. . . .

A patron may recover on a claim for restitution only if the CCC first finds the claim is meritorious, and the DGE then decides to pursue it. If the CCC summarily rejects a patron's complaint, the patron does not have the right to request a hearing before the CCC. Although the CCC has the authority to conduct investigational hearings concerning the conduct of gaming, neither the Act nor the regulations empower patrons to request a hearing if the CCC dismisses their claims. . . .

By comparison, the Nevada Gaming Act vests the State Gaming Control Board with exclusive jurisdiction over disputes between casinos and patrons over the conduct of games. If the dispute involves at least $500, the casino must immediately notify the Board; otherwise, the casino need only inform the patron of his right to a Board investigation. Nev. Rev. Stat. 463.362(1). An agent of the Board must conduct an investigation and determine within thirty days whether payment should be made. A party aggrieved by the agent's decision may request a hearing before the Board. Nev. Rev. Stat. 463.363. Until such time as the New Jersey Legislature or the CCC takes similar action, the place for patrons to file private claims for damages is in the Superior Court.

The elaborate legislative and administrative system for regulating casinos suggests, however, that the CCC should exercise primary jurisdiction over issues concerning the interpretation and application of the Act and the regulations. The doctrine of primary jurisdiction, like that requiring exhaustion of administrative remedies, promotes proper relationships between courts and regulatory agencies.

Under the doctrine of primary jurisdiction, when enforcement of a claim requires resolution of an issue within the special competence of an administrative agency, a court may defer to a decision of that agency. 3 DAVIS & PIERCE ADMINISTRATIVE LAW §14.1 (1994). Although the court may retain jurisdiction over the dispute, it defers action until receipt of the agency's views.

The pervasiveness of the regulatory scheme controlling the casino industry indicates that the Legislature intended to invest the CCC with primary jurisdiction to regulate the casino industry. To the extent that the resolution of a plaintiff's claim depends on an interpretation of the Act or administrative regulations, the CCC should have the first opportunity to provide that interpretation. A referral to the CCC should assure the resolution of the controversy consistent with the views of the entity best positioned to consider the matter. Retaining primary jurisdiction in the courts could dislocate the intricate regulatory structure governing a sensitive industry. Permitting courts and juries across the State to interpret statutory and administrative regulations could introduce confusion where uniformity is needed. The lack of uniform interpretations, in turn, could affect the stability of the industry.

## IV.

### B.

Within its delegated authority, the CCC may adopt regulations that require the uniform application of countermeasures to all players at a blackjack table or that permit the selective application of such countermeasures against card counters only. Regulations in effect in 1989 failed to state expressly whether casinos could selectively apply countermeasures against players at one table. The CCC suggests that casinos could so apply countermeasures, but at oral argument it was uncertain whether a casino could lower the limit for card counters and simultaneously allow other players to bet at the former limit or higher. Absent a regulation, a patron may not be on notice of the rules of the game.

## V.

We next turn to the question whether the Superior Court may entertain a casino patron's private damage claim. The Act does not address whether a casino patron may maintain a civil action for damages based on violations of statutory or administrative provisions. It expressly grants jurisdiction to the Superior Court only for the award of injunctive relief and treble damages arising from such nefarious activities as racketeering, loan sharking, and securities manipulation. The absence of any express provision for a cause of action for discriminatory application of CCC regulations, however, does not necessarily mean that the Legislature intended that no such actions should exist. Indeed, the presumption is against statutory abrogation of a common-law right. To abrogate a common-law right, the Legislature must speak plainly and clearly. Should a casino engage in invidious discrimination, we have no doubt that the Superior Court could entertain an appropriate action.

In the absence of a common-law basis, courts have been reluctant to imply a private right of action for money damages in favor of casino patrons. Given the elaborate regulatory scheme, we likewise decline to imply a cause of action when no such cause of action exists at common law.

Plaintiff's claim of discriminatory treatment, however, has a common-law basis. Even without statutory or regulatory support, a casino has a common-law duty to treat patrons fairly. *Uston, supra,* 445 A.2d 370. Remaining is the issue whether the CCC permits casinos to discriminate among patrons by lowering the betting limit for a card counter while retaining or raising it for other patrons. The impact of such discrete treatment is less drastic than that of the exclusion of card counters in *Uston.* Although the CCC has not adopted an express regulation, by other regulations, the CCC may have implicitly permitted casinos to apply a separate set of rules to card counters seated at the same table as other patrons. An issue of this kind is especially suited for consideration by the CCC in the exercise of its primary jurisdiction. Accordingly, the Law Division should remand the matter to the CCC so that agency may interpret its own regulations.

## VI.

The Appellate Division perceived several errors in the jury instructions on plaintiff's claim of malicious prosecution. Consequently, it reversed the entry of the judgment awarding plaintiff damages of $1,000,213.50 on that claim. We agree substantially with the Appellate Division's analysis. . . . The critical issue at trial was whether defendants had probable cause to initiate the municipal court proceeding. . . . Probable cause is a familiar, but elusive concept. Critical to a finding of probable cause is the determination of the underlying facts.

In a malicious prosecution action, when the underlying facts are in dispute, the jury bears the responsibility of making that determination. For the jury to discharge its responsibility, the trial court must provide proper instructions. Given the inconsistencies in the testimony, the trial court should have summarized the parties' versions to frame the inquiry whether a person of ordinary prudence would believe on reasonable grounds in the truth of the charges. . . . Affirmed as modified.

### NOTES

1.   Does the New Jersey Supreme Court decision in *Campione* retreat from its position in *Uston v. Resorts Iinternational?*

2. Compare the Nevada and New Jersey models for dealing with patron disputes. What are the advantages and disadvantages of each? Is New Jersey's approach likely to be more protective or less protective of patrons than the Nevada model?

3. Anthony Cabot and Robert Hannum suggest that "[a]n advantage player is simply someone who wants to be able to take advantage of another party in a private contract." Anthony Cabot & Robert Hannum, *Advantage Play and Commercial Casinos*, 74 Miss. L.J. 681, 735-738 (2005). Thus, they argue that no advantage player should have a right to play the casino game of his or her choice. If that is what an advantage player is doing, however, what is the casino doing? If the odds are stacked in favor of the casino, couldn't the casino also be characterized as "someone who wants to take advantage of another party in a private contract?" What are the contract implications of excluding advantage players?

4. Return now to Ken Uston. Though Uston's case against Resorts International in New Jersey was successful, Uston was less successful on the west coast. See the cases that follow.

## USTON v. AIRPORT CASINO, INC.
### 564 F.2d 1216 (9th Cir. 1977)

Per Curiam.

Uston's complaint alleged that the defendants, operators of a gambling casino in Las Vegas, Nevada, excluded him from their casino and denied him the opportunity to play blackjack or "21" solely because he is a "competent blackjack player." He contended that this action entitled him to recover damages under the federal civil rights laws and under the common law of innkeepers' duties. The district court dismissed for failure to state a claim upon which relief may be granted. Fed. R. Civ. P. 12(b)(6). We affirm.

It is clear from Uston's complaint and brief that there is a lack of "state action" in the discriminatory conduct he alleges. It is also clear that his complaint does not involve discrimination on the basis of race, color, religion, national origin or sex. Although there are conclusory allegations of "conspiracy," the record is devoid of specific factual allegations to support the claim. One or more of these deficiencies precludes recovery under every civil rights statute which Uston invokes.

Though the defendants in this case may be innkeepers in the common law sense, they were not acting in that capacity in their dealings with Uston. The relationship was not one of innkeeper and patron, but rather one of casino owner and prospective gambler. The policies upon which the innkeeper's special common law duties rested are not present in such a relationship.

Uston's argument based upon contract law is devoid of merit.
AFFIRMED.


*NOTE*

Given the short shrift that Uston's claims received in federal court in a case arising in Nevada, now return to the New Jersey case and try to identify the basis for Uston's claims. Why does New Jersey law protect a card counter or other blackjack player from discrimination? Does New Jersey law provide a general right to gamble? In refusing to hold that there is any obligation akin to the "innkeeper's duty" to grant a public right of access to people wishing to patronize a casino, the federal court has suggested that a casino can refuse service to anyone it chooses. What does each approach suggest about each jurisdiction's views about gambling?


## USTON v. HILTON HOTELS CORPORATION
### 448 F. Supp. 116 (D. Nev. 1978)

FOLEY, J.

This action is one of several cases filed by Kenneth Uston in this court and others over the last two years. In all, Uston has sought damages as well as injunctive relief to enjoin the respective casinos from refusing to allow him to play the game of "21". The present action arises from an event which occurred at the Flamingo Hilton Hotel casino on June 29, 1975. At approximately 6:00 P.M., Uston was approached by two security guards at a "21" table and was requested to leave the premises. The two guards escorted Uston to the hotel's entrance where Uston was read the Nevada trespass statute. Uston thereafter departed. Uston alleges that he was asked to leave because he is a "better than average black jack ("21") player." ...

Uston asserts that certain rights secured by the due process and equal protection clauses of the Fourteenth Amendment of the United States Constitution have been denied him. After having considered the pleadings, affidavits and written arguments of counsel, it is the finding of this Court that there are no pertinent genuine issues of fact. Further, it is the finding of this Court that Uston has failed to state any federally recognized cause of action.

In order to predicate an action under 42 U.S.C. §1983, it must be demonstrated, *inter alia*, that the deprivation of constitutional rights, the injury complained of, was brought about by state action, that is, took place under color of state law. It is well established that private conduct without some significant state involvement is not actionable under 42 U.S.C. §1983. In opposing the defendants' motion for summary judgment, Uston asserts that the actions of the defendants in preventing him from playing the game of "21" were tantamount to state action (1) because of the extent to which the State of Nevada regulates the gaming industry, and (2) because the State of Nevada, charged with the enforcement of the gaming laws, has refused to prohibit the discrimination against card counters. Both contentions are without merit.

Mere state regulation of a private industry in and of itself does not constitute state action. Something more, more in the nature of a substantial and direct state involvement in promoting the challenged activity, must be demonstrated in order to establish state action. In *Jackson v. Metropolitan Edison Co.*, 419 U.S. 345 (1974), a private electric utility was subject to pervasive and detailed state regulation and licensing, similar to the extent that the gaming industry is controlled by Nevada. The Court, in holding that such licensing and regulation did not constitute state action, stated, at page 358:

> Metropolitan is a privately owned corporation, and it does not lease its facilities from the State of Pennsylvania. It alone is responsible for the provision of power to its customers. In common with all corporations of the State it pays taxes to the State, and it is subject to a form of extensive regulation by the State in a way that most other business enterprises are not. But this was likewise true of the appellant club in *Moose Lodge No. 107 v. Irvis*, supra, where we said: "However detailed this type of regulation may be in some particulars, it cannot be said to in any way foster or encourage racial discrimination. Nor can it be said to make the State in any realistic sense a partner or even a joint venturer in the club's enterprise." 407 U.S. at 176-177.
>
> All of petitioner's arguments taken together show no more than that Metropolitan was a heavily regulated, privately owned utility, enjoying at least a partial monopoly in the providing of electrical service within its territory, and that it elected to terminate a service to petitioner in a manner which the Pennsylvania Public Utility Commission found permissible under state law. Under our decision this is not sufficient to connect the State of Pennsylvania with the respondent's action so as to make the latter's conduct attributable to the State for purposes of the Fourteenth Amendment.

In the case at hand, there has been no demonstration that the State of Nevada, either through its regulation and/or licensing of the

gaming industry, has to any significant degree promoted or participated in the exclusion of persons suspected by gaming establishments to be card counters or in Uston's words, "better than average
blackjack players."

Similarly, the State of Nevada is under no obligation, statutory or
otherwise, which, by its refusal to compel gaming establishments to
allow card counters to play "21", would attribute the defendants'
actions to state action. Uston has asserted that the omission by the
State of Nevada to take any affirmative action to alleviate the discrimination against card counters, in light of Nevada Revised Statutes
463.151, is akin to approval of same, and therefore state action.

NRS 463.151 requires the exclusion from gaming establishments of
certain persons named on a list compiled by the Nevada Gaming
Commission for various reasons, one of which is not card counting.
In essence, Uston argues that since the State of Nevada has enacted
measures that require the exclusion of a limited class of undesirable
persons, of which Uston is not a member, it thereby undertook the
affirmative duty to compel the admittance of all persons, such as
Uston, who were not named on the list compiled by the Nevada Gaming Commission. Such an argument strains logic. It is the judgment of
this Court that NRS 463.151 gives rise to no affirmative obligation by
the State of Nevada to compel gaming establishments to admit persons thought to be card counters. Since no duty exists, the failure to
prohibit private action is not state action. As was stated in *Cohen v.
Illinois Institute of Technology*, 524 F.2d 818 (7th Cir. 1975), at 826:

> "Finally, we are not persuaded that the omission of any affirmative
> prohibition against sex discrimination, even against the background
> of detailed State regulation of the Institute, is tantamount to express
> State approval of the objectionable policy. The holding of the Supreme
> Court in *Moose Lodge No. 107 v. Irvis*, supra, requires us to reject such an
> argument. For it is abundantly clear that the State of Pennsylvania had
> ample power to revoke the liquor license of the Lodge No. 107, and
> further that the State could not constitutionally endorse the Lodge's
> discriminatory practices. If a State's mere failure to prohibit could be
> equated with express approval, the *Moose Lodge* case would have been
> decided differently."

As such, since Uston has been unable to persuade this Court that
any of the activities involved in his removal from the casino of the
Flamingo Hilton amounted to state action, this Court concludes that
Uston has failed to state a claim under 42 U.S.C. §1983.

Next, Uston asserts that the defendants have conspired to deprive
him of the opportunity to play "21" which is actionable under 42

U.S.C. §1985. In order to state a claim under 42 U.S.C. §1985(3), it must be asserted that the defendants conspired to deprive Uston of equal protection of the laws, hence causing injury to him or his property. However, in *Griffin v. Breckenridge*, 403 U.S. 88 (1971), at 101 and 102, the Court stated that 42 U.S.C. §1985 was not "intended to apply to all tortious, conspiratorial interferences with the rights of others," but only to those which were founded upon "some racial, or perhaps otherwise class-based, invidiously discriminatory animus." In the case at hand, Uston has failed to allege that the "conspiracy" between the defendants to eliminate the class of "better than average blackjack players" was brought about by racial or any other invidiously discriminatory animus. Therefore, Uston has failed to state a claim under 42 U.S.C. §1985. [Ustons' claims should be dismissed.]

### NOTES

1. Note the strikingly different approaches to the same issue taken in New Jersey and Nevada. In light of the fact that New Jersey laws affirmatively provide access to patrons like Uston and Nevada does not, is it really true as this Nevada federal court says that in Nevada there is no "substantial and direct state involvement in promoting the challenged activity," i.e., exclusion, "to establish state action"? The court likened the State of Nevada's interest in and regulation of the Nevada gaming industry to Pennsylvania's interest in and regulation of a public electric utility in *Jackson v. Metropolitan Edison*. Are the relationships between these states and these industries analogous?

2. The New Jersey Court's ruling in favor of *Uston* was a matter of procedure, not necessarily a substantive declaration that card counters cannot be excluded from playing blackjack. What is the correct answer from a regulatory standpoint? Should casinos be authorized to exclude card counters?

### BROOKS v. CHICAGO DOWNS ASS'N, INC.
#### 791 F.2d 512 (7th Cir. 1986)

FLAUM, Circuit Judge.

This is a case of first impression on whether under Illinois law the operator of a horse race track has the absolute right to exclude a patron from the track premises for any reason, or no reason, except race, color, creed, national origin, or sex. . . .

# I

Plaintiffs are citizens of Pennsylvania who have formed a Pennsylvania partnership whose sole purpose is to pool the assets of the partners in order to place bets at horse racing tracks throughout the country. The plaintiffs are self-proclaimed expert handicappers, even though on the approximately 140 days they have bet at various race tracks they have ended up with net losses on 110 of those days. This case is about a bet they were not allowed to make.

The defendant is a private Illinois corporation licensed by the State of Illinois to conduct harness racing at Sportsman's Park race track in Cicero, Illinois. At various times during the racing season, Sportsman's Park conducts a pari-mutuel pool known as "Super Bet." In order to win the Super Bet pool, one must select the first two finishers of the fifth and sixth races and the first three finishers of the seventh race. The Super Bet pool is able to increase quickly and substantially because if the pool is not won on any given day, the total amount wagered is rolled over and added to the Super Bet purse for the next racing date. For example, in April of 1985 the plaintiffs, using their method for handicapping horses, placed bets on the Super Bet totalling $60,000. They picked the right horses and took home approximately $600,000.

In late July, 1985 the president of Chicago Downs ordered two of the plaintiffs (Jeffrey Yass and Kenneth Brodie) barred from Sportsman's Park just as they were seeking to place a $250,000 wager in the Super Bet. After the plaintiffs had been barred from Sportsman's Park, the Park's counsel informed them that they would be denied entry to all future racing dates at the Park. The plaintiffs then filed suit seeking injunctive relief that would prohibit the defendant from barring them from entering the race track premises. Sportsman's Park filed a motion to dismiss the complaint on the ground that under Illinois law the operator of a proprietary race track has the absolute right to exclude a patron from the track premises for any reason except race, creed, color, national origin, or sex. The trial court agreed with the defendants and granted their motion to dismiss, from which the plaintiffs now appeal. . . .

# II

Under the principles set forth in *Erie Railroad Company v. Tomkins*, 304 U.S. 64 (1938), as a federal court exercising diversity jurisdiction we will follow the law of the state in which the action was brought, which is in this case the law of Illinois. Because the Illinois Supreme Court has never directly confronted the issue of whether a private race track may exclude a patron without just cause, we must take what they have said, what Illinois appellate courts have said, and then the decisions of other states on the same issue, in order to formulate our holding.

The parties do not contest the Illinois Supreme Court's holding that a race track operator has the right to exclude patrons for good cause. *Phillips v. Graham*, 86 Ill. 2d 274, 56 Ill. Dec. 355, 427 N.E.2d 550 (1981). But in this case, the race track argues that it should be able to exclude a patron absent any cause at all, as long as it does not do so on the basis of race, color, creed, national origin, or sex. Under the defendant's theory, because the race track is a privately owned place of amusement it may exclude someone simply for wearing a green hat or a paisley tie. It need give no reason for excluding the patron, under its version of the common law, because it is not a state-granted monopoly, but a state-regulated licensee operating on private property.

The most recent Illinois Supreme Court case to touch on this issue was *Phillips v. Graham*, 427 N.E.2d 550 (Ill. 1981). In *Phillips* several harness racing drivers, owners, and trainers were excluded by formal Order of the State Racing Board from all race tracks in the state because they had been indicted for bribery. The Illinois Supreme Court held first that the plaintiff's were not deprived of procedural due process by their exclusion from the race tracks without a prior evidentiary hearing. Second, the Court held that the authority given organization licensees (such as race tracks) to exclude occupation licensees (such as jockeys) from their private property was not an unconstitutional delegation of legislative power. Paragraph 9(e) of the Illinois Horse Racing Act of 1975 states:

> The power to eject or exclude occupation licensees [trainers, jockeys, owners, etc.] may be exercised for just cause by the organization licensee [race track] or Board subject to subsequent hearing by the Board, as to the propriety of said exclusion.

Ill. Rev. Stat., ch. 8, par. 37-9(e) (1985). The addition of this section to the Act followed closely on the heels of *Cox v. National Jockey Club*, 323 N.E.2d 104 (Ill. 1974) and apparently codifies its holding.

The Court in *Phillips* cited the appellate court holding in *Cox* with approval and an explanation of that case is crucial to an understanding of *Phillips*. The plaintiff in *Cox* was a jockey licensed by the Illinois Racing Board. During the course of the defendant race track's annual meeting, it excluded Cox from its track, and thus foreclosed him from accepting mounts on horses he had been under contract to ride during the meet. Cox sought injunctive relief prohibiting the track from continuing to exclude him and directing that it permit him to ride unless the track could prove "just cause" for his exclusion. The race track moved to dismiss the complaint on the ground that as a private corporation it could exclude any person from its premises or deny any person racing privileges for any reason except race, color, creed, sex, or national origin. The trial court granted the relief sought by Cox and the appellate court affirmed.

The Cox court differentiated between the right of a track to exclude a licensee and its right to bar a patron. The track had argued that its common law right to exclude a patron without reason applied equally to a licensee. Although acknowledging precedent which held that the track could exclude a patron without reason or justification, the court refused to extend that authority to cover a licensee, stating:

> The defendants have also cited [cases] in which the courts upheld the right of the owners of a race track to exclude patrons from attending races without reason or justification so long as the exclusion was not based on race, creed, color or national origin. However, these cases involved patrons and not a jockey who was being arbitrarily deprived of his fundamental right to engage in his chosen occupation. We do not find [them] persuasive. 323 N.E.2d at 106.

The Illinois Supreme Court in *Phillips* found that the codification in 9(e) of the *Cox* holding was not an unconstitutional delegation of a recognized legislative power because there was in fact no attempted grant of legislative power to an administrative agency or private person. The authority to exclude came from the common law. *Phillips*, 56 Ill. Dec. 355, 427 N.E.2d at 556. The court stated:

> There is no such delegation of a recognized legislative power here. The right to exclude patrons from a private enterprise, here a racetrack, has long been recognized at common law. Though it cannot be said that section 9(e), which goes further and permits the exclusion of occupation licensees, is a precise codification of the common law right, it is clear that the authority to exclude here is not derived from some recognized legislative power, unique to the legislature, that has been delegated to organization licensees. It is simply, as the State argues, a grant of authority by the legislature. 427 N.E.2d at 556-57.

The language of *Phillips* and *Cox* lead us to conclude that Illinois follows the common law rule regarding the exclusion of patrons, as opposed to the exclusion of licensees which is governed by the "just cause" rule codified in 9(e). Of the cases cited by the Illinois courts as demonstrating the common law rule, *Madden v. Queens County Jockey*

*Club*, 296 N.Y. 249, 72 N.E.2d 697 (Ct. App.), *cert. denied*, 332 U.S. 761 (1947), is the most explicit and most cited. The plaintiff, "Coley" Madden, who claimed to be a professional "patron of the races," was barred from the defendant's Aqueduct Race Track under the mistaken belief that he was "Owney" Madden, reputed to be the fabled Frank Costello's bookmaker. Coley Madden brought suit for declaratory judgment and contended that as a citizen and taxpayer he had the right to enter the track and patronize the races. The defendant moved to dismiss on the ground that it had an unlimited right of exclusion. The trial court granted plaintiff's motion and entered an order enjoining the defendant from barring Coley Madden from its race track. The appellate division reversed, 269 App. Div. 644, 58 N.Y.S.2d 272, and the New York Court of Appeals affirmed the appellate division's reversal of the trial court. The Court of Appeals framed the question: "Whether the operator of a race track can, without reason or sufficient excuse, exclude a person from attending its races." 72 N.E.2d at 698. Its answer: "In our opinion he can; he has the power to admit as spectators only those whom he may select, and to exclude others solely of his own [volition,] as long as the exclusion is not founded on race, creed, color or national origin." 72 N.E.2d at 698.

The court went on to explain the common law:

> At common law a person engaged in a public calling, such as innkeeper or common carrier, was held to be under a duty to the general public and was obliged to serve, without discrimination, all who sought service. [Citations omitted.] On the other hand, proprietors of private enterprises, such as places of amusement and resort, were under no such obligation, enjoying an absolute power to serve whom they pleased. [Citations omitted.] A race track, of course, falls within that classification. 72 N.E.2d at 698 (emphasis added).

Madden also claimed a right to enter the track based upon the constitutional guaranty of equal protection of the laws, arguing that the track's license to conduct wagering made it an administrative agency of the state. The court answered that to adopt plaintiff's position would make it equally tenable to argue that every licensee (such as a cab driver, a barber, or a liquor dealer) is an administrative agency of the state simply because he pays a fee for his license. The court also rejected Madden's argument that a license to conduct horse racing is equivalent to a franchise or a monopoly to perform a public service and that Coley Madden, as a member of the public, could not rightfully be excluded. The court held that a race track is not a public utility but is a place of amusement—which has never been regarded as a function or purpose of government.

We too find that the defendant in this case is not a state granted franchise or monopoly. In *Cox v. National Jockey Club*, the Illinois appellate court stated:

> By virtue of Section 2 of the Horse Racing Act [Ill. Rev. Stat. ch. 8, ¶ 37(b)], the defendant, National Jockey Club, had a quasi-monopoly over thoroughbred horse racing during the period of the subject racing meet and therefore, defendants could not arbitrarily and without reason or justification deny plaintiff the opportunity of participating in its meet.

323 N.E.2d at 106. Section 2 states in essence that race tracks within 35 miles of each other may not have horse races on the same day. The defendant here is granted only a license for 75 days of racing in any one year. That license is imposed only to regulate and raise revenue, as opposed to a franchise which grants a special privilege that does not belong to an individual as a matter of common right. The court in *Cox* held that the race track had a "quasi-monopoly" only with regard to a licensee—a jockey who was alleging that he was being denied the right to earn a livelihood—rather than a patron of the offered amusement. While we pass no judgment on the language in *Cox*, we note again that the relationship between the race track and licensed jockeys is substantially different than the relationship between the race track and its patrons. Any one race track may or may not have a "quasi-monopoly" (a term that is subject to many interpretations) over opportunities available to jockeys, owners, or drivers, but they do not have a true monopoly over opportunities for the plaintiffs to bet on horses. This difference is recognized and emphasized in *Phillips, Cox,* and the Illinois statute, and is dispositive of this case.

In holding that Illinois follows the traditional common law rule we are not unmindful that several other states have questioned that rule as a matter both of law and of policy. For example, many of the states that follow the common law rule have used language broader than the facts in the case before them required. While these cases state that a proprietor has the absolute right to exclude, the facts of the case show that just cause existed to exclude the patron. *See, e.g., Silbert v. Ramsey*, 301 Md. 96, 482 A.2d 147 (1984) (patron excluded on the basis of his prior conviction for violation of state lottery laws); *James v. Churchill Downs, Inc.*, 620 S.W.2d 323 (Ky. App.1981) (excluded patron was a convicted bookmaker); *Tropical Park, Inc. v. Jack*, 374 So. 2d 639 (Fla. App. 1979) (patron alleged to have "known underworld connections" was rightfully excluded); *Burrillville Racing Association v. Garabedian*, 113 R.I. 134, 318 A.2d 469 (1974) (excluded patron had prior conviction for income tax evasion in connection with a wager messenger operation); *People v. Licata*, 28 N.Y.2d 113, 268 N.E.2d 787 (1971) (defendant had prior convictions for bookmaking); *Flores v. Los Angeles Turf Club, Inc.*, 55 Cal. 2d 736, 13 Cal. Rptr. 201, 361 P.2d 921 (1961) (plaintiff was a convicted bookmaker).

But that fact only demonstrates that proprietors of amusement facilities, whose very survival depends on bringing the public into their place of amusement, are reasonable people who usually do not exclude their customers unless they have a reason to do so. What the proprietor of a race track does not want to have to do is prove or explain that his reason for exclusion is a just reason. He doesn't want to be liable to Coley Madden solely because he mistakenly believed he was a mobster. The proprietor wants to be able to keep someone off his private property even if they only look like a mobster. As long as the proprietor is not excluding the mobster look-a-like because of his national origin (or because of race, color, creed, or sex), then the common law, and the law of Illinois, allows him to do just that.

We also choose not to follow the arguable—but not clear—abandonment of the common law rule in New Jersey in the case of *Uston v. Resorts International Hotel, Inc.*, 445 A.2d 370 (N.J. 1982). In 1959 the New Jersey Supreme Court decided *Garifine v. Monmouth Park Jockey Club*, 29 N.J. 47, 148 A.2d 1 (Sup. Ct. 1959), which was an appeal from the trial court's refusal to grant the plaintiff injunctive relief from his exclusion from Monmouth Park race track. The defendant race track, relying on *Madden*, moved to dismiss the complaint on the ground that it had "an absolute right" to exclude the plaintiff. On appeal, the plaintiff contended that the operator of a race track should not have the common law right to exclude a patron without reasonable cause and that under the New Jersey Civil Rights Act the operator did not have such authority. In a scholarly opinion the court traced the genesis of the right of race tracks to exclude patrons without justifying the exclusion:

> There was a time in English history when the common law recognized in many callings the duty to serve the public without discrimination. [Citations omitted.] With the passing of time and the changing of conditions, the common law confined this duty to exceptional callings where the needs of the public urgently called for its continuance. Innkeepers and common carriers may be said to be the most notable illustrations of business operators who, both under early principles and under the common law today, are obliged to serve the public without discrimination. [Citations omitted.] On the other hand, operators of most businesses, including places of amusement such as race tracks, have never been placed under any such common-law obligation, for no comparable considerations of public policy have ever so dictated.

No holdings contrary to the foregoing have been cited by the plaintiff; and although he has urged that the defendant's common-law right of exclusion from its race track should be limited because as a licensee "it has secured the advantage of a State monopoly" we find no force in his contention. The burden of the plaintiff's present attack is on the common-law doctrine which he states should be altered to afford to him a right of admission to the race track in the absence of affirmative legal proof by the defendant that there is good cause for his exclusion. We are satisfied that, without regard to views which may be entertained in other types of cases, there has been no showing made here for such alteration. . . .

148 A.2d at 6-7. However, in 1982 the New Jersey Supreme Court decided *Uston* in which the plaintiff was a practitioner of a strategy of playing blackjack known as "card counting." . . . The New Jersey Supreme Court held that the Casino Control Act gave the Casino Control Commission the exclusive authority to exclude patrons based upon their strategies for playing licensed casino games and that any common law right the defendant may have had to exclude Uston for these reasons was abrogated by the Act and outweighed by Uston's right of access. *Uston*, 445 A.2d at 372.

In *Marzocca v. Ferone*, 461 A.2d 1133 (N.J. 1983), the owner of a harness race horse was barred from racing that horse at Freehold Raceway in New Jersey. The appellate court determined that *Uston* overruled *Garifine v. Monmouth Park Jockey Club, sub silentio,* and remanded the case to the trial court to hear evidence as to whether the race track's exclusion was reasonable. The case was then appealed to the New Jersey Supreme Court, where the court clarified its decision in *Uston* and reversed the appellate court, stating:

> Notwithstanding the dicta in *Uston*, we must part company with the court below on the issue of Freehold's right to exclude. Without commenting on the status of the law in the amusement owner/patron context, we hold that the racetrack's common law right to exclude exists in the context of this case, i.e., where the relationship [is] between the track management and persons who wish to perform their vocational activities on the track premises.

461 A.2d at 1137. Therefore, it is clear that New Jersey has not per se abandoned the common law rule but has adapted it, in a limited fashion, to the particular needs of its casino industry. New Jersey has not gone as far as Illinois did in *Cox*, and in the Illinois Racing Statute, but they give no reason why the patron is more protected than the licensee. The law of New Jersey does not directly conflict with the law of Illinois that we inferred from *Phillips* and *Cox*, but to the extent that it is different, the differences are further evidence that Illinois follows the common law approach.

However, the New Jersey decisions do paint the wider policy picture of which our decision today is a part. As a policy matter, it is arguably unfair to allow a place of amusement to exclude for any reason or no reason, and to be free of accountability, except in cases of obvious discrimination. In this case, the general public is not only invited but, through advertising, is encouraged to come to the race track and wager on the races' outcome. But the common law allows the race track to exclude patrons, no matter if they come from near or far, or in reasonable reliance on representations of accessibility. We may ultimately believe that market forces would preclude any outrageous excesses—such as excluding anyone who has blond hair, or (like the plaintiffs) who is from Pennsylvania, or (even more outrageous) who has $250,000 to spend in one day of betting. But the premise of the consumer protection laws that the New Jersey Supreme Court alluded to in *Uston* and *Marzocca* recognizes that the reality of an imperfect market allows numerous consumer depredations. Excluding a patron simply because he is named Adam Smith arguably offends the very precepts of equality and fair dealing expressed in everything from the antitrust statutes to the Illinois Consumer Fraud and Deceptive Business Practice Act.

But the market here is not so demonstrably imperfect that there is a monopoly or any allegation of consumer fraud. Consequently, there is no such explicit legislative directive in the context of patrons attending horse races in Illinois—so the common law rule, relic though it may be, still controls. Therefore, within the prohibitions of *Erie,* the language of the Illinois cases, and the lack of language from the Illinois legislature, we hold that the common law rule is the law of Illinois. *Affirmed.*

### NOTES

1. This court suggests that the market itself will generally address problems with exclusion of customers. Since a casino generally wants to maximize the number of patrons, it will generally exclude one only when there is a legitimate reason to do so. But what is a legitimate reason for doing so?

2. Can the free market determine which casinos allow card counters and which do not? One commentator explains the market dynamics:

> Advertising a no-barring policy might be a good marketing tool for some casinos. It would fit well with high table limits, an image of courtesy and service, etc. On the other hand, casinos that orient

their product to the lower end of the market might want to retain the option since a no-barring policy will tend to penalize the very kind of customers [low stakes players] to whom they are trying to appeal.

Craig K. Lehman, The "Consumer Rights" of Card Counters, The Gambling Studies, Proceedings of the Sixth National Conference on Gambling and Risk Taking 127 (1985) (unpublished manuscript on file with the University of Nevada-Las Vegas), quoted in Anthony Cabot & Robert Hannum, *Advantage Play and Commercial Casinos*, 74 Miss. L.J. 681, 744 & n.297 (2005).

3. As the cases above suggest, gambling can be considered in contractual terms. A bet is a certain kind of contract between two parties. Consider the following excerpt.

## ANTHONY CABOT & ROBERT HANNUM, ADVANTAGE PLAY AND COMMERCIAL CASINOS
### 74 Miss L.J. 681, 682-684 (2005)

Casino-style wagering is essentially an adhesion contract between the casino and its patrons. An adhesion contract is a non-negotiable, take-it-or-leave-it contract. In terms of gaming, the casino defines the terms of the contract (the rules of the wager) and allows patrons to play the game as-is, with no possibility of changing the rules. The nature of gaming necessitates such adhesion contracts. Casinos are in the business of making money. Therefore, the casino typically only enters into contracts that have a statistical advantage favoring the casino. Altering the terms of this contract could change the statistical advantage, such, as by changing the probability of winning or losing the wager.

Because gambling is a contract, the general elements of a contract must exist before there is a binding agreement. At its simplest, the elements of a contract are: offer, acceptance, and consideration. An offer is an outward manifestation to another of a desire to enter into a contract, which confers upon the offeree the power to make a valid contract. An offer can be manifested by either words or conduct.

The terms of a gambling contract are both express and implied. The express terms are those that are stated in writing. For example, most craps tables say that if you place a bet on twelve and twelve comes up, the casino will pay thirty-one to one. Many games also have implied terms, that is, terms that are not written down but are still a part of the contract. For example, a craps table does not tell you that if you roll a seven after rolling a point, you lose; however, this rule is commonly understood and forms the basis for the game of craps. [Moreover, e]very contract contains an implied covenant of good faith and fair dealing. The covenant requires that neither party to a contract do anything that will injure the right of the other party to receive the benefits of their agreement.

### NOTES

1.  Cabot and Hannum advocate a pure contractual approach to these issues. "Advantage play that involves using superior skill in analyzing the game factors that are available to all players should never be illegal. Where gambling involves part skill, such as the games of poker and blackjack, the exercise of that skill is part of the basic contractual understanding of the parties. If one party believes that the other has too significant of an advantage based on skill or the basic house advantage, then that person has the option not to enter the contract with the other party. Once the parties enter into a contract, however, the exercise of skill by the participants consistent with the rules of the game are expected, proper and should never be considered unethical or unlawful. . . . Casinos should have the right to incorporate countermeasures to advantage play provided that the countermeasures are made part of the express terms of the contract with the player. Any person to a contract has the ability to define those terms under which he or she is willing to enter into that contract. Except for some limited overriding policy concerns unique to gambling contracts, the casino should be able to set the terms on which it is willing to accept a wager. Inherent in those terms are the ability to incorporate countermeasures that effectively reduce or eliminate the advantage sought by advantage players. . . . While the casinos should generally be permitted to set the terms and conditions of the gaming contracts that they are willing to accept, the overriding principles of gaming regulation are that the games offered are fair and honest. Based on established rules of play of the various table games, the players have all the information available to them to determine the house advantage in a given game." Anthony Cabot & Robert Hannum, *Advantage Play and Commercial Casinos*, 74 Miss. L.J. 681, 751-753 (2005). Do you agree?
2.  How should the contract be expressed to the patrons? It is unlikely that patrons would be able to negotiate the terms. Would such an adhesion contract be "fair"?
3.  If the contract metaphor is correct, is it relevant that casinos frequently provide free alcoholic beverages to patrons? Could the

patron's intoxication, particularly if it was intentionally encouraged by the casino, interfere with the competence of the patron to enter a contract under free consent? Such a claim was made in *Great Bay Hotel & Casino v. Tose*, 34 F.3d 1227 (3d Cir. 1994).

## BARTOLO v. BOARDWALK REGENCY HOTEL CASINO, INC.

### 449 A.2d 1339 (Sup. Ct. N.J. 1982)

SKILLMAN, J.

Is it permissible for a casino to detain a patron suspected of being a "card counter" for the purpose of questioning? This issue is presented in the context of a tort action brought by four patrons of a casino who allege that they were falsely imprisoned by its security personnel. Defendants are the Boardwalk Regency Hotel Casino and several of its employees. . . .

[T]he court must accept as true for the purpose of the motion the descriptions of the incident provided by plaintiffs in their depositions. Plaintiffs are two brothers and two of their friends. All four are occasional social gamblers. They arrived at the Boardwalk Regency on December 26, 1979, played various casino games, including blackjack, and lost money. They returned to the gambling area around 11 A.M. the next morning and began playing blackjack. After playing for about an hour they were approached by two casino security guards dressed in uniforms. Plaintiffs were notified that they had been identified as card counters and were directed to accompany the guards. One plaintiff was grabbed by the back of the collar and pulled away from the blackjack table. The others were grabbed by the arms and led away. This physical removal happened so quickly and so forcefully that some plaintiffs were unable even to remove their chips from the table. All four were led to a nearby area where they were joined by a games manager, who ordered them to produce identification so that they could be registered and prevented from playing blackjack. At first plaintiffs refused to produce identification, protesting that they were not card counters. However, they were threatened with arrest if they refused to cooperate, and they then acceded to the demand. When identifications were produced, the games manager wrote plaintiffs' names on a pad, told them they would not be permitted to play blackjack again at the Boardwalk Regency or any other casino and directed them to leave. During this entire confrontation the two uniformed casino security guards remained on either side of plaintiffs. The three plaintiffs who were deposed all testified that they did not feel free to leave the casino between the time they were pulled away from the blackjack table and when they produced identification.

After unsuccessfully seeking to lodge a complaint concerning the incident with an official of the New Jersey Casino Control Commission, plaintiffs arranged a meeting with the assistant manager of the casino. The assistant manager acknowledged that the casino personnel had been at fault and said that he would like to make amends by buying plaintiffs a meal and allowing them back into the blackjack game. However, plaintiffs declined the offer and departed from the casino. This lawsuit followed.

The complaint sets forth three separate theories of liability arising out of this incident: assault and battery, slander and false imprisonment. However, defendants concede that a contested material issue of fact is presented by the assault and battery claim, and plaintiffs concede that their slander claim must be dismissed due to an inability to show any damage to their business, professional or personal reputations resulting from the incident. Therefore, the sole question at this juncture is whether there is a contested material issue of fact on the false imprisonment claim.

The tort of false imprisonment is established upon showing any "unlawful restraint upon a man's freedom of locomotion." *Earl v. Winne*, 14 N.J. 119, 128 (1953). The unlawful restraint need not be imposed by physical force. As observed in *Earl v. Winne*:

> This constraint may be caused by threats as well as by actionable force, and the threats may be by conduct or by words. If the words or conduct are such as to include a reasonable apprehension of force and the means of coercion is at hand, a person may be as effectually restrained and deprived of liberty as by prison bars. [at 127]

Furthermore, the assertion of legal authority to take a person into custody, even where such authority does not in fact exist, may be sufficient to create a reasonable apprehension that a person is under restraint. *Hebrew v. Pulis*, 73 N.J.L. 621 (E. & A. 1906)[.]

There can be no serious doubt that the elements of false imprisonment would be established if plaintiffs' version of this incident were believed by a jury. According to plaintiffs, they were accosted by uniformed security guards who physically removed them from the blackjack table. They were then subjected, while surrounded by security guards, to an interrogation by a games manager, who said that they would be arrested unless identification was produced. Under these circumstances, plaintiffs reasonably could have concluded that they would be forcibly restrained if they attempted to leave the site of this interrogation without producing identification and that they were thus under confinement.

Defendants do not seriously dispute that the incident, as described by plaintiffs, contains the essential elements of a false imprisonment. However, they assert that a casino has the legal right to detain temporarily a patron suspected of being a card counter. Hence, they argue that any restraint imposed upon plaintiffs was not "unlawful." Defendants assert that they have the same right to detain a suspected card counter as a retail store owner has to detain a suspected shoplifter. See N.J.S.A. 2C:20-11e. In the words of defendants, it is their position that "a casino, in order to protect its interests, may reasonably detain a suspected card counter, and may not be held liable for false imprisonment in so doing."

[C]ard counting does not involve dishonesty or cheating. On the contrary, a card counter is simply a highly skilled player who analyzes the statistical probabilities associated with blackjack and, based upon those probabilities, develops playing strategies which may afford him an advantage over the casino. It was solely this loss of the normal "house advantage" which caused the casinos to exclude card counters from the blackjack tables.

This circumstance sharply distinguishes the detention of suspected card counters from the detention of alleged shoplifters. Shoplifting is a crime. To aid in the apprehension of shoplifters as well as to enable retail stores to protect themselves from this form of criminal activity, the Legislature has provided that "a merchant, who has probable cause for believing that a person has willfully concealed unpurchased merchandise and that he can recover the merchandise by taking the person into custody, may, for the purpose of attempting to effect the recovery thereof, take the person into custody and detain him in a reasonable manner for not more than a reasonable time." Furthermore, to ensure that merchants will be able to exercise this power without inhibition, the Legislature has specifically provided that a merchant who takes a suspected shoplifter into custody as provided by this statute shall not be "civilly liable in any manner or to any extent whatever." The decision in *Cooke v. J. J. Newberry & Co.*, 96 N.J. Super. 9 (App. Div. 1967), upon which defendants place primary reliance in support of their motion for summary judgment, simply interprets the predecessor to this statutory provision authorizing the detention of suspected shoplifters. Therefore, it obviously has no pertinency to a case where no legislation has been enacted providing immunity for conduct which otherwise would constitute false imprisonment.

However, defendants contend that N.J.S.A. 5:12-121(b) confers an immunity upon casinos comparable to that which N.J.S.A. 2C:20-11(e) confers upon retail merchants. This section provides in pertinent part:

> Any licensee or its officers, employees or agents who shall have probable cause for believing there has been a violation of sections 113 through 116 of this act in the casino by any person may take such person into custody and detain him in the establishment in a reasonable manner for a reasonable length of time, for the purpose of notifying law enforcement or commission authorities. Such taking into custody and detention shall not render such licensee or its officers, employees or agents criminally or civilly liable for false arrest, false imprisonment, slander or unlawful detention unless such taking into custody or detention is unreasonable under all of the circumstances.

To be sure, this section authorizes casino officials to detain patrons under certain circumstances and provides an accompanying qualified immunity from civil liability. However, the operation of this section can be triggered only by the existence of probable cause to believe that "there has been a violation of sections 113 through 116 of this act." These sections (N.J.S.A. 5:12-112 through 5:12-116) make it a crime of the fourth degree or a misdemeanor to use bogus chips, marked cards, loaded dice, sleight of hand tricks and a variety of other devices to cheat or swindle a casino. However, there is no basis upon which card counting can be viewed as cheating or swindling a casino and hence a violation of one of these criminal provisions. Rather, it is simply a skillful technique for playing blackjack which negates the normal advantage of the casino over the player. Therefore, N.J.S.A. 5:12-121(b) affords no authorization to a casino to detain a suspected card counter.

Absent any affirmative statutory authorization to detain suspected card counters, the plaintiffs' version of the incident at the Boardwalk Regency would constitute false imprisonment. [MOTION FOR SUMMARY JUDGMENT DENIED.]

## B.   WHAT CONSTITUTES CHEATING?

Card counting is an activity that some would characterize as cheating and others would characterize as fair play. Given that lay people could have reasonable differences of opinion as to what sorts of activity are fair and which are wrongful, some jurisdictions have sought to regulate carefully the casino environment to provide a different or more defined set of legal rules within the casino.

Other jurisdictions have contributed to the lack of clarity by increasing the stakes at issue. Several, for example, make it a felony offense to "cheat at a gambling game." The following cases explore the limits on the state's or casino's ability to define the rules of conduct inside casinos.

## CHILDS v. STATE
### 864 P.2d 277 (Nev. 1993)

STEFFEN, Justice.

This is the second time appellant Timothy John Childs has challenged, on appeal to this court, judgments of conviction for gaming crimes stemming from the exploitation of slot machines that are vulnerable to a form of play referred to as "handle popping." [*See Childs v. State*, 816 P.2d 1079 (Nev. 1991) (hereinafter *Childs I*)]. The instant appeal challenges Childs' judgment of conviction, pursuant to a bench trial, of one count of attempted fraudulent slot machine manipulation and one count of fraudulent slot machine manipulation.

Childs has developed an expertise in locating and exploiting slot machines that are vulnerable to a form of handle manipulation that substantially increases the machines' pay out. Unfortunately, Childs is not the only person to discover that certain malfunctioning slot machines may be manipulated to yield greater winnings simply by altering the pull of the handle. Moreover, the method of play may reveal itself to the novice as well as the seasoned predator. The procedure, frequently referred to as "handle popping," involves varying the motion and strength of the pull on the handle in order to stop one of the reels at a point of advantage to the player. The "handle popper" inflicts no damage to the machines and introduces no artificial device to cause the machines to malfunction. The "handle popping" player merely takes advantage of what a slot machine with a misaligned stop bracket will accommodate by skillful manipulation of the handle. *See generally Lyons v. State*, 775 P.2d 219 (Nev. 1989); *El Dorado Hotel v. Brown*, 691 P.2d 436 (Nev. 1984) (Steffen, J., dissenting).

In the instant case, Childs was observed "handle popping" a slot machine at Bill's Casino. At trial, a slot supervisor testified that he saw Childs pull down on the handle of the machine and then jerk it in such a way that one of the three reels would stop spinning prematurely. The day after the incident at Bill's Casino, Childs was seen and arrested at the High Sierra for engaging in the same method of play with the same results.

The district court found Childs guilty of attempted fraudulent slot machine manipulation and fraudulent slot machine manipulation and sentenced him to concurrent terms of five and ten years in the Nevada State Prison.

Childs is the same party who successfully sought relief from this court in *Childs I*. Although Childs was also convicted of burglary in the first case, the conduct underlying his earlier convictions is identical to the conduct that formed the basis for the convictions that prompted this appeal.

*Childs I* addressed the legislative response to our decision in Lyons that declared NRS 465.015 (cheating at gambling) unconstitutionally vague as applied to non-damaging manipulation of slot machine handles (handle popping). The new statutory provision, NRS 465.070(7),[1] which specifically grappled with the problem of defining the unlawful manipulation of a slot machine handle, was also declared invalid in *Childs I* because the new law failed to adequately define the proscribed conduct.

*Childs I* is dispositive of this appeal. There has been no transfusion of clarity in NRS 465.070(7), the slot machine statute that we declared deficient in *Childs I*, and the conduct prosecuted in that case is, as previously noted, identical to the conduct involved here.

The dissent would affirm Childs' convictions on grounds that he intended to cheat or not play by the rules. Committing a non-criminal act with criminal intent is not a crime. One of the most basic tenets of criminal law is that thoughts alone do not constitute a crime. As the venerable Blackstone explains:

> Indeed, to make a complete crime cognizable by human laws, there must be both a will and an act. For, though, *in foro conscientiae*, a fixed design or will to do an unlawful act is almost as heinous as the commission of it, yet, as no temporal tribunal can search the heart or fathom the intentions of the mind, otherwise than as they are demonstrated by outward actions, it therefore cannot punish for what it cannot know. For which reason, in all temporal jurisdictions, an overt act, or some open evidence of an intended crime, is necessary

---

1. In pertinent part, NRS 465.070(7) provides:

It is unlawful for any person:
. . . .
7. To manipulate, with the intent to cheat, any component of a gaming device in a manner contrary to the designed and normal operational purpose for the component, including, but not limited to, varying the pull of the handle of a slot machine, with knowledge that the manipulation affects the outcome of the game or with knowledge of any event that affects the outcome of the game.

in order to demonstrate the depravity of the will, before the man is liable to punishment.

4 William Blackstone, Commentaries 21. In *Childs I* we held that NRS 465.070(7) did not define the proscribed conduct. Without defining the crime in terms sufficiently clear to impart notice and understanding of the proscribed conduct to persons of ordinary intelligence, there is no prosecutable offense. *Childs I*, 107 Nev. at 585, 816 P.2d at 1079-80 (quoting from *Lyons*, 105 Nev. at 320, 775 P.2d at 221). [REVERSED.]

SPRINGER, Justice, dissenting.

I refuse to join in an opinion which would overrule *Childs v. State*, 816 P.2d 1079 (Nev. 1991) ("*Childs I*"), a case which is only two years old. I disagreed with the previous *Childs* case and registered my dissent. Once, however, that it became the law of this state, I must accept it as the law; and it is, of course, bad practice to overrule a case that has been in effect for such a short time. I am prepared to accept the adjudication of this court that the statute in question is unconstitutionally vague; nevertheless, I conclude that it is not vague when applied to the facts of this case. Childs, a professional slot machine cheat, was clearly cheating and acting in violation of NRS 465.070(7), and the conviction must be upheld.

Appellant Childs stands convicted of two felonies, both involving the cheating of slot machines. . . . There was no evidence introduced at trial. The parties stipulated that the case "be tried to the court without a jury" and that "the evidence presented at trial shall consist of the transcript of the preliminary hearing and nothing else."

To put the facts of these two convictions into proper context, it is helpful to analyze, early on, the criminal statute upon which the convictions are based. NRS 465.070(7) is set out in a footnote to the Plurality Opinion. Breaking the statute into its elements, it was unlawful for Childs:

1.   To "manipulate" the handle of a slot machine "in a manner contrary to the designed and normal operational purpose";
2.   "[W]ith the intent to cheat"; and
3.   "[W]ith knowledge that the manipulation affects the outcome of the game." NRS 465.070(7).

To be guilty of violation of this statute, Childs must have, with fraudulent intent, manipulated a slot machine handle in a manner contrary to its designed and normal purpose, with knowledge that his manipulation of the machine was going to change the designed and normal outcome of slot machine play. In the context of Childs' present criminal involvement, it appears to me that each of the elements of this statutory crime have been established.

*Attempted Fraudulent Slot Machine Operation.* The transcript of the preliminary hearing upon which this conviction is based shows that a security officer on duty at Bill's Casino on January 7, 1990, had occasion to observe Childs in the act of "obviously manipulating the reels." The officer watched Childs "pulling the handle and causing one of the reels not to spin." The manner in which Childs caused one of the reels not to spin was to pull the handle down "a little bit" and then to give it "a little pop, [a] little jerking motion." The officer testified without objection that a slot machine is not designed to have a handle pulled in that manner, that is to say, in the manner in which Childs was observed to be manipulating the machine. The officer observed that this manipulation resulted in Childs' winning money from the machine. The officer also observed that Childs was putting the money into his pocket immediately instead of leaving it in the tray; the officer considered this to be "unusual behavior" and said, "You don't see it too often."

Stating the obvious, the security officer testified that the reels are supposed to spin. Indeed, they are. When the wheels can be manipulated so that they do not spin, the slot machine "handle-popper"[1] is advantaged in at least two ways. As the security officer explained, one way is to keep a reel from spinning, holding it in the win position on a pay symbol such as a cherry. This creates a no-lose mode for the machine in which the machine "pays on cherries[;] it would pay constantly if you can get it not to spin." The witness also testified that another method of cheating is to hold the third reel so it won't spin, with a jackpot bar in the win position; and, if "it won't spin, you've got a considerable more better odds of getting three bars." There can be no question in my mind that this activity is cheating and that it is a clear and understandable violation of the statute in question.

*Fraudulent Slot Machine Manipulation.* Stephen Wegmann, a surveillance agent for the High Sierra Casino, a man trained in detecting cheating techniques by slot machine cheaters, described Childs' activities at the High Sierra. Wegmann saw Childs' way of manipulating the slot machine handle as first "slow moving and then a slam at the bottom, and the first reel held, the cherry stayed there, and then

---

1. "Handle-popper" is a well-known description of persons who cheat slot machines in the manner described by the security officer. The purpose of the jerking or "popping" is to cause a malfunction of one of the reels so that the handle popper can gain an advantage over the machine and over other players by the means explained in the text.

he received a pay off for that." Wegmann gave a very precise explanation of what is "wrong with playing the slot machine in that manner." Wegmann explained:

> Normally it's a random selection. The reels, all the reels fire, and they
> turn and a random spin, and then the—by a clock timer inside . . . it
> could stop them anywhere. So you're taking a chance of winning or not
> winning. But when . . . you hold it, there's no chance of not winning.
> You're going to win all the time.

Childs, it appears, was manipulating a slot machine, plainly and
simply, so that he could "win all the time." This is called "cheating";
slot machine players are not supposed to cheat in order to win all the
time.

This is not a difficult case. Childs was not an ordinary slot machine
player. There is more than ample evidence to support the trial judge's
almost inescapable conclusion that Childs was "manipulating" the
slot machines at the mentioned casinos with the fraudulent or cheating intent of "winning all the time." Slot machines are designed, as
pointed out by Wegmann, to be played in a manner in which the three
reels are allowed to spin freely and then be stopped by a timing device
in random fashion. When a player intentionally interferes with this
randomness, such a player is clearly manipulating the machine "in a
manner contrary to the designed and normal operational purpose" of
a slot machine. The designed and normal operation purpose is, as
Wegmann described, to pay or not to pay in accordance with the
random spinning of three reels. Childs was rather clearly intentionally
violating and interfering with this normal purpose.

When one reviews the enumerated elements of the crime set out
above, the following comes to light:

1.   Childs did "manipulate" the machines' handles "in a manner
     contrary to the designed and operational purpose." A slot
     machine is not designed to let the player win every time or even
     to give the manipulating player an advantage above that created
     by the random spin of three reels.
2.   There is ample evidence of Childs' "intent to cheat."[2] It is clear
     that Childs was cheating in the ordinary sense of the word.

---

2. "Cheat," by statute, means to alter the selection of criteria which determine
the result of a game or the amount or frequency of payment in a game. NRS 465.015.
Childs intended to and did alter the selection of criteria. The criteria for winning on
a slot machine are selected at random by three reels, consecutively stopped by a
timing device. Childs altered the selection of criteria and in doing so altered the
result and the frequency of payment.

He simply was not playing by the rules. Some of the time, at least, he could not lose.

3. Childs certainly had knowledge that what he was doing affected the outcome of his slot machine manipulation. He could not manipulate these machines without intending and knowing that he was going to profit by these activities.

All three necessary elements of the statute are well-established with reference to his activities at Bill's Casino and at the High Sierra Casino. Childs is clearly guilty of both charges.

As said, this is not a difficult case, not difficult, that is, until we collide with the case of *Childs v. State*, 816 P.2d 1079, 1081 (Nev. 1991), in which, without expressly declaring the statute in question to be unconstitutional, we ruled that, under the circumstances of that case, the resourceful and redoubtable Childs could not have understood from the statutory language just what a " 'normal' pull" was and that he had "to guess at the lawful method of pulling a slot machine handle." Well, maybe in *Childs I*, Childs had to guess as to whether his handle-popping activities at the Nugget were "lawful" or not; but he did not have to guess in the present case. He knew he could not lose. Anyone who plays a game of chance, a game based on random selection, who knows that he cannot lose, and cannot, in fact, lose, can probably be safely called a cheater. In *Childs I*, all we knew about Childs was that he would "jerk" the handle, that "one of the three reels would stop spinning prematurely" and that Childs was able to " 'freeze the reels' several times." 816 P.2d at 1079. It may be within the realm of possibility that an honest player might "jerk" a slot machine handle with the result that one or more of the reels might "freeze" from time to time and that during an honest player's play, for one reason or another, a reel might "stop prematurely"; but we know that a player who deliberately "manipulates" a machine to the extent that pay-out is guaranteed on every play is not playing in accordance with machine design and normal operation. We know that such a player is cheating, as was Childs.

The concern in *Childs I* was that unwary, innocent slot machine players might find themselves in trouble with the law because there is no description in the statute as to just what kind of handle jerking or slapping or other handle movement constituted unlawful "popping." Concern was expressed in *Childs I* about the apparent absence of a "statutory definition of the proscribed conduct." 816 P.2d at 1081. Childs has now done us the favor of providing definition to the proscribed conduct. We can now define the kind of handle manipulation that is unlawful as that which knowingly destroys the randomness of the slot machine operation. These machines are designed to operate randomly, and their normal operation requires random spinning of the reels. When a person, by "manipulating" a machine mechanically, intentionally impedes or destroys this randomness, that person is cheating.

This is not at all the same kind of activity (discussed in *Childs I*) involved in counting cards in the game of "21." In that game, properly shuffled cards come out randomly. There is a certain degree of skill involved in playing the game of "21," and the memorization of previously-dealt cards may enhance the player's chances of winning; but there is no defeating of the purpose or design of the game by engaging in the practice of card memorizing. It is true that players may believe that pulling slot machine handles slowly or rapidly may in some way give them an edge on the essential randomness of the machine. . . . What players cannot lawfully do is intentionally abuse the machine so that the randomness of the spinning reels is interrupted, thereby either making winning a sure thing or increasing the player's chances of winning in a manner that is "contrary to the designed and normal operational purpose" of the machine.

In *Childs I*, we mentioned that *Lyons v. State*, 775 P.2d 219, 222 (Nev. 1989), assumes that "handle manipulation does not alter 'the physical characteristics and potential pay offs of slot machines.'" 816 P.2d at 1081. From the record of the case before us, we now have a better and more complete understanding of what was going on, as to what Childs was really up to. We now know that Childs and others like him are quite capable of manipulating the handle of a slot machine in a way that physically guarantees success. Childs was clearly altering the machine's mechanism in such a way as to prevent one or more of the reels from performing its normal function, namely that of spinning freely and randomly until the timing mechanism brings the reel to a random stop. . . . Under these circumstances, the statute loses the vagueness that was the concern of the court in *Childs I*.

Childs is a cheater. He intended to "beat" the slot machines and was successful in doing so. The present case necessarily provides a better understanding of what these kinds of slot machine cheaters are up to. If one reel is frozen and fails, mechanically, to spin, the cheaters are altering the physical make-up of the machines and unfairly changing the pay-off, much in the favor of the cheater and contrary to the normal and designed pay-out of the machine.

As I see it, the way that Childs performed in this case, the way he manipulated the machines to his advantage, gives added meaning and understanding to the statute in question. Childs, and people who do what Childs did, are clearly violating the statute. I would, therefore, affirm the convictions.

RECANZONE, dissenting.

The majority opinion reversing the conviction against Childs is predicated on the court's prior ruling in [*Childs I*]. The dissent filed by Justice Springer, who dissented in *Childs I*, refuses to consider overruling *Childs I*, which he categorized as "a case which is only two years old." The record reflects that the appellant was arrested in January, 1990; convicted on July 9, 1990; and the appeal was filed immediately thereafter. The decision in *Childs I* was not filed until September 6, 1991, a year later. The appeal in *Childs I* had not been resolved when appellant committed the acts which resulted in this appeal being filed.

On January 7, 1990, appellant was observed "handle popping" a slot machine at Bill's Casino. A slot supervisor testified at trial that he observed appellant pull down on the handle and then jerk on it in such a way that one of the three reels would stop spinning prematurely. On January 8, 1990, appellant was observed "handle popping" at the High Sierra. A surveillance agent testified that he watched appellant pulling the handle down to a certain level and then jerking it down suddenly, at which time the first reel did not move. Appellant was detained at the High Sierra and placed under arrest. The district court found appellant guilty of both charges and sentenced appellant to serve concurrent terms of five and ten years in the Nevada State Prison. . . .

Appellant contends that his convictions must be reversed in light of this court's decision in *Childs I*. In *Childs I*, the court held that NRS 465.070(7) was unconstitutionally vague as applied to the facts of Childs' case. The court also set forth the standard to be applied to NRS 465.070(7):

> persons are deemed to have been given fair notice of a criminal offense if the statutorily proscribed conduct has been described with sufficient clarity to be understood by individuals of ordinary intelligence. . . .

*Childs*, 816 P.2d at 1079-1080. The court then concluded that the absence from NRS 465.070(7) of a definition of a "normal" pull rendered it unconstitutionally vague. Without such a definition, Childs was "left . . . to guess at the lawful method of pulling a slot machine handle." *Id.* Moreover, the court concluded, the vagueness of NRS 465.070(7) made potential felons of all "innocent, well-intentioned patrons" who "may so easily adopt various methods of handle manipulation in an attempt to change their fortune."

The general American doctrine as applied to courts of last resort is that a court is not inexorably bound by its own precedents but will follow the rule of law which it has established in earlier cases, unless clearly convinced that the rule was originally erroneous or is no longer sound because of changing conditions and that more good than harm will come by departing from precedent. It must be further noted that the doctrine of stare decisis is not applicable to statutory construction when it is decided that earlier interpretations are wanting, faulty, or even wrong. Upon careful consideration, I believe that *Childs I* was erroneously decided. I [believe that] *Childs I* should be overruled.

The doctrine of stare decisis, so vehemently supported by Justice Springer in his dissent, should not be applied. ". . . The doctrine is not ordinarily departed from where decision is of long-standing and rights have been acquired under it, unless considerations of public policy demand it. . . ." Black's Law Dictionary, Sixth Edition. *Childs I*, at the time of appellant's arrest in this case, was not long-standing, rights had not been acquired under it, and considerations of public policy demand the reversal of *Childs I*.

Our State of Nevada relies heavily on its gaming industry to maintain its economic well-being. The industry, through years of experience and tight regulation, has attained a high degree of professionalism. In view of that, it is repugnant for this court to make the assumption that each time a customer pulled the handle of a slot machine with some irregularity that management would be there charging him with manipulating the machine with "the intent to cheat." The individuals who would be apprehended are the Childs of this world who make their living "intentionally" cheating the gaming industry.

The court's principal concern in *Childs I* was that NRS 465.070(7) posed a trap for the unwary. A careful reading of NRS 465.070(7) convinces me that the court's fears are unfounded. While the statute does not define a "normal" pull of a slot machine handle, it does precisely set forth the elements of an illegal manipulation with the intent to cheat, in such a way that is "contrary to the [machine's] designed and normal operational purpose." NRS 465.070(7). Thus, patrons may pull as they choose, so long as they do not do so with both an intent to cheat[3] and knowledge that their chosen method affects the outcome of the game.

---

3. The gist of appellant's criminality is his "intent to cheat." NRS 465.070(7). The court has previously held that "cheat" as defined in Chapter 465 is not unconstitutionally vague. *Sheriff v. Martin*, 99 Nev. 336, 662 P.2d 634 (1983). There is no reason to believe that appellant could not understand the word cheat as it is used in this case.

In this case, appellant's technique is to "freeze" the first reel on the slot machine by means of a sudden force on the slot machine handle. By holding a cherry on the first reel in this manner, appellant is able to assure a winning combination on each slot machine play. Indeed, appellant may not know what constitutes a "normal pull" of a slot machine handle, but he clearly knows that his method of choice, which alters the machine's operation by freezing one of the reels, is not customary. Moreover, when appellant "interferes with the machine's 'operational purpose' by pushing, striking, jerking, or other untoward physical insult to the machine which interferes with the machine's normal operation," I consider this to be a "manipulation" which, when accompanied by an intent to cheat, constitutes a crime under NRS Chapter 465. See *Childs,* 816 P.2d at 1082 (Springer, J., dissenting). I would find that the prohibited conduct constituting the crime of fraudulent slot machine manipulation has been set forth with sufficient clarity as to be understood by individuals of ordinary intelligence.

### NOTES

1.  If the slot machine play is viewed in ordinary contractual terms, is the casino's understanding of the contract terms being met when the player "pops" the handle? Is the contractual analogy the correct way to view the question in this context? Why or why not?
2.  If there was a way to get a soda out of a vending machine without putting any money in the machine, would it be morally wrong to so do? Is that a legitimate analogy to the instant circumstance?
3.  Does the defendant's conduct in this case meet the ordinary definition of "cheating"? Are the ordinary rules of behavior different in casinos?
4.  Consider, once again, Anthony Cabot & Robert Hannum, *Advantage Play and Commercial Casinos,* 74 Miss. L.J. at 688-690:

    > Most cheating at casino games is a form of advantage play where the purpose of the cheating is to overcome the mathematical advantage that is built into every house-banked casino game. But, not all forms of advantage play are cheating.
    >     Cheating usually involves one of three major distinct situations. The first two major types of cheating involve criminalizing the player's acts to defeat the major condition of all gaming contracts, to wit, the random event. The first form is to alter the selection of outcome, by eliminating the random outcome of the event that determines the outcome of the contract. Altering the selection of outcome can be accomplished in different ways in different

games. More colorful methods may include the use of loaded dice in a craps game or marking cards in blackjack. Switching a prearranged deck of cards with a deck used in the game is another form of this type of cheating. This type of cheating, known as a cooler, usually requires the aid of at least one casino employee. A person also may attempt to alter or misrepresent the outcome of a game or event after the outcome is made sure, but before the casino reveals it to the players wagering on the game. For example, during a card game it is unlawful to switch cards with another person.

Neither the public nor the courts tend to have a problem understanding this basic form of cheating. As one court noted: "The attributes of the game—its established physical characteristics and basic rules—determine the probabilities of the game's various possible outcomes. Changing these attributes to affect the probabilities is a criminal act."

The second form is to acquire "knowledge, not available to all players, of the outcome of the game or any event that affects the outcome of the game." Types of this form of cheating include card marking and crimping. A card marker can alter the backs of cards, and figure out the value of the dealer's hole card in blackjack. Knowledge of the dealer's hole card assures the player of an advantage over the casino. Another unlawful activity relating to cards is "card crimping," which is the act of deforming a card, often by bending the corners, to make the point value of the card readable to the crimper from the back and the face of the card.

A third major form of cheating against a casino is to increase or decrease the amount of one's wager after learning the result of the random event. A skilled cheater can increase or decrease his bet after the game ends. A cheater with a losing hand in blackjack, for example, can "pinch the bet" by palming one chip in the stack wagered. If the cheater adds a chip after learning that he has a winning hand, he pressed or past-posted the bet.

Would the majority in *Childs* agree with Cabot and Hannum's definition of cheating?

5. For a different statutory approach to identifying cheating, consider provisions of the Michigan Gaming Control and Revenue Act, M.C.L.A. §432.218

Section 18 (2)—A person commits a felony punishable by imprisonment for not more than 10 years or a fine of not more than $100,000.00, or both, and, in addition, shall be barred for life from a gambling operation under the jurisdiction of the board if the person does any of the following:

(a) Offers, promises, or gives anything of value or benefit to a person who is connected with a licensee or affiliated company, including, but not limited to, an officer or employee of a casino licensee or holder of an occupational license pursuant to an agreement or arrangement or with the intent that the offer, promise, or thing of value or benefit will influence the actions of the person to whom the offer, promise, or gift was made in order to affect or attempt to affect the outcome of a gambling game, or to influence official action of a member of the board.

(b) Solicits or knowingly accepts or receives a promise of anything of value or benefit while the person is employed by or connected with a licensee, including, but not limited to, an officer or employee of a casino licensee or holder of an occupational license, pursuant to an understanding or arrangement or with the intent that the promise or thing of value or benefit will influence the actions of the person to affect or attempt to affect the outcome of a gambling game. . . .

(e) Except as otherwise provided by the board, uses or possesses with the intent to use a device to assist in doing any of the following:

(i) Projecting the outcome of a gambling game.

(ii) Keeping track of the cards played in a gambling game.

(iii) Analyzing the probability of the occurrence of an event relating to a gambling game.

(iv) Analyzing the strategy for playing or betting to be used in a gambling game.

(f) Cheats at a gambling game.

(g) Manufactures, sells, or distributes cards, chips, dice, a game, or a device that is intended to be used to violate this act.

(h) Alters or misrepresents the outcome of a gambling game on which wagers have been made after the outcome is determined but before it is revealed to the players.

(i) Places a bet after acquiring knowledge, not available to all players, of the outcome of the gambling game that is the subject of the bet or to aid a person in acquiring the knowledge for the purpose of placing a bet contingent on that outcome.

(j) Claims, collects, takes, or attempts to claim, collect, or take money or anything of value in or from the gambling games, with intent to defraud, without having made a wager contingent on winning a gambling game, or claims, collects, or takes an amount of money or thing of value of greater value than the amount won.

(k) Uses counterfeit chips or tokens in a gambling game.

(l) Possesses a key or device designed for the purpose of opening, entering, or affecting the operation of a gambling game, drop box, or an electronic or mechanical device connected with the gambling game or for removing coins, tokens, chips, or other contents of a gambling game. This subdivision does not apply to a gambling licensee or employee of a gambling licensee acting in furtherance of the employee's employment.

## ROMANSKI v. DETROIT ENTERTAINMENT, L.L.C.
### 428 F.3d 629 (6th Cir. 2005)

CLAY, Circuit Judge.

On August 7, 2001, Romanski, then 72 years old, and her friends Dorothy Dombrowski and Linda Holman, went to Defendant Detroit Entertainment's Motor City Casino in Detroit, Michigan, to gamble and enjoy lunch at the buffet. After a spate of unsuccessful tries at the slot machines, Romanski took a walk around the gaming floor. During her walk, Romanski noticed a five-cent token lying in a slot machine's tray. Seeing no chair at the machine, she picked up the token and returned to the machine at which she had earlier played, intending to use the token there. Soon a uniformed male casino employee approached and asked that she accompany him to the office. She asked why but he did not answer. Romanski then noticed there were also three female casino employees, these not in uniform, surrounding her; she felt she could not move.

One of these plain-clothed security officers was Defendant Marlene Brown, who had been assigned to patrol the casino floor at that time. Brown testified that she approached Romanski, displayed her casino security badge, and began to explain it was the casino's policy not to permit patrons to pick up tokens, which appeared to be abandoned, found at other slot machines, a practice known as "slot-walking." Romanski could not have known this at the time because the casino does not post the so-called policy anywhere. It is undisputed, therefore, that Romanski did not have—and could not have had—notice of the casino's purported policy on slot-walking.

According to Brown, Romanski became loud and belligerent, so, at the advice of Brown's supervisor, JoEtta Stevenson (a defendant below), Brown escorted Romanski to an off-the-floor room where Brown intended to explain the policy in detail. For her part, Romanski testified that Brown did not detain her because of her attitude but rather because Brown suspected her of theft.

It is undisputed that Brown and her colleagues escorted Romanski to what Defendants alternately call the "security office" and the "interview room." Whatever its name, the room is small and window-less, located off the casino's floor. According to Romanski, once they had taken their seats, Brown accused Romanski of stealing the token, whereupon Brown counted Romanski's money and removed one nickel from Romanski's winnings. Stevenson asked Romanski to turn over her social security card and driver's license; Romanski complied and these items were photocopied. Romanski was then photographed. Romanski testified that she acquiesced to these requests because Brown said she was a police officer, had a badge, and appeared to have handcuffs. Brown admitted having presented her badge and possessing handcuffs but testified that she identified herself only as a "security police officer," not as a bona fide police officer. There is no dispute that a uniformed casino security officer stood just outside the room for the duration of the questioning.

Romanski was ejected from the casino for a period of 6 months; Stevenson made the final decision to eject, or "86," Romanski. The precise ground for ejecting Romanski is unclear from the record. Although unknown to Romanski at the time, it is now undisputed that Brown and some of her colleagues on the casino's security staff were licensed under state law as "private security police officer[s]." Mich. Comp. Laws (M.C.L.) §338.1079. By virtue of being so licensed, a private security police officer has "the authority to arrest a person without a warrant as set forth for public peace officers . . . when that private security police officer is on the employer's premises." M.C.L. §338.1080. The statute additionally requires that private security police officers make arrests only when they are on duty and in "the full uniform of the[ir]employer." Id. It is undisputed that Brown was on duty during the events of this case. It is also undisputed that Brown was not wearing the uniform worn by some of the other security guards, but Defendants have never contended that this rendered Brown out of uniform for purposes of §338.1080; indeed, Defendants have conceded from the beginning that the statute applies in this case. Their argument is simply that the power admittedly conferred on Brown by the statute did not [render] her actions "under color of state law." See 42 U.S.C. §1983.

Brown was in charge of escorting Romanski to the valet parking area of the casino, where Romanski was to wait for her 3 P.M. bus home. Brown and her colleagues denied Romanski's request to meet her friends for lunch at the buffet—indeed, they did not permit Romanski to eat lunch at all. In addition, they did not permit Romanski to enter the restroom by herself; Brown accompanied Romanski into the restroom and waited outside the stall. At 3 P.M., Romanski exited the valet area to board what she thought was her bus; it turned out not to be but instead of returning to the valet area she ran into her friends and stayed outside. It was extremely hot and humid and Dombrowski and Holman persuaded Romanski to return to the casino. Upon entering, the three were confronted by casino employees, who directed them to return to the valet area, which is air-conditioned; they waited there until the bus arrived. . . .

As these facts reflect, Defendants' treatment of Romanski was inexplicable and egregious. [According to the district court,] "[t]here is sufficient evidence to allow a jury to find that after [Romanski] picked up an abandoned token that Defendants—by using the authority vested in them by the State of Michigan—surrounded her, arrested her, led her to the security office, prevented her from leaving the security office, and stole the five cents that she found from her. Afterwards, they surrounded her as they threw her out of the casino, and refused to let her use the restroom by herself. Defendants also prevented her from having lunch with her friends [and] falsely told her friends that she had stolen from them . . . . [A] jury could certainly exclaim 'Outrageous.'" *Romanski v. Detroit Entertainment, L.L.C.*, 265 F. Supp. 2d 835, 848-49 (E.D. Mich. 2003) (citations omitted). Indeed, a jury did make such an exclamation: it found in Romanski's favor and made a substantial punitive damages award.

[Romanski's action, originally brought in state court, but removed by defendants to federal court, raised the following claims: false arrest, false imprisonment, defamation, and intentional infliction of emotional distress, as well as a claim under 42 U.S.C. §1983 that Defendants had violated Romanski's Fourth Amendment rights. Specifically, Romanski alleged that Defendants, acting under color of state law, had arrested her without probable cause because the token she picked up was abandoned, i.e., not the casino's property. Among other arguments, the Defendants argued that they were not acting under color of state law.]

The district court disagreed and instructed the jury as follows: "Acting under color of law in this case simply means acting in one's capacity as a licensed security officer with powers to make an arrest on the casino premises. I instruct you as a matter of law that the defendants were acting under color of law at the time of this incident and you may find that this element has been established." The other issues in the case were submitted to the jury, which found the casino and Brown liable on the Fourth Amendment wrongful arrest claim and the casino alone liable on the state law false arrest and false imprisonment claims. The jury did not find any of the defendants liable for defamation or intentional infliction of emotional distress but, based on its verdict on Romanski's other claims, the jury awarded $279.05 in compensatory damages. Based exclusively on the verdict in favor of Romanski on her §1983 claim, the jury awarded $500 in punitive damages against Brown, and $875,000 in punitive damages against the casino.

[Defendants now contest the "state actor" ruling, the property question on whether the token was abandoned, and the damages award.]

## A. STATE ACTION

Section 1983 makes liable only those who, while acting under color of state law, deprive another of a right secured by the Constitution or federal law. 42 U.S.C. §1983. A private actor acts under color of state law when its conduct is "fairly attributable to the state." *Lugar v. Edmondson Oil Co.*, 457 U.S. 922, 947 (1982). "The Supreme Court has developed three tests for determining the existence of state action in a particular case: (1) the public function test, (2) the state compulsion test, and (3) the symbiotic relationship or nexus test." *Chapman* [*v. Higbee*], 319 F.3d [825] at 833 [(6th Cir. 2003)].

The district court concluded that Brown and any of her colleagues similarly licensed as private security police officers pursuant to M.C.L. §338.1079 were state actors under the public function test. 265 F. Supp. 2d at 841-43. . . . Under the public function test, a private entity is said to be performing a public function if it is exercising powers traditionally reserved to the state, such as holding elections, taking private property under the eminent domain power, or operating a company-owned town. See *Flagg Bros.*, 436 U.S. at 157-58 (holding elections); *Jackson v. Metropolitan Edison Co.*, 419 U.S. 345, 352-53 (1974) (exercising eminent domain); *Marsh v. Alabama*, 326 U.S. 501, 505-509 (1946) (operating a company-owned town). The Supreme Court has expressly left open the question whether and under what circumstances private police officers may be said to perform a public function for purposes of §1983. *Flagg Bros.*, 436 U.S. at 163. Nevertheless, as the district court observed, there is a growing body of case law to consult for guidance on this question.

For example, in a decision deemed by both parties and the district court to bear directly on the issue presented in this case, the Seventh Circuit held that private police officers licensed to make arrests could be state actors under the public function test. *Payton v. Rush-Presbyterian*, 184 F.3d 623, 627-30 (7th Cir.1999). To be sure, Payton was an appeal of a dismissal pursuant to Fed. R. Civ. P. 12(b)(6), but we think this distinction is of little relevance since the crucial fact in that case—assumed to be true there but indisputable here—was that by virtue of their status as on-duty special police officers, licensed by the city of Chicago, the defendants enjoyed "virtually the same power as public police officers." *Id.* at 629. Indeed, the defendants in *Payton* operated under an ordinance which provided that special police officers licensed under it "shall possess the powers of the regular police patrol at the places for which they are respectively appointed or in the line of duty for which they are engaged." *Id.* at 625 (quoting Chicago City Code §4-340-100 (1993)).

This broad delegation of power, the Seventh Circuit reasoned, distinguished *Payton* from an earlier case in which the court had held that a private security guard endowed with more limited police-type powers was not a state actor. *See Wade v. Byles,* 83 F.3d 902, 905-906 (7th Cir. 1996). The defendant in Wade was permitted to carry a handgun and to use deadly force in self-defense but could arrest someone only for "trespass pending the arrival of the police" and could exercise these powers only in the lobbies of properties owned by the public housing authority for which he worked. *Id.* at 906. The defendant was not a state actor because, as the court put it in *Payton,* "none of these powers had been exclusively reserved to the police—citizen's arrests and the rights to carry handguns and use them in self-defense are available to individuals outside of the law enforcement community." *Payton,* 184 F.3d at 629[.]

*Payton* illustrates a line that has been drawn in the case law. The line divides cases in which a private actor exercises a power traditionally reserved to the state, but not exclusively reserved to it, e.g., the common law shopkeeper's privilege, from cases in which a private actor exercises a power exclusively reserved to the state, e.g., the police power. Where private security guards are endowed by law with plenary police powers such that they are de facto police officers, they may qualify as state actors under the public function test. See *Payton,* 184 F.3d at 630; *Henderson v. Fisher,* 631 F.2d 1115 (3d Cir. 1980) (per curiam) (university policemen with plenary police authority throughout the university's campus); *Rojas v. Alexander's Dept. Store, Inc.,* 654 F. Supp. 856 (E.D.N.Y.1986) (New York City special patrolman with plenary police authority patrolling a department store). The rationale of these cases is that when the state delegates a power traditionally reserved to it alone—the police power—to private actors in order that they may provide police services to institutions that need it, a "plaintiff's ability to claim relief under §1983 [for abuses of that power] should be unaffected." *Payton,* 184 F.3d at 629[.]

On the other side of the line illustrated by *Payton* are cases in which the private defendants have some police-like powers but not plenary police authority. . . . The canonical example here is when a store avails itself of the common law shopkeeper's privilege, the privilege at issue in this Court's en banc decision in *Chapman v. Higbee Co.*, and the Fifth Circuit case upon which Chapman relied. *See Chapman*, 319 F.3d at 833-34[.]

Like the district court, we think this case falls on the *Payton* side of the line. It is undisputed that Brown (and some of her colleagues) were private security police officers licensed under M.C.L. §338.1079. This means that Brown's qualifications for being so licensed were vetted by Michigan's department of state police, *id.* §(1), and that Brown was subject to certain statutes administered by that department. *Id.* §(2); *see* M.C.L. §§338.1067, 338.1069. More critical for present purposes are the undisputed facts that Brown was on duty and on the casino's premises at all times relevant to this case. These undisputed facts lead to an inescapable conclusion of law—namely, that at all times relevant to this case, Brown "ha[d] the authority to arrest a person without a warrant as set forth for public peace officers . . . ." M.C.L. §338.1080. One consequence of Brown's possession of this authority, the authority to make arrests at one's discretion and for any offenses, is clear: at all times relevant to this case, Brown was a state actor as a matter of law.[2]

Unlike the common law privileges at issue in *Wade* (the use of deadly force in self-defense, the right to detain for trespass, and the right to carry a weapon) and *Chapman* (the shopkeeper's privilege), which may be invoked by any citizen under appropriate circumstances, the plenary arrest power enjoyed by private security police

---

2. The dissent's repeated reliance on *City of Grand Rapids v. Impens*, 414 Mich. 667, 327 N.W.2d 278 (1982), is misplaced. There, private security officers suspected the defendant and two others of shoplifting. *Id.* at 279. The officers asked the three individuals to come to the security office. *Id.* The officers searched the three and found merchandise on one of the other individuals. *Id.* The officers then elicited information from the defendant to complete a "Loss Prevention Department Voluntary Statement." *Id.* The officers read the statement to the defendant and asked the defendant to sign it, which he did. *Id.* "There was no indication that defendant would not be released if the statement were not signed." *Id.* Prior to his trial, the defendant moved to suppress the signed statement, arguing that it was obtained in violation of Miranda. *Id.* The Michigan Court held that the private security officers were not required to give Miranda warnings. *Id.* at 282.

One obvious distinction between the instant case and *Impens* is that *Impens* did not involve an arrest in any form. There, the defendant was not held against his will. He was asked to go to the security office; he was asked to sign a form. There was no indication of arrest.

The key distinction, however, is that the security officers did not exercise power exclusively reserved to the states. The contested conduct was the security officers' elicitation of the defendant's statements. Simply put, asking questions in a non-custodial setting is a power not within the exclusive province of the state.

officers licensed pursuant to M.C.L. §338.1079 is a power traditionally reserved to the state alone. . . . In contrast, the private security officers in *Wade* only had the power to "arrest people for criminal trespass . . . ." 83 F.3d at 906. As the Seventh Circuit later pointed out, the private security officers in *Wade* would have to "dial 911" if they witnessed a crime other than criminal trespass. *Payton,* 184 F.3d at 630. Under Michigan law, a private security officer has no such limitation. . . .

Consistent with the Seventh Circuit's approach in *Wade* and *Payton,* we have focused on the specific powers that Brown, in her capacity as an on-duty and duly licensed private security police officer, had at her disposal. Because at least one of these powers, the plenary arrest power, is "traditionally the exclusive prerogative of the state," *Jackson v. Metropolitan Edison Co.,* 419 U.S. at 353, 95 S. Ct. 449, and because it is undisputed that Brown was in fact duly licensed under M.C.L. §338.1079 and was in fact on duty at all times relevant to this case, the district court correctly held that Brown was a state actor as a matter of law.

## B. JURY INSTRUCTIONS

[Defendants also challenge the district court's jury instructions.] The first instruction to which Defendants object related to whether they had probable cause to arrest Romanski. Defendants apparently argued that they had probable cause to believe Romanski had stolen the five cent token from the casino, i.e., that the token was not abandoned when Romanski took it into her possession. Although the district court did conclude at the summary judgment stage that there was a bona fide jury question as to whether the token was abandoned, it nevertheless observed "that there is no other likely explanation for the token being in the tray of the slot machine." 265 F. Supp. 2d at 845. The district court's statement is an apt reflection of the record, which contains not even a scintilla of evidence supporting Defendants' contention that the token was the casino's property rather than abandoned by a prior player at the slot machine. Nor did Defendants come forward with a basis in Michigan law for their assertion that the token became the casino's property once the prior player departed. The general rule, as noted by the district court, is that playing a slot machine is the commencement of an aleatory contract between the player and the casino. In the event the player wins a round, the casino "loses its legal right to the property, and the [player] gains that right." 265 F. Supp. 2d at 845 (citing Restatement (Second), Contracts §232 cmt. c (1981)).

Against this backdrop, we cannot say the district court erred when it instructed the jury that:

> This case, as we all know, involves a token, a five-cent token. The plaintiff as the finder of a lost or abandoned token, has superior title to that token than does the Motor City Casino. In determining whether the token was lost or abandoned, you are to use your common sense and consider whether there was any other rational circumstance for that token to be in that tray. The only person who has a superior right to that token other than the plaintiff, is the person who lost it or the person who abandoned it.

We must also note the patent insignificance of a five-cent token. Assuming for the moment that Defendants genuinely suspected Romanski of theft (it appears from the record that the real motive for the poor treatment of Romanski may have been her "attitude"), Defendants' decision to deal with the situation by dispatching a team of security personnel—at least one of whom was in effect a police officer—to detain and interrogate Romanski offends the "venerable *maxim de minimis non curat lex* ('the law cares not for trifles')." *Wisconsin Dept. of Revenue v. William Wrigley, Jr., Co.*, 505 U.S. 214, 231 (1992) (citing cases). Under the circumstances of this case, the district court's instruction on abandonment was not confusing, misleading, or prejudicial.

### C. Amount of the Punitive Damages Award

The casino appeals the jury's assessment of $875,000 in punitive damages against it on the ground that the amount is unconstitutionally excessive. Whether a punitive damages award is so excessive as to offend due process depends on our assessment of the three "guideposts" first enunciated in *BMW of North America, Inc. v. Gore*, 517 U.S. 559 (1996): the degree of reprehensibility of the defendant's conduct, the punitive award's ratio to the compensatory award, and sanctions for comparable misconduct. . . . [Much of the courts' analysis is omitted, but the court had the following to say about these factors in this case.]

[Reprehensibility.] The Supreme Court has said that "[t]he most important indicium of the reasonableness of a punitive damages award is the degree of reprehensibility of the defendant's conduct." [*State Farm Mut. Auto. Ins. Co. v.*] *Campbell*, 538 U.S. [408,] at 419 [(2003)] (quoting *Gore*, 517 U.S. at 576). . . .

[T]he district court concluded that the harm caused by the casino "was primarily physical, rather than economic." The basis for this conclusion was the fact that Romanski "testified that she felt sick, embarrassed, humiliated, intimidated and scared." Romanski's economic losses totaled $9.05, the combined value of the lunch ticket revoked by the casino ($9) and the five-cent token the casino seized. The remaining $270 of the compensatory award was to make Romanski whole for the emotional distress she suffered as a result of Defendants' conduct. We think the district court was generally correct to describe Romanski's harm as primarily physical in character. Although she did not suffer actual physical injury, the jury could reasonably infer from the peculiar circumstances of Romanski's detention and questioning—a process initiated on the casino floor in front of patrons by a team of four security personnel—that the threat of physical force was apparent. Indeed, there was testimony that Brown threatened Romanski and it is undisputed that Brown had handcuffs at her disposal; in addition, it appears undisputed, so far as we can discern, that Brown and perhaps another member of the security staff accused Romanski of theft. . . .

Defendants admit that Romanski was targeted because she picked up a five-cent token. Whether Brown subsequently detained Romanski on suspicion of theft or because Romanski's "attitude" perturbed Brown, the crucial point for reprehensibility purposes is that the detention itself and the manner in which it was carried out—e.g., by a team of four security personnel surrounding Romanski—were so egregious in light of the circumstances that malice naturally comes to mind. What other motivation, a reasonable observer might ask, would cause Brown and her colleagues to detain and interrogate a 72-year-old woman in a windowless room over five cents? This is especially true in light of the jury's conclusion that Defendants lacked probable cause to arrest Romanski. . . .

But Defendants' remarkable abuse of power did not end there. It is undisputed that the casino revoked Romanski's lunch ticket and, having been ejected, she was not permitted to eat anywhere in the casino. In other words, the rather inhospitable outside (it was humid and over 90 degrees) was the 72-year-old Romanski's only choice for lunch. It is further undisputed that Defendants refused to allow Romanski to enter the restroom by herself; instead, Defendants callously forced her to endure the indignity of having Brown stand guard outside the stall. This is without question evidence of malice and of a conscious disregard for Romanski's well-being and hence is probative of reprehensibility. Finally, we must note one facet of the casino's behavior that is particularly deserving of condemnation and further indicative of malice, namely, that it dispatched someone who was in effect a police officer, with all the authority that that implies.

Apparently, the casino was not content to have an ordinary security guard—one without the power to make arrests—simply inform Romanski of the purported slot-walking policy and leave it at that. There is, consequently, a troubling element of gratuitousness in Defendants' conduct.

[According to the district court:] "[T]his case was not about the loss of a five-cent token or a nine-dollar meal ticket; it was about [Romanski's] right not to be unreasonably seized [and] unreasonably detained . . . . Defendants acted with at least indifference to the health or safety of [Romanski], an elderly woman. After Defendant Brown observed [Romanski] play the five-cent token, [Romanski] was surrounded by four security guards, led up to the security office, informed she had committed a crime, photographed, and reported to the state police . . . . [T]he Court finds the conduct of Defendant MotorCity's employees to be particularly reprehensible."

In sum, while there is no evidence of similar misconduct in the past on the casino's part, *see Gore*, 517 U.S. at 576-77, it is clear in this case that the reprehensibility guidepost weighs in favor of a substantial punitive damages award.

[Ratio of punitive to compensatory damages.] "The second and perhaps most commonly cited indicium of an unreasonable or excessive punitive damages award is its ratio to the actual harm inflicted on the plaintiff." *Gore*, 517 U.S. at 580. When considered against the broad spectrum of civil cases, the ratio in this case (3,135 to 1) is unusually high and the compensatory damages award is unusually low. *Compare Gore*, 517 U.S. at 580-81 (rejecting a 500-to-1 ratio where the compensatory award was $4000); *Campbell*, 538 U.S. at 425-26 (rejecting a 145-to-1 ratio where the compensatory award was $1 million). . . . [But t]his Court and other courts have recognized that where "injuries are without a ready monetary value," such as invasions of constitutional rights unaccompanied by physical injury or other compensable harm, higher ratios between the compensatory or nominal award and the punitive award are to be expected. *Argentine v. United Steel Workers of Am., AFL-CIO, CLC*, 287 F.3d 476, 488 (6th Cir. 2002) (sustaining a 42.5 to 1 ratio, and thus a $400,000 punitive award, where injury was a national union's sustained campaign of retaliation against a local branch because some of its members expressed disagreement with a union-promoted bargaining agreement); *see also Dean v. Olibas*, 129 F.3d 1001, 1007 (8th Cir. 1997) (sustaining a 14 to 1 ratio, and thus a $70,000 punitive award, where the unlawful arrest of the plaintiff caused him primarily a kind of harm not measurable in monetary terms). Indeed, the Second Circuit has reasoned, we think correctly, that in cases where the compensatory award is very low or nominal, "any appreciable exemplary award would produce a ratio that would appear excessive by this measure." *Lee*, 101 F.3d at 811.

These decisions in the circuits are based as much on intuition as on the only plausible interpretation of crucial dicta in *Gore* and *Campbell*; to wit, as the Court said in the first of those cases: "low awards of compensatory damages may properly support a higher ratio than high compensatory awards, if, for example, a particularly egregious act has resulted in only a small amount of economic damages. A higher ratio may also be justified in cases in which the injury is hard to detect or the monetary value of noneconomic harm might have been difficult to determine." *Gore*, 517 U.S. at 582. . . . Consistent with these principles, we think that to determine whether the punitive award in this case is within constitutional limits, the best approach is to compare it to punitive awards examined by courts "in other civil rights cases to find limits and proportions." *Lee*, 101 F.3d at 811. This approach is necessarily unscientific but aids us in identifying a ballpark within which to evaluate the $875,000 award at issue here.

We know of only one prior case in which we considered the constitutionality of a punitive damages award assessed pursuant to a finding of liability under §1983. The case, *Gregory v. Shelby County*, is quite distinguishable, however, because the plaintiff "suffered severe physical abuse, endured long hours of conscious pain and suffering, and ultimately died as a result [of a police officer's] actions." 220 F.3d 433, 445 (6th Cir. 2000). Furthermore, the compensatory award in *Gregory* was $778,000, so the $2.2 million punitive award easily satisfied *Gore*'s ratio guidepost. . . .

Our decision in *Gregory* and our review of . . . cases from other circuits leads us to two important conclusions: First, substantial punitive awards in §1983 cases, not surprisingly, tend to accompany conduct that results in physical or psychological harm. Second, in the typical §1983 case in which punitive damages are awarded, the defendant is an individual police officer, not the police department or municipality (which, odds are, have deeper pockets than the officer), let alone a deeply pocketed company, which the casino indisputably is. . . .

[A] wrinkle peculiar to this case may render appropriate an award that exceeds the average punitive award for civil rights cases involving verdicts of this type. The defendant here is a casino, which, at the time of the verdict, yielded a daily intake of nearly $1,000,000. "Since a fixed dollar award will punish a poor person more than a wealthy one, one can understand the relevance of [the defendant's financial position] to the State's interest in retribution . . . ." *Gore*, 517 U.S. at 591 (Breyer, J., concurring)[.] The defendant's financial position is equally relevant to the State's interest in deterrence, which is also a valid purpose of punitive damages.

At the same time, a defendant's wealth could heighten the likelihood of juror caprice. Thus the Supreme Court recently reiterated that "[t]he wealth of a defendant cannot justify an otherwise unconstitutional punitive damages award." *Campbell*, 538 U.S. at 427. Common sense gives us an additional reason to view skeptically the generic proposition that a high punitive award is necessary because of the wealth of the defendant. The Supreme Court said in *Gore* that "[t]he sanction imposed in this case cannot be justified on the ground that it was necessary to deter future misconduct without considering whether less drastic remedies could be expected to achieve that goal." 517 U.S. at 584. The upshot is two-fold: we must take into account the casino's wealth to ensure that the punitive damages award will further the interests it is designed to advance; but we must also ensure that our exacting appellate review results in an award that is not significantly higher than is necessary to further those interests. . . .

[Sanctions for comparable misconduct.] We have already canvassed the most comparable cases we have found; indeed, this case is an occasion where the ratio and comparable conduct guideposts substantially overlap. Still, the question here is . . . whether the casino had fair notice that conduct of the sort that occurred here might result in penalties, fines, or punitive damages on the order of $875,000. . . .

In a general sense, of course, the casino had fair notice that a verdict against a state actor for violating someone's constitutional rights might result in a punitive damages award if the conduct is sufficiently egregious. *See Smith v. Wade*, 461 U.S. 30, 56 (1983). The civil rights cases we canvassed, therefore, provided some notice as to potential punitive damages awards for §1983 liability. Accordingly, we conclude the casino had fair notice that it might face punitive damages for sanctioning the type of civil rights violation that Romanski endured here but it did not have notice that an award as high as $875,000 was likely. This guidepost militates in favor of reducing the award.

The lasting impression this case leaves is one of egregious misconduct—a de jure police officer's gratuitous abuse of power, sanctioned by a casino, that left a 72-year-old woman the victim of needless indignities and humiliation. In moral terms, the casino's conduct was significantly reprehensible; it surely was reprehensible enough to warrant a substantial punitive damages award. In comparative terms, however, because Romanski was not beaten, charged or tried, the conduct here was not as reprehensible as the defendants' conduct in some of the civil rights cases we have canvassed. . . .

However, we must consider the *Gore* guideposts in their totality and, furthermore, we must ensure that a punitive damages award actually achieves the twin purposes of punishment and deterrence. . . . [W]e think an award of no greater than $600,000—sixty percent of the casino's daily intake at the time of the verdict—would satisfy the demands of the due process clause. It cannot be seriously contended that this is an insignificant amount for the casino. Moreover, a $600,000 award is comfortably within the ballpark of the punitive damages awards in the civil rights cases we have canvassed, *see esp. Goodman*, 789 So. 2d at 171 (involving a corporate defendant); the less reprehensible conduct in this case being counteracted by the need to make the award large enough to actually punish and deter, something that is ordinarily not a challenge in civil rights cases.

Accordingly, on remand, the district court must give Romanski the option of agreeing to remit $275,000 and to accept a $600,000 punitive damages award or to proceed with a new trial on the issue of damages. We VACATE the punitive damages portion of the district court's judgment, AFFIRM the judgment in all other respects, and REMAND for proceedings consistent with this opinion.

FARRIS, Circuit Judge, dissenting.

The Michigan statute upon which the majority relies places specific limitations on private security guards that distinguish their powers of detention from those of public peace-officers. *See* M.C.L. §338.1080. Although security guards can make arrests without a warrant, M.C.L. §338.1080 emphasizes that their authority is limited by the bounds of their private employment: They can only detain individuals on company property, during their hours of employment, while wearing a company uniform.[1]

---

1. The majority relies on the holdings in *Payton v. Rush-Presbyterian* and *Henderson v. Fisher* for the proposition that the geographical limitations on security guards' authority in M.C.L. §338.1080 do not alter the "plenary" nature of their power. (Op. 647.) Those cases are distinguishable from this case. The Chicago ordinance cited in *Payton* states that private officers "possess the powers of the regular police patrol at the places for which they are respectively appointed or in the line of duty for which they are engaged." *Payton v. Rush-Presbyterian*, 184 F.3d 623, 625 (7th Cir. 1999). Unlike the Michigan statute, the Chicago ordinance grants special police officers broad police powers without specific geographical limitations. Moreover, the ordinance also forces special police officers to comply with all rules and regulations governing public officers and requires them to report directly to the superintendent of police. *Id.* Likewise, *Henderson v. Fisher* also differs significantly from this case. In *Henderson* the court held that the University of Pittsburgh, where the campus police worked, was essentially a state institution. *Henderson v. Fisher*, 631 F.2d 1115, 1118 (3d Cir.1980) ("[T]he University of Pittsburgh has lost its wholly private charter and has become an instrumentality of the Commonwealth . . ."). Furthermore, the Pennsylvania statute cited in *Henderson* extends the authority of campus officers beyond the bounds of state universities, permitting them to

The Michigan Supreme Court has specifically rejected the majority's conclusion that licensed, private security guards are necessarily state actors[, noting "We do not believe that the mere licensing of security guards constitutes sufficient government involvement to require the giving of Miranda warnings]. *City of Grand Rapids v. Impens,* 414 Mich. 667, 327 N.W.2d 278, 281 (1982).

By its own account, in granting licenses to private security guards, the State of Michigan has not attempted to, "cloak[ ] private individuals with virtually the same power as public officers." See *Payton,* 184 F.3d at 629. But even if the casino's private security guards did hold plenary arrest authority under Michigan law, it would still be necessary to establish that they actually exercised this authority during the detention of Romanski.

In applying the public interest test, it is the exercise, and not the possession, of powers belonging exclusively to the state that determines whether the action was under color of state law. *See Chapman v. Higbee Co.,* 319 F.3d 825, 834 (6th Cir. 2003) (en banc) ("Under the public function test, a private party is deemed a state actor if he or she exercised powers traditionally reserved exclusively to the state.")[.] Romanski has presented no evidence that the State of Michigan has traditionally and exclusively reserved the power to make warrantless arrests. To the contrary, the Michigan Supreme Court has held that licensed private security guards do not act as state actors in detaining shoplifting suspects. *Impens,* 327 N.W.2d at 281 ("Their [guards'] role may be viewed as an extension of the shopkeepers' privilege to detain for a reasonable period of time a person suspected of theft or failure to pay.").

Viewing the facts in the light most favorable to defendants, I am not convinced that the casino security guards acted under color of state law in detaining Romanski. The four security guards approached and then later escorted Romanski off-the-floor because they believed she had committed a crime and, as the guards contend, she had become loud and belligerent when they attempted to explain the casino's policy against "slot-walking." Even Romanski concedes that Brown detained her, not simply because of her attitude, but because she suspected Romanski of theft. (Op. 633-34.) The law on this point is very clear: Investigation of a possible crime on an employer's premises

---

"exercise those powers . . . conferred pursuant to this section within the municipality for the limited purpose of aiding local authorities in emergency situations." 71 Pa. Stat. Ann. §646 (2005). Due to M.C.L. §338.1080's comparative limitations on the authority of private security guards, I believe this case is more akin to *Wade v. Byles,* than either *Payton* or *Henderson*. See *Wade v. Byles,* 83 F.3d 902, 904 (7th Cir.1996) (finding an absence of state action where guards were not allowed to pursue individuals outside the lobby of city housing authority buildings).

"does not transform the actions of a private security officer into state action." *Chapman*, 319 F.3d at 834. That the "crime" was a "trifle," as the opinion notes, and that the guard's actions may have constituted an egregious tort, is irrelevant. . . . I respectfully dissent.

*NOTES*

1. One question presented in this case was whether the plaintiff violated the law by "slot-walking." The court viewed the question as one of abandoned property, but the Michigan statute excerpted in the notes preceding the case contains a provision that seems to make "slot-walking" illegal:

   M.C.L.A §432.218 Michigan Gaming Control and Revenue Act, Sec. 18. (2) A person commits a felony punishable by imprisonment for not more than 10 years or a fine of not more than $100,000.00, or both, and, in addition, shall be barred for life from a gambling operation under the jurisdiction of the board if the person does any of the following: . . . (j) Claims, collects, takes, or attempts to claim, collect, or take money or anything of value in or from the gambling games, with intent to defraud, without having made a wager contingent on winning a gambling game, or claims, collects, or takes an amount of money or thing of value of greater value than the amount won.

   Would the outcome of this case be different if the court had been aware of this statute? Would the jury instructions have been correct? Would there have been probable cause to believe that the plaintiff committed a crime when she removed the "abandoned" token from the slot machine tray?

2. It is common practice in the casino industry to attempt to alter the rules of "finders/keepers" in the casino environment. Just as a guest invited to a host's home for a social occasion could not reasonably claim ownership of a diamond ring found between the cushions of the host's couch, the casino presumes that any "abandoned" money on the presence of the casino belongs to its rightful owner or the casino itself. This court resists that approach, whether as a state law or only as a casino rule.

3. On the question of state action, were the casino security officers acting on behalf of the state when they "arrested" Romanski and questioned her? In another slot-walking case decided shortly after *Romanski* in which some of the suspects claimed to have been detained for several hours, a different panel of the Sixth Circuit found that casino security guards were not "state actors" for

purposes of Section 1983 because, unlike in *Romanski*, the guards were not licensed by the state under the Michigan Private Security Business and Security Guard Act, and thus were not equivalent to state actors. *Lindsey v. Detroit Entertainment*, 484 F.3d 824 (6th Cir. 2007). Given the pervasiveness of the regulation of the casino industry and that state laws and gaming regulations often require a significant security presence as a matter of law, are casino security guards often acting under the color of state law?

4. Was the punitive damage award in this case justified? Did the existing caselaw give the court adequate guidance?

# CHAPTER
# 8

# Taxation of Gambling

Gambling presents several vexing issues in the taxation context. Thinking about these issues can reveal some problems in defining and identifying the product that the casino/seller is offering and the player/patron is consuming. Is gambling a form of consumable entertainment or a profit-seeking enterprise? Is it always an avocation, or is it, for the professional gambler, a vocation? What is the player purchasing and consuming? Entertainment? An opportunity to win? Or simply the winnings themselves? Does the patron receive "the goods or services" that the casino is offering even if he walks away a loser? Different answers to these questions can produce substantially differing tax ramifications.

These uncertainties produce fundamental questions about tax rules related to gambling. One of them is whether a gambling loss is a business-related loss or a personal loss. Consider that federal rules in the United States generally allow gambling losses to be deducted from income, but only to the extent of winnings. This presumably suggests that a gambler is engaging in consumption—and thus receiving value—when he gambles, whether he wins or loses.

Because gambling is subject, in many jurisdictions, to special taxes, and is sometimes legalized and justified primarily on the basis that it can produce governmental revenue, tax issues can loom particularly large. Finally, because of the velocity of money involved in gaming transactions, the amounts in dispute, even on matters of timing, can be substantial.

## COMMISSIONER OF INTERNAL REVENUE v. GROETZINGER
### 480 U.S. 23 (1987)

Justice BLACKMUN delivered the opinion of the Court.

The issue in this case is whether a full-time gambler who makes wagers solely for his own account is engaged in a "trade or business," within the meaning of §§162(a) and 62(1) of the Internal Revenue Code of 1954, as amended, 26 U.S.C. §§162(a) and 62(1) (1976 ed. and Supp. V). The tax year with which we here are concerned is the calendar year 1978; technically, then, we look to the Code as it read at that time.

Respondent Robert P. Groetzinger had worked for 20 years in sales and market research for an Illinois manufacturer when his position was terminated in February 1978. During the remainder of that year, respondent busied himself with pari-mutuel wagering, primarily on greyhound races. He gambled at tracks in Florida and Colorado. He went to the track 6 days a week for 48 weeks in 1978. He spent a substantial amount of time studying racing forms, programs, and other materials. He devoted from 60 to 80 hours each week to these gambling-related endeavors. He never placed bets on behalf of any other person, or sold tips, or collected commissions for placing bets, or functioned as a bookmaker. He gambled solely for his own account. He had no other profession or type of employment.

Respondent kept a detailed accounting of his wagers and every day noted his winnings and losses in a record book. In 1978, he had gross winnings of $70,000, but he bet $72,032; he thus realized a net gambling loss for the year of $2,032. Respondent received $6,498 in income from other sources in 1978. This came from interest, dividends, capital gains, and salary earned before his job was terminated.

On the federal income tax return he filed for the calendar year 1978 respondent reported as income only the $6,498 realized from nongambling sources. He did not report any gambling winnings or deduct any gambling losses. He did not itemize deductions. Instead, he computed his tax liability from the tax tables.

Upon audit, the Commissioner of Internal Revenue determined that respondent's $70,000 in gambling winnings were to be included in his gross income and that, pursuant to §165(d) of the Code, 26 U.S.C. §165(d), a deduction was to be allowed for his gambling losses to the extent of these gambling gains. But the Commissioner further determined that, under the law as it was in 1978, a portion of respondent's $70,000 gambling-loss deduction was an item of tax preference and operated to subject him to the minimum tax under §56(a) of the Code, 26 U.S.C. §56(a) (1976 ed.). At that time, under statutory provisions in effect from 1976 until 1982, "items of tax preference" were lessened by certain deductions, but not by deductions not "attributable to a trade or business carried on by the taxpayer." §57(a)(1) and (b)(1)(A), and §62(1), 26 U.S.C. §57(a)(1) and (b)(1)(A), and §62(1) (1976 ed. and Supp. I). These determinations by the Commissioner produced a §56(a) minimum tax of $2,142 and, with certain other adjustments not now in dispute, resulted in a total asserted tax deficiency of $2,522 for respondent for 1978.

Respondent sought redetermination of the deficiency in the United States Tax Court. That court, in a reviewed decision, with only two judges dissenting, held that respondent was in the trade or business of gambling, and that, as a consequence, no part of his gambling losses constituted an item of tax preference in determining any minimum tax for 1978. The United States Court of Appeals for the Seventh Circuit affirmed. 771 F.2d 269 (1985). Because of a conflict on the issue among Courts of Appeals,[5] we granted certiorari.

## II

The phrase "trade or business" has been in §162(a) and in that section's predecessors for many years. Indeed, the phrase is common in the Code, for it appears in over 50 sections and 800 subsections and in hundreds of places in proposed and final income tax regulations. The slightly longer phrases, "carrying on a trade or business" and "engaging in a trade or business," themselves are used no less than 60 times in the Code. The concept thus has a well-known and almost constant presence on our tax-law terrain. Despite this, the Code has never contained a definition of the words "trade or business" for general application, and no regulation has been issued expounding its meaning for all purposes. Neither has a broadly applicable authoritative judicial definition emerged.[7] Our task in this case is to ascertain the meaning of the phrase as it appears in the sections of the Code with which we are here concerned.

5. Compare *Nipper v. Commissioner*, 746 F.2d 813 (CA11 1984), aff'g, without opinion, 47 TCM 136, ¶83, 644 P-H Memo TC (1983), and the Seventh Circuit's decision in the present case, with *Gajewski v. Commissioner*, 723 F.2d 1062 (CA2 1983), cert. denied, 469 U.S. 818, 105 S. Ct. 88, 83 L. Ed. 2d 35 (1984); *Estate of Cull v. Commissioner*, 746 F.2d 1148 (CA6 1984), cert. denied, 472 U.S. 1007, 105 S. Ct. 2701, 86 L. Ed. 2d 717 (1985); and *Noto v. United States*, 770 F.2d 1073 (CA3 1985), aff'g, without opinion, 598 F. Supp. 440 (NJ 1984). Despite the interim reversals by the Second and Sixth Circuits in *Gajewski* and *Cull, supra*, the Tax Court has adhered to its position that a full-time gambler is engaged in a trade or business. See, e.g., *Meredith v. Commissioner*, 49 TCM 318, ¶84,651 P-H Memo TC (1984); *Barrish v. Commissioner*, 49 TCM 115, ¶84,602 P-H Memo TC (1984). It has drawn no distinction between the gambler and the active market trader. See also *Baxter v. United States*, 633 F. Supp. 912 (Nev. 1986).

7. Judge Friendly some time ago observed that "the courts have properly assumed that the term includes all means of gaining a livelihood by work, even those which would scarcely be so characterized in common speech." *Trent v. Commissioner*, 291 F.2d 669, 671 (CA2 1961).

In one of its early tax cases, *Flint v. Stone Tracy Co.*, 220 U.S. 107 (1911), the Court was concerned with the Corporation Tax imposed by §38 of the Tariff Act of 1909, and the status of being engaged in business. It said: " 'Business' is a very comprehensive term and embraces everything about which a person can be employed." 220 U.S., at 171. It embraced the Bouvier Dictionary definition: "That which occupies the time, attention and labor of men for the purpose of a livelihood or profit." *Ibid.* And Justice Frankfurter has observed that "we assume that Congress uses common words in their popular meaning, as used in the common speech of men." Frankfurter, Some Reflections on the Reading of Statutes, 47 Colum. L. Rev. 527, 536 (1947).

With these general comments as significant background, we turn to pertinent cases decided here. *Snyder v. Commissioner*, 295 U.S. 134 (1935), had to do with margin trading and capital gains, and held, in that context, that an investor, seeking merely to increase his holdings, was not engaged in a trade or business. Justice Brandeis, in his opinion for the Court, noted that the Board of Tax Appeals theretofore had ruled that a taxpayer who devoted the major portion of his time to transactions on the stock exchange for the purpose of making a livelihood could treat losses incurred as having been sustained in the course of a trade or business. He went on to observe that no facts were adduced in *Snyder* to show that the taxpayer "might properly be characterized as a 'trader on an exchange who makes a living in buying and selling securities.' " *Id.*, at 139. These observations, thus, are dicta, but, by their use, the Court appears to have drawn a distinction between an active trader and an investor.

In *Deputy v. Du Pont*, 308 U.S. 488 (1940), the Court was concerned with what were "ordinary and necessary" expenses of a taxpayer's trade or business, within the meaning of §23(a) of the Revenue Act of 1928, 45 Stat. 799. In ascertaining whether carrying charges on short sales of stock were deductible as ordinary and necessary expenses of the taxpayer's business, the Court *assumed* that the activities of the taxpayer in conserving and enhancing his estate constituted a trade or business, but nevertheless disallowed the claimed deductions because they were not "ordinary" or "necessary." 308 U.S., at 493-497. Justice Frankfurter, in a concurring opinion joined by Justice Reed, did not join the majority. He took the position that whether the taxpayer's activities constituted a trade or business was "open for determination," *id.*, at 499, and observed:

> " . . . carrying on any trade or business," within the contemplation of §23(a), involves holding one's self out to others as engaged in the selling of goods or services. This the taxpayer did not do. . . . Without elaborating the reasons for this construction and not unmindful of

opposing considerations, including appropriate regard for administrative practice, I prefer to make the conclusion explicit instead of making the hypothetical litigation-breeding assumption that this taxpayer's activities, for which expenses were sought to be deducted, did constitute a "trade or business."

Next came *Higgins v. Commissioner*, 312 U.S. 212 (1941). There the Court, in a bare and brief unanimous opinion, ruled that salaries and other expenses incident to looking after one's own investments in bonds and stocks were not deductible under §23(a) of the Revenue Act of 1932, 47 Stat. 179, as expenses paid or incurred in carrying on a trade or business. While surely cutting back on *Flint*'s broad approach, the Court seemed to do little more than announce that since 1918 "the present form [of the statute] was fixed and has so continued"; that "[n]o regulation has ever been promulgated which interprets the meaning of 'carrying on a business' "; that the comprehensive definition of "business" in *Flint* was "not controlling in this dissimilar inquiry"; that the facts in each case must be examined; that not all expenses of every business transaction are deductible; and that "[n]o matter how large the estate or how continuous or extended the work required may be, such facts are not sufficient as a matter of law to permit the courts to reverse the decision of the Board." 312 U.S., at 215-218. The opinion, therefore—although devoid of analysis and not setting forth what elements, if any, in addition to profit motive and regularity, were required to render an activity a trade or business— must stand for the propositions that full-time market activity in managing and preserving one's own estate is not embraced within the phrase "carrying on a business," and that salaries and other expenses incident to the operation are not deductible as having been paid or incurred in a trade or business. It is of interest to note that, although Justice Frankfurter was on the *Higgins* Court and this time did not write separately, and although Justice Reed, who had joined the concurring opinion in *Du Pont*, was the author of the *Higgins* opinion, the Court in that case did not even cite *Du Pont* and thus paid no heed whatsoever to the content of Justice Frankfurter's pronouncement in his concurring opinion. Adoption of the Frankfurter gloss obviously would have disposed of the case in the Commissioner's favor handily and automatically, but that easy route was not followed.

Less than three months later, the Court considered the issue of the deductibility, as business expenses, of estate and trust fees. In unanimous opinions issued the same day and written by Justice Black, the Court ruled that the efforts of an estate or trust in asset conservation and maintenance did not constitute a trade or business. *City Bank Farmers Trust Co. v. Helvering*, 313 U.S. 121 (1941); *United*

*States v. Pyne*, 313 U.S. 127 (1941). The *Higgins* case was deemed to be relevant and controlling. Again, no mention was made of the Frankfurter concurrence in *Du Pont*. Yet Justices Reed and Frankfurter were on the Court.

*Snow v. Commissioner*, 416 U.S. 500 (1974), concerned a taxpayer who had advanced capital to a partnership formed to develop an invention. On audit of his 1966 return, a claimed deduction under §174(a)(1) of the 1954 Code for his pro rata share of the partnership's operating loss was disallowed. The Tax Court and the Sixth Circuit upheld that disallowance. This Court reversed. Justice Douglas, writing for the eight Justices who participated, observed: "Section 174 was enacted in 1954 to dilute some of the conception of 'ordinary and necessary' business expenses under §162(a) (then §23(a)(1) of the Internal Revenue Code of 1939) adumbrated by Mr. Justice Frankfurter in a concurring opinion in *Deputy v. Du Pont* . . . where he said that the section in question . . . 'involves holding one's self out to others as engaged in the selling of goods or services.'" 416 U.S., at 502-503. He went on to state that §162(a) "is more narrowly written than is §174."

From these observations and decisions, we conclude (1) that, to be sure, the statutory words are broad and comprehensive (*Flint*); (2) that, however, expenses incident to caring for one's own investments, even though that endeavor is full time, are not deductible as paid or incurred in carrying on a trade or business (*Higgins*; *City Bank*; *Pyne*); (3) that the opposite conclusion may follow for an active trader (*Snyder*); (4) that Justice Frankfurter's attempted gloss upon the decision in *Du Pont* was not adopted by the Court in that case; (5) that the Court, indeed, later characterized it as an "adumbration" (*Snow*); and (6) that the Frankfurter observation, specifically or by implication, never has been accepted as law by a majority opinion of the Court, and more than once has been totally ignored. We must regard the Frankfurter gloss merely as a two-Justice pronouncement in a passing moment and, while entitled to respect, as never having achieved the status of a Court ruling. One also must acknowledge that *Higgins*, with its stress on examining the facts in each case, affords no readily helpful standard, in the usual sense, with which to decide the present case and others similar to it. The Court's cases, thus, give us results, but little general guidance.

## III

Federal and state legislation and court decisions, perhaps understandably, until recently have not been noticeably favorable to gambling endeavors and even have been reluctant to treat gambling on a parity with more "legitimate" means of making a living. See, *e.g.*, §4401 *et seq.* of the Code; *Marchetti v. United States*, 390 U.S. 39, 44-46, and nn. 5 and 6 (1968).[11] And the confinement of gambling-loss deductions to the amount of gambling gains, a provision brought into the income tax law as §23(g) of the Revenue Act of 1934, 48 Stat. 689, and carried forward into §165(d) of the 1954 Code, closed the door on suspected abuses, see H.R. Rep. No. 704, 73d Cong., 2d Sess., 22 (1934); S. Rep. No. 558, 73d Cong., 2d Sess., 25 (1934), but served partially to differentiate genuine gambling losses from many other types of adverse financial consequences sustained during the tax year. Gambling winnings, however, have not been isolated from gambling losses. The Congress has been realistic enough to recognize that such losses do exist and do have some effect on income, which is the primary focus of the federal income tax. . . .

If a taxpayer, as Groetzinger is stipulated to have done in 1978, devotes his full-time activity to gambling, and it is his intended livelihood source, it would seem that basic concepts of fairness (if there be much of that in the income tax law) demand that his activity be regarded as a trade or business just as any other readily accepted activity, such as being a retail store proprietor or, to come closer categorically, as being a casino operator or as being an active trader on the exchanges.

It is argued, however, that a full-time gambler is not offering goods or his services, within the line of demarcation that Justice Frankfurter would have drawn in *Du Pont*. Respondent replies that he indeed is supplying goods and services, not only to himself but, as well, to the gambling market; thus, he says, he comes within the Frankfurter test even if that were to be imposed as the proper measure. [According to him,] "It takes two to gamble." Surely, one who clearly satisfies the Frankfurter adumbration usually is in a trade or business. But does it necessarily follow that one who does not satisfy the Frankfurter adumbration is not in a trade or business? One might well feel that a full-time gambler ought to qualify as much as a full-time trader,[12] as Justice Brandeis in *Snyder* implied and as courts have held. The Commissioner, indeed, accepts the trader result. In any event, while the offering of goods and services usually would qualify the activity as a trade or business, this factor, it seems to us, is not an absolute prerequisite.

---

11. Today, however, the vast majority of States permit some form of public gambling. The lottery, bingo, pari-mutuel betting, jai alai, casinos, and slot machines easily come to mind.

12. "It takes a buyer to make a seller and it takes an opposing gambler to make a bet." Boyle, What is a Trade or Business?, 39 Tax Lawyer 737, 763 (1986).

We are not satisfied that the Frankfurter gloss would add any help-ful dimension to the resolution of cases such as this one, or that it provides a "sensible test," as the Commissioner urges. It might assist now and then, when the answer is obvious and positive, but it surely is capable of breeding litigation over the meaning of "goods," the mean-ing of "services," or the meaning of "holding one's self out." And we suspect that—apart from gambling—almost every activity would satisfy the gloss.[14] A test that everyone passes is not a test at all. We therefore now formally reject the Frankfurter gloss which the Court has never adopted anyway.

Of course, not every income-producing and profit-making endeavor constitutes a trade or business. The income tax law, almost from the beginning, has distinguished between a business or trade, on the one hand, and "transactions entered into for profit but not connected with . . . business or trade," on the other. Congress "distin-guished the broad range of income or profit producing activities from those satisfying the narrow category of trade or business." *Whipple v. Commissioner*, 373 U.S., at 197, 83 S. Ct., at 1171. We accept the fact that to be engaged in a trade or business, the taxpayer must be involved in the activity with continuity and regularity and that the taxpayer's primary purpose for engaging in the activity must be for income or profit. A sporadic activity, a hobby, or an amusement diver-sion does not qualify.

It is suggested that we should defer to the position taken by the Commissioner and by the Solicitor General, but, in the absence of guidance, for over several decades now, through the medium of defi-nitive statutes or regulations, we see little reason to do so. We would defer, instead, to the Code's normal focus on what we regard as a common-sense concept of what is a trade or business. Otherwise, as here, in the context of a minimum tax, it is not too extreme to say that the taxpayer is being taxed on his gambling losses,[15] a result distinctly out of line with the Code's focus on income.

---

14. Each of the three cases in conflict with the Seventh Circuit's decision in the present case, see n. 5, *supra*, was a gambler's case and adopted the Frankfurter gloss. Because the same courts, in cases not involving gamblers, have not referred to the Frankfurter gloss, see *Bessenyey v. Commissioner*, 379 F.2d 252 (CA2), cert. denied, 389 U.S. 931, 88 S. Ct. 293, 19 L. Ed. 2d 283 (1967); *Gestrich v. Commissioner*, 681 F.2d 805 (CA3 1982), aff'g, without opinion, 74 T.C. 525 (1980); *Main Line Distributors, Inc. v. Commissioner*, 321 F.2d 562 (CA6 1963), it would appear that these courts in effect were creating a special class of, and with special rules for, the full-time gambler. We find no warrant for this in the Code.

15. "The more he lost, the more minimum tax he had to pay." Boyle, 39 Tax Lawyer, at 754. The Commissioner concedes that application of the goods-or-ser-vices-test here "visits somewhat harsh consequences" on taxpayer Groetzinger, Brief for Petitioner 36, and "points to . . . perhaps unfortunate draftsmanship." Ibid.

We do not overrule or cut back on the Court's holding in *Higgins* when we conclude that if one's gambling activity is pursued full time, in good faith, and with regularity, to the production of income for a livelihood, and is not a mere hobby, it is a trade or business within the meaning of the statutes with which we are here concerned. Respondent Groetzinger satisfied that test in 1978. Constant and large-scale effort on his part was made. Skill was required and was applied. He did what he did for a livelihood, though with a less-than-successful result. This was not a hobby or a passing fancy or an occasional bet for amusement. . . . AFFIRMED.

Justice WHITE, with whom THE CHIEF JUSTICE and Justice SCALIA join, dissenting.

The 1982 amendments to the Tax Code made clear that gambling is not a trade or business. Under those amendments, the alternative minimum tax base equals adjusted gross income reduced by specified amounts, including gambling losses, and increased by items not relevant here. See 26 U.S.C. §§55(b), 55(e)(1)(A), 165(d) (1982 ed. and Supp. III). If full-time gambling were a trade or business, a full-time gambler's gambling losses would be "deductions . . . attributable to a trade or business carried on by the taxpayer," and hence deductible from gross income in computing adjusted gross income, 26 U.S.C. §62(1), though only to the extent of gambling winnings, 26 U.S.C. §165(d). To again subtract gambling losses (to the extent of gambling winnings) from adjusted gross income when computing the alternative minimum tax base would be to give the full-time gambler a double deduction for alternative minimum tax purposes, which was certainly not Congress' intent.[2] Thus, when Congress amended the

---

2. Consider two single individuals filing for the tax year ending December 31, 1986: A has $75,000 in nongambling income, and $75,000 in itemized nongambling deductions; B, a full-time gambler, has $75,000 in gambling winnings, $75,000 in gambling losses, $75,000 in nongambling income, and $75,000 in itemized nongambling deductions. A's gross income and adjusted gross income are both $75,000, and so is his alternative minimum tax base. The alternative minimum tax assessed on A is 20% of the excess of $75,000 over $30,000, see 26 U.S.C. §§55(a), 55(f)(1)(B), or $9,000. Assuming that full-time gambling is a trade or business, B has gross income of $150,000, adjusted gross income of $75,000 (because his gambling losses are attributable to a trade or business), and an alternative minimum tax base of zero (because gambling losses are deducted from adjusted gross income in computing the alternative minimum tax base). Thus, if full-time gambling were treated as a trade or business, B's gambling losses would shield him against the $9,000 minimum tax that Congress clearly intended him to pay. "The Code should not be interpreted to allow [a taxpayer] 'the practical equivalent of a double deduction,' *Charles Ilfeld Co. v. Hernandez*, 292 U.S. 62, 68, 54 S. Ct. 596, 598, 78 L. Ed. 1127 (1934), absent a clear declaration of intent by Congress." *United States v. Skelly Oil Co.*, 394 U.S. 678, 684, 89 S. Ct. 1379, 1383, 22 L. Ed. 2d 642 (1969). There is no such clear declaration of intent accompanying the 1982 amendments.

alternative minimum tax provisions in 1982, it implicitly accepted the teaching of *Gentile v. Commissioner*, 65 T.C. 1 (1975), that gambling is not a trade or business. Groetzinger would have had no problem under the 1982 amendments.

One could argue, I suppose, that although gambling is not a trade or business under the 1982 amendments, it was in 1978, the tax year at issue here. But there is certainly no indication that Congress intended in 1982 to alter the status of gambling as a trade or business. Rather, Congress was correcting an inequity that had arisen because gambling is *not* a trade or business, just as 40 years earlier Congress had, by enacting the predecessor to 26 U.S.C. §212, corrected an inequity that became apparent when this Court held that a full-time investor is not engaged in a trade or business. See *Higgins v. Commissioner*, 312 U.S. 212 (1941). In neither case did Congress attempt to alter the then-prevailing definition of trade or business, nor do I think this Court should do so now to avoid a harsh result in this case.[4] In any event, the Court should recognize that its holding is a sport that applies only to a superseded statute and not to the tax years governed by the 1982 amendments. Accordingly, I dissent.

## NOTES

1.  As *Groetzinger* recognizes, under Section 165(d) of the federal tax code, deduction of losses for wagering transactions is now strictly limited to gains from the same activities. That is, gambling losses can no longer be used to offset ordinary income under any circumstances.
2.  The Court analogizes, often, to stock trading. Is the analogy apt?
3.  Many forms of entertainment and hobbies have a significant economic component. Thus, the question: is gambling any different than other such activities? Is a professional gambler engaged in a trade or business such that his losses ought be deductible against ordinary income? Does the motivation for gambling vary among gambling patrons? Should the same rule govern all gamblers? Is a rule that differentiates between professional gamblers and ordinary gamblers administrable?

---

4. While the consequences of accepting the Commissioner's position in this case may be harsh to the respondent—which is no doubt why Congress amended the relevant Code provisions in 1982—I find the Court's characterization of the result as a tax on gambling losses, ante, at 986, somewhat misleading. If gambling is not a trade or business, the practical effect of the minimum tax on tax preference items is to reduce the deduction allowed for gambling losses from an amount equal to 100% of gambling winnings to some lesser percentage of gambling winnings.

4. This question arose under state tax laws in Minnesota in *Busch v. Commissioner of Revenue*, 713 N.W.2d 337 (Minn. 2006). In *Busch*, the taxpayer was a recent retiree who "began to spend a considerable amount of time playing the slot machines at Mystic Lake Casino." Since the issue arose under a parallel provision in state law, the court discussed *Groetzinger* but held that it was not bound by the federal case. Nevertheless, it reached a similar result, holding:

> There are two ways to view Busch's gambling activities for taxation purposes. Under one theory, Busch was a serious gambler who believed she would make a profit and sought to do so, and therefore she should receive a trade or business deduction as does anyone else who is engaged in a trade or business. Under the second theory, Busch worked until retirement, then began gambling, which she enjoyed as entertainment. Under this second theory, Busch did not "lose" money; rather, she won a considerable sum and then spent it on entertainment. This type of loss is known as a "hobby loss." Hobby losses often arise from activities that appear on some level to be a "trade or business[.]" *See, e.g., Ruben v. Comm'r*, No. 87-7079, 1988 WL 79313, at *1 (9th Cir., April 4, 1988) (concluding that appellant's horse ranching operations were not a trade or business). The question before us is whether Busch's losses from her gambling activity should be treated as trade or business losses or as "hobby losses."
>
> Busch admitted she was not an expert on how slot machines worked and that she chose slot machines as a method of gambling because "it didn't take a great deal of knowledge to play a slot machine." Busch told the tax court that, for her, gambling was not entertainment, but "just plain hard work." She points to the up to 40 to 60 hours per week that she spent at a casino over a three-year period. The commissioner contends that some forms of gambling can constitute a trade or business, but Busch's gambling did not because it involved no skill and making any money via gambling on the slot machines is entirely a matter of chance. While conceding that her expectation of earning a profit might have been unreasonable, Busch claims she had such an expectation and that this expectation, in addition to the regularity of her slot machine play and her research into slot machine strategy, shows that she was engaged in gambling as a trade or business.
>
> We conclude that it is often too difficult and uncertain for courts to decide, from the safe position of hindsight, which business activities had a reasonable expectation of profit and which did not. Furthermore, if trade or business tax incentives hinged upon a court's determination of whether an activity had a "realistic" expectation of profit, valuable innovation in our entrepreneurial society could be chilled. We conclude that the taxpayer's expectation

of profit from a given activity need not always be reasonable for the activity to qualify as a trade or business.

Does the Minnesota Supreme Court's reasoning justify its conclusion?

5. Section 3402(q) of the federal tax code requires that "every person" who makes any payment of "winnings subject to withholding" must withhold taxes and remit the same to the IRS. Section 3402(q)(3) provides that the term "winnings which are subject to withholding" means, in part, proceeds from a wagering transaction, if the proceeds are more than $5,000 from a wager placed in any sweepstakes, wagering pool, or lottery. Rev. Proc. 2007-57, 2007-36 I.R.B. 547. Casinos and other purveyors of commercial gambling are required to report winnings to the IRS on a Form W-2G.

6. The next case poses a related question: What counts as gambling winnings for purposes of deductions for offsetting losses?

## LIBUTTI v. COMMISSIONER OF INTERNAL REVENUE,
### T.C. Memo. 1996-108 (U.S. Tax Ct. 1996), 71 T.C.M. (CCH) 2343, T.C.M. (RIA) 96,108, 1996 RIA TC Memo 96,108

Laro, Judge:

[W]e must decide whether petitioner can deduct gambling losses to the extent of the value of "complimentary" goods and services (comps) that he received from Trump Plaza Associates, t/a Trump Plaza Hotel and Casino (Trump). . . .

### BACKGROUND

Petitioner resided in Secaucus, New Jersey, when he petitioned the Court. He filed 1987 and 1988 Federal income tax returns on November 20, 1989. He filed a 1989 Federal income tax return shortly after April 15, 1990, and he did so without receiving an extension of time under section 6081(a). All of petitioner's returns were prepared by a certified public accountant, and petitioner filed them using the status of "Married filing separate return". On each return, petitioner reported profits from his horse brokerage business called Buck Chance Stables (the Stables), which was conducted as a sole proprietorship. Petitioner reported that the Stables' profits were $3,169,881 in 1987, $785,900 in 1988, and $796,031 in 1989.

Petitioner gambled extensively. He played mostly craps, and he gambled mainly at Trump's casino (the Casino), which was situated in Atlantic City, New Jersey. In 1987, petitioner spent 84 days at the Casino, gambled on 75 of these days, made an average bet of $14,964, and had an overall loss of $4,139,100. In 1988, petitioner spent 179 days at the Casino, gambled on 148 of these days, made an average bet of $11,526, and had an overall loss of $3,080,050. In 1989, petitioner spent 304 days at the Casino, gambled on 70 of these days, made an average bet of $9,226, and had an overall loss of $1,215,900. On many of the occasions that petitioner played craps at the Casino, his total bets for one roll of the dice ranged from $50,000 to $100,000.

As a general practice, Trump, in its sole discretion, voluntarily transferred comps to its patrons to induce them to patronize the Casino. In some instances, but not in the case of petitioner, the comps were determined by a formula that allowed each patron to receive approximately 50 percent of Trump's anticipated win with respect to him or her. The formula took into account a patron's average bet, the hours that he or she gambled at the Casino, the estimated number of hands that he or she played per hour, and a factor set by Trump to reflect the fact that the odds were in its favor. Trump's senior management determined the type and amount of petitioner's comps using their sole discretion, as opposed to a direct application of this formula. Trump's payment of the comps to petitioner was discretionary.

A summary of petitioner's comps is as follows:

1987
| | |
|---|---|
| Automobiles | $319,300 |
| Vacations | 48,778 |
| Jewelry | 75,200 |
| Total | $443,278 |

1988
| | |
|---|---|
| Automobiles etc. | 872,920 |
| Vacations | 55,560 |
| Jewelry | 46,512 |
| Total | $974,992 |

1989
| | |
|---|---|
| Automobiles etc. | 806,858 |
| Premium champagne | 40,020 |
| Entertainment tickets | 279,978 |
| Total | $1,126,856 |

The automobiles and accessories included five Rolls Royces with an aggregate value of $916,300, three Ferraris with an aggregate value of $731,400 (exclusive of additional accessories of $14,875), one Bentley

Corniche valued at $212,000 (exclusive of a $1,890 phone installed therein), one Mercedes Benz valued at $60,583, automobile repairs of $12,740, a $14,310 payment by Trump so that petitioner could trade a Bentley for a Rolls, and a $34,980 payment by Trump so that petitioner could trade a Bentley Turbo for a Bentley Corniche. The vacations included five European vacations with an average value of $17,568 and one vacation in California valued at $16,500. The jewelry included a Rolex watch and bracelet valued at $32,300, a 2.7-carat diamond valued at $30,000, a bracelet and diamond earrings valued at $23,426, a bracelet watch valued at $19,800, a tennis bracelet valued at $12,900, and a diamond bracelet valued at $3,286. The champagne included 178 bottles of Cristal Rosé, valued at $225 a bottle. The tickets were to theater and sporting events such as the Super Bowl, the NCAA basketball tournament, boxing events, and the United States Open in Flushing Meadows, New York.

Casinos in New Jersey were prohibited from transferring cash comps to patrons during the subject years.[6] Trump and petitioner used at least the automobile comps to attempt to circumvent this prohibition. Trump "purchased" the automobiles on behalf of petitioner, and petitioner contemporaneously "sold" the automobiles for

---

6. N.J. Stat. Ann. sec. 5:12-102m (West 1988) provides:
No casino licensee shall offer or provide any complimentary services, gifts, cash or other items of value to any person unless:

(1) The complimentary consists of room, food, beverage or entertainment expenses provided directly to the patron and his guests by the licensee or indirectly to the patron and his guests on behalf of a licensee by a third party; or

(2) The complimentary consists of documented transportation expenses provided directly to the patron and his guests by the licensee or indirectly to the patron and his guests on behalf of a licensee by a third party, provided that the licensee complies with regulations promulgated by the commission to ensure that a patron's and his guests' documented transportation expenses are paid for or reimbursed only once; or

(3) The complimentary consists of coins, tokens, cash or other complimentary items or services provided through a bus coupon or other complimentary distribution program approved by the commission or maintained pursuant to commission regulation; or

(4) The complimentary consists of noncash gifts, provided that such noncash gifts in excess of $2,000.00 per trip or such greater amount as the commission may establish by regulation provided directly to the patron and his guests by the licensee or indirectly to the patron and his guests on behalf of a licensee by a third party shall be supported by documentation regarding the reason the noncash gift was provided to the patron and his guests, including where applicable, a patron's player rating, to be maintained by the casino licensee. For purposes of this paragraph, all noncash gifts presented to a patron and the patron's guests within any five-day period shall be considered a single noncash gift.

cash, most (if not all) of which he gambled at the Casino. On November 22, 1991, the New Jersey Casino Control Commission, the State agency that regulates casinos, held Trump liable (and fined it $450,000) for nine separate violations of N.J. Stat. Ann. sec. 5:12-102m, stemming from Trump's "transfer" of automobiles to petitioner and his daughter. These automobiles, which had an aggregate value of $1,650,838, were the automobiles and accessories that petitioner "received" from Trump during 1988 and 1989, exclusive of the car phone, automobile repairs, and trade-in charge of $14,310.

Trump issued petitioner a 1987, 1988, and 1989 Form 1099-MISC, Miscellaneous Income, reflecting that it paid him the above-mentioned amounts of comps as "prizes and awards." [It also gave him a statement] showing that petitioner's 1987 net gambling losses at the Casino equaled $4,139,100. The amount of comps shown on the 1988 and 1989 Forms 1099-MISC were reported on petitioner's 1988 and 1989 tax returns, respectively, as "Other income" from "TRUMP PLAZA ASSOC." These returns also claimed a matching miscellaneous itemized deduction (not subject to the two percent floor) for "GAMBLING LOSSES."

[R]espondent determined that petitioner was not entitled to deduct his gambling losses in the amounts equal to the amounts of the comps. According to respondent's notice of deficiency, dated November 12, 1992, "Gambling losses are allowed only to the extent they offset gains from wagering. Income you received from Trump Plaza Associates cannot be treated as 'gains from wagering transactions' pursuant to Internal Revenue Code Section 165(d)."

## DISCUSSION

Legal gambling is a multi-billion-dollar industry that has proliferated across the country and has become a major source of adult entertainment. In an effort to attract the attention of patrons, gaming establishments routinely offer comps. In the instant case, Trump paid more than $2.5 million in comps to petitioner during the subject years. The term "comps" is generally understood to imply "free of charge." Common sense, however, makes one strongly suspicious as to whether the comps received by petitioner were free of charge. If there is any truth to the time-tested adage that there is "no free lunch," one can hardly be surprised that respondent argues that petitioner's comps are taxable to him.

Petitioner reported the subject comps as gross income on his 1987 through 1989 Federal income tax returns (including the amendment to his 1987 return). Petitioner argues that the comps are not taxable to him because they are wagering gains which may be offset by his larger wagering losses. See sec. 165(d). Respondent asserts that the comps are not wagering gains because they do not have a "strong nexus" to petitioner's wagering transactions. Petitioner bears the burden of proof.

Section 165(d) provides that an individual may deduct his or her "Losses from wagering transactions . . . to the extent of the gains from such transactions." Neither the Code nor the regulations define the phrase "gains from such transactions." We apply the "plain, obvious, and rational meaning." *Liddle v. Commissioner*, 103 T.C. 285, 293 n.4 (1994)[.]

According to WEBSTER'S NEW WORLD DICTIONARY 551 (3d coll. ed. 1988), the primary meaning of the word "gain" is "an increase; addition; specif., a) an increase in wealth, earnings, etc.; profit; winnings." A primary meaning of the word "from" is "out of; derived or coming out of." *Id.* at 542. The word "wager" means "bet," *id.* at 1500, which, in turn, connotes "an agreement between two persons that the one proved wrong about the outcome of something will do or pay what is stipulated," *id.* at 133. The word "transaction" is the noun of the infinitive "to transact," which means "to carry on, perform, conduct, or complete (business, etc.)." *Id.* at 1419.

Assuming for purposes of applying section 165(d) that the comps are gross income, petitioner's comps fit within the plain meaning of the statutory text. The comps from Trump increased petitioner's wealth, and they were derived out of his betting transactions at the Casino. The fact that petitioner's receipt of the comps bore a close nexus to his gambling transactions at the Casino cannot be denied. Petitioner would not have received the comps from Trump but for the fact that he gambled extensively at the Casino. . . . The relationship between petitioner's comps and his wagering is close, direct, evident, and strong. The comps are sufficiently related to his gambling losses for purposes of section 165(d). We hold that petitioner's comps are "gains from . . . [wagering] transactions" under section 165(d).

We recognize that the term "gains from . . . [wagering] transactions" has sometimes been equated with the term "gambling winnings." Our current holding is not in conflict with these opinions. We agree with Justice White['s dissent in *Groetzinger*] and the Court of Appeals for the Second Circuit that "gains from . . . [wagering] transactions" include "gambling winnings." We do not read those opinions, however, to suggest that "winnings" is the only meaning for the word "gains." Section 165(d) refers to "gains," not "winnings." The word "gains" is broader than the word "winnings." Not only does the word "gains" include "winnings," it also includes an "increase in wealth." WEBSTER'S NEW WORLD DICTIONARY, *supra* at 551. If the Congress had wanted to limit the income prong of section 165(d) to gambling winnings, it would have said so. . . . Given the clarity of section 165(d), the beginning and end of our inquiry is the statutory text, and we apply the plain and common meaning of that text.

We recognize the narrow interpretation that this and other Courts have given the income prong of section 165(d). Our opinion does not depart from this view. None of the prior cases dealt with the specific facts at hand; namely, a gambler who received comps to induce him to gamble. The cases dealt mostly with taxpayers who worked in gambling establishments, as opposed to placing bets in wagering transactions there, and who received compensation that was different than ordinary pay. In *Boyd v. United States, supra,* for example, the taxpayer was a professional poker player who managed a casino's poker room. The casino did not participate in the poker games, but it earned money on the games by renting its facilities to the players for a fee. The taxpayer played in the games to attract customers, and he received a portion of the fee. The Court of Appeals for the Ninth Circuit held that the taxpayer's portions of the fees were not gains from wagering transactions under section 165(d). . . . Similarly, in *Bevers v. Commissioner,* [26 T.C. 1218 (1956)] this Court faced the question of whether former section 165(d) allowed a dealer to offset his tips against his gambling losses. The Court held that it did not. According to the Court, the dealer's tips were gains from his labor as a dealer, because the tips came to him in his employment as a dealer. *Id.* at 1220-1221. Once again, the dealer did not himself place the bet in the wagering transactions; rather, it was the players who placed the bets.

In conclusion, we hold that petitioner's comps are "gains from . . . [wagering] transactions" that may be offset by wagering losses under section 165(d). . . .

### *NOTES*

1. Is *Bevers v. Commissioner,* cited within *Libutti,* correct? If gambling losses can be used to offset "wagering gains" in the form of "comps," can a taxpayer offset his gambling losses against tips he received from patrons in his job as a blackjack dealer? Are dealer tips any less related to wagering transactions than comps? Consider that dealers are often tipped more when the patron wins. *See Allen v. Commissioner,* 976 F.2d 975 (5th Cir. 1992) (also holding that such tips were not obtained as part of a "wagering

transaction."). Another way to tip a dealer is to play a hand of blackjack "for" the dealer. If the hand wins, the dealer gains the proceeds. In that instance, are the tips obtained as part of a wagering transaction?

2. Substantial taxation issues turn on timing of taxable events in an accrual based tax accounting model. The next two cases deal substantially with those timing issues.

## FLAMINGO RESORT, INC. v. UNITED STATES
### 485 F. Supp. 926 (D. Nev. 1980)

FOLEY, Chief Judge.

Flamingo Resort, Inc. (Flamingo) was incorporated on August 17, 1967, and at all times relevant to this case was the owner and operator of a gaming resort in Las Vegas, Nevada. The Flamingo kept its books and reported its taxes on the accrual basis of accounting.

Flamingo filed an income tax return for the short taxable year ended December 31, 1967. The return showed a taxable income of $22,500 and, because of certain tax credits, no tax liability. Following an audit and other administrative proceedings, the Commissioner of Internal Revenue asserted a proposed deficiency in the amount of $265,034.34. Of that amount, Flamingo agreed that $3,091.69 was properly due as the result of adjustments that raised taxable income to $31,075. Flamingo continued to object to the inclusion in income of $545,711 represented by "casino receivables." While the total "casino receivables" on the books of Flamingo amounted to $676,432, the Commissioner allowed a loss deduction of $130,721 for uncollectible accounts. The Flamingo, however, paid the entire amount of the asserted deficiency, plus interest, on December 22, 1975. Then the Flamingo filed a claim for refund of an overpayment in the amount of $261,942.65, plus interest. When the claim was denied by the Internal Revenue Service, the Flamingo timely commenced this action to recover the alleged overpayment.

From August through December 1967, the taxable period in question, Flamingo operated crap games, twenty-one games and roulette wheels in the casino portion of its business. Patrons generally gambled chips at these games. Under normal circumstances, a patron would obtain chips either through the exchange of cash or a marker, which was essentially a countercheck signed by the patron in the amount of the chips transferred to him. This exchange would take place either in the "pit" area, where the games were being conducted, or at the casino cage, where chips would be exchanged by the casino for cash or counterchecks. Before credit would be extended to a patron, Flamingo conducted extensive credit checks and then established a line of credit allowable to that patron. Extensions of credit during the course of play were subject to controls by Flamingo personnel and were recorded in the pit area and reconciled at the cashier's cage. It is estimated that sixty percent of the total play in the casino resulted from extensions of credit and, as a result, such extensions are absolutely essential to the success of the Flamingo's business.

A patron was expected to settle his liability shortly after concluding his play, and the vast majority of credit extensions were satisfied on that basis. If a patron had not satisfied his marker liability by the close of his stay at the hotel, the marker became classified as a casino receivable. Extensive collection activities were undertaken with respect to these receivables and actual payment was received on the vast majority of them. The record indicates that the Flamingo's estimates of collectibility on outstanding casino receivables ranged as high as 96 percent.

In the Flamingo operation during the period in question, the marker was in the form of a countercheck with blanks left for the name of the bank and account number. In practice, the patron only signed his name after the amount had been entered without completing the blanks for bank information. The necessary information was available, however, on the credit application kept in the casino credit office. It was thus possible for the Flamingo to complete the counterchecks and submit them for payment to the makers' banks.

Casino receivables, including markers, checks given in payment for the markers that were returned for insufficient funds, and checks given in payment for the markers that were post-dated beyond the close of the taxable period on December 31, 1967, net of a reserve for potential uncollectibility, were included on the Flamingo's financial statement as revenue and as assets.

In virtually all cases, a patron would receive chips in exchange for his marker or countercheck. But the patron could gamble both with chips and, to a limited degree, with cash. Any winnings would, however, be paid to the patron in chips. The inventory for each game at the casino consisted of chips. As the games progressed, additional chips would be transferred to the games from the cage to "fill" the inventory. The casino's net gambling revenue at a game for a given eight-hour shift would constitute the difference between the total volume of play at the table, which is called the "drop" (consisting of cash, markers and foreign chips), and the total "fill" at the table (opening chip inventory plus "fill," less closing inventory). For the short taxable period in issue, the Flamingo showed a "gross games revenue," drop minus fill, of $3,967,600 on a total play of $20,102,429. The Flamingo also accounted for and controlled calculation of its gaming revenue by reflecting adjustments in its "bankroll." This is essentially the book inventory maintained in the cage and, at the beginning of an accounting period, will consist of cash, chips, unpaid markers and chips from other casinos, foreign chips that were played in the Flamingo casino. The changing composition and amount of the bankroll gauges the casino's wins and losses, but the play of chips by gambling patrons is the activity that determines these amounts.

Chips in the patrons' hands represented outstanding obligations which the Flamingo always recognized. Once a patron obtained chips, he could expend them through gambling or by purchasing hotel, restaurant and bar services at either the Flamingo's business establishment or at other casinos in Las Vegas. In 1967 the casinos conducted a regular exchange of their chips at face value and, in addition, cash payments would be made, as necessary, to equalize the exchange.

In accordance with generally accepted accounting principles, the Flamingo prepared its financial statements on the basis of the accrual method of accounting. The amount of "casino receivables," less a reserve for doubtful accounts, was included in income. For tax purposes, however, Flamingo reduced its gross gaming receipts by excluding the face amount of the markers outstanding. The Flamingo argues that these are unenforceable gambling debts and are therefore not properly accruable as taxable income. The Government had not contested the Flamingo's claim that the markers may be legally unenforceable, but urges that the markers nevertheless represent income that is properly accruable for purposes of determining taxable income. Moreover, the Government contends that such accrual is mandated by the requirement that a taxpayer's method of accounting "clearly reflect income." Exclusion of the markers, argues the Government, allows Flamingo to distort income by postponing recognition of this income which results in a mismatching of income and expenses related thereto.

The Flamingo has moved for summary judgment with respect to that portion of the claim that relates exclusively to "pit markers." The motion seeks determination of the question of liability only, with the amount subject to subsequent determination. The Government has moved for summary judgment in its favor with respect to the entire controversy. . . .

This entire controversy arises only because of an apparent quirk of Nevada law. Despite the licensing and taxing of gaming by the State of Nevada and the state's economic dependence upon gambling, the Nevada courts have consistently refused to recognize any legally enforceable rights arising out of a gambling transaction short of the actual transfer of money.[1] The Supreme Court of the State of Nevada early held that the statute of 9 Anne, ch. 14, §1, is part of the law of Nevada. *J. E. Burke & Co. v. Buck,* 99 P. 1078, 1080 (Nev. 1909); *Evans v. Cook,* 11 Nev. 69, 75 (1876). The language of the statute is clear to the effect that any instruments or conveyances made to cover gambling losses or to advance money for betting are void and not merely voidable. The same rule applies whether the claim is asserted by a gambling establishment, *Craig v. Harrah,* 201 P.2d 1081 (1949), or against one, *Weisbrod v. Fremont Hotel, Inc.,* 326 P.2d 1104 (1958). The taint of a gambling transaction also applies to a check written to cover a gambling loss. *West Indies, Inc. v. First National Bank of Nevada,* 214 P.2d 144 (1950); *Menardi v. Wacker,* 105 P. 287 (1909). The rule also prevents an effective assignment of a negotiable instrument. *J.E. Burke & Co. v. Buck,* 99 P. 1078 (1909).

The difficult cases are those in which instruments or conveyances, valid on their face, are asserted to have been made in furtherance of a gambling purpose. The Nevada court has developed certain presumptions to aid the courts' navigation in these unsure waters.

> "In determining the purpose (behind the indebtedness), the significance and relevancy of the surrounding circumstances and environment are readily apparent. If the advancement was made in a gambling establishment in full operation, by the proprietor or his agent, to one then, or immediately prior thereto, engaged in gambling and who ran short of money, the game still being in progress, or if his conversation or the circumstances indicated he intended to resume playing, the purpose of the advancement becomes clear. On the other hand, if the advancement was at a different place than a gambling establishment, or if same was not made at a time when the recipient had been recently playing, and some other, legitimate, purpose is stated by the recipient, then no presumption or inference that the advancement was for a gambling purpose is justifiable from such circumstances."

*Craig v. Harrah,* 201 P.2d at 1084.

In *Wolpert v. Knight,* 74 Nev. 322, 330 P.2d 1023 (1958), the defendant issued a $2,500 check to cover five previously issued $500

---

1. The decisions cover a one-hundred-year period. *Corbin v. O'Keefe,* 87 Nev. 189, 484 P.2d 565 (1971) (per curiam); *Wolpert v. Knight,* 74 Nev. 322, 330 P.2d 1023 (1958); *Weisbrod v. Fremont Hotel, Inc.,* 74 Nev. 227, 326 P.2d 1104 (1958) (per curiam); *West Indies, Inc. v. First National Bank of Nevada,* 67 Nev. 13, 214 P.2d 144 (1950); *Craig v. Harrah,* 66 Nev. 1, 201 P.2d 1081 (1949); *Menardi v. Wacker,* 32 Nev. 169, 105 P. 287 (1909); *J.E. Burke & Co. v. Buck,* 31 Nev. 74, 99 P. 1078 (1909); *Evans v. Cook,* 11 Nev. 69 (1876); *Scott v. Courtney,* 7 Nev. 419 (1872).

checks, four of which had been cashed at the cashier's desk and one of which was written to obtain gambling chips. There was testimony that an undetermined amount of the money had been spent gambling, but that other amounts were used to buy drinks, were given to friends, etc. Relying on the *Craig* case, the Court upheld the determination that the defendant was liable as to the $2,000 representing the checks cashed other than at the gaming tables. Thus, the burden of proving a gambling purpose is on the party seeking to avoid liability thereon, but there is a presumption of gambling purpose where the transaction occurs in proximity to the gambling itself in terms of both time and space. . . .

Both parties accept the following rule, taken from the regulations, as the starting point for discussion of the issues in this case: "Under an accrual method of accounting, income is includible in gross income when all the events have occurred which fix the right to receive such income and the amount thereof can be determined with reasonable accuracy." Treas. Regs. §1.451-1(a).

The rule is often referred to as the "all events test." The regulation sets two criteria, both of which must be met if the taxpayer is to be required to include an item in taxable income. First, the right to receive the income must be fixed. Second, the amount of the income must be reasonably ascertainable. In this case, there is no real controversy as to the second prong of the test. Each marker is for a specific dollar amount and there are no contingencies that could alter the amount of the obligation. Moreover, the Flamingo can establish with reasonable accuracy the amount that will ultimately be collected on the markers. The controversy in this case concerns whether or not the markers represent a "fixed right" to receive income. The plaintiff contends that this means a legally enforceable right, while the defendant maintains that it means something less absolute. . . .

The "all events" test has its origin in an early Supreme Court case dealing with the availability of a deduction for taxes that had not yet been assessed and thus were not due. The Court noted that accrual basis accounting was permitted for income tax purposes to permit taxpayers to "make their returns according to scientific accounting principles," specifically the matching of revenues and expenses. *United States v. Anderson*, 269 U.S. 422, 440 (1926). Rejecting the contention that an expense for taxes could not accrue as a tax deduction until the tax became due and payable, the Supreme Court said:

> "In a technical legal sense it may be argued that a tax does not accrue until it has been assessed and becomes due; but it is also true that in advance of the assessment of a tax, all the events may occur which fix the amount of the tax and determine the liability of the taxpayer to pay it.

In this respect, for purposes of accounting and of ascertaining true income for a given accounting period, the munitions tax here in question did not stand on any different footing than other accrued expenses appearing on appellee's books. In the economic and book-keeping sense with which the statute and Treasury decision were concerned, the taxes had accrued." *Id.* at 441 (emphasis added).

At that point in time, it was clear that accounting for business purposes was essentially accepted as accounting for tax purposes. This view has changed somewhat over the years. Particularly with respect to the principle of matching revenues and expenses, business and tax accounting are recognized as obtaining divergent results in some instances. The main distinction is that tax accounting requires more certainty than does financial accounting. But it is by no means clear that this distinction turns on the existence or not of legal enforceability.

In *H. Liebes & Co. v. Commissioner*, 90 F.2d 932, 936-38 (9th Cir. 1937), the Ninth Circuit Court of Appeals reviewed the development of the accrual concept for income tax accounting purposes. Courts have used various words and phrases to describe the situation in which accrual of income is proper: "unconditional liability," a "right to payment," "fixed right to receive," "uncontested and certain," and "definitely ascertained as to its amount, and acknowledged to be due." Synthesizing the cases reviewed, the *Liebes* Court concluded: "From the above expressions, it is apparent that the general definition of (')accrued' is limited when taken in connection with income returns. We may conclude that income has not accrued to a taxpayer until there arises to him a fixed or unconditional right to receive it." 90 F.2d at 937.

What emerges from these statements is that the key concept for accrual of income is that the right to receive income must be fixed or unconditional. . . . The reference to the occurrence of "all events" seems to denote the absence of a contingency on the right to receive the income.

The plaintiff here argues that the markers do not represent an "unconditional right" to receive income because ultimate collection depends and is contingent upon a voluntary act of the maker of each obligation. . . . [It is true that] the language of *Cuba Railroad Co.*, 9 T.C. 211 (1947), seems to indicate that enforceability is necessary for the accrual of income. There, the taxpayer had fully rendered services under contract with the Cuban government, which admitted the existence of the full liability. Nevertheless, the Cuban legislature consistently appropriated an amount insufficient to cover all obligations of the government. The amount appropriated for transportation services was apportioned among various carriers. There was no means of enforcing the full amount of the debt. The Tax Court said:

> "The petitioner had an unenforceable claim. Collection was apparently at the mercy of the political whims of future Cuban administrations. The evidence as a whole shows that there was real doubt and uncertainty at the end of the taxable year as to whether any of the amount due and unpaid would ever be paid. A taxpayer, in such circumstances, is not required to accrue an item like this as income and pay income tax thereon, but is permitted to wait until the uncertainty is removed in some way." 9 T.C. at 215.

Considering the context of this reference to enforceability, however, indicates that this case falls within the area in which there is no reasonable expectancy that the contract price would be recovered. Therefore, under the *Liebes* standard, it was not accruable as income. Unenforceability was simply a factor contributing to the "doubt and uncertainty" as to the expectancy of ultimate collectibility. It is also significant that the Court spoke of "real" uncertainty.

[T]hose cases in which income was determined not to be accruable fall into three basic categories: (1) those in which the taxpayer still had to perform some act in order to bind the other party to the obligation, (2) those in which the claim to income was the subject of actual controversy, either as to liability or amount, during the taxable year in question, and (3) those in which contractual income was subject to final determination upon completion. This case fits into none of these groupings. In some cases in the last two categories, it is clear that the courts did not adequately distinguish between the two parts of the test for accrual of income. Although some cases speak in terms of "fixed rights," it is clear that the real issue in the case involves the extent to which the amount is reasonably ascertainable.

In contrast with those cases cited by the plaintiff, there are cases that have expressly held that legal enforceability is not a prerequisite to the accrual of income. . . . The case most closely analogous to the one presently before the Court involved the accrual of usurious interest. In *Barker v. Magruder*, 95 F.2d 122 (D.C. Cir. 1938), the Court held that the lender must accrue as income the amount of interest due on the face of a note, despite the fact that under the usury statute of the District of Columbia the lender was entitled only to the return of the principal and no interest whatsoever. The Court concluded that "(t)he correct answer . . . depends not so much . . . upon the legal right to enforce collection as upon the existing probability of its being received." 95 F.2d at 123. In an almost identical case, involving the same lender, the Court of Claims followed the Circuit Court and said: "(T)axability is not affected because of its illegality. If in a subsequent year the amount becomes uncollectible or a loss is sustained in respect thereof, a deduction on account thereof is then allowable."[13] *Barker v. United States,* 26 F. Supp. 1004, 1006 (Ct.Cl.1939). The Court of Claims reasoned that the usury statute was enacted as a protection for borrowers and that the taxpayer should not be permitted to invoke his own wrongdoing as a means of avoiding taxes that would be due in the absence of the statute. . . .

If anything is clear from the foregoing cases, it is that the courts have not developed a formula that can be applied mechanically to any given fact situation to determine whether accrual is proper or not. Rather, the courts have attempted to apply the "all events" test in a manner that recognizes the realities of a given transaction. As one court noted, whether a right is fixed and the amount thereof determinable depends upon "a practical rather than a legal test." *C.A. Durr Packing Co. v. Shaughnessy,* 81 F. Supp. 33, 36 (N.D.N.Y. 1948)[.]

---

13. The availability of an offsetting deduction for uncollectible accounts is important in that it satisfies the need to construe the tax law in an unoppressive way while maintaining the concept of the calendar (or fiscal) year of accounting. But even in a situation where such a deduction would have been unavailable, the Sixth Circuit Court of Appeals refused to adopt a legal enforceability requirement urged by the taxpayer. In *Knight Newspapers v. Commissioner,* 143 F.2d 1007 (6th Cir. 1944), the taxpayer argued that a dividend declared in violation of state law and contrary to the terms of the declaring corporation's preferred stock certificates was at least voidable, if not void, and therefore not properly accruable. The taxpayer had in fact been required to return the dividend during the subsequent year. Moreover, recognition of the income represented by the dividend would have resulted in the assessment of a personal holding company surtax, which would not be recoverable by deduction in a subsequent year. Nevertheless, rather than adopt the "legal unenforceability" rationale urged by the taxpayer, the Sixth Circuit invoked the constructive trust doctrine to avoid an unjust result. But the Court intimated that a different result might well inhere where there was no similar potential for injustice:

> "It was said (in *National City Bank v. Helvering,* 98 F.2d 93, 96 (2d Cir. 1938)) that 'although taxes are public duties attached to the ownership of property, the state should be able to exact their performance without being compelled to take sides in private controversies,' and also that 'collection of the revenue cannot be delayed, nor should the Treasury be compelled to decide when a possessor's claims are without legal warrant. If he holds with claim of right, he should be taxable as an owner, regardless of any infirmity of his title; no other doctrine is practically possible, and no injustice can result.'" 143 F.2d at 1009.

Of course, the *National City Bank* case stands for the familiar "claim of right" doctrine applicable to situations in which money or its equivalent is actually received, and therefore is arguably inapplicable to the issue of accrual of income. The rationale, however, is clearly applicable: in the absence of potential injustice, the administration of the tax laws of the United States should not include inquiry into the legal validity of taxpayers' claims on assets.

Aside from the recent Desert Palace case, there is only one reported federal case that has dealt directly with any tax effect of a gambling debt. *United States v. Hall*, 307 F.2d 238 (10th Cir. 1962), involved the settlement of a gambling debt incurred in a Las Vegas casino. The taxpayer had borrowed large sums of money with which to gamble on the basis of a guarantee of one of the owners of the casino. The casino owner had settled the debt with the casino and the tax-payer transferred an interest in a cattle herd to the casino owner in settlement between them. The controversy arose as to whether the taxpayer must report as income the amount by which the debt exceeded his basis in the cattle. The Court, however, treated the trans-action as if the cattle had been sold at fair market value and the cash proceeds of the sale had been used to pay off the gambling debt, the amount of which was the subject of some controversy.

The plaintiff asserts that the Tenth Circuit in *Hall* ruled that a gambling debt is a nullity for tax purposes. This characterization plainly goes too far. While the Court did say that the amount of the gambling debt had "no significance for tax purposes," that conclu-sion was expressly limited to the circumstances of that particular case. 307 F.2d at 242. . . .

In relying on the holding of *Hall*, the Government has argued that the Flamingo's income arises from the cancellation of indebtedness every time the casino wins one of the chips given out in exchange for the markers.

Despite the Government's novel, though convoluted, theory, *Hall* is simply inapplicable to the case presently before the Court. That case involved a gambling debt transaction which in no way resembles the creation of a marker. . . . [I]t is fatuous to characterize the cancella-tion of the chip "indebtedness" as a sale at fair market value of "gam-bling services," even ignoring the problems such valuation might entail. In sum, the Government's new theory stretches the "cancella-tion of indebtedness" doctrine far beyond its reasonable application. This goes directly against the rationale of *Hall* that warns against applying "mechanical standards which smother the reality of a particular transaction." 307 F.2d at 241. The use of chips in the gam-ing area is merely a convenience; the existence of any "liability" on them is, as the plaintiff points out, "transitory." The existence of this temporary debtor-creditor relationship is important only at the beginning and end of the accounting period. The method of account-ing for income employed by Flamingo completely accounts for this effect of the chips on income.[15] The most which can be said for the

---

15. The chips are important in the calculation of gross gaming revenue for two reasons. First, all bets lost by the casino are paid out in chips, and therefore revenue

Government's argument is that it shows, from another perspective, that the Flamingo's income is generated at the time the gambling occurs, not when a marker is either executed or paid. This does not, however, solve the tax accounting problem of determining at what point that income must be recognized.

The *Hall* decision does, however, provide a good starting point for the discussion of the issue before this Court. While the factual setting of *Hall* is entirely different from that here, the Tenth Circuit seized upon an important policy consideration that is applicable to the issue of accruing marker income. That principle is that the mere fact of "legal unenforceability" should not be used as a means to avoid an otherwise applicable tax incident. . . .

While the Nevada courts have never cogently explained the rationale behind their continued adherence to the old English statute regarding gambling indebtedness, and despite the fact that such a rule seems strangely incongruous in light of Nevada's economic dependence upon its gaming industry, the existence of the rule indicates that gambling on credit, or the facilitation thereof, is considered morally reprehensible and thus constitutes wrongdoing. Like the usury statute in *Barker*, the unenforceability of gambling debts is for the protection of the public. Thus, the Flamingo should not be allowed to use the rule to further shield its unsanctioned operations from the normal incidents of the United States tax laws.

On the other hand, there seems to be something inherently unfair about imposing taxes on "income" that may never be received. This objection is met, however, by the availability of a bad debt or loss deduction if the receivable actually becomes uncollectible. The Government here has allowed a deduction to create a reserve for doubtful accounts in accordance with regular accrual accounting principles. There is nothing to indicate that should the reserve prove inadequate, additional future deductions would not be allowed to eliminate the potential for injustice. Moreover, in cases of other types of wrongdoing, such as embezzlement or fraud, the "claim of right" doctrine is consistently applied to require recognition of clearly illegal

---

may be calculated without requiring all gamblers to cash the chips at the close of the accounting period. Second, chips also provide an offset against the amount of the "drop" that has not actually been won by the casino. Both of these amounts are accounted for in the calculation of the "fill." Thus, outstanding chips have no theoretical effect on the casino income. There may be an incidental effect, however, if chips are never redeemed because they are irretrievably lost, destroyed or retained as a souvenir or good luck token. The Government has not suggested how the amount of any such income due to "leakage" from the casino bankroll might be calculated.

income to which the taxpayer has no legitimate claim and indeed may have to return. . . .

[V]iewed "in the light of realism and practicality," it seems clear that the Flamingo has a fixed right to receive the income represented by the casino receivables within the meaning of the "all events" test and should be required to accrue the income represented by them. The claim is completely unconditional and there is a "reasonable expectancy" that the income will be collectible. As discussed above, it is only the actual receipt of the income that is contingent. The claim is for a sum certain, payable on demand or, in the case of some agreements between the Flamingo and certain makers, within a short period of time, usually thirty days or less. There are no events the occurrence of which could alter the amount that is due the casino or the fact of liability.[16] The markers were in the form of counter checks which would indicate to makers that their execution resulted in a binding obligation. Indeed, the evidence suggests that if the Flamingo were able to magnetically encode the counter checks, the markers would be collectible through normal banking channels unless the maker issued a stop payment order. The fact that the casino is willing to conduct a significant, even essential, portion of its gaming business on the basis of credit indicates that they expect to ultimately receive payment in the form of cash or its equivalent. The existence of this expectancy is also evidenced by the Flamingo's careful credit investigation that precedes the granting of any credit at the casino and the existence of collection procedures short of resort to the courts. The collection experience of the Flamingo, with a collection rate well in excess of ninety percent, indicates that the expectation is "reasonable." Finally, failure to include the markers in income would mean that the Flamingo's income tax return would not clearly reflect income. To the extent that the markers represent winnings of the casino, failure to include them in income would understate the revenue generated during the taxable period. To the extent that the markers are still advances,[18] the calculation of gross gaming revenues

---

16. "Liability" as it is used here simply denotes the debtor-creditor relationship between the maker of the marker and the casino. While "liability" often connotes a legally enforceable relationship, particularly when used as a legal term, it has a more general meaning that applies to less binding obligations. The word "right" has similar semantic problems that inevitably have led to some confusion in the interpretation of the "all events" test.

18. Clearly, the Flamingo's income arises only as the result of gambling transactions themselves, not by advancing money for gambling. It is only because of the nature of the casino accounting system that the markers necessarily enter the income calculation. The markers would only represent advances where the maker was still at the resort, and probably still in the gaming area.

is distorted because, whereas the "drop" is essentially reduced by the amount of the marker, there is no corresponding adjustment of the "fill" to take into account the amount that represents chips still in the hands of the gambler on account of the advance. Short of calling on all gamblers to "settle up" as part of the close of the accounting period, it would be impossible to correct this distortion.

This Court holds, therefore, that the income represented by the casino receivables is accruable under the "all events" test. In so holding, this Court determines that legal enforceability is not a necessary element of a fixed right to receive income. Such being the case and there being no genuine issues of material fact, defendant's motion for summary judgment is granted, and plaintiff's motion for partial summary judgment is denied. Let judgment be entered accordingly.

*NOTES*

1.  The case was affirmed on appeal. *Flamingo Resort, Inc. v. United States*, 664 F.2d 1387 (9th Cir. 1982). As explained in the notes following *Corbin v. O'Keefe* in Chapter 3, the Nevada legislature repealed the Statute of Queen Anne in 1983, shortly after this case was decided, thus rendering casino gambling debts legally enforceable. Commentators have suggested that the Queen Anne provision had remained a fixture of Nevada law long after the legalization of gambling only because of the apparent tax advantage it offered casinos. Once this case was decided, the tax advantage of the non-enforceability regime disappeared, and so did Queen Anne. Such is the power of tax policy.

2.  Professor Gregg Polsky explains the use of markers this way: The Flamingo booked its gaming revenue on a daily basis by comparing the "drop" with the "fill" at each table. However, for tax purposes it reduced its gaming revenue by the amount of markers outstanding. Then, when markers were paid, it increased its gaming revenue by the amount paid. The proper analysis would seem to be as follows: When the marker is signed, it represents a loan for tax purposes in the amount of the marker. No federal income tax consequences arise at that point. When the casino earns the same chips back through gambling transactions, this activity represents gambling loss for the gambler and gambling revenue for the casino. When the marker is paid, it is simply a repayment of the loan. If the marker is not paid in full, the casino gets a bad debt deduction and the gambler has cancellation of indebtedness income.

3.  The next case also addresses the application of the "all events" test.

## UNITED STATES v. HUGHES PROPERTIES, INC.
### 476 U.S. 593 (1986)

Justice BLACKMUN delivered the opinion of the Court.

This case concerns the deductibility for federal income tax purposes, by a casino operator utilizing the accrual method of accounting, of amounts guaranteed for payment on "progressive" slot machines but not yet won by playing patrons.

### I

Respondent Hughes Properties, Inc., is a Nevada corporation. It owns Harolds Club, a gambling casino, in Reno, Nev. It keeps its books and files its federal income tax returns under the accrual method of accounting. During the tax years in question (the fiscal years that ended June 30 in 1973 to 1977, inclusive), respondent owned and operated slot machines at its casino. Among these were a number of what are called "progressive" machines. A progressive machine, like a regular one, pays fixed amounts when certain symbol combinations appear on its reels. But a progressive machine has an additional "progressive" jackpot, which is won only when a different specified combination appears. The casino sets this jackpot initially at a minimal amount. The figure increases, according to a ratio determined by the casino, as money is gambled on the machine. The amount of the jackpot at any given time is registered on a "payoff indicator" on the face of the machine. That amount continues to increase as patrons play the machine until the jackpot is won or until a maximum, also determined by the casino, is reached.

The odds of winning a progressive jackpot obviously are a function of the number of reels on the machine, the number of positions on each reel, and the number of winning symbols. The odds are determined by the casino, provided only that there exists a possibility that the winning combination of symbols can appear.[1]

---

1. A 1976 study of the 24 four-reel progressive machines then in operation at respondent's casino revealed that the average period between payoffs was approximately 4 1/2 months, although one machine had been in operation for 13 months and another for 35 months without a payoff as of September 1, 1976. The payoff frequency of the other 22 machines ranged from a high of 14.3 months to a low of 1.9 months.

The Nevada Gaming Commission closely regulates the casino industry in the State, including the operation of progressive slot machines. In September 1972, the Commission promulgated §5.110 of the Nevada Gaming Regulations. See App. 55. This section requires a gaming establishment to record at least once a day the jackpot amount registered on each progressive machine. §5.110.5. Furthermore,

> "[n]o payoff indicator shall be turned back to a lesser amount, unless the amount by which the indicator has been turned back is actually paid to a winning player, or unless the change in the indicator reading is necessitated through a machine malfunction, in which case an explanation must be entered on the daily report as required in subsection 5." §5.110.2; App. 55.

The regulation is strictly enforced. Nevada, by statute, authorizes the Commission to impose severe administrative sanctions, including license revocation, upon any casino that wrongfully refuses to pay a winning customer a guaranteed jackpot. See Nev. Rev. Stat. §463.310 (1985).

It is respondent's practice to remove the money deposited by customers in its progressive machines at least twice every week and also on the last day of each month. The Commission does not regulate respondent's use of the funds thus collected, but, since 1977, it has required that a casino maintain a cash reserve sufficient to provide payment of the guaranteed amounts on all its progressive machines available to the public. Nev. Gaming Regs. §5.110(3); App. 56.

At the conclusion of each fiscal year, that is, at midnight on June 30, respondent entered the total of the progressive jackpot amounts shown on the payoff indicators as an accrued liability on its books. From that total, it subtracted the corresponding figure for the preceding year to produce the current tax year's increase in accrued liability. On its federal income tax return for each of its fiscal years 1973, 1974, 1975, and 1977, respondent asserted this net figure as a deduction under §162(a) of the Internal Revenue Code of 1954, as amended, 26 U.S.C. §162(a), as an ordinary and necessary expense "paid or incurred during the taxable year in carrying on any trade or business." There is no dispute as to the amounts so determined or that a progressive jackpot qualifies for deduction as a proper expense of running a gambling business. See Tr. of Oral Arg. 7.

On audit, the Commissioner of Internal Revenue disallowed the deduction. He did so on the ground that, under Treas. Reg. §1.461-1(a)(2), 26 CFR §1.461-1(a)(2) (1985), an expense may not be deducted until "all the events have occurred which determine the fact of the liability and the amount thereof can be determined with reasonable accuracy." In his view, respondent's obligation to pay a particular progressive jackpot matures only upon a winning patron's pull of the handle in the future. According to the Commissioner, until that event occurs, respondent's liability to pay the jackpot is contingent and therefore gives rise to no deductible expense. Indeed, until then, there is no one who can make a claim for payment. . . . [R]espondent brought this suit for refunds in the Claims Court.

Each side moved for summary judgment. . . . The Claims Court denied the Government's motion for summary judgment but granted respondent's motion. It concluded that, under the Nevada Commission's rule, respondent's liability to pay the amounts on the progressive jackpot indicators became "unconditionally fixed," at "midnight of the last day of the fiscal year[.]" The final event was "the last play (successful or not) of the machine before the close of the fiscal year, that is, the last change in the jackpot amount before the amount is recorded for accounting purposes." A contrary result would mismatch respondent's income and expenses. . . .

The Claims Court further acknowledged that its ruling was in conflict with the decision of the Court of Appeals for the Ninth Circuit in *Nightingale v. United States*, 684 F.2d 611 (1982), having to do with another Nevada casino, but it declined to follow that precedent and specifically disavowed its reasoning. The Court of Appeals for the Federal Circuit affirmed[.] Because of the clear conflict between the two Circuits, we granted certiorari.


## II


Section 162(a) of the Internal Revenue Code allows a deduction for "all the ordinary and necessary expenses paid or incurred during the taxable year in carrying on any trade or business." Section 446(a) provides that taxable income "shall be computed under the method of accounting on the basis of which the taxpayer regularly computes his income in keeping his books." Under the "cash receipts and disbursements method," specifically recognized by §446(c)(1), a taxpayer is entitled to deduct business expenses only in the year in which they are paid. Treas. Reg. §§1.446-1(c)(1)(i) and 1.461-1(a)(1), 26 CFR §§1.446-1(c)(1)(i), 1.461-1(a)(1) (1985). The Code also permits a taxpayer to compute taxable income by the employment of "an accrual method." §446(c)(2). An accrual-method taxpayer is entitled to deduct an expense in the year in which it is "incurred," §162(a), regardless of when it is actually paid.

For a number of years, the standard for determining when an expense is to be regarded as "incurred" for federal income tax purposes has been the "all events" test prescribed by the Regulations. . . . This test appears to have had its origin in a single phrase that appears in this Court's opinion in *United States v. Anderson*, 269 U.S. 422, 441 (1926) ("[I]t is also true that in advance of the assessment of a tax, all the events may occur which fix the amount of the tax and determine the liability of the taxpayer to pay it"). Since then, the Court has described the "all events" test "established" in *Anderson* as "the 'touchstone' for determining the year in which an item of deduction accrues," and as "a fundamental principle of tax accounting." *United States v. Consolidated Edison Co. of New York*, 366 U.S. 380, 385 (1961) (citing cases).

Under the Regulations, the "all events" test has two elements, each of which must be satisfied before accrual of an expense is proper. First, all the events must have occurred which establish the fact of the liability. Second, the amount must be capable of being determined "with reasonable accuracy." Treas. Reg. §1.446-1(c)(1)(ii). This case concerns only the first element, since the parties agree that the second is fully satisfied.

## III

The Court's cases have emphasized that "a liability does not accrue as long as it remains contingent." *Brown v. Helvering*, 291 U.S. 193, 200 (1934)[.] Thus, to satisfy the all-events test, a liability must be "final and definite in amount," *Security Flour Mills Co. v. Commissioner*, 321 U.S. 281, 287 (1944), must be "fixed and absolute," *Brown v. Helvering*, 291 U.S., at 201, and must be "unconditional," *Lucas v. North Texas Lumber Co.*, 281 U.S. 11, 13 (1930). And one may say that "the tax law requires that a deduction be deferred until 'all the events' have occurred that will make it fixed and certain." *Thor Power Tool Co. v. Commissioner*, 439 U.S. 522, 543 (1979).

The Government argues that respondent's liability for the progressive jackpots was not "fixed and certain," and was not "unconditional" or "absolute," by the end of the fiscal year, for there existed no person who could assert any claim to those funds. It takes the position, quoting *Nightingale v. United States*, 684 F.2d at 614, that the indispensable event "is the winning of the progressive jackpot by some fortunate gambler." It says that, because respondent's progressive jackpots had not been won at the close of the fiscal year, respondent had not yet incurred liability. Nevada law places no restriction on the odds set by the casino, as long as a possibility exists that the winning combination can appear. Thus, according to the Government, by setting very high odds respondent can defer indefinitely into the future the time when it actually will have to pay off the jackpot. The Government argues that if a casino were to close its doors and go out of business, it would not owe the jackpots to anyone. Similarly, if it were to sell its business, or cease its gaming operations, or go into bankruptcy, or if patrons were to stop playing its slot machines, it would have no obligation.

We agree with the Claims Court and with the Federal Circuit and disagree with the Government for the following reasons:

1. The effect of the Nevada Gaming Commission's regulations was to fix respondent's liability. Section 5.110.2 forbade reducing the indicated payoff without paying the jackpot, except to correct a malfunction or to prevent exceeding the limit imposed. Respondent's liability, that is, its obligation to pay the indicated amount, was not contingent. That an extremely remote and speculative possibility existed that the jackpot might never be won,[3] did not change the fact that, as a matter of state law, respondent had a fixed liability for the jackpot which it could not escape. The effect of Nevada's law was equivalent to the situation where state law requires the amounts of the jackpot indicators to be set aside in escrow pending the ascertainment of the identity of the winners. The Government concedes that, in the latter case, the liability has accrued, even though the same possibility would still exist that the winning pull would never occur.

2. The Government misstates the need for identification of the winning player. That is, or should be, a matter of no relevance for the casino operator. The obligation is there, and whether it turns out that the winner is one patron or another makes no conceivable difference as to basic liability.

3. The Government's heavy reliance on *Brown v. Helvering*, 291 U.S. 193 (1934), in our view, is misplaced. That case concerned an agent's commissions on sales of insurance policies, and the agent's obligation to return a proportionate part of the commission in case a policy was canceled. The agent sought to deduct from gross income an amount added during the year to his reserve for repayment of commissions. This Court agreed with the Commissioner's disallowance of the claimed deduction because the actual event that would create the liability—the cancellation of a particular policy in a later year—"[did] not occur during the taxable year," but rather occurred only in the later year in which the policy was in fact canceled. Here, however, the

---

3. An affidavit [submitted by respondents] in the Claims Court states that all the progressive machine jackpots unpaid as of June 30, 1977, "were subsequently won and paid to customers."

event creating liability, as the Claims Court recognized, was the last play of the machine before the end of the fiscal year, since that play fixed the jackpot amount irrevocably. That event occurred during the taxable year.

4. The Government's argument that the fact that respondent treats unpaid jackpots as liabilities for financial accounting purposes does not justify treating them as liabilities for tax purposes is unpersuasive. Proper financial accounting and acceptable tax accounting, to be sure, are not the same. Justice Brandeis announced this fact well over 50 years ago: "The prudent business man often sets up reserves to cover contingent liabilities. But they are not allowable as deductions." *Lucas v. American Code Co.*, 280 U.S. 445, 452, (1930). The Court has long recognized "the vastly different objectives that financial and tax accounting have." *Thor Power Tool Co. v. Commissioner*, 439 U.S., at 542. The goal of financial accounting is to provide useful and pertinent information to management, shareholders, and creditors. On the other hand, the major responsibility of the Internal Revenue Service is to protect the public fisc. Therefore, although §446(c)(2) permits a taxpayer to use an accrual method for tax purposes if he uses that method to keep his books, §446(b) specifically provides that if the taxpayer's method of accounting "does not clearly reflect income," the Commissioner may impose a method that "does clearly reflect income." . . .

Granting all this—that the Commissioner has broad discretion, that financial accounting does not control for tax purposes, and that the mere desirability of matching expenses with income will not necessarily sustain a taxpayer's deduction—the Commissioner's disallowance of respondent's deductions was not justified in this case. As stated above, these jackpot liabilities were definitely fixed. A part of the machine's intake was to be paid out, that amount was known, and only the exact time of payment and the identity of the winner remained for the future. But the accrual method itself makes irrelevant the timing factor that controls when a taxpayer uses the cash receipts and disbursements method.

5. The Government suggests that respondent's ability to control the timing of payouts shows both the contingent nature of the claimed deductions and a potential for tax avoidance. It speaks of the time value of money, of respondent's ability to earn additional income upon the jackpot amounts it retains until a winner comes along, of respondent's "virtually unrestricted discretion in setting odds," and of its ability to transfer amounts from one machine to another with the accompanying capacity to defer indefinitely into the future the time at which it must make payment to its customers. All this, the Government says, unquestionably contains the "potential for tax avoidance." And

the Government suggests that a casino operator could put extra machines on the floor on the last day of the tax year with whatever initial jackpots it specifies and with whatever odds it likes, and then, on the taxpayer's theory, could take a current deduction for the full amount even though payment of the jackpots might not occur for many years, citing *Nightingale*, 684 F.2d, at 615.

None of the components that make up this parade of horribles, of course, took place here. Nothing in this record even intimates that respondent used its progressive machines for tax-avoidance purposes. Its income from these machines was less than 1% of its gross revenue during the tax years in question. Respondent's revenue from progressive slot machines depends on inducing gamblers to play the machines, and, if it sets unreasonably high odds, customers will refuse to play and will gamble elsewhere. Thus, respondent's economic self-interest will keep it from setting odds likely to defer payoffs too far into the future.[5] Nor, with Nevada's strictly imposed controls, was any abuse of the kind hypothesized by the Government likely to happen. In any event, the Commissioner's ability, under §446(b) of the Code, 26 U.S.C. §446(b), to correct any such abuse is the complete practical answer to the Government's concern. If a casino manipulates its use of progressive slot machines to avoid taxes, the Commissioner has the power to find that its accounting does not accurately reflect its income and to require it to use a more appropriate accounting method. Finally, since the casino of course must pay taxes on the income it earns from the use of as-yet-unwon jackpots, the Government vastly overestimates the time value of respondent's deductions.

6. There is always a possibility, of course, that a casino may go out of business, or surrender or lose its license, or go into bankruptcy, with the result that the amounts shown on the jackpot indicators would never be won by playing patrons. But this potential nonpayment of an incurred liability exists for every business that uses an accrual method, and it does not prevent accrual. . . . And if any of the events hypothesized by the Government should occur, the deducted amounts would qualify as recaptured income subject to tax. Treas. Reg. §1.461-1(a)(2). . . . AFFIRMED.

---

5. Respondent also is unlikely to set extremely high initial jackpots on its machines, since that practice would increase the casino's risk. The initial progressive jackpot amount is the casino's money. If a patron gets the winning combination soon after the machine goes into service, the casino will not have time to recoup the initial jackpot from money gambled by the public. Thus, casinos will tend to set rather low initial jackpots, relying on a percentage of the funds gambled by previous players to contribute the bulk of the progressive jackpot.

Justice Stevens, with whom The Chief Justice joins, dissenting.

Unlike the Court, I believe that the distinction between the non-payment of an existing obligation and the nonexistence of an obligation is of controlling importance in this case. It is common ground that the taxpayer can accrue as a deduction the jackpots in its progressive slot machines only if "all the events have . . . occurred which fix the liability." The question is whether an "obligation" created by the rules of a state gaming commission and defeasible at the election of the taxpayer is "fixed" within the meaning of the Treasury Regulation. To me, the answer is clearly "no."

"Under Nevada law," if the taxpayer in this case "were to surrender its gaming license, it would no longer be subject to the gaming laws and regulations and could thus avoid the payment of the liability." Thus, "the bankruptcy of the [taxpayer], or the surrender of its gaming license could relieve it of its obligation."

On these facts, the taxpayer has no present liability to accrue. Rather, the taxpayer's obligation to pay the jackpots in this case resembles the taxpayer's obligation to pay the cost of overhauling its aircraft engines and airframes in *World Airways, Inc. v. Commissioner*, 62 T.C. 786 (1974), aff'd, 564 F.2d 886 (CA9 1977). In that case, the Tax Court held that the taxpayer, an airline, did not satisfy the "all events" test and hence could not accrue and deduct any portion of these costs—despite the existence of contracts obligating the taxpayer to pay, upon the completion of an overhaul, an amount for each hour of flight time since the previous overhaul, and a statutory obligation to overhaul its engines and airframes after a specified number of flight hours. Of critical importance to the decision before us today, the court distinguished between the nonpayment of a legal obligation and the nonexistence of an obligation by considering the taxpayer's liability in the event of a bankruptcy:

> "The bankruptcy of petitioner [the taxpayer] or the crash or permanent grounding of an aircraft might conceivably relieve petitioner of the payment of overhaul costs. The occurrences of any of these contingencies, however, would not relieve petitioner of an existing obligation to pay any overhaul costs. Rather, the occurrence would mean that no obligation to pay would ever come into existence. Petitioner has not shown that its liability for the accrued overhaul costs was absolutely fixed in the year of accrual. The contingencies referred to would act to prevent a potential liability from coming into existence." *Id.*, at 804 (emphasis in original).

The court recognized that the risk of bankruptcy or disaster was remote. But it added that "there exists another contingency whose occurrence is not unlikely": "Petitioner has sold five piston aircraft and one jet aircraft since 1965. The five piston aircraft owned by petitioner during 1965, and 1966, were sold prior to the time when major airframe overhaul was required." *Ibid.*

Here, too, the taxpayer has no obligation that could be discharged in a bankruptcy court—a fact that confirms that it has no present liability to pay the jackpots on its progressive slot machines. And there likewise exists a contingency under which it is not at all unlikely that a slot machine owner would elect to escape its liability. If the gross amount of the accruals on these machines should ever exceed the net value of the business—perhaps as a result of shrewd management—it could liquidate at a profit without having any liability to anyone for what the Court mistakenly describes as a "fixed liability." By simply tendering its gaming license the taxpayer would avoid its liability on the jackpots. This option is exercisable in the sole discretion of the taxpayer at any point in time. My research has revealed no other instance in which the Commissioner has been forced to allow accrual of a deduction when the expense deducted may be avoided entirely at the election of the taxpayer. This feature of the deduction before us unquestionably contains the "potential for tax avoidance," *Thor Power Tool Co. v. Commissioner,* 439 U.S. 522, 538, (1979), and I think it lies well within the Commissioner's authority to interpret the Regulation to forbid it[.] I respectfully dissent.

### NOTES

1.  This case hinges partially on the faith of the Court in the commitment of regulators to hold casinos to the principle that progressive slot machines must, eventually, pay.
2.  As often happens in tax policy, the Internal Revenue Service lost the battle but won the war. A new statutory provision added to the Tax Code in 1984 created a further requirement to the "all events" test: a liability meeting the all events test can be deducted no earlier than "the time of economic performance." *See generally* Erik Jensen, *Economic Performance and Progressive Slots: A Better Analysis,* 45 TAX NOTES 635 (1989). As Professor Jensen notes, however, despite this amendment, there remains a significant question: "What constitutes economic performance in the case of progressive slots?" He continues: "Section 461(h)(2)(B) states that, in the case of services and property provided by the taxpayer, "economic performance occurs as the taxpayer provides such property or services." *Id.* at 635. What activity does this provision include? "If providing entertainment constitutes the provision of

services[,] and gamblers are entertained by merely playing slot machines provided by a casino, economic performance occurs as the machines are played." Professor Jensen offers the following answer to this dilemma: "The progressive jackpot situation does not fit easily within any of the statutory definitions of economic performance. When doubt remains about the time of economic performance after legitimate attempts have been made to apply those definitions, the deduction should be deferred until payment. In other words, when in doubt, defer." *Id.* at 636. *See also* Erik Jensen, *The Supreme Court and the Timing of Deductions for Accrual-Basis Taxpayers*, 22 GA. L. REV. 229 (1988).

## ZARIN v. COMMISSIONER OF INTERNAL REVENUE
### 916 F.2d 110 (3d Cir. 1990)

COWEN, Circuit Judge.

David Zarin ("Zarin") appeals from a decision of the Tax Court holding that he recognized $2,935,000 of income from discharge of indebtedness resulting from his gambling activities, and that he should be taxed on the income. . . .

Zarin was a professional engineer who participated in the development, construction, and management of various housing projects. A resident of Atlantic City, New Jersey, Zarin occasionally gambled, both in his hometown and in other places where gambling was legalized. To facilitate his gaming activities in Atlantic City, Zarin applied to Resorts International Hotel ("Resorts") for a credit line in June, 1978. Following a credit check, Resorts granted Zarin $10,000 of credit. Pursuant to this credit arrangement with Resorts, Zarin could write a check, called a marker,[2] and in return receive chips, which could then be used to gamble at the casino's tables.

Before long, Zarin developed a reputation as an extravagant "high roller" who routinely bet the house maximum while playing craps, his game of choice. Considered a "valued gaming patron" by Resorts, Zarin had his credit limit increased at regular intervals without any further credit checks, and was provided a number of complimentary services and privileges. By November, 1979, Zarin's permanent line of credit had been raised to $200,000. Between June, 1978, and December, 1979, Zarin lost $2,500,000 at the craps table, losses he paid in full.

---

2. A "marker" is a negotiable draft payable to Resorts and drawn on the maker's bank.

Responding to allegations of credit abuses, the New Jersey Division of Gaming Enforcement filed with the New Jersey Casino Control Commission a complaint against Resorts. Among the 809 violations of casino regulations alleged in the complaint of October, 1979, were 100 pertaining to Zarin. Subsequently, a Casino Control Commissioner issued an Emergency Order, the effect of which was to make further extensions of credit to Zarin illegal.

Nevertheless, Resorts continued to extend Zarin's credit limit through the use of two different practices: "considered cleared" credit and "this trip only" credit.[3] Both methods effectively ignored the Emergency Order and were later found to be illegal.[4]

By January, 1980, Zarin was gambling compulsively and uncontrollably at Resorts, spending as many as sixteen hours a day at the craps table. During April, 1980, Resorts again increased Zarin's credit line without further inquiries. That same month, Zarin delivered personal checks and counterchecks to Resorts which were returned as having been drawn against insufficient funds. Those dishonored checks totaled $3,435,000. In late April, Resorts cut off Zarin's credit.

Although Zarin indicated that he would repay those obligations, Resorts filed a New Jersey state court action against Zarin in November, 1980, to collect the $3,435,000. Zarin denied liability on grounds that Resort's claim was unenforceable under New Jersey regulations intended to protect compulsive gamblers. Ten months later, in September, 1981, Resorts and Zarin settled their dispute for a total of $500,000.

The Commissioner of Internal Revenue ("Commissioner") subsequently determined deficiencies in Zarin's federal income taxes for 1980 and 1981, arguing that Zarin recognized $3,435,000 of income in 1980 from larceny by trick and deception. After Zarin challenged that claim by filing a Tax Court petition, the Commissioner abandoned his 1980 claim, and argued instead that Zarin had recognized $2,935,000 of income in 1981 from the cancellation of indebtedness which resulted from the settlement with Resorts.

Agreeing with the Commissioner, the Tax Court decided, eleven judges to eight, that Zarin had indeed recognized $2,935,000 of income from the discharge of indebtedness, namely the difference

---

3. Under the "considered cleared" method, Resorts would treat a personal check as a cash transaction, and would therefore not apply the amount of the check in calculating the amount of credit extended Zarin. "This trip only" credit allowed Resorts to grant temporary increases of credit for a given visit, so long as the credit limit was lowered by the next visit.

4. On July 8, 1983, the New Jersey Casino Control Commission found that Resorts violated the Emergency Order at least thirteen different times, nine involving Zarin, and fined Resorts $130,000.

between the original $3,435,000 "debt" and the $500,000 settlement. *Zarin v. Commissioner*, 92 T.C. 1084 (1989). Since he was in the seventy percent tax bracket, Zarin's deficiency for 1981 was calculated to be $2,047,245. With interest to April 5, 1990, Zarin allegedly owes the Internal Revenue Service $5,209,033.96 in additional taxes. Zarin appeals the order of the Tax Court.

The sole issue before this Court is whether the Tax Court correctly held that Zarin had income from discharge of indebtedness. Section 108 and section 61(a)(12) of the Code set forth "the general rule that gross income includes income from the discharge of indebtedness." I.R.C. §108(e)(1). The Commissioner argues, and the Tax Court agreed, that pursuant to the Code, Zarin did indeed recognize income from discharge of gambling indebtedness.

Under the Commissioner's logic, Resorts advanced Zarin $3,435,000 worth of chips, chips being the functional equivalent of cash. At that time, the chips were not treated as income, since Zarin recognized an obligation of repayment. In other words, Resorts made Zarin a tax-free loan. However, a taxpayer does recognize income if a loan owed to another party is cancelled, in whole or in part. I.R.C. §§61(a)(12), 108(e). The settlement between Zarin and Resorts, claims the Commissioner, fits neatly into the cancellation of indebtedness provisions in the Code. Zarin owed $3,435,000, paid $500,000, with the difference constituting income. Although initially persuasive, the Commissioner's position is nonetheless flawed for two reasons.

Initially, we find that sections 108 and 61(a)(12) are inapplicable to the Zarin/Resorts transaction. Section 61 does not define indebtedness. On the other hand, section 108(d)(1), which repeats and further elaborates on the rule in section 61(a)(12), defines the term as any indebtedness "(A) for which the taxpayer is liable, or (B) subject to which the taxpayer holds property." I.R.C. §108(d)(1). In order to bring the taxpayer within the sweep of the discharge of indebtedness rules, then, the IRS must show that one of the two prongs in the section 108(d)(1) test is satisfied. It has not been demonstrated that Zarin satisfies either.

Because the debt Zarin owed to Resorts was unenforceable as a matter of New Jersey state law, it is clearly not a debt "for which the taxpayer is liable." I.R.C. §108(d)(1)(A). Liability implies a legally enforceable obligation to repay, and under New Jersey law, Zarin would have no such obligation.[7]

---

7. The Tax Court held that the Commissioner had not met its burden of proving that the debt owed Resorts was enforceable as a matter of state law. *Zarin*, 92 T.C. at 1090. There was ample evidence to support that finding. In New Jersey, the extension of credit by casinos "to enable [any] person to take part in gaming activity as a

With regards to the extension of credit to Zarin after the Emergency Order of October, 1979, was issued, Resorts did not comply with New Jersey regulations. The Casino Control Commission specifically stated in 1983 "that Resorts was guilty of infractions, violations, improprieties, with the net effect that [Zarin] was encouraged to continue gambling long after, one, his credit line was reached, and exceeded; two, long after it became apparent that the gambler was an addicted gambler; three, long after the gambler had difficulty in paying his debts; and four, Resorts knew the individual was gambling when he should not have been gambling." Appendix at 325-326. It follows, therefore, that under New Jersey law, the $3,435,000 debt Zarin owed Resorts was totally unenforceable.

Moreover, Zarin did not have a debt subject to which he held property as required by section 108(d)(1)(B). Zarin's indebtedness arose out of his acquisition of gambling chips. The Tax Court held that gambling chips were not property, but rather, "a medium of exchange within the Resorts casino" and a "substitute for cash." Alternatively, the Tax Court viewed the chips as nothing more than "the opportunity to gamble and incidental services . . ." *Zarin*, 92 T.C. at 1099. We agree with the gist of these characterizations, and hold that gambling chips are merely an accounting mechanism to evidence debt.

Gaming chips in New Jersey during 1980 were regarded "solely as evidence of a debt owed to their custodian by the casino licensee and shall be considered at no time the property of anyone other than the casino licensee issuing them." N.J. Admin. Code tit. 19k, §19:46-1.5(d) (1990). Thus, under New Jersey state law, gambling chips were Resorts' property until transferred to Zarin in exchange for the markers, at which point the chips became "evidence" of indebtedness (and not the property of Zarin).

Even were there no relevant legislative pronouncement on which to rely, simple common sense would lead to the conclusion that chips were not property in Zarin's hands. Zarin could not do with the chips as he pleased, nor did the chips have any independent economic value beyond the casino. The chips themselves were of little use to Zarin, other than as a means of facilitating gambling. They could not have been used outside the casino. They could have been used to purchase services and privileges within the casino, including food, drink, entertainment, and lodging, but Zarin would not have utilized them as

---

player" is limited. N.J. Stat. Ann. §5:12-101(b) (1988). Under N.J. Stat. Ann. §5:12-101(f), any credit violation is "invalid and unenforceable for the purposes of collection . . ." In *Resorts Int'l Hotel, Inc. v. Salomone*, 178 N.J. Super. 598, 429 A.2d 1078 (App. Div. 1981), the court held that "casinos must comply with the Legislature's strict control of credit for gambling purposes. Unless they do, the debts reflected by players' checks will not be enforced. . . ." *Id.* at 607, 429 A.2d at 1082.

such, since he received those services from Resorts on a complimentary basis. In short, the chips had no economic substance.

Although the Tax Court found that theoretically, Zarin could have redeemed the chips he received on credit for cash and walked out of the casino, the reality of the situation was quite different. Realistically, before cashing in his chips, Zarin would have been required to pay his outstanding IOUs. New Jersey state law requires casinos to "request patrons to apply any chips or plaques in their possession in reduction of personal checks or Counter Checks exchanged for purposes of gaming prior to exchanging such chips or plaques for cash or prior to departing from the casino area." N.J. Admin. Code tit. 19k, §19:45-1.24(s) (1979) (currently N.J. Admin. Code tit. 19k, §19:45-1.25(o) (1990) (as amended)). Since his debt at all times equalled or exceeded the number of chips he possessed, redemption would have left Zarin with no chips, no cash, and certainly nothing which could have been characterized as property.

Not only were the chips non-property in Zarin's hands, but upon transfer to Zarin, the chips also ceased to be the property of Resorts. Since the chips were in the possession of another party, Resorts could no longer do with the chips as it pleased, and could no longer control the chips' use. Generally, at the time of a transfer, the party in possession of the chips can gamble with them, use them for services, cash them in, or walk out of the casino with them as an Atlantic City souvenir. The chips therefore become nothing more than an accounting mechanism, or evidence of a debt, designed to facilitate gambling in casinos where the use of actual money was forbidden.[8] Thus, the chips which Zarin held were not property within the meaning of I.R.C. §108(d)(1)(B).[9]

---

8. Although, as noted above, Zarin would not have been able to leave the casino with cash or chips, and probably would not have used the chips for services, these facts do not change the character of the chips. Despite the aforementioned limitations upon Zarin's use of the chips, they remain an accounting mechanism or evidence of a debt. Resorts' increased interest in Zarin's chips does not rise to the level of a property interest, since Zarin still has dominion over the chips within the casino.

9. The parties stipulated before the Tax Court that New Jersey casino "chips are property which are not negotiable and may not be used to gamble or for any other purpose outside the casino where they were issued." It could be argued that we are bound by this stipulation to accept the proposition that chips are property. We do not dispute the notion that chips are property, but as discussed above, they are only property in the hands of the casino. The stipulation is consistent with this idea. In fact, both parties agreed in their briefs that chips are property of the casino. Moreover, during oral arguments, both parties agreed that chips were not property when held by the gambler.

In short, because Zarin was not liable on the debt he allegedly owed Resorts, and because Zarin did not hold "property" subject to that debt, the cancellation of indebtedness provisions of the Code do not apply to the settlement between Resorts and Zarin. As such, Zarin cannot have income from the discharge of his debt.

Instead of analyzing the transaction at issue as cancelled debt, we believe the proper approach is to view it as disputed debt or contested liability. Under the contested liability doctrine, if a taxpayer, in good faith, disputed the amount of a debt, a subsequent settlement of the dispute would be treated as the amount of debt cognizable for tax purposes. The excess of the original debt over the amount determined to have been due is disregarded for both loss and debt accounting purposes. Thus, if a taxpayer took out a loan for $10,000, refused in good faith to pay the full $10,000 back, and then reached an agreement with the lendor that he would pay back only $7000 in full satisfaction of the debt, the transaction would be treated as if the initial loan was $7000. When the taxpayer tenders the $7000 payment, he will have been deemed to have paid the full amount of the initially disputed debt. Accordingly, there is no tax consequence to the taxpayer upon payment.

The seminal "contested liability" case is *N. Sobel, Inc. v. Commissioner*, 40 B.T.A. 1263 (1939). In *Sobel*, the taxpayer exchanged a $21,700 note for 100 shares of stock from a bank. In the following year, the taxpayer sued the bank for recision, arguing that the bank loan was violative of state law, and moreover, that the bank had failed to perform certain promises. The parties eventually settled the case in 1935, with the taxpayer agreeing to pay half of the face amount of the note. In the year of the settlement, the taxpayer claimed the amount paid as a loss. The Commissioner denied the loss because it had been sustained five years earlier, and further asserted that the taxpayer recognized income from the discharge of half of his indebtedness.

The Board of Tax Appeals held that since the loss was not fixed until the dispute was settled, the loss was recognized in 1935, the year of the settlement, and the deduction was appropriately taken in that year. Additionally, the Board held that the portion of the note forgiven by the bank "was not the occasion for a freeing of assets and that there was no gain ..." *Id.* at 1265. Therefore, the taxpayer did not have any income from cancellation of indebtedness.

There is little difference between the present case and *Sobel*. Zarin incurred a $3,435,000 debt while gambling at Resorts, but in court, disputed liability on the basis of unenforceability. A settlement of $500,000 was eventually agreed upon. It follows from *Sobel* that the settlement served only to fix the amount of debt. No income was realized or recognized. When Zarin paid the $500,000, any tax consequence dissolved.[10]

Only one other court has addressed a case factually similar to the one before us. In *United States v. Hall*, 307 F.2d 238 (10th Cir. 1962), the taxpayer owed an unenforceable gambling debt alleged to be $225,000. Subsequently, the taxpayer and the creditor settled for $150,000. The taxpayer then transferred cattle valued at $148,110 to his creditor in satisfaction of the settlement agreement. A jury held that the parties fixed the debt at $150,000, and that the taxpayer recognized income from cancellation of indebtedness equal to the difference between the $150,000 and the $148,110 value affixed to the cattle. Arguing that the taxpayer recognized income equal to the difference between $225,000 and $148,000, the Commissioner appealed.

The Tenth Circuit rejected the idea that the taxpayer had any income from cancellation of indebtedness. Noting that the gambling debt was unenforceable, the Tenth Circuit said, "The cold fact is that taxpayer suffered a substantial loss from gambling, the amount of which was determined by the transfer." In effect, the Court held that because the debt was unenforceable, the amount of the loss and resulting debt cognizable for tax purposes were fixed by the settlement at $148,110. Thus, the Tenth Circuit lent its endorsement to the contested liability doctrine in a factual situation strikingly similar to the one at issue.

The Commissioner argues that *Sobel* and the contested liability doctrine only apply when there is an unliquidated debt; that is, a debt for which the amount cannot be determined. Since Zarin contested his liability based on the unenforceability of the entire debt, and did not dispute the amount of the debt, the Commissioner would have us adopt the reasoning of the Tax Court, which found that Zarin's debt was liquidated, therefore barring the application of *Sobel* and the contested liability doctrine. *Zarin*, 92 T.C. at 1095 (Zarin's debt "was a liquidated amount" and "[t]here is no dispute about the amount [received].").

We reject the Tax Court's rationale. When a debt is unenforceable, it follows that the amount of the debt, and not just the liability thereon, is in dispute. Although a debt may be unenforceable, there still could be some value attached to its worth. This is especially so with regards to gambling debts. In most states, gambling debts are unenforceable, and have "but slight potential . . ." *United States v. Hall*,

---

10. Had Zarin not paid the $500,000 settlement, it would be likely that he would have had income from cancellation of indebtedness. The debt at that point would have been fixed, and Zarin would have been legally obligated to pay it.

307 F.2d 238, 241 (10th Cir. 1962). Nevertheless, they are often collected, at least in part. For example, Resorts is not a charity; it would not have extended illegal credit to Zarin and others if it did not have some hope of collecting debts incurred pursuant to the grant of credit.

Moreover, the debt is frequently incurred to acquire gambling chips, and not money. Although casinos attach a dollar value to each chip, that value, unlike money's, is not beyond dispute, particularly given the illegality of gambling debts in the first place. This proposition is supported by the facts of the present case. Resorts gave Zarin $3.4 million dollars of chips in exchange for markers evidencing Zarin's debt. If indeed the only issue was the enforceabilty of the entire debt, there would have been no settlement. Zarin would have owed all or nothing. Instead, the parties attached a value to the debt considerably lower than its face value. In other words, the parties agreed that given the circumstances surrounding Zarin's gambling spree, the chips he acquired might not have been worth $3.4 million dollars, but were worth something. Such a debt cannot be called liquidated, since its exact amount was not fixed until settlement.

To summarize, the transaction between Zarin and Resorts can best be characterized as a disputed debt, or contested liability. Zarin owed an unenforceable debt of $3,435,000 to Resorts. After Zarin in good faith disputed his obligation to repay the debt, the parties settled for $500,000, which Zarin paid. That $500,000 settlement fixed the amount of loss and the amount of debt cognizable for tax purposes. Since Zarin was deemed to have owed $500,000, and since he paid Resorts $500,000, no adverse tax consequences attached to Zarin as a result.[12] . . .

In conclusion, we hold that Zarin did not have any income from cancellation of indebtedness for two reasons. First, the Code provisions covering discharge of debt are inapplicable since the definitional requirement in I.R.C. section 108(d)(1) was not met. Second, the settlement of Zarin's gambling debts was a contested liability. We reverse the decision of the Tax Court and remand with instructions to enter judgment that Zarin realized no income by reason of his settlement with Resorts.

---

12. The Commissioner argues in the alternative that Zarin recognized $3,435,000 of income in 1980. This claim has no merit. Recognition of income would depend upon a finding that Zarin did not have cancellation of indebtedness income solely because his debt was unenforceable. We do not so hold. Although unenforceability is a factor in our analysis, our decision ultimately hinges upon the determination that the "disputed debt" rule applied, or alternatively, that chips are not property within the meaning of I.R.C. section 108.

STAPLETON, Circuit Judge, dissenting.

I respectfully dissent because I agree with the Commissioner's appraisal of the economic realities of this matter.

Resorts sells for cash the exhilaration and the potential for profit inherent in games of chance. It does so by selling for cash chips that entitle the holder to gamble at its casino. Zarin, like thousands of others, wished to purchase what Resorts was offering in the marketplace. He chose to make this purchase on credit and executed notes evidencing his obligation to repay the funds that were advanced to him by Resorts. As in most purchase money transactions, Resorts skipped the step of giving Zarin cash that he would only return to it in order to pay for the opportunity to gamble. Resorts provided him instead with chips that entitled him to participate in Resorts' games of chance on the same basis as others who had paid cash for that privilege.[1] Whether viewed as a one or two-step transaction, however, Zarin received either $3.4 million in cash or an entitlement for which others would have had to pay $3.4 million.

Despite the fact that Zarin received in 1980 cash or an entitlement worth $3.4 million, he correctly reported in that year no income from his dealings with Resorts. He did so solely because he recognized, as evidenced by his notes, an offsetting obligation to repay Resorts $3.4 million in cash. In 1981, with the delivery of Zarin's promise to pay Resorts $500,000 and the execution of a release by Resorts, Resorts surrendered its claim to repayment of the remaining $2.9 million of the money Zarin had borrowed. As of that time, Zarin's assets were freed of his potential liability for that amount and he recognized gross income in that amount.[2]

The only alternatives I see to this conclusion are to hold either (1) that Zarin realized $3.4 million in income in 1980 at a time

---

1. I view as irrelevant the facts that Resorts advanced credit to Zarin solely to enable him to patronize its casino and that the chips could not be used elsewhere or for other purposes. When one buys a sofa from the furniture store on credit, the fact that the proprietor would not have advanced the credit for a different purpose does not entitle one to a tax-free gain in the event the debt to the store is extinguished for some reason.

2. This is not a case in which parties agree subsequent to a purchase money transaction that the property purchased has a value less than thought at the time of the transaction. In such cases, the purchase price adjustment rule is applied and the agreed-upon value is accepted as the value of the benefit received by the purchaser; *see e.g., Commissioner v. Sherman*, 135 F.2d 68 (6th Cir. 1943); *N. Sobel, Inc. v. Commissioner*, 40 B.T.A. 1263 (1939). Nor is this a case in which the taxpayer is entitled to rescind an entire purchase money transaction, thereby to restore itself to the position it occupied before receiving anything of commercial value. In this case, the illegality was in the extension of credit by Resorts and whether one views the benefit received by Zarin as cash or the opportunity to gamble, he is no longer in a position to return that benefit.

when both parties to the transaction thought there was an offsetting obligation to repay or (2) that the $3.4 million benefit sought and received by Zarin is not taxable at all. I find the latter alternative unacceptable as inconsistent with the fundamental principle of the Code that anything of commercial value received by a taxpayer is taxable unless expressly excluded from gross income. I find the former alternative unacceptable as impracticable. In 1980, neither party was maintaining that the debt was unenforceable and, because of the settlement, its unenforceability was not even established in the litigation over the debt in 1981. It was not until 1989 in this litigation over the tax consequences of the transaction that the unenforceability was first judicially declared. Rather than require such tax litigation to resolve the correct treatment of a debt transaction, I regard it as far preferable to have the tax consequences turn on the manner in which the debt is treated by the parties. For present purposes, it will suffice to say that where something that would otherwise be includable in gross income is received on credit in a purchase money transaction, there should be no recognition of income so long as the debtor continues to recognize an obligation to repay the debt. On the other hand, income, if not earlier recognized, should be recognized when the debtor no longer recognizes an obligation to repay and the creditor has released the debt or acknowledged its unenforceability.

In this view, it makes no difference whether the extinguishment of the creditor's claim comes as a part of a compromise. Resorts settled for 14 cents on the dollar presumably because it viewed such a settlement as reflective of the odds that the debt would be held to be enforceable. While Zarin should be given credit for the fact that he had to pay 14 cents for a release, I see no reason why he should not realize gain in the same manner as he would have if Resorts had concluded on its own that the debt was legally unenforceable and had written it off as uncollectible.[5]

---

Consider the following perspectives on *Zarin*.

---

5. A different situation exists where there is a bona fide dispute over the amount of a debt and the dispute is compromised. Rather than require tax litigation to determine the amount of income received, the Commission treats the compromise figure as representing the amount of the obligation. I find this sensible and consistent with the pragmatic approach I would take.

### DANIEL SHAVIRO, THE MAN WHO LOST TOO MUCH: ZARIN v. COMMISSIONER AND THE MEASUREMENT OF TAXABLE CONSUSMPTION

45 Tax L. Rev. 215, 223-224 (1990)

Considered as a story, *Zarin* mixes personal tragedy with the sledgehammer irony of a "Twilight Zone" episode. Considered substantively, the case illuminates one of the central problems in applying an income tax: how to measure and account for the value of consumption. . . . As an element of income, consumption is relatively nonobvious. Consider a colloquial definition of income as the sum of one's cash receipts (other than from loans and gifts), plus some in-kind benefits, for example, a free European vacation won as a prize, minus business, but not personal, expenses. This colloquial definition, which very roughly corresponds to the current structure of the income tax, does not explicitly account for consumption. That it nonetheless includes consumption as a residual category becomes clear upon closer examination.

Tautologically, if spending means any diminution to one's wealth, and saving means any retained wealth, then all cash receipts must be either spent or saved. Spending and saving are definitionally the only two possible current uses of cash. If a taxpayer's income equals her cash receipts, minus business expenses, but not personal expenses, then the latter expenses, or her spending on consumption, are, in effect, a part of taxable income.

One may ask why it helps to identify consumption as an explicit component of income, instead of including it merely in a residual sense through nondeductibility. The answer is that identifying consumption helps to explain what we really mean by income, beyond the crude initial focus on cash receipts. Why should the prize of a free European vacation be included in income, whereas a business-related item (say, a free trip to Cleveland to negotiate a contract for one's employer) is not? The answer is that the vacation, but not the business trip, is something one imagines the taxpayer might have bought with her own money, specifically because it is consumption. Moreover, why should a personal expense, unlike a business expense, be nondeductible, given that both reduce the taxpayer's net worth? The answer is that the personal expense gives rise to consumption that we assume (for reasons to be discussed shortly) equals in value the amount spent. Thus, the personal expense is a wash, rather than a loss: It increases taxable consumption by the same amount as it reduces net worth.

In summary, consumption is an important part of what we mean by income. Cash is a plausible initial proxy for income solely because of its uses, consumption and saving, and not because it has any innate, uniquely income-like quality. If consumption is a part of income, however, and cash just a means to consume, then how is consumption to be measured? Must we assume that its value equals the amount spent on it?

* * *

*Zarin* is a perplexing and difficult case, both theoretically and under existing tax law. On the one hand, few would disagree that if Zarin, instead of being able to settle, had been forced to pay Resorts the entire $3,435,000, there would be no good reason to allow him any deduction. This may suggest that he did have income to the extent that he was able to do better than this and escape full liability for the nominal cost of his gambling.

On the other hand, the [position of the IRS as accepted by the Tax Court] has an undeniable Alice in Wonderland quality. [H]ow can a gambler have more pleasure from gambling the more he loses? Was Zarin really $2,935,000 better off at the end than at the beginning, or was he instead, even before being taxed, the hapless victim of a pathological disorder that was hardly less disabling and destructive than, say, an addiction to crack?

## THEODORE P. SETO, INSIDE ZARIN
### 59 SMU L. Rev. 1761, 1761-1773, 1808 (2006)

A simple model of statutory law, common among students, reads something like this: Congress enacts rules. Courts find facts and apply the rules to the facts or, at most, fill gaps in existing rules. All a student need do is to memorize the rules (or, if the exam is open book, know where to look them up) and discuss their application in the classic "on-the-one-hand, on-the-other-hand" tradition.

But law is not simply the application of rules to facts. Its goals are more profound; its means more subtle. Ultimately, law uses words, ideas, and processes to limit the exercise of power, implement norms, and create some degree of social order, legitimacy, and perceived equality. A "rule" is merely a requirement that similar situations be treated similarly; its function is to constrain. But reality is infinitely complex, and our moral and political judgments richly nuanced. To be workable, therefore, law must simplify. To this end, our legal system reduces bewildering reality to a few manageable "material facts" and complex moral and political conclusions to rote phrases. Ultimately, courts do apply rules to facts, but this is merely one step in a much more complicated process.

One might expect a legal system based on sometimes cartoonish simplification to be unsatisfactory. Legitimacy requires more than mere consistency; it also requires some adherence to intuitive notions of right and wrong. Nevertheless, in the run-of-the-mill case our system works surprisingly well. It breaks down primarily in cases for which the articulated rules were not designed. By studying how and when the system breaks down, we can better understand how it works—or, indeed, perhaps even how to make it work better. For this reason, law school texts often include atypical cases, cases in which the articulated rules do not quite work. Legal scholarship focuses disproportionately on such cases as well. *Zarin v. Commissioner* is one such case.

What is the "right" answer? A strong practical argument can be made that unenforceability should not determine whether discharged gambling debt is taxable. A strong theoretical argument can be made that losing gamblers do not receive commensurate consumption value, even if their debts are enforceable. It may also be true that the Code does not treat gambling as a consumption activity. And any tax rule governing the discharge of gambling debts must work in both market and nonmarket contexts. For all of these reasons, I suggest that the rule of *United States v. Hall* is in fact "correct"—that the discharge of gambling debts should be treated as nontaxable per se.

### NOTES

1. As *Zarin* reflects, the nature of gambling as an entertainment activity strongly tests some of the central assumptions about tax law. There may be no satisfactory answer to this problem.
2. What is the state of the law after *Zarin*? In *Rood v. Commissioner*, 71 Tax Court Memo (CCH) 3125, T.C. Memo. 1996-248 (1996), the Tax Court held that a casino gambler had discharge of indebtedness income where the debt was an enforceable debt. In *Rood*, Caesar's Palace in Las Vegas had voluntarily discharged part of the taxpayer's debt. The taxpayer claimed that it did so because the debt was disputed, but he failed to document that claim. The Tax Court held that the settlement of a debt for less than its full value is not enough, standing alone, to establish that there was a good faith dispute about the enforceability of the debt.

## COLLINS v. COMMISSIONER OF INTERNAL REVENUE
### 3 F.3d 625 (2d Cir. 1993)

CARDAMONE, Circuit Judge.

Mark D. Collins, taxpayer or appellant, appeals from a final decision of the United States Tax Court (Beghe, J.), entered October 16, 1992, determining that, as a result of unreported gross income from theft, he had an income tax deficiency for 1988 of $9,359. The theft occurred when the taxpayer, an employee of a betting parlor that accepts bets on horse races, was unable to stop himself from making wagers on his own behalf. He punched his bets on his computer without funds to pay for them. The horses Collins bet on ran like those of the bettor immortalized in Stephen C. Foster's De Camptown Races (Robbins Music Corp. 1933) (Song), some of whose horses left the racetrack, others cut across it, and one got stuck "in a big mud hole." Appellant's horses finished out of the money on most of the races he bet on and he lost heavily for the day. That which Collins had stolen is what he most feared to keep, as is so often the case; so he turned himself in. The theft precipitated a chain of events that led to the present appeal.

### BACKGROUND

#### A. THEFT AND RACETRACK BETTING

Collins was employed as a ticket vendor and computer operator at an Off-Track Betting (OTB) parlor in Auburn, New York. OTB runs a network of 298 betting parlors in New York State that permit patrons to place legal wagers on horse races without actually going to the track. Operating as a cash business, OTB does not extend credit to those making bets at its parlors. It also has a strict policy against employee betting on horse races. Collins, an apparently compulsive gambler, ignored these regulations and occasionally placed bets on his own behalf in his computer without paying for them. Until July 17, 1988 he had always managed to cover those bets without detection. On that date, appellant decided he "would like some money" and on credit punched up for himself a total of $80,280 in betting tickets.

Collins began the day by betting $20 on a horse across the board in the first race at the Finger Lakes Race Track in upstate New York, that is, he bet $20 to win, $20 to place (finish second or better), and $20 to show (finish third or better). The horse finished out of the money (not in the top three racers) and Collins lost $60. On the second race Collins again bet $40 across the board, with the same results. He was now out a total of $180. Appellant repeated this pattern, betting $600 in the third race and $1,500 in the fourth race at Finger Lakes, both of which he lost. Collins did not bet on the fifth race, but he wagered $1,500 in the sixth race, $7,500 in the seventh, and $15,000 in the eighth. Collins' luck continued to hold steady: he lost all of these races and now owed OTB $26,280.

There were only two races left that day and Collins was determined to recoup his losses. Consequently, he gambled $25,500 of OTB's money on the ninth race. This time his horse came in third, and Collins won back $8,925. He then bet $28,500 in the last or tenth race and finally picked a winner. The winning horse paid him $33,250. After this race, Collins was behind $38,105 for the day.

At the close of the races Collins put his $42,175 in winning tickets in his OTB drawer and reported his bets and his losing ticket shortfall to his supervisor, who until then had not been aware of Collins' gambling activities. She called the police, and in police custody Collins signed an affidavit admitting what he had done. On October 27, 1988 he pled guilty to one count of grand larceny in the third degree, a felony under New York law. *See* N.Y. Penal Law §155.35 (McKinney 1988). Collins was sentenced on December 1, 1988 by the Cayuga County Court in Auburn, New York, to five years of probation, 150 hours of community service, and a $100 surcharge.

Appellant's bets not only resulted in a shortfall in his till at OTB, but also had an impact on the odds of the races on which he had made those wagers. Racetrack gambling in New York is run on a "pari-mutuel" system. Under that system all bets—on each type of wager for each race—are pooled into a single so-called mutuel fund. The odds and payoffs for the first three horses in a race depend on the total amount of money in this pool. By increasing the total sum of money in the pool, Collins' bets lowered the odds and potential pay-offs on those horses on which he bet, and correspondingly increased the odds and potential payoffs on the other horses in the same race. Because Collins lost his first seven bets on July 17, his wagers increased the payout for the winners of each of those races. By contrast, Collins' last two winning bets reduced the funds available to pay off legitimate bettors who had paid cash for their winning tickets. In addition, appellant's bets increased OTB's liability to the Finger Lakes Track. Each of his bets was electronically transmitted to the racetrack via computer, and once so forwarded, OTB became liable to transfer the amount of the wager to the track.

These unauthorized actions on Collins' part resulted in OTB making a claim under its theft insurance policy with the Hartford Accident & Indemnity Co. The insurer, which paid the claim less a $5,000 deductible, sued Collins for the amount it had paid over plus costs. In December 1989 Hartford obtained a judgment against Collins for $36,601.94, and it has subsequently made attempts to enforce this judgment by garnishing Collins' wages from his new employer. The record does not reveal whether the insurer has recovered any of its money.

### B. TAX DEFICIENCY

Collins filed a timely federal income tax return for 1988 in which he reported wages of $11,980 and a corresponding tax liability of $1,054. He did not believe that his illegal activities on July 17, 1988 had any tax consequences, but the Internal Revenue Service (IRS) disagreed. On March 1, 1990 it mailed the taxpayer a deficiency notice resulting from his failure to report $38,136 in "gross income from gambling winnings during the taxable year 1988." It determined that due to this unreported income, Collins owed $9,376 in additional taxes for the calendar year 1988. Pursuant to 26 U.S.C. §§6653 and 6661, the IRS also charged Collins with penalties of $2,344 for substantial understatement of income tax and $469 for intentionally disregarding IRS rules and regulations.

The taxpayer objected to these assessments and, on June 4, 1990, filed a petition for relief with the United States Tax Court. The IRS replied to the petition by asserting, as an alternative theory of tax liability, that Collins received his $38,136 in "gross income from theft and embezzlement." The tax court, per Judge Beghe, held a one-day bench trial on November 19, 1991 and handed down an opinion on August 24, 1992 in which it found Collins liable for the unreported income, but not for any of the additional penalties.

It first determined that Collins' actions, rather than giving rise to gambling income, had resulted in a $38,105 gambling loss, arrived at by subtracting all the amounts he had earlier lost from his winnings on the last two races. Thus, contrary to the IRS' position, the taxpayer had not received any net income from his betting activities on July 17, 1988. The tax court then turned to what it deemed the more difficult question: whether the $80,280 in unpaid bets placed by Collins constituted theft or embezzlement income. It answered this query in the affirmative after undertaking a two-step inquiry that examined: (1) whether Collins realized economic value from the betting tickets he stole (the Realizable Value Test) and, if so, (2) whether Collins had sufficient control over this stolen property to derive value from it (the Control Test). The tax court found that Collins' larceny met both parts of the test because he had the opportunity to derive gratification and economic gain from using the stolen tickets.

Having concluded that Collins' theft resulted in income, the tax court calculated the amount of that income. It found a proper measure was the $80,280 value of the tickets, because Collins received from the pilfered tickets the same benefit that any legitimate purchaser would have gotten. To calculate tax liability the court then deducted from the $80,280 the $42,175 in winnings that Collins returned to his OTB till, which it characterized as a restitution payment by the taxpayer to his employer.

In sum, the tax court found Collins' unreported taxable income to be that amount which he stole on July 17 but did not return to his OTB till, a total that came to $38,105. As a consequence, it entered a final judgment on October 16, 1992 holding Collins liable for $9,359 in unpaid taxes for 1988. No additional penalties were assessed. The taxpayer has appealed contending, first, that the tax court erred by treating his illicit July 17 activities as giving rise to gross income and, second, by measuring this income by the face value of the tickets he misappropriated.

## DISCUSSION

In addressing the argument Collins raises regarding the tax treatment of his illegal actions, we believe it useful to set out initially the basic principles underlying the definition of gross income. Internal Revenue Code §61 defines gross income broadly as "all income from whatever source derived." 26 U.S.C. §61 (1988). It then categorizes 15 common items that constitute gross income, a list that includes interest, rents, royalties, salaries, annuities, and dividends, among others. Gross income, as §61 specifically states, is "not limited to" the enumerated items.

Defining gross income as "all income" is admittedly somewhat tautological. In the early days of the tax code, the Supreme Court recognized this problem and attempted to provide a more workable and perhaps somewhat more limited definition for the term. It defined income in *Eisner v. Macomber*, 252 U.S. 189, 207 (1920), " 'as gain derived from capital, from labor, or from both combined,' provided it be understood to include profit gained through a sale or conversion of capital assets. . . ."

It soon became evident that this definition created more problems than it solved. Under the *Eisner* formulation questions arose as to whether gains from cancellation of indebtedness or embezzlement— which do not fall neatly into either the labor or capital categories— constituted gross income. Acknowledging the defects in the *Eisner* definition, the Supreme Court began to steer away from it. For example, in *United States v. Kirby Lumber Co.*, 284 U.S. 1, 3, 52 S. Ct. 4, 4, 76 L. Ed. 131 (1931), it held that gains from the retirement of corporate bonds by their issuer at less than their issuing price were includable in gross income. Justice Holmes, writing for the Court, reached this conclusion despite the fact that the gains were not clearly derived from either capital or labor. In so doing he adverted to the futility of attempting to capture the concept of income and encapsulate it within a phrase. See *id.*

The Court finally abandoned the stilted capital-labor formulation of gross income and jettisoned its earlier attempts to define the term in *Commissioner v. Glenshaw Glass Co.*, 348 U.S. 426, 430-31 (1954). There the taxpayers had received treble damage awards from successfully prosecuting antitrust suits. They argued that two-thirds of these awards constituted punishment imposed on the wrongdoer and, under the gross income definition of *Eisner*, this punitive portion of the damages could not be treated as income derived from either labor or capital. See *id.* 348 U.S. at 428-30. In rebuffing this proposition, the Court ruled the damage awards taxable in their entirety. It cast aside *Eisner*'s definition of income stating that it was "not meant to provide a touchstone to all future gross income questions." *Id.* 348 U.S. at 431. Instead the Court stated, "Congress applied no limitations as to the source of taxable receipts, nor restrictive labels as to their nature." *Id.* at 429-30. The legislature intended to simply tax "all gains," which the Court effectively described as all "accessions to wealth, clearly realized, and over which the taxpayers have complete dominion." *Id.* at 430-31.

Since *Glenshaw Glass* the term gross income has been read expansively to include all realized gains and forms of enrichment, that is, "all gains except those specifically exempted." *Id.* at 430. Under this broad definition, gross income does not include all moneys a taxpayer receives. It is quite plain, for instance, that gross income does not include money acquired from borrowings. Loans do not result in realized gains or enrichment because any increase in net worth from proceeds of a loan is offset by a corresponding obligation to repay it.

This well-established principle on borrowing initially gave rise to another nettlesome question on how embezzled funds were to be treated. The Supreme Court once believed that money illegally procured from another was not gross income for tax purposes when the acquiror was legally obligated, like a legitimate borrower, to return the funds. *See Commissioner v. Wilcox*, 327 U.S. 404, 408-09, (1946). In *Rutkin v. United States*, 343 U.S. 130, 136-38, (1952), the Court partially and somewhat unsatisfactorily abandoned that view, holding that an extortionist, unlike an embezzler, was obligated to pay tax on his ill-gotten gains because he was unlikely to be asked to repay the money.

*Rutkin* left the law on embezzlement in a murky state. This condition cleared in *James v. United States*, 366 U.S. 213, 218, (1961). There the Court stated unequivocally that all unlawful gains are taxable. It reasoned that embezzlers, along with others who procure money illegally, should not be able to escape taxes while honest citizens pay taxes on "every conceivable type of income." *Id.* at 221. Thus, under *James*, a taxpayer has received income when she "acquires earnings, lawfully or unlawfully, without the consensual recognition, express or implied, of an obligation to repay and without restriction as to their disposition. . . ." *Id.* at 219. This income test includes all forms of enrichment, legal or otherwise, but explicitly excludes loans.

Distinguishing loans from unlawful taxable gains has not usually proved difficult. Loans are identified by the mutual understanding between the borrower and lender of the obligation to repay and a bona fide intent on the borrower's part to repay the acquired funds. Accordingly, in *Buff v. Commissioner*, 496 F.2d 847, 849 (2d Cir. 1974), we found an embezzler who confessed to his crime and within the same year signed a judgment agreeing to make repayment had received a taxable gain as opposed to a loan because he never had any intention of repaying the money. The embezzler's expressed consent to repay the loan, we determined, "was not worth the paper it was written on." *Id.* The mere act of signing such a consent could not be used to escape tax liability.

It is important to note, in addition, that though an embezzler must under the *James* test include as taxable income all amounts illegally acquired, the taxpayer may ordinarily claim a tax deduction for payments she makes in restitution. Such a deduction is available for the tax year in which the repayments are made. See 26 U.S.C. §165(c)[.]

With this outline of the relevant legal principles in mind, we have little difficulty in holding that Collins' illegal activities gave rise to gross income. Under the expansive definitions of income advanced in *Glenshaw Glass* and *James*, larceny of any kind resulting in an unrestricted gain of moneys to a wrongdoer is a taxable event. Taxes may be assessed in the year in which the taxpayer realizes an economic benefit from his actions. In this case, Collins admitted to stealing racing tickets from OTB on July 17, 1988. This larceny resulted in the taxpayer's enrichment: he had the pleasure of betting on horses running at the Finger Lakes Race Track. Individuals purchase racing tickets from OTB because these tickets give them the pleasure of attempting to make money simply by correctly predicting the outcomes of horse races. By punching up tickets on his computer without paying for them, Collins appropriated for himself the same benefit that patrons of OTB pay money to receive. This illegally-appropriated benefit, as the tax court correctly concluded, constituted gross income to Collins in 1988.

The taxpayer raises a series of objections to this conclusion. He first insists that such a holding cannot be correct because at the end of the day he was in debt by $38,105. He asserts that a tax is being assessed on his losses rather than on any possible gain. What may seem at first glance a rather anomalous result is explained by distinguishing between Collins' theft and his gambling activities. Collins took illegally acquired assets and spent them unwisely by betting on losing horses at a racetrack.

Although the bets gave rise to gambling losses, the taxpayer gained from the misappropriation of his employer's property without its knowledge or permission. The gambling loss is not relevant to and does not offset Collins' gain in the form of opportunities to gamble that he obtained by virtue of his embezzlement. Collins' situation is quite the same as that of any other individual who embezzles money from his employer and subsequently loses it at the racetrack. Such person would properly have his illegally-acquired assets included in his gross income. Further, taxpayer would not be able to deduct gambling losses from theft income because the Internal Revenue Code only allows gambling losses to offset gambling winnings. See 26 U.S.C. §165(d). Collins is being treated the same way.

The taxpayer next contends his larceny resulted in no taxable gain because he recognized that he had an obligation to repay his employer for the stolen tickets. He posits that recognition of a repayment obligation transformed a wrongful appropriation into a nontaxable transaction. In effect, Collins tries to revive pre-*James* law under which an embezzler's gain could be found nontaxable due to the embezzler's duty to repay stolen funds. Yet, the Supreme Court has clearly abandoned the pre-*James* view and ruled instead that only a loan, with its attendant "consensual recognition" of the obligation to repay, is not taxable. See *James*, 366 U.S. at 219. There was no loan of funds, nor was there any "consensual recognition" here: OTB never gave Collins permission to use betting tickets. To the contrary, it has strict rules against employee betting, and Collins could not have reasonably believed that his supervisors would have approved of his transactions. His unilateral intention to pay for the stolen property did not transform a theft into a loan within the meaning of *James*.

The taxpayer then avers this case is analogous to *Gilbert v. Commissioner*, 552 F.2d 478 (2d Cir. 1977), in which we found a consensual recognition of the obligation to repay despite the absence of a loan agreement. Taxpayer Edward Gilbert, as president and a director of E.L. Bruce Company, acquired on margin a substantial personal stake in the stock of a rival company, Celotex Corporation, intending to bring about a merger between Celotex and E.L. Bruce. The stock market declined after Gilbert bought these shares, and he was required to meet several margin calls. Lacking personal funds to meet these obligations, Gilbert instructed the corporate secretary of E.L. Bruce to make $1.9 million in margin payments on his behalf. A few days later, Gilbert signed secured promissory notes to repay the funds; but, the corporation's board of directors refused to ratify Gilbert's unauthorized withdrawal, demanded his resignation, and called in his notes. The board also declined to merge with Celotex, and soon thereafter the Celotex stock that Gilbert owned became essentially worthless. Gilbert could not repay his obligations to E.L. Bruce, and he eventually pled guilty to federal and state charges of unlawfully withdrawing funds from the corporation. *See id.* at 479-81.

The IRS claimed that Gilbert's unauthorized withdrawal of funds constituted income to the taxpayer. It asserted that there was no consensual recognition of a repayment obligation because E.L. Bruce Company's board of directors was unaware of and subsequently disapproved Gilbert's actions. Citing the highly atypical nature of the case, we held that Gilbert did not realize income under the *James* test because (1) he not only "fully" intended but also expected "with reasonable certainty" to repay the sums taken, (2) he believed his withdrawals would be approved by the corporate board, and (3) he made prompt assignment of assets sufficient to secure the amount he owed. *Id.* at 481. These facts evidenced consensual recognition and distinguished *Gilbert* from the more typical embezzlement case where the embezzler plans right from the beginning to abscond with the embezzled funds. *See id.* at 480-81.

Plainly, none of the significant facts of *Gilbert* are present in the case at hand. Collins, unlike Gilbert, never expected to be able to repay the stolen funds. He was in no position to do so. The amount he owed OTB was three times his annual salary—a far cry from Gilbert, where the taxpayer assigned to the corporation enough assets to cover his unauthorized withdrawals. Also in contrast to Gilbert, Collins could not have believed that his employer would subsequently ratify his transactions. He knew that OTB had strict rules against employee betting. Moreover, while Gilbert was motivated by a desire to assist his corporation, Collins embezzled betting tickets because he wanted to make some money. Collins' purpose makes this a garden variety type of embezzlement case, not to be confused with a loan. *Gilbert* is therefore an inapposite precedent.

Finally, appellant complains of the root unfairness and harshness of the result, declaring that the imposition of a tax on his July 17 transaction is an attempt to use the income tax law to punish misconduct that has already been appropriately punished under the criminal law. Although we are not without some sympathy to the taxpayer's plight, we are unable to adopt his claim of unfairness and use it as a basis to negate the imposition of a tax on his income. The Supreme Court has repeatedly emphasized that taxing an embezzler on his illicit gains accords with the fair administration of the tax law because it removes the anomaly of having the income of an honest individual taxed while the similar gains of a criminal are not. See *James*, 366 U.S. at 218; *Rutkin*, 343 U.S. at 137-38. Thus, there is no double penalty in having a taxpayer prosecuted for the crime that resulted in his obtaining ill-gotten gains and subsequently being required to pay taxes on those illegal gains. Such is not an unduly harsh result because Internal Revenue Code §165 provides that once the taxpayer makes restitution payments to OTB or its insurer, he will be able in that year to deduct the amount of those payments from his gross income. See 26 U.S.C. §165(c).

In sum, we hold that under the expansive definition of income adopted in *Glenshaw Glass* and *James*, Collins received gross income from his theft of OTB betting tickets. There is no basis upon which we may hold that the receipt of these opportunities to gamble may be excluded from a calculation of the taxpayer's income. When and if Collins repays the stolen funds, he will be entitled to a deduction from income in the year that the funds are repaid.

### VALUATION

Having determined that the July 17 transaction resulted in a taxable gain to Collins, we next consider how that gain should be measured. It is well-settled that income received in a form other than cash is taxed at its fair market value at the time of its receipt. Fair market value is defined as "the price at which the property would change hands between a willing buyer and willing seller, neither being under any compulsion to buy or to sell and both having reasonable knowledge of relevant facts." *United States v. Cartwright*, 411 U.S. 546, 551 (1973) (citing Treasury regulation definition).

Based on this measure the value of Collins' tickets was the price at which they would have changed hands between legitimate bettors and OTB. This price was the retail price or face value of the tickets. Accordingly, the tax court properly found that the stolen tickets were worth

$80,280, their retail price, and this amount was correctly included in the taxpayer's gross income, as a gain from theft. From that figure Collins was entitled to a deduction for restitution he made to OTB in 1988. Collins returned to his till on July 17 winning tickets with a face value of $42,175. Thus, the tax court correctly determined that Collins' total taxable theft income for the year was $38,105 ($80,280 minus $42,175).

Collins, relying upon the Third Circuit's decision in *Zarin v. Commissioner*, 916 F.2d 110 (3d Cir. 1990), asserts the stolen tickets were essentially valueless for tax purposes . . . It ruled that in order to demonstrate indebtedness, the IRS had to prove, under 26 U.S.C. §108(d)(1), that Zarin either (1) was liable to Resorts on the debt or (2) held "property" subject to the debt. The court found the IRS could make neither showing. Under the first part of the test, Zarin was not liable on the debt because Resorts' $3.4 million loan was issued in violation of the New Jersey Casino Control Commission's order and was not enforceable under New Jersey law. *Zarin*, 916 F.2d at 113. Under the second part, the Third Circuit held the gambling chips Zarin acquired with Resort's loan were not property because they had "no independent economic value." It reached this conclusion because the chips could not be used outside the casino, only having value as a means of facilitating gambling within the casino itself. *Id.* at 113-14.

Collins seizes on this second point, insisting that like Zarin he stole opportunities to gamble and that his stolen racing tickets—like Zarin's gambling chips—had no intrinsic economic value. He thinks therefore that his taxable gain from the theft of the tickets was zero.

In disposing of that erroneous assumption, we observe that the statement in *Zarin* regarding the value of the casino's gambling chips was offered as part of the appellate court's interpretation of the narrow income exclusion provision of §108(d) of the Code. Section 108(a) excludes from gross income the amount of the discharge of a taxpayer's indebtedness and §108(d), just discussed, defines indebtedness. We are not convinced that the Third Circuit's reasoning is applicable outside the context of §108 and the specific facts of that case where nothing was stolen and there was no embezzlement. *Cf.* Daniel Shaviro, "The Man Who Lost Too Much: *Zarin v. Commissioner* and the Measurement of Taxable Consumption," 45 *Tax L. Rev.* 215, 252-58 (1990) (criticizing the *Zarin* court for ignoring §61 of the Internal Revenue Code). *Zarin* may have been written differently had the Third Circuit been confronted with the separate question of whether to include as gross income under §61 the face value of stolen gambling opportunities.

*Zarin* we think is also inapposite because it involved a consensual transaction between Resorts Casino and the taxpayer that impacted no other parties. Zarin's gambling did not cause Resorts to transfer any money from the casino to third parties, nor did it affect other players at the gaming tables. In the instant case, Collins' wagers had external consequences beyond his tax liability. His bets affected the odds of the races at the Finger Lakes Track and impacted the payouts on those races on July 17. Further, OTB had to pay the Finger Lakes Track $38,105, the face value of the losing tickets. Hence, the betting tickets here had independent and measurable economic value, and resulted in a true loss to OTB. Consequently, we regard the fair market value of the stolen gambling tickets to be the proper measure of Collins' taxable gain in 1988. AFFIRMED.

### NOTES

1. Is the valuation analysis correct? Could Collins have resold the tickets for face value?
2. Is *Collins* consistent with *Zarin*? Did the stolen tickets in *Collins* have any more intrinsic value than the gambling chips in *Zarin*? If Collins's winnings would not have been legally enforceable, why would the IRS treat his debts as such?
3. Are *Collins* and *Zarin* based on different implicit assumptions about what each of the taxpayers received in the gambling transactions at issue? Both were losers. In gambling, does a loser nevertheless have a tangible gain?

# TABLE OF CASES

*Principal cases are indicated by italics.*

# INDEX